CW 00696376

W0006514

THE ILLUSTRATED ENCYCLOPEDIA OF

PISTOLS
REVOLVERS
and SUBMACHINE GUNS

THE ILLUSTRATED ENCYCLOPEDIA OF

PISTOLS REVOLVERS
and SUBMACHINE GUNS

WILL FOWLER, ANTHONY NORTH
& CHARLES STRONGE

LORENZ BOOKS

This edition is published by Lorenz Books,
an imprint of Anness Publishing Ltd,
108 Great Russell Street, London WC1B 3NA;
info@anness.com

www.lorenzbooks.com; www.annesspublishing.com;
twitter: @Anness_Books

Anness Publishing has a new picture agency outlet for images for
publishing, promotions or advertising. Please visit our website
www.practicalpictures.com for more information.

© Anness Publishing Ltd 2015

All rights reserved. No part of this publication may be reproduced,
stored in a retrieval system, or transmitted in any way or by any
means, electronic, mechanical, photocopying, recording or otherwise,
without the prior written permission of the copyright holder.

A CIP catalogue record for this book is available from
the British Library.

Designed and produced for Anness Publishing by
THE BRIDGEWATER BOOK COMPANY LIMITED.

Publisher: Joanna Lorenz
Editorial Director: Helen Sudell
Project Manager: Sarah Doughty
Photography: Gary Ombler
Designer: Alistair Plumb
Art Director: Lisa McCormick
Production Controller: Pirong Wang

PUBLISHER'S NOTE
Although the advice and information in this book are believed to be
accurate and true at the time of going to press, neither the authors
nor the publisher can accept any legal responsibility or liability for
any errors or omissions that may have been made nor for any
inaccuracies nor for any loss, harm or injury that comes about from
following instructions or advice in this book. The ownership and use
of firearms is regulated by law in most countries. Please ensure
that you comply with the law if owning, using or collecting firearms.
Neither the authors nor the publisher can accept any legal
responsibility or liability for failure to follow this advice.

Contents

Introduction

Although the firearm has a long history, the amount of technical progress that took place in the first 500 years is relatively small. The earliest evidence of the handgun, whether in illuminated manuscripts or as archaeological artefacts, gives us clues to its development from an unwieldy vase-shaped object to a straight-barrelled version similar to the barrel of a modern firearm. The first section of this book spans the entire history of small arms development, from the origins of gunpowder to the most up-to-date weapons of the 21st century. There then follows two unparalleled visual directories of significant pistols and submachine guns from around the world, from the 19th century to the present day.

The beginnings of arms development

The first chapter of this book, *The Early History of Arms,* is a comprehensive history of the technical development of early arms. It opens with an exploration of the very earliest inventions from the 11th century. Always improving on previous models, various techniques were subsequently developed to ignite and fire prototype guns in the most efficient way possible, while allowing the user to hold the weapon by a wooden stock (the handle). While early guns were often ignited by a burning tinder or a red-hot iron, the serpentine system allowed an arm (the holding "serpentine") a match to ignite the powder in the touch-hole. This developed into the matchlock system,

BELOW A 17th-century German flintlock pistol. The flintlock rapidly replaced earlier firearm-ignition. It continued to be in common use for over 200 years before it was replaced by the percussion cap.

whereby the arm was held clear of the powder by a spring. To fire the gun, the spring was released by means of the action of the trigger and the powder in the priming pan was lit. The wheel-lock worked very much like a flint lighter, whereby a wheelspring mechanism helped the arm to move to ignite the powder in the pan by means of friction. The 17th-century flintlock developed this idea further and a flint was struck against steel to produce a spark. The invention of the flintlock was so successful that it formed the basis of all military, naval and personal firearms for the best part of 200 years.

The percussion system was an ingenious development that saw the end of the flintlock, first by replacing the traditional locks (flintlocks or wheel-locks) on existing weapons and then by being fitted to new firearms. The percussion cap was a system using a

LEFT Handguns in use in a 15th-century siege. As technology improved, guns and cannons took over from traditional medieval weapons such as crossbows and combat became more impersonal and mechanical.

cap containing fulminate of mercury, a chemical compound which exploded when struck, that was attached to the barrel of the gun by a simple tube. The subsequent experiments with percussion caps, early cartridges and breech-loading rifles (loaded from the rear rather than the front) gave rise to the modern firearm. Different trades, influenced by increasing industrialization in Europe, contributed to its manufacture, whether lock, stock or barrel.

The 20th century and beyond

The second chapter, *Into the Modern Age,* examines the development of firearms in the modern day. Of particular significance was the invention of the revolver by Samuel Colt, which had a critical influence on American history as it was played out in both the "Wild West" (real and mythical) and the American Civil War (1861–65).

The turn of the 20th century also saw the introduction of one of the most important handgun designs of modern history, John Moses Browning's M1900 automatic pistol, later refined to become the Colt M1911. The original automatic pistols were so ingeniously designed that their derivates have remained in service with major military forces to the present day.

The beginning of World War II (1939–45) saw an acceleration of handgun and submachine-gun design. The British Sten gun was conjured up in the dark days of 1940, while the Soviet PPS-43 was born from the wreckage of Leningrad in 1942–43.

In the post-war era, further revolver, pistol and submachine-gun designs were developed, in response to international warfare, the needs of police forces, and the growing threat of international terrorism. Also covered in this section of the book is the advent of non-lethal weapons, as security forces explore the options of stunning or anaesthetizing their opponents rather than using lethal force.

ABOVE RIGHT The Micro Uzi is used for covert operations that require a weapon that can be easily concealed and deployed while providing an effective rate of fire and accuracy. While classified as a submachine gun, Micro Uzi is small enough to sometimes be designated as a pistol.

ABOVE The .45 Colt M1911, regarded as the most successful automatic pistol of all time. Adopted by the US Army in 1911, the pistol was still in service in 1985. There are many copies still in use.

The directories

The two directory chapters encompass both significant and less well-known firearms from both major and minor national producers. Organized by country and then alphabetically by manufacturer in date order (except where a chronological order shows the development of a gun), the directories provide a concise description of each firearm and its vital specifications. The weapons are mainly 20th-century firearms but the directory also includes weapons from the 19th century, as well as the latest developments in the firearms industry. The most eminent firearms manufacturers in the world today include some of the world's oldest industrial corporations. Beretta of Italy was established as far back as the 16th century, in 1526. In 1984 the company celebrated securement of one of the world's most valuable military handgun orders from the US Army. Likewise, Colt, Smith & Wesson, Remington and Ruger, all of whom helped to shape early American history, continue to produce state-of-the-art pistols and revolvers for the high-tech security forces of today. The precision engineering and high-quality manufacturing of German, Swiss and Austrian firms is catalogued in the products of firms such as Steyr Mannlicher and SIG Sauer (SIG). The directories chart their developments from the steel creations of early years to the polymer-framed modular products of the 21st century. They also include a wide range of entries from smaller manufacturers across the globe, such as the family firm Para-Ordnance of Canada, who have built on classic designs like the Browning M1911 and improved them, while developing an array of other mission-specific firearms.

RIGHT A highly decorated flintlock pistol. The flintlock quickly replaced earlier firearm technologies, such as the matchlock and wheel-lock mechanisms. It continued to be in general use for over two centuries, until the percussion cap and cartridge systems came into common use.

RIGHT This was one of the most famous revolvers of the American Wild West. Designed for the US Cavalry, it was first produced in 1873 and is often known as the "Colt 45".

The early history of arms

This chapter provides a colourful journey, from the early discoveries of chemical compounds that would explode when lit and the use of these powders to fire a projectile, through the development of ever more sophisticated systems for firing weapons. This included matchlock and flintlock mechanisms, and the early forms of today's firearms that are loaded from the rear of the barrel (the breech) and use metal cartridges containing bullet, gunpowder and primer. This section also covers such aspects as the use of firearms for duelling, examines the unique nature of handguns produced by the mostly Islamic countries of the East, and reflects on the arts of ornamentation and engraving that were to complement handgun design and development through the ages.

ABOVE From the 18th century, duels could be fought using pistols. Special sets of duelling pistols were crafted for wealthy noblemen. A pistol duel normally took place at dawn. The parties would be placed back to back with loaded weapons in hand. They would walk a set number of paces, turn to face their opponent and shoot. Many pistol duels were to first blood (such as a minor wound) rather than to death.

The first firearms

The invention of the gun was the logical consequence of the discovery of gunpowder. Once the knowledge of its powerful explosive forces had spread to Europe, probably from China via Islamic Spain, the next challenge was to contain the force and to use it to propel a missile.

The discovery of gunpowder

Gunpowder was known to the Chinese by the 11th century and the knowledge of it probably came to Europe through Moorish Spain. The earliest definite reference to guns comes from Florence in Italy in the 14th century and the earliest illustration of a gun is to be found in a 14th-century English royal manuscript. These early guns have characteristics that can be traced throughout the history of firearms.

ABOVE Roger Bacon, English experimental scientist, philosopher and Franciscan friar. His 13th-century manuscript included an anagram which contained the formula for gunpowder. Scholars such as Bacon received much knowledge from the East via Moorish Spain.

The early history of gunpowder is as confusing as it is interesting. India, China, the Arabs and Western Europe have all laid claim to its invention. Gunpowder was more widely known to consist of saltpetre, charcoal and sulphur. Sifting through the evidence reveals that, while gunpowder was known to Chinese alchemists as early as the 11th century, they were looking for a material that burned rather than propelled missiles. While alchemists of different cultures may have known about gunpowder they may not have understood the correct proportions to use to create explosions.

Early evidence

The earliest hard evidence for gunpowder is found in European manuscripts of the 13th century. There are references to gunpowder in the *Liber Ignium* of Marcus Graecus, which dates from about 1300, and in the treatise *De Mirabilium Mundi* of Albertus Magnus who died in Cologne in 1280. The best known is in a manuscript of Roger Bacon, written in about 1260. In this *Epistolae de secretis operibus artis et naturae et de nullitate magial* is a Latin anagram that, when solved, can be translated as "seven parts of saltpetre, five of new hazelwood and five of charcoal". This is an effective recipe for gunpowder. There are also references in the *Opus Majus* of 1267, and in the *Opus Tertium* of *c*.1266–68 which describes a form of firework. The method calls for the powder to be enclosed in an instrument of parchment the size of the little finger, somewhat reminiscent of later paper cartridges.

If gunpowder originated in China, it probably came to Western Europe through the alchemical works of Moorish Spain during the first half of the 13th century. The role of the Arabs in the early history of gunpowder and firearms has probably been underestimated. An Arabic treatise found in Leningrad describes arrows or bullets being fired through a tube by gunpowder, but the date of the manuscript has been disputed, so the claim that firearms were invented by the Arabs cannot, at present, be substantiated.

The Milemete gun

Some early references to guns related to military campaigns. In 14th- and 15th-century Europe, the Hundred Years' War was the most extended conflict, lasting until 1453.

In one of his early incursions into Scotland in his campaign to take the Scottish crown, Edward III of England may have had with him an early form of gun. In a manuscript dated 1326, its author, scholar Walter de Milemete, included a depiction of a vase-shaped gun supported by a trestle. This type of gun was to become more and more commonplace. Protruding from the vase was a large metal arrow. Some kind of wadding was probably placed around its shaft in order to maximize the propellent force. The vase itself would have been formed from cast iron or bronze. The weapon was fired by applying a red-hot iron or something similar to a touch-hole to ignite it. Such devices would come into ever more frequent use from this time onwards.

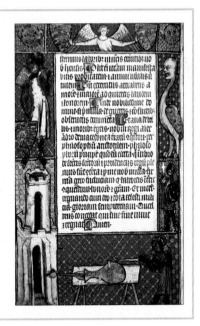

RIGHT The earliest-dated picture of a gun, from the manuscript *De Notabilitatibus, Sapientis et Prudentia* of Walter de Milemete, 1326. More efficient systems of firing guns were soon devised.

The first gun and prototypes

According to legend, the gun was invented by a German monk known as "Black Berthold", who came from Freiburg in southern Germany. While he was making gunpowder with a mortar and pestle, the mixture exploded, propelling the pestle from the mortar like a bullet, thus giving him the idea for a gun. The monk is a purely legendary figure, but this story of the introduction of firearms may contain an element of truth as it is recorded as early as the 15th century.

There are early accounts of prototype guns in both Chinese and Arab sources. From a 12th-century Chinese source is a description of a bamboo tube filled with gunpowder, which fired arrows. It was mentioned in a military treatise of the 17th century but is based on much earlier sources. Here it was described as a long copper tube containing an arrow, the stock being a short pole. A very similar primitive gun is shown in a 14th-century Arabic manuscript. Many of the early guns were designed to fire arrows rather than other missiles.

In 1326 the Council of Florence decreed that two men should be appointed to manufacture "iron bullets or arrows and metal cannon". Further references of

the same year, also from Florence, mention "cannon, iron balls and gunpowder". The earliest precisely datable illustration of a gun, the Milemete gun, also dates from 1326.

The very marked flask-shape of the gun is not just artistic licence but is based on the sound principal of reinforcing the gun at the back, where the initial explosion happens. This lesson was learned the hard way, when guns had burst at this weak point.

RIGHT Berthold Schwartz was a fictitious German monk known as "Black Berthold". He was said to have discovered gunpowder around 1320 after experimentation with solidifying quicksilver.

Early cannons and handguns

It was soon discovered that the vase-like shape of the early guns, like the Milemete gun, was not the most efficient, and that a traditional projectile like an arrow was not best suited to the new invention. A straight, metal tube was soon developed. The next step was to find the most efficient method of lighting the gunpowder. A method of absorbing "recoil" – the force of the gun going backward after the shot was fired – also needed to be found. The effectiveness of these weapons was growing – the handgun, as we know it, had arrived.

First developments

The Milemete gun demonstrated a stage in development whereby the notion of an arrow as a projectile is still in mind. The shape of the arrow, however, was not suited to maximizing the propellant effect of the explosion and, by the end of the 14th century, stone cannon balls were almost always used.

The Loshult gun

The vase-like feature occurs on the earliest known hand cannon, the Loshult gun, excavated in Sweden in 1861. Cast in bronze, it has a distinctive flask-like shape and also a simple counter-sunk pan around the touch hole to help ignition. It has been dated to the first half of the 14th century. A gun found in the sea near Morko, Sweden, has also been dated to the 14th century. Cast in bronze with a two-stage polygonal barrel, there is a cast bearded figure behind the square pan or touch-hole and a projecting hook below the breech. The hook stopped the recoil when the gun was

ABOVE An early iron gun. This long, thin hand cannon is from Vedelspang Castle, Copenhagen. Dated around 1400, it was more dangerous if used as a club.

fired, hence the name "hakenbüchs" (hook can). The surface was engraved with religious texts. The gun was very short and was clearly made as a handgun.

Another early handgun was excavated from Tannenberg Castle in Germany, destroyed in 1399. Made of cast bronze, the gun had a two-stage polygonal barrel. The bore, in front of the powder-chamber where the missile is held, has deliberately been made narrow, probably to increase the force of the explosion. The Tannenberg gun dates from about 1350.

BELOW An early gun, dated around 1350, was found near Loshult, Sweden. The Loshult gun looked like a miniature cannon and would have been fired in much the same way as the gun depicted in the Milemete manuscript, i.e. from a trestle.

BELOW The Morko gun was found on the bed of the Baltic Sea. The hexagonal barrel was similar to many of the early small arms. This gun marks an important stage in the development of the handgun – it does not have the bulbous shape of a small cannon, but instead has a "modern" straight barrel.

barrel

or twine soaked in a potassium nitrate solution. It was then left to dry. When lit, it would burn at a predictably slow rate.

It is thought that a bullet fired from a gun of this type was capable of penetrating the steel armour commonly used at the time, within a reasonable range. This was in addition to the psychological impact on the enemy of the noise and flash of the weapon. The effectiveness of these comparatively simple weapons was not underestimated and the handgun was here to stay.

Continuing development

As the understanding of the forces involved grew, so did the power and size of the weapons. In due course new designs began to appear to deal with the force of the recoil. Sometimes the handgun was supported on a tripod. Occasionally the stock was not made of wood but was instead formed of a curled metal extension to the main barrel.

Design and construction

Both the Milemete and Loshult guns looked more like cannons than handguns and they also comprised a bulbous area at the back. The Morko gun, dating from about the middle of the 14th century, was more recognizable as a handgun, with a straight firing tube, and it was designed to be fired without the use of any supports, such as a trestle. The Morko gun, like the Tannenberg gun, was a straightforward metal tube attached to a wooden stock, which was either a pole or a construction similar to that used for a crossbow. Weapons such as these may have been designed to accept a metal bolt but the Tannenberg gun when excavated was found to be loaded with a lead bullet. A variety of ancient handguns has been found in various locations, some of them in Spain, others in Switzerland, Sweden and England.

Firing the early guns

The metal tube (or barrel) of a handgun such as the Morko gun or the Tannenberg gun was about 300mm/12in in length. The bore (the interior diameter of the barrel) was about 17mm/0.67in. A handgun had a powder chamber, which was linked to a small hole drilled at right angles. The gunpowder and propellant would have been inserted through the muzzle (the forward end). The gun was probably fired by inserting a red hot wire poker into the touch-hole. Another way of firing would have been to use a slow-burning match fuse. The slow match was usually made up of cord

ABOVE Use of handguns in the 15th century as depicted in *Rudimentum Noviciorum*, Lubeck, 1475. This gun was mounted on a pole and appeared to be lit through a touch-hole.

Matchlocks

The matchlock was the first major step forward in developing an efficient firing mechanism that would allow the user to concentrate on holding his weapon with both hands and aiming it effectively. As the power and efficiency of the handgun increased, the wooden stock began to be developed, so that the recoil could be effectively absorbed. Increased weight meant that a pike or forked support between the weapon and ground were used.

The serpentine lock

The method of manually igniting the charge by means of a rod that held a piece of metal or glowing tinder, was superseded in the early 15th century by a device known as a serpentine (an angled arm) or serpentine lock. The first mechanical firing mechanism was the matchlock, the basis of which was the serpentine. The mechanism had to be both efficient and robust.

The early matchlock was operated by pressing the lever up to the stock so the match or tinder was pushed into the touch-hole. Since the pole stock could be placed under the arm at the shoulder, the gun could now be aimed properly. This development led to changes in the shape of the stock, which became polygonal. Some handguns, however, retained the pole-stock until well into the 15th century. It is possible that the serpentine lock was suggested by the

BELOW A drawing of parts of a matchlock. The simple mechanism could work well as long as match and powder were dry.

trigger action of a crossbow, which, like the serpentine, was a long lever under the stock which was pressed upwards to release the cord. The polygonal profile of some early gun stocks also resembles those of crossbows. The crossbow was the most powerful hand-held missile weapon then in use, so it was logical for early gunmakers to copy its features.

Serpentine development

The first recorded illustration of a serpentine lock is from a manuscript dated 1411 (Codex Vindobana 3069) which can be found in the Austrian National Library. This shows the simplicity of the serpentine system, and the straightforward operation of the lever mechanism. The man firing the weapon is able to keep both hands on the stock making aiming and firing easier. It is known that stocks grew in length in order to absorb recoil from firing, and they ranged between just under a metre to 1.5 metres (1.64 yards) in length. As stocks developed, different methods of holding the weapon also evolved.

LEFT The gun-wielder from this 14th-century manuscript is firing the weapon from under his arm, but over time firing from the shoulder became more common. The kneeling figure is in the process of casting bullets.

Some matchlock serpentines included a spring, which would move the arm holding the match more rapidly into the pan. The "match" was normally a length of woven hemp cord boiled in a solution of saltpetre and then allowed to dry. It was literally looped around the fingers. It was carried lit, smouldering ready to ignite the gunpowder. The invention of the matchlock allowed mechanical means to press the glowing end into the touch-hole. In addition the matchlock was a simple mechanism, easy to make and repair and reasonably reliable. It did not, however, resolve the problem of how to ignite the powder without having to carry a constantly glowing match. It also could give away the position of the user to the enemy.

Fifteenth-century improvements

During the 15th century a number of improvements were made. The touch-hole was moved from the top of the barrel to the side. This led to an improved pan, which was mounted on the side of the barrel and had a hinged cover to protect the powder. As the arm holding the match descended, the flash pan cover moved aside exposing the powder in the pan. Once the powder had been ignited and the gun fired, the pan cover would return to its original position. This ingenious system gave the powder in the pan much greater protection from the effects of wind or rain or from being inadvertently tipped out of the pan. It also meant that the weapon was safeguarded against sparks inadvertently firing the gun before the

firer was ready. More rapid action was achieved by the development of the "snap-matchlock" in which the serpentine arm was replaced by a curved match-holder driven by a spring.

ABOVE A handgun being discharged. This is a matchlock handgun with a pike rest. Some matchlocks had a disproportionately large stock requiring a support to take the weight.

BELOW An ornate matchlock mechanism from the 18th century. Despite the ornate design, the matchlock was operated by the simple process of a lit match igniting the gunpowder.

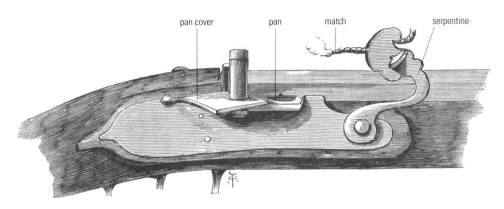

pan cover   pan   match   serpentine

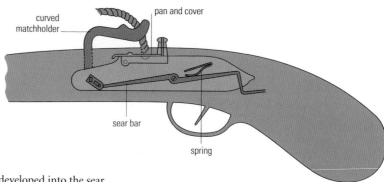

RIGHT Cross-section through a firearm showing the internal workings of the snap-matchlock: when the trigger lever was pressed the lighted match fell into the powder in the pan and ignited the charge. The curved matchholder was drawn back against a spring so that when the trigger was pulled the match came down very quickly to the powder.

curved matchholder

pan and cover

sear bar

spring

The snap-matchlock

By about 1470 the system had developed into the sear, or snap-matchlock. The serpentine was replaced by a curved matchholder driven by a spring. When the trigger lever was pressed, the lighted match fell into the powder in the pan and ignited the charge. The match was held down in the pan through the action of springs and levers mounted on the inside of the lock-plate. The matchholder was then pulled back manually and was held by the sear (a lever or catch). When the trigger was pulled, the sear was withdrawn and the matchholder snapped back into the pan. The mechanism was soon superseded by new inventions in Europe, but was taken to Japan by Portuguese traders in the 16th century and used in Japan until the 19th century. The Japanese snap-matchlock pistol is a scaled-down version of a long arm, fitted with a wide barrel and the matchlock on the side of the stock.

Advances in gunpowder

The gunpowder used at the time was also known as serpentine. One defect of serpentine powder was that its different constituents, of different mass, tended to separate over time or during movement. The saltpetre and sulphur would settle at the bottom and the charcoal element at the top. This was likely to make ignition less efficient. It was only with the invention of "corned" powder in the early 15th century that this problem was addressed. In this process, the ingredients were all ground and mixed together and then sieved to make sure that all the constituent particles were the same size.

The matchlock in warfare

By the 15th century firearms were used to an increasing extent on the battlefield. Improved systems of ignition such as the serpentine lock and the snap-matchlock, together with changes in the shape of guns, made them lighter and easier to use. Improved methods of making barrels included the introduction of rifling within the barrel of the firearm. Rifling refers to the grooves that were created in the barrel of a firearm to produce a spin on the projectile to improve accuracy of the shot.

By the end of the 15th century firearms were playing an increasing role in warfare. The matchlock musket gave the common footsoldier a much better chance of bringing down a swordsman without either of them having to be in contact. The weapon stock began to change to a flattened form that could be placed against the shoulder, one hand gripping the butt and operating the trigger while the other supported the barrel. Assuming the powder did not simply "flash in the pan" (the explosion of gunpowder in the pan), but ignited the charge, in the breech, the bullet was propelled in a cloud of smoke and with a loud bang.

However, the disadvantage was that the matchlock musket was much better suited to use by the infantry than the cavalry. The cavalry needed pistols that could be fired on horseback and could be lit without using a

LEFT An early 17th-century musketeer fires a matchlock musket. The musket replaced the arquebus, a firearm used from the 15th to the 17th centuries. The matchlock gradually became lighter and more compact in design and more efficient to use.

ABOVE Matchlock musket from around the late 17th century as painted by the circle of the Master of Calamarca.

constantly glowing match that was exposed to the weather. However, matchlocks were cheap and simple to produce, and so stayed as part of armed warfare on the battlefield for over 200 years. Although considered obsolete in the 16th century, some matchlocks were still being used during the 18th century.

Fire-lock mechanisms
Throughout history gunmakers have attempted to improve their weapons and make them easier to hold and shoot. After the development of the matchlock there was a move towards producing something more elegant with a more effective method of ignition. What was required was a device to produce a fire on demand. In the 16th century matchlocks were replaced by fire-lock mechanisms (so-named because they created fire by striking pyrite against steel). Early versions used the wheel-lock mechanism, but the more efficient flintlock mechanism soon followed.

Development of the pistol

Although some of the early matchlocks were small, essentially they were not "small arms". They were more closely aligned with small shoulder – or long arms. Early pistols were often referred to as "small arquebusses". The arquebus was a small firearm used during the 15th to 17th centuries, using the matchlock mechanism. The arquebus would later slowly be succeeded by the larger musket, a muzzle-loading shoulder gun with a long barrel, beginning in the 16th century. Surviving examples of small handguns or pistols fitted with matchlocks are extremely rare and were not widely used, except in Japan where the snap-matchlock was in common use. The term "pistol" did not come into general use before the 16th century. Its origins are unclear. It may have developed from the word *pistolet* which in the 14th century meant both a dagger and a firearm.

ABOVE A Japanese matchlock musket from the 18th century. The snap-matchlock mechanism was used in Japan until the 19th century.

The wheel-lock

In the early years of the 16th century there came an invention that was a milestone in the history of firearms – the wheel-lock. The matchlock had relied on a lighted match which was awkward to hold and entirely susceptible to the weather. It was normally held between the fingers and was dangerous to use. Seventeenth-century accounts tell of careless gunners going to replenish powder, forgetting that they were holding a match, and as a result blowing up entire powder magazines. The wheel-lock solved this problem, as the gun could simply be aimed and fired. It remained in use until about 1650.

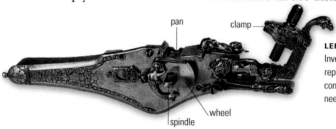

pan clamp wheel spindle

LEFT An example of the revolutionary wheel-lock mechanism. Invented in the early 16th century, this development represented a firearm milestone. It was safer and more convenient than a matchlock, since there was no longer a need to keep a smouldering match close to loose gunpowder.

How a wheel-lock worked

The wheel-lock worked like a giant cigarette lighter. A wheel cut with slots turned against a piece of iron pyrite, producing a shower of sparks that ignited the powder in the pan. The wheel was turned by a short chain. Protruding from the wheel was a spindle. A spanner was used to wind the mechanism and this depressed the spring and wound the chain round the spindle. When the wheel was fully wound it was locked by a series of levers. Pulling the trigger withdrew the locking lever and the wheel then revolved around the pyrite. The pyrite was held in jaws at the end of a curved arm, which was lowered manually against the wheel. The pan had a sliding cover operated by a button. In later wheel-locks the pan-cover slid back automatically when the trigger was pulled.

An Italian invention

Recent research by arms historian Claude Blair has established that the wheel-lock was almost certainly invented and first used in the province of Friuli in north-east Italy, in the early years of the 16th century. The letters of Luigi da Porto (1485–1529), an author and military commander in Venice, provided the evidence. In 1510 he was on campaign in Friuli and visited the city of Cividale where he observed some of the citizens using handguns for "shooting little birds high in flight" and also fish in clear water. He also describes an action between Venetian and Imperial German forces in which "little guns", which resembled iron maces, were used to great effect. He describes the guns as being "three spars long", although this does not translate to any known measurement.

RIGHT Cross-section through a firearm showing the workings of the wheel-lock. A spring was connected to the wheel's axle by a short length of chain. The axle was wound back to put the spring under tension. When ready to fire, the trigger was pulled. The wheel was released and would spin rapidly, scraping against the pyrite. White-hot particles from the pyrite fell into the flash pan, igniting its powder and then the main charge.

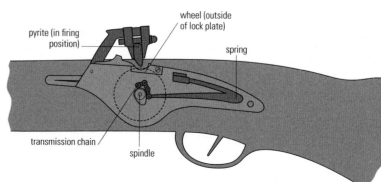

pyrite (in firing position)

wheel (outside of lock plate)

spring

transmission chain

spindle

BELOW French wheel-lock pistol. The elaborate engraving and high-quality materials are typical of French pistol manufacture. They reflect the complexity of the wheel-lock mechanism, which required a high level of craftsmanship.

RIGHT Wheel-lock six-shot revolver from Germany, dated around 1600. This multi-barrelled firearm has a six-chambered cylinder that needs to be rotated by hand.

It is almost impossible to shoot birds in flight or fish in water with a matchlock, as the "flash in the pan" (the explosion of gunpowder in the pan) acted as a warning. This led inevitably to the conclusion that the little guns must have been wheel-locks. As Friuli province belonged to Venice, it also explains why some of the earliest examples of the wheel-lock are to be found in the Doge's armoury in the Palazzo Ducale, Venice. Two of these are horseman's axes, perhaps the "iron maces" that Luigi da Porto saw in Cividale. These have been dated to about 1520.

The wheel-lock in Germany

German gunsmiths also seem to have adopted the wheel-lock early in the 16th century, as there is an account in 1507 of a servant being given money by the steward of Cardinal Ippolite d'Est to go to Germany and buy "a gun of the type that is ignited with a stone". Another reference dating from 1515 describes a young German accidentally shooting a girl in the neck with a gun that "fired itself". An indication of how novel and dangerous wheel-locks were considered to be in the early 16th century is the edict issued in 1517 by Maximilian I (1459–1519) banning their use in the Habsburg empire.

The earliest-dated wheel-lock pistol was made for the Emperor Charles V (1519–56), almost certainly

by a German gunsmith. It is dated 1534 and has a stock shaped like the grip of a dagger. It still has its original key. Although the mechanism remained basically the same, there were changes to the shape of the stock of wheel-lock pistols. By the end of the 16th century the stock was angular; one type of German wheel-lock, the "puffer", which was fashionable in the 1580s, had a stock terminating in a large ball. This allowed it to be drawn from large holsters, which were then fashionable. Wheel-locks were in use until the last quarter of the 17th century, but were being superseded by other forms of ignition by the 1650s.

RIGHT A horse soldier with a wheel-lock pistol, from the *Kunstbuchlin* by Jost Amman, Frankfurt, 1599. Although the development of the wheel-lock was not widely adopted because they were expensive to produce, they allowed pistols to be aimed and fired with one hand.

The snaphance

An important development in the history of firearms, the snaphance led directly to the invention of the flintlock. The snaphance was an improvement on most of the previous systems of ignition. It was almost certainly a German invention based on the snap-matchlock. Invented in the 1540s, it was rapidly adopted throughout Europe. Local variants of the snaphance lock were developed throughout the 17th century.

Early snaphance designs

In the 16th century a suitable replacement for the wheel-lock needed to be found for military use. It required something cheaper and simpler than the wheel-lock. The snaphance lock was invented in about 1540. A Florentine ordnance dated 1547 describes some guns having locks of this form. The earliest snaphance lock known is to be found on a gun in the Royal Armoury, Stockholm. This is one of a group of thirty-five documented as having been fitted with these new locks at the Royal workshops at Arboga in central Sweden in 1556. The miquelet was a Mediterranean version of the snaphance lock. Both the snaphance lock and the miquelet played an important part in the development of the flintlock, the next step

BELOW Part of a snaphance lock from about 1580. The action of the mechanism was likened to a cock or hen pecking at grain, possibly the origin of the word "cock" for the arm of the mechanism.

forward in the development of firearms.

The name of the snaphance lock probably derived from a Dutch expression describing its action – like that of a pecking hen or cock ("snap haan"). Although this suggested a Dutch origin for the lock, the evidence seems to contradict this, as some of the earliest known snaphances are German and this type of lock was almost certainly a German improvement on the earlier snap-matchlock.

The workings of the snaphance

In the snaphance lock, the cock was fitted with jaws that hold flint or iron pyrite. The cock was pulled back against a large spring and when the trigger was pulled the cock fell and the pyrites or flint struck a pivoted arm known as the steel plate (or battery). This produced sparks which ignited the powder in the pan. In its earliest form the pan-cover had to be opened before pressing the trigger. There were variations of the lock throughout Europe.

BELOW Cross-section through a firearm showing the workings of the snaphance lock. The lock was invented in around 1540. In the snaphance system, the flint was held in a clamp at the end of the cock. Once the trigger was pulled, the cock was released and, under strong pressure, the flint struck against the steel plate (or battery). White-hot steel shavings were produced that fell into the flash pan and ignited the priming powder. The steel could be retained in a "safe" position, forward of the pan if required. The cock could not then cause a spark if accidentally released.

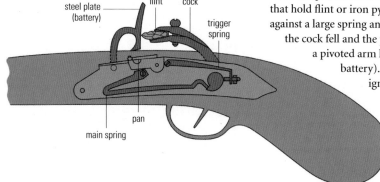

The miquelet or patilla

Another form of snaphance was the Mediterranean lock or miquelet, widely used in southern Europe and northern Africa. The Spanish version of this lock was known as a patilla lock. At least one writer on Spanish firearms in the late 18th century declared that the miquelet was a Spanish invention, although the evidence contradicts this. The snaphance was probably introduced to Spain in the 1570s. The main characteristics of the Spanish snaphance were the large external mainspring, which acted on the heel of the cock, and the steel plate (battery) made in two parts so that the front could be replaced. The steel plate was cut with a series of vertical grooves. The most noticeable feature, however, is the form of the jaws, which were long and rectangular and held together by a screw with a large open ring at the top.

The snaphance was most widely used in Italy. It had its own local variation – the Roman lock – which had a mainspring operating on the end of the cock, and two sears to allow for the half-cock and full-cock position. It had a horizontal sear and the usual separate pan-cover and steel plate. This type of lock possibly derived from English locks, which were very popular in Italy in the 17th century.

The Baltic lock

Snapping-lock guns were mechanically simpler and much more reliable than wheel-locks. One of the earliest forms of snaphance was known as the Baltic lock, characterized by prominent jaws held by a screw, a cock formed as a long bar with shallow downward curve and an extension at the back. This extension caught on a sear which operated horizontally through the lock. The mainspring was mounted on the outside of the lock-plate.

The Netherlandish lock

There were local variations of the snaphance produced in the Low Countries, and in England and Scotland. The Netherlandish lock had a cock with a projection at the rear, which connected with a sear. The pan-cover opened automatically when the lock fell and the steel was attached to the end of a pivoting arm. The Netherlands developed a trade in the lock.

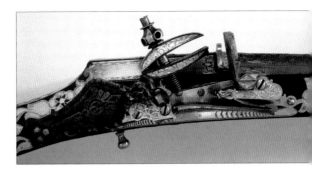

ABOVE A miquelet lock sporting gun from Algeria. Sometimes known as the Mediterranean lock, the miquelet was characterized by large jaws that held the flint, and by a large main spring.

The Scottish lock

There is some evidence to show that the snaphance was known in the early 17th century as a Scottish lock. With their engraved brass stocks and locks, Scottish firearms have always been appreciated as curiosities and enjoyed wide distribution in the 16th and 17th centuries. The two earliest Scottish snaphances known are a pair with left- and right-handed locks in the armoury of the Electors of Saxony in Dresden. They are dated 1598.

The English lock

A type of snaphance found on English firearms of the 1630s is known as the English lock. This could be engaged at the half-cock position. This was a safety device for the lock. Like the Baltic lock, the English lock has a back-catch, which is caught in a notch cut into the back of the cock.

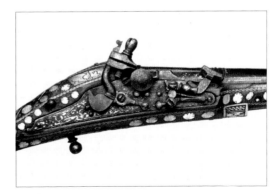

ABOVE A highly decorated 16th-century snaphance. The pistol shows the mechanism's high level of sophistication. The flintlock that was developed during the 17th century was less complex to produce.

The early flintlock

The invention of the flintlock in the early 17th century brought together the best features of the local snaphance designs. The flintlock was comparatively simple and very efficient, and was widely used on pistols and long guns. It originated in France but, by the middle of the 17th century, it was in use in most European countries. Because of its popularity the flintlock was in service for over 200 years and was still being made in the 1830s.

The first flintlocks

The flintlock was a development of the earlier snaphance. The early mechanism, sometimes called a doglock, has the steel and pan-cover made as one unit. The sear moves vertically, engaging in two notches cut in the tumbler (a steel cam attached to the axis shaft of the cock). These notches give either half-cock or full-cock as required, the safety position being half-cock.

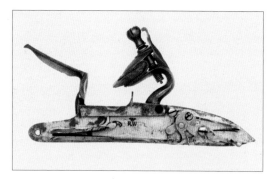

ABOVE An English flintlock mechanism from London of around 1775. The flintlock mechanism was relatively straightforward and reliable. It became the primary means of ignition for muskets and pistols for the best part of 300 years.

To fire the weapon the cock was pulled back to full-cock and the trigger was pulled. The flint struck the steel, which opened the pan lid and created a spark which fell into the powder. The powder ignited and set off the main charge of powder which was placed in the barrel, with the propellant, such as a ball.

The flintlock was almost certainly invented by a member of the le Bourgeoys family who worked in Lisieux, Normandy. Jean, Pierre and Marin le Bourgeoys had a workshop which specialized in the production of mechanical devices such as locks and watches, and Marin was mechanic to the king. The earliest datable flintlock mechanism is to be found on a French royal gun from the famous cabinet d'armes of Louis XIII. The stock was inlaid with the royal cipher and the barrel was stamped with the mark of Pierre le Bourgeoys. As Pierre died in 1627, the flintlock is likely to have originated sometime in the 1620s.

The earliest recorded pistol using the flintlock system is a revolver in the Kremlin armoury, Moscow. It was made by a Russian gunmaker named Pervusha Isaev who worked in the Kremlin armoury around 1625 and had clearly come across contemporary French flintlocks.

RIGHT Cross-section through a firearm showing the workings of the flintlock. The flash pan, or frizzen, is filled with priming powder and then closed to protect it. The cock holding the flint is then drawn back to half-cock. In this mode the weapon cannot be fired. To fire the weapon the cock is pulled back to full-cock. When the trigger is pulled the flint strikes the steel, which opens the pan lid and creates a spark which falls into the powder. The powder ignites and sets off the main charge, which has been placed in the barrel.

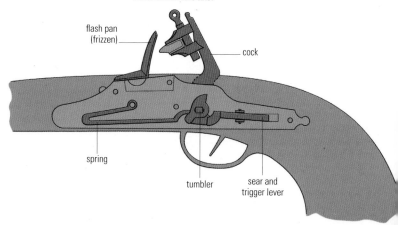

flash pan (frizzen)

cock

spring

tumbler

sear and trigger lever

Common features

Flintlocks dating from the first half of the 17th century have several easily recognizable characteristics. The lock-plate was flat, attached to the stock by two screws, and the upper and lower edges were usually parallel. In early examples the lock-plate extended downwards at the centre, revealing a feature found on the earlier wheel-locks. The cock was flat, with a long, curved narrow neck and forward jaws to hold the flint. Early flintlock pistols were very long, the barrels supported by a full stock which was flat and curved gently at the butt-end, which made the early pistols appear very graceful. Initially the butt-cap (its base) had a short spur extending down the stock. By the end of the 17th century this spur extended almost to the lock-plate. In about 1630 a lock-plate and cock of concave section were introduced, for added strength. After 1660 the profile of the lock-plate became concave. It is these features that enable the specialist to date flintlock pistols accurately.

National characteristics

With the spread of the flintlock across Western Europe after the 1630s, national characteristics began to emerge. Each workshop had its own special, easily recognizable style. France dominated the firearms trade in the early 17th century and many fine flintlock pistols that are preserved in the famous armouries of Europe were made by the gunmakers of Paris.

In Scotland the true flintlock was not introduced until about 1700, the earlier snaphance being preferred. The shape of Scottish pistols was always very distinct and the flintlock is found on pistols with the characteristic heart-shape and ram's horn butt.

By the middle of the 17th century the form of the flintlock was fully developed and it changed little over the next century. One technical feature that was found on some later flintlocks was the *detent*. This was a small, hinged lever attached to a tumbler, the mechanism which held or released the power of the mainspring on the cock. The *detent* stopped the sear from going to the half-cock position as the cock fell.

Decoration

The stock of a flintlock pistol could be elaborately carved and decorated. One very distinctive group of pistols made by the gunmakers of Maastricht in the Low Countries in the 1650s have stocks of carved ivory, the butt-caps terminating in carved classical heads with helmets in the Baroque style.

Italian flintlock pistols of the latter part of the 17th century are also very distinctive. Gunmaking centres like Brescia in northern Italy were famous for their firearms. A feature of their work is the use of chiselled, engraved and pierced steel to decorate the stock. The locks are chiselled in low relief with flowers and animals, and the butt-plates are decorated with finely pierced and engraved mounts. Engraving was a decorative technique widely used on the mounts and locks of firearms because it did not weaken the working parts by removing too much metal from the structure.

Compared to the work of continental gunsmiths, the products of English makers during the 17th century were comparatively modest, the decoration being usually limited to rather naïve engraving, although pierced silver butt-caps are occasionally found on late 17th-century English flintlocks.

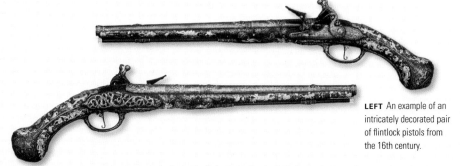

LEFT An example of an intricately decorated pair of flintlock pistols from the 16th century.

Breech-loaders and early revolvers

As the development of the handgun continued, the minds of both craftsmen and gun-users turned to the problem of how to fire more shots while taking the least amount of time to reload. Both the breech-loading system for pistols and early revolvers were attempts to improve efficiency in this area.

BELOW A flintlock breech-loading magazine pistol from 1780. The use of breech-loading mechanisms demonstrated the continual quest to increase the speed of reloading; however, with powder and ball they were rarely successful.

Breech-loading

There are early documentary references to breech-loading guns by the middle of the 14th century. A late 15th-century manuscript from the University Library at Evlangen in Germany illustrates some breech-loading handguns with separate reloadable chambers. The earliest surviving breech-loading firearms date from the early 16th century. These generally have a hinged section at the breech which can be opened to allow a reloadable chamber containing powder and ball to be inserted. A carbine (a small firearm) made for Henry VIII of England, dated 1537, is of this type.

The turn-off barrel

Another form of breech-loader used a system in which the barrel could be unscrewed. This was widely used in England during the 17th and 18th centuries, particularly on "Queen Anne"-style flintlock pistols. It became apparent that greater accuracy could be achieved if a large ball was used with a rifled barrel that unscrewed. A rifled barrel had a number of grooves that have been cut, pressed or forged into the barrel of the weapon to stabilize the projectile. It is recorded that Prince Rupert hit the weathercock of St Mary's church in Stafford, England in 1642, twice in succession, using rifle-barrelled pistols.

Barrels could also be hinged so that they "broke" rather like a modern shotgun. When the trigger-guard was pulled back it revealed a locking-catch on the top of the barrel. The charge and ball were located in a separate reloadable chamber. The best breech-loading systems relied on a vertical plug which could be unscrewed by turning the trigger-guard. Patents were taken out in the 18th century for this system but they were used almost entirely on long guns rather than pistols. Patents were also taken out in the 19th century for barrels that swivelled and chambers that pivoted.

The Roman-candle system

The problem of making a firearm that could fire a series of shots was solved initially by increasing the number of barrels. However, by the 16th century the idea of the super-imposed load was developed. It was known as the "Roman-candle system", named after a firework that threw out a series of burning balls. A series of charges were placed next to each other, the bullets being pierced and loaded with fuse. In theory, when the first charge was fired, the ignition should have passed to the one behind it, firing the charges in a measured series. This system was used on specially designed wheel-lock pistols which fired three shots, but needed three separate locks.

French four-shot repeater

In the 1630s a clockmaker of Grenoble in France produced a repeater that could fire four shots from a single barrel. In order to prevent all the charges going off together – a major problem with superimposed loads – the pistol had to be carefully loaded with tight-fitting wads and balls to separate each charge.

The sliding lock
Another system developed in the 1780s for flintlock pistols was known as the sliding lock. Four shots could be fired from four touch-holes, the lock being slid along the lock plate on a bar to connect with each touch-hole.

Magazine systems
Before the invention of the cartridge that contained powder, ball and primer, a repeater had to have separate "magazines" for the powder and ball. In the mid-17th century a Florentine gunmaker, Michele Lorenzoni, developed a repeating system for pistols that used separate magazines for the powder and ball. It also had a priming magazine on the lock. The pistol was primed and cocked by means of a lever on the side, powder and ball passing into the chamber when the pistol was raised and lowered. Versions of this system were made in England as late as 1800.

The magazine system developed by the Kalthoff family in the 1640s is only found on long guns, although a version was used on pistols made by the German gunsmith Sigmund Klett.

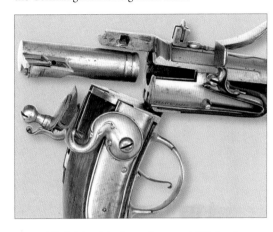

ABOVE A flintlock breech-loading gun from around 1690. Breech-loading of the powder and ball led the way to new developments such as the metal cartridge, shown above, which would replace the powder, ball and primer and eventually make the flintlock mechanism obsolete.

The early revolver

LEFT The seven-barrel revolving flintlock. The introduction of revolving barrels meant it was no longer necessary to reload after each shot, though the primer had to be replaced in the flash pan. The system would work better with the percussion cap lock.

The earliest example of a revolver is generally accepted to be a three-barrelled matchlock pistol in the Palazzo Ducale, Venice, which dates from about 1540. The barrels are turned manually and locked in place by a spring catch. Another early revolver is the three-barrelled wheel-lock pistol etched with devices associated with the Emperor Charles V. The pistol is of steel and fires steel darts from small-calibre barrels. A wing-nut at the end of the stock allows the barrels to be moved and locked. Firearms with revolving cylinders and single barrels were known by 1600, and the 17th and 18th centuries

saw several ingenious versions. One of the best known is the six-chambered snaphance revolver made by John Dafte in the 1680s. It has a brass barrel and cylinder and six chambers, each of which aligns with the barrel when the pistol is cocked. The Swiss gunsmith James Gorgo also made a revolver in the late 17th century with three chambers, the cylinder being released by pulling up the trigger guard. The late 18th century saw the development of the pepperbox (an early form of revolving repeating pistol), but it had been anticipated in the 1730s with the five-barrel pistol made by Johan Gottfried Kolbe. It was manually cocked for each shot, the barrels rotating when the pistol was cocked.

Flintlock development

The invention of the flintlock was to have a transforming effect on world history. Although imperfect in many ways and liable to misfire, the flintlock's success was based on its essential simplicity and ease of maintenance. The testament to its success was that the flintlock remained the basic ignition system for a pistol or musket for over 200 years.

RIGHT A Royal Navy Sea Service pistol from 1805. A typical pistol of this kind would have a walnut stock and be fitted with a brass trigger guard and a brass butt cap. The elegant simplicity of the design also speaks of reliability, essential for seamen in battle.

Flintlock pistols

The flintlock pistol had a comparatively short range and, as it was often not rifled, it was also not very accurate. It was normally used as a close-range back-up to the sword or cutlass, as a self-defence weapon, or for duelling.

During the 18th century, a pattern of Sea Service pistols began to emerge in the Royal Navy, and these were often used by boarding parties, in addition to the cutlass, or they could be used to repel boarders. These pistols, some of which were manufactured by Richard Wilson in England, were either produced in 300mm/12in long form or 225mm/9in short form, the latter being better suited to the mêlée of a boarding

ABOVE The flintlock pistol was highly regarded by pirates and carried when boarding ships. However, reloading was so slow that pirates often used the pistol's butt as a club.

party. A typical Sea Service pistol would have a walnut stock, fully stocked to the muzzle, and would be fitted with both a brass trigger guard and a brass butt cap. It would have a pipe for the ramrod (which was inserted into the gun's barrel). The ramrod itself was made of wood and had a brass tip. The pistol would have a steel trigger and there was also a steel belt hook fitted on the side. The hook would have made the pistol easy to carry and to replace on the belt when it had been fired.

Apart from its use by the navy, the flintlock pistol was also used by cavalry in the 18th and 19th centuries. It was, of course, impossible to reload while in the midst of a charge or a mêlée with the enemy, so the pistol would normally be fired in the first instance when reasonably close to the enemy lines, to cause as much damage and confusion as possible, and the cavalry cutlass (a short, curving sword) would then be used for close-quarter action.

Like the Sea Service Pistol, the British also introduced a standard type of cavalry pistol in 1796. Called the New Land Cavalry Pistol, it was designed for units such as the Royal Horse Artillery. Fitted with a flat butt and a ring to make it easy to carry when not in use, it also had a ramrod that swivelled to make it easier and quicker to reload when on horseback.

Huguenot gunmakers in England

Compared with guns made in France, which was one of the chief centres of gunmaking in Europe, English guns were relatively plain in design. Strangely enough, this characteristic may not be entirely native to England for many Huguenot gunmakers came to England as refugees in the 17th century and they would have had a significant influence on the design of English guns.

Pocket pistols

Flintlock pistols, however, were not all designed for the derring-do of the battlefield or the high seas. Gunmakers were also conscious of a market that continues to be lively today – for discreet, elegant weapons to be used in self-defence. In the days of highwaymen, this was a useful asset. Bunney of London, for example, is known to have manufactured a 150mm/6in ladies' gold pistol with an elegantly worked stock. Such a weapon could be easily concealed about the person and used to devastating effect if necessary. There is also a man's version in plainer style of the same proportions.

The box lock

Concealment of a flintlock pistol threw up an obvious difficulty. The mechanism was large and unwieldy and would be liable to get snagged, making quick deployment difficult. Gunmakers therefore developed what is known as the "box lock". This was a system whereby the cock and frizzen were removed from the sides and concealed in the body of the pistol, only emerging once the trigger was pulled. The pan was taken away leaving only a saucer-shape depression surrounding the touch-hole. In some versions, the

ABOVE A pair of 18th-century lady's muff pistols made by Charles Gourley of Glasgow. The length of each gun was under 125mm/5in so could be carried easily. They were also louder than the average pistol to frighten off assailants, but would be unlikely to cause serious damage.

trigger and trigger guard were also concealed in the body of the weapon, making it a very easy armament to carry. In this case the trigger was revealed once the weapon was cocked.

Flintlocks in America

The flintlock mechanism in Europe was the mainstay of military forces both on land and at sea for several centuries. It was also hugely important, as a musket or rifle, in colonial America. Although the flintlock mechanism was complex, it was also relatively easy to manufacture, maintain and highly reliable. For the colonists who lived in America in the 17th century it had a huge influence on their ability to survive and to expand westwards. They were used to kill game to feed their families, defend the homestead and to exert dominance over the native American population.

The American flintlock musket evolved from the colonists' weapons. It was effectively used by US forces in the American War of Independence (1775–83) and in the War of 1812, against the English army where it was nicknamed the "Kentucky rifle". The rifle was also the friend of the solitary backwoodsman.

ABOVE *Trade from the Monongahela* by Gayle Hoskins, showing American backwoodsmen buying and testing Kentucky rifles. Whereas blacksmiths had previously been concerned exclusively with horseshoes and similar requirements, the growing importance of firearms led to the development of a skilled cottage industry.

The percussion system

Although the flintlock was a successful mechanism, it also had its limitations. Two factors led to the replacement of the flintlock by a more efficient system. One was the creation of fulminate of mercury and the other was the ingenuity of a Scottish pastor, Alexander John Forsyth, who developed its use in the new percussion system.

Early gunpowder experiments

From the early 17th century, chemists and military specialists had been experimenting with ways to increase the explosive power of gunpowder. Giuliano Bossi, writing in 1625, recommended adding antimony or mercury precipitated with acid. A German alchemist, Johann Kunchel (1630–1703), is thought to have discovered fulminate of mercury,

ABOVE An example of a percussion pistol with a scent-bottle lock made by Alexander John Forsyth. Although Forsyth's percussion system was a big advance, there were a number of teething problems before the system was perfected.

which was later used in the percussion system. There were a number of experiments by French chemists in the 18th century that replaced gunpowder with fulminate of mercury. These were unsuccessful as the fulminates were highly volatile and either detonated too quickly or burst the cannon or firearm in which they were used.

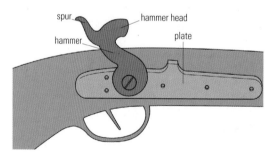

spur — hammer head
hammer — plate

ABOVE Diagram showing the external view of the percussion system. The system was developed to overcome the disadvantages of the flintlock ignition. Many flintlocks were converted to the percussion system. The system is exactly the same as the flintlock in terms of its internal mechanisms and, like the flintlock, the hammer used could be held in uncocked, half-cocked and fully-cocked positions.

RIGHT Wall tablet memorial to Alexander John Forsyth, inventor of the firearm percussion system, in 1807, Tower of London. Forsyth invented the system as a result of a logical necessity to reduce the delay in setting off the main charge.

The work of Forsyth

In 1800 Edward Howard published a paper on mercury fulminate in the *Philosophical Transactions of the Royal Society*. His work came to the notice of an amateur chemist and mechanic of Aberdeen, the Reverend Alexander John Forsyth (1768–1843). Forsyth was also a keen sportsman. Although the flintlock was reliable, it had its faults. The priming powder was easily affected by damp, but more serious from the sporting point of view was the problem of the delay between the priming powder being ignited in the pan and the main charge in the barrel being set off. The puff of smoke from the priming powder frequently alerted the game as well.

Using fulminate

Forsyth realized that if fulminate could be used instead of priming powder, a gun could be fired very quickly once the trigger had been pulled. He had already written a paper on fulminate in 1799 and by 1805 had developed a lock, which used fulminate of mercury instead of priming powder to detonate the main charge. The old flintlock mechanism could be converted to the new percussion system very easily and cheaply. The cock was replaced by a hammer, the steel and spring were removed. The priming pan would be replaced by the circular plug around which the scent-bottle magazine revolved. It was not necessary to alter the interior working of the lock as the hammer, like a cock, was operated by the mainspring.

Forsyth was cousin to the influential characters Henry and James Brougham, who introduced him to Sir Joseph Banks, a patron of science and Member of Parliament. This led to an introduction to Lord Moira, Master General of the Ordnance. Moira realized how useful firearms using the new percussion system would be to the British army, and arranged for Forsyth to have a workshop at the Tower of London. Although initially he received some financial support, Forsyth had difficulty in getting anyone to make the new lock, and also in obtaining sufficient fulminate. A gun-lock and a lock for a small cannon were tried out at Woolwich but the results were disappointing, and an unfavourable report about the new lock was made to the Board of Ordnance. Forsyth was aware that the military potential of his invention could not be immediately realized, especially when a new Master of the Ordnance stopped his work at the Tower.

The 1807 patent

On 11 April 1807 Forsyth took out a patent for the new lock and in 1808, established a business with James Brougham in London at the Forsyth Patent Gun Co. Much of his later career was spent protecting his patent from infringement by competitors.

The scent-bottle lock

To hold the fulminate powder, Forsyth used a container shaped like a flat scent-bottle. It held enough to prime 30 shots. At the top was a striking pin operating against a spring. The container was attached to the lock by a round plug, which allowed it to rotate, and had a channel that led to the touch-hole. The scent-bottle magazine was rotated to drop some fulminate into a cavity on the top of the plug. It was then returned to its original position so that the striker was at the top. Instead of a cock with jaws holding flint, Forsyth devised a hammer that hit the striking pin when the trigger was pulled.

RIGHT The scent-bottle lock was an ingenious device but also potentially dangerous, as the contents could ignite and explode.

The percussion cap

In Britain the percussion lock took some time to establish itself and it was not until about 1820 that it began to replace the flintlock on a large scale. On the Continent, however, the virtues of the new lock were immediately recognized and Parisian gunmakers were soon making copies and taking out patents based on the design of the Forsyth lock. One of the problems of the new percussion lock was how to control the rate of flow of the fulminate, and this led to another significant development – the percussion cap.

The tube lock

The London gun trade was initially very reluctant to accept the new percussion lock, principally because its craftsmen had spent their working lives on flintlocks and the change constituted an upheaval in manufacturing. However, in 1816 British gunsmith Joseph Manton took out a patent for a percussion lock in which the fulminate was contained in a tube set in the hammer. The tube could be taken out and reloaded. The disadvantage of the lock was that it was necessary to carry a number of loaded tubes when shooting, as a new one was needed for every shot.

The problem of the volatile fulminate, however, remained unsolved. One solution was to put the fulminate between two paper discs. Another was to make the fulminate into pellets covered with wax or iron oxide. Fulminate was very susceptible to damp and deteriorated quickly, so it had to be carefully stored.

In 1818 Joseph Manton took out another patent, this time for a tube lock in which the fulminate was contained in a copper tube. A section of the tube went directly into the touch-hole, and the hammer fell on

ABOVE AND BACK A Belgian percussion pistol and small copper and brass percussion caps. There is a small amount of fulminate of mercury in each cap, which is attached to the nipple and tube leading into the barrel. The cap ignites the gunpowder in the barrel. The hammer is shaped to strike the cap on the nipple and cover it so the nipple is not blown off. A striker hits the outside of the cap, which bends, and the primer is crushed, so it explodes.

the exposed section. This was held in place on a flat pan by a cover and spring. The detonation was very rapid but it tended to blow the tube to fragments – a danger to both the shooter and his immediate neighbours.

The problem of safely housing the fulminate was only solved with the invention of the percussion cap. This was made in the form of a small cylinder shaped like a top hat, which contained the fulminate. The lock was fitted with a nipple which was adjacent to the barrel, and had a channel leading directly into it. The cap fitted over the nipple and was detonated by the hammer when it fell.

Various claims for the invention

The percussion cap was so successful that many of the prominent sportsmen and gunmakers of the day claimed to have invented it. Colonel Hawker wrote an account in *Instructions to Young Sportsmen*, published

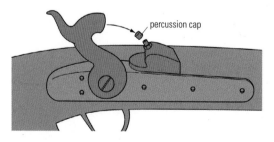

percussion cap

ABOVE Diagram showing the positioning of the percussion cap. The percussion system was relatively straightforward. The hammer struck a nipple on top of which was placed a copper cap containing the priming charge. This exploded on impact and set off the main charge.

in 1830, saying it was his idea and that the gunmaker Joe Manton had altered a pellet-lock gun to his design. Gunmaker Josef Egg claimed to have made a copper cap out of an old penny piece while James Purdey claimed a cap out of the brass ferrule of an umbrella. The most likely inventor, however, is English-born Joshua Shaw (1776–1860), who claimed to have made a series of percussion caps, first in steel, then in pewter, then in copper, in 1816. He went to America in 1817 and was finally granted a patent in 1822. The patent office must have believed his claim because in 1847 Congress awarded him $18,000 for the invention.

The earliest European patent for a percussion cap was granted to François Prelat, a Parisian gunmaker, in 1820 as an addition to another patent issued in 1818. However, as Prelat is known to have copied other gunmakers' discoveries, it is unlikely that he actually invented it, and Joshua Shaw is the most likely inventor.

ABOVE Shooting was to become a fashionable activity. This is a shooting gallery in a smart part of London, c.1825–1830.

Adopting the new system

One of the reasons why the percussion cap was slow to be adopted was the composition of the fulminate. The most commonly found priming powder used in early percussion locks was made from potassium chlorate, sulphur and charcoal, along with some other ingredients. The mixture gave very variable results and it also quickly corroded the nipple and the gun barrel.

In 1824 a London chemist took up the manufacture of percussion caps. He based the priming on fulminate of mercury, following a paper published in the *Philosophical Magazine and Journal* by E. Goode Wright, who advocated the use of fulminate of mercury because of its ease of manufacture and relative stability compared with other methods.

The under-hammer lock

The development of the percussion lock led to major changes in the design of firearms. One result was the under-hammer lock. The percussion lock was usually located on the top of the firearm, but on the under-hammer lock it was located on the underside. Under-hammer locks, however, were rare. Their advantage was that during shooting, the flash did not impair vision.

RIGHT Under-hammer box lock percussion pistol, of around 1850 with a turn-off rifled barrel. New designs allowed for a cleaner exterior and greater ease of concealment.

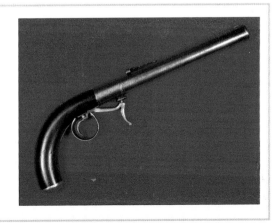

The development of cartridges

As with many handgun developments, there was one overriding criterion. This was the time it took to reload. Soldiers under fire were under pressure to reload as quickly as possible before the enemy was upon them. Sportsmen also needed to reload quickly before their prey escaped. The answer was the cartridge, where all the elements required for firing were contained in a single package.

Loading the gunpowder

In the early days of firearms, gunpowder was loaded into the muzzle of a barrel, followed by cloth and wadding, and then a lead ball. Hunters carried a powder flask, while the military used paper cartridges. The cartridge began as a thick paper tube, which contained both powder and the ball. When it was used with a muzzle loader, the base of the cartridge would be ripped off and the powder poured down through the muzzle into the barrel. The ball would then be inserted and the paper would be shoved down on top of the ball with the use of a ramrod, in order to keep powder and ball in place.

In the days before the flintlock, serpentine powder was used to prime the pan. Later, serpentine was no longer used and the user would prime the pan with some of the powder from the cartridge before pouring the remainder down the barrel. The flintlock

ABOVE 17th-century English powder flasks. The ritual of loading a flintlock musket, or pistol, with powder from a flask and a separate bullet came to an end with the invention of the cartridge.

Priming the flintlock

To prime the flintlock with a cartridge, the lock was half-cocked. The cartridge was torn open and enough powder was used to half fill the pan, away from the touch-hole. The pan was then shut and the remaining charge was poured down the barrel, followed by the paper and ball pushed into position by a ramrod. Once ignited, the flash shot through the touch-hole into the main charge in the barrel. The flintlock was a fairly reliable system, but it could fail in adverse weather.

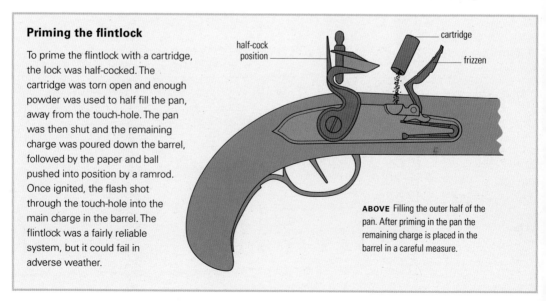

half-cock position

cartridge

frizzen

ABOVE Filling the outer half of the pan. After priming in the pan the remaining charge is placed in the barrel in a careful measure.

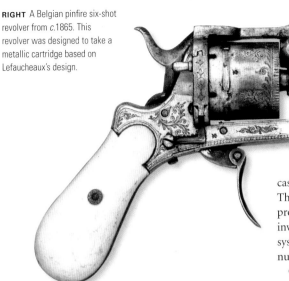

RIGHT A Belgian pinfire six-shot revolver from *c.*1865. This revolver was designed to take a metallic cartridge based on Lefaucheaux's design.

mechanism obviated the need to prime the pan as a separate operation, as a certain amount of powder would run through from the base of the barrel into the covered pan. This system was to prevail during most of the extensive flintlock era, and was mostly reliable as long as the powder in the flash pan stayed dry. This, of course, was not always the case, and on average three out of ten times the flash-pan powder would fail to ignite or the flash pan would ignite without setting off the main charge in the barrel.

After the development of the percussion system by John Forsyth and others, and the parallel development of fulminate of mercury, the next logical step was to contain all the various elements – the ignition, the main charge and the bullet – in one package. There were various experiments with different forms of cartridge, and there were also different schools of thought about the position of the percussion cap in the cartridge.

The pinfire cartridge

Johannes Pauly was a Swiss gunmaker working in Paris. In 1812 he developed and patented a breech-loading firearm and a new kind of cartridge, which was the early development of the pinfire cartridge. These designs were very well thought out, but for various reasons, gunmakers of the time did not follow up his ideas. Work continued in this field, and the pinfire cartridge was invented by a Frenchman called Casimir Lefaucheaux in 1835. The cartridge consisted of a brass case containing a percussion cap and a powder charge. The bullet filled the end of the brass case. A metal pin protruded from the side of the case and when knocked inwards it would ignite the percussion cap. This system proved to be popular and successful, and a number of different weapons were built around it.

One drawback of the Lefaucheaux system was that the protruding pin made the round less convenient to handle than the later rimfire or centrefire cartridges. The pin needed to be aligned correctly in a slot in the chamber, and it could cause the round to detonate if it were accidentally knocked. Lefaucheaux's son Eugene continued to improve both the cartridge and the design of the weapon after his father died in 1852. The system was refined and patented by another Frenchman, Clément Pottet, in 1855, and further work was carried out in London by Colonel Edward Boxer, who patented a centrefire cartridge with a metal base and coiled brass body.

BELOW The kit of an American Civil War cavalryman included French pinfire pistols and a cartridge case.

Paris gunsmiths such as Lefrancheaux were influential in the development of composite cartridges comprising paper and brass. A similar version was successfully used by gunsmith Johann Nikolaus van Dreyse for a needle gun – so named because of the extended pin that ran through the centre of the bolt to ignite the percussion cap. The most notable development was the placement of the percussion cap in the centre of the base of the brass cartridge, which is the same system used in modern centrefire cartridges.

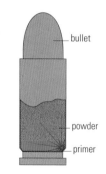

ABOVE The first rimfire cartridge was essentially just a percussion cap with a projectile pressed in the front, and a rim to hold it securely in the chamber.

The rimfire cartridge

The rimfire cartridge developed in the 1830s, although it was not started commercially until 1845. The rimfire cartridge was essentially a large percussion cap which contained not only the priming compound, but also the propellant powder and bullet. One disadvantage of the rimfire system was that the cartridge is rendered useless by the impact of the hammer and it could not be re-used (unlike other cartridges which could be reused by replacing the primer, gunpowder and bullet). It also had a shorter range. Due to the thin case they are limited to light, low pressure calibres (calibres relate the diameter of the inside of the barrel). If the calibre measurement is in inches then the calibre is quoted as decimal of an inch, so a gun with a diameter of 0.22in is a .22 or "twenty-two calibre". In the past, rimfire calibres up to .44 were common. Today's rimfires are of calibre .22 (around 5.5mm) or smaller.

The centrefire cartridge

In 1854 Charles Lancaster invented a cartridge which was sealed in a brass case. The brass at the base was thin enough for the pin to activate the percussion cap contained in the base of the cartridge.

ABOVE Pinfire pistols were used during the American Civil War (1861–65), although they were not always highly regarded because of their low power compared with other percussion revolvers, such as Colts, which were widely used on the battlefield.

This was a centrefire cartridge, which proved to be the most successful cartridge type and is one of the most commonly used for all large-calibre weapons today. There is some discussion as to the original patent for the centrefire cartridge, which is in itself an indication of the significance of the invention. It is said to have been invented in 1861 by the English gunmaker G. H. Daw, but Clément Pottet of Paris is also mentioned, and a London firm, the Eley Brothers, successfully won the patent.

In 1867 an Eley–Boxer centrefire cartridge was adopted by the British War Office for use in Enfield rifles. The original Eley–Boxer cartridge was made of solid brass. In 1870, Colonel Hiram Berdan of the US Ordnance Department developed a bottle-shaped brass cartridge with a cap and chamber at the base and flash holes drilled on either side. Modern cartridges are made from a brass and metal alloy. Centrefires today also are generally capable of higher-powered loads than rimfire.

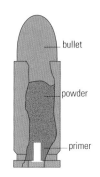

ABOVE A centrefire cartridge has the primer located in the centre of the base. Centrefires are generally capable of high-powered loads.

bullet

powder

primer

The advantages of a metal cartridge

The beauty of a metal case for some types of cartridges was that it expanded under the heat of the explosion and thus created a seal in the chamber. This increased the energy of the bullet towards the muzzle of the gun. It also prevented the gun user from being injured by escaping high-pressure gases as the trigger was pulled. The brass case of a centrefire cartridge could also be re-used once it had been ejected from the chamber. It had to be precisely manufactured to suit the dimensions of the particular gun for which it was intended. This entailed precision machining to fine tolerances of the parts integral to the gun and the cartridge itself. Different cartridges would be designed to carry different loads, and it would be important to match the right cartridge load to the pistol, otherwise the pistol would be liable to explode when it was fired. Cartridges are manufactured and named in imperial or metric sizes.

The needle gun

Johann Nikolaus Dreyse was a Prussian gunsmith who invented a military breech-loading needle gun. The system involved the use of a bolt which was used to open and close the breech, through which the cartridge was loaded. The bolt was locked by pulling it down in front of a lug in the frame. The "needle" was an extended firing pin that passed through the centre of the bolt. When released by the trigger, the needle would fly forward, pass through the paper cartridge and ignite a percussion cap at the base of the bullet. The cartridge used in this system was made up of four separate elements: the paper case itself, the powder charge, the priming cap and the bullet. The primer was placed between the bullet and the main powder charge so that the needle passed through the powder charge before igniting the primer.

Although it was a clever design and was highly effective for its time, the needle gun also had some inherent weaknesses. The fact that the needle had to pass through the bolt meant that, unless the parts were extremely well fitted and sealed, a certain amount of gas would leak through the bolt. Also, as the needle was present when the explosion took place, it was quickly subjected to wear and tear and would sometimes break.

ABOVE German needle-fire bolt-action military rifle from around 1851. The effectiveness of the needle and cartridge system was soon shown on the battlefield when the Prussian army succeeded in producing a more rapid rate of fire than its enemies. Other countries, such as France, soon caught up.

Manufacture, proof and trade

The term "lock, stock and barrel" is a reminder that the firearm was made up of several different components, each of which required different materials and different craftsmanship skills. The inherent and increasing complexity of the firearm was to pose a growing technological challenge to gunmakers, while the organization of the different trades was to become both a stimulus to and a sign of the growing process of industrialization, first in Europe and then elsewhere.

Craftsmanship

The manufacture of a firearm was a complex process and involved a number of different specialist trades relevant to the different parts of the firearm. The 16th-century origins of the firearm manufacturer Beretta, for example, lie in precision forging of steel barrels. As firearms became more complex, they not only called on the skills of metalworkers and forgers but also of woodworkers to develop the stock and experts in precision mechanisms to create the trigger and lock systems.

Each part of the lock mechanism for a flintlock pistol would have been hand-made. The trigger, powder pan, springs and screws would have been individually forged and filed.

ABOVE A gun is assembled at the Beretta gun factory in Italy. Craftsmanship skills would prove to be compatible with the advent of the machine age, and successful firearms manufacturers would find the right balance between the two.

Although early stocks for such weapons as the arquebus or matchlock were fairly rudimentary, later stocks for flintlocks, percussion weapons and breech-loaders were an integral part of the weapon. These needed to be worked with skill so that the metal parts fitted correctly and in alignment with each other, and so that the stock itself was strong enough to both support the weapon and absorb recoil.

Stocks were often made of well-seasoned hardwoods such as English walnut, although this did not necessarily always come from England. In addition to their utilitarian value, stocks were sometimes engraved to underline their fine workmanship. The barrel itself was often forged from a flat wrought-iron bar. Metalworking skills that included heating, hammering and boring would result in a smooth-bore interior. A separate process was used for rifling.

The quality of weapons depended to a large extent on developments in metallurgy. Weapons could not be made to fine tolerances if the metal could not be worked precisely. Due to the high pressures involved when a weapon was fired, this was of some significance.

The art of gunmaking had to take many factors into account. It needed to be fitted to its purpose, to have the right balance and "feel", and such details as the quality of the trigger pull would also be noticed. The craftsmanship of the gun evolved in the manufacture of finely weighted barrels, the creation of smooth-functioning locks and triggers and the sculpting of a fine stock. Alongside this individual craftsmanship came the advent of the machine age. Machines were designed to produce parts in greater volumes, though without the individual touch. The two processes could be successfully combined by bespoke gunmakers while volume manufacturers could claim that their products were often on a par with their handmade competitors.

The Birmingham Gun Quarter

The different skills required in the manufacture of a firearm were part and parcel of the process of industrialization in England. Different craftsmen focused on their individual products and they were brought together by the gun manufacturers to assemble the finished product. It made sense to keep the different trades as close together as possible in order to cut down on time and expense and as a result areas such as Birmingham's Gun Quarter became recognized as specialist areas for gunmaking. Not all of the parts were produced in the Gun Quarter, however. Locks, for example, often came from elsewhere.

In 1767 Birmingham in England had 35 gun and pistol manufacturers, 8 gun barrel manufacturers and filers, 5 gun barrel polishers and finishers, 11 gun lock manufacturers, forgers and finishers, and three gun-swivel and stock makers. The different parts were often sent to London to be made up by "fabricators" who assembled and sold the weapons.

LEFT Manufacture of arms around 1862. The organization of craftsmen and machinery to satisfy the demand for firearms was a significant stage in the Industrial Revolution.

Proving

The Birmingham Proof House is evidence of another important stage in gunmaking – the proving (testing) of barrels. The gun barrel would have a charge fired through it that was significantly more powerful than the one it was designed to fire. If there was any sign of weakness, such as distortion or cracking, the gun would fail the test. Otherwise, it would be awarded an official proof mark to prove its worthiness. The Birmingham Proof House was established in 1813 by Act of Parliament, and it became illegal to trade in arms without the award of a proof mark.

Due to the particular nature of gunmaking, it both thrived upon and contributed to the greater sophistication of the nascent industrial age. With the growth of large cities and, in the case of England, with labourers beginning to leave the land to seek work in the towns and cities, there was great scope for the development of a thriving gun trade.

The United States

In colonial America, gunsmiths also sprang up, though initially many of these would either assemble or repair firearms imported from England and elsewhere. In due course, the United States would be the pioneer of some of the most important small-arms designs of all time and would develop its own thriving gun trade.

ABOVE Smith & Wesson's revolver factory: *Scientific American* 24 January, 1880. Like Colt, Smith & Wesson soon became a major industrial concern with growing markets both at home and overseas.

Duelling pistols

As firearms became more accurate, they were used for hunting and for sport. In due course, the handgun in particular came to be used in duelling, a practice that had its roots in a warped code of honour. While an "honourable scar" might be obtained from the slash of a sword, firearms were inherently less difficult to control and the results were almost invariably fatal. In order to meet the ongoing demand, specialist manufacturers began to emerge who prided themselves in the sophistication and accuracy of their products.

A code of honour

Duelling has had a long and undistinguished history that pre-dates the medieval era. The throwing down of a gauntlet was the traditional challenge that would be followed in the pre-firearms era by a fight with swords. In England there was such a thing as a judicial duel, dating from the 11th century, which was only abolished by English law in 1819.

The nature of duelling, however, is such that it tells us less about the law of the state than it does about individual codes of honour. So precarious was the notion of honour that the offended person was "honour bound" to demand satisfaction for even the smallest slight, or risk a disastrous decline in his status. Similarly, the accused would either have to accept the challenge or risk being branded a coward. It was the direct opposite of the Christian teaching of "turn the other cheek".

ABOVE A matched pair of flintlock duelling pistols made by London gunmakers in 1805. Duelling pistols were designed to be identical in every way to give both contestants an even chance.

The use of pistols for duelling became more common from about the middle of the 18th century and, in order to ensure that the duellists should have an equal chance, the pistols were often designed as matching pairs and presented in a box. In some cases the box also contained miniature pistols to be used by the "seconds" (trusted representatives of each party who may stand in for the dueller). This would allow the seconds to defend themselves or to intervene if there should be any unorthodox behaviour.

Early makers of duelling pistols

The first set of duelling pistols was probably made in England, to very high specifications. As duelling was supposedly the preserve of "gentlemen", it was appropriate that the design and finish of duelling pistols should be suitably lavish, and this was particularly the case for French pistols. It was also important that the pistols should be both reliable and accurate. In the days of flintlocks, great care was taken to minimize the chances of a misfire by careful loading.

There were a number of pistol makers in both Europe and America who acquired considerable reputations for the quality of their products. These included Durs Egg, John Manton, John Twigg and Robert Wogdon of England; Gastinne Renette, Le Page and Nicolas Beutet of France; Auguste Francotte of Belgium; Continner of Vienna; and Simeon North, James Haslett and R. Constable of America.

Early duelling pistols tended to be lightweight designs, but heavier designs began to emerge. Part of the extra weight was in the barrel, which was designed to reduce recoil and improve accuracy. As with many flintlock firearms, duelling pistols were often converted to the percussion system, which radically increased their reliability.

Code Duello

Duelling was controlled by elaborate codes, which included the French Renaissance code, and an Irish code agreed at the Clonmel Summer Assizes in 1777 which was to some extent based on the French code. The Irish code had over 25 rules that stipulated how a duel should be managed and what constituted satisfaction for an insult.

The basis of any code was that, once an insult had been made, a challenge would be given and a place agreed where the duel could take place. Normally the contestants would bring seconds as well as a physician. The seconds might try to arrange a reconciliation between the parties and, if an apology was accepted, the duel would be called off.

The duel would be carried out on a piece of measured ground and details such as the number of paces between the contestants would be agreed.

ABOVE Pistols were increasingly used for duelling from the mid-18th century.

RIGHT Normally duels were carefully stage-managed. The "quick draw" from a holster belonged to the Wild West.

Sometimes the contestants would "delope", which meant firing into the air so as not to wound the other party. This practice was, however, forbidden in the Irish code.

Famous duels

There have been a number of notable duels through the ages. In 1598 the playwright Ben Jonson killed the actor Gabriel Spenser. In 1796 William Pitt the Younger had a duel with George Tierney. In 1809 George Canning had a duel with Lord Castlereagh and, in 1829, the Duke of Wellington had a duel with the 10th Earl of Winchelsea.

The duel between the duke and the earl followed public criticisms of the duke by the earl. The two met in Battersea Fields and the duke fired wide. Winchelsea returned the compliment, after which he agreed to publicly retract his accusations. The duel damaged the reputation of the Duke of Wellington and underlined public distaste for the practice of duelling. It is a good indication of the level to which the code of honour had become ingrained that, in two countries where the practice of duelling had been declared illegal, the Prime Minister of Great Britain and two leading American politicians should use the duel to seek their satisfaction. At the height of its notoriety, hundreds of duels per year were fought between less well-known individuals.

The Hamilton–Burr duel

In 1804 the United States Vice-President, Aaron Burr, fought a duel with the former United States Treasury Secretary, Alexander Hamilton, in which Hamilton was killed. By the time the Hamilton-Burr duel was fought, duelling had been declared illegal in New York, so the two men and their accomplices secretly crossed the Hudson River to a remote rocky ledge in New Jersey.

It is said that Hamilton may have deliberately aimed wide with his first shot, though another view is that, the bullet from Hamilton's gun was launched too early and went high. Burr is also said to have tried a non-fatal shot, but it did enough damage to Hamilton's internal organs to kill him.

ABOVE The 1804 duel between Aaron Burr and Alexander Hamilton in which Hamilton was killed. This duel was fought despite legislation in New York that prohibited duelling.

Eastern pistols and handguns

Firearms from the East have a rich and distinctive history. They are recognizable, both for their unique shapes and also for the characteristically rich decoration that distinguish them from more sober European products. Although some of these firearms were decorated European derivatives, many fine and original products were also developed in the East.

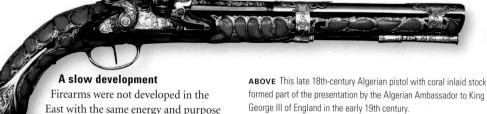

A slow development

Firearms were not developed in the East with the same energy and purpose as they were in Europe. The military tactics that flowed from the appearance of firearms were slow to develop. Codes of honour and concepts of how a warrior should behave meant that the sword was often preferred to the firearm. Moreover, unlike Europe, where a process of industrialization complemented firearms development, the manufacture and maintenance of firearms in the East was not as well developed.

However, it is almost certain that gunpowder was invented in the East, and the knowledge of its secrets are said to have been transmitted to Europe via Iran and India, where they are likely to have been recorded in Sanskrit, and then to the Maghrib (the West), which included Moorish Spain. In the 13th century the Arab alchemist Hasan al-Rammah wrote a description of how to make gunpowder, and Roger Bacon and Albertus Magnus visited the Spanish-based centres of learning to find out about it.

Despite its Eastern origins, the conservatism of the Ottoman Empire was such that little was done to take the next logical step – to develop the means by which the gunpowder could be used. It is said, however, that the Arabs fired a missile from a sealed tube of bamboo, filled with black powder, and the Chinese are believed to have developed one of the first metal handguns.

By the time of the Siege of Algeciras in southern Spain by Alfonso XI in 1343, the Christians discovered to their cost that the Muslims were armed with cannon.

ABOVE This late 18th-century Algerian pistol with coral inlaid stock formed part of the presentation by the Algerian Ambassador to King George III of England in the early 19th century.

The Balkans

The transfer of firearms technology from the West to the East largely took place via the Balkans. The Venetians are said to have taken firearms to the Balkans in 1352 and the Ottomans used firearms to defeat Christian crusaders at battles such as the Battle of Kosovo (1448).

Due to the ongoing threat of Muslim expansion, a Papal Bull of 1444 banned the trade of firearms with the Ottomans, but this and other bulls do not appear to have had much effect. After the dissolution of the monasteries in England in 1541, lead and bronze from the destroyed buildings were sold to the Turks, some of which may have been used for making weapons and ammunition.

The elite Ottoman corps known as the janissaries were the soldiers most likely to be equipped with firearms. The janissaries included a large proportion of young, originally Christian men from the Balkans who had converted to Islam, and they largely replaced the traditional cavalry, the spahis, as footsoldiers.

By the beginning of the 16th century, handguns were widely in use in the Ottoman Empire, but many of these were of European origin or were inspired by European designs and it is said that European-sourced firearms were preferred to the local variety by those who could afford them. It was soon discovered that when they malfunctioned there was little or no native expertise or backup from armourers to put them right.

ABOVE Siege of Belgrade, 1521, from *The Military Campaigns of Suleyman I*. The exchange between East and West in the Balkans would also include the transfer of knowledge about firearms.

A pistol might become little more than an ornate and expensive club. As in Europe, homemade firearms were made by different craftsmen and there was a system of testing and approval among the Turks, with the appropriate mark made on the pistol once it had been passed.

In the 18th and 19th centuries firearms continued to be imported into the Ottoman Empire in ever-greater numbers, and it provided a valuable market as the Industrial Revolution gathered pace. English firms such as the Birmingham Small Arms Company won substantial orders from the Ottoman Government.

The Maghrib

As European nations such as Portugal pushed down the west African coast in their quest for the route to India, and as France and Spain extended their influence in North Africa, the development of firearms in the Maghrib was duly influenced by European designs. Again, innate conservatism led to the retention of certain archaisms in design, and local influence was seen largely in the style of decoration,

which might include gold and silver wire or gold and silver damascene. In some parts, notably Algeria, coral was also widely used. Again, different craftsmen would produce parts of the firearm, and often these were manufactured to a high standard.

The Caucasus

Like the Balkans, the Caucasus is a link between Europe and Asia, and the region has its own tradition of weapon-making which speaks of a high level of craftsmanship and enjoys a high reputation. Typical pistols from the region from the beginning of the 19th century would have ivory ball butts and black, leather-covered stocks. Decoration with niello (an alloy used as an inlay in a design) was common.

Japan

Firearms were first introduced into Japan in 1542 by the Portuguese. The local warlords were keen to trade for more arms, and they also ordered local swordsmiths to copy the weapons. By 1575, at the Battle of Nagashino, Japanese battle tactics had changed to suit the introduction of firearms. By 1587, however, it was thought they might give too much power to the peasantry. Under the military dictatorship of the Tokugawa Shogunate, which lasted until 1868, firearms were believed to have been suppressed as part of a wider plan to maintain stability, but this was mostly notional, and on the whole they continued to be used.

ABOVE *Geijutsu Hideu Hue* (Accomplishments in the Secret Arts) by Japanese Ohmori Sakou, illustrated by Kuniyoshi, reveals the Japanese use of firearms in the mid-19th century.

The art of the gunmaker

Early firearms were sophisticated pieces of workmanship and the owners of these treasured possessions were invariably wealthy. Alongside the craftsmanship required to produce a firearm there grew the craft of decoration. The more complex the firearm was, the more elaborate was the decoration. The level of decoration, however, varied between different countries, with France producing some of the most lavish handguns and England the most sober. Gunmaking centres created their own styles.

Early decorated handguns

Even in their very earliest forms, firearms were sometimes decorated. The barrel of the late 14th-century cast-bronze handgun from Morko is roughly engraved with religious texts on the barrel and has the bust of a bearded man adjacent to the touch-hole. Bronze barrels were made in late medieval times, by founders used to producing decorated bronze wares, so it was no wonder the barrels were often ornate.

The earliest examples of decorated handguns date from the 1530s, including wheel-locks made for the Emperor Charles V (1519–56). The number of finely decorated wheel-lock guns far outnumbers those with matchlock mechanisms – this expensive, complicated mechanism was deemed to deserve rich decoration. Craftsmen from various traditions, specializing in decoration, therefore found themselves practising their skills on firearms. Barrels were chiselled and gilded, and wooden stocks inlaid with engraved staghorn.

ABOVE A pair of pistols by N. Boulet made for Murat in 1805, Musée de L'Armée, Paris. France produced some of the most lavishly decorated firearms, with French gunmakers dominating the trade in the 17th and early 18th centuries. It was a celebration of craftsmanship.

There has always been a link between the craftsmen who worked on gun-stocks and those who worked on small items of furniture such as cabinets and desks, because of the use of materials such as staghorn and ebony which were widely used for inlaid wood in the 16th and 17th centuries. The craftsmen who decorated high-quality firearms were careful to avoid techniques that would weaken either the stock or the barrel. For this reason, in the 16th century, etched decoration was always preferred to chiselling, and inlaid decoration to carving.

Sources of ornament

It seems from surviving examples that highly decorated firearms first began to be produced in quantity in the first quarter of the 16th century. Elaborate decoration was based upon the engraved sheets of designs which circulated in the workshops of different gunmakers. The craftsmen employed on the decoration of a gun would reflect elements of an engraved design, fitting them into the space available on a gun-stock or barrel. It is possible therefore to see the influence of artists such as German artist Virgil Solis and French goldsmith Etienne Delaune on firearms decoration.

A finely decorated firearm was the work of several craftsmen. The wooden stock was made by the stock-maker, the barrel maker produced the barrel, and the lock was made by yet another craftsman. Engraved designs made specifically for firearms were not apparent before the last quarter of the 16th century. After this period they become common.

It is from the 17th and 18th centuries that most surviving pattern books date, and it is possible to relate engraved and chiselled work from these periods to the pattern books of particular artists. Among the more notable are François Marcou (c.1657), Jean

Berain (c.1650) and De Lacollombe (c.1730). All three artists were French, but as French gunmakers dominated the trade in the 17th and early 18th centuries this is not surprising.

Gunmaking centres

Various gunmaking centres had their own particular decorative styles. Northern Italy, especially Brescia, used pierced steel and chiselled work; French gunmakers used chased gold; and the gunmakers of Tula in Russia used blued steel overlaid with tiny flowers in gold. By contrast, the best English makers used decoration very sparsely – the maker's name and some simple engraved scroll-work is often the only ornament. Silver mounts are frequently found on firearms, usually cast from moulds and applied to the stock. For the highest-quality work cast gold was used. The neo-classical presentation pistols by the French gunmaker Boutet are often mounted in gold. Five pistols made for the 19th-century exhibitions of 1851 and 1882 also by French gunmakers, were highly decorative and cannot have been intended for use. Some fine early Colt revolvers are richly engraved, but had the overall sense of design of the earlier periods.

Decorative techniques

A variety of techniques was used over the centuries to decorate firearms. The metal parts such as the barrel, lock, butt-cap and mounts were etched and gilded, damascened (inlaid) in gold and silver and chiselled. Some of the first chiselled work was done by Daniel and Emmanuel Sadeler, who worked for the Elector of Bavaria in the 1620s. The designs were usually based on the engravings of Etienne Delaure and were in low relief against a gold background, the relief decoration being coloured dark blue to make a vivid colour contrast. The stocks of pistols were inlaid with a variety of metals, especially brass and silver.

The subjects were drawn from mythology or from the chase. Firearms were widely used for hunting, especially in the 16th and 17th centuries.

Gunmakers followed contemporary ornamental styles extremely closely. French Rococo and Neo-classical styles are all found on firearms and there are even pistols made for presentation in the 19th century that are decorated in the style of the gothic revival, the stocks being set with medieval knights in architectural niches of carved ivory.

BELOW Dutch gunsmiths at work, c.1695.

Combined weapons

The somewhat unpredictable nature of early firearms, added to the elaborate and lengthy process of reloading, gave rise to the notion that the firearm should be combined with an edged weapon or another form of defence.

Early inventions

The idea of combining the mechanism of a firearm with another weapon was thought of as early as the 15th century. Some of the earliest wheel-locks were found on three crossbows in the Arsenale at Venice, dating from about 1510. Another interesting group of combined weapons are the gun-shields from the armoury of Henry VIII of England, many of which are preserved in the Tower of London and Windsor Castle, in England. Supplied in 1544 by an Italian merchant in Ravenna, these consisted of a steel-faced circular shield, fitted in the centre with a short, heavy, breech-loading pistol operating on the matchlock principle.

In addition to guns combined with maces and axes, firearms were also combined with a dagger. The wheel-lock mechanism was mounted on the face of the blade and the barrel was formed of the central section of the blade. The dagger became a gun when the tip of the blade was pulled out to reveal the barrel.

Different gunmaking centres produced their own distinctive combination arms. One such was the *fokos*, an axe with a small blade, mounted on an elaborately inlaid wooden shaft, on which is set a flintlock mechanism. The *fokos* was a speciality of the gunmakers of Teschen in Silesia and was popular in the late 17th century, mainly in Eastern Europe.

Hunting swords

Where combined weapons were most widely used was in the hunting-field. Hunting was a most important occupation, especially before the 19th century. Elaborate costumes and equipment were designed specifically for the chase. Included in this equipment were combined arms. These included spears combined with guns and, in particular, sword gun combinations. There are a number of short hunting swords dating from the 18th century which have short barrels mounted on the blade with a small flintlock set near

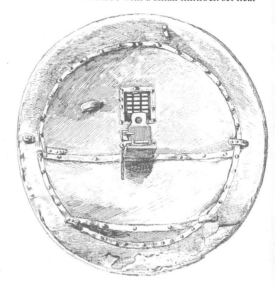

ABOVE Gunshield with a short barrelled breech-loading matchlock gun in its centre. Stored in the Tower of London since the 16th century, the shield was mentioned in an inventory dated 1547.

ABOVE Rear view of a 15th-century English shield with a gun. The small trellised window would have been used for aiming. Such designs were impractical and short-lived.

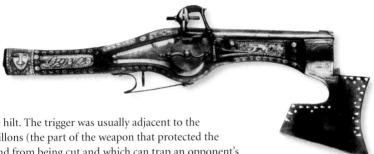

LEFT A German 17th-century wheel-lock pistol with battleaxe. Apart from the sword or knife, most combination weapons such as these were clumsy and inefficient and have never been very successful in use.

the hilt. The trigger was usually adjacent to the quillons (the part of the weapon that protected the hand from being cut and which can trap an opponent's blade). Mention should also be made of the series of flintlock firearms produced at the end of the 18th century that had a bayonet folded under the barrel which snapped forward into place when the trigger guard was pulled back.

Combining with furniture

One of the most unusual examples of a firearm combined with a piece of furniture is a 19th-century steel chest made to contain valuables which has four percussion pistols mounted inside. If the lid is opened without setting a special catch, the pistols fire. An examination of the barrels of the steel chest indicated that all four pistols had been fired at some time.

Other combinations

Pistols have been combined with keys, with knives, forks and spoons, and with truncheons. An inventor from Barnstaple in Devon, England, patented a metal truncheon with a percussion lock in 1823. An American patent of 1837 obtained by George Elgin of Georgia was a single-shot percussion pistol combined with the blade of a Bowie knife (a stout hunting knife). These were made in some quantity and were clearly very popular. In Sheffield a knife-pistol known as the "self protector" was made by the cutlery firm of Unwin and Rogers. These were made from about 1845 and were large pen-knives set with a barrel.

Wheel-lock combination axe and pistol

This was possibly a novelty or curiosity weapon, which fired from five barrels from the axe-edge end of the weapon. The muzzles of these five barrels were concealed by a hinged cover which formed the edge of the axe-blade at the right. The topmost barrel was ignited by a matchlock (not visible) fitted on the left side – the mechanism was concealed by a brass plate. The second barrel was visible from the right side of the weapon and ignited by a wheel-lock. This mechanism occupied most of the outer surface of the axe-head on the right side. The gunpowder in the pan was ignited by the pyrites held in the jaw. There was a tubular extension to the pan of the wheel-lock to hold a length of match which would be ignited by the flash of the priming and then withdrawn to ignite the remaining three barrels. The remaining three barrels were ignited by the hand-held match, as was the sixth barrel forming the handle or shaft.

RIGHT This unusual weapon is believed to be Iberian or German, dating from the early 17th century.

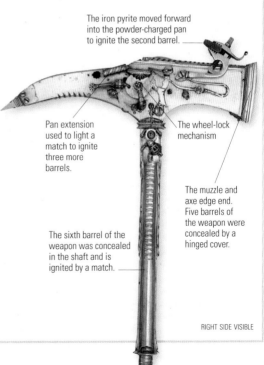

The iron pyrite moved forward into the powder-charged pan to ignite the second barrel.

Pan extension used to light a match to ignite three more barrels.

The wheel-lock mechanism

The muzzle and axe edge end. Five barrels of the weapon were concealed by a hinged cover.

The sixth barrel of the weapon was concealed in the shaft and is ignited by a match.

RIGHT SIDE VISIBLE

"The gun that won the West"

The handgun most widely associated with the opening up of the American West in the mid and late 19th century, and the books and films that have been based on this period, will always be the Colt revolver in its various forms. If this was the gun used by the "good guy" in a Hollywood Western movie, the weapon of choice of the villain was the pocket sized Deringer pistol. In the 1890s Smith & Wesson, a company with a fine pedigree in small-arms design would produce the revolver that would replace the Colt for the US Navy and Army.

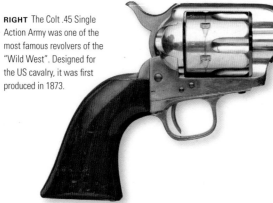

RIGHT The Colt .45 Single Action Army was one of the most famous revolvers of the "Wild West". Designed for the US cavalry, it was first produced in 1873.

Samuel Colt's innovation

The style of revolver that was popular in the 1840s and 1850s had six bored holes in the barrel. It could be loaded with six shots in one go, which could be fired one after the other. It continued to be used until the 1860s in both Europe and the United States. In 1835 Samuel Colt took out a patent for a weapon with a rotating cylinder. He established the standard of a cylinder with multiple chambers, each of which successively locked in position behind the barrel and was discharged by pressure on the trigger. In Colt's early revolvers, the cylinder revolved as the hammer was cocked manually. Later revolvers, in which the hammer was cocked and the cylinder revolved as the trigger was pulled, were developed soon afterwards.

The .44/40 Colt

Colt initially produced the same gun in a variety of calibres and barrel lengths, ranging from a stubby 4.75in/120mm up to 12in/305mm for the civilian market. The .44/40 Colt was particularly popular because the ammunition was compatible with that of the Winchester carbine (known as "the gun that won

the West"). The US Army bought about 37,000 Artillery and Cavalry Colt pistols between 1873 and 1893. Commercial production continued, but ceased in 1941. The Colt model 1873 revolver, known as the Colt Single Action, Peacemaker or Frontier was developed by 1872, based on the patents granted to Charles B. Richards and W. Mason. In 1873, the US Army adopted this revolver along with its black powder centrefire .45 Long Colt cartridge, and issued the Army or Cavalry model with two different lengths of barrel.

The advent of films and television Westerns in the 1950s prompted the Colt company to bring the Single Action back into production for the commercial market in 1956. The 1957 film *Gunfight at the O.K. Corral*, depicting a fight on a chilly day in 1881, is an interesting example of the realities of gunfights in the Wild West. Handguns were notoriously difficult to fire at close range. The accepted wisdom is the classic pose of a gun at arm's length and shoulder height. The quick-firing hero fanning the hammer of his Colt as he "shoots from the hip" and hits his adversaries with lethal shots is pure Hollywood.

Deringer pocket pistols

At the far end of the scale from the Colt revolver was the little single-shot pocket pistol developed by Henry Deringer of Philadelphia. Versions of the Deringer were made by numerous gunsmiths, including Colt. It achieved its greatest popularity in the United States in the years leading up to the Civil War. It was a favourite of men and women who wanted a compact, easily concealed firearm for personal defence, and so 15,000 were produced between 1850 and 1866.

The Colt factory

Samuel Colt, the son of a factory owner, was born in Hartford, Connecticut, on 19 July 1814. After leaving school, Colt worked at his father's textile mill. He was fascinated with machinery and spent his spare time disassembling and reassembling his father's guns. When only 16, he designed a fireworks display for the Fourth of July celebrations. Unfortunately, the school building burned to the ground. Fearing expulsion, Colt ran away to sea in 1829. While at sea Colt got the idea of designing a handgun with a revolving cylinder containing several bullets which could be fired through a single barrel. On his return he continued his work and the five-shot revolver was patented in the mid-1830s. In 1836 Colt established his Patent Arms Manufacturing company in Paterson, New Jersey.

However, sales were generally slow, and in 1842 he was forced to close down his factory. In 1847 Colt designed a six-shot Walker revolver. Soon afterwards the US government ordered 1,000 revolvers for use in the Mexican War. Colt was now in a position to establish a new factory in Hartford, Connecticut. By 1856 Colt had the largest private arms' manufacturing facility in the world. Colt, who skilfully promoted the gun culture that endures in America to this day, died on 14 January 1862. The Colt industry thrived and its handguns would arm the US Armed Forces and Police for many years.

LEFT The inventor and industrialist Samuel Colt. By 1856 Colt owned the largest private arms manufacturing facility in the world.

Although the .41 Deringer pistol was somewhat limited by its single-shot capacity, its light weight and small size gave it a distinct advantage over bulkier weapons like the 1873 Colt. To compensate for the single shot, many people simply carried two pistols. The Deringer became notorious when it was used in a number of Californian murders in the 1850s, as well as its later use in the assassination of President Lincoln. In Hollywood films about the West the little pistol would be used by sneaky gamblers, though in John Ford's 1939 classic film *Stagecoach* the southern gambler produced a Deringer as an act of mercy to kill the wife of a US Cavalry officer and spare her from capture by Apache Indians.

The test of war

In 1892 the US Army retired the Colt .45 Single Action Army Model revolver and decided to re-equip with a more modern revolver. They selected a .38 revolver built on a robust frame and both Colt and Smith & Wesson made versions of these firearms. In 1889 the US Navy adopted the revolver, followed by the US Marine Corps in 1905.

However it was during the Philippine Insurrection of 1899–1900 that showed that the .38in cartridge was not powerful enough. To rectify this, in 1908 a .38 Special cartridge was developed and the .38 Army Special revolver. Though it was superseded by a .45 model of similar design in 1909 the Special remained in production until 1928 for the commercial market and police, with some 220,000 being made.

LEFT *Gunfight at the O.K. Corral,* 1881, as depicted in a painting by Terence Cuneo. It gives a good idea of the close range at which many of these shootouts took place. In this gunfight one participant – John "Doc" Holliday – used a shotgun that he had kept hidden under his coat.

Innovations

The final years of the 19th century saw innovations in the way pistols and revolvers were designed. Among them were firearms made by Leopold Gasser who operated factories across Europe, which reputedly turned out 100,000 revolvers annually in the 1880s and 1890s. In 1907 the Austrian Roth-Steyr self-loader was the first such weapon to be adopted for military service. The huge British Gabbet-Fairfax Mars semi-automatic (also called self-loading) pistol, though novel, was destined never to be used by the British Army.

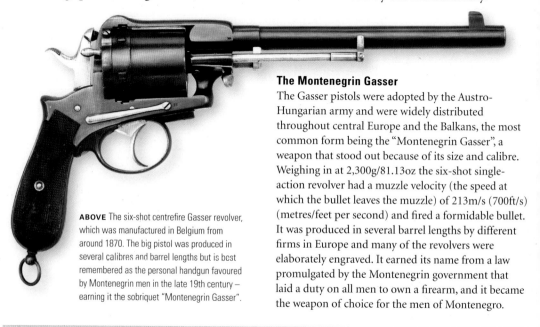

ABOVE The six-shot centrefire Gasser revolver, which was manufactured in Belgium from around 1870. The big pistol was produced in several calibres and barrel lengths but is best remembered as the personal handgun favoured by Montenegrin men in the late 19th century – earning it the sobriquet "Montenegrin Gasser".

The Montenegrin Gasser

The Gasser pistols were adopted by the Austro-Hungarian army and were widely distributed throughout central Europe and the Balkans, the most common form being the "Montenegrin Gasser", a weapon that stood out because of its size and calibre. Weighing in at 2,300g/81.13oz the six-shot single-action revolver had a muzzle velocity (the speed at which the bullet leaves the muzzle) of 213m/s (700ft/s) (metres/feet per second) and fired a formidable bullet. It was produced in several barrel lengths by different firms in Europe and many of the revolvers were elaborately engraved. It earned its name from a law promulgated by the Montenegrin government that laid a duty on all men to own a firearm, and it became the weapon of choice for the men of Montenegro.

The single-and double-action revolver

A revolver works by having several firing chambers arranged in a circle in a cylindrical block. These are brought into alignment with the firing mechanism and barrel one at a time. In early revolvers, a shooter had to pull the hammer back before each shot and then pull the trigger to release the hammer. These are called single-action revolvers.

An innovation in lock-work arrived in the 1850s, which allowed firing by single- or double-action. The hammer could either be cocked and then released by a light trigger pressure, or the trigger could be pulled right back in a "long pull" action to rotate the cylinder and raise and release the hammer. This meant it did

not need to be manually cocked between shots. Double-action is used on most present day revolvers. The first revolvers used gunpowder, balls and caps like the early percussion-cap pistols. The shooter would load each of the six chambers in the cylinder with gunpowder and a projectile, and fire using the percussion caps. In the 1870s, these early models were replaced by revolvers that used bullet cartridges instead of gunpowder and caps. Revolvers passed through the pinfire and rimfire stages to use the centrefire metallic cartridge case. The breech-loading revolver has a gate in the rear part of the frame (which backs up the cylinder) for loading and ejecting.

Young cannon

In the world of big self-loaders, the British Gabbet-Fairfax Mars reigned supreme. Different marks designed by H.W. Gabbet-Fairfax could fire 8.5mm, 9mm or .45 calibre ammunition. However, it was the .45 that really had a punch. It had a muzzle velocity of 381m/s (1,250ft/s) while the 8.5mm produced an incredible 533m/s (1,750ft/s). It was rejected by the British War Office as a service weapon because of the requirement for special ammunition and the excessive recoil caused by the powerful cartridges and complex long recoil mechanism, which did not lend itself to cost-effective production. Another drawback of the design was that the cases were ejected out of the back of the pistol directly into the face of the firer. The design did not prove to be a commercial success. It is not known exactly how many Mars pistols were manufactured, most estimates being around 70, although one pistol is known with a serial number of 195. It is an indication of the rarity of these weapons that the starting price for one that came up at auction in 2006 was set between £8,000 and £12,000.

ABOVE Different designs of the Gabbet-Fairfax Mars could fire 8.5mm, 9mm or .45 ammunition. The recoil force from the .45 round was such that the firer found his arm jerked vertically upright on firing.

receiver · breech · bolt

butt (holds magazine)

ABOVE The Roth-Steyr Model was developed by George Roth and first issued to the Austro-Hungarian cavalry in 1907. The design included a bolt that extended the full length of the receiver.

Cavalry pistols

The Roth-Steyr Model is an early 20th-century pistol. It was the first self-loader to be adopted by a major power as a service weapon when it entered service with the cavalry arm of the Austro-Hungarian army in 1907. It was a large and heavy pistol that fired a unique rimless 8mm cartridge. The barrel and breech were locked together and are separated during recoil by a cam action that rotated the barrel through 90 degrees to unlock the bolt. Though the pistol had 10-rounds of ammunition, this was not housed in a removable magazine and they had to be loaded into the butt (grip) from the top using a charger (a device to load a

magazine). The pistol had a rather complex safety system: the pistol would reload after it had been fired, but would not recock. The bolt had to be pulled back by hand to reset the mechanism if there was a misfire. This was a deliberate feature as a pistol with a conventional pull would have been too light and prone to accidental discharge if the horse shied or bucked.

ABOVE The 1908 Bergmann-Bayard. German industrialist, Theodor Bergmann, hired a gun designer and developed a series of automatic pistols at the turn of the 20th century. It used its own 9mm Bergmann-Bayard cartridge.

ABOVE The 1935 Browning 9mm GP or Grand Puissance (High-Power) pistol. The pistol had been designed a decade earlier in 1925 by the weapons engineer John Moses Browning.

Into the modern age

During the 20th century technological improvements in weapons design meant that they became more reliable, faster and ultimately more deadly. Although revolvers maintained a steady following, the automatic handgun, initially designed by John Moses Browning, became standard issue for police and security forces around the world. Many have become classics: the Luger, Beretta and Browning High-Power remain highly regarded weapons. Two world wars and countless smaller conflicts have only encouraged arms manufacturers to produce lighter, quieter and more powerful weapons. From the Mauser and Tommy gun, via the Sten gun to the Uzi, successive generations have produced ever more efficient weapon systems. In the early years of the 21st century, the wheel seems to have gone full circle. Fail-safe firepower is still critical, but there is now a demand for non-lethal ammunition that will fell an opponent without causing permanent damage.

ABOVE Weapons training for women in 1941. The submachine gun in the foreground is a Sten Mark III and the Sten in the background is a Mark I. The Mark I had a wooden foregrip and forward handle. The Mark III is a simplified version of the Mark I and II.

Guns of the Empire

The weapons of empire used by soldiers and adventurers were often large-calibre revolvers that could be used quickly in a confined space such as a tent or cabin, and long-range rifles used in engagements on the North-West Frontier of India or the open veldt of South Africa. A classic example was the British Webley .455 revolver developed by Webley & Son (Webley & Scott Revolver and Arms Company Ltd from 1897) in the 1870s. A few years later the French Army adopted an 8mm revolver, the Modèle d'Ordonnance (Lebel); it was a revolver that would be taken into the 20th century.

Webley revolvers

The British Webleys were the first "top-break" revolvers with a two-piece frame, which hinged (or broke) at the forward low end for the ejection of cartridge cases and loading. The ejector operated automatically when the frame was broken open and all six empty cases were ejected simultaneously from the cylinder. The cartridges could then be inserted by hand. Designers of revolvers in all calibres adopted the top-break system, as it made for quick reloading – crucial in a short-range firefight. Webleys that had been rechambered for the .45 ACP (a calibre known as .45 Automatic Colt Pistol) round used two three-round half-moon clips (to hold enough ammunition to half-fill the cylinder). This further speeded up reloading.

six-chamber cylinder

hammer

bird's-head hand grip

LEFT The Webley Mark I, adopted by the Royal Navy in 1887, was the first in a series of revolvers produced by this British company.

BELOW The last stand of a British officer at the Battle of Isandlwana in 1879. He has only six rounds in his Webley revolver and little scope to reload quickly.

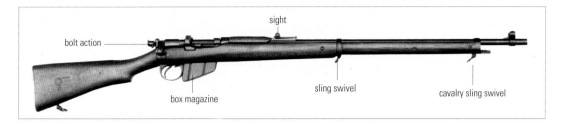

sight

bolt action

box magazine

sling swivel

cavalry sling swivel

ABOVE The British eight-round .303 Lee Metford, the first repeater rifle. Adopted by the British military in 1888, it encouraged development in small-arms design which, in the case of the Lee Metford, resulted in the introduction of the No. 4 Rifle.

Personal choice

British Army officers and colonial administrators of the Empire would often buy private weapons – handguns that were either superior in design or more convenient to use than standard-issue weapons.

The penalty for this personal choice could be finding ammunition if the weapon was of an unusual calibre. In a remote outpost of the Empire this could literally be a matter of life and death and persuasive words of a salesman in a London gunsmith would ring hollow as the officer looked at his emptying ammunition pouch in a firefight.

In 1887, the British Army and Royal Navy took the first Webley revolver as its official service revolver. This six-shot, double-action revolver was engineered to take the black powder .455 British service cartridge. This cartridge fired a large lead bullet, but because it used black powder it had a relatively slow muzzle velocity of 180m/s (590.55ft/s). Although a smokeless cartridge was then developed, the velocity remained low and could also be fired in early revolvers.

All Webley revolvers were double-action or double-action-only, with a very distinctive barrel shape, a frame lock with lock lever on the left side of the frame, and V-shaped lock spring at the right side.

Trench raids

The generals and political leaders who took Europe to war in August 1914 had not anticipated the possibility of trench warfare, but as the stalemate on the Western Front continued, compact and handy weapons such as the Webley became highly valued by the combatants.

The long bolt-action rifles carried by most infantry in European armies (the exception was the British, with their compact Short Magazine Lee Enfield), were ideal for long-range engagements in open country, but were impractical in the confines of a trench. In the quick, violent fighting patrols known as "trench raids" soldiers carried clubs, knuckle-dusters and knives – silent weapons that could be used in hand-to-hand combat. The revolver or semi-automatic pistol were the only useful firearms in these confined spaces. This was the battleground that would spawn a new weapon: the submachine gun.

The French army revolver

The French 8mm Modèle d'Ordonnance (Lebel) 1892 revolver enjoyed a remarkable longevity in service with the French Army. Adopted in 1892, it was still in service in World War II. The pistol had a conventional swing-out cylinder, with the release button on the right, which made it a user-friendly weapon for left-handed shooters. It had an ingenious system that allowed the left-hand plate to swing forward on a hinge to expose the mechanism for cleaning. Like many weapons developed in the late 19th century the revolver used its own special 8mm ammunition.

hinge

squared-style hand grip

LEFT The Webley Mark VI was first produced in 1915 and remained in service until World War II. The revolver, similar in many ways to the Mark V Webley, was issued to British and Commonwealth forces.

Classic revolvers

Revolvers were the classic handguns of the 19th and early 20th centuries. Although they were reliable and robust, reloading under pressure always presented a problem, and the weapon could become clogged by dirt or grit.

The Nagant Model 1895

Widely regarded as a Russian revolver, the Nagant Model 1895G was actually designed in the early 1890s by the Belgian brothers Emile and Leon Nagant. It was first manufactured and used in Russia and adopted by other countries, including Sweden and Poland and, later, the USSR. Local production began in 1898 after the Imperial Russian government had received shipments from Belgium. Technically, the Nagant was almost obsolete when it was adopted in 1895, since revolvers like the American Smith & Wesson Hand Ejectors and Colts with side-opening cylinders were much faster to reload. However, it was not until 1930 that the Nagant Model 1895 finally became obsolete in Russia, enduring as the standard sidearm for more than thirty years. It was widely used and manufactured during World War II, and production finally ceased in the 1950s. The Nagant Model 1895 had some distinctive features, such as the gas-sealed cylinder, which, almost uniquely, made it a revolver suitable for mounting a

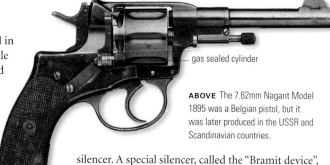

gas sealed cylinder

ABOVE The 7.62mm Nagant Model 1895 was a Belgian pistol, but it was later produced in the USSR and Scandinavian countries.

silencer. A special silencer, called the "Bramit device", was designed by the Mitin brothers, and was used by the Russian NKVD secret police and some Red Army special forces during World War II.

The Webley-Fosbery model 1901

Designed by George Fosbery, a Victorian hero who at the age of 31 had won the Victoria Cross, the Webley-Fosbery is a remarkable weapon. In effect it is an automatic revolver. It opens, loads and unloads like other contemporary Webley revolvers. However, when the pistol is fired, the recoil from the cartridge moves the receiver back in its frame. At this point a cam pin

RIGHT The original caption for this American poster reads: "Cowboy spurring on horse to escape Indians, while shooting it out with a Smith and Wesson pistol." The poster was created in the late 19th century in order to promote Smith & Wesson revolvers.

fixed in the frame engages in zigzag slots in the outer surface of the pistol cylinder, and revolves it half-way toward the next chamber.

front sight

zig-zag cylinder tracks

Simultaneously the pistol's hammer is moved into the cocked position. As the frame-mounted spring returns the receiver forward, the cam pin forces the cylinder to revolve the rest of the way, and the weapon is cocked and ready to fire its next shot. Because of this feature the Webley-Fosbery is fitted with a safety catch – an unusual feature in revolvers.

ABOVE The Webley-Fosbery .455 Model 1902, a revised version of the 1901 automatic revolver, an ingenious weapon that harnessed recoil to revolve the cylinder.

The weapon was popular with British officers before World War I, who could purchase a revolver made to order. The Webley was available in .455 calibre for the British service cartridge, and later in .38 ACP. With a ready supply of six-round clips, a marksman could attain a rate of fire of 70 rounds per minute (rpm).

The Colt model 1917

With the United States' entry into World War I, manufacturers of the Colt 1911 with the .45 ACP cartridge could not keep up with the demand of the US Army. Two pistols were chosen as a stopgap measure:

the Colt New Service pistol and the Smith & Wesson New Century, both of which had been used in action by the British Army on the Western Front. In the light of this combat experience the design of the Smith & Wesson was modified. The Colt New Service was chambered in the .45 ACP cartridge and known as the Colt Model 1917. It could be quickly loaded or unloaded by either three-round stamped metal half-moon clips or six-round full-moon clips.

The "Three Eight"

six-chamber cylinder   barrel   front sight

After World War I the British War Department decided that tank crews and other service personnel who required a sidearm needed a more compact handgun. The result was the Enfield No. 2 Mark I .38 revolver developed at the Royal Small Arms Factory in Enfield between 1926 and 1927. The design was a scaled-down Webley Mark VI with its "break-top" frame and cylinder chambered for six rounds and firing a heavy-grain bullet. The hammer/trigger group was redesigned, with a manual hammer safety lock added, as well as a separate cylinder lock. This revolver was adopted for British military service in 1932 as the Enfield revolver, .38 No. 2 Mark I. After 1938, almost all No. 2 Mark Is were converted into No. 2 Mark I* configuration.

The Enfield No. 2 Mark I* was developed in the late 1930s for the British Tank Corps (part of the Royal Armoured Corps) and was distinguished from the early Mark I by a spurless, double-action-only

ABOVE The early Enfield No. 2 Mark I revolver. This was modified in the late 1930s for the British Army and remained in service until the late 1960s.

hammer, lighter mainspring and reshaped grip side plates. The spurless hammers, which were required by the Royal Armoured Corps, meant that the weapon could be carried in an open holster without snagging on controls or cabling inside the tank.

The Enfield No. 2 Mark I** appeared in 1942 as a simplified, wartime design. These revolvers were similar to the No. 2 Mark I*, but without the hammer stop. After 1945, all the Enfields were recalled and converted into No. 2 Mark I* configuration. Known informally as the "Three Eight" in the British army, the revolver was robust and comfortable to fire.

Enter the semi-automatic

To men who carried revolvers, the semi-automatic pistol initially seemed over-engineered and too complex. It would, however, supersede the revolver in almost all roles in the 20th century. Among its attractions were a more compact shape and ease of reloading.

The John Moses Browning

The first semi-automatic pistol, the FN Browning M1900, was designed by American firearms maker J.M. Browning in c.1896, and followed by an improved version in 1897. In 1898, Browning's design was accepted by the Belgian firearms manufacturer Fabrique Nationale de Herstal (FN), who began production of the 1899 model. A year later, in 1900, Belgium adopted the FN Browning M1900, a modified version with a shorter barrel. Use of the Browning Number 1 pistol, as it was also known, spread across Europe as a civilian and police sidearm. The chamber was designed for the 7.6mm x 17mm round, which is also known in the Americas as the .32 AC, a new smokeless round. Manufactured until about 1911, more than 700,000 FN Browning M1900 pistols were made.

An Austrian aristocrat

The 7.63mm Austrian Mannlicher Model 1900 has all the elegance of a duelling pistol from an earlier century. Designed by Ferdinand Ritter von Mannlicher,

ABOVE The 7.63mm Austrian Mannlicher Model 1900, designed by Ferdinand Ritter von Mannlicher, has a mechanism which has been likened to that of a fine watch.

hammer   barrel

ABOVE The FN Browning M1900 was one of the most commercially successful semi-automatic pistols produced before World War I. It was widely used by police forces and bodyguards.

Blowback and recoil operations

Semi-automatic pistols use either blowback, recoil, or other systems to work the mechanisms that fire, expel and reload ammunition:

Blowback-operated weapons use the pressure created from the fired round to push a bolt, located directly behind the round, back and forth against a spring. Its pressure pushes the bolt backwards against the spring and also ejects the spent round from the gun. A new round enters the weapon, and as the compressed spring pushes the bolt forward, the bolt pushes the round into the breech. A pin on the end of the bolt strikes the round and fires it, beginning the cycle again. Blowback weapons are simple and reliable, but they do not form a complete seal at the breech when firing.

Recoil-operated weapons push the barrel and the breech backwards as a unit, along with the bolt. The ejection and reloading cycles are completed during this recoil, and the breech remains sealed during firing. Recoil-operated have more moving parts than blowback-operated weapons. The weapons are heavy but very reliable. As a result, they have relatively low rates of fire.

it is a well-balanced, light pistol with a mechanism that has been likened to that of a fine watch for its precision and action. Von Mannlicher had a good design but knew that it could be improved. The 1900 model was followed by the 1901 with a longer barrel and a repositioned rear sight. In 1903 he produced a model with a box magazine (a device for holding ammunition via a slot on the receiver) in front of the trigger guard and a new mechanism. Although European armies did not take up the 1900 and 1901 models, they became popular in South America. One of the drawbacks of this pistol was that it used a special cartridge made only in Austria, and, to add to the logistic problems, the 1903 pistol had its own specialized ammunition.

hammer

magazine

LEFT The Bergmann-Bayard (1908 model) had a six or ten-round detachable magazine but could also be loaded with a stripper clip.

The Bergmann-Bayard

This German pistol was one of the first pistols developed to use 9mm calibre ammunition, although this was not Parabellum but a round with a larger cartridge unique to the Bergmann-Bayard. Produced in 1903, the pistol was adopted by the Danish army in 1905, and later by the Belgian and Spanish armies. It was made at the Bergmann works in Germany and also mass-produced by Peiper of Herstal in Belgium. Although the pistol looks like a Mauser, it has a simpler trigger mechanism and the magazine can be removed. To reload, the magazine can either be filled by hand or, with the action open, a charger can be inserted and the rounds pushed into the magazine – an obvious advantage in a military pistol. Like other weapons of this period it could be fitted with a holster stock that was clipped to the bottom of the butt to convert it into a light carbine (automatic rifle).

The Luger Model 1908

The German Luger self-loading pistol, known in German army service as the Pistole 08 from its year of adoption, was named after George Luger, a designer at the Ludwig Löwe small-arms factory in Berlin. Hugo Borchardt based the Luger's design on an earlier idea, but Luger re-designed the Borchardt locking system (called lock-out) into a much smaller package. The toggle-lock mechanism was complex, but it made the weapon comfortable to fire and therefore more accurate. The first military Lugers were made in 1900 to a Swiss order. The original calibre was 7.65mm, but in 1902 at the request of the German navy, the firm of Deutsche Waffen und Munitionsfabriken (DWM), along with Luger, designed a bigger round. By re-necking the case of the 7.65mm Luger round the 9mm Luger/Parabellum was developed. The standard pistol had an eight-round box magazine and fired the Parabellum round with a maximum effective range of 70m/230ft.

rear sight (flip-up)

toggle link hinge

magazine release

ABOVE The Luger Model 1908, also known as the Pistole 08.

In the 1920s the British firm Vickers manufactured Lugers for export to the Netherlands. The shortest pistol had a 103mm/4.06in barrel, an overall length of 222mm/8.75in and weighed 875g/30.9oz.

The Naval Luger weighed 1,043g/36.8oz, had a 198mm/7.8in barrel, a tangent sight, and could be fitted with a 32-round "snail" magazine, effectively making it a light submachine gun.

Semi-automatic innovation

The German Luger was an elegant design. However, the first .455in self-loading pistol produced in 1904 by the prolific British firm Webley & Scott Revolver and Arms Company Ltd did not have the same appeal, nor was it a commercial success. The American Colt M1911 self-loading pistol, however, proved to be the era's great survivor: with its rugged design and reliability in the front line it remained in service until the Vietnam War.

The .455 Webley & Scott 1910

An improved version of the .455 Webley & Scott pistol introduced in 1910 proved a real success. It was the Royal Navy's standard pistol until the end of World War II and was used by the Royal Air Force, the Metropolitan Police and throughout the Empire. The pistol had a grip safety (a safety mechanism that prevents a gun from being fired, unless the grip is held firmly). On firing the ejection port threw the empty cases upwards and forwards. An ingenious system with the magazine allowed a user to fire hand-loaded single shots with the magazine partially inserted – if he needed a full magazine he simple had to push it completely home and six rounds were immediately available.

bolt   cross key

LEFT The Italian Glisenti Model 1910, sometimes referred to in early records as the Brixia, fired a low-powered 9mm round.

At the same time, the Italian Glisenti M1910 became the first semi-automatic pistol to be adopted by the Italian military. Although a later version was chambered to use the same cartridge case as the 9mm Luger, it was largely replaced by the 9mm Beretta Model 1915 in World War I.

Introduced in 1912, the Austro-Hungarian forces in World War I preferred the Steyr Model 1912 pistol over the range of other standard issue pistols. It was also used by the Romanians and Germans. Officially named "Selbstiade Pistol M12" by the Austrian Army, the pistol was also informally known as the Steyr-Hahn ("Steyr with a hammer") to distinguish it from the Roth-Steyr. During World War II, a number of weapons were re-barrelled for use by the German Army to take the 9mm Parabellum cartridge. About 250,000 of the pistols were made before production ceased in 1919.

The .45 Colt 1911

The giant in the world of self-loading or semi-automatic pistols is the .45 Colt 1911, a US government model developed from a Browning design. It is a much more reliable pistol under muddy or sandy conditions than weapons like the Luger, because it does not have so much of its working mechanism exposed. The United States adopted this

ABOVE A British sergeant armed with a Colt .45 M1911A1 semi-automatic pistol stalks a German sniper in Italy, 1943. The American-made Colt was widely issued to Allied forces and was a popular sidearm. Its .45 rounds made it highly effective at short range.

pistol in 1911 and modified it in 1921. It was redesignated the M1911A1. American servicemen carried the .45 Colt through World War II, the wars in Korea and Vietnam, and it was also widely issued to Allied forces. It was 215mm/8.46in long, weighed 1,105g/39oz, had a seven-round magazine, and a muzzle velocity of 262m/s (860ft/s). Ammunition from the Colt 1911A1 was compatible with the Thompson submachine gun Model 1928A1.

ABOVE The Austrian Steyr Model 1912 was converted by the Germans in World War II to take 9mm Parabellum.

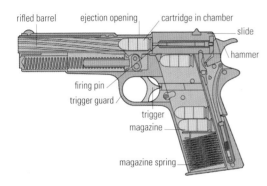

ABOVE A cross-section of a .45 Colt pistol. The rounds are held under compression in the magazine and each time the slide moves to the rear – either on firing or when the pistol is cocked, a round is fed into the chamber. Pressing the trigger releases the mechanism that allows the spring-loaded hammer to hit the firing pin.

Soviet TT pistols

About this time in the Soviet Union, Fedor V. Tokarev began developing a series of pistols with the prefix TT for Tula-Tokarev, or Tulskiy Tokarev (meaning Tokarev from Tula). The 7.62mm TT-33 was developed in 1930 and adopted by the Soviet Army the same year. In 1933, the pistol was improved with a new locking system and a different disconnector (used to prevent the gun from firing unless a magazine is inserted). It looked rather like the 1903 Colt .38 Pocket Automatic Pistol and could be disassembled (field stripped) in a similar way to the Colt 1911. The pistol was single-action, and recoil-operated in the same way as the Browning design, with an eight-round single-stack magazine.

Japanese Nambu Type 14

Across the Pacific, the 14th Year Pistol designed by Japanese General Kijiro Nambu was an improved and cheaper version of an earlier, similar Japanese pistol. Externally it looked like a Luger, but the locking system was based on a different system. The Imperial Japanese Army adopted it in 1925 as the official sidearm with the designation Type 14 Pistol. One unusual version, nicknamed "Kiska", had a very large trigger guard designed for use by a soldier wearing thick gloves in the bitter winters of northern Japan, mainland China and Korea.

The Nambu Type 14 was maligned as a very poorly designed weapon. It fired an underpowered 8mm cartridge with a muzzle velocity of 290m/s (950ft/s). It was difficult to reach and operate the safety catch, and if the magazine release catch became clogged it

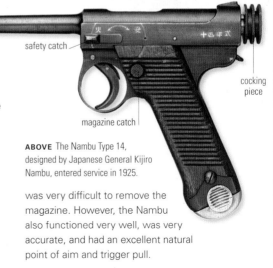

ABOVE The Nambu Type 14, designed by Japanese General Kijiro Nambu, entered service in 1925.

was very difficult to remove the magazine. However, the Nambu also functioned very well, was very accurate, and had an excellent natural point of aim and trigger pull.

The submachine gun

The need for a submachine gun had its origins in World War I, as a method of clearing the enemy trenches of soldiers at close-range. Fast-firing semi-automatic pistols fitted with a detachable stock pointed the way to the introduction of the first submachine gun (SMG). By the close of that war the Germans and Italians had produced the first submachine guns – the German weapon being a classic design.

ABOVE The Italian 9mm Glisenti Twin Villar Perosa. Though this unusual-looking weapon is a world away from modern submachine guns, it was in fact the world's first submachine gun. The Italians failed to see its potential at first and used it as a static light machine gun.

The Mauser pistol

Known as the "Military Model", the German 1895 Broomhandle Mauser pistol was never an official issue weapon, although it was popular with officers as a private-purchase sidearm. Although it had been made in 7.63mm with a special 9mm Mauser cartridge, by 1914 many had been converted to 9mm Parabellum (the most standard calibre). The standard model had a built-in ten-round magazine, fed by a clip from the top. A fully automatic type was also produced in limited numbers and used by German troops as a light machine pistol – a submachine gun by any other name.

ABOVE A German Waffen-SS soldier takes aim with a private-purchase Mauser military pistol, converted from the original 7.63mm model to 9mm Parabellum. Fitted with a shoulder stock, this weapon could be fired very accurately by experienced shots, particularly against static targets.

The first submachine guns

In 1915 Italy became the first country to adopt a submachine gun, known as either the "Villar Perosa", or the "Fiat" depending on its place of manufacture, or the "Revelli" after the designer Abiel Revelli. The original production had no stock, and two barrels with two 25-round box magazines and thumb-type triggers. Like all other early Italian submachine guns, it was chambered for 9mm Glisenti ammunition, basically a low-powered 9mm Parabellum cartridge. Although it was portable, it was largely used as a static machine gun. By 1918 Italian soldiers were re-equipped with a Beretta modification of the design and began to use the submachine gun in an assault role.

The German Bergmann MaschinenPistole 18 or MP18 was designed by Louis Schmeisser in 1917 and incorporated many of the features that would become standard in early submachine guns. The German army ordered 50,000 and around 10,000 had been delivered in time for the *Kaiserschlacht*, the 1918 offensive on the Western Front. After the war, stocks of the gun were taken over by the French Army which substituted a 20- or 32-round box magazine that loaded from the left. This feed mechanism was adopted when production recommenced in 1928 under licence in Belgium.

At the close of World War I the Beretta M1918 (or strictly the Beretta Moschetto Automatico 1918) was designed by the talented young engineer Tullio

adjustable sights

drum magazine

LEFT The Soviet PPD-34/38 was produced at the Tula and Sestrorjetsk arsenals until 1940, when it was replaced by the simpler but well-made PPD-40.

folding spike bayonet

LEFT The elegant Beretta Model 1918 was still in service with the Italian Army in World War II. A 25-round curved magazine fitted in the top of the receiver and it had a folding spike bayonet.

Marengoni, who used the Villar Perosa action, barrel, body and feed system for the cartridges. A new trigger and stock were added, with an ejection chute under the ejection slot. Finally, the bayonet catch and folding bayonet, two components from the Carcano military carbine, were added. It was issued to *Arditi* (assault troops) in the Italian army.

The PPD (Pistolet-Pulemyot Degtyarova) was developed by the Russian small arms designer Vassili A. Degtyarov in 1934 and adopted by the Red Army a year later. With a 25-round box magazine, it went into limited production with the designation PPD-34. Following modifications in 1938, it was produced until 1939 as the PPD-34/38 with a newly developed 71-round drum magazine. Although a new version was developed in 1940 with a two-part stock designed to accept a new pattern of 71-round drum magazine, by June 1941 it became clear that the PPD-40 was not suited to wartime mass production, and it was replaced by the more efficient and inexpensive PPSh-41.

The French 7.65mm Mitraillette MAS 38 submachine gun introduced in 1938 had evolved from the experimental MAS 35 and was an accurate short-range weapon machined from solid metal. It fired from a 32-round box magazine with a cyclic rate of between 600 and 700 rpm. Following the fall of France in 1940 the Germans kept production going at Manufacture d'Armes de St Etienne for their own use until 1944.

Tullio Marengoni and Pietro Beretta

Firearms historians have described Tullio Marengoni as Europe's John Browning since his designs that began with a hammerless shotgun in the early 1900s continued to dominate every significant Beretta weapon for the next sixty years. Beretta and Marengoni had a unique working relationship, and would often work together all through the night. Marengoni came up with the concepts and Beretta engineered the working weapons from his designs. Their wide-ranging output included the monobloc breech for shotgun barrels, the classic Beretta over/under shotgun line, and the pistol design that would evolve into the official US military sidearm, the modern Model 92/M9. Marengoni remained a consultant for Beretta for several years after his official retirement in 1956.

BELOW The early 32-round "snail" magazine designed for the 9mm German MP18 submachine gun proved complex and prone to stoppages.

barrel jacket   magazine housing

RIGHT The MP18 would have been issued on a scale of six guns per company, with gunners supported by a second soldier carrying extra ammunition. However, though World War I ended before this could be fully tested, it was a pointer to the future.

The trench broom

The American M1928, the Thompson Model 1928 "Trench Broom" or "Tommy Gun", was the brainchild of John T. Thompson, who helped develop the M1903 Springfield rifle and the .45 M1911 pistol (shortly after his retirement from the army in 1918). He began work on a handy, fast-firing weapon for use in attacks through field fortifications.

ABOVE The Thompson M1928A1 with 20-round box magazine. Although heavy, at 4,880g/172oz, this was a robust and reliable weapon that was popular with US and Allied soldiers, particularly British Commandos.

The Thompson submachine gun

Drawing on experience of fighting on the Western Front, John T. Thompson recognized that the .45 bullet used in the M1911 pistol would transform a fully automatic weapon. Early in 1920, a prototype capable of firing 800 rpm was produced by Thompson's company, Auto-Ordnance.

Despite its performance in trials, neither the US Army nor the Marine Corps adopted the Thompson. Nevertheless, Thompson was able to sign a contract with Colt for 15,000 "Thompson Submachine Gun, Model of 1921".

ABOVE A French soldier, armed and equipped by the US Army, on guard in 1945 with his Thompson M1A1. Weighing 4,740g/167.2oz, this was the final simplified version of the submachine gun, with a fixed firing pin.

There were no further orders for submachine guns until the eve of the United States' entry into World War II. From 1942, the orders were huge. The reliability of the Thompson to outperform other submachine guns in adverse conditions such as dirt, mud and rain was one of its main assets. British Commandos retained their Thompsons after the Sten had become more widely available, and went ashore at D-Day in 1944 armed with them. The main drawbacks of the gun were weight, inaccuracy at ranges over 45m/50yd, and lack of penetrating power. However, as a close-range weapon it was devastating.

The "Tommy Gun"

In 1940 the British Government rushed to purchase the Model 1928A1, Thompson Machine Carbine (TMC) or "Tommy Gun". Senior staff officers in the British army had referred to submachine guns disparagingly as "gangster weapons" because of their gangland reputation in Prohibition America, but the reservations of the British War Office were forgotten in the face of the threat of German invasion, and orders were placed for the Model 1928.

This gun saw service in North Africa and Italy. It weighed 4,800g/172oz was 857mm/33.75in long, had sights set out to 548m/1,800ft, and had a cyclic rate of 600 to 725 rpm with a 20- or 30-round box or a 50-round drum magazine. Most soldiers favoured the 20-round magazine that fitted into a pouch and made for easier movement in close country.

In 1942 the original Thompson M1928 had the cocking handle (which compresses the spring behind the bolt) on top of the receiver and utilized the Blish Lock system of operation. The Blish Lock system worked on a principle of static friction in a delayed-blowback breech lock. The gun was redesigned as the Thompson M1A1. The M1A1 used a simple blowback system of operation and the cocking handle was moved to the side. To cut manufacturing costs, the Cutts compensator (a device which alleviates the tendency of the muzzle to rise when firing on full automatic), the finned barrel, the fingered fore-grip, and the flip-up adjustable rear-sight were either simplified or eliminated. The M1A1 did not accept the drum magazine, which was abandoned for reasons including the fact that it was bulky and that the rounds rattled, a noise that could be fatal on night patrols. By the end of World War II, more than one million M1 and M1A1 submachine guns had been made.

RIGHT A sales brochure for the Thompson submachine gun, published by the Auto-Ordnance Corporation. The "Tommy Gun" was used by police and gangsters in the 1920s and 1930s. This led the British War Office to describe them as gangster weapons and reject them in the 1930s.

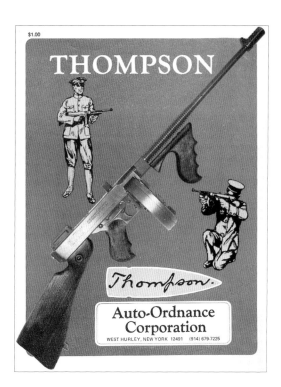

$1.00

THOMPSON

Auto-Ordnance Corporation
WEST HURLEY, NEW YORK 12491   (914) 679-7225

Gangster weapons

Compared with the thousands of Thompson submachine guns used properly by law-abiding Americans in the course of their duty, only a very small number of Thompsons were misused by Depression and Prohibition-era gangsters in the United States. Despite this, the weapon got a bad name in the late 1920s and 1930s.

The best-known front-page crime remains the notorious "St. Valentine's Day Massacre" of 1929 when henchmen of the gang-leader Al Capone, who had conveniently left town for Florida, shot down seven members of the "Bugs" Moran gang in a Chicago garage.

On a summer night in 1933, Oklahoma City oilman Charles Urschel was kidnapped from his home by gangster George Kelly. Kelly was armed with a Thompson submachine gun and this crime earned him the nickname "Machine Gun" Kelly.

"Public Enemy No.1" John Dillinger stole Thompsons from small-town police stations. Both the Dillinger–Nelson gang and Charles Arthur "Pretty Boy" Floyd customized their Thompsons, making them easier to conceal and fire one-handed. This was done by removing the butt and replacing the 50-round drum magazine with a 20-round box magazine.

Hollywood also played its part in giving the gun a bad reputation, with Jimmy Cagney and Edward G. Robinson playing Thompson-toting hard men in violent movies like *The Public Enemy* and *Little Caesar*.

LEFT John Dillinger, "Public Enemy No. 1", one of the American Prohibition-era gangsters who used the Thompson M1928 submachine gun with a 20-round box magazine.

The 1930s: rearmament

When Adolf Hitler came to power in Germany in 1933, he introduced a vast programme of rearmament, in contravention of the Versailles Treaty of 1919. Some superb designs and concepts were developed in the late 1930s and early 1940s that have long outlasted the life of the Third Reich. The 9mm Walther Pistole 38 or P38 was designed to replace the P08 Luger and the compact PP and PPK pistols were introduced. In Italy Beretta produced the elegant Pistol Automatica Beretta Modello 1934/38 and the 8mm Mitra Beretta MAB38 submachine guns. However, the Browning 9mm High-Power pistol developed in the 1930s would be one of the most successful pistols of the period.

The Walther pistole 38 (P38)

The German Walther P38 was safe, easy, and cheap to manufacture. The P38 has the distinctive feature of a positive safety catch that prevents accidental firing, even when cocked with a round in the breech. A pin indicator, which could be felt in the dark, showed if a round was loaded. The magazine held eight rounds that could be fired in 20 seconds with an effective range of 50m/164ft. Between 1939 and 1945 over one million P38s were made and it is widely acknowledged to have been the best military pistol of World War II.

ABOVE The German wartime Walther P38 would return after 1945 as the lightweight Bundeswehr Model P1 pistol.

The Walther PPK

In 1928, before the Nazis came to power, Walther produced the Model PP or Polizei Pistole, a compact weapon with an eight-round magazine designed for police use. The PPK or Polizei Pistole Kriminal was only 150mm/5.91in long compared to the PP's 170mm/6.7in, and was intended for police working in plain clothes. During World War II it was the personal weapon of choice for senior officers in the German armed forces, and it remained in service after the war, later becoming famous as the weapon of Agent 007, Ian Fleming's fictional spy James Bond.

Italian designs

In Italy another small-arms manufacturer with a worldwide reputation was producing new designs. The Pistol Automatica Beretta Modello 1934/38 was a handy blowback-operated weapon that weighed 616g/21.76oz. The finish was excellent and it became one of the most prized war trophies for the Allies.

The 8mm Mitra Beretta MAB38 submachine gun introduced in 1938 was based on the Villar Perosa. It had two triggers, one for semi-automatic and one for automatic fire. It fired from 10-, 20- or 40-round magazines that could be loaded by hand or by specific

ABOVE A British sergeant proudly displays the FN Browning 9mm High-Power pistol, captured during fighting in north-west Europe. The Brownings were popular with Allied and German soldiers because of their capacious double-stacked 13-round magazine.

tools. The maximum range for the pistol-sized bullet (the same as the Beretta 34 pistol) was allegedly 1,000m/ 3,281ft; in reality the effective range was around 100m/328ft.

The Browning high-power

In 1935 the Belgian firm of Fabrique National (FN) began production of the Browning 9mm GP or Grand Puissance (High-Power) pistol. They offered two versions: the standard with fixed sights and the "Adjustable Rearsight Model" with tangent rear sights, graduated up to 500m/1,640ft and a slot in the pistol grip to take a detachable wooden stock. The pistol had been designed a decade earlier by the weapons engineer John Moses Browning, and granted a US patent in February 1927 three months after his death. This superb weapon, with its double-stacked 13-round magazine, would be produced in Canada by Inglis for use by Allied troops,

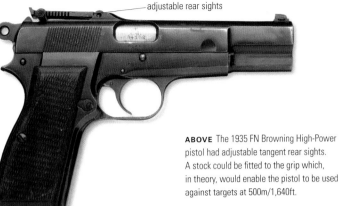

adjustable rear sights

ABOVE The 1935 FN Browning High-Power pistol had adjustable tangent rear sights. A stock could be fitted to the grip which, in theory, would enable the pistol to be used against targets at 500m/1,640ft.

while the FN weapons were eagerly taken up by the Germans following the occupation of Belgium in 1940. Prior to 1939 the pistol had already been adopted as a service sidearm in Belgium, Denmark, Holland, Lithuania and Romania. In the late 20th century it remained in service in more than 55 countries and the improved 9mm Browning High-Power Mark 3 was still in production at FN.

ABOVE The 9mm Walther PPK, a compact automatic that was favoured as a sidearm by senior German officers in World War II.

ABOVE The compact Beretta M1934, one in a line of superb weapons designed by Tullio Maregoni for the Italian Beretta company. It fired a low-powered 9mm Short or .38 Auto round.

9mm Parabellum

This is a world standard for pistol and submachine gun ammunition used and manufactured throughout the world. The 9mm Parabellum cartridge was developed in 1902 by George Luger. "Parabellum" was taken from the ancient Latin saying *Si vis pacem, para bellum*, meaning "If you want peace, prepare for war".

The original cartridge used an 8g full metal or a semi-jacketed truncated-cone bullet. The jackets were nickel-plated steel, although later copper was used. The charge (0.35g) of smokeless powder gave a muzzle velocity of 310m/s (1,017ft/s).

The name "9mm Luger" was never an official designation but the Luger name was registered in 1923 as a marketing ploy by A.F. Stoeger, the American company who imported the ammunition in the years between the wars.

RIGHT The term Parabellum has been used in the naming of a number of cartridges. However, a Parabellum is most likely to refer to a 9mm cartridge.

German submachine guns

The origins of the submachine gun in German service during World War II date back to 1916 when the Imperial German Army tasked the small-arms designer Hugo Schmeisser to produce a short-range rapid-fire weapon. It was ready for the 1918 offensive and was designated the Machine Pistol 18 or MP18. The first German submachine gun, the 9mm MP34/35, was designed by Bergmann. However, it was the MP38 and MP40 (the "Schmeisser") that would be seen as the classic German submachine gun of World War II.

bolt retracting handle

double-acting trigger

ABOVE The MP34, designed in Germany by Theodor Bergmann. A prototype was produced in small numbers in Denmark in 1932 and the MP34 was issued to the Danish army, as the BMK 32.

ABOVE A dramatic propaganda poster featuring a highly decorated German officer leading an assault armed with an MP38.

The MP34/35

Production of the MP34/35 began in Germany in 1934. The bulk of the stock made by Junker & Ruh AG at Karlsruhe went to the Waffen-SS, the Nazi's fighting force. The trigger was unusual: a partial pull produced single shots, and automatic followed if it was pulled fully to the rear. Its most distinctive feature was that the magazine loaded from the right and, when fired on automatic, had a fearsome cyclic rate of 650 rpm.

The Erma

The 9mm MP Erma (or EMP) was developed from an earlier Heinrich Vollmer design from the 1920s and was designed by Heinrich Vollmer and Berthold Giepel, both co-directors of Erma Werke. It remained in front line service until 1942. A silenced variant of the EMP was used to equip the Milice (the French security police who operated under German control) between 1940 and 1944. It had a lower muzzle velocity and rate of fire. The Erma submachine gun has unfairly become known by the name of "Schmeisser" after the senior designer at Haenel of Suhl. Haenel manufactured the weapon, and perhaps that is why Hugo Schmeisser has received the credit for the MP38, 38/40 and 40.

It was the first submachine gun to have a folding metal butt, which reduced its size from 833mm/32.8in to 630mm/24.8in and made it ideal for paratroops and vehicle crews. It had a distinctive lug called a "resting

tunnel foresight

resting bar

folding butt

ABOVE The MP38, first
produced by the Erma Werke
at Erfurt, included a folding metal
butt and was also unusual in its
use of plastic.

plastic grip

bar" below the muzzle so that it could be fired on automatic through weapons ports or over the side of vehicles with no danger of the vibration causing it to slip back inside. From the resting bar a metal fin called a "cooling strip" ran back to the receiver. The pistol grip and trigger combination drew on the US Thompson M1928 for inspiration – earlier submachine guns retained a carbine-style wooden stock. It was the first submachine gun to use plastic in the form of Bakelite in its construction.

The MP 38 went into production, and in the campaign in Poland in 1939 it soon emerged that the weapon had a dangerous fault. When the submachine gun was cocked the bolt could easily be knocked forward, accidentally causing it to fire. An improvised solution was a leather collar that fitted over the barrel with a strap that held the cocking handle. At the factory a simple safety catch was produced and these modified weapons were designated MP38/40.

Cost cutting and fire power

The drive to cut production costs and speed manufacture led to the MP40. This weapon had many of the external features of the MP38/40. In the new weapon, machining was reduced to a minimum and steel pressings and welds used wherever possible. In Russia, German soldiers armed with the MP40 found themselves out-gunned by the Soviet PPSh-41 submachine gun with its 71-round magazine. To address this problem, late in 1943 Erma introduced the MP40/1. This consisted of a special housing which took two 30-round magazines fitted side by side. While this effectively produced a 60-round weapon, it also increased the weight to 5,402g/190.56oz.

By the end of World War II, some 1,047,000 MP40s had been manufactured. It is reported that an MP40 was the weapon that was used to kill the Italian fascist leader Benito Mussolini when Communist partisans captured him in 1945. After the war it was used by the French, and remained in service as the Maskin 9mm M40 with the Norwegian Army into the 1980s.

"The Schmeisser"

The MP38 and MP40 submachine guns, known loosely by the Allies in World War II as the "Schmeisser", were issued to German Non-Commissioned Officers (NCOs) commanding MG34 and MG42 machine-gun crews. This ensured that if the gun crew was suddenly attacked by an enemy they had a weapon that could produce a high volume of short-range fire. Powerful as the machine gun was it could be difficult to handle in a confined space, unlike the handy submachine gun. The NCO was also issued with binoculars that allowed him to locate distant targets for the machine-gun crew.

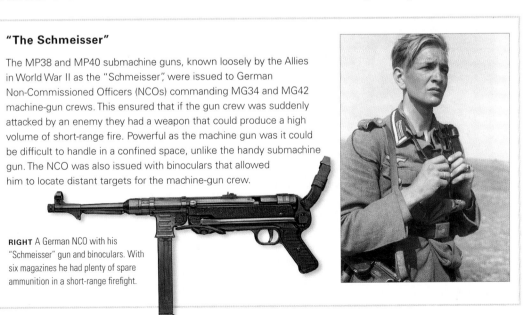

RIGHT A German NCO with his "Schmeisser" gun and binoculars. With six magazines he had plenty of spare ammunition in a short-range firefight.

Fast and cheap

During World War II some weapons were developed at short notice, while others were refined for faster, cheaper production. The definitive examples are the British Sten and the Soviet PPSh-41. The distinctive Owen gun was produced in Australia, and would serve from World War II until Vietnam, while the US developed the UD M42 or Marlin gun and the highly successful M3 "grease gun".

The Owen gun

By 1939 in Australia, Evelyn Owen had developed his first automatic weapon, chambered for the .22 Long Rifle (LR) cartridge, and offered it to the Australian army, which rejected the curious-looking weapon. However, Owen persisted and by 1941 the Lysaghts Newcastle Works in New

sights

retractable butt

barrel

box magazine

ABOVE The American .45 M3 or "grease gun", introduced in 1943, incorporated several innovative design features.

South Wales had produced several more prototypes in different calibres, including .45 ACP, 9mm Parabellum and even .38 Special revolver cartridges. The 9mm prototype weapon was tested successfully against the Thompson and Sten submachine guns. The Owen gun was adopted in 1942 and manufactured until 1945 in three basic versions: Mark 1-42, Mark 1-43 (or Mark 1 Wood Butt), and Mark 2. About 45,000 Owen submachine guns were made by Lysaghts, and these remained in service with Australian forces until the 1960s, through World War II, Korea and Vietnam. Although rather heavy, the robust, reliable and simple Owen gun was well liked by Australian soldiers.

The Marlin gun

The American 9mm submachine gun that would be widely known as the Marlin gun, but had the official designation United Defense M42, was designed between 1941 and 1942 by Carl G. Swebilius, a small-arms designer working for the High Standard

LEFT An Australian soldier armed with an Owen Mark 1. The weapon was well-made and robust and the bolt was protected against mud and dirt. The vertical 33-round magazine ensured a reliable feed, combining gravity and a spring, that compared favourably with the Thompson.

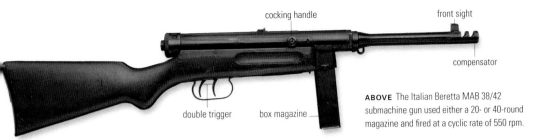

ABOVE The Italian Beretta MAB 38/42 submachine gun used either a 20- or 40-round magazine and fired at a cyclic rate of 550 rpm.

cocking handle

front sight

compensator

double trigger   box magazine

Manufacturing Company. The first UD M42 submachine guns were made by High Standard and Marlin to a Dutch order, and most were shipped to the Dutch East Indies just prior to the Japanese invasion. The remaining 15,000 guns made by the company were purchased by the US government and mostly used by Office of Strategic Services (OSS) operatives and supplied to Resistance groups, notably in Crete. The UD M42 was a somewhat complicated but well-made weapon that fired from a 20-round magazine. In an unusual development, twin reversed magazines were produced for quick reloading.

The M3 "grease gun"
The American M3, a submachine gun produced in 1943 as a low-cost substitute for the Thompson, with several updated design features. Accessories were included, such as an oiler in the weapon's pistol grip and the ingenious wire stock that could be used as a screwdriver, a spanner to unscrew the barrel, a cleaning rod and a magazine filling tool. Though the M3 only fired on full automatic, the cyclic rate was notably low at 450 rounds per minute and the straight line of recoil thrust made it easier to control. An experienced soldier could fire single shots. Before firing, the ejection port cover had to be opened manually by the operator; this also functioned as the weapon's safety catch.

The exterior of the weapon was formed from two pressed-metal shells, welded together, while the barrel of the M3 was secured by a simple nut, and the bolt rode on two guide rods inside the receiver.

This provided clearance between the bolt and receiver, preventing dirt from jamming the weapon, and making it a "soldier friendly" weapon in combat. Its main drawback was that the magazine had a tendency to jam or fall out of the housing if the magazine catch was accidentally depressed. Its unusual appearance earned it the nickname the "grease gun".

The M3 had a 30-round single position feed box magazine and fired the .45 ACP cartridge used in the M1911A1 pistol and Thompson submachine gun. It remained in service with the US Army in Korea, Vietnam and even with some units in the First Gulf War of 1990–91.

MAB38
The Italian MAB38, known as the Moschetto Automatico, was manufactured in the Beretta factory at Brescia. Until 1943, it was only available to parachute units, Carabinieri and Polizia Africa Italiana. It became more widespread in the Armed Forces of the Republic of Salò, partisans and Italian units fighting under Allied command. A later version, the MAB 38/42, was lighter, shorter and had a higher rate of fire. It remained in service well into the 1970s with the Carabinieri and police.

BELOW The UD M42 submachine gun, also known as the Marlin Gun, had a double 20-round magazine and fired at a cyclic rate similar to the Thompson M1 and M1A1 of 700 rpm.

grip

double 20-round magazine

ejection bolt

The Sten gun

Following the fall of France and the evacuation at Dunkirk in 1940, the British faced the prospect of imminent invasion by a well-armed German Army, and urgently needed an inexpensive automatic weapon. The answer was a British submachine gun designed by Major R.V. Shepherd and H.J. Turpin at the Royal Small Arms Factory at Enfield. It was named the "S.T.EN" as a tribute to Shepherd's and Turpin's ingenuity and to the factory.

Powerfully simple

The Sten went into mass production and, by the end of the war, an estimated 3.25 million had been made in Britain and Canada. The guns were cheap and easy to make. The Sten weighed about 3,500g/123oz and all marks of the weapon were blowback operated, with a cyclic rate of 540 rpm and a muzzle velocity of 366m/s (1,201ft/s). Magazine capacity was 32 rounds, but since there were always feed problems this was normally kept down to 30. Between 1940 and 1945 the Sten was modified and improved, going through numerous marks.

flash hider and compensator — rear sights — wire frame butt — forward grip

ABOVE The Sten Mark II entered service in the summer of 1941, but was not well received by soldiers on account of its rough and crudely made appearance.

The development of the Sten

The Sten Mark I, which featured a flash hider (a device to reduce muzzle flash on firing), wooden furniture, and folding hand grip, was quickly replaced by the Sten Mark II, which saw widespread issue. The fact that the Mark II was compact and easy to take apart made it easy to hide, and it was a weapon of choice for many European Resistance groups. It was also very useful that the similarity of the magazine to the German MP40 meant that it could use captured German 9mm ammunition. However, as with the German MP40, jamming could sometimes be a problem. Easy to manufacture, it was a simply built weapon composed of 47 steel parts that were welded, riveted or pushed together. The bolt and barrel were the only machine-made components. Two million Sten Mark II weapons were manufactured.

One of the requirements in the original design of the Sten was that it could be made by manufacturers who were not specialist gunsmiths. This was exemplified by the Mark III, with its fixed barrel and all-in-one body and casing welded shut along the top. It was built by a firm of toy makers, Lines Brothers. The Sten Mark III was issued to troops in time for the Normandy landings in 1944. Surprisingly, although this was possibly the best Sten version of all, it was not produced in large numbers.

ABOVE Home Guard weapons training for women in 1941. The gun in the foreground is a Sten Mark III and the other is a Mark I. The weapons are not cocked as the women are practising the basic techniques of holding and aiming.

cocking handle

silencer

wire frame butt

fabric grip

ABOVE The Sten Mark II (S) was introduced in 1943. It was popular with the Resistance and was designed to be fired on single shot. Although it was possible to fire it on automatic, the silencer was burned out when bullets were fired at 450 rpm.

Although the Sten was issued to vehicle crews, despatch riders, and those who had no need for a long-range weapon, it was principally issued to infantry battalions, especially platoon commanders, platoon sergeants, and section commanders. Although senior officers could carry a pistol as a personal weapon, many preferred the extra firepower of a Sten.

The Sten was not popular among troops because, besides jamming, it could be fired accidentally if the cocking handle snagged on clothing, or if it was dropped. This happened to Corporal Proctor of the Somerset Light Infantry during operations in Holland in 1944. A soldier slipped, dropped his Sten, and the weapon hit the ground and fired a single shot that hit Proctor in the groin. The platoon commander, Lt. Jary, condemned the weapon as "designed with little but cheap mass production in mind…. It had no locking device at the moment of firing and consequently, if the weapon was jolted sufficiently for the bolt to slide back and engage the stop round in the magazine, this would be fed into the breech and fired."

Stens in action

The Sten first saw action at the disastrous raid at Dieppe in August 1942. In the weeks prior to the raid, Canadian soldiers had to constantly adjust and test their Stens to make sure they worked properly. The first raid, Operation *Jubilee*, was cancelled in July and the Stens were withdrawn. A day before the remounting of the raid, now called Operation *Rutter*, brand new Stens, still in their crates and packed in grease, were issued to some unimpressed soldiers.

German copies

Despite these deficiencies, its ease of manufacture and low cost encouraged the Germans to copy it in 1944–45, producing weapons designated variously as the 9mm MaschinenPistole 3008, VolksmaschinenPistole, Gerät Potsdam and MaschinenPistole 749 (e). Having been so widely produced, the Sten had a lethal afterlife post-1945. The US Army technical manual *Unconventional Warfare Devices and Techniques* includes an example of a copy of the Mark II captured from the Viet Cong in 1964 during the war in Vietnam.

ABOVE Captain Brian Priday, second-in-command of 2nd Batallion of the Oxford and Bucks Light Infantry, armed with a Sten Mark V with fixed bayonet, Normandy 6 June 1944. Two key bridges had been captured across the river Orne and Orne Canal.

Soviet firepower

The weapon that would influence Soviet submachine-gun design and so eventually the war on the Eastern Front was the Suomi ("Finland") submachine gun. Used by the Finnish army in 1931 as the Suomi-KP Model 1931, it was produced by Finnish arms-designer Aimo Lachti between 1920–30. It would shape the design of the hugely successful Soviet PPSh-41 submachine gun.

bolt handle

drum magazine
(various sizes used)

ABOVE The Finnish Suomi-KP M/31 submachine gun was an exceptionally well made weapon. It weighed 4.676kg/10.3lb because many of its components were made from solid metal. As a result it was very robust and would remain in service for many years.

The Suomi

The Finnish Suomi-KP Model 1931 was also known simply as the KP-31, KP – *Konepistooli* or Automatic Pistol – and was manufactured in Finland by Tikkakoski Oy, licensed to Denmark, Sweden and Switzerland, and also widely exported. The Suomi was used very effectively during the Winter War of 1939–40 when the Soviet Union attacked Finland, and the experience of coming under fire from submachine guns with 71-round magazines had a profound impact on Soviet forces. Manufacture of the Suomi ceased in Finland in 1944, but it was used well into the 1990s when it was replaced in the Finnish army by assault rifles.

The PPSh-41

Following the German invasion of the Soviet Union in 1941 when the Russians lost huge quantities of small arms and much of their engineering capability, there was an urgent demand for a light and simple weapon capable of a high volume of fire. The answer to this was the robust and very effective Pistolet-Pulemet Shpagina 1941g or PPSh-41 7.62mm submachine gun, designed by Georgii Shpagin. It was much cheaper and quicker to make than earlier Soviet submachine guns because there were no screws or bolts on it, and all metal parts were stamped or brazed. It weighed 3,500g/123oz and had a 71-round drum magazine based on the Suomi submachine gun, or a 35-round box magazine. It fired at 900 rpm, a rate of fire that in Korea would earn it the nickname the "burp gun".

During World War II Soviet soldiers knew their submachine gun affectionately as the *Pah-pah-shah*, or *Shpagin*. The gun used barrels taken from bolt-action Mosin Nagant M1891/30 rifles that were chromed to reduce corrosion and wear. Stripping was simple, as the receiver hinged open to reveal the bolt and spring.

LEFT A Finnish soldier in a trench on the Eastern Front, holding a Suomi with a 20-round magazine. The gun had a 318mm/12.5in barrel, which made it very accurate over longer ranges.

There was no selector lever (for single shots or automatic) on some of the late models, when the gun was capable of only automatic fire, and though this was high, a rudimentary compensator and muzzle brake helped to reduce muzzle climb (the upward movement of a gun as a result of recoil). The weapon had a few drawbacks: if dropped, it could accidentally discharge, reloading was difficult and the drums were prone to jamming, something which didn't occur with the box magazines.

About five million PPSh-41s had been made by 1945, and the Soviets adapted their infantry tactics to take full advantage of such huge numbers, often equipping complete units, notably "tank descent" infantry, with the submachine gun. The standard equipment load for a soldier seems to have been the one drum and five- or six-box magazines. Before magazines were introduced, it appears that soldiers would have been equipped with two drums. The short range of these weapons meant that these units had to close with their enemy in something of the style of a bayonet charge – a tactic that terrified the enemy on the Eastern Front. The Finns captured a little over 4,000 Soviet 7.62mm submachine guns during World War II. This was too small a number to justify retooling to

ABOVE The 7.62mm PPSh-41 submachine gun, one of the weapons that was mass produced in the USSR during World War II that armed Soviet tank-riding infantry fighting on the Eastern Front.

sights

angled barrel jacket acts as compensator

71-round drum magazine

make Soviet 7.62mm ammunition and posed an added logistic burden for Finnish front-line troops. However, the demand for more submachine guns remained high and, although Finnish army HQ explored the possibilities of modifying the gun to accept Finnish 9mm ammunition and Suomi magazines, production of this modified gun was never started.

The MP717(r)

The Germans themselves were very impressed by the PPSh-41, and would use the guns as often as they captured them. Since the 7.62mm and 9mm Parabellum cartridges shared similar dimensions, only a 9mm barrel and a magazine housing adaptor was needed to convert the PPSh-41 to fire from MP38/40 32-round magazines. The Wehrmacht (the German armed forces) officially adopted the converted PPSh-41 as the MP717(r).

The Leningrad gun

During the siege of Leningrad (1941–44), there were working munitions factories, but basic materials were in short supply. In these conditions A.I. Sudarev designed the PPS-42. It was soon improved and resulted in the Pistolet-Pulemet Sudareva 1943g or PPS-43 submachine gun, an all-metal weapon with a folding stock and a compact 35-round curved box magazine. This modern design remained in production after the war. The folding stock reduced the weapon's length and made it ideal for tank crews, paratroopers, and reconnaissance units. While the weapon had a slightly slower firing rate of 700 rpm, it more than made up for this with its lighter weight, small size and greater ease of manufacture. About 500,000 were made. Captured PPS-43s were used by the Germans, with the designation MP719(r).

folding butt

35-round curved magazine

LEFT The PPS-43 had a folding stock that reduced its length to a compact 622mm/24.48in, making it an ideal weapon for Armoured Fighting Vehicle (AFV) crews and paratroops.

Submachine gun design advances

Following World War II many countries produced submachine guns for their armed forces and police. Many looked at the design features of wartime weapons, and with the leisure of peacetime production refined and improved on these combat-tested submachine guns. Some, like the Swedish Kulsprutpistole Model 45, French MAT-49 and Czech Model 61 Skorpion took on what could be called cult status. In Italy the 9mm Beretta Model 12 submachine gun proved to be a reliable weapon that enjoyed a long operational life.

sight

hinged wire butt

magazine

ABOVE The Smith & Wesson Model 76, a licence-built version of the Swedish Carl Gustaf Model 45 9mm submachine gun. The US version was a popular weapon with the CIA in Vietnam in the 1960s and 1970s. It was also produced in Egypt by the Maadi Company as the Port Said.

"The Swedish K"

The Kulsprutpistole Model 45 submachine gun was developed by Swedish state-owned Carl Gustaf Arms company in 1945 and was manufactured under licence in Indonesia, and in Egypt under the name of "Port Said", and sold to Ireland.

An almost exact copy of the Model 45 was also produced in the United States by the Smith & Wesson company in the early 1970s as the S&W Model 76. The Model 45 was not adopted by the US navy, army or police forces, but known colloquially as "the Swedish K" it did gain fame or notoriety when the Central Intelligence Agency (CIA) and special forces used it in South-east Asia during the Vietnam War. A silenced version was used in covert operations. The CIA and other agencies were able to buy these weapons without going through US military sources and men in civilian clothes seen in Vietnam carrying a Swedish K were easily recognizable as "spooks" (secret agents or spies).

The weapon had an excellent 36-round two-column magazine that was very reliable and has therefore been copied or type developed in Czechoslovakia (as it was then), Scandinavia and Germany. Uncomplicated and reliable overall, loading and maintainance are generally problem-free. It is easy to field strip and clean, and has a quick-change barrel. Partly due to the "in-line" design of the stock the Swedish K is a good shooting weapon: it is balanced, easy to handle and control for

long bursts of fire. A compact gun, the rigid stock is folding and the cartridges push directly into the body, so the magazine does not need a loader.

The MAT 49

The French state arms factory MAT (Manufacture Nationale d'Armes de Tulle) developed the MAT 49 submachine gun in the late 1940s. Adopted by the French army in 1949, the MAT 49 was widely used by the French army and police for nearly 30 years, and it also saw action in Indo-China and Algeria. It is a solid, well-made submachine gun with a magazine that hinges forward to clip under the muzzle when the weapon is not in use. The retractable wire butt can be slipped forward to reduce the length to a compact 460mm/18in. During the Vietnam War the Viet Cong produced a local copy of the MAT 49, chambered for Soviet 7.62mm ammunition.

The Beretta Model PM 12 and PM 12 S

In 1959 the 9mm Beretta Model PM 12 submachine gun was developed by the venerable Italian small-arms manufacturer Pietro Beretta Spa. Designed by Domenico Salza, it went through a number of prototypes. The weapon was made from heavy sheet steel stampings spot-welded together to form the

tunnel foresight

retractable wire butt

grip safety

hinged housing and hand grip

RIGHT The French MAT 49 has a 32- or 20-round box magazine that fits into a hinged housing. The telescopic wire butt is similar to that on the US M3 submachine gun. The MAT 49 fires at a cyclic rate of 600 rpm.

receiver and magazine housing. The receiver, forward pistol grip, magazine housing, trigger housing and pistol grip are all one unit. It has two safety catches. The Model 12 was adopted by the Italian army in 1961 and sold under licence to Brazil. It was also sold in Gabon, Libya, Nigeria, Saudi Arabia and Venezuela. The company followed the Model 12 with the Model PM 12 S. The Model PM 12 S included a number of modifications and improvements, among which was an epoxy-resin finish resistant to corrosion and wear. The Model PM 12 S had a safety catch that when applied blocked the grip safety and trigger. Both weapons had a cyclic rate of fire of 550 rpm. The Model PM 12 and the Model PM 12 S were designed for mass production but are compact and well made.

ABOVE Promotional literature from Beretta for the PM 12 S. The compact 9mm submachine gun has a 32-round detachable box magazine with options for a 20- or 40-round magazine. This model has a folding metal stock, but it is also available with a wooden butt stock.

Skorpion's sting

The design philosophy behind the 7.65mm Model 61 Skorpion (Czech vz.61) was an almost futuristic concept in 1952. It was intended to replace the pistol, but could also be used as a close-combat assault weapon, as well as for personal defence. At 270mm/10.63in long with the butt folded, its small size makes it easy to conceal in a holster and can be used in confined spaces, such as cars or aircraft. Although it became popular with both police and security units in the 1960s, it was also used by terrorist groups.

The Skorpion has also been manufactured in Serbia as the Model 84, and police and security forces in Afghanistan, Angola, Egypt, Libya, Mozambique and Uganda have adopted it. The Skorpion was produced for export chambered for the 9mm Makarov cartridge and the Browning 9mm Short. The CZ91S is a semi-automatic version with very high "collector's" finish in black enamel.

folding butt

10- or 20- round curved magazine

ABOVE The Model 61 Skorpion was intended to be a dual-purpose weapon, combining the functions of pistol and submachine gun. Since it had a stock and can be held with two hands it was effective against targets that were beyond the range of a conventional pistol, and had greater firepower.

Invention and innovation

In 1950, Uzi Gal, an engineer with Israel Military Industries (IMI), developed a very effective 9mm submachine gun, which would become known as the "Uzi". The British L2A3 9mm Sterling submachine gun entered service with the British Army in 1957 and would see action in the numerous campaigns fought from Borneo to the Falklands. The compact American MAC 10 and MAC 11 submachine guns have proved popular with undercover formations around the world.

The Uzi

Since it entered service with the Israeli Army in 1951, the Uzi has been adopted by the police and armed forces of more than 90 countries, including Israel, Germany and Belgium. The more compact versions, the Mini and Micro Uzi, are used by many police, special operations and security units around the world, including the Israeli Sayeret and the US Secret Service.

The Uzi was based on the Czech M23 and 25 submachine guns, but with a completely different receiver (rectangular instead of round in cross-section) and other changes. It is a recoil-operated, select-fire submachine gun, firing from the open bolt (the bolt is the part of a firearm that blocks the rear of the

cocking handle

grip safety

hinged butt

ABOVE The Israeli 9mm Mini Uzi is a compact weapon that is ideal for close protection teams because it can be concealed inside a jacket. It can be fitted with a 20-, 25- or 32-round magazine.

ABOVE An officer "checks clear" to see that the breech is clear of rounds on the L2A3 Sterling submachine guns of a section of Gurkha soldiers during training in a Fighting In Built Up Area (FIBUA) complex in the 1980s.

Uziel Gal (1923–2002)

Uziel "Uzi" Gal was born Gotthard Glass on 15 December 1923 in the town of Weimar in Germany. When Hitler came to power, the ten-year-old Glass moved with his school to England. In 1936, he moved to Kibbutz Yagur in what was then the British Mandate of Palestine. In Palestine he joined Palmach, the underground infantry arm of the Hagana, working as an armourer.

In 1948 Gal began work on the Uzi submachine gun shortly after Israel became a nation. In 1951 the submachine gun was adopted by the Israel Defence Force (IDF) and though Gal did not want the weapon to be named after him, his request was ignored. In 1958, for his work on the Uzi, Gal became the first person to receive the Israel Security Award, presented to him by Prime Minister David Ben-Gurion.

cocking handle

sights

folding butt

magazine housing

RIGHT The L2A3 9mm Sterling submachine gun entered service with the British Army in the 1950s. It was used around the world until the Gulf War.

chamber while the powder burns). The bolt "sleeves" around the rear part of the barrel, reducing the overall length of the gun. The Uzi has a cyclic rate of fire of 600 rpm, while the Mini's rate is 1,500 to 1,900 and the Micro's is 1,200 to 1,400 rpm.

The Sterling submachine gun

The L2A3 9mm Sterling submachine gun entered service with the British Army in 1957 and soldiered on for almost 35 years. It would be used by officers, vehicle crews and radio operators in operations around the world until the Gulf War of 1990–91. It weighed 3,500g/123.46oz and was 690mm/27in long with its butt extended and 483mm/19in with it folded. The effective range was about 200m/654ft with a muzzle velocity of 390m/s (1,279ft/s) and cyclic rate of fire of 550 rpm. The standard magazine held 34 rounds, but was usually loaded with 28 to reduce pressure on the spring.

For covert operations stubby 10- and 15-round magazines, "stacked" for a quick change, were available. This arrangement proved efficient in use. Canada produced the Sterling submachine gun as the C1 and Spain as the C2.

American genius

When weapons designer Gordon B. Ingram returned to the United States at the end of World War II he began working on submachine gun designs. In the late 1960s he came up with the tiny MAC 10 and MAC 11 submachine guns built at his Military Armament Company (hence the name MAC) at Powder Springs, Georgia. Also known as the Ingram, the versions of the MAC 10 and MAC 11 without stocks are respectively 267mm and 222mm/10.5in and 8.75in long. If the wire stock is extended, the guns are 548mm/21.5in and 460mm/18.11in long. These compact guns have a phenomenal rate of fire: the MAC 10 fires at 1,145 rpm, the 9mm MAC 10 at 1,090 rpm and the 9mm MAC 11 at 1,200 rpm. These small submachine guns are popular with security forces on covert operations since their external thread muzzle can be fitted with a MAC suppressor.

BELOW The Ingram MAC 10 is in service with the US navy and several Central American countries but, despite being excellent weapons, the .45 and 9mm MAC 10 and 11 have never been widely adopted.

thread for suppressor

hinged butt

grip safety

magazine integral to grip

The Colt M4 carbine

One American weapon that falls between a rifle and a submachine gun is the Colt M4 Carbine, the most compact of the Colt range of 5.56mm weapons. It features a four-position telescopic butt, a barrel length of 292mm/11.5in, and is designed for use wherever lightness, speed of action, mobility and close-quarters combat are required. It uses the same 30-round magazine as the M16 rifle. One veteran of the Vietnam War carried an M4 Carbine that had developed a reputation as a "jinxed" weapon since its previous users had been killed. Far from being jinxed, he said, it was a very handy weapon. It did, however, have a different signature when it was fired and consequently had attracted hostile fire when its former users had been caught in a firefight. As he explained, what had killed them was not the weapon, but their field craft and low-level tactics.

Assault rifles to submachine guns

One of the most influential submachine guns of the post-war period was the Heckler & Koch MP5, but it was rivalled by the Soviet AKSU-74, a modified AK-74 assault rifle. In Chile, Fabricas y Maestranzas del Ejercito (FAMAE) produced a modular range of submachine guns under the designation SAF, and during the 1970s Russian Evgenij Dragunov designed the Kedr, a submachine gun that departed from the AK format.

The HK54

The West German Heckler & Koch MP5 submachine gun was first produced in the mid-1960s as the HK54. It was designated Machine Pistol 5, (MP5), when it was adopted by the West German government for use by its police and border guards. It was a lightweight, air-cooled, magazine-fed, select-fire weapon with delayed blowback operation. It could be shouldered or hand-fired in semi-automatic, with two- or three-round bursts, and sustained fire modes. It is a very accurate weapon that has a cyclic rate of fire of 800 rpm.

The modular design of the weapon consisted of six assembly groups and provided an unmatched degree of flexibility, as these groups can be exchanged with optional parts to create various styles of weapons for

tactical light

retractable butt

magazine

ABOVE The Heckler & Koch MP5 mechanism is used in six different submachine guns including three silenced versions and the compact easy-to-conceal MP5K that is popular with counter-terrorist teams.

numerous operational requirements. The metal surfaces of the MP5 were phosphated and coated with a black lacquer finish that is highly resistant to salt-water corrosion and surface wear. The MP5 is made or has been made under licence in the United States, UK, Turkey, Pakistan, Mexico, Iran and Greece.

The AKS-74U

Modified from the Russian 5.45mm AK-74 assault rifle, the AKS-74U was specifically designed for vehicle crews who needed a weapon with a much shorter barrel. The overall length of the submachine gun is only 492mm/19.37in with the metal stock folded, or 728mm/28.66in with extended stock. The AKS-74U has other advantages over the AK-74 assault rifle, as its loaded weight of 3,100g/109.34oz makes it significantly lighter and it also has a somewhat higher cyclic rate of fire at 650 to 735 rpm. The rear sight is a flip-type U-notch, while the front sight is a cylindrical post. At the end of the barrel, there is a device which operates as an expansion chamber to bleed off gases that could otherwise cause a violent recoil. It is also produced in Poland as the ONYX and in Serbia as the Zastava M85.

ABOVE The AKSU-74 has become notorious as a weapon favoured by terrorist and dissident groups in Afghanistan. Its compact length of 492mm/19.37in makes it an ideal weapon for such purposes as it fires powerful 5.45mm rounds from a 30-round magazine.

rear sight

cocking handle

sling swivel

hinged butt

magazine

ABOVE The Spanish Star 9mm Model Z-84 submachine gun has a cyclic rate of 600 rpm. It is constructed using stampings and investment castings that helps to speed production and keep costs down.

Compact Chilean

Fabricas y Maestranzas del Ejercito or FAMAE, the Chilean arms manufacturer, took the Swiss SIF 540 assault rifle that they were manufacturing under licence and developed it into the SAF and Mini-SAF submachine gun. The 9mm submachine gun comes in several forms: the standard with a fixed butt stock, standard with folding stock, silenced and Mini-SAF. They employ 20- or 30-round box magazines, and the 30-round is made from translucent plastic so a quick visual check can establish how much ammunition is available. The SAF submachine gun is in service with Chilean armed forces and police.

Russian police weapons

In the early 1970s, Evgenij Dragunov, the designer of famous SVD sniper rifle, designed the Kedr submachine gun (then known as the PP-71). The project was shelved, but was revived in the early 1990s. The PP-71 was slightly modified and went into

production in limited numbers, and was issued to Russian police units. New, more powerful ammunition was developed to replace the original 9mm Makarov ammunition. This new round, the PMM, while retaining the same dimensions, had a slightly lighter bullet and heavier charge, which increased its performance. In 1994 the Kedr was slightly strengthened to take this new ammunition, and the weapon was marketed as the submachine gun.

The Spanish Z-84

Despite being compact and lightweight, the Spanish Z-84 is a powerful submachine gun which was developed in the mid-1980s by Star Bonifacio Echeverria SA. It fires soft point and semi-jacketed bullets, as well as full metal jacket military ammunition, from 25- or 30-round magazines. Once it has been cocked the submachine gun has no external moving parts, which is one of the reasons that it has been adopted by special forces in the Spanish army and police units.

Guns of the Special Air Service (SAS)

When six armed revolutionaries besieged the Iranian Embassy in London on 30 April 1979, Prime Minister Margaret Thatcher authorized the use of elite SAS counter-terrorist troops to neutralize them.

On 5 May, two SAS troopers clad in hooded black overalls were spotted outside the embassy as they positioned a frame charge against an upper-floor window. The large explosion that followed ten seconds later was a signal for the assault by teams at the front and rear, who moved nimbly across the balconies and through the smashed window.

The SAS weapon was the Heckler & Koch MP5, which they had encountered during joint training with the West German GSG9 counter-terrorist force, and which the SAS nicknamed the "Hockler".

ABOVE SAS troopers armed with Heckler & Koch MP5 submachine guns storm through the blasted windows at the front of the Iranian Embassy at Princes Gate, London, on 5 May, 1980.

Silenced guns

In World War II Britain pioneered some silencer concepts, notably with the Sten Mark VI (S) which was the world's first silenced submachine gun when it was introduced in 1943. Britain also produced the hybrid De Lisle Silent Carbine for use by covert forces. After the war the British developed the L34A1 silenced Mark 5 Sterling submachine gun. The Chinese made two rather bulky silenced pistols in the 1960s: the Type 64 and Type 67.

rear sight

sling swivel

magazine
housing

Wartime innovations

The Sten Mark VI (S) submachine gun was intended for single shots only, though it could be fired on automatic in an emergency. With the silencer the weapon was 908mm/35.75in long, compared to the 762mm/30in of a standard weapon. It was also popular with Resistance groups, and German counter-intelligence officers were greatly impressed by captured weapons. Silenced weapons have been improved since 1945 so that the silencers have a longer life even if the gun is fired in bursts.

ABOVE The Sten Mark VI (S) submachine gun was almost completely silent. It had a lower muzzle velocity compared with conventional Stens and lower cyclic rate of 450 rpm to reduce wear.

De Lisle Carbine

The British De Lisle Silent Carbine is hard to pigeonhole – is it a bolt-action pistol or a pistol-calibre rifle? What it definitely is, is a silent weapon. To work effectively with a silencer a weapon has to generate a muzzle velocity below the speed of sound, around 330m/s (1,082.67ft/s) depending on altitude and air temperature. The De Lisle Carbine, developed for British Commandos and special forces in World War II, took a .303 Lee Enfield bolt-action rifle but chambered it for the standard .45 ACP from the Colt 1911 pistol. A massive silencer gave it a 210mm/ 8.25in barrel. The first examples used the standard

Lee-Enfield wooden stock but a paratroop version with a folding stock was also produced. The signature or noise when the De Lisle Carbine was fired was a quiet "plop", a sound that would not arouse suspicion. However, although the carbine was reportedly accurate to over 300m/984.25ft, the velocity of around 260m/s (853ft/s), combined with a relatively light round-nosed bullet, produced a curved trajectory at long range, making accurate range estimation crucial.

The L34A1 Mark V Silent Sterling

The British L34A1 Mark V Sterling was a silent version of the 9mm L2A3 Sterling. It weighed 4,300g/151.68oz, and was 864mm/34in long with the butt extended. It had an effective range of 152m/500ft, with a muzzle velocity of 292–310m/s (958–1,017ft/s). The basic

cocking handle

rear sight

forward facing
hinged butt

LEFT The Silent Sterling L34A1 uses an ingenious silencing system that allows gases to escape through radial holes into an expansion chamber and then through a series of baffles. It fires standard 9mm cartridges, unlike other silenced weapons that require subsonic ammunition.

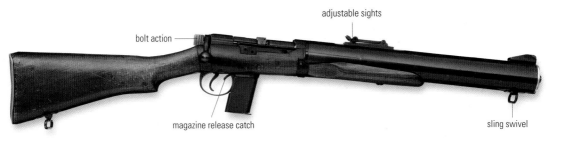

bolt action

adjustable sights

magazine release catch

sling swivel

mechanism was the same as the Sterling but the Silent Sterling has a fixed silencer allied to a special barrel. In the barrel, 72 radial holes are drilled through allowing for the hot propellent gases that follow the bullet out of the muzzle to enter an "expansion chamber". Here these gases expand to dissipate some of their energy. The gases pass through a series of metal baffles, with a central hole to allow the passage of the bullet. The baffles deflect and slow the flow of gas emerging from the expansion chamber. By the time the gases emerge from the silencer, they are cooler, slower and silenced.

Compared to the standard Sterling the L34A1 Mark V appears clumsy and unbalanced. In fact, while it is not as compact, it handles well since the silencer is not intrinsically very heavy. However, it is recommended the silenced weapon should only be fired on single shots and automatic used only in an emergency. The standard Sterling submachine gun is not a noisy weapon when it is fired, but with the

ABOVE The De Lisle Carbine made by the Royal Small Arms Factory at Enfield, with a ten-round magazine. It was fitted with a .45 barrel forming part of a large, and very efficient silencer.

silencer fitted it is almost inaudible at 30m/100ft. Before the Heckler & Koch MP5 SD became more widely available on the world market, the L34A1 Mark 5 was very popular. Ironically, while it was used by British Special Forces, it was also bought by Argentina. The L34A1 Mark V was issued to the Special Forces who spearheaded the invasion of the Falkland Islands in 1982.

Chinese silenced pistols

China had initially looked to the Soviet Union for weapons and copied these designs. However, in the Type 64 and its successor the Type 67, Chinese small arms designers came up with ingenious silenced weapons. The nine shot Type 67 and 64 pistols are built around an integral silencer. The Type 64 silencer is a light steel cylinder that contains steel mesh and several baffles that slow down and cool the gases from the muzzle blast. It could not fire standard ammunition. Instead it fires a relatively low-powered 7.65mm ammunition developed for the weapon that has a muzzle velocity of 241m/s (790ft/s). Though this helps to keep the sound down, the penalty is a short effective range of between 9–18 m /30–60ft. The pistol can also be fired manually using a lock system that prevents the semi-automatic action from operating.

The Type 67 silenced pistol is a further development of the Type 64 and has replaced the Type 64 in Chinese service. It provides the users with the same combat characteristics, but weighs 1,050kg/37.04oz in contrast to the 1,810g/63.85oz of the Type 64, and the shape of the silencer has been changed to make carrying easier.

Silent Sterling

There are few times when British Special Forces are on public view – and fewer still of the L34A1 Mark V Sterling. Ironically, the greatest exposure that the weapon received was on the morning of 2 April 1982 on news reports. It was slung from the shoulder of Sergeant I.M. Batista, the Argentine commando who escorted the Royal Marine naval party who had surrendered after their overnight defence of Government House in Port Stanley on the Falkland Islands. Batista's imperious manner and the glum Royal Marines with their hands raised in surrender did much to galvanize public opinion in Britain to back the despatch of a Task Force to the Falklands.

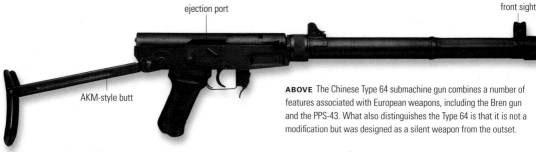

ejection port   front sight

AKM-style butt

ABOVE The Chinese Type 64 submachine gun combines a number of features associated with European weapons, including the Bren gun and the PPS-43. What also distinguishes the Type 64 is that it is not a modification but was designed as a silent weapon from the outset.

Chinese submachine guns

Though the Chinese Type 64 was one of the first indigenously designed weapons it incorporated a number of features taken from European weapons. The bolt action comes from the Soviet PPS-43, the folding butt from the AKM and the trigger mechanism from the British Bren LMG. The silencer is integral to the SMG. It is said to be reasonably effective and to reduce any muzzle flash, and the use of the subsonic 7.62mm Type 64 round further reduces the firing signature. The gun can fire conventional 7.62mm TT ammunition but the higher velocity wears out the silencer. For a submachine gun, the Type 64 has a surprisingly high rate of fire at 1,315 rpm – however, it is a selective fire SMG and would probably be used for single shots.

The Type 85 produced by China North Industries Corporation (NORINCO) is a simplified and lighter version of the Type 64 that has been produced for the export market. The silencer is similar to that on the Type 64.

ABOVE A silenced MP5, part of the series SD1–6. The silencer requires no maintenance except rinsing in an oil-free cleaning agent.

It is most effective firing Type 64 ammunition with its heavy, subsonic bullet, but it can also fire standard 7.62mm ammunition, although there is an increased noise level. The Type 85 uses the same 30-round box magazines as the Type 64 submachine gun.

Silenced German submachine guns

The German Heckler & Koch MP5 SD submachine gun series (SD1–SD6), introduced in 1974, was a superb weapon widely favoured by Western special forces. It had an integrated suppressor and a specially made barrel that has 30 2.5mm ports that reduce the muzzle velocity of its ammunition to subsonic and the the bullet crack and muzzle blast are much reduced. The result is that the MP5 SD series is almost inaudible at distances of more than 15m/49.21ft. Because of this remarkable sound reduction and the almost invisible muzzle flash, the gun has been selected by many police and military units around the world.

Silent Soviet killers

The Soviet two-shot MSP pistol does not use a silencer, but instead has an ingenious type of ammunition, making it well suited to close-range assassination operations. The pistol was developed around 1972, intended as an easily concealed, short-range assassination weapon for the KGB, GRU, Spetznatz and other covert organizations. Because of its specially designed SP-3 silent ammunition, which encapsulates all powder gases within the cartridge case, the pistol does not require a silencer.

The MSP pistol is a two-barrel, non-automatic pistol. Two barrels are in an "over-under" configuration, and are tipped up at the rear for loading and unloading. The two cartridges come clipped together which makes reloading quicker. The trigger is single-action, with the manual safety catch just behind the trigger on the left side of the grip. The enclosed hammers are cocked manually using the cocking lever at the bottom of

The sound of silence

No automatic weapon fired in bursts is completely silent, and Heckler & Koch have the correct description when they describe the MP5 SD as *Schalldämpfer*, literally "sound dampened".

When a gun is fired there are actually two noises – the explosion of the cartridge and the high-velocity crack of the bullet if it breaks the sound barrier. In a firefight, timing the interval between "crack and thump" gives both an indication of range and also whether the rounds are being aimed at the listener. If there is a distinct delay between the crack and thump then the weapon is being fired at long range and consequently the shooting may not be very accurate. If, however, the sounds almost run together the marksman is nearby and this is the time to be worried. If all that is heard is the thump of the exploding cartridge the rounds are being fired in a different direction.

RIGHT A "night vision" view of a special forces operative clearing a room using a silent submachine gun, the MP5 SD, to dampen the sound in an enclosed area.

A suppressor, widely called a silencer, will reduce the speed of the bullet so that it is travelling below the speed of sound, thus removing the "crack" noise. The thump of the exploding cartridge can also be reduced so the sound is something like that of a pneumatic stapling gun or the rattle of machinery.

the trigger guard. Surprisingly, given that engagement ranges would probably be measured in a few feet, the pistol has small open sights.

Designed in the mid-to-late 1970s, the Soviet S-4 and S-4M pistols further developed the concept of the MSP, and were used in Afghanistan, as well as in many counter-terror operations closer to home. However, possibly because it was seen as a military weapon, the bigger S-4 pistol sacrificed ease of concealment for greater range and hitting power from the powerful silent PZ cartridges.

Adopted around 1983, the Soviet 7.62mm PSS Pistolet Spetsialnyj Samozaryadnyj or Special Self-loading Pistol is a sophisticated design that is a significant improvement on the MSP and S-4M silent pistols in performance and particularly firepower.

It has a six-round box magazine and is much more compact and silent in action than conventional silenced pistols like the Soviet PB or Chinese Type 67. Currently, most elite Russian anti-terrorist teams use the PSS.

RIGHT The Russian PSS is a compact silent weapon that has a six-round magazine. The special SP-4 ammunition has an internal piston that encapsulates the propellent gases in the cartridge case. The breech block can also be locked closed to prevent the empty case being ejected to rattle to the ground, so ensuring complete silence.

Specialist and personal defence

Some Personal Defence Weapons (PDWs) are almost novelty guns, while others, such as the classic Belgian FN P90 5.7mm, have a useful role as back-up weapons and are compact enough to be carried and concealed easily. The Personal Defence Weapon falls somewhere between a submachine gun and a handgun, and the Chinese and Soviet Union have both developed gun/knife combinations, an idea that actually dates back to the Frank Wesson dagger-pistol from the 1860s in the United States.

Guns and knives

Introduced around 1994, the Chinese Firing Combat Knife falls outside the PDW category but merits description. Its blade is 40mm/1.58in long and it has four barrels chambered for .22 LR rounds built into the cylindrical handle. The barrels are positioned so that there are two on either side of the blade, with the muzzle at the base of the blade. By pressing a spring-loaded cap at the rear of the grip, the hilt cap is removed and rounds can be inserted into the chambers. The safety catch is a serrated ring in front of the handle. If it is rotated clockwise this locks the trigger, which doubles as a handguard. With the catch on, the combat knife can be used in knife mode. Twist the safety catch to the "off" position and the Combat Knife is ready to fire. The Firing Combat Knife has an effective range of 18m/60ft, although it is probably more useful at shorter ranges.

Although the Russian 7.62mm Scouting Knife fires only one round, this is a 7.62mm silent cartridge. Unlike the Chinese weapon, the muzzle of the Russian knife is in the hilt – so to fire it the knife is reversed and fired by pressing the trigger bar in the handle. A sliding safety catch prevents accidental firing. The effective range is 23m/75ft. The blade of the Scouting Knife is electrically insulated and is 152mm/6in long and 25mm/1in wide – substantial enough to cut heavy cables. A screwdriver is also incorporated.

Small but deadly

The Heckler & Koch MP5K introduced in 1976 was a dumpy, short-barrelled version of the MP5 that had no shoulder stock and used a small 15-round magazine. It was adopted by German special forces, and police and military forces throughout the world.

In 1991 H&K in the United States produced a version with a special hinged shoulder stock that was renamed "MP5K-PDW," which could fire from 15- or 30-round magazines. Only 368mm/14.5in long with the butt folded, it became a much more stable weapon to fire from the shoulder or the hip once it was extended.

The Finnish 9mm Jati-Matic/GG-95 PDW has an unusual barrel location that allows the bolt to recoil up an inclined plane at an angle to the barrel and so reduce muzzle climb when fired on automatic. It has a select-fire trigger and a (rudimentary) folding foregrip. It fires from a 20- or 40-round box magazine and has a cyclic rate of 600 to 650 rpm. Although it is very compact, the fact that it fires 9mm ammunition puts it up against more proven systems like the Hecker & Koch MP5K-PDW. Despite this the Jati-Matic is manufactured under licence in China.

ABOVE Due to its compact size the MP5K has high mobility. However, it is not as popular as the PDW version of the MP5K which has a shoulder stock making control of the weapon much easier.

ABOVE Packed ready for transport, the SPP-1M Russian underwater pistol. It can be fired underwater, and on land when the diver has reached the shore, making it a truly amphibious weapon.

Combat beneath the waves

The Russian Tsniitochmash organization produced the *Spetsialnyj Podvodnyj Pistolet* – the Special Underwater Pistol or SPP-1 – in the late 1960s for combat divers working in the Soviet navy. The SPP-1 is a four-barrelled, non-automatic weapon that fires 115mm/4.5in-long drag-stabilized darts that are lethal at 45m/147.5ft in the air and 15.5m/51ft under water. It is also lethal at greater depths than this, although at closer ranges. The sealed ammunition is loaded from the rear and the self-cocking mechanism fires one round with each pull of the trigger. The SPP-1 has been modified and upgraded as the SPP-1M and is still used by the Russian navy special forces.

The definitive PDW

The Belgian P90 5.7mm PDW designed by Fabrique Nationale de Herstal (FN Herstal) entered service in 1994. It is a truly innovative weapon built around a new FN round that is a cross between a rifle and pistol bullet. PDWs are now required in service because existing pistol calibre cartridges are becoming increasingly ineffective at disabling troops equipped with body armour.

It is a lightweight and completely ambidextrous weapon with a compact, translucent 50-round magazine that runs horizontally across the top of the P90, and empty cases are ejected downwards, well away from the operator. Only the bolt and barrel are made of steel, the rest being from high-impact plastic material. It fires from a closed bolt, giving it outstanding accuracy and making it easy to keep on target. It has a cyclic rate of fire of 900 rpm and a combat range of 137m/450ft.

BELOW The FN P90 fires a new type of 5.7mm ammunition that uses dense plastic in place of conventional lead and can penetrate 48 layers of body armour, making it particularly lethal.

Magnum force

Although the compact convenience and large magazines of automatic pistols seemed to spell the end of the revolver, the weapon still had its advocates after World War II and was much favoured by police. These guns include the .44 American Smith & Wesson Magnums, the .357 Colt Python and the .357 Ruger Blackhawk Magnum. The Russian 12.3mm Udar is a different type of revolver, but it still delivers a formidable punch.

hammer
spur

ABOVE The Smith & Wesson Model 29, with cartridge, is powerful enough to have made handgun hunting a recognized sport in the United States.

Classic revolvers

One American handgun, the S&W Model 29, would become something of a film star in the 1970s. From 1955 to 1957 the big Smith & Wesson revolver was simply called "the .44 Magnum", but when in 1957 S&W standardized the model numbering of their products it became the S&W Model 29. Smith & Wesson .44 Magnum revolvers have heavyweight steel frames produced in blue or stainless-steel finishes. The blue and nickel models are called the Model 29, while the stainless-steel version is the Model 629. Versions such as the "629 Classic", "629 DX", "629 Classic Hunter" have specialized features such as interchangeable front sights, full lug barrels, and special grips. *Jane's Infantry Weapons* sums up the reputation of the .44 Magnum: "When the utmost power is required from a handgun, the Model 29 is the obvious answer, delivering upwards of 1600 J of muzzle energy with the longer barrels."

The revolver revival

When it was introduced in 1955, the hand-made Colt Python .357 revolver immediately became one of the most popular personal weapons for US Law Officers.

It was available either blued or nickel plated, however, the nickel plated finish was replaced by satin or polished stainless steel finish. Uniformed officers carried the service revolver with its 101mm/4in or 152mm/6in barrels, while their colleagues in plain clothes tucked the self-defence versions with their stubby 64mm/2.5 in or 101mm/4in barrels underneath jackets. Hunters and target shooters opted for the big 101mm/4in and 203mm/8in versions.

The weapons were well made, comfortable to fire and since they had originally been intended to be a big calibre target revolver – very accurate. The foresights were conventional with a red polymer dot insert, the rear sights adjustable for both windage and elevation and had a white edging. Production stopped in 1998 when the Python was replaced by the Kingcobra, however, individual revolvers were made until 2003.

ABOVE The discharge of a Magnum revolver at a shooting range. The target is aimed at using an optical scope. Large-calibre weapons are best suited to target shooting and hunting,

In 1955 the American gunmaker William Ruger, who had noted popular interest in single-action revolvers seen in Western films, produced a single-action gun that quickly became the flagship for all his single-action handguns – the .357 Blackhawk Magnum. This was followed by the .44 Magnum Blackhawk in 1956. Three years later the largest of the single action Rugers appeared, the Super Blackhawk, which had an all steel frame and could fire either .44 Magnum or .45 Colt ammunition. However, Ruger revolver designs were also innovative. The compact SP 101 is a stainless steel five shot weapon in various calibres and capable of handling powerful modern ammunition. In 1993 a double action pistol with a spurless hammer was introduced that was ideal for covert use as there was no risk of the spur snagging on clothing. It was available in 0.38 Special and 0.357 Magnum chambering.

ABOVE The Colt Python was originally made in a nickel-plated finish. This was changed when stainless-steel became available, supplementing the existing blued carbon-steel.

The Udar revolver

If a modern version of the film *Dirty Harry* were produced, the hero might choose the Russian 12.3mm Udar or "Blow". This compact weapon is a double- and single-action revolver designed to fire a range of special cartridges built around the 32-gauge hunting round, and has been developed for police and security forces. Clips are preloaded with different ammunition types that can be quickly replaced according to the tactical situation.

The armour-piercing round has a sub-calibre steel bullet that can penetrate a 5mm/0.2in steel plate at 45m/147.64ft, as well as conventional body armour. A plastic round is available for non-lethal operations, and a pyroliquid (coloured ink) bullet for training exercises and for marking offenders. The pistol fires conventional ball ammunition and a high-noise blank round. Empty cases are ejected simultaneously. Three filled reserve clips are carried in the box, together with the holster.

"Do you feel lucky?"

Don Siegel's 1971 film *Dirty Harry* was considered sensational because of its overt violence. The duelling combatants, Clint Eastwood's unconventional cop and the pathological sadistic criminal, share traits of brutal violence and insanity.

When the film was being made, the .44 Model 29 Magnum was not in production, so strings had to be pulled to get a few made especially for the film. Eastwood spent time on the range prior to undertaking the role, so that he could properly replicate the .44's recoil when firing blank cartridges in the film. The blanks also had to be specially made, as the traditional Hollywood blanks would not fit the .44 chamber. In the film, Harry uses a light special load that gives better control because of its reduced recoil.

RIGHT Clint Eastwood in *Dirty Harry*. In the film he describes the S&W Model 29 as "The most powerful handgun in the world". This, together with "Do you feel lucky, punk?", are among the memorable lines uttered by the ruthless detective in the film.

Post-war pistols

Pistol design expanded vastly after World War II in Europe, when the major users were police and the armed forces, with only a small number of private owners. In the United States, however, there was a large domestic market, too. Many designers took the best features of existing pistols, notably the German P38 and FN Browning 9mm High-Power and incorporated them into their pistols.

ABOVE The Czech 9mm CZ75 is a handy weapon that incorporates features like the safety from the P38 and the double stack magazine from the Browning HP.

French service

The French 9mm MAS Model 1950 pistol was developed in the late 1940s by Manufacture d'Armes de Saint Etienne (MAS) in France, and manufactured by MAS and also by Manufacture d'Armes de Chatellerault (MAC) until 1970. The pistol was a development of the pre-war SACM Model 1935A pistol, designed by Swiss engineer Charles Petter. This recoil-operated, locked breech, semi-automatic pistol, uses a single-action trigger with slide-mounted safety. This locks the firing pin, which, by pressing the trigger with the safety engaged, enables the hammer to be lowered. The MAS Model 1950 has fixed sights and a single-stack nine-round magazine.

Czech copies

Although the 9mm CZ75 pistol developed by the brothers Josef and Frantisek Koucky, seemed an ideal military pistol, it was only adopted by police forces. It would, however, prove to be a very influential design. It first appeared in 1975, with production beginning a year later. Obviously intended for the export market, it looked good, was comfortable to handle and shoot, and was quite accurate and reliable.

The CZ75 design had drawn on the best features of previous pistols such as the P38 and the Browning High Power, and in turn was widely copied and cloned. Israel's IMI produced the Jericho-941; in Italy Tanfoglio made the TZ75, TZ90 and T95; in Turkey Sarsilmaz manufactured the M2000; in Switzerland ITM the AT-88; while in China Norinco designed the NZ-75.

Spanish designs

Two years after Llama-Gabilondo y Cia of Vitoria produced their 9mm M-82 pistol it was adopted by the Spanish Army. It has a 15-round magazine and is a recoil operated, locked breech pistol with a short recoiling barrel like the Walther P-38 or Beretta 92. To load with the safety "on", a magazine is inserted, the slide operated, a round is fed in, but the hammer drops in a safe condition. To fire, push the safety to "fire" and pull the trigger – this cocks and releases the hammer. For greater accuracy, the hammer can also be manually cocked for the first shot. With a steel frame and slide, the M82 is relatively heavy at 1,110g/39.15oz, but it is also strong; an alloy frame version weighs in at 875g/30.86oz.

ABOVE The Spanish Star Model 30M has a 15-round magazine and an ambidextrous safety catch. The trigger guard is shaped for a double-handed grip.

The 9mm Spanish Star Model 30M and 30 PK was developed and manufactured by Star Bonifacio Echeverria SA. It appeared in 1990 and is now in service with the Spanish army and police. An updated version of the earlier Star 28M, they are recoil-operated, locked-breech pistols, that use Browning-designed, linkless locking. Safety features include a magazine safety that prevents firing without a magazine, as well as a chamber loaded indicator.

Safety and weapons handling

ABOVE The pistol is safe when the breech is empty of ammunition and the safety catch applied.

A firearm is a lethal tool that requires very little skill to use. To prevent accidents there are two simple safety rules. The first is to ensure that a weapon is unloaded. Remove the magazine while pointing the weapon in a safe direction. Then operate the action, which will eject a round that might be in the breech. Then, and only then, is the trigger pulled.

The weapon can then be "made safe" with the full magazine in place, but with the safety catch applied and no rounds in the breech. If it is unloaded, the magazine is removed and any rounds that may have been ejected are stowed back in the magazine, which is then put in a pocket or pouch.

If a weapon is handed from one user to another, he should, in British military parlance, "show clear", that it has been unloaded. A revolver is broken to show the empty cylinders, while the magazine is removed from an automatic weapon and the action pulled to the rear to show that the breech is empty. The second safety rule is never to point a weapon at anyone in fun.

In 1993 the Heckler & Koch Universal Self-loading Pistol (USP) – was marketed initially in 9mm and .40 S&W. With a modified Browning linkless locked-breech action with patented recoil reduction system, it is a very accurate pistol to fire since it is easy to recover the sight picture between shots. The USP has a moulded polymer frame with special grooves for the quick mounting of laser-aiming modules or tactical lights.

Italian style on trial

Beretta 92 pistols first began production in 1976 and were based on the early Beretta model 1951. Developed by the Italian company Armi Pietro Beretta Spa, the Model 92 was adopted by the Italian army as well as being manufactured under licence in Egypt. It is a blowback operated, locked-breech semi-automatic pistol which has a vertically tilting locking block system and an external trigger bar on the right side of the frame similar to the Walther P38. It also has a double-action trigger with a frame-mounted safety. Aluminium alloy is used for the frame and steel for the slide. Although the original Beretta 92 is no longer being made, it has served as the basis for numerous modifications and improvements.

In 1985 the Beretta model 92F was submitted as the XM9 for US Army Pistol Trials. Improvements and modifications included a chromed barrel, a trigger guard designed for a double-handed grip, new grip panels and a trigger bar disconnect safety. There was considerable controversy in the United States when it was finally adopted as the 9mm M9 pistol. It is manufactured in Italy, and in the United States by Beretta United States.

ABOVE The Italian Beretta 92 was adopted by the US Army as the M9. It is available in several configurations, all of which have a Browning HP-style 15-round magazine.

New guns, new materials

The attraction of new materials such as alloys and glass-reinforced plastic (GRP) in weapons construction is that they are lighter, sometimes stronger and do not rust or corrode. With a lower metallic content, they can be harder to detect by conventional security systems (found at airports for example), although some weapons developed using these new technologies have attracted controversy in the trade over materials and design.

The Glock

Glock Gmbh of Austria had an established reputation for its combat knives and entrenching tools when its 9mm Glock 17 won at the Austrian army pistol trials. The gun was subsequently adopted in the early 1980s under the designation P-80 by Austrian police and military forces. Since then, the Glock 17 and its subsequent derivatives have become very popular firearms, being exported to more than 50 countries. Among the features that have attracted users are the small number of working parts (only 33 including the magazine), and the use of highly resistant polymer materials. The Glock was probably the first handgun to be made successfully using polymers.

Currently, Glocks are chambered for all major pistol calibres, and are available in full-size service models, semi-compact models, compact models for concealed/backup use, and in longslide competition models. The Glock Selective-Fire Submachine Pistol has fitted a fire selector and 19- or 33-round magazine to the basic pistol and produced a weapon with an awesome rate of fire of around 1,300 rpm. It is possible

ABOVE A Colt .357 Python revolver receives the hands-on treatment on the production line at the factory at Hartford, Connecticut, United States. The company introduced the pistol in the early 1960s. While new guns and materials are introduced, older versions are still popular.

to obtain training versions, which fire non-lethal practice ammunition. To avoid confusion, the frame colour of "live" guns is red while guns that fire non-lethal ammunition are coloured blue.

Special operations

The Heckler & Koch Mark 23 SOCOM pistol was developed to a requirement from the US Special Operations Command for a pistol of a calibre of no less than .45 with a 12-round magazine. The gun must have a service life of 30,000 rounds before major maintenance, and be capable of being fired when wet,

ABOVE The revolutionary Glock 17 pistol has been adopted by the Austrian army and the forces of 45 other countries.

ABOVE The Heckler & Koch Mark 23 originated in 1991 when Heckler & Koch began development of a pistol for the US Special Operations Command (SOCOM). It finally passed all their rigorous tests and was issued by SOCOM in 1996.

dirty, icy or not maintained. A silencer and laser-aiming device were added to the specifications, which had to be instantly removable without tools and which would not adversely affect the accuracy of the gun upon refitting. Both Colt and Heckler & Koch entered the trials.

The H&K pistol had several parts (the slide and 12-round box magazine) made from polymers, and a mechanical recoil-suppression system that reduced recoil forces by 30 per cent. As well as the required flash and noise suppressor, it also had a laser-aiming module that could be attached to give an infrared or visual aiming spot. The H&K gun finally passed all the tests and became the .45 MK23 SOCOM offensive handgun and was issued in 1996.

Police and civilian guns
The 9mm Vektor Compact pistol (CP1) manufactured by the DENEL Corporation of South Africa was another weapon built using a polymer frame and a stainless-steel barrel. Introduced during the late 1990s, it was intended as a concealed-carry weapon for police and civilian use. Magazines are double-stack and the Compact's 12-round magazine fits flush with the bottom of the grip, while the 13-round has extended finger rests at the bottom.

Weighing 720g/25.4oz with the 13-round magazine, the CP1 seemed a useful little handgun. However, controversy struck when the US gun enthusiast press published a recall notice in October 2000 warning that the loaded pistol could fire if bumped or dropped, and advised users not to load the gun under any circumstances.

Hollow point or full metal jacket (FMJ)

The name "dum-dum" was used to describe a British military bullet that was developed at the Dum-Dum Arsenal, on the North-West Frontier of India in the late 1890s. It consisted of a jacketed .303 rifle bullet with the jacket nose open to expose its lead core. The aim was to improve the bullet's effectiveness by increasing its expansion upon impact; what this actually meant was terrible injuries to the victim. The phrase "dum-dum" was later expanded to include any soft-nosed or hollow-pointed bullet. The Hague Convention of 1899 outlawed the use of these bullets.

However, although soldiers are required to fire bullets that have a full metal jacket (FMJ), the police are not. While hollow-point rounds can make big holes when they hit human tissue, the rounds simply flatten if they hit a building, and will not ricochet off with the consequent chance of injuring innocent people in the vicinity.

ABOVE The hollow-point round causes extreme expansion or disintegration on impact.

Controversy
In 1994 Smith & Wesson introduced the Sigma series of pistols with the Sigma 40F in .40 S&W, and this was followed by a 9mm version. S&W had taken ten years to develop the pistol, which was the first to be made using polymer for both the gun frame and slide. However, the Sigma pistol was so similar to a Glock, that some referred to the Sigma series as "Swocks", a play on words between S&W and Glock. Glock sued Smith & Wesson, and although Smith & Wesson were obliged to pay an undisclosed sum to Glock for breach of patents, they received the rights to continue production of the Sigma line, with some amendments.

Modern handgun mechanisms

By the early years of the 20th century, the semi-automatic pistol and revolver had established themselves as viable weapons although the basic principles have not changed greatly since the 1930s. There are dozens of different operating methods for firearms, but the same basic principle applies to all: the firearm must be loaded, the hammer cocked for firing, and the firing pin must strike the primer of the cartridge for it to fire.

Single-action mechanism

Single-action (SA) pistols have a single-action trigger mechanism. The hammer is cocked and the trigger fired to discharge a bullet. A semi-automatic pistol such as the Colt M1911 is an example of a pistol that must be cocked for the first shot, but after the first shot has been fired, it is cocked automatically. These types of pistols typically have a very light trigger pull, and are very accurate. The pistol mechanism is always partially cocked while being carried and during firing, but cannot discharge a cartridge before it is fired.

Double-action mechanism

Traditional double-action (TDA) pistols have a mechanism that can be used in two ways. They can either be pre-cocked, like the single-action gun, or they can be fired with the gun uncocked. In this case, the gun has an additional mechanism added to the trigger that will cock the gun as the trigger is pulled. The hammer is released and the gun fired once the trigger is pulled far enough. For autoloading pistols, the self-loading mechanism will also recock the hammer after the first shot so that subsequent shots are fired single-action. Double-action-only (DAO) pistols do not use the motion of the slide to recock the hammer. Rather, both for the initial shot and all subsequent shots, the hammer is cocked by releasing the trigger.

Firing a gun

When a single or semi-automatic pistol is fired the hammer is cocked to draw back the slide. Pulling the trigger then discharges the cartridge. This causes the slide to recoil backwards. As the slide recoils it opens the breech, ejecting the casing. At the same time the slide recocks the hammer for the next shot. The spring-loaded slide mechanism automatically returns to its position and a new cartridge is fed into the magazine.

How the modern revolver works

A revolver has several firing chambers arranged in a circle in a cylindrical block. When the trigger of the revolver is pulled, the cartridge in the chamber is aligned with the barrel. At the same time the hammer is released and a compressed spring drives the hammer forward. The firing pin on the hammer extends through the body of the gun and hits the primer. The primer explodes, igniting the propellant. The propellant burns, releasing a large volume of gas, which drives the bullet down the barrel. The pressure of the gas also expands the cartridge case which has the effect of temporarily sealing the breech. At the same time the trigger is pulled, a mechanism attached to the trigger pushes on a ratchet to rotate the cylinder. This positions the next breech chamber in front of the gun barrel ready for firing.

ABOVE When the spent shells have been removed from the cylinder, individual cartridges can be placed in the chambers.

How a semi-automatic pistol works

A semi-automatic pistol works by extracting and ejecting a fired cartridge automatically from a chamber, which then loads an unfired cartridge from a magazine into the chamber to be ready for the next trigger pull. This cycle uses the energy of the explosive discharge of each cartridge that is fired.

1. A magazine is loaded with 9mm cartridges, and then placed into the pistol's grip. The slide is pulled back. This cocks the hammer and is then released and is pushed forward by the recoil spring. The breech block feeds the first round of ammunition from the magazine into the barrel's chamber. The next round in the magazine is moved into position.

2. Now the pistol is loaded, the trigger is pulled. This draws the trigger bar forward. This pivots the safety lever, raising the firing pin safety block so the firing pin can move. Simultaneously, the trigger bar pulls the sear forwards, releasing the hammer. The main spring pushes the hammer forwards so that it strikes the back of the firing pin. This hits the cartridge and the primer causes the gun to fire.

3. The force of driving the bullet out of the barrel also presses the empty cartridge case backwards as a result of recoil. The force also pushes the slide to the back. The firing pin safety block is activated by its separation from the safety lever. As it moves backwards the slide forces the trigger bar downwards and away from the safety lever. The slide also takes the barrel with it as it travels backward. The locking insert stops the backward motion and moves it down and away from the slide.

4. As the slide returns, the sear and safety lever go back to their starting points. The empty cartridge case is pushed upwards out of the ejection port. As the slide recoils to its stop, it cocks the hammer. The slide is pushed forward by the recoil spring, and the next round is fed into the chamber of the barrel as the slide locks up with the barrel again. The pistol can be fired again.

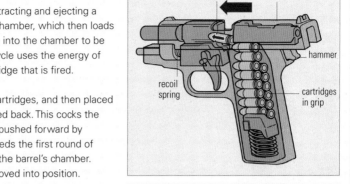

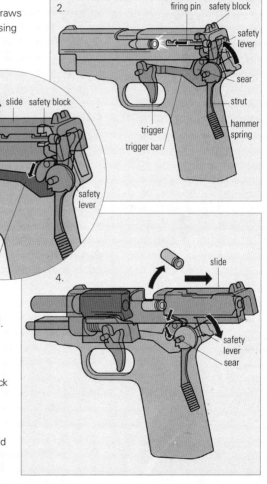

The 21st century and the future

Non-lethal hand-held guns are now regarded as useful weapons, whereas 20 years ago a handgun was used simply to kill an assailant. Research continues into how to produce weapons that will stop an aggressive person without killing or severely injuring them. On a larger scale, riots present a different but related challenge. Arms manufacturers have produced a variety of solutions, from incapacitating gases that generate coughing and disorientation, but not lasting injury, to rubber bullets and anaesthetizing darts.

CS gas and baton rounds

In 1928 two American scientists, Ben Carson and Roger Staughton, discovered 2-chlorobenzalmalononitrile, and the first two letters of the scientists' surnames were used to name the substance. This CS gas was developed and tested secretly at the British Chemical and Biological Warfare Establishment at Porton Down, Wiltshire, during the 1950s and 1960s. CS is actually a solid chemical and in order to deliver it to a human target it must be converted into a smoke or aerosol. In powder form it can be incorporated into

ABOVE Police firing rubber bullets and tear gas as they struggle to stop supporters of Venezuelan President Hugo Chavez from clashing with opposition protesters, Caracas, 4 November 2002.

riot-control munitions like baton rounds. The 12-gauge Ferret barricade round from Mace Security of the United States is designed to punch through barriers such as car windshields or wooden doors and scatter a quick-acting liquid irritant agent inside. However, unlike a baton round, the Ferret breaks up on impact with a barrier.

The British developed baton rounds in the late 1960s, when colonial police in Hong Kong used 51mm/2in wooden cylinders fired from large-bore weapons to disrupt riots. The aim was to replicate the effect of using a truncheon on demonstrators, without the police actually having to engage in hand-to-hand combat with the rioters.

The rounds were expected to fall a few feet short of rioters, to ricochet off the ground at about ankle height. However, the police found the wooden rounds often split, had unpredictable characteristics, and could prove lethal if fired at close range. When the "troubles" began in Northern Ireland in the 1970s, British troops were equipped with baton-round guns that fired tough rubber bullets, which were later replaced by PVC rounds. The use of baton rounds became increasingly controversial as injuries and deaths were linked to close-range hits.

Rubber bullets

The French company Manurhin, with a well-respected reputation for its small arms, devised the MR-35 Punch. This is a 35mm five-shot weapon that uses a small powder charge to fire a soft rubber ball. A hit will not kill, but it does deliver the sort of impact that you would feel if hit by a .38 Special bullet. Five balls can be fired from the MR-35 Punch in as many seconds and it can hit a 17cm^2 target at 7m (6in^2 at 20ft). Made largely from polymers, the MR-35 weighs only 1,500g/53oz loaded.

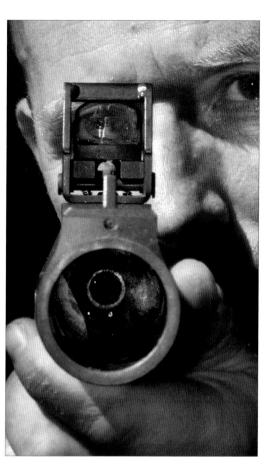

A similar concept is reflected in the American RB rubber ball series of 12-gauge cartridges. These contain nine small hard rubber balls that are designed to ricochet off the ground. Again, this firearm will knock down, wind and deter a hostile individual without causing fatal injury.

The anaesthetic gun

The Chinese BBQ-901 anaesthetic gun system is a slightly sinister device for neutralizing an assailant and is probably derived from game conservancy dart rifles. It is a single-shot hand-held weapon that fires a projectile, that on impact, injects a liquid anaesthetic. Depending on the type of anaesthetic used, this will render the target unconscious in one to three minutes. The effects of the anaesthetic wear off in three to four minutes – which gives enough time for the subject to have been handcuffed.

The grenade launcher

The South African MGL Mark 1 40mm grenade launcher is a six-shot shoulder or hip-fired revolver that fires baton rounds or tear gas cartridges. It has a minimum range of 30m/98ft and maximum of 400m/1,312ft. Like gun fighters in the Wild West, a skilled operator can fire six rounds in just three seconds.

LEFT A Metropolitan Police firearms officer with a L104AL baton gun. This weapon can be deployed at a distance no closer than 1 metre from a suspect. The L104AL fires a high-velocity plastic round.

Knock down

One of the most effective non-lethal systems available to police and security services is the Taser, developed by Taser Inc. in the United States. The hand-held device fires two probes up to 5m/16ft carrying a lightweight wire. Once the probes have attached themselves to an assailant, an electrical signal is transmitted causing him to lose neuromuscular control. Once he has been knocked down, a series of pulses keeps him down and ensures that he cannot remove the probes. The Taser has become an ideal device for controlling aggressive or dangerous individuals. Unlike a CS spray that must be directed at the face, or a handgun that has to be fired at a head or torso, the Taser works on whatever part of the body it hits.

ABOVE British Police used a non-lethal Taser at Manchester Airport in September 2005 to immobilize a man who was acting suspiciously and resisting arrest.

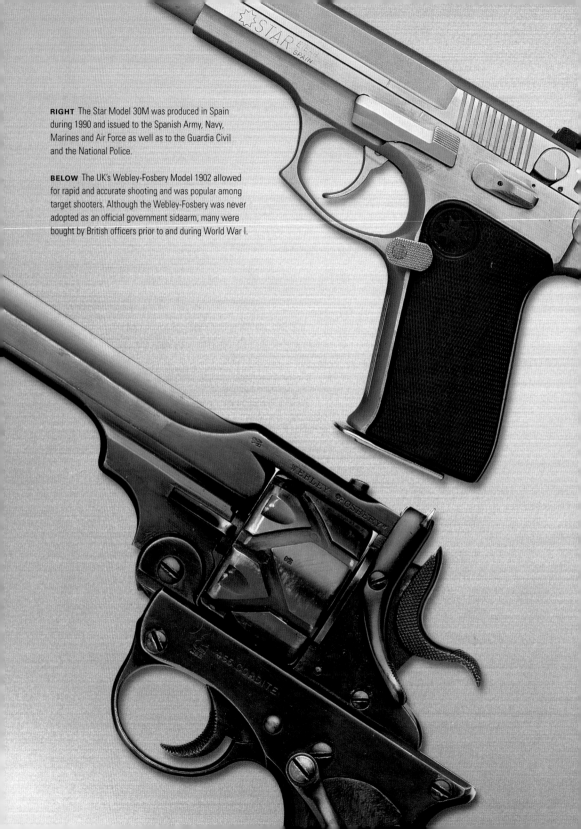

RIGHT The Star Model 30M was produced in Spain during 1990 and issued to the Spanish Army, Navy, Marines and Air Force as well as to the Guardia Civil and the National Police.

BELOW The UK's Webley-Fosbery Model 1902 allowed for rapid and accurate shooting and was popular among target shooters. Although the Webley-Fosbery was never adopted as an official government sidearm, many were bought by British officers prior to and during World War I.

A directory of pistols and revolvers from around the world

A variety of countries around the world produce and manufacture firearms. Some produce arms that are unique, while others produce or import versions of firearms from other countries under licence, sometimes with different fittings and specifications. This directory is a cross-section of selected countries of the world, west to east – and some of the firearms that are available in those countries and their main features. Within each country guns are organized alphabetically by manufacturer except where its historical development is shown more clearly chronologically or a company changes its name. Each firearm has a description and a specification that lists its vital measurements, including its calibre.

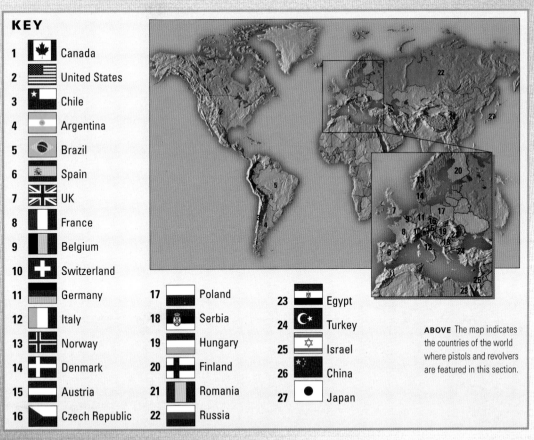

KEY

1	Canada
2	United States
3	Chile
4	Argentina
5	Brazil
6	Spain
7	UK
8	France
9	Belgium
10	Switzerland
11	Germany
12	Italy
13	Norway
14	Denmark
15	Austria
16	Czech Republic
17	Poland
18	Serbia
19	Hungary
20	Finland
21	Romania
22	Russia
23	Egypt
24	Turkey
25	Israel
26	China
27	Japan

ABOVE The map indicates the countries of the world where pistols and revolvers are featured in this section.

Note on specification boxes: Traditionally guns developed in the United States have been given calibres in inches, while European countries have designated calibre in metric. Guns have retained this designation in this book. Calibre is given different names in different parts of the world – for example .380 ACP is called the 9mm Browning Short in Belgium, 9mm Corto in Italy, and 9mm Kurtz in Germany, and 9 x 17mm by many countries. Dimensions refer to the weapon shown, where illustrated. Weights and measurements are approximate.

 Canada

Having previously relied largely on imports or copies of weapons from countries in Europe and the United States, Canada now has a small but highly reputable small-arms industry. The company Para-Ordnance, founded in 1985, has been credited with some of the most significant improvements on Browning's original M1911 design and since then has developed a wide range of pistols for the military, law enforcement, sports and competition markets. Para-Ordnance works in coordination with Colt Canada.

Browning M1935, John Inglis version

The M1935 was an improvement on the earlier and hugely successful M1911 pistol, first produced in Belgium in the early 20th century. The Browning M1935 was a semi-automatic 9mm pistol conceived by firearms inventor John Browning and produced in Belgium in 1935. It was the most advanced military pistol available. During World War II, John Inglis and Company in Ontario produced a Canadian version of the Browning M1935 for use by Allied Forces, including the British, Canadians and Greeks. The pistol was widely used by the British Special Air Service (SAS) as well as by the US Office of Strategic Services (OSS).

SPECIFICATION

MANUFACTURER John Inglis Ltd.
CALIBRE 9mm Parabellum
MAGAZINE CAPACITY 13
ACTION Recoil/single
TOTAL LENGTH 197mm/7.75in
BARREL LENGTH 118mm/4.65in
WEIGHT UNLOADED 920g/32.5oz

Para-Ordnance P14-45

hammer

Introduced in 1990, this was the first pistol in the Para range – an updated version of the classic pistol, the M1911, which became the standard issue handgun used in the United States between 1911 and 1985. The .45 ACP (Automatic Colt Pistol) P14-45 is a single-action pistol that can be carried "cocked and locked" – this means a round can be carried in the chamber while the external hammer is checked and the thumb safety applied. Favoured by competition shooters, this is an effective combat weapon with a good reliability record.

SPECIFICATION

MANUFACTURER Para-Ordnance
CALIBRE .45 ACP
MAGAZINE CAPACITY 14
ACTION Recoil/single
TOTAL LENGTH 216mm/8.5in
BARREL LENGTH 127mm/5in
WEIGHT UNLOADED 1,334g/40oz

Para-Ordnance Carry

grip
safety

When this pistol was introduced in 1992, it was the world's smallest double-action-only (DAO) pistol in .45 ACP and the first in the Carry Option range. The safety system allows the pistol to be carried with the hammer down, ready for action ("cocked and locked"). It remains flush with the pistol when not firing and each subsequent trigger pull produces a smooth shot (Para call this light double-action or LDA). Before firing, the grip safety needs to be depressed before the gun can operate. Standard features of the Carry include night sights, which are used to acquire targets in poor light.

SPECIFICATION

MANUFACTURER Para-Ordnance
CALIBRE .45 ACP
MAGAZINE CAPACITY 6
ACTION Recoil/LDA
TOTAL LENGTH 165mm/6.5in
BARREL LENGTH 76mm/3in
WEIGHT UNLOADED 850g/30oz

Para-Ordnance CCW (Concealed Carry Weapon)

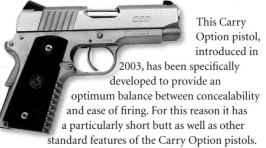

SPECIFICATION	
MANUFACTURER	Para-Ordnance
CALIBRE	.45 ACP
MAGAZINE CAPACITY	7
ACTION	Recoil/LDA
TOTAL LENGTH	196mm/7.7in
BARREL LENGTH	108mm/4.25in
WEIGHT UNLOADED	850g/30oz

This Carry Option pistol, introduced in 2003, has been specifically developed to provide an optimum balance between concealability and ease of firing. For this reason it has a particularly short butt as well as other standard features of the Carry Option pistols.

ABOVE Light double-action (LDA) Para triggers allowed a hammer-down carry for instant readiness, and a smooth trigger pull to keep the shot on target.

Para-Ordnance Carry 12

The Carry 12, developed in 2004, is a high-capacity carry pistol. It is slim and compact enough to be easily concealed while providing a high level of firepower. The Carry 12 has all the standard features of the Carry range, with sophisticated night sights to help with targeting in poor light. It has a high-capacity magazine with 12 rounds of ammunition, while much of the recoil from firing the pistol is absorbed by its solid stainless-steel construction.

SPECIFICATION	
MANUFACTURER	Para-Ordnance
CALIBRE	.45 ACP
MAGAZINE CAPACITY	12
ACTION	Recoil/LDA
TOTAL LENGTH	178mm/7in
BARREL LENGTH	89mm/3.5in
WEIGHT UNLOADED	963g/34oz

Para-Ordnance 1911 SSP

SPECIFICATION	
MANUFACTURER	Para-Ordnance
CALIBRE	.45 ACP
MAGAZINE CAPACITY	7
ACTION	Recoil/single
TOTAL LENGTH	216mm/8.5in
BARREL LENGTH	127mm/5in
WEIGHT UNLOADED	1,105g/39oz

This pistol, introduced in 2004, was the first in the Para range to feature the new "power extraction" mechanism for extracting and feeding the cartridge within the pistol. One weakness of the original M1911 was that if the extractor did not maintain the proper tension, it could fail to extract the empty cartridge. A revised design and an improved "claw" ensures positive extraction and feeding of the cartridge, found in all Para pistols since 2004. The SSP also has an adjustable rear sight. The model includes extras such as competition triggers and hammers. It has a single-stack frame for cartridges.

Para-Ordnance S12-45 Limited

SPECIFICATION	
MANUFACTURER	Para-Ordnance
CALIBRE	.45 ACP
MAGAZINE CAPACITY	10 or 12
ACTION	Recoil/single
TOTAL LENGTH	180mm/7.1in
BARREL LENGTH	89mm/3.5in
WEIGHT UNLOADED	963g/34oz

Built for the accuracy of competition, this pistol developed in 2004 was designed to incorporate a high level of durability. It has a competition trigger that prevents backlash when shooting and ambidextrous safety features that allows the pistol to be well supported in use by both hands. It also includes an adjustable rear sight, which can be altered for windage and elevation. It is equipped with a 12-round magazine, and a 10-round magazine is also available.

Para-Ordnance S14-45 Limited

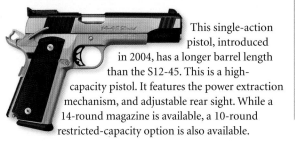

This single-action pistol, introduced in 2004, has a longer barrel length than the S12-45. This is a high-capacity pistol. It features the power extraction mechanism, and adjustable rear sight. While a 14-round magazine is available, a 10-round restricted-capacity option is also available.

Chamber-loaded
The Para-Ordnance range has a "chamber-loaded" indicator on top of the barrel that is visible through the ejection port.

SPECIFICATION

MANUFACTURER Para-Ordnance
CALIBRE .45 ACP
MAGAZINE CAPACITY 10 or 14
ACTION Recoil/single
TOTAL LENGTH 216mm/8.5in
BARREL LENGTH 127mm/5in
WEIGHT UNLOADED 1,134g/40oz

Para-Ordnance OPS (Operations)

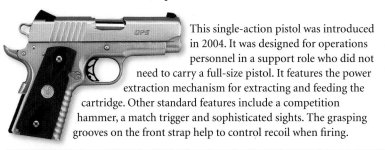

This single-action pistol was introduced in 2004. It was designed for operations personnel in a support role who did not need to carry a full-size pistol. It features the power extraction mechanism for extracting and feeding the cartridge. Other standard features include a competition hammer, a match trigger and sophisticated sights. The grasping grooves on the front strap help to control recoil when firing.

SPECIFICATION

MANUFACTURER Para-Ordnance
CALIBRE .45 ACP
MAGAZINE CAPACITY 7
ACTION Recoil/single
TOTAL LENGTH 180mm/7.1in
BARREL LENGTH 89mm/3.5in
WEIGHT UNLOADED 907g/32oz

Para-Ordnance 1911 LTC (Lieutenant Colonel)

This pistol, introduced in 2004, is a full-size, single-action pistol. It has a steel frame which helps absorb recoil from firing the shot. The LTC features the power extraction mechanism for extracting and feeding the cartridge, which is a standard of the Para-Ordnance range. It has a competition hammer, match trigger and an adjustable rear sight. There is also an all-weather stainless-steel version of the same pistol.

SPECIFICATION

MANUFACTURER Para-Ordnance
CALIBRE .45 ACP
MAGAZINE CAPACITY 7
ACTION Recoil/single
TOTAL LENGTH 197mm/7.75in
BARREL LENGTH 108mm/4.25in
WEIGHT UNLOADED 992g/35oz

Para-Ordnance TAC-S

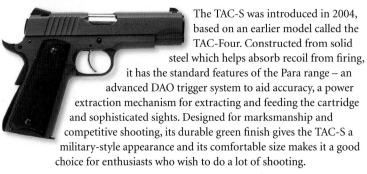

The TAC-S was introduced in 2004, based on an earlier model called the TAC-Four. Constructed from solid steel which helps absorb recoil from firing, it has the standard features of the Para range – an advanced DAO trigger system to aid accuracy, a power extraction mechanism for extracting and feeding the cartridge and sophisticated sights. Designed for marksmanship and competitive shooting, its durable green finish gives the TAC-S a military-style appearance and its comfortable size makes it a good choice for enthusiasts who wish to do a lot of shooting.

SPECIFICATION

MANUFACTURER Para-Ordnance
CALIBRE .45 ACP
MAGAZINE CAPACITY 7
ACTION Recoil/LDA
TOTAL LENGTH 184mm/7.25in
BARREL LENGTH 108mm/4.25in
WEIGHT UNLOADED 992g/35oz

Para-Ordnance Colonel

SPECIFICATION

MANUFACTURER Para-Ordnance
CALIBRE .45 ACP
MAGAZINE CAPACITY 14
ACTION Recoil/LDA
TOTAL LENGTH 197mm/7.75in
BARREL LENGTH 108mm/4.25in
WEIGHT UNLOADED 1,048g/37oz

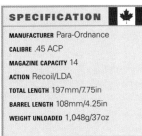

This high-capacity DAO pistol was introduced in 2004. It has a shortened slide and barrel and a lighter weight than other high-capacity models but still supplies 14 rounds of .45 ACP firepower. The pistol includes the standard power extraction mechanism for extracting and feeding the cartridge. The Colonel has sophisticated sights which can be adjusted for windage. The rear sight is rounded in order to prevent snagging when the pistol is drawn. The finish is black except for the non-reflective military-style olive surface for the frame and slide.

Para-Ordnance Hi-Cap (High-Capacity)

SPECIFICATION

MANUFACTURER Para-Ordnance
CALIBRE .45 ACP
MAGAZINE CAPACITY 14
ACTION Recoil/LDA
TOTAL LENGTH 216mm/8.5in
BARREL LENGTH 127mm/5in
WEIGHT UNLOADED 1,134g/40oz

Safety features
The Para-Ordnance range has three vital safety features to accompany the trigger action: a thumb safety disengages the trigger, a grip safety locks the hammer assembly and an internal firing-pin block guards against the possibility of accidental discharge.

This DAO pistol was introduced in 2004 – a full-size high-capacity model chambered for .45 ACP and capable of delivering 14 rounds. It includes the standard power extraction mechanism for extracting and feeding the cartridge.

Para-Ordnance Covert Black Hi-Cap 9

SPECIFICATION

MANUFACTURER Para-Ordnance
CALIBRE 9mm Parabellum
MAGAZINE CAPACITY 18
ACTION Recoil/LDA
TOTAL LENGTH 216mm/8.5in
BARREL LENGTH 127mm/5in
WEIGHT UNLOADED 1,134g/40oz

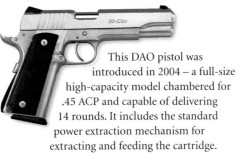

Para-Ordnance feature several high-capacity pistols that are chambered for the 9mm cartridge. Finished with a durable black surface, this DAO pistol is useful for covert operations. It has the standard power extraction mechanism of the Para-Ordnance range and includes 18 rounds of 9mm firepower and a light DAO trigger system. It is designed to be smooth and reliable, which is important when doing undercover work. The pistol is also available in a brushed stainless steel.

SPECIFICATION

MANUFACTURER Para-Ordnance
CALIBRE .45 ACP
MAGAZINE CAPACITY 7
ACTION Recoil/LDA
TOTAL LENGTH 180mm/7.1in
BARREL LENGTH 89mm/3.5in
WEIGHT UNLOADED 907g/32oz

Para-Ordnance Black Watch Companion

The Black Watch Companion is a slimline pistol that is also suitable for defence when undertaking covert operations. It incorporates the standard power extraction and light double-action trigger mechanism of the Para-Ordnance rang. It is designed to be smooth and reliable – essential when doing undercover work.

Para-Ordnance Nite-Tac 9

light rail

Introduced in 2005, the Nite-Tac 9 is an addition to the Para-Ordnance range of Nite-Tac pistols, available in .40 and .45 ACP calibre. They were created for law enforcement duty and defence. Nite-Tacs have the standard features of this range of pistols with the addition of a light rail that can be set up with optional light accessories (such as a mini light or laser sight) to illuminate targets when shooting.

SPECIFICATION

MANUFACTURER Para-Ordnance
CALIBRE 9mm Parabellum
MAGAZINE CAPACITY 18
ACTION Recoil/LDA
TOTAL LENGTH 216mm/8.5in
BARREL LENGTH 127mm/5in
WEIGHT UNLOADED 1,134g/40oz

Para-Ordnance Warthog

The single-action Warthog pistol was introduced in 2005. It is one of the world's smallest .45 ACP pistols, and easy to carry in any situation. The contoured hand grip is designed to maximize control, despite the small size of the weapon. The match-grade trigger is designed to prevent backlash. The receiver of the standard Warthog is made from alloy. This range of pistols incorporates the standard power extraction mechanism and safety mechanisms of the Para-Ordnance range.

ABOVE There is a clean, crisp release of the skeletonized spur hammer on pressing the trigger. This allows for a precise shot when the shooter comes on target.

SPECIFICATION

MANUFACTURER Para-Ordnance
CALIBRE .45 ACP
MAGAZINE CAPACITY 10
ACTION Recoil/single
TOTAL LENGTH 165mm/6.5in
BARREL LENGTH 76mm/3in
WEIGHT UNLOADED 680g/24oz

Stainless steel
An all-weather stainless-steel version of this pistol is also available. The added weight reduces the level of recoil.

Para-Ordnance Nite Hawg

This single-action pistol, introduced in 2005, has similar features to the standard Warthog except that it has a non-reflective all-black finish for covert concealment. It is also fitted with sophisticated night sights. The contoured hand grip is designed to maximize control, although the weapon is small. The match-grade trigger is designed to eliminate backlash. It has a lightweight alloy frame.

SPECIFICATION

MANUFACTURER Para-Ordnance
CALIBRE .45 ACP
MAGAZINE CAPACITY 10
ACTION Recoil/single
TOTAL LENGTH 165mm/6.5in
BARREL LENGTH 76mm/3in
WEIGHT UNLOADED 680g/24oz

Para-Ordnance Hawg 9

This high-capacity pistol is capable of carrying 12 rounds in a micro-compact frame. It is chambered for the popular 9mm Parabellum cartridge and was developed for those who do not need the stronger firepower of the .40 or .45 cartridges. The contoured hand grip is designed to maximize control, and the match-grade trigger reduces backlash. It has a lightweight alloy frame.

SPECIFICATION

MANUFACTURER Para-Ordnance
CALIBRE 9mm Parabellum
MAGAZINE CAPACITY 12
ACTION Recoil/single
TOTAL LENGTH 165mm/6.5in
BARREL LENGTH 76mm/3in
WEIGHT UNLOADED 680g/24oz

Para-Ordnance Lite Hawg

SPECIFICATION	
MANUFACTURER	Para-Ordnance
CALIBRE	.45 ACP
MAGAZINE CAPACITY	10 or 12
ACTION	Recoil/single
TOTAL LENGTH	165mm/6.5in
BARREL LENGTH	76mm/3in
WEIGHT UNLOADED	893g/31.5oz

The Lite Hawg, introduced in 2006, is a single-action pistol. It has a light rail to attach accessories such as a mini light or laser sight in order to provide target identification in low light conditions or at night. The Lite Hawg is made of carbon steel rather than stainless steel and has a compact frame. It carries ten rounds of .45 ACP in the magazine but can also be used with 12 rounds of 9mm ammunition.

Para-Ordnance Slim Hawg

SPECIFICATION	
MANUFACTURER	Para-Ordnance
CALIBRE	.45 ACP
MAGAZINE CAPACITY	6
ACTION	Recoil/single
TOTAL LENGTH	165mm/6.5in
BARREL LENGTH	76mm/3in
WEIGHT UNLOADED	850g/30oz

The Slim Hawg, introduced in 2006, is a single-action pistol that is both light and slim, combined with the very small frame of the Warthog. It is made of stainless steel. It has grasping grooves to help control recoil and make every shot as accurate as possible (although this may not have featured on all shipped Slim Hawgs). The match-grade trigger is designed to eliminate backlash. The pistol is small enough to be easily concealed, light enough to carry for extended periods, very accurate for its small size and very reliable.

Para-Ordnance Nite-Tac

SPECIFICATION	
MANUFACTURER	Para-Ordnance
CALIBRE	.40 S&W
MAGAZINE CAPACITY	16
ACTION	Recoil/double
TOTAL LENGTH	216mm/8.5in
BARREL LENGTH	127mm/5in
WEIGHT UNLOADED	1,134g/40oz

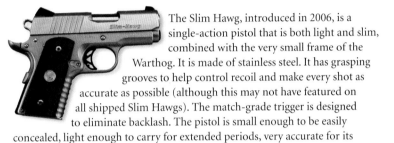

This pistol, introduced in 2006 is a modernized version of the P14-45, chambered for the popular .40 S&W (Smith & Wesson) cartridge. This pistol is specifically designed for night-time operations by the inclusion of a light rail to attach accessories in order to provide target identification in low light conditions and at night. It is available in classic stainless steel or black.

Para-Ordnance Todd Jarrett USPSA, Limited Edition

SPECIFICATION	
MANUFACTURER	Para-Ordnance
CALIBRE	.45 ACP
MAGAZINE CAPACITY	16
ACTION	Recoil/single
TOTAL LENGTH	216mm/8.5in
BARREL LENGTH	127mm/5in
WEIGHT UNLOADED	1,134g/40oz

This competitive model was designed by world-class shooter Todd Jarrett and named after the United States Practical Shooting Association (USPSA). It is aimed at those who were wishing to take part in competitive sport such as the USPSA Limited Nationals or their local club matches. It includes features such as an ambidextrous thumb safety, adjustable rear sight and fibre-optic front sight, and 16-round magazines.

Para-Ordnance Tac-Five

The Tac-Five, introduced in 2006, was designed to meet the needs of those "special operations" teams that used the 9mm cartridge, with a capacity of 18 rounds. Its barrel is designed to achieve high-speed velocity. The pistol is made of stainless steel covered in a resistant and durable black coating. Other features include polymer grips and an adjustable rear sight with a dovetailed front blade.

SPECIFICATION	
MANUFACTURER	Para-Ordnance
CALIBRE	9mm Parabellum
MAGAZINE CAPACITY	18
ACTION	Recoil/LDA
TOTAL LENGTH	216mm/8.5in
BARREL LENGTH	127mm/5in
WEIGHT UNLOADED	1,063g/37.5oz

Para-Ordnance SSP-SE (Special Edition) 1

This pistol, introduced in 2006, is a special-edition high-performance single-action pistol, chambered for the powerful .45 ACP cartridge. A full-size pistol, it includes features such as an ambidextrous safety, sophisticated sights with an adjustable rear sight. The special-edition pistols were limited production because the stocks were made of high-quality cocobolo wood. This is expensive and difficult to find – and is twice the density of walnut. Some Para-Ordnance models feature this stock with a double-diamond pattern for grip.

SPECIFICATION	
MANUFACTURER	Para-Ordnance
CALIBRE	.45 ACP
MAGAZINE CAPACITY	7
ACTION	Recoil/single
TOTAL LENGTH	216mm/8.5in
BARREL LENGTH	127mm/5in
WEIGHT UNLOADED	1,105g/39oz

Para-Ordnance Tac-Forty

Introduced in 2007, the new Para Tac-Forty is designed to meet the needs of those in law enforcement who use the .40 S&W cartridge. The barrel is a popular length for duty pistols and the light, double-action trigger system provides instant first-shot capability when security forces are on active duty in difficult circumstances or in poor weather conditions. This gives consistency to the shot. Made of rust resistant stainless steel, the Tac-Forty has the standard feature of the Carry Option range, including an adjustable rear sight.

SPECIFICATION	
MANUFACTURER	Para-Ordnance
CALIBRE	.40 S&W
MAGAZINE CAPACITY	15
ACTION	Recoil/single
TOTAL LENGTH	196mm/7.7in
BARREL LENGTH	108mm/4.25in
WEIGHT UNLOADED	1,020g/36oz

Para-Ordnance Carry (GAP)

The Carry and the Companion Carry Option (CCO) were chambered for the .45 GAP (Glock Automatic Pistol) cartridge introduced in 2007. Modern technology has made it possible to achieve the ballistics of the .45 ACP in a cartridge that has the shorter overall length of a round of 9mm ammunition. Using the shorter cartridge means that the grip of the pistol does not need to be increased in size to accommodate it. The shooter can keep grip on a smaller pistol without having to give up any of the power of the .45 ACP cartridge. A better grip translates into greater accuracy and control for the shooter.

SPECIFICATION	
MANUFACTURER	Para-Ordnance
CALIBRE	.45 GAP
MAGAZINE CAPACITY	6
ACTION	Recoil/LDA
TOTAL LENGTH	163mm/6.4in
BARREL LENGTH	76mm/3in
WEIGHT UNLOADED	822g/29oz

United States

Perhaps like no other country in the world, small-arms manufacture in the United States is bound up with its history and identity. The invention of the revolver by Samuel Colt, and the succession of designs by Colt, Smith & Wesson, Remington and other manufacturers, played a key part in the establishment of European settlers in the Native American territories, the independence of Texas in 1836, the Mexican War (1846–48) and the American Civil War (1861–65). Another American, John Moses Browning, was to design the definitive pistol of modern times, the M1911. The right to carry a firearm as an aspect of personal freedom has remained deeply ingrained in the American psyche.

Colt Paterson

SPECIFICATION	
MANUFACTURER	Colt Patent Arms Manufacturing Co.
CALIBRE	.36
CYLINDER	5
ACTION	Percussion/single
TOTAL LENGTH	292mm/11.5in
BARREL LENGTH	190mm/7.5in
WEIGHT UNLOADED	1,134g/40oz

The Colt Paterson was an iconic revolver, not only in the history of the percussion revolver and the Colt firearms manufacturing company but also in the history of Texas and the Wild West. This handgun with a revolving cylinder and .36 calibre lead ball was invented by Samuel Colt in 1831. It was patented in 1836 and manufactured until 1842. As manufacturing took place at Paterson in New Jersey, this was the name given to one of these early types. The .36 Paterson was used not only by the Texas Navy but also by mounted Texas Rangers. In both scenarios, it proved to be remarkably successful.

Colt Walker

This revolver, produced in 1847, was officially designated a pistol because the Army Ordnance Department had never come across a revolver before. The Colt Walker revolver was named after a hero of the Mexican War, Captain Samuel Hamilton Walker, who was instrumental in ensuring that Colt secured an official US Government contract, so avoiding the company's bankruptcy. The Walker was a development of the existing Paterson design that had already seen success on the US western frontier. It was reputed to have firepower similar to that of a rifle and that made US cavalrymen formidable opponents. It could take up to 50 grains of powder and a .44 or .45 calibre lead ball.

loading lever

cylinder to hold powder charge

SPECIFICATION	
MANUFACTURER	Colt Patent Arms Manufacturing Co.
CALIBRE	.44 or .45
CYLINDER	6
ACTION	Percussion/single
TOTAL LENGTH	400mm/15.75in
BARREL LENGTH	229mm/9in
WEIGHT UNLOADED	2,040g/72oz

Colt Dragoon M1848

SPECIFICATION	
MANUFACTURER	Colt Firearms Co.
CALIBRE	.44
CYLINDER	6
ACTION	Percussion/single
TOTAL LENGTH	355mm/14in
BARREL LENGTH	190mm/7.5in
WEIGHT UNLOADED	1,871g/66oz

The Colt Dragoon was slightly smaller than the Colt Walker. Designed for use in the Mexican War, the Walker had proved effective but also heavy and sometimes prone to accidental explosion. The Dragoon had a shorter cylinder, shorter barrel and an improved loading lever. Changes were made to the metal used in manufacture. It was produced from 1848 to 1863. The Dragoon became a popular weapon in the 1850s and continued the upward spiral in Colt's fortunes. It was produced in three different models and the US Government ordered over 8,000 of them.

Colt Single Action Navy 1851

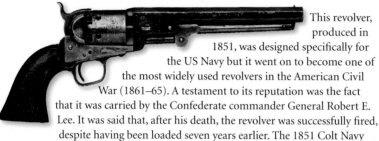

This revolver, produced in 1851, was designed specifically for the US Navy but it went on to become one of the most widely used revolvers in the American Civil War (1861–65). A testament to its reputation was the fact that it was carried by the Confederate commander General Robert E. Lee. It was said that, after his death, the revolver was successfully fired, despite having been loaded seven years earlier. The 1851 Colt Navy revolver was in use for many years after the Civil War in the hands of such men as "Wild Bill" Hickock and "Buffalo Bill" Cody. With over a quarter of a million manufactured between 1851 and 1873, it was one of the most popular and long-lived revolvers in the Wild West.

SPECIFICATION

MANUFACTURER Colt Firearms Co.
CALIBRE .36
CYLINDER 6
ACTION Percussion/single
TOTAL LENGTH 305mm/12in
BARREL LENGTH 190mm/7.5in
WEIGHT UNLOADED 907g/32oz

British forces copies
Thousands of the Colt Navy Model were produced for the British forces in the Crimea War.

Colt New Army Model 1860

This revolver was introduced in 1860 by Colt as the ultimate single-action percussion combat handgun. The frame was based on the Colt 1851 Navy model and the cylinder was adapted to fit. The weapon featured a ratcheting loading lever and could take up to 35 grains of powder and a .44 calibre lead ball. The Colt 1860 was widely used in the American Civil War by officers, cavalrymen and artillerymen. It had a fine, streamlined profile and quickly won favour with the military. Some variants were supplied with a detachable rifle stock which was said to improve accuracy. Over 200,000 1860 Army revolvers were produced between 1860 and 1873. The first 1,000 Army revolvers were equipped with seven-inch barrels, but they quickly gave way to the eight-inch barrel the Army preferred, and the style of the cylinder was also updated.

SPECIFICATION

MANUFACTURER Colt Firearms Co.
CALIBRE .44
CYLINDER 6
ACTION Percussion/single
TOTAL LENGTH 356mm/12.5in
BARREL LENGTH 203mm/8in
WEIGHT UNLOADED 1,077g/38oz

Colt copies
This revolver was so popular with Confederate armies that they went on to produce southern-made copies of the weapon.

Colt Richards-Mason 1860 cartridge conversion

This revolver was a conversion carried out first by an employee of Colt, Charles Richards, in 1871. He was awarded a patent for converting Colt percussion models to breech-loading cartridge revolvers. Another colleague, William Mason, was awarded a patent for an improvement to the original Richards patent in 1872. The 1860 revolver was converted, along with the 1851 Navy model. The conversion entailed cutting off the cap-and-ball cylinders at the back and installing a conversion ring that would accept cartridges. The Richards-Mason conversions gave a new lease of life to some of the classic Colt revolvers and had the effect of improving their efficiency and safety, obviating the dangers of the old ball-and-powder system which could sometimes result in the simultaneous explosion of all six cylinders.

SPECIFICATION

MANUFACTURER Colt Firearms Co.
CALIBRE .44
CYLINDER 6
ACTION Percussion/single
TOTAL LENGTH 356mm/14in
BARREL LENGTH 203mm/8in
WEIGHT UNLOADED 1,134g/40oz

Colt Single Action Army

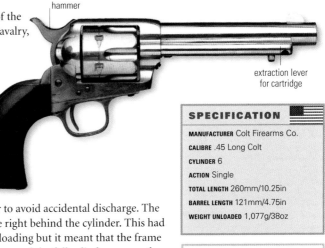

hammer

extraction lever
for cartridge

This was one of the most famous revolvers of the American Wild West. Designed for the US Cavalry, it was first produced in 1873 and was often known as the "Colt 45". The Single Action Army (SAA) used .45 Long Colt cartridges (which were not the same as the .45 ACP cartridge commonly used in semi-automatic pistols). This revolver had no conventional safety so in theory a round could be discharged if the hammer was to receive a hard blow. As a precaution, one chamber was often left empty while the revolver was being carried in order to avoid accidental discharge. The revolver was loaded by opening a gate on the right behind the cylinder. This had disadvantages in terms of speed and ease of loading but it meant that the frame was rigid and strong, with no break points to reveal the full cylinder, as on other weapons. Various Colt SAA models were built from 1873 to 1940, and again from 1976 in a variety of calibres and barrel lengths. Famous names given to variants of the SAA include the Peacemaker. The Single Action Army has been copied by numerous makers both in America and in Europe including Aldo Uberti in Italy, and United States Firearms Mfg. Co. in Hartford, Connecticut.

SPECIFICATION

MANUFACTURER Colt Firearms Co.
CALIBRE .45 Long Colt
CYLINDER 6
ACTION Single
TOTAL LENGTH 260mm/10.25in
BARREL LENGTH 121mm/4.75in
WEIGHT UNLOADED 1,077g/38oz

Original value
Among the most valuable to the collector are original, good condition, first generation Single Action Army revolvers (produced before 1940).

Colt M1877 Lightning

SPECIFICATION

MANUFACTURER Colt Firearms Co.
CALIBRE .38 Colt. .41 Colt
CYLINDER 6
ACTION Double
TOTAL LENGTH 228mm/9in
BARREL LENGTH 114.3mm/4.5in
WEIGHT UNLOADED 652g/23oz

This was Colt's first production double-action revolver, with the mechanism designed by inventor William Mason. It was produced from 1877 to 1909. The Lightning is known to have been used in some famous gunfights in the Wild West. It was still early days for the double-action system and the M1877 Lightning had some problems in this respect with fragile mechanisms and complicated actions, so was not reliable. One explanation may be that users, familiar with single-action pistols, attempted to cock and fire the pistol in the old way, which may have damaged the mechanism. Few surviving examples of the revolver are said to work smoothly. Remaining revolvers that saw action are often in poor condition because the original finish was thin and has worn away.

SPECIFICATION

MANUFACTURER Colt Firearms Co.
CALIBRE .45 Colt
CYLINDER 6
ACTION Double
TOTAL LENGTH 250mm/9.85in
BARREL LENGTH 121mm/4.75in
WEIGHT UNLOADED 1,020g/36oz

Colt M1878 Double Action Army

The Double Action Army revolver was a development of the New Model Double Action, itself based on the Single Action Army revolver. The Army version was much more robust than the New Model and it found favour with the US Army who purchased 4,500 in 1902. It was available in a variety of barrel lengths. The M1878 was used in action on America's frontier and throughout the world until production ceased in 1905. There proved to be some problems, however, with the mainspring which meant the Army did not repeat their order.

Colt New Army and Navy Model

The model of 1889 was a significant leap forward by Colt. Before this, all Colt revolvers had fixed cylinders, loaded one chamber at a time. Colt introduced the "swing-out" cylinder. It was an immediate success. The cylinder swung out on a crane which was connected to a pin that entered a recess in the centre of a rotating ratchet at the rear of the cylinder, and was locked back in position with a latch. The Navy Department ordered over 5,000 of these revolvers, followed by the Army three years later, and there were strong civilian sales. Some of the most ornate finishes produced by Colt appeared on the 1889s. The revolver was very solidly built. However, one problem was that the trigger did not always return to its original position after firing, due to a weak spring.

SPECIFICATION	
MANUFACTURER	Colt Firearms Co.
CALIBRE	.38 Colt, .41 Colt
CYLINDER	6
ACTION	Double
TOTAL LENGTH	292mm/11.5in
BARREL LENGTH	152mm/6in
WEIGHT UNLOADED	940g/33.16oz

Colt New Service

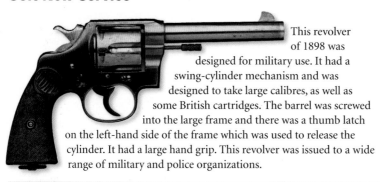

This revolver of 1898 was designed for military use. It had a swing-cylinder mechanism and was designed to take large calibres, as well as some British cartridges. The barrel was screwed into the large frame and there was a thumb latch on the left-hand side of the frame which was used to release the cylinder. It had a large hand grip. This revolver was issued to a wide range of military and police organizations.

SPECIFICATION	
MANUFACTURER	Colt Firearms Co.
CALIBRE	.45 Colt, .44 Special, .38-40
CYLINDER	6
ACTION	Double
TOTAL LENGTH	275mm/10.83in
BARREL LENGTH	140mm/5.50in
WEIGHT UNLOADED	1,162g/41oz

Colt Model 1900

This was a semi-automatic, self-loading pistol which was developed from designs made by Browning in the 1890s. The Model 1900 was a key development in the history of pistol design as it heralded the introduction of John Browning's invention, a method of returning a weapon to position, loaded and ready to fire on each time the trigger was pulled. This mechanism was to be copied in just about every effective pistol from then on and was certainly key to the continued development and success of Browning's own pistol designs that were to result in the famous M1911.

SPECIFICATION	
MANUFACTURER	Colt Firearms Co.
CALIBRE	.38 ACP
MAGAZINE CAPACITY	7
ACTION	Recoil/single
TOTAL LENGTH	228.6mm/9in
BARREL LENGTH	152mm/6in
WEIGHT UNLOADED	992g/35oz

Colt Model 1903 Pocket Hammer

This semi-automatic pistol was a derivative of the Colt Model 1900. It was developed from a sporting model introduced in 1902 but had a shorter barrel and slide. The 1903 model did not prove to be very successful and only a few models were produced, partly because it fell between categories as it was neither a pocket nor a full-size model.

SPECIFICATION	
MANUFACTURER	Colt/FN, Herstal
CALIBRE	.38 ACP
MAGAZINE CAPACITY	7 or 8
ACTION	Recoil/single
TOTAL LENGTH	205mm/7in
BARREL LENGTH	127mm/5in
WEIGHT UNLOADED	930g/24oz

Colt Model 1905

SPECIFICATION

MANUFACTURER Colt Firearms Co.
CALIBRE .45 ACP
MAGAZINE CAPACITY 7
ACTION Recoil/single
TOTAL LENGTH 203mm/8in
BARREL LENGTH 127mm/5in
WEIGHT UNLOADED 921g/32.5oz

The Model 1905 was a single-action semi-automatic pistol, an adapted version of the earlier autoloading model including Browning's method of returning a weapon to position, loaded and ready to fire on each time the trigger was pulled. It also included modifications suggested by the US authorities, making a crucial model in the development process that was to result in the world's longest-serving and most famous pistol, the M1911. Over 6,000 pistols were produced and were sold between 1905 and 1911. It had an external hammer, a grip safety at the back of the hand grip and also a manual safety.

Colt Police Positive

SPECIFICATION

MANUFACTURER Colt Firearms Co.
CALIBRE .32 S&W, .38 Colt New
Police
CYLINDER 6
ACTION Double
TOTAL LENGTH 216mm/8.5in
BARREL LENGTH 102mm/4in
WEIGHT UNLOADED 565g/20oz

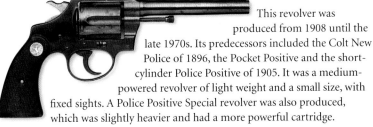

This revolver was produced from 1908 until the late 1970s. Its predecessors included the Colt New Police of 1896, the Pocket Positive and the short-cylinder Police Positive of 1905. It was a medium-powered revolver of light weight and a small size, with fixed sights. A Police Positive Special revolver was also produced, which was slightly heavier and had a more powerful cartridge.

Colt Model 1908 (Vest Pocket)

SPECIFICATION

MANUFACTURER Colt Firearms Co.
CALIBRE .25 ACP
MAGAZINE CAPACITY 6
ACTION Recoil/single
TOTAL LENGTH 114mm/4.5in
BARREL LENGTH 53mm/2.1in
WEIGHT UNLOADED 386g/13.6oz

This was a pocket pistol designed to be easily concealable in a handbag or somewhere about the person. It was a small, striker-fired (no hammer), single-action pistol. The firing pin was spring-loaded and when the trigger was pulled the firing pin was released. The pistol was provided with both a manual safety and a grip safety in the hand grip. The grip needed to be fully depressed before the gun would fire. It is often confused with the "Baby Browning". The European version was introduced first as the FN Model 1905.

Colt Model 1911A1 and Government Model

SPECIFICATION

MANUFACTURER Colt/Various
CALIBRE .45 ACP, .38 Super
MAGAZINE CAPACITY 7
ACTION Recoil/single
TOTAL LENGTH 216mm/8.5in
BARREL LENGTH 127mm/5in
WEIGHT UNLOADED 1,130g/39.86oz

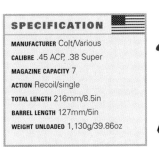

This is simply the most successful semi-automatic pistol of all time. Designed by John Moses Browning and initially produced by Colt, it was adopted by the US Army in March 1911, and was still in service in 1985. At least 2.7 million units were issued by the US Government to various parts of their armed forces during that period. The M1911 was single-action, with short-recoil operation. On recoil, the barrel dipped downwards, disengaging from the inner surface of the slide. Once the breech had re-chambered a round, the rear of the barrel moved back to its normal operating position. The weapon also featured a hammer, a grip safety at the back of the hand grip and a manual safety.

Colt Model 1917

This revolver was a variant of the New Service model that had been introduced in 1898. It was a swing-cylinder design of substantial size. The 1917 model was designed with the US Army in mind, at a time when it was short of pistols. The revolver had a shortened cylinder and used the .45 ACP rimless cartridge which was loaded by means of two half-moon spring clips, holding three cartridges each. The weapon featured a positive hammer lock and a pivoted firing pin. It remained in production until after World War II.

SPECIFICATION

MANUFACTURER Colt Firearms Co.
CALIBRE .45 ACP
CYLINDER 6
ACTION Double
TOTAL LENGTH 275mm/10.83in
BARREL LENGTH 140mm/5.5in
WEIGHT UNLOADED 1,162g/41oz

Colt Commando Special

The .38 revolver had been the standard US forces sidearm prior to the introduction of the M1911 semi-automatic pistol. The Colt Commando revolver was a development of the Official Police revolver for the military, which in turn evolved from the Army Special of 1908. The Commando was largely issued to security personnel and factory guards, though some were ordered by the undercover organization, Office of Secret Services (OSS). Only about 1,800 Commandos went to the US Navy, although there had been requests for the revolver, Colt was not always able to keep up with demand. However, about 45,000 Colt Commandos were produced in 1945 alone.

SPECIFICATION

MANUFACTURER Colt Firearms Co.
CALIBRE .38 Special
CYLINDER 6
ACTION Double
TOTAL LENGTH 285mm/11.22in
BARREL LENGTH 152mm/6in
WEIGHT UNLOADED 1,030g/36.3oz

Colt Python

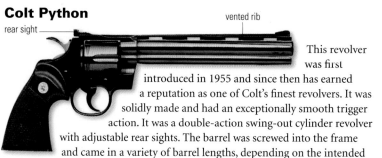

vented rib

rear sight

This revolver was first introduced in 1955 and since then has earned a reputation as one of Colt's finest revolvers. It was solidly made and had an exceptionally smooth trigger action. It was a double-action swing-out cylinder revolver with adjustable rear sights. The barrel was screwed into the frame and came in a variety of barrel lengths, depending on the intended use. It was distinguished by a vented upper rib (to expel gases from the cartridge) and it also had a full-length bottom rib with extractor rod.

SPECIFICATION

MANUFACTURER Colt Firearms Co.
CALIBRE .357 Magnum
CYLINDER 6
ACTION Double
TOTAL LENGTH 343mm/13.5in
BARREL LENGTH 203mm/8in
WEIGHT UNLOADED 1,360g/48oz

Colt Anaconda

Similar in design to the .357 Colt Python, but chambered for a more powerful round, the Anaconda .44 Magnum first appeared in 1990. Since then it has been described as one of the most accurate revolvers of its type. It came in various lengths of barrel with a vented top rib. The revolver was manufactured from stainless steel and was generally considered too unwieldy for regular police and military use, though it may have been used when extra firepower was required. Otherwise it was used for sport and hunting.

SPECIFICATION

MANUFACTURER Colt Firearms Co.
CALIBRE .44 Magnum
CYLINDER 6
ACTION Double
TOTAL LENGTH 330mm/13in
BARREL LENGTH 152mm/6in
WEIGHT UNLOADED 1,700g/52oz

Colt Commander

SPECIFICATION

MANUFACTURER Colt Firearms Co.

CALIBRE .45 ACP

MAGAZINE CAPACITY 7

ACTION Single

TOTAL LENGTH 197mm/7.75in

BARREL LENGTH 108mm/4.25in

WEIGHT UNLOADED 765g/27oz

Colt developed a series of compact versions of its full-sized guns, which had shortened barrels and slides. Proposed at the end of 1949, the Commander was intended to fill a military need for a lighter handgun which would be issued to officers. While it was not selected for the armed forces, it was produced commercially and it proved to be a popular and successful design. The modern Colt Commander semi-automatic had the power and performance of a full-sized pistol in a compact, lightweight carry format. It was comparatively small, accurate and reliable, with excellent sights. It was produced up to the 1960s when it was replaced by the Combat Commander.

Remington Army Model 1858

SPECIFICATION

MANUFACTURER Remington

CALIBRE .44

CYLINDER 6

ACTION Percussion/single

TOTAL LENGTH 342mm/13.5in

BARREL LENGTH 203mm/8in

WEIGHT UNLOADED 1,106.7g/39oz

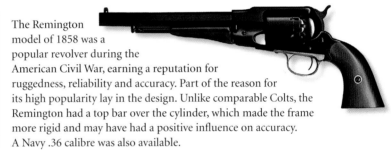

The Remington model of 1858 was a popular revolver during the American Civil War, earning a reputation for ruggedness, reliability and accuracy. Part of the reason for its high popularity lay in the design. Unlike comparable Colts, the Remington had a top bar over the cylinder, which made the frame more rigid and may have had a positive influence on accuracy. A Navy .36 calibre was also available.

SPECIFICATION

MANUFACTURER Remington

CALIBRE .44 Remington, .45 Colt

CYLINDER 6

ACTION Percussion/single

TOTAL LENGTH 305mm/12in

BARREL LENGTH 305mm/7.5in

WEIGHT UNLOADED 1,220g/43oz

Remington New Model Army 1875

The Remington 1875 was manufactured for the US Army from 1875 to 1889. It was solidly built, with the Remington trademark top bar that gave added strength to the frame. The revolver had a brass trigger guard and a wooden hand grip. Over 25,000 New Model Army revolvers were produced by Remington. They were high-quality, very strong and accurate revolvers. Although widely appreciated, the Remington 1875 could not compete with the Single Action Army model, and the company was soon bought out.

Remington 51

SPECIFICATION

MANUFACTURER Remington

CALIBRE .32 ACP, .380 ACP

MAGAZINE CAPACITY 7

ACTION Blowback/single

TOTAL LENGTH 168mm/6.63in

BARREL LENGTH 82.5mm/3.25in

WEIGHT UNLOADED 595g/21oz

This pistol was designed by Remington arms-designer John Pedersen and mainly produced between 1918 and the late 1920s, with a few being made in the 1930s. It was Remington's first self-loading pistol. The operating system was a complex system of delayed blowback, developed by Pedersen. The Remington 51 also featured a grip safety visible at the rear of the butt, which acted as a slide stop and release and it had a manual safety as well. The Remington 51 was expensive to produce, and despite critical acclaim, no government or private agency is known to have adopted the weapon for issue.

Savage 1907

SPECIFICATION

MANUFACTURER Savage Arms
CALIBRE .32 ACP, .380 ACP
MAGAZINE CAPACITY 10 or 9
ACTION Delayed blowback/single
TOTAL LENGTH 168mm/6.62in
BARREL LENGTH 90mm/3.5in
WEIGHT UNLOADED 652.04g/23oz

This pistol was invented by Major Searles (formerly of Springfield Armouries) and was manufactured in both .32 and .380 calibre, the latter introduced in 1913. The pistol featured a serrated hammer-like device at the rear of the slide. It had the unusual feature of a locking action for the barrel. When the breech block moved backwards, the barrel turned. The spin of the bullet travelling through the barrel resisted this turn and helped to hold the breech locked. Another selling feature of the pistol was its large magazine capacity: the .32 could hold ten rounds and the .380 nine rounds.

SPECIFICATION

MANUFACTURER Smith & Wesson Inc.
CALIBRE .22 Rimfire
CYLINDER 6
ACTION Single
TOTAL LENGTH 171mm/6.75in
BARREL LENGTH 81mm/3.18in
WEIGHT UNLOADED 284g/10oz

Smith & Wesson Model 1

Although Colt was making American history with its early revolver designs, Smith & Wesson had a large claim to fame as well. The Model 1 was in many respects a leap into the future. Horace Smith and Daniel B. Wesson, all too aware of the time-consuming nature of the traditional ball and powder designs, devised a revolver that would take a self-contained metallic cartridge. Their first design was patented as the Model 1, First Issue Revolver in 1857. It was the first revolver to combine using a .22 Rimfire cartridge and a bored-through cylinder. The revolver was in high demand because of its easily-loaded rimfire cartridge and was highly significant in the history of firearms.

Smith & Wesson Model 2

SPECIFICATION

MANUFACTURER Smith & Wesson Inc.
CALIBRE .32 Rimfire
CYLINDER 6
ACTION Single
TOTAL LENGTH 254mm/10in
BARREL LENGTH 127mm/5in
WEIGHT UNLOADED 595g/21oz

Once the Civil War began in 1861, a new design called the Model 2 was brought out. This immediately caught on with the Army, and the Army name became associated with the weapon. One of the reasons for its popularity was that the Model 2 could be loaded in just 25 seconds. That was over two minutes faster than the reload time for comparable weapons available at the time, and in battle could have meant the difference between life and death.

Smith & Wesson Model 3

This revolver was first produced in the 1870s and was an immediate success. Smith & Wesson had devised a top-break design, whereby when the revolver was broken open the barrel tipped downwards. At the same time, an ejector system ejected spent cases from all six cylinders simultaneously. This made reloading much quicker. About 2,000 Smith & Wesson Model 3s were issued to the Army and many more were bought by individuals. The weapon was also used in engagements with Native Americans. A variant of the Model 3 was adopted by the Russian military and made in large quantities.

SPECIFICATION

MANUFACTURER Smith & Wesson Inc.
CALIBRE .44 S&W American, .44 S&W
CYLINDER 6
ACTION Single
TOTAL LENGTH 305mm/12in
BARREL LENGTH 165mm/6.5in
WEIGHT UNLOADED 1,134g/40oz

Smith & Wesson New Century

SPECIFICATION

MANUFACTURER Smith & Wesson Inc.

CALIBRE .44 Special, .455 Eley

CYLINDER 6

ACTION Double

TOTAL LENGTH 300mm/11.75in

BARREL LENGTH 165mm/6.5in

WEIGHT UNLOADED 1,079g/37.9oz

This revolver is often regarded as a high point in revolver design. It had a triple-lock system: a side-swing cylinder which was anchored by an additional latch in the front of the frame to make for positive alignment. For the first time the ejector rod was enclosed in a shroud under the barrel. The revolver was precisely engineered and manufactured throughout, which made it a reliable weapon to use in the heat of battle. The .455 Eley model was made for the British Army and over 5,000 were delivered.

Smith & Wesson Hand Ejector 2nd Model

SPECIFICATION

MANUFACTURER Smith & Wesson Inc.

CALIBRE .44 Special, .45 ACP, .455 Eley

CYLINDER 5

ACTION Double

TOTAL LENGTH 300mm/11.75in

BARREL LENGTH 165mm/6.5in

WEIGHT UNLOADED 1,079g/37.9oz

This was the replacement for the New Century triple-lock. The shroud around the ejector rod and the triple-lock feature were removed because the British military felt that it would make the revolver less vulnerable to fouling from mud and dirt, as was being encountered in the trenches. About 5,500 revolvers in .455 Eley were supplied to the British during World War I. A .45 ACP version of this revolver was used by the US military as the M1917.

Smith & Wesson Model 36

SPECIFICATION

MANUFACTURER Smith & Wesson Inc.

CALIBRE .38 Special, .357 Magnum

CYLINDER 5

ACTION Double

TOTAL LENGTH 216mm/8.5in

BARREL LENGTH 102mm/4in

WEIGHT UNLOADED 566g/20oz

This revolver, originally designated the Model 388, was also described as the "Chief's Special", as it was launched at the International Association of Chiefs of Police (IACP) conference in 1950. The Model 36 was a small-frame revolver that could take a powerful cartridge. It became the basis of many different variations that followed.

Smith & Wesson Model 39

SPECIFICATION

MANUFACTURER Smith & Wesson Inc.

CALIBRE 9mm Parabellum

MAGAZINE CAPACITY 8

ACTION Recoil/double

TOTAL LENGTH 190mm/7.5in

BARREL LENGTH 102mm/4in

WEIGHT UNLOADED 780g/27.52oz

This was the first double-action pistol to be produced in the United States, in 1955. It was a recoil-operated, locked-breech pistol with a double-action trigger and a Browning-style locking system. The safety catch was mounted on the side of the receiver. The spent cartridge case was ejected from a gap on the right side of the receiver and the profile of the pistol from the left showed no gap. The hand-grip furniture was normally wood with a chequered effect for improved grip.

Smith & Wesson Model 29

SPECIFICATION

MANUFACTURER Smith & Wesson Inc.

CALIBRE .44 Magnum

CYLINDER 6

ACTION Double

TOTAL LENGTH 357mm/14in

BARREL LENGTH 210mm/8.27in

WEIGHT UNLOADED 1,374g/48.5oz

Introduced in 1955, this has been described as the most powerful revolver in the world, though more powerful revolvers are now currently available. The Model 29 was part of a series of Smith & Wesson's largest frame revolvers and it was designed to handle the most powerful cartridges. The Model 29 achieved notoriety through the film *Dirty Harry*, starring Clint Eastwood. A modern version, the 629, is currently in production.

Smith & Wesson Model 19

There were two calibres of the Model 19 produced, the .38 Special and the .357 Magnum revolver. The Model 19 had a medium frame and adjustable sights. This revolver proved to be an instant success and was highly regarded for its power as well as its good balance and accuracy. It was easy to carry and handled well. Introduced in 1955, the Model 19 was eventually replaced by the Model 66.

SPECIFICATION

MANUFACTURER Smith & Wesson Inc.

CALIBRE .38 Special, .357 Magnum

CYLINDER 6

ACTION Double

TOTAL LENGTH 203mm/8in

BARREL LENGTH 64mm/2.5in

WEIGHT UNLOADED 865g/30.5oz

Smith & Wesson Model 10

The Smith & Wesson Model 10 was one of the most successful revolver designs ever. The first model came out in 1899 and was known as the "Military and Police". With Smith & Wesson's new numbering system, from 1958 it was known as the Model 10. Since then, the design of the revolver has remained fundamentally unchanged since it was first invented. About a million or so revolvers were supplied to the US Government during World War II. The success of the Model 10 was such that about six million were produced to cover demand from most US police departments. The pistol was also exported to some British Commonwealth countries.

SPECIFICATION

MANUFACTURER Smith & Wesson Inc.

CALIBRE .38 Special

MAGAZINE CAPACITY 6

ACTION Double

TOTAL LENGTH 254mm/10in

BARREL LENGTH 102mm/4in

WEIGHT UNLOADED 865g/30.5oz

Smith & Wesson Model 15

Introduced in 1957, the Model 15 revolver was a combat weapon. As part of the Smith & Wesson "Military and Police" series, this was a successful product. It was a double-action revolver with a swing-out cylinder with a dual-locked six-chamber cylinder. It had fixed front and rear sights.

SPECIFICATION

MANUFACTURER Smith & Wesson Inc.

CALIBRE .38 Special

CYLINDER 6

ACTION Double

TOTAL LENGTH 203mm/8in

BARREL LENGTH 51mm/2in

WEIGHT UNLOADED 1,020g/36oz

Smith & Wesson Model 59

SPECIFICATION

MANUFACTURER Smith & Wesson Inc.
CALIBRE 9mm Parabellum
MAGAZINE CAPACITY 8
ACTION Recoil/double
TOTAL LENGTH 192mm/7.55in
BARREL LENGTH 102mm/4in
WEIGHT UNLOADED 840g/30oz

The Model 59, introduced in 1971, was a development of the Model 39 and the first high-capacity double-action pistol for the 9mm cartridge. It was recoil operated with a double-action trigger and Browning-style locking system. The safety catch was mounted on the side of the receiver. The spent cartridge case was ejected from a gap on the right side of the receiver. The hand-grip furniture was plastic and the back of the hand grip had a straight edge, as opposed to the curved back on the Model 39.

Smith & Wesson 686

SPECIFICATION

MANUFACTURER Smith & Wesson Inc.
CALIBRE .357 Magnum, .38 Special
CYLINDER 6
ACTION Double
TOTAL LENGTH 292mm/11.5in
BARREL LENGTH 152mm/6in
WEIGHT UNLOADED 1,250g/44oz

This revolver was introduced by Smith & Wesson in 1981 and it had a considerable impact. Made from stainless steel, it was a double-action revolver designed to take .357 Magnum cartridges and .38 Special cartridges. In due course a number of variations of the 686 were produced, aimed at specialized users, such as national security officers or target shooters. Smith & Wesson had intended this revolver to be light enough for extended carry by uniformed officers while providing considerable firepower.

Smith & Wesson 624 ("Horton Special")

SPECIFICATION

MANUFACTURER Smith & Wesson Inc.
CALIBRE .44 Special
MAGAZINE CAPACITY 6
ACTION Double
TOTAL LENGTH 197mm/7.8in
BARREL LENGTH 76mm/3in
WEIGHT UNLOADED 1,134g/40oz

The Lew Horton Special was introduced in 1985. It was based on popular earlier models of S&W revolvers and was chambered for a .44 Special cartridge. The weapon became known as the "Horton Special" because it was put in production following the order of a Massachusetts gun distributor, Lew Horton. It had a solid frame with a cylinder that swung out to the left, a chrome-plated finish and a "birdshead"-shaped grip. The revolver is considered to be technologically outdated because of its low-pressure calibre.

Smith & Wesson Model 581

SPECIFICATION

MANUFACTURER Smith & Wesson Inc.
CALIBRE .357 Magnum
CYLINDER 6
ACTION Double
TOTAL LENGTH 216mm/8.5in
BARREL LENGTH 102mm/4in
WEIGHT UNLOADED 1,134g/40oz

This was part of a lightweight series of Smith & Wesson revolvers and made from carbon steel. Introduced in 1981, it had a double-action trigger mechanism and the firing pin mounted on the hammer. The cylinder was double-locked to the frame with a lock at the rear of the cylinder and another on the under-barrel lug. Revolvers in this series proved popular with police forces and other security services as they were easy to carry and conceal while providing considerable power in emergencies.

Smith & Wesson 645

SPECIFICATION	🇺🇸
MANUFACTURER	Smith & Wesson Inc.
CALIBRE	.45 ACP
MAGAZINE CAPACITY	8
ACTION	Recoil/double
TOTAL LENGTH	225mm/10in
BARREL LENGTH	127mm/5in
WEIGHT UNLOADED	1,247g/44oz

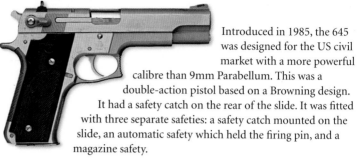

Introduced in 1985, the 645 was designed for the US civil market with a more powerful calibre than 9mm Parabellum. This was a double-action pistol based on a Browning design. It had a safety catch on the rear of the slide. It was fitted with three separate safeties: a safety catch mounted on the slide, an automatic safety which held the firing pin, and a magazine safety.

Starr Model Army Revolver 1858

SPECIFICATION	🇺🇸
MANUFACTURER	Starr
CALIBRE	.44
CYLINDER	6
ACTION	Percussion/double
TOTAL LENGTH	296mm/11.67in
BARREL LENGTH	152mm/6in
WEIGHT UNLOADED	1,360g/48oz

This pistol, designed by Ebenezer Townsend Starr, was issued to the US Army during the American Civil War and was also used by individuals on the Western Frontier. The Starr Model Army Revolver was an innovative double-action design, as for the first time, a revolver could be fired without having first to be manually cocked. This was achieved in two stages. First, the pull on the trigger would rotate the cylinder and cock the hammer. Second, the trigger pressed on an actuator at the back of the trigger guard that fired the weapon. The Starr also had a hinged frame and the cylinder could be changed for ease of reloading. It was, however, more prone to breaking than single-action revolvers.

Ruger Mark I

SPECIFICATION	🇺🇸
MANUFACTURER	Sturm, Ruger & Co. Inc.
CALIBRE	.22 Long Rifle
MAGAZINE CAPACITY	9
ACTION	Blowback/single
TOTAL LENGTH	276mm/10.87in
BARREL LENGTH	175mm/6.89in
WEIGHT UNLOADED	1,190g/42oz

In 1949 the Ruger company based in Southport, Connecticut, produced the Ruger Standard pistol. This pistol was modelled on the iconic German Luger/Parabellum pistol. The Mark I version was first produced in the early 1950s and was a target-shooting version of the successful Ruger Standard. It was fitted with a heavy barrel and had fully adjustable sights. The models and variations that followed, to the present day, were very successful.

Ruger Security Six

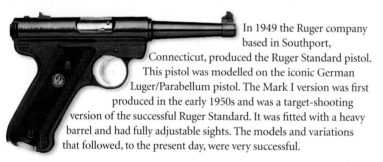

SPECIFICATION	🇺🇸
MANUFACTURER	Sturm, Ruger & Co. Inc.
CALIBRE	.357 Magnum
CYLINDER	6
ACTION	Double
TOTAL LENGTH	235mm/9.25in
BARREL LENGTH	102mm/4in
WEIGHT UNLOADED	950g/33.5oz

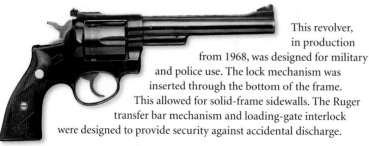

This revolver, in production from 1968, was designed for military and police use. The lock mechanism was inserted through the bottom of the frame. This allowed for solid-frame sidewalls. The Ruger transfer bar mechanism and loading-gate interlock were designed to provide security against accidental discharge.

Ruger Police Service Six

SPECIFICATION

MANUFACTURER Sturm, Ruger & Co. Inc.
CALIBRE .357 Magnum
CYLINDER 6
ACTION Double
TOTAL LENGTH 254mm/10in
BARREL LENGTH 102mm/4in
WEIGHT UNLOADED 950g/33.5oz

This revolver was based on the Security Six. It had slightly modified grips and a sighting groove in the backstrap (instead of a separate rear sight). This modification was intended to provide adequate sights for quick combat firing at short range but also to avoid catching the sight on a holster or clothing as it was drawn. The Service Six was a successful handgun, strongly built and reliable. It was widely used by US police forces. The manufacture of the Service Six was discontinued in the late 1980s. Another police revolver, the Ruger Speed Six, with a shorter barrel was also available until replaced by the Ruger GP-100.

Ruger Redhawk

SPECIFICATION

MANUFACTURER Sturm, Ruger & Co. Inc.
CALIBRE .44 Magnum, .45 Long Colt
CYLINDER 6
ACTION Double
TOTAL LENGTH 330mm/13in
BARREL LENGTH 190mm/7.5in
WEIGHT UNLOADED 1,502g/53oz

The Ruger Redhawk was first introduced in 1979 and was one of the most powerful handguns in the world. It was based on previous Ruger models, with square butt grip, adjustable sights and two barrel lengths. The Redhawk was a conventional double-action revolver with a triple-locking cylinder, locked into the frame at the front, rear and bottom, and a mechanism that made for a lighter trigger pull than earlier models. It also had a one-piece frame, rather than a removable sideplate, which gave it better strength.

Ruger GP-100

SPECIFICATION

MANUFACTURER Sturm, Ruger & Co. Inc
CALIBRE .357 Magnum, .38 Special
CYLINDER 6
ACTION Double
TOTAL LENGTH 248mm/9.75in
BARREL LENGTH 102mm/4in
WEIGHT UNLOADED 1,200g/42oz

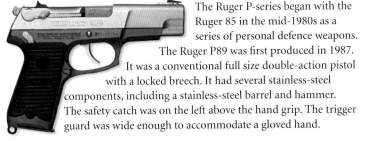

The GP-100, introduced in 1986, was a medium-sized revolver that replaced the Security Six and Police Service Six as the standard police revolver. It incorporated a number of improvements. It was a double-action revolver with a swing-out cylinder and fitted with a dual-cylinder crane lock, operated by a pushbutton. Chambered for the .357 Magnum round, the series was also available in .38 Special. The trigger mechanism was easily removable for maintenance. There was an option for either adjustable or fixed rear sights.

Ruger P89

The Ruger P-series began with the Ruger 85 in the mid-1980s as a series of personal defence weapons. The Ruger P89 was first produced in 1987. It was a conventional full size double-action pistol with a locked breech. It had several stainless-steel components, including a stainless-steel barrel and hammer. The safety catch was on the left above the hand grip. The trigger guard was wide enough to accommodate a gloved hand.

SPECIFICATION

MANUFACTURER Sturm, Ruger & Co. Inc.
CALIBRE 9mm Parabellum
MAGAZINE CAPACITY 10 or 15
ACTION Short recoil/double
TOTAL LENGTH 200mm/7.87in
BARREL LENGTH 114mm/4.49in
WEIGHT UNLOADED 907g/33.5oz

Ruger Super Redhawk

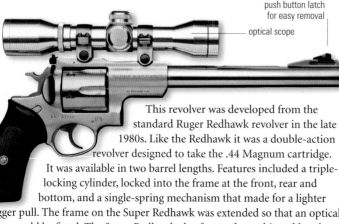

push button latch
for easy removal

optical scope

This revolver was developed from the standard Ruger Redhawk revolver in the late 1980s. Like the Redhawk it was a double-action revolver designed to take the .44 Magnum cartridge. It was available in two barrel lengths. Features included a triple-locking cylinder, locked into the frame at the front, rear and bottom, and a single-spring mechanism that made for a lighter trigger pull. The frame on the Super Redhawk was extended so that an optical scope could be fitted. The Super Redhawk also featured a cushioned hand grip. The stainless-steel finish was available with a low glare option that was corrosion resistant. The Ruger Super Redhawk was more than capable of carrying more powerful cartridges and within a few years it was chambered for new cartridges such as the .480 Ruger.

SPECIFICATION	
MANUFACTURER	Sturm, Ruger & Co. Inc.
CALIBRE	.44 Magnum
CYLINDER	6
ACTION	Double
TOTAL LENGTH	343mm/13.5in
BARREL LENGTH	190mm/7.5in
WEIGHT UNLOADED	1,474g/52oz

Redhawk models
Sturm, Ruger & Co.'s double-action Redhawk models are based on the first double-action revolvers, such as the Security Six, Police Six and Speed Six, manufactured between 1972 and 1988.

Ruger SP101

This small-frame revolver was introduced as a compact revolver that could be used for concealed carry. It was introduced in the late 1980s and was capable of taking the powerful .357 Magnum cartridge and was also chambered for other rounds. It was available in a number of different barrel lengths and options for fixed or adjustable sights. The sidewalls of the revolver were solid and integral to the rest of the frame. It had a triple-locking cylinder: this was locked into the frame at the front, rear and bottom in order to ensure positive alignment, and it had a forward latch mechanism to open it.

SPECIFICATION	
MANUFACTURER	Sturm, Ruger & Co. Inc.
CALIBRE	.22 Long Rifle, .38 Special,
	9mm Parabellum, .357 Magnum
CYLINDER	5
ACTION	Double
TOTAL LENGTH	181mm/7.12in
BARREL LENGTH	57mm/2.25in
WEIGHT UNLOADED	694.56g/24.5oz

Ruger P90

The Ruger P90, introduced in the early 1990s, had typical characteristics of this series of pistols, including a rugged build and overall durability. It was also capable of firing a high-pressure round. The P90 featured a firing pin block safety which was only disengaged once the trigger was fully depressed. The frame was manufactured from aluminium alloy, and other parts from stainless steel. It was designed to be easily disassembled. The P90 was found to be a very accurate and reliable pistol, though somewhat cumbersome compared to some other weapons of its calibre and/or power.

SPECIFICATION	
MANUFACTURER	Sturm, Ruger & Co. Inc.
CALIBRE	.45 ACP
MAGAZINE CAPACITY	8
ACTION	Recoil/double and DAO
TOTAL LENGTH	200mm/7.75in
BARREL LENGTH	114mm/4.5in
WEIGHT UNLOADED	963g/34oz

Ruger P94

SPECIFICATION

MANUFACTURER Sturm, Ruger & Co. Inc.
CALIBRE 9mm Parabellum
MAGAZINE CAPACITY 10
ACTION Recoil/double and DAO
TOTAL LENGTH 190mm/7.5in
BARREL LENGTH 108mm/4.25in
WEIGHT UNLOADED 930g/27oz

This pistol featured a hard-coated, aircraft-quality aluminium frame, a rugged steel slide and polycarbonate grip panels. It was fitted with a manual ambidextrous safety that, when engaged, prevented firing unless the lever was returned to the "fire" position. It has been developed by Ruger to reduce the impact of recoil when firing. The pistol has been fitted with high-visibility front and rear sights. Pistols in this series were designed to be easily maintained and could be field stripped into five major subassemblies for cleaning, without the need for special tools.

Ruger P95

SPECIFICATION

MANUFACTURER Sturm, Ruger & Co. Inc.
CALIBRE 9mm Parabellum
MAGAZINE CAPACITY 10
ACTION Recoil/double and DAO
TOTAL LENGTH 184mm/7.25in
BARREL LENGTH 99mm/3.9in
WEIGHT UNLOADED 765g/27oz

The P95 from the mid-1990s built upon the success of the earlier pistols in the P-series. The newest versions of the pistol had a non-slip, textured grip area, a contoured, rounded trigger guard, a matt-finished reinforced-polymer frame, and Picatinny rail (a bracket used for mounting accessories such as sights and lights, placed directly on the receiver). The P95 has a good reputation for being trouble free and good value.

Ruger 22/45 Mark III bull barrel

SPECIFICATION

MANUFACTURER Sturm, Ruger & Co. Inc.
CALIBRE .22 Long Rifle
MAGAZINE CAPACITY 10
ACTION Recoil/double and DAO
TOTAL LENGTH 203mm/8in
BARREL LENGTH 102mm/4in
WEIGHT UNLOADED 878.84g/31oz

This pistol was designed to provide the feel of a 1911 pistol. It was fitted with both front and rear sights. It had a molded polymer grip frame with a serrated front strap and chequered grip panel area. A cylindrical bolt construction ensured better accuracy than other moving-slide designs. An internal lock maintained the safety in the "safe" position. The pistol was fitted with a magazine disconnect to prevent accidental discharge when the magazine had been removed. A bull barrel is an unusually thick walled barrel that adds weight to the muzzle of the pistol and reduces recoil.

Ruger P345

manual safety

SPECIFICATION

MANUFACTURER Sturm, Ruger & Co. Inc.
CALIBRE .45 ACP
MAGAZINE CAPACITY 8
ACTION Recoil/double and DAO
TOTAL LENGTH 190mm/7.5in
BARREL LENGTH 108mm/4.25in
WEIGHT UNLOADED 822g/29oz

The P345 pistol has been available since 2002. As with all of the P-series, this is a double-action, recoil-operated semi-automatic pistol. Its slim profile, smooth edges and rounded contours make it a useful pistol for concealed carry. The combination of stopping power and controlled penetration make the .45 ACP practical for police use. It has a dovetailed, three-dot sight system for faster, more precise targeting, and a slim contoured slide and frame.

Taurus PT92 B-17

The PT92 (or Model 92) was first developed in the early 1980s. It is based on the Italian Beretta 92, with which it shares a large number of features – both are recoil operated with a locked-breech system. Like the Beretta it also has a double-action trigger and an ambidextrous frame-mounted manual safety with three positions (which can also be used as a de-cocking lever). This means the weapon can be carried "cocked and locked". The compact version of this model was introduced in 1991.

SPECIFICATION	
MANUFACTURER	Taurus Int. MFG, Inc.
CALIBRE	9mm Parabellum
MAGAZINE CAPACITY	17
ACTION	Recoil/double or single
TOTAL LENGTH	216mm/8.5in
BARREL LENGTH	127mm/5in
WEIGHT UNLOADED	964g/34oz

Taurus PT99 SS

The PT99 (or Model 99) was developed in 1982. Like the PT92, the design is based on the Beretta 92, with which it shares a large number of features. It has a double-action trigger and an ambidextrous frame-mounted manual safety with three positions (which can also be used as a de-cocking lever). This means the weapon can be carried in "cocked-and-locked" mode. The PT99 has many similar features to the PT92 except that the rear sights are micrometer-click adjustable making target acquisition more accurate. The PT99 has been extensively tested and widely used. It has proved to be well made and finished, and reasonably reliable.

SPECIFICATION	
MANUFACTURER	Taurus Int. MFG, Inc.
CALIBRE	9mm
MAGAZINE CAPACITY	17
ACTION	Short recoil/double
TOTAL LENGTH	216mm/8.5in
BARREL LENGTH	127mm/5in
WEIGHT UNLOADED	964g/34oz

Taurus PT100 SS11

The PT100 (or Model 100), introduced in 1991, was also based on the Beretta 92. It is chambered for the larger cartridge in an attempt to capitalize on the popularity of the .40 S&W cartridge with US police departments. It has a double-action trigger and an ambidextrous frame-mounted manual safety with three positions (which can also be used as a de-cocking lever). This means the weapon can be carried in "cocked-and-locked" mode. It has a fixed two-dot rear sight and fixed one-dot front sight.

SPECIFICATION	
MANUFACTURER	Taurus Int. MFG, Inc.
CALIBRE	.40 S&W
MAGAZINE CAPACITY	11
ACTION	Recoil/double
TOTAL LENGTH	216mm/8.5in
BARREL LENGTH	127mm/5in
WEIGHT UNLOADED	964g/34oz

Taurus PT22 BGR

hinged barrel

Introduced in 1992, the PT22 (or Model 22) is a small frame pistol easily concealed in a handbag or about the person. The barrel is hinged at the muzzle end so that it is easy to unload and also easy to carry out inspection and maintenance. The design of the gun was based on that of the Beretta M21. The pistol incorporates a magazine safety which prevents a round being fired if there is no magazine inserted.

SPECIFICATION	
MANUFACTURER	Taurus Int. MFG, Inc.
CALIBRE	.22 Long Rifle
MAGAZINE CAPACITY	8
ACTION	Blowback/DAO
TOTAL LENGTH	133mm/5.25in
BARREL LENGTH	65mm/2.56in
WEIGHT UNLOADED	349g/12.3oz

Taurus PT25 N

SPECIFICATION

MANUFACTURER Taurus Int. MFG, Inc.

CALIBRE .25 ACP

MAGAZINE CAPACITY 9

ACTION Blowback/DAO

TOTAL LENGTH 133mm/5.25in

BARREL LENGTH 70mm/2.75in

WEIGHT UNLOADED 349g/12.3oz

Produced as a small but powerful pistol for self-defence, the PT25 (or Model 25) is virtually the same as the PT22. The main difference between them is that the PT25 takes the .25 ACP cartridge. Like the PT22, it is designed to be easily concealed, and has the tip-up barrel feature. The PT25 has a DAO trigger system and a manual safety.

Brazil and the USA
Forjas Taurus was originally a small-arms manufacturer based in Port Alegre, Brazil. An affiliated company was set up in Miami, Florida, in 1982 and today, Taurus produces weapons in both Brazil and the United States.

Taurus PT940 SSPRL (Special)

SPECIFICATION

MANUFACTURER Taurus Int. MFG, Inc.

CALIBRE .40 S&W

MAGAZINE CAPACITY 10

ACTION Recoil/double

TOTAL LENGTH 178mm/7in

BARREL LENGTH 95mm/3.75in

WEIGHT UNLOADED 799g/28.2oz

The first of the Taurus 900 series pistols, the .40 S&W-calibre PT940 was introduced in 1992. It was produced to provide civilians and police with a pistol that is both substantial and compact, yet powerful enough to be used on primary duty or as self-defence weapon. The ambidextrous three-position safety allows the pistol to be carried "cocked and locked". The hand grips of the special edition are mother-of-pearl composite.

Taurus PT908

SPECIFICATION

MANUFACTURER Taurus Int. MFG, Inc.

CALIBRE 9mm Parabellum, .357 SIG

MAGAZINE CAPACITY 10

ACTION Recoil/double

TOTAL LENGTH 178mm/7in

BARREL LENGTH 95mm/3.75in

WEIGHT UNLOADED 770g/27.2oz

Introduced in 1993, the medium-sized PT908 is a modification of the PT92 and was designed for US combat duties. It is sturdy, reliable and easy to conceal. It has a double-action trigger and a three-point ambidextrous frame-mounted manual safety. The pistol is also available in .357 SIG. Despite a good performance, the PT908 ceased to be manufactured after 1997.

Taurus PT945 B

SPECIFICATION

MANUFACTURER Taurus Int. MFG, Inc.

CALIBRE .45 ACP

MAGAZINE CAPACITY 8

ACTION Recoil/double and single

TOTAL LENGTH 190mm/7.5in

BARREL LENGTH 108mm/4.25in

WEIGHT UNLOADED 836g/29.5oz

The PT945 B is a medium-framed steel and alloy pistol with chequered rubber grips. It is chambered for the .45 ACP cartridge. It is fitted with a manual safety and de-cocker, a firing-pin block automatic safety and a chamber-loaded indicator. The ambidextrous three-position safety allows the pistol to be carried "cocked and locked". The PT945 is a sturdy pistol, well suited as a duty gun and powerful, while being relatively easy to shoot.

Taurus Millennium PRO PT145 SSP

The lightweight polymer frame with chequered polymer grips makes this pistol a useful weapon for law enforcement. It is also aimed at the personal safety market in some countries. It is a compact-size pistol that has been produced to a high standard. It carries three safety features which consist of a manual safety lever, trigger-block mechanism and a firing-pin block.

SPECIFICATION

MANUFACTURER Taurus Int. MFG, Inc.
CALIBRE .45 ACP
MAGAZINE CAPACITY 10
ACTION Recoil/double and single
TOTAL LENGTH 158mm/6.2in
BARREL LENGTH 83mm/3.25in
WEIGHT UNLOADED 629g/22.2oz

Taurus Millennium Model PT111 B

The Millennium Model PT111B l is constructed from both polymer and steel and is ergonomically designed for optimum grip. Its lightweight frame makes it a useful weapon for law enforcement. It is also intended as a concealed carry defensive weapon for civilians. Like the other pistols in the range, it is a locked breech pistol that uses modified Browning-type locking, with single lug on the barrel which engages the ejection port in the slide. Similarly, the pistol is DAO and fitted with a manual safety as well as a firing-pin block safety.

SPECIFICATION

MANUFACTURER Taurus Int. MFG, Inc.
CALIBRE 9mm Parabellum
MAGAZINE CAPACITY 10
ACTION Recoil/DAO
TOTAL LENGTH 158mm/6.2in
BARREL LENGTH 83mm/3.25in
WEIGHT UNLOADED 530g/18.7oz

Taurus Millennium PRO PT140 SSP

The Millennium Pro PT140 SSP is a compact polymer frame pistol. Its modern design and materials offers good ergonomics and strong performance. The magazine is relatively high capacity, carrying 10 rounds in a double magazine. This DAO pistol is lightweight and easy to handle, which makes it suitable for both law enforcement and the personal defence market. The PT140 carries three safety features including a manual safety lever, trigger-block mechanism and a firing-pin block. Like the other Millennium pistols, the Taurus PT140 SSP is known for good reliability and reasonable firepower, despite its relatively compact size.

SPECIFICATION

MANUFACTURER Taurus Int. MFG, Inc.
CALIBRE .40 S&W
MAGAZINE CAPACITY 10
ACTION Recoil/DAO
TOTAL LENGTH 159mm/6.25in
BARREL LENGTH 83mm/3.25in
WEIGHT UNLOADED 530g/18.7oz

Taurus PT24/7 40BP

The PT24/7 is a large polymer- and steel-framed pistol with advanced ergonomics. It also includes features such as a chamber-loaded indicator, manual safety, internal trigger safety, and a comfortable moulded rubber grip offering a positive grasp under recoil. The pistol is DAO. It has a lightweight frame with integral accessory rail system. Its features make it suitable for use in law enforcement and for the personal defence market.

SPECIFICATION

MANUFACTURER Taurus Int. MFG, Inc.
CALIBRE .40 S&W
MAGAZINE CAPACITY 15
ACTION Recoil/DAO
TOTAL LENGTH 181mm/7.12in
BARREL LENGTH 102mm/4in
WEIGHT UNLOADED 771g/27.2oz

Taurus 65 SS4

SPECIFICATION

MANUFACTURER Taurus Int. MFG, Inc.
CALIBRE .357 Magnum
CYLINDER 6
ACTION Double and single
TOTAL LENGTH 268mm/10.5in
BARREL LENGTH 102mm/4in
WEIGHT 1,077g/38oz

The Taurus 65 SS4 (or Model 65) is made of steel with a rubber grip, and has a medium frame. It was designed largely for use by security personnel. It holds six rounds of the powerful Magnum load. The transfer bar mechanism prevents the hammer from striking the firing pin unless the trigger is pulled fully to the rear.

Taurus 444 SS6 Raging Bull

ported barrel

SPECIFICATION

MANUFACTURER Taurus Int. MFG, Inc.
CALIBRE .44 Magnum
CYLINDER 6
ACTION Double and single
TOTAL LENGTH 305mm/12in
BARREL LENGTH 165mm/6.5in
WEIGHT UNLOADED 1,502g/53oz

The 444 SS6 Raging Bull features a double-lockup cylinder which gives it strength where it is needed. It also has telescope mount bases along the barrel to fix a mini light or laser sight. It holds six rounds of the powerful .41 Magnum cartridge. The barrel is ported to expel gases from the cartridge and to allow for quick target acquisition.

Taurus 44 Tracker 4SS

SPECIFICATION

MANUFACTURER Taurus Int. MFG, Inc.
CALIBRE .44 Magnum
CYLINDER 5
ACTION Double and single
TOTAL LENGTH 228mm/9in
BARREL LENGTH 102mm/4in
WEIGHT UNLOADED 964g/34oz

This 44 Tracker 4SS is designed to give the best combination of weight, durability and power for protection on hunting or fishing trips. It holds five rounds of the powerful .41 Magnum cartridge. The barrel is ported to allow gases to escape from the cartridge and so control muzzle flip, making target shooting more accurate. The transfer bar mechanism prevents the hammer from striking the firing pin unless the trigger is pulled fully to the rear.

Taurus 444 Multi-4 Ultra-Lite

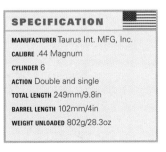

SPECIFICATION

MANUFACTURER Taurus Int. MFG, Inc.
CALIBRE .44 Magnum
CYLINDER 6
ACTION Double and single
TOTAL LENGTH 249mm/9.8in
BARREL LENGTH 102mm/4in
WEIGHT UNLOADED 802g/28.3oz

The 444 Multi-4 Ultra-Lite revolver was designed around the Raging Bull frame and has a powerful .44 Magnum cartridge. It was produced for hunting trips. The cushioned insert grip pillows the recoil, making shooting more comfortable. The revolver is made entirely from titanium and alloy so is exceptionally lightweight, easy to fire and control.

Taurus 605 B2

This concealable revolver
is made of steel and is
designed primarily for
personal defence. For a small frame
it fires the powerful .357 Magnum
load. It is a very finely tuned model
in terms of design, fabrication, fitting and
performance. While the hammer is visible in this
model, it is also available with a concealed hammer.

SPECIFICATION	
MANUFACTURER	Taurus Int. MFG, Inc.
CALIBRE	.357 Magnum
CYLINDER	5
ACTION	Double and single
TOTAL LENGTH	165mm/6.5in
BARREL LENGTH	51mm/2in
WEIGHT UNLOADED	680g/24oz

Taurus 607

Introduced in 1995, this weapon was the first ever standard-production
revolver to have a seven-round cylinder. The longest barrel length is
165mm/6.5in, with a full-length underlug, adjustable sights, and a vent rib on
top. The long-barrel model comes with an integral compensator (a device to
reduce recoil). Immediately, the US manufacturer Smith & Wesson produced
their own seven-round revolver by issuing a variant of their popular Model
686 revolver as the Model 686 Plus. Within a year the 607 was eclipsed by the
Taurus Model 608 which featured an eight-round cylinder.

SPECIFICATION	
MANUFACTURER	Taurus Int. MFG, Inc.
CALIBRE	.357 Magnum
CYLINDER	7
ACTION	Double and single
TOTAL LENGTH	301mm/11.87in
BARREL LENGTH	165mm/6.5in
WEIGHT UNLOADED	1,418g/52oz

Taurus 608 SS6

The Taurus 608 SS6
was produced in 1997 in
response to Smith & Wesson's .357 Model 686
Plus, which was chambered for seven rounds.
Taurus re-chambered their large-frame 607 to hold
eight rounds. This revolver was designed to achieve smooth
trigger action. The rear sight is adjustable. It has factory porting for
release of gases, so reducing recoil. The Model 608 SS6 is available in
three different barrel lengths. Scope mount bases are available to match
the finish for the larger models.

SPECIFICATION	
MANUFACTURER	Taurus Int. MFG, Inc.
CALIBRE	.357 Magnum
CYLINDER	8
ACTION	Double and single
TOTAL LENGTH	295mm/11.62in
BARREL LENGTH	165mm/6.5in
WEIGHT UNLOADED	1,446g/51oz

Taurus 650 SS2 "CIA" hammerless

This revolver was designed primarily
as a backup weapon for law enforcement
or for concealed carry and personal
protection. It has a small, lightweight, steel
construction with a rubber grip. Despite its
diminutive size, it is chambered for five rounds
of the .357 Magnum cartridge and is also available
chambered for the .35 Special cartridge as the Model 850.

SPECIFICATION	
MANUFACTURER	Taurus Int. MFG, Inc.
CALIBRE	.357 Magnum, .35 Special
CYLINDER	5
ACTION	DAO
TOTAL LENGTH	165mm/6.5in
BARREL LENGTH	51mm/2in
WEIGHT UNLOADED	678g/23.9oz

Taurus Model 651 SS2 Protector

SPECIFICATION

MANUFACTURER Taurus Int. MFG, Inc.
CALIBRE .357 Magnum, .38 Special
CYLINDER 5
ACTION Double and single
TOTAL LENGTH 165mm/6.5in
BARREL LENGTH 51mm/2in
WEIGHT UNLOADED 709g/25oz

The Taurus Protector is a small revolver designed particularly for personal protection. The revolver features a hammer that is hidden and can be manually cocked or de-cocked in single-action operation. The revolver is also designed to function smoothly in full double-action. The Protector is available in .357 Magnum or .38 Special, both versions hold five rounds. It is produced in both matt stainless steel and titanium.

Taurus 817S SUL

SPECIFICATION

MANUFACTURER Taurus Int. MFG, Inc.
CALIBRE .38 Special
CYLINDER 7
ACTION Double and single
TOTAL LENGTH 165mm/6.5in
BARREL LENGTH 51mm/2in
WEIGHT UNLOADED 595g/21oz

This revolver is unusual in providing an extra round in the cylinder, chambered for seven shots. The soft rubber grip and low-profile sights are provided to make the revolver more comfortable to use and easy to draw. It is ultra-light making it suitable for either law enforcement or personal defence.

Taurus Model 851 B2 "CIA" Protector

SPECIFICATION

MANUFACTURER Taurus Int. MFG, Inc.
CALIBRE .38 Special, .357 Magnum
CYLINDER 5
ACTION Double and single
TOTAL LENGTH 165mm/6.5in
BARREL LENGTH 51mm/2in
WEIGHT UNLOADED 595g/21oz

This small, ultra-light stainless steel or all-titanium model was designed for the home defence market. It is a double-action revolver that has a fully shrouded hammer that can be manually cocked or de-cocked in single-action operation when needed. The Protector is available in .38 Special and .357 Magnum holding five rounds. The recoil of strong ammunition is cushioned to a certain extent by the rubber grip.

Taurus 905 SS2

SPECIFICATION

MANUFACTURER Taurus Int. MFG, Inc.
CALIBRE 9mm Parabellum, .45 ACP
CYLINDER 5
ACTION Double and single
TOTAL LENGTH 165mm/6.5in
BARREL LENGTH 51mm/2in
WEIGHT UNLOADED 630g/22.2oz

Designed for law enforcement professionals at close range, this is a small-frame, lightweight revolver with rubber grips chambered for five rounds of the popular 9mm cartridge (and is also available for the .45 ACP round). The idea is that should users wish to carry both a revolver and a pistol then they need to carry and use just one calibre of ammunition.

Taurus/Rossi 351 02

The small-frame Rossi 351 02 revolver is chambered for the .38 Special cartridge. With five rounds and a 2-inch/51-mm barrel, it is ideal for concealed carriage in undercover work as well as for personal defence. It is reliable and simple to use. The Rossi 351 02 is finished in blue steel and the hand grip is rubber, contoured for optimum finger grip.

SPECIFICATION
MANUFACTURER Taurus Int. MFG, Inc.
CALIBRE .38 Special
CYLINDER 5
ACTION Double and single
TOTAL LENGTH 165mm/6.5in
BARREL LENGTH 51mm/2in
WEIGHT UNLOADED 680g/24oz

Taurus/Rossi 352 02

This small-frame revolver is similar to the 351 model but has a slightly different shaped frame and grip and is finished in stainless steel. It is chambered for the .38 Special cartridge and is accurate and well balanced. It is ideal for concealed carriage as well as for personal defence. The 352 02 fits most hands comfortably.

Rossi and Taurus
The Rossi company was founded by Amadeo Rossi in Brazil in 1889. Taurus Int. MFG, Inc. bought the rights and the tooling equipment to manufacture Rossi handguns in 1997. Taurus Int. MFG, Inc. makes a selection of revolvers under contract with Rossi.

SPECIFICATION
MANUFACTURER Taurus Int. MFG, Inc.
CALIBRE .38 Special
CYLINDER 5
ACTION Double and single
TOTAL LENGTH 165mm/6.5in
BARREL LENGTH 51mm/2in
WEIGHT UNLOADED 680g/24oz

Taurus/Rossi R461 02

The .357 Magnum round is widely regarded as an ideal round for use in revolvers that are created for self-defence. The Rossi R461 02 was built to handle the .357 Magnum cartridge and it can also fire the popular .38 Special rounds. It has a fixed front sight but no rear sight, and a contoured rubber grip.

SPECIFICATION
MANUFACTURER Taurus Int. MFG, Inc.
CALIBRE .357 Magnum, .38 Special
CYLINDER 6
ACTION Double
TOTAL LENGTH 165mm/6.5in
BARREL LENGTH 50.8mm/2in
WEIGHT UNLOADED 737.09g/26oz

Taurus/Rossi 851 04

SPECIFICATION
MANUFACTURER Taurus Int. MFG, Inc.
CALIBRE .38 Special
CYLINDER 6
ACTION Double and single
TOTAL LENGTH 216mm/8.5in
BARREL LENGTH 102mm/4in
WEIGHT UNLOADED 908g/32oz

The Rossi 851 04 was designed for service and duty use. It carries six rounds of the popular .38 Special calibre cartridge in an easy-to-handle medium frame. It also has a telescope mount base along the barrel to fix a mini light or laser sight. The model 851 has an adjustable rear sight and a rubber grip, contoured for optimum finger grip.

Taurus/Rossi 971 04

SPECIFICATION	
MANUFACTURER	Taurus Int. MFG, Inc.
CALIBRE	.357 Magnum, .38 Special
CYLINDER	6
ACTION	Double
TOTAL LENGTH	216mm/8.5in
BARREL LENGTH	102mm/4in
WEIGHT UNLOADED	907.18g/32oz

The model 971 04 is a double-action .357 Magnum revolver with a steel barrel. The revolver can also fire the .38 Special round. It has a solid sighting ridge along the barrel and an adjustable rear sight. This revolver is made from solid steel and the grip is made of contoured rubber, for optimum finger grip.

Taurus/Rossi R972 06

SPECIFICATION	
MANUFACTURER	Taurus Int. MFG, Inc.
CALIBRE	.357 Magnum, .38 Special
CYLINDER	6
ACTION	Double
TOTAL LENGTH	268mm/10.5in
BARREL LENGTH	152mm/6in
WEIGHT UNLOADED	992g/35oz

The Rossi R972 06 is a double-action, stainless steel .357 Magnum revolver. It has a long barrel for long-distance accuracy and adjustable rear sights for better target acquisition. While it can handle .357 Magnum cartridges, the 972 can also fire the popular .38 Special cartridge.

★ Chile

Chilean small-arms manufacture is centred round the firm of FAMAE (Las Fábricas y Maestranzas del Ejército), which was founded in 1811 and is said to be the oldest company of its type in South America.

Small-arms production is largely focused on assault rifles (in association with Swiss Arms, known as SIG, the oldest manufacturer of arms in Switzerland) and submachine guns, which are developed by FAMAE.

Steyr Hahn Model 1911

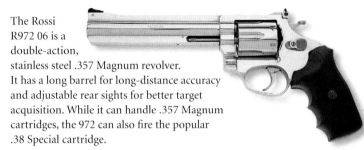

SPECIFICATION	
MANUFACTURER	Osterreichische Waffenfabriks-Gesellschaft Steyr
CALIBRE	9mm Steyr
MAGAZINE CAPACITY	8
ACTION	Recoil/single
TOTAL LENGTH	216mm/8.5in
BARREL LENGTH	128mm/5.04in
WEIGHT UNLOADED	1,134g/40oz

This was a Chilean version of a famous pistol designed by Bohemian Karel Krnka and developed in Austria for military use. It was adopted by Austro-Hungarian forces towards the end of World War I, and exports to countries such as Chile were an important part of the production run. The pistol achieved a high reputation for robustness and reliability. On recoil, the barrel turned about 20 degrees and was then brought to a halt by lugs, while the rest of the slide continued rearward. The magazine was integral to the butt and was loaded with a charger. The Chilean versions had the coat of arms on the left of the slide and the words "Ejército de Chile" on the right, above the grip.

Argentina

In Argentina the firm of Ballester-Molina dates back to 1929 when two Spaniards, Arturo Ballester and Eugenio Molina, set up an engineering firm to provide parts for Hispano-Suiza cars. In due course they were commissioned by the Argentine Army to produce small arms. In the early to mid-1960s the firearms company Bersa began production and it still remains in business today.

Bersa Model 64

Bersa's earliest pistols were simple, blowback-operated single-action designs chambered for the .22 Long Rifle cartridge. A trigger-blocking manual safety was placed just behind the trigger and a magazine catch was located near the heel of the grip. The Bersa model line has run since the 1960s and this pistol was one of the basic designs from which others were developed for the first generation of pistols.

safety

SPECIFICATION	
MANUFACTURER	Bersa S.A.
CALIBRE	.22 Long Rifle
MAGAZINE CAPACITY	7
ACTION	Blowback/single
TOTAL LENGTH	168mm/6.63in
BARREL LENGTH	90mm/3.54in
WEIGHT UNLOADED	794g/28oz

Bersa Model 62

guide rod

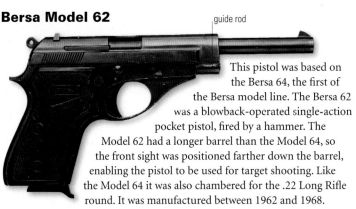

This pistol was based on the Bersa 64, the first of the Bersa model line. The Bersa 62 was a blowback-operated single-action pocket pistol, fired by a hammer. The Model 62 had a longer barrel than the Model 64, so the front sight was positioned farther down the barrel, enabling the pistol to be used for target shooting. Like the Model 64 it was also chambered for the .22 Long Rifle round. It was manufactured between 1962 and 1968. Bersa's first generation of pistols were produced until the end of the 1970s, when modifications were made for the next generation.

The guide rod
A separate recoil spring guide rod is inserted under the barrel. Guide rods are said to improve reliability and moderate recoil.

SPECIFICATION	
MANUFACTURER	Bersa S.A.
CALIBRE	.22 Long Rifle
MAGAZINE CAPACITY	10
ACTION	Blowback/single
TOTAL LENGTH	229mm/9in
BARREL LENGTH	152mm/6in
WEIGHT UNLOADED	695g/24.5oz

Bersa Model 97

Produced between 1978 and 1982, the single-action Model 97 represented a second-generation model and Bersa's first pistol in .380 ACP. Like previous Bersa models, it was a blowback-operated single-action pistol. Unlike previous models it did not have a recoil spring guide, as the barrel itself was used for this purpose. A slide-mounted hammer-blocking safety and a magazine disconnect safety were added as new features. A dedicated barrel pin was used as the trigger pin, freeing up the slide catch. The pistol featured windage-adjustable rear sights. After four years of production, the Model 97 was replaced in 1983 by the Model 383.

SPECIFICATION	
MANUFACTURER	Bersa S.A.
CALIBRE	.380 ACP
MAGAZINE CAPACITY	7
ACTION	Blowback/single
TOTAL LENGTH	168mm/6.63in
BARREL LENGTH	90mm/3.54in
WEIGHT UNLOADED	Not known

Bersa Model 383

SPECIFICATION

MANUFACTURER Bersa S.A.
CALIBRE .380 ACP
MAGAZINE 7
ACTION Blowback/single
TOTAL LENGTH 168mm/6.63in
BARREL LENGTH 90mm/3.54in
WEIGHT UNLOADED 680g/24oz

manual safety   magazine release

The Model 383 succeeded the Model 97 and was produced from 1983 to 1985. It was a compact, single-action blowback-operated pistol, part of the third generation. The Model 383 was designed to be easily concealed. It had a large magazine release located just above the hand grip on the right side, and the manual safety was above and to the rear of this. It also had a recurved trigger-guard with a finger rest. The double-action version of the 383 (called the 383A) was produced between 1986 and 1988 with various modifications of the fourth generation of Bersa pistols. The Model 383A was produced in polished blue or nickel with walnut grips.

SPECIFICATION

MANUFACTURER Bersa S.A.
CALIBRE 9mm Parabellum
MAGAZINE 15
ACTION Blowback/double
TOTAL LENGTH Not known
BARREL LENGTH Not known
WEIGHT UNLOADED 695g/24.5oz

Bersa Model 90

The Model 90 was part of the range of Bersa models from the early 1990s and was chambered for the 9mm Parabellum cartridge. The fifth generation of Bersa pistols was similar to previous models, but used new materials. The external slide catch was removed (although later reinstated on the Model 90). Instead of a slide catch, the pistol used an internal mechanism which allowed it to be released from slide-lock using the slide. High-capacity magazines were introduced. However, when legislation was introduced in the United States in 1994 to reduce magazine capacity, Bersa designs were modified.

SPECIFICATION

MANUFACTURER Bersa S.A.
CALIBRE 9mm Parabellum
MAGAZINE 17
ACTION Recoil/double
TOTAL LENGTH 192mm/7.56in
BARREL LENGTH 110mm/4in
WEIGHT UNLOADED 870g/30oz

Bersa Thunder 9

This semi-automatic pistol was available from 1994. It had a substantial trigger guard that was designed to accommodate a gloved finger. The rear sight was dovetailed and the front sight was incorporated in the slide. The pistol was fitted with a firing-pin safety. The Thunder 9 was imported into the United States only after the lifting of the ban on high-capacity magazines in 2004. Bersa Thunder 9 pistols are standard issue pistols for the Argentine Federal Police and the Buenos Aires Province Police.

Bersa Thunder 380

SPECIFICATION

MANUFACTURER Bersa S.A.
CALIBRE .380 ACP
MAGAZINE 7 or 9
ACTION Blowback/double
TOTAL LENGTH 168mm/6.63in
BARREL LENGTH 90mm/3.54in
WEIGHT UNLOADED 567g/19.75oz

This small, lightweight semi-automatic pistol was introduced in 1995. Intended primarily for civilian use, the weapon was also used by a variety of security and military forces. It had a safety switch mounted on the slide and a magazine safety that prevented the weapon firing if a magazine was not inserted. It was not possible to carry the pistol "cocked and locked". It also featured a trigger lock, operated by a key. Although the .380 ACP cartridge was comparatively weak, the light and convenient setup of this weapon made it a convenient pistol to carry. In the United States, the Thunder 380 was known as the Firestorm 380. It was a popular model with a long production run.

Bersa Thunder 45 Ultra-Compact

This pistol was produced from 2002 and designed for concealed carriage by civilians as well as for law enforcement and military personnel. It was a compact double-action pistol with a locked breech. Much attention has been paid to ergonomics. The safety catch was ambidextrous, as was the slide-release lever. The magazine release could be mounted on either side of the hand grip. The trigger could be locked with a key. Some versions had a rail attachment for a laser or light below the barrel.

SPECIFICATION

MANUFACTURER Bersa S.A.
CALIBRE .45 ACP
MAGAZINE CAPACITY 7
ACTION Recoil/double
TOTAL LENGTH 173mm/6.81in
BARREL LENGTH 92mm/3.62in
WEIGHT UNLOADED 780g/27.5oz

Ballester-Molina

This pistol was originally made by a Spanish automotive company, Hispano-Suiza. The Argentine section of the company, Hispano Argentino de Automóviles S.A. (HAFDASA), was contracted by the Argentine government to manufacture small arms. The company set about adapting designs of existing weapons, one of which included the Colt M1911A1. Produced in the late 1930s, the .45 Ballester-Molina was similar in appearance to the Colt. However, there were a number of significant differences between the two weapons, including the design of the hammer strut, safety lock, firing-pin stop and mainspring housing. The success of the modified design was such that the pistol was adopted by the Argentine Police and Army and was also ordered by the British for use by members of the Special Operations Executive (SOE).

The Hafdasa
This pistol is sometimes known as the "Hafdasa" from the initials of the manufacturer (Hispano Argentino Fábrica de Automóviles S.A.).

SPECIFICATION

MANUFACTURER Hispano Argentino Fábrica de Automóviles S.A.
CALIBRE .45 ACP
MAGAZINE CAPACITY 7
ACTION Recoil/single
TOTAL LENGTH 216mm/8.5in
BARREL LENGTH 127mm/5in
WEIGHT UNLOADED 1,077g/38oz

Modelo 1905

The Mannlicher 1905 pistol was originally made in Austria. It was known in Europe as the M1901 and was purchased by the Argentine Army in 1905. It was a semi-automatic pistol and had an unusually elegant appearance, with a gentle curve from the hand grip up over the trigger-guard area. The Modelo 1905 had an open-topped slide and the barrel was screwed into the breech. The slide was a short breech-block section behind the barrel and incorporated both the extractor and the firing pin. The pistol had a delayed blowback mechanism. The magazine was integral to the butt and was loaded via a charger through the action mechanism. This pistol remained popular and in use in South America long after it had been discontinued in Europe.

SPECIFICATION

MANUFACTURER Osterreichische Waffenfabriks Gesellschaft
CALIBRE 7.63mm Mannlicher
MAGAZINE CAPACITY 8
ACTION Blowback/single
TOTAL LENGTH 246mm/9.69in
BARREL LENGTH 160mm/6.3in
WEIGHT UNLOADED 910g/32oz

 # Brazil

Small-arms manufacture in Brazil is largely centred around Industria de Material Bélico (IMBEL), which is government-owned and has close links with the Ministry of Defence and the Army. It was established in 1975 and brought together a number of ammunition factories in Brazil.

IMBEL M973

SPECIFICATION

MANUFACTURER Indústria de Material Bélico do Brasil (IMBEL)
CALIBRE 9mm Parabellum, .45 ACP
MAGAZINE CAPACITY 9
ACTION Short recoil/single
TOTAL LENGTH 216mm/8.5in
BARREL LENGTH 128mm/5.04in
WEIGHT UNLOADED 1,010g/35.6oz

First produced in 1973, this pistol was a 9mm version of the Colt M1911A1. It was chambered in .45 ACP as the standard IMBEL. It was standard issue to the Brazilian Army and has also been widely exported. It was a semi-automatic pistol, based on the short-recoil system. The Colt M1911 was the longest-serving service weapon in the world. Like many others throughout the world, the Brazilian security forces chose a classic design as their weapon of choice due to its rugged design, robustness and reliability. The only drawback for its future service is the development of modern body armour that is resistant even to the 9mm Parabellum round.

IMBEL MD1

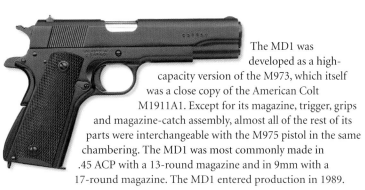

SPECIFICATION

MANUFACTURER Indústria de Material Bélico do Brasil (IMBEL)
CALIBRE .45 ACP, 9mm Parabellum
MAGAZINE CAPACITY 13 or 17
ACTION Short recoil/single
TOTAL LENGTH 216mm/8.5in
BARREL LENGTH 128mm/5.04in
WEIGHT UNLOADED 1,060g/37.4oz

The MD1 was developed as a high-capacity version of the M973, which itself was a close copy of the American Colt M1911A1. Except for its magazine, trigger, grips and magazine-catch assembly, almost all of the rest of its parts were interchangeable with the M975 pistol in the same chambering. The MD1 was most commonly made in .45 ACP with a 13-round magazine and in 9mm with a 17-round magazine. The MD1 entered production in 1989.

SPECIFICATION

MANUFACTURER Indústria de Material Bélico do Brasil (IMBEL)
CALIBRE .45 ACP, 9mm Parabellum
MAGAZINE CAPACITY 13 or 17
ACTION Short recoil/single
TOTAL LENGTH 216mm/8.5in
BARREL LENGTH 128mm/5.04in
WEIGHT UNLOADED 1,060g/37.4oz

IMBEL MD2

This was a compact version of the high capacity MD1 in .45 ACP and 9mm Parabellum. Because of its flat design, the original Colt M1911A1-based models were surprisingly easy to carry concealed and this reduced-size model was even more so. This made it a good choice for police, military and civilian concealed carry.

Colt .45-based models
Brazil has a number of models based on the Colt .45, available in .45, .40 and 9mm calibres, for use by military and police (M1911A1, M973, IMBEL and variants), and .38 calibre for civilian use.

 # Spain

Spain produced a wide variety of pistols and revolvers throughout the 20th century, mostly centred on the firms of Astra-Unceta y Cia. S.A. and Star Bonifacio Echeverría S.A. Although these were primarily designed to meet the requirements of the Spanish armed forces, the police and the Guardia Civil, a number of designs were also exported as far afield as China. Both of these companies went out of business in the late 1990s, but a new firm, Astra, was formed, which produces a range of firearms.

Military Model

This pistol was based on the style of the Mannlicher pistols and the ten-round magazine would be positioned in front of the trigger guard. The bolt itself was rectangular and the top rear part of the receiver was squared off to house it. There was an external hammer which struck a firing pin in the bolt. It had a removable plate on the left side and a separate barrel return spring. Although its history was not well documented, the Military Model was produced before World War I. It was a well-made pistol that was exported in large numbers. It was also issued to Spanish security forces.

SPECIFICATION	
MANUFACTURER Star Bonifacio Echeverría S.A.	
CALIBRE 7.65mm (.32 ACP)	
MAGAZINE CAPACITY 10	
ACTION Recoil/single	
TOTAL LENGTH 312mm/12.3in	
BARREL LENGTH 160mm/6.3in	
WEIGHT UNLOADED 646g/23oz	

Star Model 1920

The Model 1920 was produced solely for the Guardia Civil, the Spanish police. This was the first Star pistol designed in the style of the Colt M1911. The 1920 model was made in at least four variants, produced between 1920 and 1921. Although it had the general outline of the Colt and was locked via a Browning-style tipping barrel and link system, there were other changes. The safety was an all-new rotating lever, but it was mounted high at the extreme rear of the slide. These changes indicated that it was not simply copied from the Colt-Browning, but was a new design in its own right. Subsequent models continued to be produced to meet the needs of the Guardia Civil, known as the "military model".

SPECIFICATION	
MANUFACTURER Star Bonifacio Echeverría S.A.	
CALIBRE 9mm Largo	
MAGAZINE CAPACITY 8	
ACTION Recoil/single	
TOTAL LENGTH 200mm/7.87in	
BARREL LENGTH 122mm/4.8in	
WEIGHT UNLOADED 1,100g/38.8oz	

Star Model 1921

Shortly after adopting the 1920 pistol, the Guardia Civil decided that they were not completely satisfied with the design. They felt that the slide-mounted safety was not appropriate for a service pistol. The safety was moved to the frame and a grip safety was added. This became the Star Modelo Militar 1921. Star next removed the grip safety from the Model 1921 and redesignated it as the Model 1922.

SPECIFICATION	
MANUFACTURER Star Bonifacio Echeverría S.A.	
CALIBRE 9mm Largo	
MAGAZINE CAPACITY 8	
ACTION Recoil/single	
TOTAL LENGTH 200mm/7.87in	
BARREL LENGTH 122mm/4.8in	
WEIGHT UNLOADED 1,100g/38.8oz	

Star Model B

SPECIFICATION

MANUFACTURER Star Bonifacio Echeverría S.A.

CALIBRE 9mm Parabellum

MAGAZINE CAPACITY 9

ACTION Recoil/single

TOTAL LENGTH 215mm/8.46in

BARREL LENGTH 122mm/4.8in

WEIGHT UNLOADED 1,085g/38.27oz

Star's Model B series was a continuation of the Model A series of pistols designed in the style of the M1911 for the Guardia Civil in the early 1920s. The first Model B pistol was introduced in 1924 and was a variation of the Model A. The first version of the Model B is quite rare today and an upgraded version was introduced in 1931. The style of the frame was updated and a larger safety as well as more rugged and higher-visibility sights were fitted. This model was to remain in service until 1983. Some specially designated Model B pistols were issued to German forces during World War II.

Star Model D

SPECIFICATION

MANUFACTURER Star Bonifacio Echeverría S.A.

CALIBRE 9mm Corto (.380 ACP)

MAGAZINE CAPACITY 6

ACTION Blowback/single

TOTAL LENGTH 145mm/5.7in

BARREL LENGTH 80mm/3.15in

WEIGHT UNLOADED 420g/14.28oz

The Model D series was designed both as a weapon for personal self-defence and also as a concealable weapon for security forces. It was first produced in the 1920s and issued to the Guardia Civil. A number of variants have been produced. This version of the pistol, from 1928, featured a slide stop over the trigger and it had a thumb safety on the left-hand side of the receiver. One version of the pistol was produced in collaboration with Colt in the United States, but the partnership did not last very long and few pistols were produced.

Star Model E

SPECIFICATION

MANUFACTURER Star Bonifacio Echeverría S.A.

CALIBRE 6.35mm (.25 ACP)

MAGAZINE CAPACITY Not known

ACTION Blowback/single

TOTAL LENGTH 102mm/4in

BARREL LENGTH 51mm/2in

WEIGHT UNLOADED Not known

Starlite

A series of pistols, known as Starlite, were produced in the 1990s and have similar features to the Model E series.

Pistols in the Star Model E series were the smallest of the Star "vest pocket" pistols. This subcompact pistol was first introduced in 1925 and was in production for nearly ten years. Unusually for a pistol of this size, it had an external hammer, which could cause snagging problems for a pistol designed to be concealed around the body. The slide was designed so that it did not fully hide the barrel (which keeps the weight down). A safety catch was positioned just behind the trigger guard. It had quite basic round-section front sights. The magazine release catch was also positioned behind the trigger guard, which was also very unusual for a pistol of this size. The Model E series was produced until the mid-1930s.

Star Model F

The first Model F series of Star pistols appeared in 1932. The series was updated to the second series in 1942. This pistol was a .22 Long Rifle-calibre target pistol and a variant of the Star pocket pistols. Designed primarily for sport and target shooting, pistols in the F series had barrels of varying lengths, depending on the model (which include variations such as Target or Sport). All versions had adjustable rear sights. Instead of being just behind the trigger, the second Model F series had more conventional safeties, situated behind the gripframe, just behind the hammer pin.

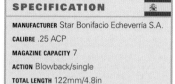

SPECIFICATION

MANUFACTURER Star Bonifacio Echeverría S.A.
CALIBRE .22 Long Rifle
MAGAZINE CAPACITY 10
ACTION Blowback/single
TOTAL LENGTH 255mm/10.04in
BARREL LENGTH 180mm/7in
WEIGHT UNLOADED 895g/32oz

The end of an era
In 1983, when Star stopped producing the classic series, the whole of the model F series went out of production.

Star Model CO

The Model CO series of pistols were small, "vest pocket" pistols produced between 1930 and the mid-1950s. In 1956 they were replaced with the Model CU series, which were manufactured up until the early 1970s. The CO and the CU were produced as single-action pistols with a fixed barrel. The layout of the Model CO was very typical of small pocket pistols. The magazine release was positioned on the left side behind the trigger guard instead of on the butt, and the safety was a small lever behind the trigger. Although numerous small changes were made to bring the Model CU up to date, the main change was to incorporate a conventional thumb safety. The gripframe was lengthened and slightly widened at the bottom and the magazine release was enlarged. The Model CK was introduced in 1973 and was in production for about ten years.

SPECIFICATION

MANUFACTURER Star Bonifacio Echeverría S.A.
CALIBRE .25 ACP
MAGAZINE CAPACITY 7
ACTION Blowback/single
TOTAL LENGTH 122mm/4.8in
BARREL LENGTH 60mm/2.36in
WEIGHT UNLOADED 420g/14.8oz

Model COE
The model COE ("engraved") was manufactured from mother of pearl.

Star Model BM

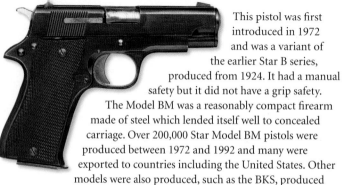

This pistol was first introduced in 1972 and was a variant of the earlier Star B series, produced from 1924. It had a manual safety but it did not have a grip safety. The Model BM was a reasonably compact firearm made of steel which lended itself well to concealed carriage. Over 200,000 Star Model BM pistols were produced between 1972 and 1992 and many were exported to countries including the United States. Other models were also produced, such as the BKS, produced slightly earlier than the BM, and the BKM. Both were alloy framed and generally have not remained in as good condition as the Model BMs.

SPECIFICATION

MANUFACTURER Star Bonifacio Echeverría S.A.
CALIBRE 9mm Parabellum
MAGAZINE CAPACITY 8
ACTION Recoil/single
TOTAL LENGTH 182mm/7.17in
BARREL LENGTH 99mm/3.9in
WEIGHT UNLOADED 965g/34oz

A popular choice
Despite being rather heavy, the Model BM is a relatively popular handgun as it is reasonably inexpensive to purchase.

Star Model PD Compact

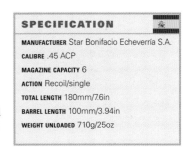

The Model P series was started in the 1920s and a number of variants have since been produced. This included the Model PKM in 1974, on which the Model PD is based. The Model PD was produced between 1975 and today. It was designed to be easily carried and concealed while providing considerable power. The pistol had a locking system similar to a Browning design but with only one interlocking lug between barrel and slide. An internal plastic buffer had been added to reduce the effects of recoil. The frame was of light alloy and the rear sight was adjustable. The pistol had a manual safety but no grip safety.

<table>
<tr><td colspan="2">SPECIFICATION</td></tr>
<tr><td>MANUFACTURER</td><td>Star Bonifacio Echeverría S.A.</td></tr>
<tr><td>CALIBRE</td><td>.45 ACP</td></tr>
<tr><td>MAGAZINE CAPACITY</td><td>6</td></tr>
<tr><td>ACTION</td><td>Recoil/single</td></tr>
<tr><td>TOTAL LENGTH</td><td>180mm/7.6in</td></tr>
<tr><td>BARREL LENGTH</td><td>100mm/3.94in</td></tr>
<tr><td>WEIGHT UNLOADED</td><td>710g/25oz</td></tr>
</table>

Star Firestar M43

<table>
<tr><td colspan="2">SPECIFICATION</td></tr>
<tr><td>MANUFACTURER</td><td>Star Bonifacio Echeverría S.A.</td></tr>
<tr><td>CALIBRE</td><td>9mm Parabellum</td></tr>
<tr><td>MAGAZINE CAPACITY</td><td>7</td></tr>
<tr><td>ACTION</td><td>Recoil/single</td></tr>
<tr><td>TOTAL LENGTH</td><td>165mm/6.5in</td></tr>
<tr><td>BARREL LENGTH</td><td>86mm/3.4in</td></tr>
<tr><td>WEIGHT UNLOADED</td><td>855g/30.2oz</td></tr>
</table>

The Firestar series was a group of small, compact pistols designed for concealed carry. The M43 had a short-barrel recoil and Browning-style locking. It was fitted with an automatic firing-pin safety and a magazine disconnect safety. It also had a frame-mounted ambidextrous safety lever. The pistol could be carried "cocked and locked". It was, however, quite heavy being manufactured from solid steel. There were two other pistols in the Firestar series – the M40 and the M45 – which were double-action pistols with a similar frame-mounted ambidextrous safety that also allowed for "cocked-and-locked" carry. The M40 was chambered for the .40 S&W cartridge and the M45 for the .45 ACP cartridge, and both carried six rounds.

Star Model 30M

<table>
<tr><td colspan="2">SPECIFICATION</td></tr>
<tr><td>MANUFACTURER</td><td>Star Bonifacio Echeverría S.A.</td></tr>
<tr><td>CALIBRE</td><td>9mm Parabellum</td></tr>
<tr><td>MAGAZINE CAPACITY</td><td>15</td></tr>
<tr><td>ACTION</td><td>Recoil/double</td></tr>
<tr><td>TOTAL LENGTH</td><td>205mm/8.1in</td></tr>
<tr><td>BARREL LENGTH</td><td>119mm/4.69in</td></tr>
<tr><td>WEIGHT UNLOADED</td><td>1,140g/40.21oz</td></tr>
</table>

Use in the services
The Model 30M was issued to the Navy, Marines and Air Force as well as to the Guardia Civil and the national police.

The Star Model 30M was the main pistol in a series beginning with the Model 28. This pistol was a recoil-operated locked-breech pistol that featured Browning-style locking. It had a slide-mounted ambidextrous safety that locked the firing pin, and also a magazine safety. It also had a chamber-loaded indicator and fixed front sights and adjustable rear sights. It was made from solid steel and had a reputation for solidity and reliability. The Star Model 30M was produced in 1990. The Model 31 was an updated version of the 30M and incorporated a number of both external and internal modifications, for example to the safety lever and to the extractor mechanism.

Campo-Giro Model 1913

This pistol was a development of a design first conceived by Venancio Lopez de Ceballos y Aguirre, a retired Lieutenant-Colonel and Count of Conde del Campo Giro. The first demonstration model was produced in Oviedo in 1903. In 1910, 25 prototypes were completed and in 1912 the pistol was adopted as the 9mm Campo-Giro pistol, known as the Model 1913 and issued to the Army. Various modifications had been made to the design and it was revised again in 1921. The pistol had some design failings and in due course it was thoroughly revised and renamed the Astra 400.

SPECIFICATION

MANUFACTURER Esperanza y Unceta
CALIBRE 9mm Largo
MAGAZINE CAPACITY 8
ACTION Blowback/single
TOTAL LENGTH 237mm/9.33in
BARREL LENGTH 165mm/6.5in
WEIGHT UNLOADED 950g/33.5oz

Astra Model 400

In 1920 the Campo-Giro Model 1913 was phased out as the Army issue model. The Astra 400, an improved version of this pistol, was selected to replace it. The Astra 400 was produced between 1921 and 1950. It was an adaptable pistol that could fire the powerful 9mm Largo cartridge as well as a variety of other 9mm cartridges, which made it unique. It had a safety catch on the left just behind the trigger guard. The Astra 400 was used by both sides in the Spanish Civil War (1936–39) and by German forces in World War II.

SPECIFICATION

MANUFACTURER Esperanza y Unceta
CALIBRE 9mm Largo
MAGAZINE CAPACITY 8
ACTION Blowback/single
TOTAL LENGTH 225mm/8.86in
BARREL LENGTH 150mm/5.91in
WEIGHT UNLOADED 1,140g/40.21oz

Astra Model 300

This pistol was essentially a smaller version of the Astra 400 and was produced in 1922. It had the same tubular slide which also acted as a breech block, and it had three lugs on the barrel. It was fitted with a grip safety and had an internal hammer. The Astra 300 was largely issued to security guards in Spain, and large numbers were also purchased by the German armed forces.

SPECIFICATION

MANUFACTURER Esperanza y Unceta
CALIBRE 7.65mm (.32 ACP)
MAGAZINE CAPACITY 8
ACTION Blowback/single
TOTAL LENGTH 162mm/6.38in
BARREL LENGTH 102mm/4in
WEIGHT UNLOADED 623.69g/22oz

Astra Model 600

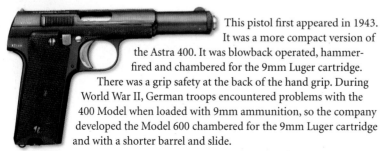

This pistol first appeared in 1943. It was a more compact version of the Astra 400. It was blowback operated, hammer-fired and chambered for the 9mm Luger cartridge. There was a grip safety at the back of the hand grip. During World War II, German troops encountered problems with the 400 Model when loaded with 9mm ammunition, so the company developed the Model 600 chambered for the 9mm Luger cartridge and with a shorter barrel and slide.

SPECIFICATION

MANUFACTURER Astra-Unceta y Cia S.A.
CALIBRE 9mm Luger
MAGAZINE CAPACITY 8
ACTION Blowback/single
TOTAL LENGTH 205mm/8.1in
BARREL LENGTH 133mm/5.25in
WEIGHT UNLOADED 905g/31.92oz

Astra Model 900

SPECIFICATION

MANUFACTURER Astra-Unceta y Cia S.A.

CALIBRE 7.63mm

MAGAZINE CAPACITY 10

ACTION Recoil/single

TOTAL LENGTH 310mm/12.1in

BARREL LENGTH 160mm/6.3in

WEIGHT UNLOADED 1,360g/48oz

This pistol was first introduced in 1927 and was said to have been inspired by the model 1896 "Broomhandle". It had a separate barrel-return spring that lay in a frame below the chamber. The bolt lock was pinned to the barrel extension and engaged the bolt via a spring-loaded bar. Both bolt and barrel recoil together and the bolt cocked the hammer. On its movement back into position, the bolt chambered a new round. The Astra Model 900 was issued to Spanish internal forces such as the Guardia Civil and it had some success abroad.

Astra 2000 (Cub)

SPECIFICATION

MANUFACTURER Astra-Unceta y Cia S.A.

CALIBRE 6.35mm (.25 ACP)

MAGAZINE CAPACITY 6

ACTION Blowback/single

TOTAL LENGTH 112mm/4.41in

BARREL LENGTH 57mm/2.24in

WEIGHT UNLOADED 354g/12.5oz

This pistol was a development of the Astra Model 200, a small-calibre pistol first introduced in 1920 that remained in service for about 70 years. The Astra 2000 was made after World War II and was sturdy and reliable. It had an external hammer and, unlike the Model 200, it had no grip safety.

Astra Model 4000

SPECIFICATION

MANUFACTURER Astra-Unceta y Cia S.A.

CALIBRE 7.65mm (.32 ACP)

MAGAZINE CAPACITY 7

ACTION Blowback/single

TOTAL LENGTH 164mm/6.46in

BARREL LENGTH 99mm/3.9in

WEIGHT UNLOADED 646g/22.79oz

This pistol was introduced after World War II and was designed primarily as a personal defence weapon or for use in the second line of defence. The design was rooted in the Campo-Giro 1913, with its distinctive round barrel and receiver. The return spring was coiled round the barrel and the pistol had a visible hammer. The Model 4000 was fitted with a manual safety behind the trigger guard and also had a magazine safety.

Llama Model 8

SPECIFICATION

MANUFACTURER Llama-Gabilondo y Cia S.A.

CALIBRE 9mm

MAGAZINE CAPACITY 15

ACTION Recoil/single

TOTAL LENGTH 209mm/8.23in

BARREL LENGTH 114mm/4.5in

WEIGHT UNLOADED 875g/30.86oz

This pistol was first produced in 1986 and issued to the Spanish armed forces. It had a similar system to the German Walther P38, whereby breech locking was performed by a dropping block. The barrel remained fixed and the safety catch was mounted on the slide. The pistol was loaded with the safety in the "safe" position, the magazine was then inserted and the slide drawn back to feed a round into the chamber. Once the safety was moved to "fire", the movement on the trigger cocked and released the hammer. Subsequent shots were fired in single-action mode.

United Kingdom

Small-arms manufacture in the UK in the late 19th and early 20th centuries was centred largely around the independent firm of Webley, later Webley & Scott, and the British Government's Royal Small Arms Factory at Enfield. Webley started producing weapons for the British Army from 1887 and continued to supply a variety of revolvers through the hey-day of the Empire. Between World War I and World War II, production moved to Enfield, which created some friction over what Webley claimed as their own designs. The Enfield No. 2 revolver, based on the Webley Mark VI, remained the standard British service sidearm until the advent of the Browning High-Power automatic pistol.

Lancaster Oval Bore

four barrels

This pistol was designed and produced by London barrel-maker Charles Lancaster in the 1870s. It had four fixed barrels, each of which had a firing pin behind it. The striker rotated behind the firing pin at each pull of the trigger, striking each pin in turn. The pistol could be broken open on a hinge for reloading.

SPECIFICATION

MANUFACTURER Charles Lancaster
CALIBRE .455 Webley
MAGAZINE CAPACITY 4
ACTION Double
TOTAL LENGTH 248mm/9.75in
BARREL LENGTH 152mm/6in
WEIGHT UNLOADED 1,247g/44oz

Webley RIC (Royal Irish Constabulary) 1872

James Webley set up a business making revolvers in Birmingham in the 1830s. Webley's first official contract was for the Royal Irish Constabulary (RIC), which was adopted by police and military forces throughout Europe. The 1872 model was a civilian version of this revolver. It was a solid-frame revolver and the cylinder was loaded through a gate on the left-hand side. An ejector rod was positioned underneath the barrel. The revolver was designed to be easily concealed and had a short barrel. The .450 Webley built a reputation for reliability, in both its service and commercial models.

SPECIFICATION

MANUFACTURER P. Webley & Sons
CALIBRE .450 Eley
CYLINDER 6
ACTION Double-action only (DAO)
TOTAL LENGTH 203mm/8in
BARREL LENGTH 82mm/3.23in
WEIGHT UNLOADED 700g/24.7oz

Enfield Mark II

cylinder lock

front sight

spur

SPECIFICATION

MANUFACTURER Royal Small Arms Factory, Enfield
CALIBRE .476 Eley
CYLINDER 6
ACTION Double
TOTAL LENGTH 805mm/12in
BARREL LENGTH 152mm/6in
WEIGHT UNLOADED 1,150g/40.6oz

The first models of this revolver, the Mark I and Mark II, were official British military sidearms from 1880–87. The Enfield Mark II was a double-action revolver with a hinged frame. It had a novel extraction mechanism whereby the extractor plate remained in place while the barrel and cylinder tilted forwards (a feature also found on Webleys). A rounded front sight and a cylinder lock prevented movement of the cylinder when the revolver was in its holster.

Webley Mark I

short barrel

This revolver, first manufactured in 1887, could be distinguished by its hinged frame, bird's beak butt and four-inch barrel. When the frame was broken open, the ejector automatically ejected the empty cases. New cartridges were then inserted by hand. Webley revolvers were either double action or double-action only (DAO). Adopted in 1895, the Webley Mark II was almost the same as the Mark I, but with hammer and grip modifications.

SPECIFICATION	
MANUFACTURER	P. Webley & Sons
CALIBRE	.455 Webley
CYLINDER	6
ACTION	Selective double
TOTAL LENGTH	260mm/10.23in
BARREL LENGTH	102mm/4in
WEIGHT UNLOADED	995g/36oz

Webley Mark III

short barrel

LEFT The Mark III was an updated edition of Mark I with an an improved cylinder-to-frame lock.

This was a revised version of the Webley Mark II revolver which was produced in the mid-1890s. Alterations included a barrel and cylinder borrowed from the 1892 Webley Green revolver (a version of Webley Mark I used in military service). The lock between the cylinder and the frame was also improved. The cylinder could be removed for maintenance. The introduction of Mark IV (1899), known as the "Boar War" model, and Mark V (1913) made further small improvements in design and materials including changes to accept smokeless (cordite) ammunition.

SPECIFICATION	
MANUFACTURER	P. Webley & Sons
CALIBRE	.455 Webley
CYLINDER	6
ACTION	Selective double
TOTAL LENGTH	260mm/10.23in
BARREL LENGTH	102mm/4in
WEIGHT UNLOADED	995g/36oz

Webley Mark VI

SPECIFICATION	
MANUFACTURER	P. Webley & Sons
CALIBRE	.455 Webley
CYLINDER	6
ACTION	Selective double
TOTAL LENGTH	286mm/11.25in
BARREL LENGTH	152mm/6in
WEIGHT UNLOADED	1,075g/37.9oz

This version of the Webley was first produced in 1915 and remained in service through to World War II. In many respects, it was similar to the Webley Mark V, first produced in 1913. The Mark VI was a top-breaking revolver, opened by a pivoting lever on the side of the receiver. The hand grip was altered from a bird's beak design to a squared style. This revolver was issued to the British and Commonwealth forces. It was used throughout World War I and stood up well to the mud and dirt in the trenches. A short bayonet was also designed and proved useful, although it was never officially adopted. The Webley Mark VI was considered the ultimate Webley until the arrival of the Enfield No. 2 Mark I in the 1930s. The Mark VI was manufactured until 1921 but became obsolete during the next decade.

Webley-Fosbery Model 1901

The Webley-Fosbery was designed by Lieutenant-Colonel George Vincent Fosbery, VC, and was based on patents from 1896. It was produced by the Webley & Scott company from 1901 to 1915. The revolver was a mixture of ideas between Webley and Fosbery and it incorporated ideas that had appeared in the semi-automatic pistol, particularly making use of the recoil energy to both turn the cylinder and recock the weapon. During this movement a stud on the frame was engaged in the grooves on the cylinder; the movement caused the cylinder to be rotated during each stroke. The turning of the cylinder was completed by the return movement of the barrel unit, operated by a spring, and a new round was aligned for firing. The recoil action had the effect of absorbing recoil and therefore improving accuracy. The revolver was reliable, but proved expensive to produce.

SPECIFICATION	
MANUFACTURER Webley & Scott Revolver Arms Co.	
CALIBRE .455	
CYLINDER 6	
ACTION Recoil/single	
TOTAL LENGTH 267mm/10.5in	
BARREL LENGTH 152mm/6in (various available)	
WEIGHT UNLOADED 1,155g/40.8oz	

Webley-Fosbery Model 1902

This was a revised version of the Webley-Fosbery 1901. The Webley-Fosbery models had quickly proved popular among target-shooters. The trigger mechanism did not rotate, which meant that the cylinder shots were smooth and consistent. This allowed rapid and accurate shooting. The Webley-Fosbery was never adopted as an official government sidearm, although many were privately purchased by British officers before and during World War I. However, production of the model ceased during this time.

cylinder

8 chambers

SPECIFICATION	
MANUFACTURER Webley & Scott Revolver Arms Co.	
CALIBRE .38 ACP	
CYLINDER 8	
ACTION Single	
TOTAL LENGTH 267mm/10.5in	
BARREL LENGTH 152mm/6in	
WEIGHT UNLOADED 1,065g/37.6oz	

Webley & Scott 1905/1906

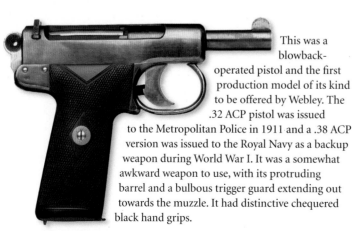

This was a blowback-operated pistol and the first production model of its kind to be offered by Webley. The .32 ACP pistol was issued to the Metropolitan Police in 1911 and a .38 ACP version was issued to the Royal Navy as a backup weapon during World War I. It was a somewhat awkward weapon to use, with its protruding barrel and a bulbous trigger guard extending out towards the muzzle. It had distinctive chequered black hand grips.

SPECIFICATION	
MANUFACTURER Webley & Scott Revolver Arms Co.	
CALIBRE .32 ACP	
MAGAZINE CAPACITY 8	
ACTION Blowback/single	
TOTAL LENGTH 159mm/6.25in	
BARREL LENGTH 89mm/3.5in	
WEIGHT UNLOADED 565g/20oz	

Webley & Scott Mark I

SPECIFICATION

MANUFACTURER Webley & Scott Revolver Arms Co.
CALIBRE .455 Webley Auto
MAGAZINE CAPACITY 7
ACTION Recoil/single
TOTAL LENGTH 216mm/8.5in
BARREL LENGTH 127mm/5in
WEIGHT UNLOADED 1,110g/39.2oz

This was a recoil-operated automatic pistol produced in the early 20th century. It was fitted with a safety system that could hold the hammer at full cock. It could be fitted with a shoulder stock for greater control when aiming and firing. The pistol was issued to members of the Royal Flying Corps, the theory being that pilots would occasionally have the opportunity to fire at their opponents with a handgun. It was also issued to the Royal Horse Artillery, although it was said that the mechanism was prone to jamming in dirty conditions, which made it an impractical weapon for combat duties.

Webley & Scott Mark IV

SPECIFICATION

MANUFACTURER Webley & Scott Revolver Arms Co.
CALIBRE .38/200 (.38 S&W)
CYLINDER 6
ACTION Double
TOTAL LENGTH 257mm/10.12in
BARREL LENGTH 152mm/6in
WEIGHT UNLOADED 735g/26oz

This revolver was a British double-action military revolver first designed in 1923. The revolver used the same extraction system as the Webley .455 service revolvers, and this was produced as a scaled-down version of these models. The Webley .38 Mark IV was produced until 1945 and was in service with the British Army from 1929 to 1956 becoming obsolete in the 1960s. The demands of manufacturing guns for World War II were too great for the three factories making the Enfield revolver and the army bought supplies of the Mark IV from Webley & Scott.

Enfield No. 2 Mark I

SPECIFICATION

MANUFACTURER Royal Small Arms Factory, Enfield
CALIBRE .38/200 (.38 S&W)
CYLINDER 6
ACTION Double-action only (DAO)
TOTAL LENGTH 260mm/10.23in
BARREL LENGTH 127mm/5in
WEIGHT UNLOADED 780g/27.5oz

Modified Webley
The vast majority of Mark I revolvers were modified to Mark I*. They reverted to a spurless hammer to make them more serviceable in action.

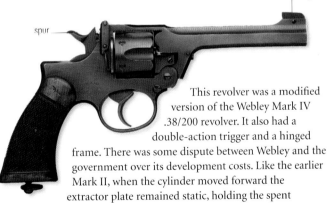

blade foresight

spur

This revolver was a modified version of the Webley Mark IV .38/200 revolver. It also had a double-action trigger and a hinged frame. There was some dispute between Webley and the government over its development costs. Like the earlier Mark II, when the cylinder moved forward the extractor plate remained static, holding the spent cartridges. The hammer spur was removed to prevent it catching on the controls or cables inside armoured fighting vehicles in versions called Mark I* (1938). The .38 Enfield No. 2 Mark I was in service from 1932 and large numbers were sent to Free French Forces during World War II. The Mark I** version appeared between 1942 and 1945.

 France

The French small-arms industry has a long and distinguished history. Development and production have taken place across a number of state factories, including Manufacture d'Armes de St Etienne (MAS), Manufacture d'Armes de Bayonne (MAB), Manufacture des Machines du Haut-Rhin (Manurhin). The French police were issued with the Manurhin MR-93 from 1993.

Automatique Française

This pistol, first produced before 1914, was based on a Mannlicher design and had a slide with arms that lay alongside the barrel. At the front the arms joined and held the return spring. The barrel was mostly exposed. The pistol had an unusual appearance, with a deep butt, which was fitted with a heavily stylized grip. The hand grip included a grip safety and there was a magazine release button at the base. The manufacturer, the Société Française d'Armes Automatiques de Saint Etienne, went out of business before the end of World War I.

SPECIFICATION

MANUFACTURER Société Française d'Armes Automatiques de Saint Etienne
CALIBRE 6.35mm (.25 ACP)
MAGAZINE CAPACITY 6
ACTION Blowback/single
TOTAL LENGTH 120mm/4.72in
BARREL LENGTH 60mm/2.36in
WEIGHT UNLOADED 315g/11.1oz

MAB D

The company Manufacture d'Armes de Bayonne brought into production in 1933 a pistol based on the Browning 1910. This was a blowback-operated pistol with a recoil spring set around the barrel. It had a single-action trigger. After the occupation of France by the Germans in 1939, some MAB Ds were issued in considerable numbers to German forces. The German-issue pistols were marked "Pistole MAB Kaliber 7.65 m". The MAB D had been designed primarily for police use but it was regarded as a robust and accurate weapon that could be used for relatively short-range defence in military operations.

SPECIFICATION

MANUFACTURER Manufacture d'Armes de Bayonne (MAB)
CALIBRE 7.65mm (.32 ACP)
MAGAZINE CAPACITY 9
ACTION Blowback/single
TOTAL LENGTH 176mm/6.9in
BARREL LENGTH 103mm/4.06in
WEIGHT UNLOADED 725g/25.57oz

SACM M1935A

The development of the M1935A followed a protracted series of trials by the French authorities, begun in 1922, to find a replacement for the obsolete weapons then in service. Pistol trials held in 1933 yielded no satisfactory candidates. The process was repeated in 1935 with four contenders, out of which the SACM pistol was selected. The M1935 was essentially a modified Browning Colt M1911. It featured a removable unit comprising the hammer, hammer spring, ejector and sear. A safety catch was also added on the side as well as a magazine safety. One factor that limited distribution of this weapon outside France was the unique 7.65mm Long French cartridge, which was not compatible with weapons manufactured outside France.

SPECIFICATION

MANUFACTURER Société Alsacienne de Construction Mécanique (SACM)
CALIBRE 7.65mm Long French
MAGAZINE CAPACITY 8
ACTION Short recoil/single
TOTAL LENGTH 189mm/7.45in
BARREL LENGTH 109mm/4.29in
WEIGHT UNLOADED 730g/25.75oz

MAC M1935S

SPECIFICATION

MANUFACTURER Manufacture d'Armes de Châtellerault (MAC)
CALIBRE 7.65mm French Long
MAGAZINE CAPACITY 8
ACTION Short recoil/single
TOTAL LENGTH 189mm/7.45in
BARREL LENGTH 109mm/4.29in
WEIGHT UNLOADED 730g/25.75oz

Following the introduction of the M1935A, demand from the French military was such that SACM was unable to meet it on its own. The military therefore ordered one of the unsuccessful contenders in the competition, Manufacture d'Armes de Châtellerault (MAC), to produce its pistol, designated the M1935S. In this version the locking system on the barrel was changed. The visible difference was that the butt was straight and the muzzle slightly protruded. By 1938, the M1935S was the primary production model, although SACM continued to manufacture the M1935A. Although 10,000 of the M1935S were ordered, with production starting in February 1939, France was overtaken by invasion before anything like this number could be produced. Only about 1,400 came off the production line and none was manufactured during the Occupation (1940 to 1944).

Unique Kriegsmodell

SPECIFICATION

MANUFACTURER Manufacture d'Armes des Pyrénées d'Hendaye
CALIBRE 7.65mm (.32 ACP)
MAGAZINE CAPACITY 10
ACTION Blowback/single
TOTAL LENGTH 150mm/5.91in
BARREL LENGTH 80mm/3.15in
WEIGHT UNLOADED 652g/23oz

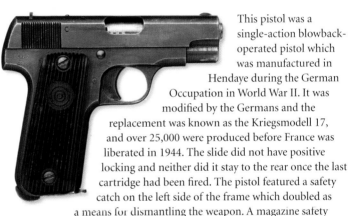

This pistol was a single-action blowback-operated pistol which was manufactured in Hendaye during the German Occupation in World War II. It was modified by the Germans and the replacement was known as the Kriegsmodell 17, and over 25,000 were produced before France was liberated in 1944. The slide did not have positive locking and neither did it stay to the rear once the last cartridge had been fired. The pistol featured a safety catch on the left side of the frame which doubled as a means for dismantling the weapon. A magazine safety prevented the pistol from being fired unless a magazine was inserted. The magazine release catch was located at the back of the frame.

Kriegsmodell 17
Developed by the Germans, the Kriegsmodell 17 had the addition of a hammer and a curved grip frame.

MAC M1950

SPECIFICATION

MANUFACTURER Manufacture d'Armes de St Etienne (MAS) & Châtellerault (MAC)
CALIBRE 9mm Parabellum
MAGAZINE CAPACITY 9
ACTION Short recoil/single
TOTAL LENGTH 195mm/7.67in
BARREL LENGTH 112mm/4.41in
WEIGHT UNLOADED 860g/30.34oz

In 1946 the French Army General Staff called for a new pistol to replace all current in-service pistols, partly in order to rationalize the various calibres. After a series of tests, the pistol submitted by Manufacture d'Armes de Saint Etienne (MAS) was adopted. This pistol was a development of the M1935S, with a short-recoil operation. The new pistol retained the cross-bolt safety as well as the magazine safety of the M1935S. The hammer could be lowered when the pistol was set to "safe" as the safety prevented the hammer from striking the firing pin. Although the pistol was originally designed by Manufacture d'Armes de Saint Etienne (MAS), much of the initial production run came from Manufacture d'Armes de Châtellerault (MAC). From 1961, however, production reverted to MAS.

MAB PA-15

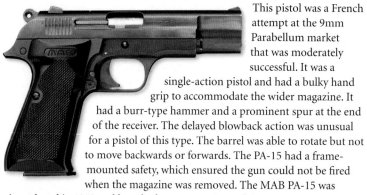

This pistol was a French attempt at the 9mm Parabellum market that was moderately successful. It was a single-action pistol and had a bulky hand grip to accommodate the wider magazine. It had a burr-type hammer and a prominent spur at the end of the receiver. The delayed blowback action was unusual for a pistol of this type. The barrel was able to rotate but not to move backwards or forwards. The PA-15 had a frame-mounted safety, which ensured the gun could not be fired when the magazine was removed. The MAB PA-15 was introduced in 1952 and bought for some sections of the French Army and the Finnish Border Police. It went out of production in the late 1980s.

SPECIFICATION

MANUFACTURER Manufacture d'Armes de Bayonne (MAB)
CALIBRE 9mm Parabellum
MAGAZINE CAPACITY 15
ACTION Delayed blowback/single
TOTAL LENGTH 203mm/8in
BARREL LENGTH 114mm/4.5in
WEIGHT UNLOADED 1,090g/38.45oz

No competition
Because of its single action the PA-15 was not able to be a potential competitor to the Czech CZ75.

Manurhin MR73

Special operations
This revolver was issued not only to the French Police but also to elite units that undertook special operations.

This was an adaptable, compact double-action revolver, which could fire two types of round, a replacement cylinder being fitted for the Parabellum cartridge. Developed in 1973, it was produced with a range of barrel lengths, to suit the requirements of either military, police or competition shooting. This revolver soon achieved a high reputation, whether in service or sporting use, being equally valued by competition shooters and by elite military and police units. The action was regarded as one of the smoothest and lightest available and the construction was of high quality. The cold-hammering production process of the barrel, for instance, was said to produce longer wear as well as improving precision.

SPECIFICATION

MANUFACTURER Manufacture des Machines du Haut-Rhin (Manurhin)
CALIBRE .357 Magnum, 9mm Parabellum
CYLINDER 6
ACTION Double
TOTAL LENGTH 195mm/7.67in
BARREL LENGTH 64mm/2.5in
WEIGHT UNLOADED 1,090g/38.45oz

MAS GI

This pistol was essentially the same as the Beretta M92, which used a short recoil operating system. Produced in the 1970s it had a double-action trigger system, and a short recoil system. This system used a falling locking block which was driven down to disengage the slide from the barrel and arrest the barrel as it moved backwards. Unlike the Italian Beretta M92, it did not have a manual safety using a decking lever instead. The magazine release was located at the bottom of the hand grip. A controversial issue for the MAS GI was the material used in the manufacture of the slide. For the MAS GI, this included a mineral called tellurium, which was hard though brittle and prone to cracking and breaking.

SPECIFICATION

MANUFACTURER Manufacture d'Armes de Saint Etienne
CALIBRE 9mm Parabellum
MAGAZINE CAPACITY 10, 15 or 17
ACTION Short recoil/single or double
TOTAL LENGTH 217mm/8.54in
BARREL LENGTH 125mm/4.92in
WEIGHT UNLOADED 945g/32.63oz

Belgium

The Belgian small-arms industry is centred on the Fabrique Nationale de Herstal, otherwise known as FN Herstal, which was originally set up in 1889 to manufacture Mauser rifles. Through a highly profitable association with the American arms-designer John Moses Browning, FN Herstal went on to produce some of the most famous and long-lasting pistols of all time, including the FN Browning High-Power, designed in the first decade of the 20th century. Versions of that pistol are still current issue to various armed forces throughout the world, including Great Britain, in the first decade of the 21st century.

Pieper Bayard 1908

extractor   front sight

SPECIFICATION

MANUFACTURER Anciens Établissements Pieper (AEP), Herstal

CALIBRE 7.65mm (.32 ACP)

MAGAZINE CAPACITY 6

ACTION Blowback/single

TOTAL LENGTH 125mm/4.92in

BARREL LENGTH 57mm/2.25in

WEIGHT UNLOADED 481.94g/17oz

This compact pistol was designed by Bernard Clarus of the Anciens Établissements Pieper (AEP) company and was based on a system developed by John Browning. Clarus introduced ideas of his own, including a novel design for the hammer and sear, with the sear being suspended in the slide behind the hammer. The slide, hammer and sear moved simultaneously to the rear during recoil and the recoil energy was absorbed by ramps and a leaf spring. There were several variations of the 1908 pistol but the size remained identical for different calibres.

Pieper Bayard 1923

SPECIFICATION

MANUFACTURER Anciens Établissements Pieper (AEP), Herstal

CALIBRE 7.65mm (.32 ACP)

MAGAZINE CAPACITY 6

ACTION Blowback/single

TOTAL LENGTH 149mm/5.88in

BARREL LENGTH 85mm/3.35in

WEIGHT UNLOADED 340.2g/12oz

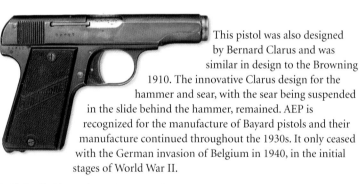

This pistol was also designed by Bernard Clarus and was similar in design to the Browning 1910. The innovative Clarus design for the hammer and sear, with the sear being suspended in the slide behind the hammer, remained. AEP is recognized for the manufacture of Bayard pistols and their manufacture continued throughout the 1930s. It only ceased with the German invasion of Belgium in 1940, in the initial stages of World War II.

Clement 1907

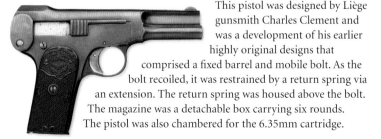

This pistol was designed by Liège gunsmith Charles Clement and was a development of his earlier highly original designs that comprised a fixed barrel and mobile bolt. As the bolt recoiled, it was restrained by a return spring via an extension. The return spring was housed above the bolt. The magazine was a detachable box carrying six rounds. The pistol was also chambered for the 6.35mm cartridge.

SPECIFICATION

MANUFACTURER Charles Ph. Clement

CALIBRE 7.65mm (.32 ACP), 6.35mm

MAGAZINE CAPACITY 6

ACTION Blowback/single

TOTAL LENGTH 150mm/5.91in

BARREL LENGTH 75mm/2.95in

WEIGHT UNLOADED 584g/20.6oz

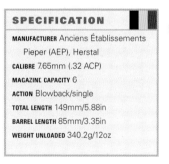

FN Browning M1900

This was a single-action handgun that was designed by John Browning for FN Herstal of Belgium in 1898. A slightly modified version was produced in 1900, which had a slightly shorter barrel. The success of the design was testified to by the fact that by 1911 at least 700,000 pistols had been manufactured. One reason for this success was the ingenious simplicity of the design which reduced the number of parts to be manufactured and assembled. A feature of the pistol was a recoil spring located above the barrel and connected to the breech block by a lever.

Model names
This model is known by several names, including the FN M1900, FN Mle.1900 Browning M1900 and Browning No.1.

SPECIFICATION

MANUFACTURER FN Herstal
CALIBRE 7.65mm (.32 ACP)
MAGAZINE CAPACITY 7
ACTION Blowback/single
TOTAL LENGTH 170mm/6.75in
BARREL LENGTH 102mm/4in
WEIGHT UNLOADED 620g/21.87oz

FN Browning M1903

This was an improvement on the design of the M1900 and it was manufactured not only by FN Herstal but also by Colt in the United States and by Husqvarna Vapenfabriks of Sweden. The pistol had a simple blowback mechanism and its comparatively long barrel contributed to a high level of accuracy. It had a safety catch on the left-hand side above the pistol grip. This model was produced in large numbers and became standard issue for various armed forces, including those of the United States, Belgium and Sweden.

SPECIFICATION

MANUFACTURER FN Herstal
CALIBRE 9mm Browning Long
MAGAZINE CAPACITY 7
ACTION Blowback/single
TOTAL LENGTH 203mm/8in
BARREL LENGTH 127mm/5in
WEIGHT UNLOADED 910g/32oz

FN Browning M1910

grip safety

This pistol was a development of both the M1900 and M1903 versions. A classic design, it was to continue in almost uninterrupted production until 1983. In this model the recoil spring was mounted round the barrel, which gave the weapon a different appearance to its two predecessors. In addition to the safety catch on the left side of the frame, the M1910 also had a grip safety at the back of the grip. Comparatively lightweight and relatively small, the M1910 was often used as a personal weapon and was also issued by several armed forces around the world.

SPECIFICATION

MANUFACTURER FN Herstal
CALIBRE 7.65mm (.32 ACP), 9mm Browning
Short (.380 ACP)
MAGAZINE CAPACITY 7
ACTION Blowback/single
TOTAL LENGTH 152mm/6in
BARREL LENGTH 89mm/3.5in
WEIGHT UNLOADED 600g/21oz

Assassination
An FN M1910 was used by Gavrilo Princip to assassinate Archduke Franz Ferdinand of Austria in Sarajevo on 28 June 1914.

FN Browning M1922

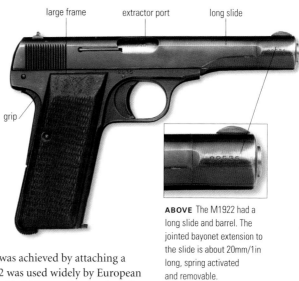

large frame   extractor port   long slide

grip

SPECIFICATION

MANUFACTURER FN Herstal

CALIBRE 7.65mm (.32 ACP), 9mm Browning Short (.380 ACP)

MAGAZINE CAPACITY 9

ACTION Blowback/single

TOTAL LENGTH 178mm/7.01in

BARREL LENGTH 114mm/5in

WEIGHT UNLOADED 730g/25.75oz

The M1922 pistol was a development of the 1910 model. For the M1922, the barrel was lengthened in order to improve accuracy and velocity. The frame size was increased and the slide lengthened. The lengthening of the slide was achieved by attaching a removable extension or nose piece. The M1922 was used widely by European military and police forces, including the Greek, Turkish, Dutch, French and Yugoslav armies. Between the two World Wars these pistols became very popular across Europe as police, military and self-defence guns. Production continued throughout World War II (where several hundred thousand were made for the Germans during their occupation of Belgium).The exceptionally long production run of this successful design lasted until 1983. In the United States both the M1910 and M1922 were imported as the Browning 380 pistol, chambered in .380 ACP. After 1971, these guns had adjustable target-type sights and bigger grips to meet US gun laws.

ABOVE The M1922 had a long slide and barrel. The jointed bayonet extension to the slide is about 20mm/1in long, spring activated and removable.

Grip safety
The grip safety of these models was primarily introduced to prevent accidental discharge – such as to prevent the gun from being fired if accidentally dropped.

FN Browning Baby

SPECIFICATION

MANUFACTURER FN Herstal

CALIBRE 6.35mm (.25 ACP)

MAGAZINE CAPACITY 6

ACTION Blowback/single

TOTAL LENGTH 103mm/4.06in

BARREL LENGTH 54mm/2.13in

WEIGHT UNLOADED 275g/9.70oz

Early Browning Baby
An early version of the Browning Baby was produced in 1905, but this pistol was not manufactured officially until 1932.

This pistol was first officially produced in 1932 and was largely based on the compact 1906 model. It could be identified by its squared-off appearance, due to the fact that the frame was the same length as the slide. Its sights were fixed. Early models could also be easily identified by the name "Baby" engraved on both sides of the hand grip at the base. This version did not have a grip safety, though it had a manual safety lever under the grip. The pistol was normally used two-handed due to a very strong recoil. It was first imported into the United States in 1954.

FN Browning High-Power M1935 (Grand Puissance 35)

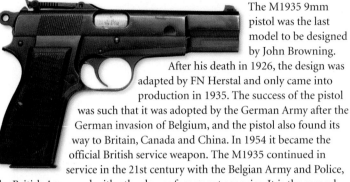

The M1935 9mm pistol was the last model to be designed by John Browning. After his death in 1926, the design was adapted by FN Herstal and only came into production in 1935. The success of the pistol was such that it was adopted by the German Army after the German invasion of Belgium, and the pistol also found its way to Britain, Canada and China. In 1954 it became the official British service weapon. The M1935 continued in service in the 21st century with the Belgian Army and Police, the British Army, and with other law enforcement agencies. It is the second-longest-serving service pistol after the Colt 1911, also designed by Browning. Plans are underway to replace it in the UK because the 9mm Parabellum round is no longer effective against the latest body armour technology.

SPECIFICATION

MANUFACTURER FN Herstal
CALIBRE 9mm Parabellum
MAGAZINE CAPACITY 13
ACTION Recoil/single
TOTAL LENGTH 197mm/7.75in
BARREL LENGTH 118mm/4.64in
WEIGHT UNLOADED 990g/34.92oz

Today's High-Powers
Despite its age, and the many copies and modified versions that have been produced, original Browning High-Powers are still manufactured.

FN Browning Mark II

This is an adaptation of the Browning High-Power, one of the classic pistol designs of all time. Although it was essentially an improvement on the previous model, with a new grip and an ambidextrous safety catch, the Mark II did not go far enough in its revisions to enable it to be competitive against modern pistol designs that were coming into the market. It fell between two stools – the classic High-Power and a requirement for a truly revised version. The production run was relatively short – from about 1980 to 1987.

SPECIFICATION

MANUFACTURER FN Herstal
CALIBRE 9mm Parabellum
MAGAZINE CAPACITY 13
ACTION Short recoil/single
TOTAL LENGTH 200mm/7.87in
BARREL LENGTH 118mm/4.64in
WEIGHT UNLOADED 930g/28oz

FN Browning Mark III

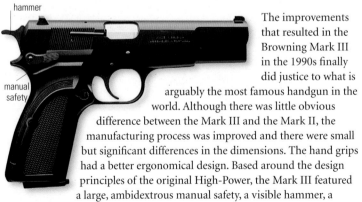

hammer

manual safety

The improvements that resulted in the Browning Mark III in the 1990s finally did justice to what is arguably the most famous handgun in the world. Although there was little obvious difference between the Mark III and the Mark II, the manufacturing process was improved and there were small but significant differences in the dimensions. The hand grips had a better ergonomical design. Based around the design principles of the original High-Power, the Mark III featured a large, ambidextrous manual safety, a visible hammer, a half-cock notch that prevented the weapon firing if the hammer accidentally slipped, a firing-pin safety and a magazine safety that disengaged the trigger when the magazine was removed. Sight improvement made for quick aiming.

SPECIFICATION

MANUFACTURER FN Herstal
CALIBRE 9mm Parabellum
MAGAZINE CAPACITY 13
ACTION Short recoil/single
TOTAL LENGTH 197mm/7.75in
BARREL LENGTH 118mm/4.64in
WEIGHT UNLOADED 990g/34.92oz

Modern techniques
FN Herstal combined computer technology with a classic design to produce a weapon that was very competitive.

FN BDA 380

SPECIFICATION

MANUFACTURER FN Herstal/Italy

CALIBRE .380 ACP

MAGAZINE CAPACITY

ACTION Blowback/double

TOTAL LENGTH 173mm/6.81in

BARREL LENGTH 50mm/1.97in

WEIGHT UNLOADED 640g/22.58oz

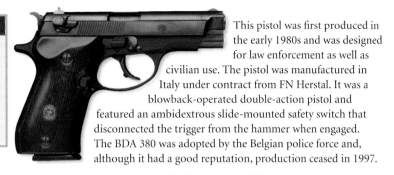

This pistol was first produced in the early 1980s and was designed for law enforcement as well as civilian use. The pistol was manufactured in Italy under contract from FN Herstal. It was a blowback-operated double-action pistol and featured an ambidextrous slide-mounted safety switch that disconnected the trigger from the hammer when engaged. The BDA 380 was adopted by the Belgian police force and, although it had a good reputation, production ceased in 1997.

FN BDA (Browning Double Action)

SPECIFICATION

MANUFACTURER FN Herstal

CALIBRE 9mm Parabellum

MAGAZINE CAPACITY 15

ACTION Short recoil/double

TOTAL LENGTH 200mm/7.87in

BARREL LENGTH 118mm/4.65in

WEIGHT UNLOADED 875g/30.86oz

This pistol, produced in the 1990s, was derived from the FN High-Power and its essential mechanics were the same. The main differences were a double-action trigger and a hammer de-cocking lever which replaced the safety catch. The de-cocking lever was on both sides of the frame and could be operated by either hand. The magazine release could be fitted for either left- or right-hand use. The most obvious difference in the BDA was the extended trigger guard. A further development of this weapon was the BDA0, developed for law enforcement duties. The trigger was modified to reduce the likelihood of involuntary discharge.

SPECIFICATION

MANUFACTURER FN Herstal

CALIBRE .40 S&W

MAGAZINE CAPACITY 10

ACTION Recoil/single

TOTAL LENGTH 197mm/7.75in

BARREL LENGTH 118mm/4.64in

WEIGHT UNLOADED 885g/31.32oz

FN Browning High-Power

The .40 High-Power was produced for the civilian market. It had a redesigned and strengthened slide in order to accommodate the more powerful cartridge and the magazine capacity was reduced to ten rounds. Only High-Powers specifically built for these rounds could be used to fire them. Like the other Brownings, the .40 pistol was recoil operated with a locked breech. It had linkless barrel-to-slide locking, a mechanism invented by John Browning. The trigger was single-action, with an external hammer.

FN Five-SeveN

This pistol was developed in the 1990s to cope with modern battlefield conditions and, with the 5.7mm cartridge, was able to penetrate most of the latest battlefield armour. The pistol was extremely light due to the use of modern synthetic materials in its construction. It had a very low recoil, thus increasing the accuracy of follow-up shots. The high-capacity magazine carried 20 rounds. The Five-SeveN was designed to be fully safe through the use of a double-action firing mechanism. The pistol had been designed to have an extremely smooth exterior, with very few protrusions. It could be fitted with accessories, including a laser target designator and tactical light.

SPECIFICATION

MANUFACTURER FN Herstal

CALIBRE 5.7mm FN

MAGAZINE CAPACITY 20

ACTION Delayed blowback/double

TOTAL LENGTH 208mm/8.23in

BARREL LENGTH 123mm/4.84in

WEIGHT UNLOADED 620g/21.87oz

FN Browning PRO-9

This pistol, otherwise known as the FNP-9, was designed for law enforcement. It had a polymer frame that was 30 per cent lighter than a steel-frame pistol. It could be set in either single-action or double/single-action mode, the first for quick reaction and the second for greater safety and requiring a more deliberate pull on the trigger. The hammer housing was removable for maintenance or replacement. The hammer was visible in its cocked modes and there was also a red indicator under the extractor to indicate a chambered round. Interchangeable back straps could be fitted to the hand grip to allow for different hand sizes.

SPECIFICATION

MANUFACTURER FN Herstal
CALIBRE 9mm Parabellum
MAGAZINE CAPACITY 15
ACTION Short recoil/single and
   double/single
TOTAL LENGTH 180mm/7.1in
BARREL LENGTH 102mm/4in
WEIGHT UNLOADED 709g/25oz

 Switzerland

With their worldwide reputation for exceptional manufacturing quality, especially with regard to mechanisms with small moving parts and fine tolerances, it is no surprise that the Swiss also produce high-quality handguns. Schweizerische Industrie Gesellschaft (SIG), partnered with J.P. Sauer & Sohn of Germany, continue to manufacture pistols that are used by elite and other armed forces as well as a wide range of police and security units throughout the world.

SIG-Sauer P220 (Pistole/Model 75)

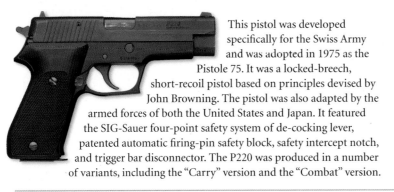

This pistol was developed specifically for the Swiss Army and was adopted in 1975 as the Pistole 75. It was a locked-breech, short-recoil pistol based on principles devised by John Browning. The pistol was also adapted by the armed forces of both the United States and Japan. It featured the SIG-Sauer four-point safety system of de-cocking lever, patented automatic firing-pin safety block, safety intercept notch, and trigger bar disconnector. The P220 was produced in a number of variants, including the "Carry" version and the "Combat" version.

SPECIFICATION

MANUFACTURER SIG Arms/
   J.P. Sauer & Sohn GmbH.
CALIBRE 9mm Parabellum and
   45 ACP
MAGAZINE CAPACITY 9
ACTION Short recoil/double
TOTAL LENGTH 198mm/7.8in
BARREL LENGTH 112mm/4.41in
WEIGHT UNLOADED 830g/29.3oz

SIG-Sauer P225

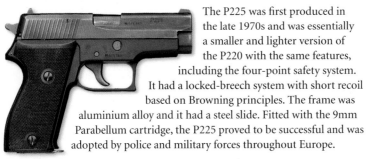

The P225 was first produced in the late 1970s and was essentially a smaller and lighter version of the P220 with the same features, including the four-point safety system. It had a locked-breech system with short recoil based on Browning principles. The frame was aluminium alloy and it had a steel slide. Fitted with the 9mm Parabellum cartridge, the P225 proved to be successful and was adopted by police and military forces throughout Europe.

SPECIFICATION

MANUFACTURER SIG Arms/
   J.P. Sauer & Sohn GmbH.
CALIBRE 9mm Parabellum
MAGAZINE CAPACITY 8
ACTION Short recoil/double
TOTAL LENGTH 180mm/7.1in
BARREL LENGTH 98mm/3.86in
WEIGHT UNLOADED 740g/26.1oz

SIG-Sauer P230

SPECIFICATION

MANUFACTURER SIG Arms/
J.P. Sauer & Sohn GmbH.

CALIBRE .380 ACP, .32 ACP

MAGAZINE CAPACITY 7 or 8

ACTION Blowback/double or single
or DAO

TOTAL LENGTH 168mm/6.63in

BARREL LENGTH 92mm/3.62in

WEIGHT UNLOADED 460g/16.2oz

Introduced in the 1970s, the P230 was a blowback-operated pistol which could be used in either single or double-action modes. The hammer could be lowered by depressing the hammer de-cocking lever. It had an automatic firing-pin lock. There was no manual safety, but the only way the pistol could be fired was by fully pulling through the trigger. The pistol could be dropped with the hammer cocked and the pistol would not fire. The SIG-Sauer P230 achieved a reputation for reliability and good build quality. It was also available in .32 ACP (8-round magazine).

SIG-Sauer P226

SPECIFICATION

MANUFACTURER SIG Arms/
J.P. Sauer & Sohn GmbH.

CALIBRE 9mm Parabellum

MAGAZINE CAPACITY 15

ACTION Short recoil/single or double

TOTAL LENGTH 196mm/7.7in

BARREL LENGTH 112mm/4.41in

WEIGHT UNLOADED 964g/34oz

fixed sights (some adjustment available)

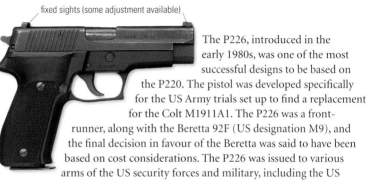

The P226, introduced in the early 1980s, was one of the most successful designs to be based on the P220. The pistol was developed specifically for the US Army trials set up to find a replacement for the Colt M1911A1. The P226 was a front-runner, along with the Beretta 92F (US designation M9), and the final decision in favour of the Beretta was said to have been based on cost considerations. The P226 was issued to various arms of the US security forces and military, including the US Navy SEALs (Air, Sea and Land), as well as to special operations teams in other countries, including the British SAS (Special Air Service).

SIG-Sauer P228

SPECIFICATION

MANUFACTURER SIG Arms/
J.P. Sauer & Sohn GmbH.

CALIBRE 9mm Parabellum

MAGAZINE CAPACITY 13

ACTION Blowback/double, single or
DAO

TOTAL LENGTH 180mm/7.1in

BARREL LENGTH 98mm/3.8in

WEIGHT UNLOADED 825g/29.1oz

The P228, introduced in the late 1980s, was a more compact version of the P226. It was a blowback-operated, locked-breech pistol with a linkless locking system based on Browning principles. It also featured the four-point SIG-Sauer safety system. The frame was constructed from aluminium alloy. While the Beretta 92F had been favoured over the P226 on cost grounds at the US Army trials, in the 1980s the more compact P228 (US designation M11) was selected as the sidearm of choice for aircrew and any other personnel who required a more compact pistol than the M9. While .40 calibre pistols became popular in the United States, many intelligence agencies still use the 9mm Parabellum P228 as a weapon of choice. One of its advantages is that recoil is near-negligible with the P228. The 9mm Parabellum round is more easily controlled than the .40 or .45 ACP rounds.

US imports
SIG Arms was established in 1985 to import and distribute SIG firearms into the States.

Sig-Sauer P229

This pistol, introduced in the early 1990s, was almost identical to the P228 but was developed with law-enforcement officers in mind, chambered for the .40 S&W cartridge. It was fitted with high-contrast sights and had a stainless-steel slide with a different design to that of the P228. There was a high level of use for this pistol and similar SIG-Sauer types by top-level security agencies in the United States, such as the FBI (Federal Bureau of Investigation) and DEA (Drug Enforcement Administration).

SPECIFICATION	
MANUFACTURER	SIG Arms/ J.P. Sauer & Sohn GmbH.
CALIBRE	.40 S&W
MAGAZINE CAPACITY	12
ACTION	Short recoil/double or single or DAO
TOTAL LENGTH	180mm/7.1in
BARREL LENGTH	98mm/3.86in
WEIGHT UNLOADED	865g/30.51oz

SIG-Sauer P232

This was the smallest and lightest pistol in the SIG-Sauer range, and was developed in the late 1990s. Featuring a fixed-barrel blowback action, the P232 was designed to be a reliable back-up pistol. It was well balanced and its smooth shape and rounded, snag-free edges were designed to make it easy to deploy quickly for personal protection. The compact size allows the pistol to be easily concealed whether in a discreet holster, handbag or on the ankle. The hand grip was ergonomically designed to allow for a secure hold. The P232 was said to be a widely used off-duty gun carried by federal agents and law enforcement professionals.

SPECIFICATION	
MANUFACTURER	SIG Arms/ J.P. Sauer & Sohn GmbH.
CALIBRE	.380 ACP
MAGAZINE CAPACITY	7
ACTION	Blowback/double or single
TOTAL LENGTH	168mm/6.63in
BARREL LENGTH	92mm/3.62in
WEIGHT UNLOADED	499g/17.6oz

SIG-Sauer P239

The P239 was similar in design and concept to the P228 but it was a more compact version. It was designed for ease of concealment, perhaps in undercover operations, and could be used as a secondary weapon for emergencies. The frame was aluminium alloy while the slide was solid steel. The P239 was a recoil-operated, locked-breech weapon and incorporated the linkless locking system based on Browning's ideas. Chambered for the 9mm Parabellum cartridge, it was also available in larger calibres. The P239 has become quite popular in the United States as a concealed carry pistol.

SPECIFICATION	
MANUFACTURER	SIG Arms/ J.P. Sauer & Sohn GmbH.
CALIBRE	9mm Parabellum
MAGAZINE CAPACITY	8
ACTION	Recoil/double or single or DAO
TOTAL LENGTH	167mm/6.6in
BARREL LENGTH	92mm/3.62in
WEIGHT UNLOADED	775g/27.34oz

SIG-Pro SP2022

This pistol was designed to provide optimum safety, reliability and accuracy and to resist corrosion. The trigger guard had a serrated finger rest for better control when firing. It was fitted with a chamber-loaded indicator that provided both visual and tactile control of the gun status. A variety of trigger sizes and systems, grips, floor plates and calibre options have been devised to accommodate individual requirements. In 2003, the largest European post-war order for law-enforcement service pistols was awarded to Swiss Arms, formerly SIG-Sauer (acquired by German investors in 2000). The SP2022 is the standard service and law-enforcement weapon in France.

SPECIFICATION	
MANUFACTURER	Swiss Arms/ J.P. Sauer & Sohn GmbH.
CALIBRE	9mm Parabellum
MAGAZINE CAPACITY	15
ACTION	Short recoil/double or DAO
TOTAL LENGTH	187mm/7.36in
BARREL LENGTH	99mm/3.9in
WEIGHT UNLOADED	760g/26.8oz

Germany

From the late 19th to the early 21st century, the most significant developments in Germany have been in pistols, as opposed to revolvers. German design ingenuity, backed up by high-quality manufacturing, has resulted in such key designs as the 9mm Luger by George Luger (inspired by earlier designs) and the 7.65mm Walther PP of 1929. Firms such as Carl Walther and Heckler & Koch continue to uphold this reputation today with innovative and highly successful designs.

Bergmann Model 1896

front sight

hammer

SPECIFICATION

MANUFACTURER V.C. Schilling, Suhl

CALIBRE 5mm Bergmann

MAGAZINE CAPACITY 5

ACTION Blowback/single

TOTAL LENGTH 175mm/6.89in

BARREL LENGTH 80mm/3.15in

WEIGHT UNLOADED 470g/16.6oz

Theodor Bergmann
This is one of the earliest pistol designs commissioned by Theodor Bergmann.

ABOVE The pistol was loaded from the right side by opening the casing by the trigger-guard. A magazine clip was placed inside and the cover shut. A lifter spring pushes up the round one by one and, when empty, the clip was removed downwards.

This was a blowback-operated pistol developed by Theodor Bergmann (the founder of Bergmann in Suhl) with the probable involvement of Louis Schmeisser, a technical designer, who often played a role in realizing Bergmann-inspired designs. The 1894 model was unusual in having a folding trigger and no extractor. The empty case was simply ejected when it hit a protrusion, though this system did not always work. This rather hit-and-miss approach did not prove to be a success and the 1894 version was soon replaced with the 1896. Although the first 1896 had the same extraction system, this was soon replaced with a conventional extractor. The Bergmann 1896 never gained any real popularity as the Mauser models were found to be more effective.

SPECIFICATION

MANUFACTURER Anciens Établissements Pieper
  (AEP)

CALIBRE 9mm Bergmann-Bayard (9mm Largo)

MAGAZINE CAPACITY 6

ACTION Recoil/single

TOTAL LENGTH 250mm/9.84in

BARREL LENGTH 102mm/4in

WEIGHT UNLOADED 1,015g/35.8oz

Bergmann-Bayard 1908

This pistol incorporated the design patented by Bergmann for a gun with a vertically moving locking piece which locked the breech block. The bolt extracted and ejected the spent cartridge casing and cocked the hammer on the recoil strike. It then pulled a round from the magazine and chambered it on the return. The Bergmann-Bayard was supplied to the Danish, Belgian and Spanish armed forces, where it was designated the Modelo 1908. This was the start of a long history of servicing the Spanish military and police.

Luger 1900

fixed barrel   cocking grip rear toggle link

This pistol was an important stage in the development of the famous Luger. Based on the ideas of designers Hiram Maxim and Hugo Borchardt, this was a toggle-lock pistol operating on a short-recoil principle. As the barrel moved to the rear, it opened a toggle lock. The breech block then compressed a mainspring which returned the breech block to its original position, closing the toggle lock as it did so. The pistol was precisely engineered, using high-quality materials, and it would function efficiently if maintained properly. However, it was very sensitive to dirt and this could be a problem in combat conditions. The 1900 had a grip safety in the rear of the butt as well as a manual safety on the left-hand side of the frame. The 1900 was issued to the Swiss Army.

grip safety

SPECIFICATION

MANUFACTURER Deutsche Waffen und Munitions Fabrik (DWM)
CALIBRE 7.65mm Luger
MAGAZINE CAPACITY 8
ACTION Short recoil/single
TOTAL LENGTH 211mm/8.31in
BARREL LENGTH 122mm/4.8in
WEIGHT UNLOADED 840g/29.6oz

Luger accuracy
A feature of the Luger is that the barrel remains aligned or fixed with the frame axis, said to improve accuracy.

Luger P08

The 9mm P08 model followed several Luger updates. However, unlike the earlier models this model did not have a grip safety. Like all Lugers, its fixed barrel meant the pistol was extremely accurate. As with the previous models, this pistol was operated by a toggle action. Each pistol was manufactured to a high standard but it is generally thought that the fine tolerances of all moving parts, though an indication of excellent craftsmanship, still made the pistol susceptible to jamming in combat conditions.

SPECIFICATION

MANUFACTURER DWM
CALIBRE 9mm Parabellum
MAGAZINE CAPACITY 8
ACTION Short recoil/single
TOTAL LENGTH 223mm/88.78in
BARREL LENGTH 102mm/4in
WEIGHT UNLOADED 850g/30oz

Heckler & Koch HK4

Heckler & Koch grew up out of the ashes of the Mauser firm, which had been damaged and closed down as part of reparations after World War II (and remained closed for a number of years). The HK4 was the first pistol to be manufactured by the company, mass produced from the late 1960s. It was a double-action pistol based on the design of the Mauser HSc of 1937. The internal workings are made from stamped steel but are as precisely engineered as individually machined parts. The frame was made from a lightweight alloy. A variety of calibres were available in addition to the .380 with 7 rounds. The calibre could be altered by changing the barrel and the magazine, and different barrels could be purchased with the weapon. The pistol was issued to German customs police and was produced until the mid-1980s as the P11.

SPECIFICATION

MANUFACTURER Heckler & Koch GmbH.
CALIBRE .380 ACP, 7.65mm (.32 ACP), 6.35mm (.25 ACP), .22 Long Rifle
MAGAZINE CAPACITY 7 (.380 ACP) or 8
ACTION Blowback/double
TOTAL LENGTH 157mm/6.18in
BARREL LENGTH 85mm/3.35in
WEIGHT UNLOADED 480g/16.9oz

Alex Seidel
The HK4 was devised by Alex Seidel, a co-founder of Heckler & Koch and former employee of the Mauser company.

Heckler & Koch HKP9

SPECIFICATION

MANUFACTURER Heckler & Koch GmbH.

CALIBRE 9mm Parabellum, .45 ACP

MAGAZINE CAPACITY 9

ACTION Delayed blowback/double (P9), single (P9S)

TOTAL LENGTH 192mm/7.56in

BARREL LENGTH 102mm/4in

WEIGHT UNLOADED 880g/31oz

The HKP9 was a delayed-blowback pistol designed in the 1960s and released in the early 1970s. It had a roller-locked breech-block inertia system similar to that used on the G3 rifle. A two-part breech block incorporated a roller mechanism that was designed to create inertia in recoil and to enable the return for rechambering the next round. The HKP9 incorporated an internal hammer and there was a de-cocking lever on the left-hand side of the receiver. The HKP9S (a sporting version of the P9) differed from the HKP9 in having a double-action lock and a polygonal rifled barrel. Despite its sophisticated design, the HKP9 did not sell large quantities. The HKP9S was more successful then the HK P9, but has now been discontinued. The licenced version of the HKP9S is manufactured in Greece as EP9S.

9mm Heckler & Koch HKP7

SPECIFICATION

MANUFACTURER Heckler & Koch GmbH.

CALIBRE 9mm Parabellum

MAGAZINE CAPACITY 8

ACTION Delayed blowback/single

TOTAL LENGTH 171mm/6.75in

BARREL LENGTH 105mm/4.13in

WEIGHT UNLOADED 780g/27.5oz

grip safety

The first version of the HKP7, the PSP (Police Self-loading Pistol), was produced between 1976 and 1979. The HKP7 was primarily designed for use by police forces but it was also entered for trials with the US Army to replace the Colt M1911A1. It was a single-action pistol with a grip safety on the front of the hand grip. This had to be squeezed before the weapon could be cocked. The blowback system was gas delayed, in other words the gases from the exploded cartridge were released into a cylinder and slow down the recoil. The HKP7 was one of the most accurate 9mm service pistols available. The HKP7 ceased production in 2005.

Heckler & Koch MK23 (SOCOM pistol)

SPECIFICATION

MANUFACTURER Heckler & Koch GmbH.

CALIBRE .45 ACP

MAGAZINE CAPACITY 12

ACTION Short recoil/double and single

TOTAL LENGTH 245mm/9.65in

BARREL LENGTH 149mm/5.87in

WEIGHT UNLOADED 1,097g/38.72oz

This was a short-recoil operated, locked-breech pistol, which originated in 1991 when Heckler & Koch began development for the US Special Operations Command (SOCOM), and finally passed all the tests and was issued by SOCOM in 1996. The barrel locked into the slide with a single lug. It had a one-piece machined steel slide and a frame-mounted de-cocking lever and a separate ambidextrous lever. The pistol could be carried "cocked and locked" when the safety was applied. The extractor doubled as a chamber-loaded indicator. The pistol was fitted with an oversize trigger guard so that it could be fired with gloves. It was also fitted with grooves for mounting accessories such as a laser pointer.

Special operations
This pistol was developed for special units such as the US Navy SEALs and Green Berets.

Heckler & Koch USP (Universal Self-loading Pistol)

This USP was introduced in the early 1990s as a modular concept, adaptable to the requirements of different security forces. The pistols incorporated a Browning linkless locked-breech action, similar to the system used in the Browning High-Power. It also featured a "cocked and locked" system for safe carriage. The USP was developed alongside the MK23 for US Special Operations Command (SOCOM). The pistol that won the US contract had a longer slide than the USP and special mountings for a laser-aiming module (LAM). The barrel was also extended so that a suppressor could be screwed on. This pistol was available in a variety of calibres.

SPECIFICATION

MANUFACTURER Heckler & Koch GmbH.
CALIBRE 9mm Parabellum, .40 S&W, .45 ACP
MAGAZINE CAPACITY 13
ACTION Recoil/double or single
TOTAL LENGTH 194mm/7.64in
BARREL LENGTH 108mm/4.25in
WEIGHT UNLOADED 830g/29.3oz

Heckler & Koch USP Compact

Based on the full-sized USP models, the Compact version of the USP combined a handy size with good performance. The USP Compact was smaller and lighter than the large-frame USP and the slide and barrel were reduced in length. The reduction in trigger reach and a smaller grip made it easier to conceal. Unlike some subcompact semi-automatic pistols that used a difficult-to-hold two-finger grip frame, the USP Compact used a narrow, full-hand grip frame. The gun was supplied with two magazines. One had a magazine extension, which aided in firing the gun, while the other magazine set flush with the grip, when inserted, for better concealment.

SPECIFICATION

MANUFACTURER Heckler & Koch GmbH.
CALIBRE 9mm Parabellum, 40 S&W, .45 ACP
MAGAZINE CAPACITY 13
ACTION Short recoil/double or single
TOTAL LENGTH 173mm/6.81in
BARREL LENGTH 91mm/3.58in
WEIGHT UNLOADED 667g/23.52oz

Heckler & Koch HKP8

This was a recoil-operated pistol chambered for the 9mm NATO cartridge. It had a locked breech and tilting barrel introduced in 1994, and was a modified version of the standard USP. It was introduced to replace the Walther P1 that had been in service with the German armed forces for 35 years. The hand grip was made of glass-fibre reinforced polymer with corrosion-proof metal inserts. The pistol had a safety lever on the left for safety and de-cocking function. There was an integrated support rail so that scopes could be attached. The P8 included the mechanical recoil reduction system, which meant the handgun absorbed some of the recoil, reducing the amount felt by the user. The magazine was transparent and also made of glass-fibre reinforced polymer. The pistol had an open square notch rear sight with contrast points.

safety/de-cocking lever

SPECIFICATION

MANUFACTURER Heckler & Koch GmbH.
CALIBRE 9mm Parabellum
MAGAZINE CAPACITY 15
ACTION Recoil/double and single
TOTAL LENGTH 194mm/7.64in
BARREL LENGTH 108mm/4.25in
WEIGHT UNLOADED 780g/27.51oz

Standard sidearm
The P8 is the standard sidearm of the *Bundeswehr* (German armed forces).

Heckler & Koch HKP10

The P10 was a USP Compact with a spurred hammer, and the firing control mechanism of the P8. It was chambered for the 9mm Parabellum cartridge. This pistol was recoil operated with a locked breech and tilting barrel. The hand grip was made of glass-fibre reinforced polymer with corrosion proof metal inserts. It had a single/double-action trigger with a de-cocking lever that could be positioned either on the left or the right of the pistol. There was an integrated support rail to which a scope or other device could be fitted. It had an open square notch rear sight with contrast points. This was the first pistol to meet and be certified to the requirements of the Technical Guidelines on pistols of the German Police Staff College. It has also been issued to a number of police forces outside Germany.

SPECIFICATION

MANUFACTURER Heckler & Koch GmbH.
CALIBRE 9mm Parabellum
MAGAZINE CAPACITY 13
ACTION Recoil/double or single
TOTAL LENGTH 173mm/6.81in
BARREL LENGTH 91mm/3.58in
WEIGHT UNLOADED 648g/22.86oz

Police forces
The Heckler & Koch HKP10 combines some of the best attributes of both the P8 and the USP in order to meet the stringent requirements of police forces.

Heckler & Koch USP Tactical

SPECIFICATION

MANUFACTURER Heckler & Koch GmbH.
CALIBRE .45 ACP, 9mm Parabellum
MAGAZINE CAPACITY 13
ACTION Short recoil/double or single
TOTAL LENGTH 219mm/8.64in
BARREL LENGTH 129mm/5in
WEIGHT UNLOADED 862g/30.4oz

adjustable sights

The USP .45 ACP Tactical met the requirements of the US military but in a smaller model. The differences between a Tactical and a standard USP included the adjustable sights, a threaded and extended barrel for a suppressor (silencer) and a match trigger. It also had an adjustable micrometer sight. The Tactical was soon issued by SOCOM (Special Operations Command) and became the preferred choice of the special operations units. The USP Tactical has undergone testing in extreme conditions. It was available in .45 ACP and 9mm Parabellum as USPSD.

Heckler & Koch USP Expert

SPECIFICATION

MANUFACTURER Heckler & Koch GmbH.
CALIBRE 9mm Parabellum, .40 S&W, .45 ACP
MAGAZINE CAPACITY 10
ACTION Short recoil/double or single
TOTAL LENGTH 221mm/8.74in
BARREL LENGTH 132mm/5.2in
WEIGHT UNLOADED 1,043g/36.8oz

Introduced in 1998, this version incorporated most of the features of the Tactical with all the design advantages of a target-shooting pistol, focusing on extreme precision. It could be used by security forces as a highly accurate weapon, or as a competition pistol. It had an elongated steel slide and was recoil operated with a locked breech and tilting barrel. The hand grip and magazine were manufactured from glass-like polymer with metal inserts. In addition to 9mm Parabellum, the USP Expert was available in .40 S&W and .45 ACP. In order to convert from one calibre to another, the slide, barrel, recoil spring, guide rod and magazine could be changed.

Heckler & Koch HKP2000

The design brief for this pistol was that it should offer a high level of safety for police and special units undertaking operations. Attention was also paid to improving the hit-rate capabilities of the user during reflexive firing. The manufacturers set out to achieve the highest possible safety and operational reliability under all conditions. It was designed to be adaptable to individual users and had a simple and easy operation by both right- and left-handed shooters. Due to its modular design, the HKP2000 could be fitted to the individual needs of the shooter. The requirements of the user could be met due to a variety of trigger and de-cocking systems. The HKP2000 had a safety trigger with concealed cocking piece in the hammer and centrally arranged de-cocking lever for firing in either single or double action mode. The P2000 V1 also had a safety trigger with concealed cocking piece in the hammer, with a constant trigger pull from the first shot to the last, without de-cocking.

LEFT The HKP2000 has a square notch rear sight. The long glowing contrast points allow accurate shooting in poor lighting conditions.

SPECIFICATION

MANUFACTURER Heckler & Koch GmbH.
CALIBRE 9mm Parabellum
MAGAZINE CAPACITY 13 or 16
ACTION Recoil/single and double
TOTAL LENGTH 173mm/6.81in
BARREL LENGTH 93mm/3.66in
WEIGHT UNLOADED 620g/21.87oz

Heckler & Koch HKP30

This pistol was designed primarily for police forces and it incorporated a high level of safety as well as being quick to deploy. The open square notch rear sight with long glow contrast points was designed to allow fast and accurate target acquisition in all light conditions. The pistol was said to have a good weight balance and the hand grip was made of high-grade fibre-reinforced polymer. The grip was ergonomically moulded in order to maximize accuracy during reflexive firing. The grip also incorporated an ambidextrous magazine release and captive slide release. There was automatic hammer and firing pin safety. It was also fitted with a chamber-loaded indicator. The HKP30 featured a modular trigger and de-cocking system capable of being individually tailored to various requirements. It had a safety trigger with a concealed cocking piece in the hammer with spur. There was a central de-cocking latch, with a constant double-action trigger pull, without operation of the de-cocking latch, and defined let-off point.

LEFT Magazine removal is equally easy for right- and left-handed shooters. It can be operated by the thumb/index finger of either hand.

HKP3000/HKP30

The HKP30 is a refinement of the HKP2000 pistol and was to be known as the HKP3000. It is a state-of-the-art design with highly moulded hand grips.

SPECIFICATION

MANUFACTURER Heckler & Koch GmbH.
CALIBRE 9mm Parabellum
MAGAZINE CAPACITY 15
ACTION Recoil/double, single and DAO
TOTAL LENGTH 177mm/6.96in
BARREL LENGTH 98mm/3.86in
WEIGHT UNLOADED 740g/26.1oz

Korth Combat

SPECIFICATION

MANUFACTURER Korth
CALIBRE .357 Magnum, .38 Special
CYLINDER 6
ACTION Double or single
TOTAL LENGTH 168mm/6.63in
BARREL LENGTH 75mm/3in
WEIGHT UNLOADED 936g/33oz

The Korth Combat revolver was in many respects a Rolls-Royce of revolvers. No expense was spared in its design, development and manufacture. It was a precision-engineered weapon manufactured using very high-quality steel and with a walnut hand grip to finish it off. Its owners were those prepared to pay for this level of excellence. It was a six-shot double-action revolver with a single-action option. The trigger had a telescoped, coil-type mainspring. The cylinder could be released and, if necessary, exchanged to change calibres. It had a full-length ejector rod shroud. The sights were adjustable. The Korth was usually chambered in .357 Magnum or .38 Special, with optional 9mm cylinders and a variety of barrels.

Borchardt 1893

SPECIFICATION

MANUFACTURER Ludwig Loewe & Co.
CALIBRE 7.63mm Borchardt
MAGAZINE CAPACITY 8
ACTION Recoil/single
TOTAL LENGTH 279mm/10.98in
BARREL LENGTH 165mm/6.5in
WEIGHT UNLOADED 1,160g/40.9oz

hand grip with magazine

leather holster

shoulder stock

ABOVE The original pistol would have been supplied with a leather holster for storage, integrated with the shoulder stock.

This extraordinary looking pistol was designed by firearms inventor and engineer Hugo Borchardt and manufactured by Ludwig Loewe. Part of the reason for the pistol's strange appearance was the toggle lock and clock-style return spring housed in the rear overhang. The magazine was inserted into the hand grip, which was at the centre of the weapon. Despite the bizarre appearance, the pistol was technically accomplished and regarded with some respect by connoisseurs. It could not compete, however, with more modern and utilitarian designs.

SPECIFICATION

MANUFACTURER Gebr. Mauser & Co.
CALIBRE 9mm Mauser
CYLINDER 6
ACTION Double
TOTAL LENGTH 270mm/10.63in
BARREL LENGTH 136mm/5.35in
WEIGHT UNLOADED 750g/26.5oz

Mauser Model 1878

This is sometimes known as the "zig zag" revolver due to the method for moving the cylinder onwards. The cylinder was grooved in a zig zag pattern and a stud followed the groove and moved the cylinder round. Once the movement was completed, the stud acted as a brake on the cylinder. The M1878 also had an unusual way of opening. The revolver broke open and pivoted from a position just forward of the base of the cylinder and was locked by a ring catch in front of the trigger guard. These innovative design ideas were not considered entirely practical by the German High Command and sales were limited.

Mauser Model 1896 ("Broomhandle")

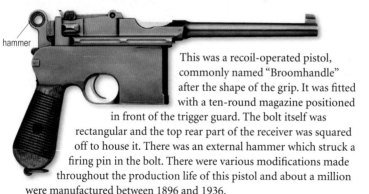

hammer

This was a recoil-operated pistol, commonly named "Broomhandle" after the shape of the grip. It was fitted with a ten-round magazine positioned in front of the trigger guard. The bolt itself was rectangular and the top rear part of the receiver was squared off to house it. There was an external hammer which struck a firing pin in the bolt. There were various modifications made throughout the production life of this pistol and about a million were manufactured between 1896 and 1936.

SPECIFICATION

MANUFACTURER Waffenfabrik Mauser AG.
CALIBRE 7.63mm Mauser
MAGAZINE CAPACITY 10
ACTION Recoil/single
TOTAL LENGTH 295mm/11.62in
BARREL LENGTH 140mm/5.51in
WEIGHT UNLOADED 1,045g/36.9oz

Mauser records
All records from the Mauser plant were destroyed in 1945.

Mauser Model 1914

This was a blowback-operated pistol which was striker-fired. It had a fixed barrel and an open-top slide. Early versions had a short extractor and later versions a long one. The 1934 version was much the same as the 1914 with a revised hand grip. These Mauser pistols were issued in considerable numbers to the German Army in World War I but eventually they would be superseded by designs from Walther.

SPECIFICATION

MANUFACTURER Waffenfabrik Mauser AG.
CALIBRE 7.65mm (.32 ACP)
MAGAZINE CAPACITY 8
ACTION Blowback/single
TOTAL LENGTH 153mm/6.02in
BARREL LENGTH 87mm/3.43in
WEIGHT UNLOADED 600g/21oz

Mauser HSc

The Mauser HSc (Self-cocking Hammer pistol, model C) was a blowback-operated pistol with a fixed barrel, from 1937. The hand grip shape provided optimum hold. The pistol was designed primarily for military use and saw service in the German Luftwaffe.

SPECIFICATION

MANUFACTURER Waffenfabrik Mauser AG.
CALIBRE 7.65mm (.32 ACP)
MAGAZINE CAPACITY 8
ACTION Blowback/double
TOTAL LENGTH 162mm/6.38in
BARREL LENGTH 86mm/3.39in
WEIGHT UNLOADED 640g/22.6 oz

Dreyse 1907

This pistol was designed by Louis Schmeisser, one of the best-known technical designers in Europe at the beginning of the 20th century. It was a blowback pistol with a breech block that surrounded the barrel. It was striker-fired. The frame and slide could be broken open, pivoting on a pin in front of the trigger guard, and this was essential for maintenance. The Dreyse 1907 proved to be quite a popular pistol and it was issued to some German police forces.

SPECIFICATION

MANUFACTURER Rheinische Metallwaaren und Maschinefabrik
CALIBRE 7.65mm (.32 ACP)
MAGAZINE CAPACITY 7
ACTION Blowback/single
TOTAL LENGTH 160mm/6.3in
BARREL LENGTH 93mm/3.66in
WEIGHT UNLOADED 710g/25oz

Sauer Model 13

screw cap

SPECIFICATION

MANUFACTURER J.P. Sauer & Sohn GmbH.
CALIBRE 7.65mm (.32 ACP)
MAGAZINE CAPACITY 7
ACTION Blowback/double and single
TOTAL LENGTH 144mm/5.67in
BARREL LENGTH 75mm/2.95in
WEIGHT UNLOADED 570g/20.1oz

This was a blowback pistol with a fixed barrel and a tubular slide. The breech block was retained in the slide by a screw-cap at the back. It had a safety catch just behind the trigger guard. The pistol was a successful design and quickly caught on. Due to its compact size it was often favoured by military officers as a personal defence weapon and it was also issued more widely to police and military forces. The magazine was inserted in the butt.

Sauer Model 38

SPECIFICATION

MANUFACTURER J.P. Sauer & Sohn GmbH.
CALIBRE 7.65mm (.32 ACP)
MAGAZINE CAPACITY 8
ACTION Blowback/single and double
TOTAL LENGTH 171mm/6.73in
BARREL LENGTH 84mm/3.31in
WEIGHT UNLOADED 720g/25.4oz

This blowback-operated pistol was based on earlier models and became available near the end of 1939. It was produced almost entirely for the German armed forces. The pistol was produced to a high standard. It had a fixed barrel and the recoil spring was positioned round the barrel. The breech block was connected to the slide. There was a decocking lever on the side of the frame and a safety catch which locked the hammer. The pistol also featured a magazine safety, whereby the pistol would not function unless the magazine was loaded.

Schwarzlose 1908

fixed sight

SPECIFICATION

MANUFACTURER A.W. Schwarzlose GmbH.
CALIBRE 7.65mm (.32 ACP)
MAGAZINE CAPACITY 6
ACTION Blow forward/single
TOTAL LENGTH 143mm/5.63in
BARREL LENGTH 121mm/4.76in
WEIGHT UNLOADED 532.69g/18.79oz

grip safety

This pocket pistol was a blow forward-operated service pistol as devised by Ferdinand Ritter von Mannlicher, a German-born engineer and small-armaments designer who worked for most of his life in Austria. The German company, A.W. Schwarzlose of Berlin, began marketing the 1908 pistol in 1909. In the United States the Schwarzlose was imported and assembled by the Warner Arms Company of Brooklyn, New York, until the model stopped being manufactured in 1911. The Schwarzlose was not an altogether successful design – the pistol was prone to jam and it was uncomfortable for the shooter to use. The grip safety was on the front of the grip frame and was squeezed before firing. Alternatively the grip safety could be locked with a push button. As it was made for only a short time, the Schwarzlose 1908 was a relatively rare model.

Mannlicher

Although Mannlicher's designs for pistols were relatively successful, his greater success was with his bolt-action rifles.

Walther Model 4

barrel
extractor port

This was a striker-fired blowback-operated pistol with a fixed barrel. It had a full-length slide with an extraction port on its left and an internal hammer. The hand grip on the Model 4 was larger than on previous models in order to accommodate a larger magazine. There was a manual safety catch in the rear of the receiver, behind the hand grip. The Model 4 was ordered in large numbers by the German Army and saw extensive use in World War I.

SPECIFICATION
MANUFACTURER Carl Walther GmbH. Waffenfabrik
CALIBRE 7.65mm (.32 ACP)
MAGAZINE CAPACITY 8
ACTION Blowback/single
TOTAL LENGTH 152mm/6in
BARREL LENGTH 85mm/3.35in
WEIGHT UNLOADED 550g/19.4oz

Walther PP

This pistol set a new standard in double-action design. It had a double-action lock and an external hammer, and a signal pin indicated whether the chamber was loaded. There was a safety catch on the side of the receiver. First produced in 1929, the PP was issued to German police, and to panzer troops and the Luftwaffe during World War II. It was both reliable and easily concealed. The Walther PP continued in production to the end of the 20th century and was purchased by security forces and individuals in many countries.

SPECIFICATION
MANUFACTURER Carl Walther GmbH. Waffenfabrik
CALIBRE 7.65mm (.32 ACP), .380 ACP
MAGAZINE CAPACITY 8
ACTION Blowback/double
TOTAL LENGTH 160mm/6.7in
BARREL LENGTH 98mm/3.86in
WEIGHT UNLOADED 695g/24.5oz

Walther PPK

The Walther PPK was first produced in 1931. It was a more compact version of the Walther PP and it was designed to be easily concealed and carried. The internal workings of the PPK were the same as those of the PP. Apart from the different dimensions, the only real external design alteration was the hand grip. Otherwise the PPK had the same smooth lines as the PP, which was to make it one of the most iconic of pistol designs. A PPK is thought to have been carried by Adolf Hitler. It was also made famous by Ian Fleming's character James Bond in *Dr No*, who later updated to the P99.

SPECIFICATION
MANUFACTURER Carl Walther GmbH. Waffenfabrik
CALIBRE 7.65mm (.32 ACP), .380 ACP
MAGAZINE CAPACITY 8
ACTION Blowback/double
TOTAL LENGTH 154mm/6.06in
BARREL LENGTH 84mm/3.31in
WEIGHT UNLOADED 580g/20.5oz

Walther P38

This short-recoil pistol was issued to German forces in 1938 as a replacement for the Luger. It had a locked breech and was the first pistol of this type to have a double-action mechanism. The weapon could therefore be carried fully loaded, with a round chambered, in considerable safety. The weapon would only fire if the trigger was fully pulled through. At the height of demand, other manufacturers were brought in to produce individual parts.

SPECIFICATION
MANUFACTURER Carl Walther GmbH. Waffenfabrik
CALIBRE 9mm Parabellum
MAGAZINE CAPACITY 8
ACTION Short recoil/double
TOTAL LENGTH 213mm/8.38in
BARREL LENGTH 127mm/5in
WEIGHT UNLOADED 960g/33.86oz

SPECIFICATION

MANUFACTURER Carl Walther GmbH.
Waffenfabrik

CALIBRE 9mm Parabellum

MAGAZINE CAPACITY 8

ACTION Short recoil/double or single

TOTAL LENGTH 180mm/7.1in

BARREL LENGTH 90mm/3.54in

WEIGHT UNLOADED 795g/28oz

Walther P5

Developed in 1979, the P5 was a revised
version of the classic P38. It was a recoil-operated
pistol with a double-action trigger system and the
same breech-locking system as the P38. The ejector was moved
to the left of the receiver. The main differences between the P5
and the P38 are in the safety system. The safety catch was moved
left side of the frame and used as a de-cocking lever. The weapon
would not be fired by a fall of the external hammer unless the trigger had been
pulled. The pistol was issued widely to the German Police.

Walther P88

SPECIFICATION

MANUFACTURER Carl Walther GmbH.
Waffenfabrik/Sportwaffen

CALIBRE 9mm Parabellum

MAGAZINE CAPACITY 15

ACTION Recoil/double

TOTAL LENGTH 187mm/7.36in

BARREL LENGTH 102mm/4in

WEIGHT UNLOADED 900g/31.7oz

This pistol was first produced
in 1988 and continued in production until
1996. It was a highly regarded recoil-operated,
locked-breech pistol. Instead of a locking wedge, it
used a variation of the Browning cam system. With this system
the barrel block lug locked into an ejection port in the slide.
It also featured an ambidextrous frame-mounted de-cocking
lever. It was fully ambidextrous, with magazine release and
de-cocking lever on both sides of the frame. The P88 was
designed for both military and law-enforcement use.

SPECIFICATION

MANUFACTURER Carl Walther GmbH.
Sportwaffen

CALIBRE 9mm Parabellum

MAGAZINE CAPACITY 16

ACTION Recoil/double or single

TOTAL LENGTH 180mm/7.1in

BARREL LENGTH 102mm/4in

WEIGHT UNLOADED 630g/22.22oz

Walther P99

This pistol was produced in 1996. The main aim was to develop a new,
modern-style police and self-defence pistol. The P99 used an internal striker
rather than an external hammer, and had a chamber-loaded indicator on the
right side of the slide. There was a quick-action trigger system in which the
striker was partially pre-cocked. Then, when the trigger was pulled, the striker
was fully cocked and released, firing the pistol. It also featured four internal
safeties, a de-cocking button and adjustable sights. There was an ambidextrous
magazine release incorporated into the trigger guard.

SPECIFICATION

MANUFACTURER Carl Walther GmbH.
Sportwaffen

CALIBRE .22 Long Rifle

MAGAZINE CAPACITY 10

ACTION Blowback/double and single

TOTAL LENGTH 160mm/6.3in

BARREL LENGTH 86mm/3.4in

WEIGHT UNLOADED 430g/15.17oz

Walther P22

Although this was a compact pistol, it was said to retain all of the features of
a full-sized version. The P22 could be adapted to several different equipment
configurations. The compact design and light weight have been achieved by
the use of a polymer frame. It featured ambidextrous controls for both left-
and right-handed shooters. There was an integrated trigger lock, chamber-
loaded indicator, as well as a magazine disconnect, hammer safety and firing-
pin safety. The fixed barrel was said to improve accuracy. The rear sight was
adjustable for windage and elevation while the front sight was interchangeable.

 Italy

Italian gun manufacturers, including Beretta and Bernadelli, have long and distinguished histories going back to the 16th and 18th centuries. As such, they form part of the history of gunmaking, and they are also renowned manufacturers of both traditional and modern firearms. Beretta won the contract to replace the longest-serving pistol in history, the Colt M1911, with the Beretta 92F (designated the M9 in the US). The contract was updated in 2005 for Beretta to produce the M9A1.

Benelli MP90S

Benelli is a long-established Italian firm of gunmakers who have specialized in producing target pistols. The MP90S was produced in the 1980s. It was operated by delayed blowback and had a fully adjustable, single-action trigger release and a square-section sight. The sight line was extremely close to the barrel axis. This minimized movement caused by wrist torsion, which in turn allowed for better control of the pistol for target shooting. The sights were fixed and adjustable for windage and elevation.

SPECIFICATION

MANUFACTURER Benelli Armi SpA.
CALIBRE .32 S&W Wadcutter
MAGAZINE CAPACITY 5
ACTION Delayed blowback/single
TOTAL LENGTH 218mm/8.58in
BARREL LENGTH 110mm/4.33in
WEIGHT UNLOADED 1,180g/41.62oz

Beretta Model 1915

This was a historic design for Beretta, as it was their first ever pistol. Beretta designed a simple blowback pistol, fired by a concealed hammer. Although most were chambered for either .32 or .38 ACP, a few were chambered to fire the 9mm Glisenti cartridge. During World War I there was increased demand for firearms. The Model 1915 was produced in large numbers during these years, while other manufacturers such as Carl Walther were on standby to fill the gap in arms production. The Model 1915 was produced between 1915 and 1945 and was later used for the military and the police.

SPECIFICATION

MANUFACTURER Pietro Beretta SpA.
CALIBRE .32 ACP, .38 ACP, 9mm Glisenti
MAGAZINE CAPACITY 7
ACTION Blowback/single
TOTAL LENGTH 149mm/5.87in
BARREL LENGTH 83mm/3.25in
WEIGHT UNLOADED 570g/20.1oz

Beretta Model 1915/19

slide cutaway

This pistol was an improved version of the Model 1915. It had a revised ejection port and a smaller safety catch than the earlier model. This design also had a larger cutaway in the slide, extending halfway towards the rear sight. The entire weapon was also slightly shorter, yet had a longer barrel. It was not produced primarily for military purposes, but small numbers were manufactured for the services and were known as the Model 1922. The hand grip plates were made from sheet metal instead of the usual wood.

SPECIFICATION

MANUFACTURER Pietro Beretta SpA.
CALIBRE .32 ACP
MAGAZINE CAPACITY 7
ACTION Blowback/single
TOTAL LENGTH 145mm/5.7in
BARREL LENGTH 85mm/3.35in
WEIGHT UNLOADED 670g/23.63oz

Beretta Model 1923

The Model 1923 pistol was designed to consolidate the improvements of the 1915/19 model and to take the 9mm Glisenti round. However, the Model 1923 Glisenti cartridge was not powerful enough to be fully effective. There were also misunderstandings over use of the 9mm Parabellum cartridge, which was a much more powerful round than the Glisenti. If the pistol was loaded and fired with this ammunition, it could damage the pistol as it was not designed to handle this round. Only about 10,000 of these pistols were produced.

SPECIFICATION
MANUFACTURER Pietro Beretta SpA.
CALIBRE 9mm Glisenti
MAGAZINE CAPACITY 7
ACTION Blowback/single
TOTAL LENGTH 177mm/6.96in
BARREL LENGTH 87mm/3.43in
WEIGHT UNLOADED 800g/28.22oz

SPECIFICATION
MANUFACTURER Pietro Beretta SpA.
CALIBRE 7.65mm (.32 ACP)
MAGAZINE CAPACITY 7
ACTION Blowback/single
TOTAL LENGTH 177mm/6.96in
BARREL LENGTH 87mm/3.43in
WEIGHT UNLOADED 800g/28.22oz

Beretta Model 1931

This weapon was an adaptation of the Model 1923 and a precursor of the Model 1934. The main difference between this pistol and the Model 1923 was that it was chambered for the .32 ACP round, rather than the 9mm Glisenti round and so did not have its associated problems with its cartridges. The Model 1931 was issued to the Italian Navy and could be instantly recognized by the Regia Marina emblem on the hand grip.

Beretta Model 1934

SPECIFICATION
MANUFACTURER Pietro Beretta SpA.
CALIBRE 9mm Corto (.380 ACP)
MAGAZINE CAPACITY 7
ACTION Blowback/single
TOTAL LENGTH 152mm/6in
BARREL LENGTH 94mm/3.7in
WEIGHT UNLOADED 660g/23.28oz

This blowback-operated pistol was first introduced in 1936. It was essentially an improved version of the 1915/19 pistol. Although it was chambered for the 9mm round, it used a short Corto cartridge to keep the pressure within safe limits. The only real drawback with the Model 1934 was that the round was underpowered. The pistol was designed for the Italian armed forces and many were issued to officers. The Model 1934 proved to be a reliable weapon, partly due to its rugged manufacture and relatively few parts.

Beretta Model 1951

SPECIFICATION
MANUFACTURER Pietro Beretta SpA.
CALIBRE 9mm Parabellum
MAGAZINE CAPACITY 8
ACTION Short recoil/single
TOTAL LENGTH 203mm/8in
BARREL LENGTH 115mm/4.53in
WEIGHT UNLOADED 890g/31oz

This pistol went into production in 1953 and was made under licence in Egypt for many years. Its mechanism was based on a system designed for the German Walther P38. It was a recoil-operated, locked-breech pistol with a short recoiling barrel, which was locked to the slide by a wedge under the barrel. The magazine release was located at the base of the hand grip. The original pistol was made from light alloy, but was soon found not to be sturdy enough and a steel frame was developed.

Beretta Model 76

This was a blowback-operated single-action pistol. The frame, slide and barrel were made from heavy steel. The pistol had a safety lever on the left-hand side of the frame. Although this was designed as a target pistol, its rugged and angular appearance meant that it could easily be mistaken for a full combat pistol.

SPECIFICATION

MANUFACTURER Pietro Beretta SpA.
CALIBRE .22 Long Rifle
MAGAZINE 10
ACTION Blowback/single
TOTAL LENGTH 233mm/9.17in
BARREL LENGTH 150mm/5.91in
WEIGHT UNLOADED 930g/32.8oz

Beretta Model 81

This pistol first went into production in 1976. It was a blowback-operated weapon. It had an ambidextrous safety catch on the frame. The sights were fixed. The pistol took a 12-round magazine. It had a reversible magazine release button and could be fitted with an optional magazine safety. The frame was made from a light alloy, and the slide from steel. The hand grips were wood or plastic. The M81 formed the basis of several later models, such as the Model 82, Model 84 and Model 85.

SPECIFICATION

MANUFACTURER Pietro Beretta SpA.
CALIBRE .32 ACP
MAGAZINE 12
ACTION Blowback/single or double
TOTAL LENGTH 172mm/6.77in
BARREL LENGTH 97mm/3.82in
WEIGHT UNLOADED 670g/21.54oz

Beretta Model 84

This was a blowback-operated, hammer-fired weapon produced from 1976 to 1995. It had an ambidextrous safety catch on the frame and fixed sights. The pistol took a 13-round magazine which was designed for staggered loading. It had a reversible magazine-release button. It could also be fitted with an optional magazine safety. The frame was manufactured from a light alloy and the slide from steel.

SPECIFICATION

MANUFACTURER Pietro Beretta SpA.
CALIBRE .380 ACP
MAGAZINE 13
ACTION Blowback/single or double
TOTAL LENGTH 172mm/6.77in
BARREL LENGTH 97mm/3.82in
WEIGHT UNLOADED 660g/21.22oz

Beretta Model 89

adjustable rear sights

SPECIFICATION

MANUFACTURER Pietro Beretta SpA.
CALIBRE .22 Long Rifle
MAGAZINE 8
ACTION Blowback/single
TOTAL LENGTH 240mm/9.45in
BARREL LENGTH 152mm/5.98in
WEIGHT UNLOADED 1,160g/40.92oz

This was a simple blowback-operated pistol, manufactured specifically for target practice. It had a heavy barrel mounted on a mixed alloy frame. The pistol was fitted with an external hammer, an ambidextrous safety catch and a magazine safety device. It had fully adjustable rear sights and a front sight that could be changed. The trigger pull was finely set. As a target pistol, the Model 89 did not have a safety hammer de-cocking device. This meant the hammer did not have been pulled back first if there was a round in the chamber.

Beretta Model 92

SPECIFICATION

MANUFACTURER Pietro Beretta SpA.

CALIBRE 9mm Parabellum

MAGAZINE 15 (10 civilian)

ACTION Short recoil/single and double

TOTAL LENGTH 217mm/8.54in

BARREL LENGTH 125mm/4.92in

WEIGHT UNLOADED 950g/33.51oz

This pistol was first manufactured in 1976. It used a short-recoil system of operation instead of the blowback system of Beretta's smaller designs. This reduced recoil and allowed it to fire the more powerful 9mm Parabellum cartridge. The Model 92 was single-action pistol with a double-action capability. About 5,000 Beretta Model 92 pistols were produced. This model proved to be a highly successful design and the forerunner of many successful variants.

Beretta Model 92SB Compact

SPECIFICATION

MANUFACTURER Pietro Beretta SpA.

CALIBRE 9mm Parabellum

MAGAZINE 13

ACTION Short recoil/single or double

TOTAL LENGTH 211mm/8.31in

BARREL LENGTH 119mm/4.69in

WEIGHT UNLOADED 915g/32.28oz

The full-size Beretta 92SB was introduced in 1981, a development of the base Beretta Model 92. The Model 92 had been modified by adding a slide-mounted combined safety and de-cocking lever and replacing the frame-mounted manual thumb safety. The Model 92SB won the approval of the US armed forces during trials which resulted in formal issue by the US Government. The Model 92SB Compact was also produced from 1981, and had a shorter barrel and slide. It was chambered for 13 rounds rather than the 15 of the Model 92SB.

SPECIFICATION

MANUFACTURER Pietro Beretta SpA.

CALIBRE 9mm Parabellum

MAGAZINE 15 (10 civilian)

ACTION Short recoil/single or double

TOTAL LENGTH 211mm/8.31in

BARREL LENGTH 119mm/4.69in

WEIGHT UNLOADED 915g/32.28oz

Beretta Model 92F

The Model 92F was a slightly modified version of the Beretta 92SB. It was first called the Model 92SB-F and the minor modifications of the "F" version were later included in the standard issue pistol as it evolved during US trials. It operated on the short-recoil, delayed-block system. The Model 92F was designed to have parts that were interchangeable with all Model 92 variants, to ease maintenance. It also had a redesigned trigger guard, a chromed barrel inside and a renewed finish on the outside. At least 500,000 were produced.

Beretta Model 92FS

The Model 92FS was introduced in the late 1980s as a further modification of the Model 92. Improvements included an ambidextrous manual safety that also functioned as a de-cocking lever. There was a chamber-loaded indicator that was visible and could be felt to the touch, and a firing-pin block that secured the firing pin. It also had a rotating firing-pin striker. These modifications were designed to prevent over-travel of the slide, which could be dangerous to the user if the slide failed.

SPECIFICATION

MANUFACTURER Pietro Beretta SpA.

CALIBRE 9mm Parabellum

MAGAZINE 15

ACTION Short recoil/single or double

TOTAL LENGTH 211mm/8.31in

BARREL LENGTH 119mm/4.69in

WEIGHT UNLOADED 915g/32.28oz

Beretta Model 93R

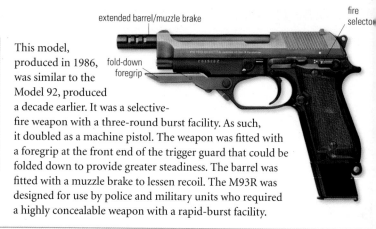

extended barrel/muzzle brake

fire selector

fold-down foregrip

SPECIFICATION

MANUFACTURER Pietro Beretta SpA.
CALIBRE 9mm Parabellum
MAGAZINE 20
ACTION Short recoil/single/rapid burst
TOTAL LENGTH 240mm/9.45in
BARREL LENGTH 156mm/6.16in
WEIGHT UNLOADED 1,120g/39.51oz

This model, produced in 1986, was similar to the Model 92, produced a decade earlier. It was a selective-fire weapon with a three-round burst facility. As such, it doubled as a machine pistol. The weapon was fitted with a foregrip at the front end of the trigger guard that could be folded down to provide greater steadiness. The barrel was fitted with a muzzle brake to lessen recoil. The M93R was designed for use by police and military units who required a highly concealable weapon with a rapid-burst facility.

Beretta Model 8000 Cougar

SPECIFICATION

MANUFACTURER Pietro Beretta SpA.
CALIBRE 9mm Parabellum
MAGAZINE CAPACITY 13
ACTION Short recoil/single
TOTAL LENGTH 180mm/7.1in
BARREL LENGTH 92mm/3.62in
WEIGHT UNLOADED 800g/28.2oz

This pistol was first produced in 1994 to meet a requirement for a more compact pistol than the full-size Model 92F (US M9). The weapon was intended for police duties, personal defence and covert operations. It was a recoil-operated, locked-breech pistol with a rotating barrel locking system. The pistol had an ambidextrous safety de-cocking lever, a rotating firing-pin striker, an automatic firing-pin block and a chamber-loaded indicator. The trigger guard was designed for double-handed use.

Beretta 9000S

SPECIFICATION

MANUFACTURER Pietro Beretta SpA.
CALIBRE 9mm Parabellum
MAGAZINE CAPACITY 12
ACTION Recoil/single or double
TOTAL LENGTH 168mm/6.63in
BARREL LENGTH 88mm/3.46in
WEIGHT UNLOADED 755g/26.63oz

This was the most compact pistol in the Beretta range, launched in 2000. Its lightness in weight was partly achieved through the use of glass-reinforced fibre (GRP) materials and polymers. The hand grips were made from a soft polymer and provide a high level of grip. The 9000S featured a patented locking system that incorporated a tilting barrel and open slide. The pistol developed in two versions. The version "F" was both single and double action, with a manual safety lever that also worked as de-cocker. The version "D" was a double-action only (DAO) pistol, without manual safety, and did not have a de-cocking feature.

Bernadelli Model 60

SPECIFICATION

MANUFACTURER Vincenzo Bernadelli SpA.
CALIBRE .22 Long Rifle, 7.65mm, .380 ACP
MAGAZINE CAPACITY 8
ACTION Blowback/single
TOTAL LENGTH 165mm/6.5in
BARREL LENGTH 90mm/3.54in
WEIGHT UNLOADED 685g/24.2oz

This pistol was introduced in 1959 and manufactured during the late 1950s and 1960s. It was a blowback-operated pistol with twin return springs to decrease the effect of recoil on the user. It had a locked-breech system and was made of steel throughout. The barrel was forged together with the frame and the pistol could be dismantled by releasing a spring catch, after which the slide could be removed. The pistol was available in three calibres, .22 LR, 7.65mm (.32 ACP) and .380 ACP.

Bernardelli P6

SPECIFICATION

MANUFACTURER Vincenzo Bernadelli SpA.
CALIBRE .22 Long Rifle, 7.65mm
(.32 ACP), .380 ACP
MAGAZINE 10, 8 and 7
ACTION Blowback/double
TOTAL LENGTH 168mm/6.63in
BARREL LENGTH 89mm/3.5in
WEIGHT UNLOADED 505g/17.8oz

This pistol was designed to be a light and easy-to-carry pocket and defence pistol with external hammer and lightweight alloy frame. It was similar in style to the German Walther PP. The Bernardelli P6 was available in versions that chamber .22 Long Rifle, 7.65mm and .380 ACP rounds with a magazine capacity of 10, 8 and 7 rounds respectively. It could be fitted with either plastic or walnut hand grips designed to absorb and distribute recoil between the wooden or plastic components. The pistol featured a chamber-loaded indicator and adjustable rear sights.

Bernardelli P8 Compact

SPECIFICATION

MANUFACTURER Vincenzo Bernadelli SpA.
CALIBRE .22 Long Rifle, 7.65mm, .380 ACP
MAGAZINE 10
ACTION Blowback/double
TOTAL LENGTH 168mm/6.63in
BARREL LENGTH 89mm/3.5in
WEIGHT UNLOADED 507g/17.88oz

This was a lightweight, compact pistol designed for home defence and backup. The hand grip was fitted with plastic target grips. It had manual thumb, half-cock, magazine and auto-locking firing-pin safeties as well as a loaded-chamber indicator and click-adjustable rear sight.

Safety mechanisms
The P6 and P8 Compact were largely identical, with the P8 adding safety mechanisms to comply with arms regulations in some countries.

Bernardelli P90

SPECIFICATION

MANUFACTURER Vincenzo Bernadelli SpA.
CALIBRE .22 Long Rifle, 7.65mm, .380 ACP
MAGAZINE 10 and 7
ACTION Blowback/double
TOTAL LENGTH 228mm/9in (full size)
BARREL LENGTH 152mm/6in
WEIGHT UNLOADED 693g/24.5oz

This pistol was designed as a precision shooting pistol for both sport shooting and police and military use. In many ways similar to the P6, the P90 was manufactured with three different barrel lengths with a choice of three different calibres, .22 Long Rifle, 7.65mm (.32 ACP) and .380 ACP. The P90 frame was lightweight and the pistol had a fixed barrel outside the muzzle with a front sight screwed on to the end of the barrel. The rear sight was adjustable. The hand grip was ergonomically designed for ease of use and had either plastic or walnut grips.

Bernadelli Model P0-18

SPECIFICATION

MANUFACTURER Vincenzo Bernadelli SpA.
CALIBRE 9mm Parabellum, 7.65mm
(.32 ACP)
MAGAZINE 16
ACTION Short recoil/double
TOTAL LENGTH 213mm/8.38in
BARREL LENGTH 122mm/4.8in
WEIGHT UNLOADED 1,010g/35.6oz

Introduced in 1984, this was a selective double-action pistol with a Browning-style short-recoil system and a locking breech. There was a safety catch mounted on the side of the frame. The P0-18 was first introduced in the mid-1980s and was bought by some police forces. There was also a .32 ACP version for use by civilians in locations where military calibres were prohibited. The PO-18 has had considerable commercial success. A compact model is also available and variations of this were chambered for both rounds of ammunition.

Bernardelli POne

Successor to the P0-18, this double-action pistol was designed to achieve accuracy, stability, shooting speed and reliability. Produced in the 1980s, it was intended for use by law enforcement and military professionals as well as for personal defence or sport shooting. The pistol had a forged steel frame, slide and barrel, and it was designed to be durable, light and reliable. The hand grip was slim and was fitted with plastic or walnut grips. Full-length slide rails were designed to achieve both stability and accuracy.

SPECIFICATION

MANUFACTURER Vincenzo Bernadelli SpA.
CALIBRE 9mm Parabellum
MAGAZINE 15
ACTION Blowback/double
TOTAL LENGTH 212mm/8.35in
BARREL LENGTH 122mm/4.8in
WEIGHT UNLOADED 971g/34.25oz

Glisenti Model 1910

This pistol was derived from a design by the Italian inventor Bethel Abiel Revelli. He assigned the patent to the manufacturers, Glisenti. After further development, the design was first accepted by the Italian Army as a 7.65mm pistol. In due course, the Italian Army requested a 9mm pistol and, having passed it on to another manufacturer, it was adapted to become the Glisenti Model 1910. The pistol was used in World War I and was also used by Italian forces during World War II.

SPECIFICATION

MANUFACTURER Metallurgica Brescia gia Tempini; Societa Siderurgica Glisenti
CALIBRE 9mm Glisenti
MAGAZINE CAPACITY 7
ACTION Short recoil/single
TOTAL LENGTH 207mm/8.15in
BARREL LENGTH 100mm/3.94in
WEIGHT UNLOADED 820g/29oz

Tanfoglio TA90

The TA-90 was inspired by the design of the Czech CZ75 pistol. Production of the TA90 started in 1984. It was a blowback-operated, locked-breech pistol with a durable steel frame. The pistol had a good reputation for quality and attention to detail. The barrel, for example, was carefully rifled. The pistol had fixed sights and rubber grips. It had a "cocked and locked" safety mounted on the frame as well as an automatic firing-pin safety. The pistol was bought commercially and had also been issued to some security forces.

SPECIFICATION

MANUFACTURER Fratelli Tanfoglio SNC.
CALIBRE 9mm Parabellum
MAGAZINE 15
ACTION Short recoil/double
TOTAL LENGTH 202mm/7.96in
BARREL LENGTH 120mm/4.72in
WEIGHT UNLOADED 1,015g/36oz

Tanfoglio Standard

Production of the Standard started in the mid-1980s. It was designed as a blowback-operated, locked breech self-defence pistol based on features of the Browning High-Power. It featured a hammer-drop ambidextrous safety, a de-cocking system located on the slide, a double-action trigger, a standard reversible magazine catch, a standard hammer, rubber hand grips, three-dot sights and a compact magazine with a high capacity. A compact version was also available as a pocket-sized model.

SPECIFICATION

MANUFACTURER Fratelli Tanfoglio SNC.
CALIBRE 9mm Parabellum, .40 S&W, .45 ACP
MAGAZINE CAPACITY 16, 12, 10
ACTION Blowback/double
TOTAL LENGTH 210mm/8.27in
BARREL LENGTH 113mm/4.45in
WEIGHT UNLOADED 1,150g/40.57oz

Tanfoglio Combat

SPECIFICATION

MANUFACTURER Fratelli Tanfoglio SNC.
CALIBRE 9mm Parabellum
MAGAZINE CAPACITY 16, 12, 10
ACTION Blowback/double
TOTAL LENGTH 210mm/8.27in
BARREL LENGTH 113mm/4.45in
WEIGHT UNLOADED 1,150g/40.57oz

Production of this pistol started in the mid-1980s and it was the basic model for the Tanfoglio combat range of pistols. It was designed primarily for self-defence and sport shooting. It could be carried "cocked and locked" and it also had an automatic firing-pin safety, a double-action trigger, standard reversible magazine catch, standard hammer, rubber hand grips, three-dot sights and a standard magazine. The Combat was available in blued, chromed or duotone finish.

SPECIFICATION

MANUFACTURER Fratelli Tanfoglio SNC.
CALIBRE .22 Long Rifle, .32 ACP, .380 ACP
MAGAZINE CAPACITY 7
ACTION Blowback/single
TOTAL LENGTH 160mm/6.3in
BARREL LENGTH 83mm/3.25in
WEIGHT UNLOADED 700g/24.69oz

Tanfoglio GT22

This was a blowback-operated pistol developed in 1992. It had an external hammer and an open-top slide. A target-shooting version of this pistol was also developed. It had a longer barrel and featured an adjustable rear sight. The magazine featured a finger rest at the base to improve the user's grip.

Tanfoglio
Tanfoglio models G22 and G27/GT28 were available worldwide from 1992. Some models are not available in the USA.

Tanfoglio GT27 and GT28

SPECIFICATION

MANUFACTURER Fratelli Tanfoglio SNC.
CALIBRE .25 ACP (GT27), 8mm (GT28)
MAGAZINE CAPACITY 6
ACTION Blowback/single
TOTAL LENGTH 120mm/4.72in
BARREL LENGTH 63mm/2.48in
WEIGHT UNLOADED 350g/12.35oz

Production of the GT27 was started by Tanfoglio in 1992. This was a super-compact self-defence pistol with fixed barrel and single-action trigger, available in only .25 ACP. It had a trigger safety, a single-column magazine. The hand grips were finished in wood or plastic and it was available in either blued or chromed finish. There was also a GT28 version available. This was a signal pistol, chambered to fire an 8mm blank cartridge (containing an explosive charge but no bullet).

Tanfoglio Professional Defence

SPECIFICATION

MANUFACTURER Fratelli Tanfoglio SNC.
CALIBRE 9mm Parabellum, .40 S&W, .45 ACP
MAGAZINE CAPACITY 16, 12, 10
ACTION Blowback/double
TOTAL LENGTH 210mm/8.27in
BARREL LENGTH 133mm/5.25in
WEIGHT UNLOADED 1,150g/40.57oz

This was a pistol specially made for professional use by special operations and law enforcement agencies. Production of the pistol started in 1994. The Professional Defence had a stainless-steel frame with a rounded trigger guard, and stainless-steel compact slide. There were chequered straps on both the front and rear of the hand grip and rubber side grips. The double-action trigger was an extended beavertail design. The pistol had a dovetail front night sight on the slide and carried a standard magazine. The barrel had a compensator to reduce recoil. It was available in a variety of chamberings including 9mm Parabellum.

Tanfoglio Carry

This self-defence pistol was designed as a carry pistol for special operations and law enforcement agencies. Production started in 1994. Its frame had a large rounded trigger guard suitable for a gloved hand, with a double-action trigger. It had a compact slide, a standard reversible magazine catch and high-capacity magazine, a standard safety and hammer. The pistol also had rubber grips and three-dot sights. It was available in a blued, chromed or duotone.

SPECIFICATION

MANUFACTURER Fratelli Tanfoglio SNC.
CALIBRE 9mm Parabellum, .40 S&W, .45 ACP
MAGAZINE CAPACITY 16, 12, 10
ACTION Blowback/double
TOTAL LENGTH 185mm/7.28in
BARREL LENGTH 93mm/3.66in
WEIGHT UNLOADED 1,100g/38.8oz

Tanfoglio Force

This pistol, introduced in 1996, was designed primarily for personal defence and in particular for use by the police. The Force had a light polymer frame for ease of carriage and a high-capacity magazine. The pistol could be carried "cocked and locked". Features included a double-action trigger, standard reversible magazine catch, standard hammer and three-dot sights.

Tanfoglio
This Italian company is based in the Gardone valley in Brescia. Firearms have been produced at Tanfoglio for over 500 years.

SPECIFICATION

MANUFACTURER Fratelli Tanfoglio SNC.
CALIBRE 9mm Parabellum, .40 S&W, .45 ACP
MAGAZINE CAPACITY 16, 12, 10
ACTION Blowback/double
TOTAL LENGTH 210mm/8.27in
BARREL LENGTH 113mm/4.45in
WEIGHT UNLOADED 850g/29.98oz

Tanfoglio Force Compact

This was a pocket-size version of the Force model, produced in 1996. It had a shorter barrel and a shorter grip. It was designed to be easily carried by police on duty or as a personal-defence weapon. It also featured a high-capacity magazine. It had a "cocked and locked" safety on the frame with an automatic firing-pin safety, double-action trigger, standard reversible magazine catch, standard hammer, three-dot sights and a compact magazine.

SPECIFICATION

MANUFACTURER Fratelli Tanfoglio SNC.
CALIBRE 9mm Parabellum, .40 S&W, .45 ACP
MAGAZINE CAPACITY 13, 10, 8
ACTION Blowback/double
TOTAL LENGTH 195mm/7.67in
BARREL LENGTH 93mm/3.66in
WEIGHT UNLOADED 750g/26.45oz

Tanfoglio Stock

This pistol was designed for either self-defence or target shooting. It was known as the Stock in Europe and the Witness in the United States, where it is sold by European American Armory Corporation (EAA). Among its features it had a custom reversible magazine catch and extended safety. It had a steel frame and slide and specially designed polygonal barrel and was available in several calibres.

Witness brand
In the USA the brand is known as "EAA Witness". This includes a variety of individual models that can be customized with optional features.

SPECIFICATION

MANUFACTURER Fratelli Tanfoglio SNC.
CALIBRE 9mm Parabellum, .40 S&W, .45 ACP
MAGAZINE CAPACITY 16, 12, 10
ACTION Blowback/double
TOTAL LENGTH 210mm/8.27in
BARREL LENGTH 113mm/4.45in
WEIGHT UNLOADED 1,150g/40.57oz

Norway

Norway does not have a tradition of designing and manufacturing pistols and revolvers, and weapons in this category issued to its armed forces were mainly imported. Some, however, such as the US Colt and the Russian Nagant (originally Belgian), were manufactured under licence in Norwegian factories.

Colt 1914

SPECIFICATION	
MANUFACTURER	Kongsberg Arsenal
CALIBRE	.45 ACP
MAGAZINE	7
ACTION	Short recoil/single
TOTAL LENGTH	216mm/8.5in
BARREL LENGTH	127mm/5in
WEIGHT UNLOADED	1,130g/39.86oz

This pistol was manufactured under licence in Norway at the Kongsberg Arsenal. It was effectively the same weapon as the Colt M1911, apart from different markings, and identification on the receiver, namely "11.25mm Aut. Pistol. M/1914". The pistol was produced in large numbers at Kongsberg from 1919.

Nagant Model 1893

SPECIFICATION	
MANUFACTURER	Manufacture d'Armes Nagant Freres/Tula Arsenal
CALIBRE	7.5mm Nagant
CYLINDER	7
ACTION	Single or double action
TOTAL LENGTH	229mm/9.06in
BARREL LENGTH	110mm/4.35in
WEIGHT UNLOADED	790g/27.87oz

This revolver was one of many versions of the Russian Nagant revolver and many were imported, though some may have been assembled in Norway. It was replaced by the .45 ACP Colt Model of 1911.

— seven-shot cylinder

Use in Europe
The Nagant was provided for the military in Sweden, Denmark, Belgium and Luxembourg.

Denmark

Danish pistol and revolver design, production and manufacture have included both entirely home-grown developments and adaptations of foreign designs. Some of these designs, such as the Schouboe of 1907, were innovative, but unfortunately ingenious designs such as these did not always find a ready market.

Bergmann-Bayard Model 1910

SPECIFICATION	
MANUFACTURER	Anciens Établissements Pieper (AEP)
CALIBRE	9mm Bergmann-Bayard
MAGAZINE	6
ACTION	Recoil/single
TOTAL LENGTH	250mm/9.84in
BARREL LENGTH	102mm/4in
WEIGHT UNLOADED	1,015g/35.8oz

This pistol incorporated the design patented by Bergmann for a machine-gun with a vertically moving locking piece which locked the breech block. The bolt extracted and ejected the spent cartridge casing and cocked the hammer on the recoil strike. It then pulled a round from the magazine and chambered it on the return. The Bergmann-Bayard 1910 was made in Belgium and supplied to the Danish armed forces.

Schouboe M1907

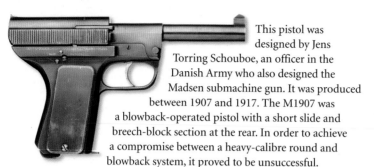

SPECIFICATION

MANUFACTURER Dansk Rekylriffel
Syndikat AS
CALIBRE 11.35mm Schouboe
MAGAZINE CAPACITY 6
ACTION Blowback/single
TOTAL LENGTH 203mm/8in
BARREL LENGTH 130mm/5.12in
WEIGHT UNLOADED 690g/24.3oz

This pistol was designed by Jens Torring Schouboe, an officer in the Danish Army who also designed the Madsen submachine gun. It was produced between 1907 and 1917. The M1907 was a blowback-operated pistol with a short slide and breech-block section at the rear. In order to achieve a compromise between a heavy-calibre round and blowback system, it proved to be unsuccessful. Schouboe used an extremely light bullet to minimize recoil. The problem with this was that the bullet proved to be too light to be accurate.

Austria

Austria has a tradition of producing world-class small arms that continue to be used by armed forces throughout the world. Ferdinand Ritter von Mannlicher was one of the most famous armaments designers of all time and lends his name to the current firm of Steyr-Mannlicher. Another leading small arms producer in Austria is Glock, which was founded in 1963.

Glock 17

SPECIFICATION

MANUFACTURER Glock GmbH.
CALIBRE 9mm Parabellum
MAGAZINE CAPACITY 17
ACTION Recoil/double – Safe Action (SA)
TOTAL LENGTH 186mm/7.32in
BARREL LENGTH 114mm/4.5in
WEIGHT UNLOADED 625g/22.04oz

This was the first Glock handgun, introduced in 1983. It was innovative both for its pure polymer frame and for the "Safe Action" safety system – a semi-double-action trigger system along with a striker instead of a hammer and firing pin which allowed for several trigger pulls. Glock pistols had three independent and automatic safeties – trigger safety, firing-pin safety and drop safety – which sequentially disengaged when the trigger was pulled and which re-engaged as the pistol fired and the trigger returned to its forward position. Glock pistols are said to have about half the number of components as comparable handguns. The Glock 17 had only 33 parts and could be disassembled and reassembled with one tool. The synthetic material used to construct the frame of a Glock handgun was stronger than steel and much lighter. The metal components were finished with a hardening surface treatment which was also said to be more corrosion resistant than stainless steel. The Glock 17 was issued to the Swedish Army in 1988 (as the Pistole 88).

Glock 17L
The Glock 17 appeared in 1983 in 9mm Parabellum, suitable for the military. The next Glock, the G17L was the first "long slide" Glock which was intended for competition use only.

Glock 19

Developed in 1988, the Glock 19 was essentially the same as the Glock 17 but of reduced size, designed for ease of concealment. Compared with the original Glock 17, the Glock 19 had a slide and grip that were slightly shorter. The advantage of the Glock 19 was the magazine capacity of 15 for 9mm Parabellum calibre rounds, which was more common in larger pistols. The Glock 19 is used for law enforcement and self-defence.

ABOVE Glocks have a small lever set in the face of the trigger locking it until the pistol is properly engaged.

SPECIFICATION
MANUFACTURER Glock GmbH.
CALIBRE 9mm Parabellum
MAGAZINE CAPACITY 15
ACTION Recoil/double (SA)
TOTAL LENGTH 174mm/6.85in
BARREL LENGTH 102mm/4in
WEIGHT UNLOADED 595g/20.99oz

Glock 20

SPECIFICATION
MANUFACTURER Glock Ges.mbH
CALIBRE 10mm Auto
MAGAZINE CAPACITY 15
ACTION Recoil/double (SA)
TOTAL LENGTH 193mm/7.59in
BARREL LENGTH 117mm/4.61in
WEIGHT UNLOADED 785g/27.68oz

This pistol, produced in 1990, was similar in most respects to the Glock 17, but was both longer and wider in dimensions and had a significantly increased calibre. The slide and barrel of the Glock 20 was heavier than the lighter 9mm Parabellum pistols such as the Glock 17. The pistol was carried by some police departments. It provided the same accuracy and power as a Magnum hunting revolver.

Glock 21

SPECIFICATION
MANUFACTURER Glock Ges.mbH
CALIBRE .45 ACP
MAGAZINE CAPACITY 13
ACTION Recoil/double (SA)
TOTAL LENGTH 193mm/7.59in
BARREL LENGTH 117mm/4.61in
WEIGHT UNLOADED 745g/26.28oz

This was a large-frame Glock, produced in 1990. It was based on the Glock 20 and fired the .45 ACP cartridge. It had a modified Glock 20 frame, slide and magazine, but these difference were quite minor. This pistol was designed to fulfil the requirement for a personal defence handgun and was also used for law enforcement. Because of its frame size, its grip was too large for many people, but well suited for those with bigger hands.

Glock 22

SPECIFICATION
MANUFACTURER Glock Ges.mbH
CALIBRE .40 S&W
MAGAZINE CAPACITY 15
ACTION Recoil/double (SA)
TOTAL LENGTH 186mm/7.32in
BARREL LENGTH 114mm/4.59in
WEIGHT UNLOADED 650g/22.92oz

This pistol, produced in 1990, was distinguished by the novel .40 S&W-calibre cartridge and was popular for self-defence and law-enforcement. Otherwise it was essentially the same as the Glock 17, apart from its modified slide, frame, barrel size and magazine. In 2006, the Glock 22 was the most popular sidearm in use in the United States. It was used by law enforcement agencies, the military, security personnel and also by private citizens.

Glock 23

This pistol was essentially the same as the Glock 19 in size, with modified slide, frame and .40 S&W cartridge, with the size reduced for ease of concealment. In the United States many police patrol officers carry full-size Glock 22s, while detectives, officers and supporting staff carry the slightly smaller Glock 23. This pistol had the benefit of being the size of a 9mm pistol while having the ballistics of the bigger cartridge.

SPECIFICATION
MANUFACTURER Glock GmbH.
CALIBRE .40 S&W
MAGAZINE CAPACITY 13
ACTION Recoil/double (SA)
TOTAL LENGTH 174mm/6.85in
BARREL LENGTH 102mm/4.02in
WEIGHT UNLOADED 600g/21.16oz

Glock 24

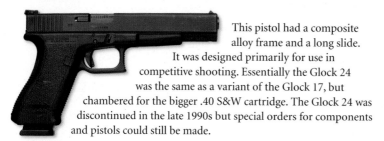

This pistol had a composite alloy frame and a long slide. It was designed primarily for use in competitive shooting. Essentially the Glock 24 was the same as a variant of the Glock 17, but chambered for the bigger .40 S&W cartridge. The Glock 24 was discontinued in the late 1990s but special orders for components and pistols could still be made.

SPECIFICATION
MANUFACTURER Glock GmbH.
CALIBRE .40 S&W
MAGAZINE CAPACITY 10, 15, 29
ACTION Recoil/double (SA)
TOTAL LENGTH 225mm/8.86in
BARREL LENGTH 153mm/6.02in
WEIGHT UNLOADED 757g/26.7oz

Glock 25

Introduced in 1995, the Glock 25 was marketed for countries that do not allow standard military calibres for private use. Although the Glock 25 was the same size as the more powerful Glock 19, it had the more compact .380 chambering. The Glock 25 was a blowback pistol with no barrel lock-up as this is not required with the .380 ACP round.

The .380 ACP cartridge
This was a rimless, straight-sided cartridge that was designed by John Browning. It was specifically designed for pistols that did not have a barrel lock-up mechanism and therefore had a low breech pressure.

SPECIFICATION
MANUFACTURER Glock GmbH.
CALIBRE .380 ACP
MAGAZINE CAPACITY 15
ACTION Blowback/double (SA)
TOTAL LENGTH 174mm/6.85in
BARREL LENGTH 102mm/4.02in
WEIGHT UNLOADED 570g/20.11oz

Glocks 26, 27 and 28

The Glock 26 and Glock 27 were introduced in 1996. They shared the same exterior dimensions and were smaller Glock pistols, though retained many of the features of the larger Glocks. They were small enough to fit in the palm of the hand and could be easily concealed in a jacket pocket or an ankle holster. The Glock 28, introduced a year later, was a blowback-operated system designed for use in countries that did not allow standard military calibres for private use, and was slightly lighter in unloaded weight than the Glock 26 and Glock 27.

SPECIFICATION
MANUFACTURER Glock GmbH.
CALIBRE 9mm Parabellum (G26), .40 S&W (G27) and .380 ACP (G28)
MAGAZINE CAPACITY 9 to 33
ACTION Blowback/double (SA)
TOTAL LENGTH 160mm/6.3in
BARREL LENGTH 88mm/3.46in
WEIGHT UNLOADED 560g/19.75oz (G26/27), 529g/18.66oz (G28)

Glocks 29 and 30

SPECIFICATION

MANUFACTURER Glock GmbH.
CALIBRE 10mm (G29), .45 ACP (G30)
MAGAZINE CAPACITY 9 to 15
ACTION Recoil/double action
TOTAL LENGTH 172mm/6.77in
BARREL LENGTH 96mm/3.78in
WEIGHT UNLOADED 700g/24.69oz
  (G29), 680g/23.99oz (G30)

The Glock 29 and 30 were subcompact pistols, although they were only slightly smaller than the Glock 19. They retained plenty of power for their size and were very popular for self-defence in the United States. The Glock 30 was identical to the Glock 29, except for a different calibre, and slightly lighter unloaded weight.

10mm calibre
The Glock 29 used 10mm calibre ammunition that was comparatively powerful, especially for a subcompact pistol. These pistols featured a double recoil spring that absorbed the recoil energy.

Glock 31

SPECIFICATION

MANUFACTURER Glock GmbH.
CALIBRE .357 SIG
MAGAZINE CAPACITY 15, 17
ACTION Recoil/double (SA)
TOTAL LENGTH 186mm/7.32in
BARREL LENGTH 114mm/5in
WEIGHT UNLOADED 660g/23.28oz

With the growing popularity of the new .357 SIG calibre, Glock decided to develop a new pistol in this calibre. The Glock 31 was almost identical to the Glock 22 in appearance. It had a modified slide, frame, larger barrel and magazine. It also had a magazine capacity of 15 rounds and was chambered for the .357 SIG cartridge, which was preferred by many shooters. This pistol was designed primarily for law enforcement duties. It was not as comfortable to shoot as the Glock 22 as it had a sharper recoil.

Glock 32

SPECIFICATION

MANUFACTURER Glock GmbH.
CALIBRE .357 SIG
MAGAZINE CAPACITY 13, 15, 17
ACTION Recoil/double (SA)
TOTAL LENGTH 174mm/6.85in
BARREL LENGTH 102mm/4in
WEIGHT UNLOADED 610g/21.52oz

The Glock 32 was a compact Glock, almost identical to the Glock 19 and the Glock 23. They were identical in barrel length and external dimensions. The Glock 32 was slightly heavier in unloaded weight, which may have been due to a wider barrel width, used a .357 cartridge and used a modified slide and frame. It was designed for law enforcement duties. The Glock 32 could be converted to .40 S&W.

Wear resistant
Glock pistols are treated with Tenifer in the final stage of hardening to improve corrosion and wear resistance. The process involves what is known as carbonitriding, whereby the metal absorbs both carbon and nitrogen.

Glocks 33, 34 and 35

Introduced in 1997, this pistol was a subcompact version and about the same size as the Glock 26 and Glock 27, and the smallest Glock available in .357 chambering. It had a magazine with a capacity of 9 rounds, with a legal limit of 10 rounds, which could be acquired through a magazine extension kit. More innovations were made in the same year by developing the International Practical Shooting Federation (IPSF)-sized Glock 34 in 9mm Parabellum and the Glock 35 in .40 ACP.

SPECIFICATION

MANUFACTURER Glock GmbH.
CALIBRE .357 SIG (G33), 9mm
  Parabellum (G34), .40 ACP (G35)
MAGAZINE CAPACITY 9 to 33
ACTION Recoil/double (SA)
TOTAL LENGTH 160mm/6.3in
BARREL LENGTH 88mm/3.46in
WEIGHT UNLOADED 560g/19.75oz

Glock 36

Introduced in 1999, this pistol was distinguished from the others in the Glock family by its slimline design, for ease of concealment. It was flatter than the other Glocks so had a more comfortable hold on the trigger. It had a single stack (rather than a double stack) magazine. It was a popular model for personal defence, providing a potency of firepower with ease of handling.

SPECIFICATION

MANUFACTURER Glock GmbH.
CALIBRE .45 ACP
MAGAZINE CAPACITY 6
ACTION Recoil/double (SA)
TOTAL LENGTH 172mm/6.77in
BARREL LENGTH 96mm/3.78in
WEIGHT UNLOADED 570g/20.1oz

Glock 37

The G37 first appeared in 2003 and in most respects was similar to the Glock 17, but it had a wider slide and a 10-round magazine. It was designed for law enforcement and self-defence use. Its larger calibre offered improved single-shot stopping power, while avoiding the larger frame-size problems of the Glock 21. The new .45 GAP round added to its appeal.

GAP/ACP
The .45 GAP (Glock Automatic Pistol) is a round specifically devised by Glock. It is slightly shorter than the .45 ACP round designed by John Browning and it is said to have comparable performance.

SPECIFICATION

MANUFACTURER Glock GmbH.
CALIBRE .45 GAP
MAGAZINE CAPACITY 10
ACTION Recoil/double (SA)
TOTAL LENGTH 186mm/7.32in
BARREL LENGTH 114mm/4.5in
WEIGHT UNLOADED 735g/25.92oz

Glock 38

This pistol was first produced in 2005 and featured the .45 GAP cartridge. Designed by Glock, the .45 GAP cartridge had the same performance as the .45 ACP cartridge but was short enough to fit into smaller-framed pistols. In law enforcement and self-defence, the large calibre of this pistol was intended to offer improved single-shot stopping power, while maintaining the benefits of a smaller frame for easier concealed carry.

SPECIFICATION

MANUFACTURER Glock GmbH.
CALIBRE .45 GAP
MAGAZINE CAPACITY 8, 10
ACTION Recoil/double (SA)
TOTAL LENGTH 174mm/6.85in
BARREL LENGTH 102mm/4in
WEIGHT UNLOADED 685g/24.16oz

Glock 39

The Glock 39 was released in 2005. Like the Glock 37 it used the .45 GAP cartridge. The Glock 39 had the same frame size as the Glock 26 (in 9mm) and the Glock 27 (.40 S&W). It was one of the lightest of all Glock pistols when unloaded, which made it ideal for self-defence by a concealed weapons carrier. It was designed for law enforcement and self-defence use. Its large calibre offered considerable single-shot stopping power, while the smaller frame made it easier for concealed carry.

SPECIFICATION

MANUFACTURER Glock GmbH.
CALIBRE .45 GAP
MAGAZINE CAPACITY 6, 8, 10
ACTION Recoil/double (SA)
TOTAL LENGTH 160mm/6.3in
BARREL LENGTH 88mm/3.46in
WEIGHT UNLOADED 548g/19.33oz

Mannlicher M1900

barrel — front sight

hammer

SPECIFICATION

MANUFACTURER Osterreichische
  Waffenfabrik Steyr
CALIBRE 7.63mm Mannlicher
MAGAZINE CAPACITY 8
ACTION Delayed blowback/single
TOTAL LENGTH 246mm/9.69in
BARREL LENGTH 160mm/6.3in
WEIGHT UNLOADED 910g/32.1oz

This was a delayed-blowback pistol with a heavy spring and large external hammer. The barrel was screwed into the breech. The slide included the extractor and the firing pin. As it moved back, the slide cocked the hammer. After recoil, the slide re-chambered a fresh round as it moved back into position. The magazine was integral to the hand grip and was loaded with a charger. This innovative pistol possibly did not achieve the success it deserved in Europe, but it was adopted by the Argentine armed forces as the Modelo 1905 and produced in considerable numbers.

Roth-Steyr M1907

barrel — breech — bolt

SPECIFICATION

MANUFACTURER Osterreichische
  Waffenfabrik Steyr
CALIBRE 8mm Steyr
MAGAZINE CAPACITY 10
ACTION Recoil/single
TOTAL LENGTH 233mm/9.17in
BARREL LENGTH 131mm/5.16in
WEIGHT UNLOADED 1,030g/36.3oz

This pistol, developed by George Roth, was first issued to the Austro-Hungarian Cavalry in 1907. The unusual design included a bolt that extended the full length of the receiver. The front part of the bolt was hollow and this part surrounded the barrel, while the rear part was solid, apart from the area round the striker. On recoil, the barrel rotated until lugs engaged with the breech and stopped the movement. The spent round was ejected through the top of the receiver casing and a new round was chambered. These pistols were also issued to the Italian Army.

Steyr Hahn M1911/M1912

SPECIFICATION

MANUFACTURER Osterreichische
  Waffenfabriks-Gesellschaft
CALIBRE 9mm Steyr
MAGAZINE CAPACITY 8
ACTION Recoil/single
TOTAL LENGTH 216mm/8.5in
BARREL LENGTH 128mm/5.04in
WEIGHT UNLOADED 1,020g/35.98oz

Steyr Hahn
"Hahn" is a German word that means hammer. The hammer on this pistol is clumsy but workable.

The M1911 was designed by firearms designer Karel Krnka, and was believed to be based on an earlier work by George Roth. It was a recoil-operated pistol that was developed primarily for military use. Both the slide and barrel moved back during recoil and the barrel rotated through approximately 20 degrees. When the slide stopped, the barrel continued backwards, extracting the empty case. When the barrel returned, it chambered a new round. It worked well and was both a notable mechanism and a fine example of precision machining. The M1911 had a fixed blade front sight, while the M1912, produced a year later, was identical except for a dovetailed front sight. Numbers of these weapons were taken over by the German Army after the annexation of Austria by Germany in 1938. The Germans standardized many of these weapons to 9mm Parabellum (named P-08) at the Mauser firm.

Rast & Gasser M1898

This was an eight-chamber revolver first made by Rast & Gasser of Vienna in the 1870s. The M1898 was used widely by Austrians in World War I, and many were in the hands of Italians in World War II.

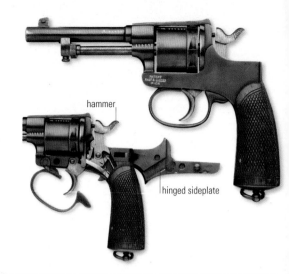

hammer

RIGHT The M1898 had a hinged sideplate that could be opened to allow access to the internal workings of the revolver. When the gun was opened the trigger was disconnected from the hammer.

hinged sideplate

SPECIFICATION

MANUFACTURER Rast & Gasser
CALIBRE 8mm Rast & Gasser
CYLINDERS 8
ACTION Single/double
TOTAL LENGTH 220mm/8.66in
BARREL LENGTH 116mm/4.57in
WEIGHT UNLOADED 1,077g/38oz

Steyr Mannlicher M1894

The first version of this pistol was produced in 1894 in Switzerland by the Austrian firm Mannlicher and several years of development followed. The pistol was a departure in pistol design as it used a concept known as "blow forward" whereby the barrel was moved forward against a spring positioned around the barrel to extract the empty cartridge and to strip off a new cartridge. The hammer was manually cocked by the user. Rounds were loaded via a clip into the receiver and the cartridges could then be pressed into the magazine.

SPECIFICATION

MANUFACTURER Schweizerische Industrie-Gesellschaft (SIG)
CALIBRE 6.5mm Mannlicher
MAGAZINE CAPACITY 5
ACTION Blow forward/single
TOTAL LENGTH 215mm/8.46in
BARREL LENGTH 165mm/6.5in
WEIGHT UNLOADED 850g/30oz

Steyr GB (Gas Break)

de-cocking lever

In the early 1970s, Austria decided to replace the standard army issue P38 pistol and the Browning High-Power with a new model. A new pistol was developed, originally known as the P1-18, which later came to be known as the Steyr GB. Production for the GB ran from 1981 to 1988 and up to 20,000 pistols were thought to have been produced. The GB was manufactured from carbon steel and the chrome-lined barrel was attached solidly to the frame. The pistol was gas-retarded and blowback-operated, which produced a minimal amount of recoil. It was fitted with a double-action trigger and included a slide-mounted de-cocking lever.

SPECIFICATION

MANUFACTURER Steyr Mannlicher AG & Co. KG.
CALIBRE 9mm Parabellum
MAGAZINE CAPACITY 18
ACTION Blowback/double
TOTAL LENGTH 216mm/8.5in
BARREL LENGTH 136mm/5.35in
WEIGHT UNLOADED 845g/29.81oz

Barnitzke
The GB uses a gas-delayed blowback action developed by a German engineer and known as the Barnitzke system.

Steyr SPP (Special Purpose Pistol)

SPECIFICATION

MANUFACTURER Steyr Mannlicher
AG & Co. KG.

CALIBRE 9mm Parabellum

MAGAZINE CAPACITY 15 or 30

ACTION Delayed blowback/single

TOTAL LENGTH 282mm/11.1in

BARREL LENGTH 130mm/5.12in

WEIGHT UNLOADED 1,300g/45.86oz

The 9mm Steyr SPP, developed in 1993, was a civilian semi-automatic version of the Steyr TMP (Tactical Machine Pistol), categorized as a submachine gun. The Steyr SPP used the same frame and receiver as the TMP. It allowed for a two-handed hold, with one hand on the grip and the other on a spur at the front of the pistol. The SPP was supplied with a 15-round magazine, but 30-round magazines were also available. It had a delayed-blowback operating system, and a locked-breech design with rotating barrel. This design provided more accuracy during rapid fire than simple blowback pistols.

Steyr M40

SPECIFICATION

MANUFACTURER Steyr Mannlicher
AG & Co. KG.

CALIBRE .40 S&W

MAGAZINE CAPACITY 12

ACTION Short recoil/double

TOTAL LENGTH 180mm/7.1in

BARREL LENGTH 102mm/4in

WEIGHT UNLOADED 794g/28oz

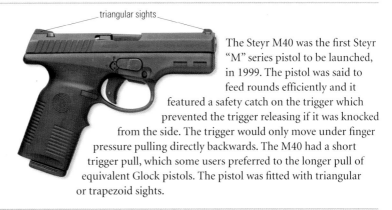

triangular sights

The Steyr M40 was the first Steyr "M" series pistol to be launched, in 1999. The pistol was said to feed rounds efficiently and it featured a safety catch on the trigger which prevented the trigger releasing if it was knocked from the side. The trigger would only move under finger pressure pulling directly backwards. The M40 had a short trigger pull, which some users preferred to the longer pull of equivalent Glock pistols. The pistol was fitted with triangular or trapezoid sights.

Steyr M9

SPECIFICATION

MANUFACTURER Steyr Mannlicher
AG & Co. KG.

CALIBRE 9mm Parabellum

MAGAZINE CAPACITY 14

ACTION Short recoil/single

TOTAL LENGTH 180mm/7.1in

BARREL LENGTH 102mm/4in

WEIGHT UNLOADED 794g/28oz

Variations
Since the M9 pistol came on to the market a number of variations have also been introduced, including the M40, M357 and smaller models called the S9, S40 and S357.

This pistol, launched in 1999, featured a number of innovations and was manufactured using advanced polymer synthetics, typical of the Steyr brand. The M9 pistol was the result of careful development by Steyr in order to match the highly successful Glock pistols. It had the first integrated limited-access key-lock safety for use when the gun was cocked – and also featured triangular or trapezoid sights, designed for rapid target acquisition. The pistol also had a chamber-loaded indicator that could be both seen and touched. The pistol was developed mainly for law enforcement duties, although some earlier models were thought to have too light a trigger; the trigger resistance was increased in later models.

triangular sight

triangular sight (inverted v-shape)

Manual safety catch

Key-operated safety lock

ABOVE The manual safety can be used when the gun is cocked. It is activated by pulling down one of the little catches on either side of the gun just above the front of the trigger guard.

Sweden

With regard to the specific manufacture of pistols and revolvers, Sweden has relied almost exclusively on imports or weapons manufactured in Sweden under licence. Until 1943, a copy of the Browning 1903 was the standard service weapon, after which a copy of the Finnish Lahti pistol was brought in.

Nagant 1887

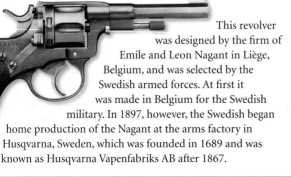

This revolver was designed by the firm of Emile and Leon Nagant in Liège, Belgium, and was selected by the Swedish armed forces. At first it was made in Belgium for the Swedish military. In 1897, however, the Swedish began home production of the Nagant at the arms factory in Husqvarna, Sweden, which was founded in 1689 and was known as Husqvarna Vapenfabriks AB after 1867.

SPECIFICATION

MANUFACTURER E & L Nagant, Liège/ Husqvarna Vapenfabriks AB.
CALIBRE 7.5mm Nagant
CYLINDER 6
ACTION Double
TOTAL LENGTH 235mm/9.25in
BARREL LENGTH 114mm/4.5in
WEIGHT UNLOADED 770g/27.2oz

Browning 1907

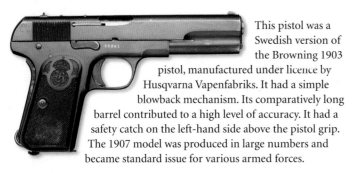

This pistol was a Swedish version of the Browning 1903 pistol, manufactured under licence by Husqvarna Vapenfabriks. It had a simple blowback mechanism. Its comparatively long barrel contributed to a high level of accuracy. It had a safety catch on the left-hand side above the pistol grip. The 1907 model was produced in large numbers and became standard issue for various armed forces.

SPECIFICATION

MANUFACTURER Husqvarna Vapenfabriks AB.
CALIBRE 9mm Browning Long
MAGAZINE CAPACITY 7
ACTION Blowback/single
TOTAL LENGTH 203mm/8in
BARREL LENGTH 127mm/5in
WEIGHT UNLOADED 910g/32oz

Lahti Husqvarna Model 40

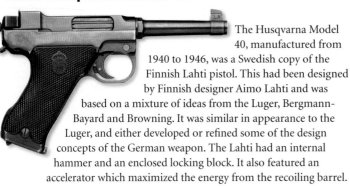

The Husqvarna Model 40, manufactured from 1940 to 1946, was a Swedish copy of the Finnish Lahti pistol. This had been designed by Finnish designer Aimo Lahti and was based on a mixture of ideas from the Luger, Bergmann-Bayard and Browning. It was similar in appearance to the Luger, and either developed or refined some of the design concepts of the German weapon. The Lahti had an internal hammer and an enclosed locking block. It also featured an accelerator which maximized the energy from the recoiling barrel.

SPECIFICATION

MANUFACTURER Husqvarna Vapenfabriks AB.
CALIBRE 9mm Parabellum
MAGAZINE CAPACITY 8
ACTION Short recoil/single
TOTAL LENGTH 240mm/9.45in
BARREL LENGTH 120mm/4.72in
WEIGHT UNLOADED 1,250g/44oz

Czech Republic

The Czech Republic has a tradition of quality arms manufacturing, centred around the Skoda works. The largest producer of small arms is the firm of Ceská Zbrojovka. Founded in 1936, the firm has established an excellent reputation for well-designed and rugged sidearms. One pistol in its line-up, the CZ75B, is said to be the most widely issued pistol to military and police forces around the world.

Ceská Zbrojovka CZ22

SPECIFICATION

MANUFACTURER Ceská Zbrojovka
CALIBRE 9mm Vzor 22
MAGAZINE CAPACITY 8
ACTION Short recoil/single
TOTAL LENGTH 152mm/5.98in
BARREL LENGTH 91mm/3.58in
WEIGHT UNLOADED 700g/24.69oz

This pistol was initially developed by Josef Nickel for German arms company Mauser, who decided not to take it up. When Nickel moved to the Czech arms factory at Brno to deliver new machinery, he discovered that the Czechs were seeking a pistol and he continued to develop it there. The design was complex, involving a rotating barrel which locked the breech, and the pistol was expensive. Although a new version was introduced in 1922, only about 35,000 of the type were produced before production ceased in 1926. Unfortunately the 9mm Vzor 22 cartridge was not widely used.

Ceská Zbrojovka CZ24

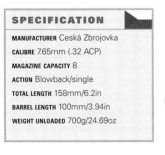

SPECIFICATION

MANUFACTURER Ceská Zbrojovka
CALIBRE 7.65mm (.32 ACP)
MAGAZINE CAPACITY 8
ACTION Short recoil/single
TOTAL LENGTH 152mm/5.98in
BARREL LENGTH 91mm/3.58in
WEIGHT UNLOADED 700g/24.69oz

The CZ24 pistol was a development of the CZ22 and finally achieved what the CZ22 had not in 1925: acceptance by the Czech Army. Although there were some minor visible differences between the CZ24 and its predecessor, such as a magazine safety, the crucial change was the adoption of the more popular 7.65mm (.32 ACP) cartridge. Production began in June 1926 in a new factory and by 1937 some 190,000 had been delivered. However, the complicated mechanism was expensive and inefficient to produce. This would be resolved to some extent in the CZ27.

Ceská Zbrojovka CZ27

SPECIFICATION

MANUFACTURER Ceská Zbrojovka
CALIBRE 7.65mm (.32 ACP)
MAGAZINE CAPACITY 8
ACTION Blowback/single
TOTAL LENGTH 158mm/6.2in
BARREL LENGTH 100mm/3.94in
WEIGHT UNLOADED 700g/24.69oz

Despite the relative success of the CZ24, its complex design meant that the development of a simplified version was just a matter of time. Designer Frantishek Myshka took on the task before 1939 and came up with the CZ27, that was outwardly similar to the CZ24 but radically different under the surface. The CZ27 had a conventional blowback mechanism and used the reduced calibre 7.65mm round. It was easier and cheaper to produce than the CZ24. The CZ27 was adopted by the German Army when it occupied Czechoslovakia and renamed it the Pistole 2727(t).

Ceská Zbrojovka CZ38

Although this double-action pistol from 1936 was sturdily made, it was difficult to shoot with one hand and the trigger heavy to pull, due to the self-cocking mechanism. The physical effort required made accurate shooting difficult. However, the pistol was easy to dismantle and clean, with a hinge at the muzzle that allowed the barrel and slide to be raised. Limited production meant the pistol never found its way into the Czech Army before the German invasion in 1939.

SPECIFICATION	
MANUFACTURER	Ceská Zbrojovka
CALIBRE	.380 ACP
MAGAZINE CAPACITY	8
ACTION	Blowback/double
TOTAL LENGTH	206mm/8.11in
BARREL LENGTH	118mm/4.65in
WEIGHT UNLOADED	940g/33.16oz

Ceská Zbrojovka CZ50

The Czech Ministry of the Interior ordered a new pistol based on the Walther PP in the late 1940s. The basic mechanics of the Walther PP were maintained, including the double-action mechanism, but otherwise there were a number of minor modifications. It proved to be an undistinguished and somewhat unreliable weapon. The CZ50 was produced through to the late 1960s when development of a replacement, the CZ70, took place.

SPECIFICATION	
MANUFACTURER	Ceská Zbrojovka
CALIBRE	7.65mm, .32 ACP
MAGAZINE CAPACITY	8
ACTION	Blowback/double
TOTAL LENGTH	167mm/6.6in
BARREL LENGTH	94mm/3.7in
WEIGHT UNLOADED	660g/23.28oz

Ceská Zbrojovka CZ52

This pistol was first produced in 1952. It was single-action with a recoil mechanism which involved the barrel and slide being interlocked by two rollers, upon which they recoiled together. The rollers then moved together again which released the slide. Once the barrel stopped moving, the slide continued rearwards to eject an empty case and strip off a new round. The pistol featured a three-position manual safety and could be carried "cocked and locked".

SPECIFICATION	
MANUFACTURER	Ceská Zbrojovka
CALIBRE	7.62mm Tokarev
MAGAZINE CAPACITY	8
ACTION	Short recoil/single
TOTAL LENGTH	209mm/8.23in
BARREL LENGTH	120mm/4.72in
WEIGHT UNLOADED	950g/33.51oz

Ceská Zbrojovka CZ70

The CZ70 was developed in order to remedy the problems that had emerged in the CZ50, mostly with regard to reliability. The internal dimensions were modified and some of the construction materials were changed. One of the visible differences between the CZ50 and the CZ70 was that the latter had a hollow circle in the hammer, while the hammer of the CZ50 was solid. The pistol was manufactured from 1970 to 1984.

SPECIFICATION	
MANUFACTURER	Ceská Zbrojovka
CALIBRE	.32 ACP
MAGAZINE CAPACITY	8
ACTION	Blowback/double
TOTAL LENGTH	167mm/6.6in
BARREL LENGTH	94mm/3.7in
WEIGHT UNLOADED	660g/23.28oz

Ceská Zbrojovka CZ75

Introduced in 1975, this pistol soon became an established favourite among many armed forces around the world. The CZ75 was a pistol that used the locked-breech principle. It was recoil-operated and chambered for the 9mm Parabellum cartridge. It had a double-action trigger system, with the safety catch on the left side of the frame, locking the hammer linkage. It was similar to the Browning High-Power.

SPECIFICATION

MANUFACTURER Ceská Zbrojovka
CALIBRE 9mm Parabellum
MAGAZINE CAPACITY 8
ACTION Short recoil/double
TOTAL LENGTH 203mm/8in
BARREL LENGTH 120mm/4.7in
WEIGHT UNLOADED 1,000g/35.27oz

Ceská Zbrojovka CZ83

SPECIFICATION

MANUFACTURER Ceská Zbrojovka
CALIBRE .45 Makarov and .380 ACP
MAGAZINE CAPACITY 15
ACTION Blowback/double or single
TOTAL LENGTH 173mm/6.81in
BARREL LENGTH 96mm/3.78in
WEIGHT UNLOADED 650g/22.93oz

The CZ83, developed in 1983, was a blowback pistol with a double-action trigger mechanism. An automatic safety system ensured that the hammer would not operate unless the trigger was fully pressed. There was also an ambidextrous safety catch and a magazine safety. The CZ83 was widely issued to security forces in former Czechoslovakia. The CZ83's compact design meant that it was useful for undercover duties and also for personal defence. The ergonomics, calibre and light weight lend themselves to an easy-to-operate weapon.

Ceská Zbrojovka CZ85

SPECIFICATION

MANUFACTURER Ceská Zbrojovka
CALIBRE 9mm Parabellum
MAGAZINE CAPACITY 16
ACTION Short recoil/double
TOTAL LENGTH 206mm/8.11in
BARREL LENGTH 120mm/4.72in
WEIGHT UNLOADED 1,000g/35.27oz

This pistol was derived from the successful CZ75 and was made from the mid-1980s. The pistol featured a firing-pin safety to enhance the drop-safety advantages of this firearm. It also had an ambidextrous manual safety lever and slide stop. The pistol was designed for maximum comfort in either hand, with a well-proportioned rubber-lined hand grip. It had a three-dot illuminated sight system and in the Combat version of this pistol, the rear sights are adjustable.

Ceská Zbrojovka CZ92

SPECIFICATION

MANUFACTURER Ceská Zbrojovka
CALIBRE .25 ACP
MAGAZINE CAPACITY 8
ACTION Short recoil/DAO
TOTAL LENGTH 126mm/4.94in
BARREL LENGTH 64mm/2.52in
WEIGHT UNLOADED 309g/10.9oz

This was a subcompact handgun designed for maximum ease of concealment, either for personal defence or for covert operations. Although it did not have a manual safety, the hammer returned to its position after each discharge as a protection against unintentional discharge. The pistol also had a magazine safety, which meant that the trigger mechanism would not operate if a magazine was not fitted. The pistol was ergonomically designed and ambidextrous.

Ceská Zbrojovka CZ97

First introduced in 1997, this was a more powerful version of the successful CZ75 and is described as one of the best combat handguns of the 20th century. The construction was all steel and the barrel was hammer forged, which is said to provide greater accuracy. It also featured a chamber-loaded indicator and an ergonomic grip. The gun used the locked-breech principle and was double action. The slide remained locked open when the last magazine from the cartridge had been fired. The pistol also incorporated a firing-pin safety to prevent accidental discharge when it was dropped. The weapon was said to be well balanced and to have a high level of accuracy. It had a long service life and was both rugged and reliable.

SPECIFICATION

MANUFACTURER Ceská Zbrojovka
CALIBRE .45 ACP
MAGAZINE CAPACITY 10
ACTION Short recoil/double
TOTAL LENGTH 212mm/8.35in
BARREL LENGTH 123mm/4.84in
WEIGHT UNLOADED 1,150g/40.57oz

Ceská Zbrojovka CZ100

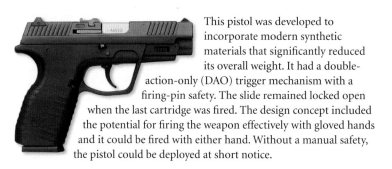

This pistol was developed to incorporate modern synthetic materials that significantly reduced its overall weight. It had a double-action-only (DAO) trigger mechanism with a firing-pin safety. The slide remained locked open when the last cartridge was fired. The design concept included the potential for firing the weapon effectively with gloved hands and it could be fired with either hand. Without a manual safety, the pistol could be deployed at short notice.

SPECIFICATION

MANUFACTURER Ceská Zbrojovka
CALIBRE 9mm Parabellum
MAGAZINE CAPACITY 13
ACTION Short recoil/DAO
TOTAL LENGTH 180mm/7.1in
BARREL LENGTH 98mm/3.86in
WEIGHT UNLOADED 665g/23.46oz

Poland

Poland produced a high-quality pistol known as the Radom before World War II. It was an ingenious design and proved popular with its users. Manufacture of the Radom was taken over by the Germans after the invasion of Poland. Subsequent production of pistols in Poland was based around designs such as the Soviet Makarov. More recent designs have been produced by the Polish firm Zaklady Metalowe.

Radom or VIS Model 1935

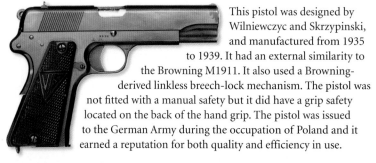

This pistol was designed by Wilniewczyc and Skrzypinski, and manufactured from 1935 to 1939. It had an external similarity to the Browning M1911. It also used a Browning-derived linkless breech-lock mechanism. The pistol was not fitted with a manual safety but it did have a grip safety located on the back of the hand grip. The pistol was issued to the German Army during the occupation of Poland and it earned a reputation for both quality and efficiency in use.

SPECIFICATION

MANUFACTURER Fabryka Broni Radom
CALIBRE 9mm Parabellum
MAGAZINE CAPACITY 8
ACTION Short recoil/single
TOTAL LENGTH 205mm/8.1in
BARREL LENGTH 115mm/4.53in
WEIGHT UNLOADED 1,025g/36.16oz

M48

SPECIFICATION

MANUFACTURER Radom
CALIBRE 7.62mm Tokarev
MAGAZINE CAPACITY 8
ACTION Recoil/single
TOTAL LENGTH 193mm/7.59in
BARREL LENGTH 116mm/4.57in
WEIGHT UNLOADED 830g/29.28oz

This pistol, produced in 1930, was a Polish version of the Russian Tokarev TT33. The design was influenced by the 1903 Colt .38. It had a single action with recoil operation. One difference from the Browning design was that certain parts of the mechanism, including the hammer and lockwork, were removable, which made for ease of maintenance or replacement. In Poland, Hungary and the former Yugoslavia, locally produced TT33s were all known as the M48.

P64

triangular hammer

serial number and date of manufacture

double-action trigger

SPECIFICATION

MANUFACTURER State Arsenals
CALIBRE 9mm Makarov
MAGAZINE CAPACITY 6
ACTION Blowback/single or double
TOTAL LENGTH 155mm/6.1in
BARREL LENGTH 84mm/3.31in
WEIGHT UNLOADED 636g/22.43oz

The Makarov round
The 9mm Makarov round was widely used by Soviet armed forces and by Soviet Bloc allies. For size and power it fell between the .38 ACP and 9mm Parabellum.

This pistol was a replacement for the Pistolet TT, which in turn was based on the Tokarev TT33 pistol. The P64 was developed in the late 1950s. It was a blowback-operated pistol which appeared to have been influenced by both the Makarov and the Walther PP pistol designs. It had a double-action mechanism and the safety catch was located on the slide. It could also be fired in single-action mode and this involved pulling back the external hammer. The P64 was relatively small and light and could be easily concealed.

P83

SPECIFICATION

MANUFACTURER State Arsenals
CALIBRE 9mm Makarov
MAGAZINE CAPACITY 8
ACTION Blowback/single or double
TOTAL LENGTH 165mm/6.5in
BARREL LENGTH 90mm/3.54in
WEIGHT UNLOADED 730g/25.75oz

The P83 featured various improvements over the previous P64 service pistol in terms of both manufacturing cost and effectiveness in combat. It also had a larger magazine. This was a blowback-operated pistol manufactured largely from stamped steel parts. It had a double-action trigger and a safety/de-cocking device was mounted on the slide. Unlike the P64, the magazine release catch was located at the bottom of the plastic hand grip. It had fixed sights, with the rear sight dovetailed into the slide. The pistol was issued to Polish military and police forces in the early 1980s and proved to be rugged and reliable.

Serbia

Since before World War II, small-arms production in the former Yugoslavia has been based at the firm of Zavodi Crvena Zastava (meaning "Red Flag"). It is located 138 km (86 miles) south-east of Belgrade and still produces a wide range of both civilian and military small arms today, based on Russian or German designs.

Zastava M57 and M57 Lux

This pistol, introduced in 1957, had a short-recoil barrel and a locked breech. The design was based on the Soviet Tokarev TT33. The basic version of the M57 had an old-fashioned look which was very similar to the original Russian pistol, except that its grip frame and magazine were longer and it held one more round of ammunition. Zastava also produced the M57 Lux version, which had an ergonomic hand grip and a stainless-steel finish to the receiver. The M57 was primarily designed as a personal defence weapon and was easy to handle and maintain.

SPECIFICATION	
MANUFACTURER Zastava Arms Co.	
CALIBRE 7.62mm Tokarev	
MAGAZINE CAPACITY 9	
ACTION Short recoil/single	
TOTAL LENGTH 200mm/7.87in	
BARREL LENGTH 116mm/4.57in	
WEIGHT UNLOADED 850g/29.98oz	

Zastava M70 and M70A

Like the M57, the M70 had a short-recoil barrel and a locked breech. The design was also based on the Tokarev TT33, and its operation was based on the Browning swing-link system. The M70, and improved version the M70A, were very similar to the M57. The main difference is that they were chambered for the 9mm Parabellum cartridge and had improved rifling in the barrel. The change of calibre made the pistol slightly easier and more comfortable to handle and more attractive for export.

SPECIFICATION	
MANUFACTURER Zastava Arms Co.	
CALIBRE 9mm Parabellum	
MAGAZINE CAPACITY 9	
ACTION Short recoil/single	
TOTAL LENGTH 200mm/7.87in	
BARREL LENGTH 116mm/4.57in	
WEIGHT UNLOADED 850g/29.98oz	

Zastava M70 and M70(k) Pocket Pistol

Like the M57, this pistol had a short recoil barrel and a locked breech, but chambered for .32 ACP. The design was also based on the Tokarev TT33, and the Browning swing-link system. The M70 Pocket Pistol was was primarily designed as a personal defence weapon and for police use, and was easy to handle and maintain. A variant, known as the M70(k) was chambered for the 9mm cartridge. Apart from the difference in calibre, these pistols were otherwise the same.

SPECIFICATION	
MANUFACTURER Zastava Arms Co.	
CALIBRE .32 ACP	
MAGAZINE CAPACITY 9	
ACTION Short recoil/single	
TOTAL LENGTH 200mm/7.87in	
BARREL LENGTH 94mm/3.7in	
WEIGHT UNLOADED 740g/26.1oz	

Police and military use
For many years this pistol was used by the Yugoslavian Police and military officers. They are still sold worldwide.

Zastava M83/84

SPECIFICATION

MANUFACTURER Zastava Arms Co.

CALIBRE .357 Magnum, .38 Special

CYLINDER 6

ACTION Double

TOTAL LENGTH 254mm/10in

BARREL LENGTH 64mm/2.52in

WEIGHT UNLOADED 900g/31.75oz

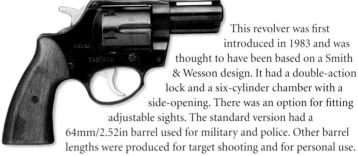

This revolver was first introduced in 1983 and was thought to have been based on a Smith & Wesson design. It had a double-action lock and a six-cylinder chamber with a side-opening. There was an option for fitting adjustable sights. The standard version had a 64mm/2.52in barrel used for military and police. Other barrel lengths were produced for target shooting and for personal use.

Zastava CZ99

The design is thought to be influenced by the SIG-Sauer P220. It was a double-action, locked-breech semi-automatic pistol with a forged-steel barrel. It had an ambidextrous safety lever and de-cocking lever, the latter positioned underneath the grip on the left. The pistol also had a chamber-loaded indicator and an indicator to show when there are only three rounds left in the magazine. The pistol was ergonomically designed and had a visible hammer. There is also a .40 S&W version and a compact version (CZ99G Compact). The Zastava CZ999 was the most recent addition to the Zastava range.

SPECIFICATION

MANUFACTURER Zastava Arms Co.

CALIBRE 9mm Parabellum, .40 S&W

MAGAZINE CAPACITY 10 (9mm Parabellum) or 15 (.40 S&W)

ACTION Short recoil/double

TOTAL LENGTH 198mm/7.8in

BARREL LENGTH 108mm/4.25in

WEIGHT UNLOADED 920g/32.45oz

Hungary

The Hungarian Army's requirements in the early 20th century were satisfied by Rudolf Frommer, George Roth and Karel Krnka designs. The Frommer Stop pistol was unusual for having a long-recoil system.

This design tradition is continued by the company known today as FÉGArmy Arms Manufacturing Ltd, in Budapest. It specializes in precision engineering, mostly for arms manufacturing.

Frommer M1910

SPECIFICATION

MANUFACTURER Fegyver es Gepgyar Reszvenytarsasag (FÉG)

CALIBRE .32 ACP

MAGAZINE 8

ACTION Recoil/single

TOTAL LENGTH 186mm/7.32in

BARREL LENGTH 100mm/3.94in

WEIGHT UNLOADED 635g/22.4oz

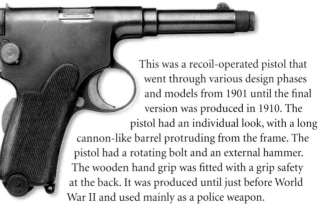

This was a recoil-operated pistol that went through various design phases and models from 1901 until the final version was produced in 1910. The pistol had an individual look, with a long cannon-like barrel protruding from the frame. The pistol had a rotating bolt and an external hammer. The wooden hand grip was fitted with a grip safety at the back. It was produced until just before World War II and used mainly as a police weapon.

Frommer Stop 1912

This pistol was an unusual design as it operated on the long-recoil system. The Frommer Stop 1912 was developed by Rudolf Frommer and was issued to the Austro-Hungarian Army and Police. When the pistol was fired, the bolt and the barrel lock recoiled together. Two recoil springs were compressed, one for the barrel and one for the bolt. The bolt was temporarily held by a catch while the barrel-recoil spring pushed the barrel back to its original position. The barrel released the catch and the bolt was also returned to position by its spring. As they returned, the barrel stripped out the empty case while the bolt chambered the next round. The bolt rotated to lock the breech.

SPECIFICATION

MANUFACTURER Fegyver es Gepgyar Reszvenytarsasag (FÉG)
CALIBRE 7.65mm Frommer, .380 ACP
MAGAZINE 7
ACTION Long recoil/single
TOTAL LENGTH 186mm/7.32in
BARREL LENGTH 100mm/3.94in
WEIGHT UNLOADED 635g/22.4oz

Frommer Baby 1912

The Frommer Stop and Frommer Baby were patented in 1912. Most of the early guns produced were the Frommer Baby, in both 7.65mm (similar to but not intechangeable with .32 ACP) and .380 ACP calibres. The Frommer Baby was produced in small quantities at first, probably because the Fegyver es Gepgyar factory in Budapest was also producing the Roth Steyr pistol for service between 1911 and 1914. The Frommer Baby was mainly produced for the civilian market in .32 ACP, but a small number was produced for the Hungarian Air Force. It is thought that the Frommer Baby and Frommer Stop were made until the end of the 1920s.

SPECIFICATION

MANUFACTURER Fegyver es Gepgyar Reszvenytarsasag (FÉG)
CALIBRE 7.65mm Frommer, .380 ACP
MAGAZINE 5 or 6
ACTION Recoil/single
TOTAL LENGTH 122mm/4.8in
BARREL LENGTH 58mm/2.3in
WEIGHT UNLOADED 500g/17.6oz

Rudolph Frommer

This Hungarian designer was born in Budapest in 1868. During his lifetime he registered over 100 patents for pistols and machine guns.

Frommer Model 1937

SPECIFICATION

MANUFACTURER Femaru es Szerszamgepgyar NV
CALIBRE 7.65mm Frommer
MAGAZINE 7
ACTION Blowback/single
TOTAL LENGTH 182mm/7.17in
BARREL LENGTH 110mm/4.33in
WEIGHT UNLOADED 770g/27.2oz

This pistol was a development of an earlier model from 1929. It was a blowback-operated pistol with a Browning operation whereby the barrel was retained in the frame. The Model 1937 had an external hammer and there was an extended finger rest at the base of the hand grip. There was a grip safety at the back of the hand grip and the model had a manual safety, as requested by the German Luftwaffe. The marking on the slide indicates the model was part of a contract between the Hungarians and the German government.

Tokarev Tokagypt/48M

This pistol was an adapted version of the Tokarev TT33. The design was influenced by the .38 Colt from 1903. It was recoil operated with a single-action trigger. One difference from the Browning design was that some parts of the mechanism, including the hammer and lockwork, were removable, which made for ease of maintenance or replacement. The Tokagypt had a new safety catch and a revised plastic hand grip. The pistol was designed for the Egyptian armed forces but many ended up on the open market.

SPECIFICATION

MANUFACTURER Femaru es Szerszamgepgyar NV
CALIBRE 9mm Parabellum
MAGAZINE CAPACITY 7
ACTION Recoil/single
TOTAL LENGTH 192mm/7.56in
BARREL LENGTH 115mm/4.53in
WEIGHT UNLOADED 910g/32.1oz

FÉG PA-63 and AP9

SPECIFICATION

MANUFACTURER FÉG
CALIBRE 9mm Makarov (PA-63), .32 ACP, .380 ACP (AP9)
MAGAZINE 8
ACTION Blowback/double
TOTAL LENGTH 170mm/6.7in
BARREL LENGTH 98mm/3.86in
WEIGHT UNLOADED 695g/24.5oz

This pistol was based on the famous Walther PP. It had a double-action lock, and an external hammer and signal pin indicated whether the chamber was loaded. There was a safety catch on the side of the receiver. The return spring was positioned around the fixed barrel. The PA-63 was issued to the Hungarian Army as its official pistol. A civilian version, the AP9, was chambered in .32 ACP and .380 ACP. It had an aluminium frame and had all the same operating features as the PA-63.

SPECIFICATION

MANUFACTURER FÉG
CALIBRE 9mm Parabellum
MAGAZINE 13
ACTION Short recoil/single
TOTAL LENGTH 198mm/7.8in
BARREL LENGTH 118mm/4.64in
WEIGHT UNLOADED 950g/33.51oz

FÉG FP9

This pistol was a copy of the classic FN Belgium M1935 Browning High-Power pistol. It was recoil-operated with a locked breech. The only significant difference was the addition of a ventilated rib to the slide as a cosmetic feature and an aiming aid for sport shooting. Although some guns were used by the police, these pistols were not widely used as service guns in Hungary and were manufactured mainly for export. In Europe, the FP9 pistol was also sold under the name of Mauser, and was known as the Mauser 80SA pistol.

SPECIFICATION

MANUFACTURER FÉG
CALIBRE 9mm Parabellum
MAGAZINE 13
ACTION Short recoil/double
TOTAL LENGTH 234mm/9.21in
BARREL LENGTH 150mm/5.91in
WEIGHT UNLOADED 1,008g/35.56oz

FÉG P9L

This was a competition version of the FP9 and P9M. It was a Browning High-Power copy with a longer barrel and slide and match-type adjustable rear sights. The configuration was suitable for target shooters because it resulted in better ballistic performance, lower recoil, and a longer sighting radius. This pistol also varied from standard Browning High-Power and the FP9 and P9M because it did not have a magazine safety. This allowed the round in the chamber to be fired with the magazine removed.

FÉG P9M

This was FÉG's primary single-action service pistol. The P9M is a short recoil operated, locked breech-pistol. This is a near-exact copy of the FN Belgium M1935 Browning High-Power pistol in its standard version and had all the features of that pistol. The only difference is that the frame-mounted safety lever is longer than the original GP-35 safety lever. The frame and slide are made from carbon steel. The P9M was not used in Hungary as the pistols were intended for export, but may be used as service pistols in other Eastern European countries.

SPECIFICATION

MANUFACTURER FÉG
CALIBRE 9mm Parabellum
MAGAZINE 13
ACTION Short recoil/single
TOTAL LENGTH 198mm/7.8in
BARREL LENGTH 118mm/4.64in
WEIGHT UNLOADED 910g/32.1oz

FÉG P9R

The P9R was FÉG's primary double-action service pistol produced in the early 1990s. This pistol had a steel frame and a double-action firing mechanism with an external hammer. It had a slide-mounted rotating safety that de-cocked the hammer and allowed a round to be chambered with the safety engaged. If carried with the hammer down and the safety off the first shot could be fired double action or the hammer could be manually cocked first. The front sight was permanently fixed to the slide, while the rear sight was dovetailed. In Europe the FÉG P9R was known as the Mauser 90DA, as it was distributed through Mauser. The 90DA was almost identical to the Mauser 90SA except for the double action, larger trigger guard and a safety/de-cocking lever.

SPECIFICATION

MANUFACTURER FÉG
CALIBRE 9mm Parabellum
MAGAZINE 10 or 14
ACTION Short recoil/double
TOTAL LENGTH 203mm/8in
BARREL LENGTH 118mm/4.64in
WEIGHT UNLOADED 1,000g/35.27oz

Romania

Romania produced the Austrian Steyr Hahn M12 under licence and has produced other weapons particularly for Soviet countries. It has been increasing its arms exports in recent years. It exports semi-automatic weapons to the main civilian markets for firearms, Switzerland and the USA.

Steyr Hahn M12

This pistol was adopted by the Austro-Hungarian Army in 1912 and was the official Austrian sidearm during World War I. It had a locked-breech mechanism operated by a rotating barrel with a special 9mm Steyr cartridge, loaded through the top by a charger clip. The pistol was also adopted in Chile and Romania under licence until war caused the Romanian contract to be discontinued. A large number of the Romanian Steyr Hahn pistols were later captured by the Austrians during World War I and pistols with both Romanian parts and Austrian proof marks were common at the time. During World War II many Romanian and Austrian pistols were captured by Germans and converted to 9mm Parabellum.

SPECIFICATION

MANUFACTURER Osterreichische Waffenfabriks-Gesellschaft
CALIBRE 9mm Steyr
MAGAZINE CAPACITY 8
ACTION Recoil/single
TOTAL LENGTH 216mm/8.5in
BARREL LENGTH 128mm/5.1in
WEIGHT UNLOADED 990g/34.92oz

 # Finland

Although Finland has produced relatively few individual pistol and revolver designs, some of them have been outstanding. Some of the most successful, including the Lahti L35, were designed by the famous Finnish master-armourer and self-taught weapons designer, Aimo Johannes Lahti.

Ahlberg

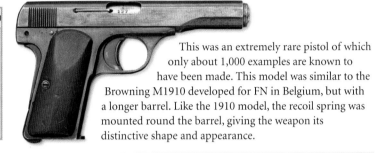

SPECIFICATION

MANUFACTURER Ahlberg	
CALIBRE 7.65mm (.32 ACP)	
MAGAZINE CAPACITY 7	
ACTION Blowback/single	
TOTAL LENGTH 167mm/6.6in	
BARREL LENGTH 95mm/3.75in	
WEIGHT UNLOADED 623.68g/22oz	

This was an extremely rare pistol of which only about 1,000 examples are known to have been made. This model was similar to the Browning M1910 developed for FN in Belgium, but with a longer barrel. Like the 1910 model, the recoil spring was mounted round the barrel, giving the weapon its distinctive shape and appearance.

Lahti L35

bolt

SPECIFICATION

MANUFACTURER Valtion Kivaaritehdas	
(VKT), Jyvastalyla/Valmet Oy	
Tourula Factories	
CALIBRE 9mm Parabellum	
MAGAZINE CAPACITY 8	
ACTION Short recoil/single	
TOTAL LENGTH 245mm/9.68in	
BARREL LENGTH 120mm/4.72in	
WEIGHT UNLOADED 1,220g/43oz	

magazine catch

Disassembly
The Lahti could only be disassembled or stripped for cleaning or repairs by an armourer with access to the correct tools.

This pistol was designed by Aimo Lahti and issued to the Finnish Army during the late 1930s and 1940s. A recoil-operated, single-action, locked-breech pistol with a recoiling barrel, it fired with a concealed hammer. A manual safety was located on the left-hand side. The pistol was fitted with an accelerator which maximized the movement of the bolt to the rear. The pistol earned a reputation for being solid and reliable, although it was very heavy. The Lahti was said to be exceptionally well sealed against the intrusion of dirt and reliable in freezing conditions. However, the use of submachine ammunition (often used by Finnish troops) could cause the slide to crack and many new slides were produced in the 1950s as replacements. The complexity of the design meant that it could not be easily maintained in the field, but was reliable enough to make this situation unusual. The production of the Lahti started in 1936 and over half of the 9,000 pistols produced were issued to the Finnish armed forces. After World War II, the pistols was produced more commercially and also sold abroad. However, after several revisions it was clear that the pistol was too costly and complicated to continue production. Replacement parts for the L35 were manufactured until the 1970s. In 1985, Valmet Oy Tourula Factories made a 50-year commemoration series of L35 pistols. This was the last production series of the pistol.

Russia

Russia and the Soviet Union have produced a wide variety of arms over the 19th and 20th century and competitive designs continue to be produced. In the 1920s the Tokarev TT33 was one of the mainstays, while the the 9mm Makarov was introduced in the 1950s and issued to both Soviet and Warsaw Pact forces. A number of more recent designs have been developed for police, security services and military use.

Nagant Revolver M1895

This revolver was developed in Belgium by Leon Nagant in 1894. It was to become most identified, however, with the Soviet armed forces who bought not only the Nagant M1895 but also the production rights. Unusually for a revolver, the Nagant featured a gas-sealed cylinder which reduced the amount of escaping gas to which many revolvers are prone and thus maximized the propellent force on the round. This mechanism required a uniquely designed round in order to work properly. The Nagant had a solid frame and loading was accomplished via a loading gate on the right side of the frame. It was produced in both single-action and double-action models.

SPECIFICATION	
MANUFACTURER	L. Nagant & Co., Liège/Imperial Russian Arms Factory, Tula
CALIBRE	7.62mm Nagant
CYLINDER	7
ACTION	Double and single
TOTAL LENGTH	229mm/9.33in
BARREL LENGTH	110mm/4.33in
WEIGHT UNLOADED	790g/27.87oz

Korovin TK (Tula Korovin)

manual safety

The Korovin TK was the first semi-automatic pistol produced in the Soviet Union. It was designed by Sergey Korovin in 1926 and, due to its relatively small size, was used both commercially and by military officers as a personal defence weapon. It was a blowback, single-action pistol fired by a striker. It was fitted with a manual safety above the trigger guard and it had fixed sights.

SPECIFICATION	
MANUFACTURER	Soviet Tula Arms Factory
CALIBRE	.25 ACP
MAGAZINE	8
ACTION	Blowback/single
TOTAL LENGTH	127mm/5in
BARREL LENGTH	688mm/27.09in
WEIGHT UNLOADED	423g/14.9oz

Tokarev TT30

This pistol was designed by Fedor V. Tokarev, who also designed a range of weapons for the Soviet Army, including the SVT-1938 automatic rifle and the MT1925 pistol. The TT30 appears to have been based on the Browning Colt M1911, though it incorporated some changes that made for ease of manufacture and replacement, including a modular hammer and lockwork mechanism. It is chambered for the 7.62mm Tokarev cartridge, which is similar to the 7.63mm Mauser round. A modified version, the TT33, was to entirely replace the TT30.

SPECIFICATION	
MANUFACTURER	Soviet Tula Arms Factory
CALIBRE	7.62mm Tokarev
MAGAZINE CAPACITY	8
ACTION	Short recoil/single
TOTAL LENGTH	193mm/7.59in
BARREL LENGTH	116mm/4.57in
WEIGHT UNLOADED	830g/29.28oz

Tokarev TT33

Adopted in 1933, this pistol was a development of the Tokarev TT30. Certain parts of the mechanism, including the hammer and lockwork, were removable, which made for ease of maintenance or replacement. The TT33 had slight modifications in the design of the barrel and also a new locking system and disconnector. Large numbers were produced during World War II and manufacturing continued until the 1950s.

SPECIFICATION

MANUFACTURER Soviet Tula Arsenal
CALIBRE 7.62mm Tokarev
MAGAZINE CAPACITY 8
ACTION Short recoil/single
TOTAL LENGTH 193mm/7.59in
BARREL LENGTH 116mm/4.57in
WEIGHT UNLOADED 830g/29.28oz

Pistolet Makarova (PM)

SPECIFICATION

MANUFACTURER Izhevsk Mechanical Plant (IZHMECH)
CALIBRE 9mm Makarov
MAGAZINE CAPACITY 8
ACTION Recoil/double and single
TOTAL LENGTH 160mm/6.3in
BARREL LENGTH 91mm/3.58in
WEIGHT UNLOADED 663g/23.39oz

This pistol was designed at the end of the 1940s by Nikolai Fyodorovich Makarov and it became standard issue to Soviet armed forces. It was developed as a replacement for the Tokarev TT33. It had a blowback operation, although it was based around a new 9mm round devised by Makarov, which was incompatible with NATO firearms. The weapon had a free firing pin and was designed to have very few parts. It was a double-action, single-action (DA/SA) pistol. The first shot was fired with the hammer down after loosening the safety catch and required a long, heavy trigger pull. All shots after the first were single shots with a light trigger pull.

Pistolet Makarova Modified (PMM)

SPECIFICATION

MANUFACTURER IZHMECH
CALIBRE 9mm Makarov
MAGAZINE CAPACITY 12
ACTION Blowback/double and single
TOTAL LENGTH 169mm/6.65in
BARREL LENGTH 94mm/3.7in
WEIGHT UNLOADED 760g/26.81oz

This, as its name designation suggests, is simply a modified version of the original Makarov PM (Pistolet Makarova) pistol. Steps were taken by a design team in the early 1990s to adapt the existing pistol to take a larger load within the existing cartridge. The magazine size was also increased so that the revised Makarov could take a 12-round magazine instead of the previous 8-round magazine. The design of the hand grip was also changed to make it more comfortable for the user.

Makarov PM silenced

SPECIFICATION

MANUFACTURER IZHMECH
CALIBRE 9mm Makarova
MAGAZINE CAPACITY 8
ACTION Short recoil/double and single
TOTAL LENGTH 160mm/6.3in
BARREL LENGTH 91mm/3.58in
WEIGHT UNLOADED 663g/23.39oz

silencer

The Makarov PM (silenced) was a blowback-operated double-action pistol. The hammer could be cocked manually for a single-action shot. Alternatively, when the trigger was pulled all the way through, the pistol was both cocked and fired automatically. The pistol had a manual safety on the left of the slide and a magazine catch at the base of the hand grip. This silenced version of the Makarov was designed for undercover work and stealth operations.

Baikal-442 pistol

This pistol was a modified version of the Makarov PMM, designed for the export market: it could take both the Russian 9mm Makarov cartridge and the 9mm Luger cartridge and an 8, 10 or 12-round magazine. Like the Makarov PMM, the Baikal had a delayed-blowback system.

IZMECH
Two large arsenals in Izhevsk in Russia are better known as IZHMASH and IZHMECH. IZHMASH was founded in 1807, while IZHMECH was founded as a separate production facility in 1942, known for its Makarov and Stechkin pistols, and owned the "Baikal" trademark.

SPECIFICATION
MANUFACTURER IZHMECH
CALIBRE 9mm Makarov or Luger
MAGAZINE CAPACITY 8 or 12
ACTION Delayed blowback/double
TOTAL LENGTH 161mm/6.34in
BARREL LENGTH 94mm/3.7in
WEIGHT UNLOADED 730g/25.75oz

Stechkin

safety and fire mode selector

This weapon was designed by Igor Stechkin in Tula after World War II to fulfil the requirement for a large, semi-automatic pistol. In production from 1951, it had a conventional blowback operation and could be set to either single shot or full automatic fire. The weapon was supplied with an optional shoulder stock, which provided an insight into the difficulties of weapon control when firing in full automatic mode. Due to the fact that it was difficult to categorize, the Stechkin was withdrawn from Russian service.

SPECIFICATION
MANUFACTURER State Arsenals
CALIBRE 9mm Makarov
MAGAZINE CAPACITY 20
ACTION Blowback/double
TOTAL LENGTH 225mm/8.86in
BARREL LENGTH 127mm/5in
WEIGHT UNLOADED 1,030g/36.33oz

Stechkin silenced

This was a silenced version of the somewhat unsuccessful Stechkin pistol. During the 1970s, some of the Stechkin pistols were modified and issued with quickly detachable silencers which reduced the crack of the weapon.

detachable silencer

The AK47
The Stechkin was withdrawn after the introduction of the shortened AK47 rifle. The Stechkin was less easy to control than a submachine gun.

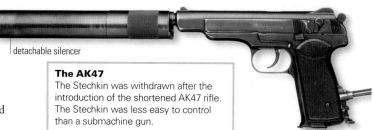

Margolin MT

back sight (adjust for windage)

front sight (adjust for elevation)

This was a specialist target pistol designed by Mikhail Margolin, a blind Russian designer. It was a blowback-operated pistol with advanced target sights used since the 1950s, adjustable for windage and elevation. The Margolin was quite easy to manage because of its light weight and slim barrel, although recoil movement could be stronger than expected.

SPECIFICATION
MANUFACTURER IZHMECH
CALIBRE .22 Long Rifle
MAGAZINE CAPACITY 6
ACTION Blowback/single
TOTAL LENGTH 310mm/12.2in
BARREL LENGTH 160mm/6.3in
WEIGHT UNLOADED 1,180g/41.6oz

PSM (small self-loading pistol)

SPECIFICATION

MANUFACTURER IZHMECH

CALIBRE 5.45mm PSM

MAGAZINE CAPACITY 8

ACTION Recoil/double

TOTAL LENGTH 155mm/6.1in

BARREL LENGTH 85mm/3.35in

WEIGHT UNLOADED 460g/16.2oz

This pistol became standard issue to police and security forces in Russia in the 1970s. It was designed around the newly developed small bore 5.45mm cartridge and was slim and compact and could be easily concealed. It had conventional recoil operation with a double-action mechanism. The cartridge was of relatively low power but it had high penetrative qualities. The safety catch was positioned to the rear of the slide.

MP-443

SPECIFICATION

MANUFACTURER TSINIITOCHMASH

CALIBRE 9mm Parabellum

MAGAZINE CAPACITY 18

ACTION Blowback/double

TOTAL LENGTH 205mm/8.1in

BARREL LENGTH 132mm/5.2in

WEIGHT UNLOADED 900g/31.75oz

This was a self-loading pistol with a floating barrel, firing from a closed bolt. It has a conventional blowback action. The weapon is designed for a high level of penetration and was said to be effective against fragmentation vests at 50m/164ft or against steel plate at 30m/98ft. The military index "6P35" was given to all the handguns which were submitted at the "Grach" (meaning "rook") trials which took place in the 1990s, aimed at replacing military pistols. This pistol, initially known as the 6P35 or as MP-443 "Grach", is now officially adopted by the Russian Government for the military and for law enforcement.

"Udar" revolver

SPECIFICATION

MANUFACTURER TSINIITOCHMASH

CALIBRE 12.3mm/pyroliquid/noise

CYLINDER 5

ACTION Double

TOTAL LENGTH 210mm/8.27in

BARREL LENGTH 56mm/2.2in

WEIGHT UNLOADED 950g/33.51oz

This revolver was developed as a specialist weapon for police and special forces and it was designed as a defensive weapon to achieve a variety of tasks that might be encountered in a crowd-control emergency or other crisis. The weapon was supplied with a number of alternative cartridges, some of which were entirely different to a standard round. It took a 12.3mm cartridge with a plastic bullet; a pyroliquid cartridge; or a noise cartridge. These cartridges enabled the weapon user to deal with threats with different levels of deterrent. It was unlikely that this revolver could do very much physical harm when fired.

SPECIFICATION

MANUFACTURER TSINIITOCHMASH

CALIBRE 7.62mm special, noiseless cartridge

CYLINDER CAPACITY 6

ACTION Blowback/double

TOTAL LENGTH 165mm/6.5in

BARREL LENGTH 60mm/2.36in

WEIGHT UNLOADED 700g/24.7oz

PSS (silent self-loading pistol)

This small pistol was devised for covert use by special forces and was sometimes known as the "Vul". In production from 1995, it was designed to be silent and to deliver a high-impact round that would penetrate a steel helmet at 25m/82ft. The pistol automatically reloaded after each shot. It was equipped with a safety catch to prevent accidental firing. The pistol was not fitted with a silencer; instead the silencing effect was derived from the design of the cartridge.

Egypt

The Egyptian defence industry is spread across a number of engineering factories which together contribute to making Egypt one of the primary arms producers in the Arab world. The Helwan pistol was a licenced version of a Beretta design. It is named after the local industrial area in which it was produced.

Helwan

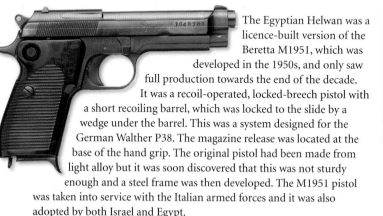

The Egyptian Helwan was a licence-built version of the Beretta M1951, which was developed in the 1950s, and only saw full production towards the end of the decade. It was a recoil-operated, locked-breech pistol with a short recoiling barrel, which was locked to the slide by a wedge under the barrel. This was a system designed for the German Walther P38. The magazine release was located at the base of the hand grip. The original pistol had been made from light alloy but it was soon discovered that this was not sturdy enough and a steel frame was then developed. The M1951 pistol was taken into service with the Italian armed forces and it was also adopted by both Israel and Egypt.

SPECIFICATION

MANUFACTURER Local Egyptian manufacturer
CALIBRE 9mm Parabellum
MAGAZINE CAPACITY 8
ACTION Recoil/single
TOTAL LENGTH 203mm/8in
BARREL LENGTH 115mm/4.53in
WEIGHT UNLOADED 890g/31.41oz

Turkey

Turkey was the first country to adopt and issue a pistol from another country. They purchased over a thousand German Mauser M1896 pistols in 1896. Turkey then adopted the Belgian FN Browning M1903 pistol before World War I. Turkey manufactured a copy of the famous Walther PP pistol, which was known as the Kirikkale, although minor alterations were made to suit Turkish production methods.

Kirikkale MKE

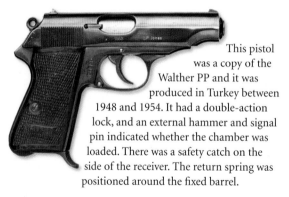

This pistol was a copy of the Walther PP and it was produced in Turkey between 1948 and 1954. It had a double-action lock, and an external hammer and signal pin indicated whether the chamber was loaded. There was a safety catch on the side of the receiver. The return spring was positioned around the fixed barrel.

ABOVE The double-action trigger was a feature of the Walther PP and its clones. The pistol was considered easy to handle and control.

SPECIFICATION

MANUFACTURER Local Turkish manufacturer
CALIBRE .380 ACP, .32 ACP
MAGAZINE 8
ACTION Blowback/double
TOTAL LENGTH 170mm/6.7in
BARREL LENGTH 98mm/3.86in
WEIGHT UNLOADED 695g/24.5oz

 # Israel

Israeli small-arms production is most famous for the Uzi submachine gun. The smallest of these can arguably be categorized as a pistol, though some might say this is stretching a point. Otherwise Israeli Military Industries developed the Desert Eagle, a Magnum Pistol which has earned some fame for its sheer size and power. KSN Industries and Ta'as Israel Industries also have products in the pistols category.

Desert Eagle

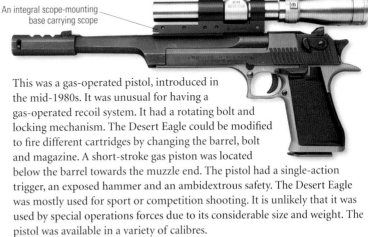

An integral scope-mounting base carrying scope

SPECIFICATION	✡
MANUFACTURER Magnum Research Inc/Israel Military Industries (IMI)	
CALIBRE .44 Magnum, .357 Magnum, .50 Action Express	
MAGAZINE 9	
ACTION Gas recoil/single	
TOTAL LENGTH 260mm/10.3in	
BARREL LENGTH 152mm/6in	
WEIGHT UNLOADED 1,715g/62oz	

This was a gas-operated pistol, introduced in the mid-1980s. It was unusual for having a gas-operated recoil system. It had a rotating bolt and locking mechanism. The Desert Eagle could be modified to fire different cartridges by changing the barrel, bolt and magazine. A short-stroke gas piston was located below the barrel towards the muzzle end. The pistol had a single-action trigger, an exposed hammer and an ambidextrous safety. The Desert Eagle was mostly used for sport or competition shooting. It is unlikely that it was used by special operations forces due to its considerable size and weight. The pistol was available in a variety of calibres.

 # China

The Chinese small-arms industry is centred on the state-owned China North Industries Corporation (Norinco). This company produces a number of small arms, though currently the production is focused largely on automatic rifles, submachine guns and heavy machine guns.

Makarov Type 59

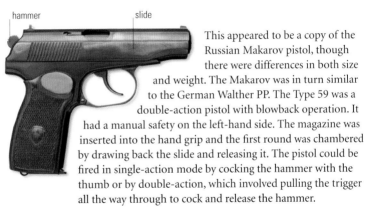

hammer   slide

SPECIFICATION	✶
MANUFACTURER China North Industries Corp.	
CALIBRE 9mm Makarov	
MAGAZINE CAPACITY 8	
ACTION Blowback/double or single	
TOTAL LENGTH 162mm/6.38in	
BARREL LENGTH 94mm/3.7in	
WEIGHT UNLOADED 730g/25.75oz	

This appeared to be a copy of the Russian Makarov pistol, though there were differences in both size and weight. The Makarov was in turn similar to the German Walther PP. The Type 59 was a double-action pistol with blowback operation. It had a manual safety on the left-hand side. The magazine was inserted into the hand grip and the first round was chambered by drawing back the slide and releasing it. The pistol could be fired in single-action mode by cocking the hammer with the thumb or by double-action, which involved pulling the trigger all the way through to cock and release the hammer.

Tokarev Type 51

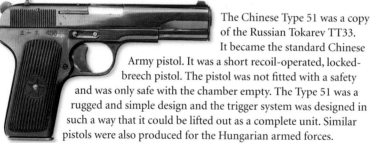

The Chinese Type 51 was a copy of the Russian Tokarev TT33. It became the standard Chinese Army pistol. It was a short recoil-operated, locked-breech pistol. The pistol was not fitted with a safety and was only safe with the chamber empty. The Type 51 was a rugged and simple design and the trigger system was designed in such a way that it could be lifted out as a complete unit. Similar pistols were also produced for the Hungarian armed forces.

SPECIFICATION

MANUFACTURER State Arsenals
CALIBRE 7.62mm Tokarev
MAGAZINE CAPACITY 8
ACTION Short recoil/single
TOTAL LENGTH 196mm/7.7in
BARREL LENGTH 116mm/4.57in
WEIGHT UNLOADED 830g/29.28oz

Norinco Tokarev Type 54

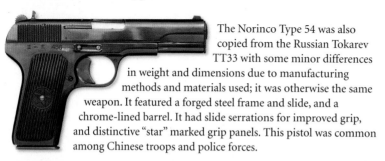

The Norinco Type 54 was also copied from the Russian Tokarev TT33 with some minor differences in weight and dimensions due to manufacturing methods and materials used; it was otherwise the same weapon. It featured a forged steel frame and slide, and a chrome-lined barrel. It had slide serrations for improved grip, and distinctive "star" marked grip panels. This pistol was common among Chinese troops and police forces.

SPECIFICATION

MANUFACTURER Norinco
CALIBRE 7.62mm Tokarev
MAGAZINE CAPACITY 8
ACTION Short recoil/single
TOTAL LENGTH 196mm/7.7in
BARREL LENGTH 116mm/4.57in
WEIGHT UNLOADED 900g/31.75oz

Norinco Tokarev Type 213

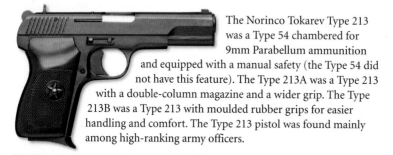

The Norinco Tokarev Type 213 was a Type 54 chambered for 9mm Parabellum ammunition and equipped with a manual safety (the Type 54 did not have this feature). The Type 213A was a Type 213 with a double-column magazine and a wider grip. The Type 213B was a Type 213 with moulded rubber grips for easier handling and comfort. The Type 213 pistol was found mainly among high-ranking army officers.

SPECIFICATION

MANUFACTURER Norinco
CALIBRE 9mm Parabellum
MAGAZINE CAPACITY 8
ACTION Short recoil/single
TOTAL LENGTH 195mm/7.67in
BARREL LENGTH 115mm/4.53in
WEIGHT UNLOADED 830g/29.28oz

QSZ-92

The QSZ-92 was a state-of-the-art pistol that had been adopted by the Chinese People's Liberation Army. It was a short recoil-operated, locked-breech pistol with a polymer frame. It incorporated a rotating barrel system which unlocked the slide during recoil. The pistol was fitted with an accessory rail which could accept either laser sights or lighting systems. The pistol was available in two versions, one the more common 9mm Parabellum cartridge and one for the Chinese type 5.8mm bottle-necked cartridge. Development of the pistol was thought to have started in 1994.

SPECIFICATION

MANUFACTURER Norinco
CALIBRE 9mm Parabellum
MAGAZINE CAPACITY 15
ACTION Short recoil/double
TOTAL LENGTH 190mm/7.5in
BARREL LENGTH 111mm/4.37in
WEIGHT UNLOADED 760g/26.8oz

Japan

Early 20th century Japanese pistols and revolvers were centred on the designs of Colonel Kijiro Nambu. Not all of these were world-class – and some were bedevilled by poor manufacture. In the post-World War II era, Japan was to prove itself a world leader in the quality of its manufacturing processes but it was also a nation dedicated to putting the past behind it and the development of small arms was definitely not a priority.

Nambu Baby

<table>
<tr><td colspan="2">SPECIFICATION ●</td></tr>
<tr><td>MANUFACTURER</td><td>Koishikawa Arsenal</td></tr>
<tr><td>CALIBRE</td><td>7mm Nambu</td></tr>
<tr><td>CYLINDER</td><td>7</td></tr>
<tr><td>ACTION</td><td>Short recoil/single</td></tr>
<tr><td>TOTAL LENGTH</td><td>171mm/6.75in</td></tr>
<tr><td>BARREL LENGTH</td><td>83mm/3.25in</td></tr>
<tr><td>WEIGHT UNLOADED</td><td>650g/22.93oz</td></tr>
</table>

cocking knob

This pistol was a smaller-size version of the Nambu Model 1904, and was produced in the early 20th century. The intention was to overcome some of the criticisms of the M1904 mainly regarding size and weight. However, the pistol did not prove to be a great success, partly due to high production costs. The magazine base was originally wood and was then changed to aluminium, and it had a rounded cocking knob. The 1904 pistol had two variations, the Type 4 and the Type 14.

Nambu Type 14

safety catch   bolt   cocking piece

trigger guard

magazine guard

<table>
<tr><td colspan="2">SPECIFICATION ●</td></tr>
<tr><td>MANUFACTURER</td><td>Nagoya Arsenal</td></tr>
<tr><td>CALIBRE</td><td>8mm Nambu</td></tr>
<tr><td>CYLINDER</td><td>8</td></tr>
<tr><td>ACTION</td><td>Short recoil/single</td></tr>
<tr><td>TOTAL LENGTH</td><td>227mm/8.9in</td></tr>
<tr><td>BARREL LENGTH</td><td>121mm/4.76in</td></tr>
<tr><td>WEIGHT UNLOADED</td><td>900g/31.75oz</td></tr>
</table>

The Nambu Type 14 was essentially an improved version of the Nambu Type 4. It was a locked-breech pistol, the breech being locked by a floating locking block attached to the barrel extension. Unlike the Type 4 Model, the pistol featured a safety catch. This pistol was adopted by the Japanese Army, though there continued to be problems with removing the magazine which made the Type 14 a tricky weapon to maintain in adverse circumstances.

Nambu Type 94

<table>
<tr><td colspan="2">SPECIFICATION ●</td></tr>
<tr><td>MANUFACTURER</td><td>Nagoya Rifle Mfg Co.</td></tr>
<tr><td>CALIBRE</td><td>8mm</td></tr>
<tr><td>CYLINDER</td><td>6</td></tr>
<tr><td>ACTION</td><td>Short recoil/single</td></tr>
<tr><td>TOTAL LENGTH</td><td>183mm/7.2in</td></tr>
<tr><td>BARREL LENGTH</td><td>96mm/3.78in</td></tr>
<tr><td>WEIGHT UNLOADED</td><td>765g/26.98oz</td></tr>
</table>

This was a totally revised pistol, designed by Nambu to try to overcome the problems experienced with some of the previous designs, including size and weight. After design input from the Japanese Army, however, the pistol turned out to be even more expensive than its predecessor. The ugly outward appearance was an accurate reflection of the internal workings. The pistol was awkward and inefficient to use and it could be fired accidentally if a sear on the side of the receiver were knocked or pushed. The design seemed to show scant regard for the convenience or safety of the user.

KEY

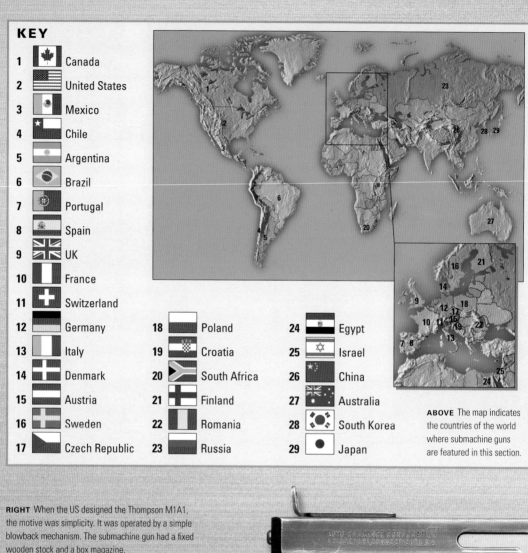

1 Canada
2 United States
3 Mexico
4 Chile
5 Argentina
6 Brazil
7 Portugal
8 Spain
9 UK
10 France
11 Switzerland
12 Germany
13 Italy
14 Denmark
15 Austria
16 Sweden
17 Czech Republic

18 Poland
19 Croatia
20 South Africa
21 Finland
22 Romania
23 Russia

24 Egypt
25 Israel
26 China
27 Australia
28 South Korea
29 Japan

ABOVE The map indicates the countries of the world where submachine guns are featured in this section.

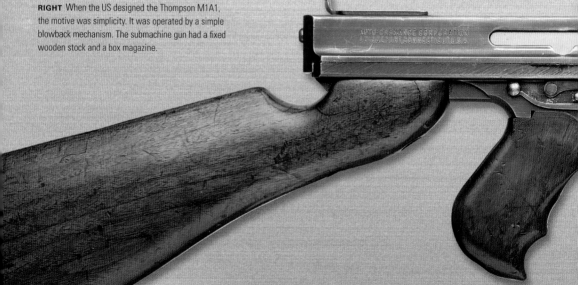

RIGHT When the US designed the Thompson M1A1, the motive was simplicity. It was operated by a simple blowback mechanism. The submachine gun had a fixed wooden stock and a box magazine.

A directory of submachine guns from around the world

Submachine guns are manufactured in many parts of the world. Some manufacturers produce unique firearms, while others produce or import versions of arms from other countries under licence. Taking a cross-section of selected countries of the world, west to east, this directory aims to feature a broad selection of the firearms that are available in those countries and detail their main features. Within each country's entry submachine guns are organized alphabetically by manufacturer except where its historical development is shown more clearly chronologically or a company changes its name. Each firearm has a description and a specification that lists its vital measurements, including its calibre.

BELOW The rugged-looking MAT-49 was developed in France during the late 1940s.

ABOVE Israel's Uzi submachine gun is an extremely efficient weapon of its type.

 # Canada

Canada does not have a tradition of designing weapons in the submachine gun category, and those that have been used in the past have been derived from other parts of the world. The Canadian military has used the Thompson, the Sten and the MP5 and produced a version of the C1.

C1 SMG

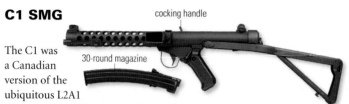

cocking handle

30-round magazine

The C1 was a Canadian version of the ubiquitous L2A1 Sterling submachine gun. As the Sterling L2A1 was a reliable weapon with a good performance record, there was not much requirement for change. The small changes that were made included a reduction in magazine capacity (from 34 rounds), which also involved a change to the feed mechanism. The C1 was a blowback-operated weapon with selective fire and a folding butt. It was used by the Canadian military in the 1950s.

SPECIFICATION

MANUFACTURER Canadian Arsenals Ltd.
CALIBRE 9mm Parabellum
MAGAZINE CAPACITY 30 or 10
ACTION Blowback
TOTAL LENGTH (STOCK EXTENDED) 686mm/27in
TOTAL LENGTH (STOCK RETRACTED) 493mm/19.41in
BARREL LENGTH 198mm/7.8in
WEIGHT UNLOADED 2,950g/104oz

United States

The most famous submachine gun produced in the United States was the Thompson submachine gun. It has iconic status among submachine guns and this gun is probably the most easily identified model ever produced, later replaced by the more workman-like M3A1 "grease gun". Today, Smith & Wesson and Ruger produce submachine guns, and weapons are manufactured for American forces and for export.

American 180

flat-pan magazine

The American 180 (AM180) was imported from Austria by American Arms International (AAI) in 1972 before being manufactured domestically. The original design was by US designer Richard Casull, who devised a series of small-calibre rifles. It was a conventional blowback-operated submachine gun fired from an open bolt in either full automatic or single-shot mode. After AAI went out of business in 1986, the Illinois Arms Company (Ilarco) produced the weapon with some modifications, such as reducing the magazine capacity from 177 rounds to 165. It was fitted with an extremely high-capacity magazine, not unlike those fitted to fighter aircraft. The magazine was unusual because it was in a flat pan of layered ammunition. The .22 Long Rifle cartridge gave the user the advantages of low recoil, good accuracy and a high rate of fire. It was used mainly by police departments for riot-control duties. The gun had a high standard of manufacture, with solid machined steel parts, and a solid wooden stock and forehand grip.

SPECIFICATION

MANUFACTURER American Arms International/Illinois Arms Co.
CALIBRE .22 Long Rifle
MAGAZINE CAPACITY 177 or 165
ACTION Blowback
TOTAL LENGTH 900mm/35.43in
BARREL LENGTH 470mm/18.5in
WEIGHT UNLOADED 2,600g/91.7oz

Thompson M1921

SPECIFICATION	
MANUFACTURER	Auto-Ordnance Corp.
CALIBRE	.45 ACP
MAGAZINE CAPACITY	18, 20 or 30 box;
	50 or 100 drum
ACTION	Delayed blowback
TOTAL LENGTH	857mm/33.74in
BARREL LENGTH	267mm/10.51in
WEIGHT UNLOADED	4,690g/165oz

hand grip

detachable buttstock

drum magazine

This weapon was developed by John Thompson, the founder of the Auto-Ordnance Corporation. It had a delayed-blowback mechanism fed from a round box or round drum magazine. The 1921 version was developed from the 1920 version (which in turn followed the 1918 and 1919 models). Although it was the first production model, the M1921 was not adopted by any of the US armed services. The M1921 proved to be the defining model in terms of appearance for the Thompson submachine gun, losing the barrel jacket that had been a feature of earlier models. It had a forward hand grip and a detachable buttstock.

SPECIFICATION	
MANUFACTURER	Auto-Ordnance Corp./
	Savage Arms Corp./Colts Patents
	Firearms Corp.
CALIBRE	.45 ACP
MAGAZINE CAPACITY	18, 20 or 30 box;
	50 or 100 drum
ACTION	Delayed blowback
TOTAL LENGTH	857mm/33.74in
BARREL LENGTH	267mm/10.51in
WEIGHT UNLOADED	4,880g/172oz

Thompson M1928A1

This version of the Thompson submachine gun was the same in many respects as the M1921 version. However, it was under the M1928 designation that the weapon achieved its first major orders by the US armed forces, especially the US Navy and US Marine Corps. It was also ordered by Britain and France in considerable numbers. With the start of World War II in 1939, these commissions saved the manufacturer from bankruptcy. The A1 version had some minor modifications. This variant entered mass production before the attack on Pearl Harbor in December 1941, and replaced stocks of the M1928. Only two factories supplied M1928A1 Thompson submachine guns during the early years of World War II. It was used mainly in the Pacific by the US military.

Thompson M1A1

SPECIFICATION	
MANUFACTURER	Auto-Ordnance Corp./
	Savage Arms Corp.
CALIBRE	.45 ACP
MAGAZINE CAPACITY	20 or 30
ACTION	Blowback
TOTAL LENGTH	813mm/32in
BARREL LENGTH	266mm/10.47in
WEIGHT UNLOADED	4,820g/170oz

stick magazine

In 1942 the Thompson M1928 was redesigned and called the Thompson M1A1. The design motive behind the M1A1 was simplicity. The earlier Thompsons all incorporated the "Blish" mechanism, which relied on friction to delay the opening of the breech. This mechanism was complex, of questionable value and time-consuming, and therefore expensive to produce. The M1A1 incorporated a simple blowback mechanism which helped to radically reduce production time. The cocking handle was moved to the side. It also came with a fixed stock and simplified sights. The trademark drum magazine was replaced with a simpler stick magazine. The M1A1 was differentiated from the M1 by the design of the firing pin.

Calico M961A

helical magazine

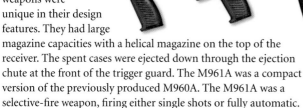

First produced in
the 1990s, Calico
weapons were
unique in their design
features. They had large
magazine capacities with a helical magazine on the top of the
receiver. The spent cases were ejected down through the ejection
chute at the front of the trigger guard. The M961A was a compact
version of the previously produced M960A. The M961A was a
selective-fire weapon, firing either single shots or fully automatic.
It was distinguished from the M960A by a shorter barrel.

SPECIFICATION

MANUFACTURER Calico, Oregon
CALIBRE 9mm Parabellum
MAGAZINE CAPACITY 50 or 100
ACTION Delayed blowback
TOTAL LENGTH (STOCK EXTENDED) 835mm/32.87in
TOTAL LENGTH (STOCK RETRACTED) 647mm/25.47in
BARREL LENGTH 330mm/12.99in
WEIGHT UNLOADED 2,170g/76.54oz

Colt

This weapon was based on the design of the M16A2/A4 rifle and
was first produced in 1987. It had a closed-bolt mechanism and
relatively low recoil, which improved accuracy. The weapon had a
sliding, heavy-duty buttstock. The major working parts were the
same as on the M16 rifle, making it easy for troops to cross between
the two weapons. Due to its compact size, it was relatively easy to
conceal and it was well suited to operations in environments with
restricted space, such as vehicles, ships and buildings. It was
adopted by the US armed forces and various law enforcement
agencies, and has also been exported around the world.

SPECIFICATION

MANUFACTURER Colt Firearms
CALIBRE 9mm Parabellum
MAGAZINE CAPACITY 20 or 32
ACTION Blowback
TOTAL LENGTH (STOCK EXTENDED) 730mm/28.74in
TOTAL LENGTH (STOCK RETRACTED) 650mm/25.59in
BARREL LENGTH 260mm/10.23in
WEIGHT UNLOADED 2,610g/92oz

M3

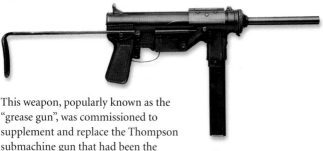

This weapon, popularly known as the
"grease gun", was commissioned to
supplement and replace the Thompson
submachine gun that had been the
mainstay of US forces. Although an efficient weapon, the Thompson
was expensive and inefficient to produce. The M3 was first produced
in December 1942 and it was manufactured from stampings rather
than machining operations. It had a comparatively low rate of fire
and moderate recoil but it proved to be somewhat unreliable. The
bolt-retracting handle was awkward to operate and the magazine
had a tendency to jam. A later version had a modified bolt-retracting
system. The weapon had a retractable butt. It was deployed
throughout the Korean War, in Vietnam and in the first Gulf War.

SPECIFICATION

MANUFACTURER Guide Lamp Division,
General Motors Corp.
CALIBRE .45 ACP
MAGAZINE CAPACITY 30
ACTION Blowback
TOTAL LENGTH (STOCK EXTENDED) 757mm/29.8in
TOTAL LENGTH (STOCK RETRACTED) 579mm/22.8in
BARREL LENGTH 203mm/8in
WEIGHT UNLOADED 3,668g/129oz

M3 design
Although the design was a combined effort,
George Hyde was the main designer of the
M3. The designers studied the way the
British Sten gun was made with a view
to making a similar weapon. Designs were
prepared and specifications submitted to
the Guide Lamp Division of GM for approval.

M3A1

An improved version of the M3, the M3A1, was developed during the 1940s. By the end of 1944 the M3A1 was standardized, and some of the weaknesses corrected. The bolt-retracting mechanism was removed completely and the revised design involved pulling the bolt back by inserting a finger into a machined recess. The magazine remained but a transparent, plastic dust cap was provided for the magazine in order to reduce stoppages caused by dirt. A silencer could be fitted to the barrel, reducing 80 per cent of the sound. By the end of World War II it was decided to phase out the Thompson and the M3A1 replaced the Thompson as the standard submachine gun of the United States military.

SPECIFICATION

MANUFACTURER Guide Lamp Division, General Motors Corp.

CALIBRE .45 ACP

MAGAZINE CAPACITY 30

ACTION Blowback

TOTAL LENGTH (STOCK EXTENDED) 757mm/29.8in

TOTAL LENGTH (STOCK RETRACTED) 579mm/22.8in

BARREL LENGTH 203mm/8in

WEIGHT UNLOADED 3,368g/129oz

Reising Model 50

SPECIFICATION

MANUFACTURER Harrington and Richardson

CALIBRE .45 ACP

MAGAZINE CAPACITY 12 or 20

ACTION Delayed blowback

TOTAL LENGTH 959mm/37.76in

BARREL LENGTH 279mm/10.98in

WEIGHT UNLOADED 3,100g/109oz

Drawbacks of the Reising
Although the Reising was well-designed and manufactured, it was quite a complex weapon and fine tolerances made it liable to jam. Large-scale production ceased in 1945.

The Reising Model 50 was designed in the 1940s by Eugene Reising (a US designer who had previously worked with John Browning) and entered service with the US armed forces, primarily the US Navy. The Model 50 was brought in to supplement supplies of the Thompson submachine gun, which was proving costly and time-consuming to manufacture. Unlike most other submachine guns it had a closed-bolt mechanism. It proved accurate and reliable in trials. However, perhaps due to the intricacy of the design, it was unreliable in combat conditions and it rapidly became unpopular with servicemen. In the later stages of World War II the weapon was largely issued to personnel in non-combat roles.

Reising Model 55

wire folding stock

SPECIFICATION

MANUFACTURER Harrington and Richardson

CALIBRE .45 ACP

MAGAZINE CAPACITY 12 or 20

ACTION Delayed blowback

TOTAL LENGTH (STOCK EXTENDED) 787mm/31in

TOTAL LENGTH (STOCK RETRACTED) 570mm/22.44in

BARREL LENGTH 279mm/10.98in

WEIGHT UNLOADED 2,889g/101.92oz

This was an adapted version of the Reising Model 50 which could be identified immediately by the use of a wire stock in place of the wooden stock of the Model 50. Since the wooden furniture under the receiver was retained, the M55 had a somewhat unbalanced appearance and the wire stock did not prove strong enough to provide a secure firing platform. The rest of the weapon remained the same as its predecessor and retained all of its problems. Like the Reising M50, the M55 could only be operated effectively in a clean, non-combat environment. The gun was withdrawn from frontline service in 1943.

UD M42

double magazine

SPECIFICATION

MANUFACTURER High Standard Mfg. Co./Marlin Firearms Co.
CALIBRE 9mm Parabellum
MAGAZINE CAPACITY 20
ACTION Blowback
TOTAL LENGTH 820mm/32.28in
BARREL LENGTH 279mm/10.98in
WEIGHT UNLOADED 4,110g/144.96oz

This weapon was designed for the High Standard Manufacturing Company in the United States and produced in 1942. It was also manufactured by Marlin. It was a conventional blowback-operated weapon, firing from an open bolt, while an independent hammer engaged the firing pin. The slide handle acted independently of the bolt. The M42 was ordered by Dutch forces in the East Indies and was also issued to some OSS (Office of Strategic Services) forces, but it could never challenge the Thompson submachine gun in popularity.

Interdynamic USA KG9

This automatic pistol originated in Sweden as the TEC-9. It was devised as an inexpensive weapon manufactured largely from polymers. However, due to relative lack of interest from potential customers, a subsidiary company, Interdynamic USA (later renamed Intratec), was set up in the United States. The weapon was redesignated the KG9. Initially it had an open-bolt mechanism but the US authorities ruled that it should only be produced in closed-bolt form due to the ease with which earlier versions could be converted to full automatic. The KG9 was intended for use by special forces and has consistent and reasonable power for a small-barrelled gun.

SPECIFICATION

MANUFACTURER Intratec
CALIBRE 9mm
MAGAZINE CAPACITY 10, 20, 32, 36 or 50
ACTION Blowback
TOTAL LENGTH 241mm/9.49in
BARREL LENGTH 76mm/3in
WEIGHT UNLOADED 1,230g/43oz

Intratec USA
Intratec was an arms company based in Miami, Florida until it went out of business in 2001. Intratec's most famous firearm was the TEC-9.

Intratec DC9

The Intratec DC9 differs in some ways from the Intratec KG9: the DC9 had a closed bolt and separate firing pin, while the KG9 had an open bolt and a fixed firing pin. The receiver on the DC9 was manufactured from steel while the lower part of the frame was polymer. It was a blowback-operated, semi-automatic weapon and had no manual safety. It was fitted with fixed, open sights. Like the KG9, the DC9 was said to be used by criminal gangs, and it was banned in its first production form in the United States.

SPECIFICATION

MANUFACTURER Intratec
CALIBRE 9mm Parabellum
MAGAZINE CAPACITY 10, 20, 32, 36 or 50
ACTION Blowback
TOTAL LENGTH 241mm/9.49in
BARREL LENGTH 76mm/3in
WEIGHT UNLOADED 1,230g/43oz

Barrel extension
The DC9 could be fitted with a screw-on barrel extension, designed to provide better balance or to make the weapon look more powerful.

Ingram Model 6

SPECIFICATION

MANUFACTURER Police Ordnance Co.
CALIBRE 9mm Parabellum
MAGAZINE CAPACITY 30
ACTION Blowback
TOTAL LENGTH 762mm/30in
BARREL LENGTH 228mm/9in
WEIGHT UNLOADED 3,290g/116oz

This weapon was similar in appearance to the Thompson submachine gun and was first produced in the early 1950s. It was one of the first weapons to use a two-stage trigger whereby initial pressure would produce single shots and sustained pressure would produce automatic fire. Considerable thought went into manufacturing the weapon as cheaply and efficiently as possible. In the event, however, there was not enough of a market for the weapon in either the United States or Europe.

Smith & Wesson Model 76

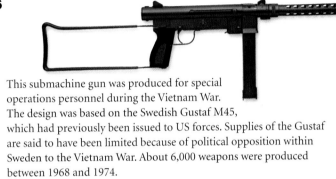

SPECIFICATION

MANUFACTURER Smith & Wesson Inc.
CALIBRE 9mm Parabellum
MAGAZINE CAPACITY 36 or 50
ACTION Blowback
TOTAL LENGTH (STOCK EXTENDED) 806mm/31.73in
TOTAL LENGTH (STOCK RETRACTED) 552mm/21.73in
BARREL LENGTH 203mm/8in
WEIGHT UNLOADED 3,430g/121oz

This submachine gun was produced for special operations personnel during the Vietnam War. The design was based on the Swedish Gustaf M45, which had previously been issued to US forces. Supplies of the Gustaf are said to have been limited because of political opposition within Sweden to the Vietnam War. About 6,000 weapons were produced between 1968 and 1974.

Ruger MP-9

SPECIFICATION

MANUFACTURER Sturm, Ruger & Co. Inc.
CALIBRE 9mm Parabellum
MAGAZINE CAPACITY 32
ACTION Blowback
TOTAL LENGTH (STOCK EXTENDED) 556mm/21.89in
TOTAL LENGTH (STOCK RETRACTED) 376mm/14.8in
BARREL LENGTH 173mm/6.81in
WEIGHT UNLOADED 2,700g/95oz

This weapon, originally known as the Gal-Tech, was produced in the 1980s and was the result of an attempt by the Ruger Company to improve the Uzi submachine gun. It was a compact, blowback-operated weapon that fired from a closed bolt. It had a fire-selector for single or automatic fire. The trigger guard was placed forward of the second hand grip. The magazine was inserted into the pistol grip at the centre of the weapon, which provided a good balance. It had a folding buttstock which fitted neatly against the back of the receiver and the rear hand grip when folded.

Ingram MAC 10

SPECIFICATION

MANUFACTURER Various
CALIBRE 9mm Parabellum, .45 ACP
MAGAZINE CAPACITY 30
ACTION Blowback
TOTAL LENGTH (STOCK EXTENDED) 548mm/21.6in
TOTAL LENGTH (STOCK RETRACTED) 269mm/10.59in
BARREL LENGTH 146mm/5.75in
WEIGHT UNLOADED 2,840g/100oz

This weapon was designed by Gordon B. Ingram in the 1960s and set new standards for compact submachine gun design. It was short and made from rugged steel pressings and incorporated a wrap-around bolt with the firing pin placed well back in order to envelop the breech. The cocking handle could be locked by rotating it. On the right of the trigger guard there was a safety catch. The weapon featured a telescopic stock. Although it did not achieve general-issue status, the Mac 10 was used by special forces units in various parts of the world.

Mexico

Small-arms manufacture in Mexico goes back to the Mexican Revolution, and the firm of Mendoza began producing arms in 1911. Due to restrictions imposed by the Mexican Government in the 1970s, Mendoza has branched out into other areas, but still retains the impressive HM-3 submachine gun in its catalogue.

Mendoza HM-3

This was a lightweight, blowback-operated weapon of all-steel construction, produced in the 1990s. The magazine slid into the pistol grip which incorporated a grip safety. The HM-3 had a selector on the right-hand side of the weapon and the stock could either be folded or unfolded. The HM-3 has achieved a good reputation for its quality of construction and over 6,000 have been produced for the Mexican armed forces. The weapon can be dismantled and put back together again without the use of tools. It had an indicator to show when a round had been chambered. The manufacturers claimed the weapon was well balanced and that it achieved a high level of accuracy.

SPECIFICATION

MANUFACTURER Productos Mendoza S.A.
CALIBRE 9mm Parabellum
MAGAZINE CAPACITY 32
ACTION Blowback/selective fire
TOTAL LENGTH (STOCK EXTENDED) 635mm/25in
TOTAL LENGTH (STOCK RETRACTED) 395mm/15.55in
BARREL LENGTH 255mm/10.04in
WEIGHT UNLOADED 2,690g/94.89oz

Chile

FAMAE (Las Fábricas y Maestranzas del Ejército), the oldest manufacturer of firearms in South America, produces a range of submachine guns and assault rifles. The submachine guns are original designs and the assault rifles are made under licence from the Swiss firm SIG.

FAMAE SAF

FAMAE is the Chilean Government small-arms factory. The FAMAE SAF was a development of the SIG 540 rifle. The SIG 540 rifle was produced under licence in Chile in the 1980s. The FAMAE SAF was produced in 1996. In general, the design was a shortened version of the SIG 540 rifle, but the rifle's rotating bolt had been replaced with a simple blowback bolt. The submachine gun had a closed-bolt mechanism with a hammer and floating-pin firing mechanism. The upper and lower parts of the receiver could be separated by removal of two pins, allowing access to the internal mechanism. A safety selector switch allowed the operator to select safe, single shot or three-round burst or fully automatic mode. The weapon was available with either folding or fixed stocks. Translucent magazines could be clipped together for speed of interchange. This gun has been issued not only to the Chilean security forces but more widely in South America. There is also a Mini-SAF available that has a forward hand grip, a much shorter barrel and no shoulder stock. It can use the standard 30-round magazine but has a special 20-round magazine that makes it more compact.

SPECIFICATION

MANUFACTURER Las Fábricas y Maestranzas del Ejército (FAMAE)
CALIBRE 9mm Parabellum
MAGAZINE CAPACITY 20 or 30
ACTION Blowback/closed bolt/selective fire
TOTAL LENGTH (STOCK EXTENDED) 640mm/25in
TOTAL LENGTH (STOCK RETRACTED) 410mm/16.14in
BARREL LENGTH 200mm/7.87in
WEIGHT UNLOADED 2,700g/95oz

FAMAE variations
The FAMAE submachine guns come in four versions: the SAF Standard, for police and special forces; the Mini SAF, for security personnel and VIP work; the silenced SAF, for special units; and the MT-40, primarily designed for the police.

Argentina

Argentina produced some original submachine-gun designs as well as some derived from other makes. In the first category was the Halcón, a design which proved to be easy to manufacture and to maintain, and in the second the PAM, PA and FMK – designs loosely based on the US M3A1.

Halcón ML43

SPECIFICATION

MANUFACTURER Fábrica de Armas de Halcón
CALIBRE 9mm Parabellum
MAGAZINE CAPACITY 17 or 30
ACTION Blowback
TOTAL LENGTH 848mm/33.39in
BARREL LENGTH 292mm/11.5in
WEIGHT UNLOADED 4,080g/143.9oz

Developed in the early 1940s, this gun was issued to the Argentine Gendarmería Nacional (GNA) which is primarily a frontier guard force but it was also issued for other roles. This was a blowback-operated weapon with a simple design concept that made it easy to manufacture. Its mechanism also kept it fairly light for its intended purpose. The 1946 model was known as the Modelo Aeronáutica and was issued to the Argentine Air Force. In 1949 a new version was brought out in 9mm Parabellum. This version had a curved magazine and was issued to the Army.

Halcón ML63

SPECIFICATION

MANUFACTURER Fábrica de Armas de Halcón
CALIBRE 9mm Parabellum
MAGAZINE CAPACITY 42
ACTION Blowback
TOTAL LENGTH 848mm/33.39in
BARREL LENGTH 292mm/11.5in
WEIGHT UNLOADED 4,380g/154.10oz

An updated version of the Halcón design, simplified in a way that reduced the manufacturing costs of producing the model. It had two triggers which could shoot the weapon in automatic form or a single shots. However, its heavier weight has made the weapon difficult to handle for the functions that it was designed for – such as by air force personnel and for operations by armed forces on the ground.

PAM1/PAM2

SPECIFICATION

MANUFACTURER Fábrica de Armas de Halcón
CALIBRE 9mm Parabellum
MAGAZINE CAPACITY 17 or 30
ACTION Blowback
TOTAL LENGTH (STOCK EXTENDED) 725mm/28.54in
TOTAL LENGTH (STOCK RETRACTED) 535mm/21.06in
BARREL LENGTH 200mm/7.87in
WEIGHT UNLOADED 2,990g/105.47oz

The PAM1 and 2 submachine guns were directly inspired by the successful US M3A1 "grease gun".
The M3A1 was blowback operated and fully automatic. It had a retractable stock, made from steel wire, which could double as a cleaning rod and it also had a magazine loading tool. The PAM1 and PAM2 were slightly shorter and were issued widely to the Argentine Army and Police from 1950 to the mid-1960s.

PA-3DM

This weapon was a development of the PAM1 and appeared in two models: one with a fixed butt and the other with a sliding butt. The barrel could be released by unscrewing a cap at the end of the gun body. The magazine slid into the pistol grip, which incorporated a grip safety. There was a cocking handle on the left of the receiver. The wrap-around bolt was a design influence from the Israeli Uzi submachine gun. The PA-3DM was manufactured up to 1978 and about 15,000 were made. This weapon is no longer in active service in Argentina, but may still be found among paramilitary groups and police.

SPECIFICATION

MANUFACTURER Fábrica Militar de Armas Portátiles "Domingo Matheu", Rosario

CALIBRE 9mm Parabellum

MAGAZINE CAPACITY .25

ACTION Blowback

TOTAL LENGTH 523mm/20.59in

BARREL LENGTH 290mm/11.42in

WEIGHT UNLOADED 3,400g/120oz

FMK-3 Model 2

This machine gun was a development of the PA-3DM and has become the new standard Argentine submachine gun. It was mostly produced with the sliding stock reminiscent of the US M3A1 "grease gun", although the fixed-stock version is occasionally seen. Like its predecessor, the FMK-3 was blowback operated. The magazine slid into the pistol grip, which incorporated an automatic safety. On the left side, above the pistol grip, there was a manual safety selector. The front and back sights could be flipped up when required.

SPECIFICATION

MANUFACTURER Fábrica Militar de Armas Portátiles "Domingo Matheu", Rosario

CALIBRE 9mm Parabellum

MAGAZINE .25

ACTION Blowback

TOTAL LENGTH (STOCK EXTENDED) 693mm/27.3in

TOTAL LENGTH (STOCK RETRACTED) 523mm/20.5in

BARREL LENGTH 290mm/11.42in

WEIGHT UNLOADED 3,170g/112oz

Brazil

Brazilian industry has developed a wide range of submachine guns over the years, one of which was an adaptation of the Danish Madsen. The company Indústria de Material Bélico do Brasil (IMBEL) developed a couple of submachine gun types, and another was developed and produced by Mekanika Indústria e Comércio Lda, known as the Uru Mekanika.

INA MB50

The Madsen submachine gun had been developed by Madsen in Denmark after World War II. One of its most notable characteristics was that it could be opened in two halves, pivoting on a hinge at the rear. The barrel, bolt, return spring and trigger unit could all be accessed easily once the gun was opened. The weapon was manufactured under licence in Brazil as the INA MB50, initially in .45 ACP and later in 9mm Parabellum. A muzzle compensator was added to improve performance and in general the weapon was easy to control. The revised weapon was issued to the Brazilian Army and Police.

SPECIFICATION

MANUFACTURER Indústria de Material Bélico do Brasil (IMBEL)

CALIBRE .45 ACP, 9mm Parabellum

MAGAZINE 30

ACTION Blowback

TOTAL LENGTH (STOCK EXTENDED) 800mm/31.5in

TOTAL LENGTH (STOCK RETRACTED) 530mm/20.87in

BARREL LENGTH 200mm/7.87in

WEIGHT UNLOADED 3,170g/112oz

Uru Mekanika

SPECIFICATION

MANUFACTURER Mekanika Indústria e Comércio Lda.

CALIBRE 9mm Parabellum

MAGAZINE 30

ACTION Blowback

TOTAL LENGTH (STOCK EXTENDED) 670mm/26.38in

TOTAL LENGTH (STOCK RETRACTED) 425mm/16.73in

BARREL LENGTH 175mm/6.89in

WEIGHT UNLOADED 2,580g/91oz

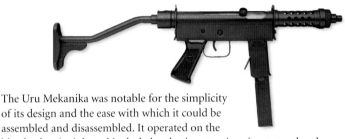

The Uru Mekanika was notable for the simplicity of its design and the ease with which it could be assembled and disassembled. It operated on the blowback principle and included a plastic rear grip, trigger guard and a metal forward grip into which the magazine was inserted. On the left-hand side there was a fire selector with settings for safe, semi-automatic and automatic modes. The Uru went into production in the late 1970s. Since then large numbers have been delivered to the Brazilian security forces. Sales have also been achieved elsewhere in South America as well as in Africa and the Middle East. The Brazilian company Bilbao bought the rights from Mekanika in 1988. In 1997 Mekanika Indústria e Comércio re-acquired the rights to the Uru Mekanika.

Portugal

Portugal did not produce any submachine guns of its own until 1948. With its ongoing colonial commitments that carried on into the early 1970s, Portugal developed some highly serviceable submachine guns, some of which were based on previous designs and others which were innovative.

FBP M948

SPECIFICATION

MANUFACTURER Fábrica Militar de Braço de Prata

CALIBRE 9mm Parabellum

MAGAZINE CAPACITY 32

ACTION Blowback

TOTAL LENGTH (STOCK EXTENDED) 812mm/32in

TOTAL LENGTH (STOCK RETRACTED) 635mm/25in

BARREL LENGTH 250mm/9.84in

WEIGHT UNLOADED 3,740g/122.4oz

The design for this weapon is said to be derived from both the German MP-40 and the American M3. The MP-40 inspired the design of the internal workings, such as the bolt, return spring and telescopic guide, and the M3 inspired the design of the receiver and general exterior appearance. The wire stock was also based on the M3 design. Produced in 1948, this weapon was manufactured largely from steel pressings and it was issued widely to Portuguese forces, also finding its way into the hands of various guerrilla groups in Portuguese colonial Africa.

FBP M976

SPECIFICATION

MANUFACTURER Indústrias Nacionais de Defesa

CALIBRE 9mm Parabellum

MAGAZINE CAPACITY 32 or 36

ACTION Blowback

TOTAL LENGTH (STOCK EXTENDED) 850mm/33.45in

TOTAL LENGTH (STOCK RETRACTED) 657mm/25.87in

BARREL LENGTH 250mm/9.84in

WEIGHT UNLOADED 3,120g/110oz

The M976 was a development of the M948 submachine gun and continued the emphasis on ease of manufacture through the use of stamped-steel parts. As the M948 had questionable accuracy, efforts were made to improve this in the M976 through the use of a cold-forged steel barrel and a perforated barrel jacket. The trigger mechanism was designed as one unit, which can be removed for maintenance or replacement. There was a safety selector as well as a grip safety. The weapon was mostly issued to Portuguese colonial forces.

INDEP Lusa

The INDEP Lusa was an all-new design which replaced the M976. It was possibly influenced by the Italian Franchi submachine gun. Much more compact than its predecessors, the INDEP incorporated an overhanging bolt and a double-cylinder receiver. The clever design included a space for the sliding buttstock to slide between the two curves on the receiver. There was a fire selector above the trigger on the left-hand side. The front magazine housing also acted as the forward hand grip. A1 and A2 versions were produced, one with a removable barrel and the other with a perforated barrel cover.

SPECIFICATION

MANUFACTURER Fábrica Militar de Braço de Prata
CALIBRE 9mm Parabellum
MAGAZINE CAPACITY 30
ACTION Blowback
TOTAL LENGTH (STOCK EXTENDED) 600mm/23.6in
TOTAL LENGTH (STOCK RETRACTED) 445mm/17in
BARREL LENGTH 160mm/6.3in
WEIGHT UNLOADED 2,500g/88.18oz

Spain

Spanish production of submachine guns ranges from somewhat rudimentary designs urgently produced at the time of the Spanish Civil War (1936–39), adaptations of the German MP40, to original and successful weapons like the Z84 produced by Star Bonifacio Echeverría.

Astra Model 901

The Model 901 was the first of three Astra machine pistols which were copies of a design made by Peter Paul Mauser in 1885. Manufacturers such as Unceta y Cia. (known today as Astra), located in the city of Eibar (Gipuzkoa province) copied this design and made improvements. The Model 901 was a development of the Model 900 and could be set to automatic fire. It had a 10-round magazine. The Model 902 differed only in being able to take a 20-round magazine. The Model 903 could take either a 10-round or a 20-round magazine and was also fitted with a fire selector for single or automatic fire. Some versions could be fitted with a stock.

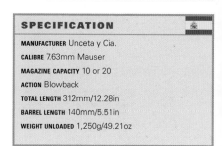

SPECIFICATION

MANUFACTURER Unceta y Cia.
CALIBRE 7.63mm Mauser
MAGAZINE CAPACITY 10 or 20
ACTION Blowback
TOTAL LENGTH 312mm/12.28in
BARREL LENGTH 140mm/5.51in
WEIGHT UNLOADED 1,250g/49.21oz

Labora

There is some uncertainty over the initial development of this weapon, although it was probably initiated by the Comisión de Industrias de Guerra de la Generalitat. It appears to have been manufactured to a very high standard using machined steel parts as opposed to steel stampings. The magazine was inserted into the forward hand grip and the cocking handle was located on the right of the receiver. Despite its effectiveness, the weapon does not appear to have been used extensively in the Spanish Civil War (1936–39) and few examples remain.

SPECIFICATION

MANUFACTURER Industrio de Guerra de Cataluña
CALIBRE 9mm Largo
MAGAZINE CAPACITY 36
ACTION Blowback
TOTAL LENGTH 806mm/31.75in
BARREL LENGTH 260mm/10.3in
WEIGHT UNLOADED 4,250g/149.9oz

Largo Star S135

SPECIFICATION

MANUFACTURER Star Bonifacio Echeverría S.A.

CALIBRE 9mm Largo

MAGAZINE CAPACITY 10, 30 or 40

ACTION Delayed blowback

TOTAL LENGTH 900mm/35.45in

BARREL LENGTH 269mm/10.59in

WEIGHT UNLOADED 3,740g/131.9oz

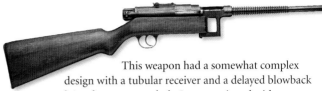

This weapon had a somewhat complex design with a tubular receiver and a delayed blowback system firing from an open bolt. It was equipped with two multi-position selectors that had to be co-ordinated in order to achieve single-shot or automatic fire. This unnecessary complexity was to ruin the weapon's chances of being selected for major production contracts and it was rejected by both the British and the Americans. It saw limited service in the Spanish Civil War. It had a conventional full wooden stock.

Largo Star Z45

SPECIFICATION

MANUFACTURER Star Bonifacio Echeverría S.A.

CALIBRE 9mm Largo

MAGAZINE CAPACITY 10 or 30

ACTION Blowback

TOTAL LENGTH (STOCK EXTENDED) 840mm/33.1in

TOTAL LENGTH (STOCK RETRACTED) 580mm/22.83in

BARREL LENGTH 192mm/7.56in

WEIGHT UNLOADED 3,870g/136.5oz

Tried and tested
In 1942 Star received blueprints and plans for the MP40 through a German engineer working at the plant. As it was based on a proven design, the Z45 could hardly fail.

The Z45, which was introduced in 1945, appeared in a number of forms, some of which had full wooden stocks, some with pistol grips and a wooden piece under the receiver, and some in full metal with folding metal stocks. It was based on the German MP40 and, with its proven design, was adopted by the Spanish armed forces as well as by some other countries. One difference with the MP40 was that the Z45 had a two-mode trigger which could fire single shots, or automatic fire with finger pressure. It also incorporated a barrel-change feature, whereby the barrel and compensator could be removed together by twisting. By simply changing the barrel another calibre of cartridge could be used.

Star Z62

SPECIFICATION

MANUFACTURER Star Bonifacio Echeverría S.A.

CALIBRE 9mm Largo

MAGAZINE CAPACITY 20, 30 or 40

ACTION Blowback

TOTAL LENGTH (STOCK EXTENDED) 701mm/27.60in

TOTAL LENGTH (STOCK RETRACTED) 480mm/18.9in

BARREL LENGTH 201mm/7.9in

WEIGHT UNLOADED 2,870g/101oz

The Z62 was designed as a replacement for the Z45 in 1953. It was issued to the Spanish armed forces and remained in service until 1971. In many respects, the Z62 was a conventional blowback weapon with a cocking handle on its left-hand side and a folding stock. It did, however, have an unusual trigger mechanism which was designed to fire single shots by pressing the lower part of the trigger and automatic shots by pressing the upper half. The weapon was manufactured from stamped steel parts and plastics. Created for the 9mm Largo cartridge, it was offered for export using the 9mm Parabellum cartridge. The Z62 was later replaced by the Z70B, which had a more conventional trigger mechanism and a selector lever for the choice of single fire or automatic.

STAR Model Z-70

SPECIFICATION	
MANUFACTURER Star Bonifacio Echeverría S.A.	
CALIBRE 9mm Parabellum	
MAGAZINE CAPACITY 20, 30 or 40	
ACTION Blowback	
TOTAL LENGTH (STOCK EXTENDED) 700mm/27.56in	
TOTAL LENGTH (STOCK RETRACTED) 450mm/17.72in	
BARREL LENGTH 200mm/7.87in	
WEIGHT UNLOADED 2,870g/101.24oz	

This weapon was a development of the Z62 and it came about due to problems with the trigger mechanism of the Z62. Designed in 1971, it had a conventional trigger mechanism that was installed with a selector on the left of the receiver for single-shot or automatic fire. Otherwise, it is a blowback-operated weapon with a folding buttstock. It is constructed from metal pressings and plastics.

STAR Model Z84

The Z84 was an all-new weapon designed to be easy and efficient to manufacture. It was blowback operated with an open-bolt system and it had a wrap-around breech block, allowing maximum barrel length without extending the exterior length of the weapon. The pistol grip was located centrally below the receiver and also acts as the magazine housing. Due to the central location of the pistol grip, the weapon was well balanced. On the left of the receiver there was a fire selector for single or automatic fire. There was a separate safety catch within the trigger guard. The Z84 entered service with Spanish forces in 1985. It has also been sold to other forces.

SPECIFICATION	
MANUFACTURER Star Bonifacio Echeverría S.A.	
CALIBRE 9mm Parabellum	
MAGAZINE CAPACITY 25 or 30	
ACTION Blowback	
TOTAL LENGTH (STOCK EXTENDED) 615mm/24.21in	
TOTAL LENGTH (STOCK RETRACTED) 410mm/16.14in	
BARREL LENGTH 410mm/16.4in	
WEIGHT UNLOADED 3,000g/105.8oz	

Bergmann MP28 copy

The German MP28 was a development of the MP18 and manufactured between 1928 and 1938. It was widely produced in Germany and was used in the Spanish Civil War, on both sides of the conflict, by Nationalists and Republicans alike. Copies were produced in Spanish factories. The success of the weapon in the Spanish Civil War is said to have influenced the German high command in encouraging further developments of the design.

ABOVE The Spanish copies of the Bergmann MP28 are distinguishable by the large retracting handle that does not appear on the German model.

SPECIFICATION	
MANUFACTURER Various	
CALIBRE 9mm Largo	
MAGAZINE CAPACITY 32	
ACTION Blowback	
TOTAL LENGTH 812mm/31.97in	
BARREL LENGTH 196mm/7.7in	
WEIGHT UNLOADED 4,190g/147.8oz	

United Kingdom

British submachine-gun design began with a copy of the German MP28, which was a solid option in the dark days of 1940. Later, Messrs Shepherd and Turpin of the Royal Small Arms Factory at Enfield came up with what was to prove to be the ubiquitous British submachine gun of World War II and the immediate post-war era: the Sten. In its various forms, the Sten was to remain in service until the 1960s, when it was replaced by the Sterling. This in turn was phased out with the arrival of the SA80 assault rifle.

Sten Mark I

SPECIFICATION
MANUFACTURER Birmingham Small Arms Co./ Royal Ordnance Factory
CALIBRE 9mm Parabellum
MAGAZINE CAPACITY 32
ACTION Blowback
TOTAL LENGTH 895mm/35.25in
BARREL LENGTH 196mm/7.7in
WEIGHT UNLOADED 3,260g/115oz

The Sten gun was named after its designers, Major-General Reginald Sheperd and Harold Turpin and the location Enfield, where the Royal Small Arms Factory was located, hence S.T.EN. The Sten gun was a quick solution to Britain's desperate need for a submachine gun after British troops were rescued at Dunkirk in France in 1940. The Sten prototype was first put forward in 1941. The Sten gun's rudimentary design proved to be ideal for use by resistance fighters who required a simple, rugged weapon that was easy to assemble, maintain and conceal. However, it was less popular among British regular forces, who were used to better-quality weapons.

Sten Mark II

SPECIFICATION
MANUFACTURER Birmingham Small Arms Co./ Royal Ordnance Factory
CALIBRE 9mm Parabellum
MAGAZINE CAPACITY 32
ACTION Blowback
TOTAL LENGTH 762mm/30in
BARREL LENGTH 196mm/7.7in
WEIGHT UNLOADED 2,950g/104oz

This version of the Sten was produced between 1942 and 1944 in large numbers. The Mark II was basically a stripped-down version of the Mark I. It had some small improvements in both technical design and safety features, but the aim was to simplify the manufacturing process. It had a removable barrel and a tubular or skeleton stock, which meant the gun could be easily stowed and concealed. The magazine housing rotated around the receiver, allowing it to be used as a dust cover for the ejection port.

Silent Sten Mark II (S)

SPECIFICATION
MANUFACTURER Birmingham Small Arms Co./ Royal Ordnance Factory
CALIBRE 9mm Parabellum
MAGAZINE CAPACITY 32
ACTION Blowback
TOTAL LENGTH 908mm/35.75in
BARREL LENGTH 89mm/3.5in
WEIGHT UNLOADED 3,520g/124oz

insulating cover to protect hands from heat of silencer

This version of the Sten gun was fitted with an integral silencer, as opposed to a removable one. The silencer and barrel were screwed on together. The silencer was formed of a series of baffles which had the effect of slowing down the gases so that they emerged from the end of the muzzle without making a noise. The baffles proved to be sensitive to wear and later the Mark II (S) was used almost exclusively in single-shot mode.

Sten Mark III

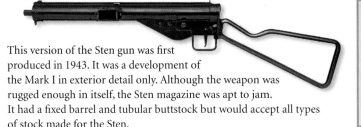

This version of the Sten gun was first
produced in 1943. It was a development of
the Mark I in exterior detail only. Although the weapon was
rugged enough in itself, the Sten magazine was apt to jam.
It had a fixed barrel and tubular buttstock but would accept all types
of stock made for the Sten.

SPECIFICATION	
MANUFACTURER Birmingham Small Arms Co./	
Royal Ordnance Factory	
CALIBRE 9mm Parabellum	
MAGAZINE CAPACITY 32	
ACTION Blowback	
TOTAL LENGTH 762mm/30in	
BARREL LENGTH 196mm/7.7in	
WEIGHT UNLOADED 3,180g/112oz	

Sten Mark V

This gun was introduced in 1944
and saw service until well into the 1950s.
It was essentially the same as the Mark II but
with a more elaborate stock and hand grip. It was issued to the British
Parachute Regiment and was famously used in the ill-fated World War II
Arnhem campaign on the Dutch/German border in 1944.

SPECIFICATION	
MANUFACTURER Birmingham Small Arms Co./	
Royal Ordnance Factory	
CALIBRE 9mm Parabellum	
MAGAZINE CAPACITY 32	
ACTION Blowback	
TOTAL LENGTH 762mm/30in	
BARREL LENGTH 196mm/7.7in	
WEIGHT UNLOADED 3,860g/136oz	

Silent Sten Mark VI

Produced during World War II,
this version of the Sten was a mixture
of the Sten Mark V and the Sten Mark II (S).
The Sten Mark VI can be distinguished by a
wooden butt, as opposed to the folding metal butt of other versions,
and a pistol grip behind the trigger guard. The silencer was a different
design from that of the Mark II (S).

SPECIFICATION	
MANUFACTURER Birmingham Small Arms Co./	
Royal Ordnance Factory	
CALIBRE 9mm Parabellum	
MAGAZINE CAPACITY 32	
ACTION Blowback	
TOTAL LENGTH (SILENCED) 908mm/35.8in	
BARREL LENGTH 196mm/7.7in	
WEIGHT UNLOADED 4,450g/157oz	

Lanchester

The Lanchester was named after
George Lanchester who developed the
weapon as a direct copy of the German
MP28 with some essential modifications. In 1940, after the evacuation
of British troops at Dunkirk, there was little time to design a new
submachine gun from scratch and therefore this adaptation of an
existing design seemed to be a sensible way round the problem. The
Lanchester proved to be a well-made weapon with a solid wooden stock,
brass fittings and high-quality working parts. In use from 1941 to 1960,
the Lanchester saw service in the Royal Navy and Royal Air Force, both
during and after World War II.

SPECIFICATION	
MANUFACTURER Sterling Armament Co.	
CALIBRE 9mm Parabellum	
MAGAZINE CAPACITY 50	
ACTION Blowback	
TOTAL LENGTH 85mm/33.5in	
BARREL LENGTH 203mm/8in	
WEIGHT UNLOADED 4,340g/153oz	

Sterling L2A3

SPECIFICATION

MANUFACTURER Sterling Armament Co./
Royal Ordnance Factory, Fazakeley

CALIBRE 9mm Parabellum

MAGAZINE CAPACITY 34

ACTION Blowback

TOTAL LENGTH (STOCK EXTENDED) 690mm/27.16in

TOTAL LENGTH (STOCK RETRACTED) 483mm/19in

BARREL LENGTH 198mm/7.8in

WEIGHT UNLOADED 2,720g/95.95oz

This version of the Sterling submachine gun first appeared in 1956 and proved to be the last version to be produced by Sterling/Royal Ordnance and issued to the British Army. The magazine was inserted into the left side of the receiver and there was a selector lever above the trigger which was used to select rapid fire, single shots or safe mode. There were also versions of the L2A3 which fired single shots only. The weapon had a successful sales record, being sold to about 90 countries around the world, including Canada, Ghana, India, Libya, Malaysia, Nigeria, Tunisia and some Arabian Gulf states. The Sterling L2A3 was replaced from 1988 by the SA80 assault rifle.

Sterling L2

SPECIFICATION

MANUFACTURER Sterling Armament Co./
Royal Ordnance Factory, Fazakeley

CALIBRE 9mm Parabellum

MAGAZINE CAPACITY 34

ACTION Blowback

TOTAL LENGTH (STOCK EXTENDED) 690mm/27.16in

TOTAL LENGTH (STOCK RETRACTED) 483mm/19in

BARREL LENGTH 198mm/7.8in

WEIGHT UNLOADED 2,720g/95.95oz

The Sterling L2 was the official designation for what was originally known as the Patchett gun. This design was one of a few under consideration by the British Government, including the Sten, a BSA design and an Australian contender. The Sterling L2 prototype was introduced in the 1960s. The weapon was blowback operated and the action incorporated a steel spring that caught the bolt on recoil. The bolt incorporated ribs that were designed to clear any dirt out of the casing. The weapon was manufactured from steel and plastic and its basically simple mechanism left little to go wrong.

Sterling L34A1

SPECIFICATION

MANUFACTURER Sterling Armament Co./
Royal Ordnance Factory, Fazakeley

CALIBRE 9mm Parabellum

MAGAZINE CAPACITY 34

ACTION Blowback

TOTAL LENGTH (STOCK EXTENDED) 864mm/34in

TOTAL LENGTH (STOCK RETRACTED) 660mm/26in

BARREL LENGTH 198mm/7.8in

WEIGHT UNLOADED 3,600g/126.97oz

In production from 1966 to 1985, this weapon was the silenced version of the Sterling L2A3 submachine gun. Its design was based on the Silent Sten as a guide, but the technology was improved. The barrel was perforated in order to allow gases to escape into a diffuser. Movement of the gases was controlled through a system of metal wrappings and spirals that ensured that the gas emerging from the end of the silencer was travelling at a reduced rate. Apart from the silencer, the basic mechanics of the L34A1 were the same as those of the L2A3.

France

A variety of submachine guns have been produced in France over the years by Manufacture d'Armes de St Etienne (MAS), Manufacture d'Armes de Tulle (MAT) and Groupement Industriel des Armaments Terrestres (GIAT). Latterly, submachine guns issued to French forces have been replaced by the FAMAS assault rifle.

Hotchkiss "Universal"

This submachine gun was first produced shortly after the end of World War II. It was designed to fold into a compact size for ease of carriage by military personnel such as paratroopers or other units. Both the butt and the pistol grip could be folded underneath the receiver, the magazine and its housing underneath the barrel, and the barrel itself could be telescoped into the receiver. Despite these convenient design features, it was over-complicated and was not sold in large numbers.

SPECIFICATION

MANUFACTURER Hotchkiss et Cie.

CALIBRE 9mm Parabellum

MAGAZINE CAPACITY 32

ACTION Blowback

TOTAL LENGTH (STOCK EXTENDED) 776mm/30.6in

TOTAL LENGTH (STOCK RETRACTED) 538mm/21.2in

BARREL LENGTH 270mm/10.63in

WEIGHT UNLOADED 3,400g/120oz

MAS 38

This model was produced just before the start of World War II and could be recognized by its curved appearance. This was due to the fact that the receiver and butt sloped away from the axis of the barrel. A tube ran into the butt to allow room for the bolt to travel on recoil. Instead of a conventional safety catch, the bolt could be locked by pushing the trigger forward. Uniquely for this kind of weapon, it had a buffered sear to prevent wear. Production of the MAS 38 was taken over by the Germans after the invasion of France in 1940 and some weapons were issued to the German army.

SPECIFICATION

MANUFACTURER Manufacture d'Armes de St Etienne (MAS)

CALIBRE 7.65mm French Long

MAGAZINE CAPACITY 32

ACTION Blowback

TOTAL LENGTH (STOCK EXTENDED) 623mm/24.5in

BARREL LENGTH 224mm/8.8in

WEIGHT UNLOADED 2,870g/101oz

MAT 49

The MAT 49 was developed in the late 1940s. It had a rugged design which was possible to produce in large numbers due to an efficient machine-stamping process. The weapon was blowback operated and had a novel system whereby the magazine housing could be locked flat against the barrel, which also prevented the weapon being fired. The magazine housing doubled as a forward hand grip and, when the magazine was in the firing position, the weapon was also protected by a grip safety. It had flip-up sights and was provided with a sliding wire stock that could be locked at different lengths.

SPECIFICATION

MANUFACTURER Manufacture d'Armes de Tulle (MAT)

CALIBRE 9mm Parabellum

MAGAZINE CAPACITY 32

ACTION Blowback

TOTAL LENGTH (STOCK EXTENDED) 720mm/28in

TOTAL LENGTH (STOCK RETRACTED) 460mm/18in

BARREL LENGTH 228mm/9in

WEIGHT UNLOADED 3,630g/128oz

Gevarm D4

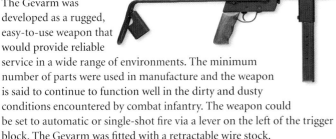

The Gevarm was developed as a rugged, easy-to-use weapon that would provide reliable service in a wide range of environments. The minimum number of parts were used in manufacture and the weapon is said to continue to function well in the dirty and dusty conditions encountered by combat infantry. The weapon could be set to automatic or single-shot fire via a lever on the left of the trigger block. The Gevarm was fitted with a retractable wire stock.

SPECIFICATION

MANUFACTURER	Société Gevarm et Gevelot
CALIBRE	9mm Parabellum
MAGAZINE CAPACITY	32
ACTION	Blowback
TOTAL LENGTH	500mm/19.69in
BARREL LENGTH	220mm/8.66in
WEIGHT UNLOADED	3,200g/112.9oz

Belgium

In 1945 Belgium produced a successful submachine gun designed by a retired Belgian army officer, Colonel Vigneron. With its exceptionally long barrel, the Vigneron could not be in greater contrast to the foreshortened FN Herstal P90, which was designed as a reserve weapon for non-frontline personnel.

Vigneron M2

SPECIFICATION

MANUFACTURER	Société Anonyme Précision Liégeoise, Herstal
CALIBRE	9mm Parabellum
MAGAZINE	32
ACTION	Blowback
TOTAL LENGTH (STOCK EXTENDED)	886mm/34.9in
TOTAL LENGTH (STOCK RETRACTED)	706mm/27.8in
BARREL LENGTH	305mm/12in
WEIGHT UNLOADED	3,290g/116oz

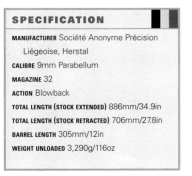

Designed by Colonel Vigneron, the 9mm Vigneron M2 was issued to the Belgian Army from 1953. The Vigneron appeared in the Belgian Congo and was also issued by the Portuguese Army for operations in Angola and Mozambique. The Vigneron was a blowback-operated weapon with a telescopic steel stock. The pistol grip had an integrated safety and it also incorporated a three-position safety catch which could select full safety, single fire and automatic fire. The weapon also incorporated a variable-pressure trigger that could produce either single shots or automatic fire.

FN P90 Personal Weapon

SPECIFICATION

MANUFACTURER	FN Herstal
CALIBRE	5.7mm FN
MAGAZINE	50
ACTION	Blowback
TOTAL LENGTH	500mm/19.69in
BARREL LENGTH	150mm/5.91in
WEIGHT UNLOADED	1,400g/49.40oz

The P90 was developed in the late 1980s. It was an unusual design with the trigger well forward along the receiver and close to the barrel muzzle. The stock was integrated with the rear portion of the receiver. Designed as a personal defence weapon, it could also be used by special forces and law-enforcement units in close combat. The FN90 had a smooth design to minimize the chances of snagging. The magazine sat over the front portion of the barrel. There was a rail on the top designed to take sights and side rails will take tactical lights and lasers. There was a cocking handle on each side of the weapon, contributing to its ambidextrous qualities.

Switzerland

Switzerland has produced some successful submachine-gun designs, although some have proved too complicated for easy manufacture. In a market full of simpler serviceable weapons, Swiss designs

such as the SIG MP310 did not achieve the recognition they deserved. As a result companies such as SIG focused their design and development on such armaments as pistols and assault rifles.

MP43/44

When the invasion of Switzerland by Germany seemed likely in the early 1940s, the Swiss Army was issued with the Furrer MP41/44 developed at Waffenfabrik in Bern, which was a complex weapon with expensive machining. It soon became apparent that the M41/44 could not be produced fast enough to satisfy demand and the Swiss Army procured a tried and tested weapon to replace it. A licence was obtained from Suomi of Finland to reproduce their 1931 Suomi submachine gun almost identically, with just minor modifications known as the MP43/44. It succeeded the MP41 as the standard submachine gun of Switzerland. It proved to be a success and remained in service through to the 1960s.

SPECIFICATION

MANUFACTURER Hispano-Suiza SA., Genf
CALIBRE 9mm Parabellum
MAGAZINE CAPACITY 50
ACTION Blowback
TOTAL LENGTH 890mm/33.9in
BARREL LENGTH 315mm/12.4in
WEIGHT UNLOADED 4,760g/167.9oz

Rexim "Favor" Mk 4

This weapon was developed in the 1950s by Swiss small arms company Rexim in Geneva. The Rexim was a conventional blowback-operated weapon with a somewhat complex firing mechanism incorporating an independent hammer. As with other complex designs, the weapon was not accepted by major armed forces. The parent company eventually went out of business in 1957. A version continued to be made for a period of time by the manufacturers in Spain at La Coruna and several thousand weapons were produced.

bayonet

ABOVE The bayonet was stored underneath the barrel and was fitted to a holder just behind the muzzle when required.

Rifle characteristics
The Rexim Mk 4 had rifle-like characteristics – such as a long barrel and a bayonet. This made it a fearsome weapon even without ammunition.

SPECIFICATION

MANUFACTURER Rexim SA., Geneva
CALIBRE 9mm Parabellum
MAGAZINE CAPACITY 32
ACTION Blowback
TOTAL LENGTH (STOCK EXTENDED) 873mm/34.37in
TOTAL LENGTH (STOCK RETRACTED) 617mm/24.3in
BARREL LENGTH 340mm/13.38in
WEIGHT UNLOADED 4,670g/164.7oz

Germany

In 1916, German designers and manufacturers created the first true submachine gun, the 9mm MP18. Almost a century later they are producing some of the most widely used and respected submachine guns, with weapons such as the Heckler & Koch MP5 and the HK UMP40 (Universal Machine Pistol).

Bergmann MP18/I

SPECIFICATION

MANUFACTURER Theodor Bergmann Waffenfabrik

CALIBRE 9mm Parabellum

MAGAZINE CAPACITY 32

ACTION Blowback

TOTAL LENGTH 812mm/31.97in

BARREL LENGTH 196mm/7.75in

WEIGHT UNLOADED 4,190g/81.13oz

This weapon, devised by Hugo Schmeisser (son of Louis Schmeisser) had a strong influence on the design and development of the submachine gun. Arguably the first true submachine gun, the MP18/I was developed at Spandau (a district of Berlin) and featured a revolutionary blowback mechanism. Construction of the weapon was to the highest standards and the inherent simplicity of the design contributed to a high level of reliability. The weapon was fed from a snail-drum magazine and was set to constant automatic mode. Later versions would be designed to fire single shots as well.

Bergmann MP28/II

firing selector

SPECIFICATION

MANUFACTURER C.G. Haenel Waffenfabrik

CALIBRE 9mm Parabellum

MAGAZINE CAPACITY 20, 32 or 50

ACTION Blowback

TOTAL LENGTH 812mm/31.97in

BARREL LENGTH 196mm/7.75in

WEIGHT UNLOADED 3,970g/140oz

The MP28/II was a derivative of the MP18 and similar in appearance. It also incorporated the high-quality machined parts that made the MP18 the first truly successful submachine gun. A fire selector was added for single shots or automatic fire and it was also fitted with a box magazine to replace the snail-drum used in the MP18. The fire selector was a cross-bolt, push-button device. When pushed from the right-hand side two Ds, denoting *Dauerfeuer* or duration firing, were shown on the left of the selector. When pushed the other way, two Es, denoting *Einzelfeuer* or single-shot firing, were shown. The MP28 also had a larger-diameter operating spring than the MP18.

Bergmann MP34/I and MP35/I

SPECIFICATION

MANUFACTURER Carl Walther GmbH. Waffenfabrik/Junker & Ruth AG

CALIBRE 9mm Parabellum

MAGAZINE CAPACITY 24 or 32

ACTION Blowback

TOTAL LENGTH 840mm/33.1in

BARREL LENGTH 196mm/7.75in

WEIGHT UNLOADED 4,050g/142.86oz

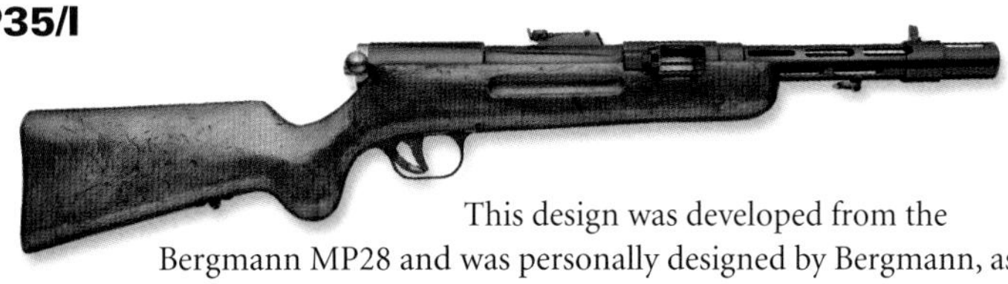

This design was developed from the Bergmann MP28 and was personally designed by Bergmann, as opposed to Schmeisser. It had a different bolt-handle design to the MP28 which was located at the rear of the receiver, as opposed to on the side. It also featured a double-action trigger that could fire either single shots or automatic fire, depending on the amount of pressure placed on the trigger. It was produced in both long and short versions. The MP35/I had minor modifications.

Vollmer Erma Machine Pistol (EMP)

This weapon was developed by Henrich Vollmer (the chief designer at Erma in Erfurt) and was in production for most of the 1930s. It was issued to German forces and saw widespread use until about 1942, when it was replaced by the MP40. It had conventional blowback operation. It was easily identified by its full wooden stock and forward wooden hand grip.

SPECIFICATION

MANUFACTURER Erfurter Maschinenfabrik Berthold Geipel GmbH. (Erma Werke)
CALIBRE 9mm Parabellum
MAGAZINE CAPACITY 25 or 32
ACTION Blowback
TOTAL LENGTH 902mm/35.5in
BARREL LENGTH 254mm/10in
WEIGHT UNLOADED 4,400g/155.2oz

MP38

The MP38 was first introduced in 1938. Designed by Heinrich Vollmer at Erma, it proved to be one of the most successful submachine-gun designs of all time. The mechanics of the weapon were unremarkable – it was a simple blowback design. However, its overall appearance, with a folding metal stock and no wooden fittings, helped to define the new generation of submachine guns. The manufacturing processes of the MP38 were, however, inefficient and its magazine had a tendency to jam.

SPECIFICATION

MANUFACTURER Erfurter Maschinenfabrik Berthold Geipel GmbH. (Erma Werke)
CALIBRE 9mm Parabellum
MAGAZINE CAPACITY 32
ACTION Blowback
TOTAL LENGTH (STOCK EXTENDED) 832mm/32.75in
TOTAL LENGTH (STOCK RETRACTED) 630mm/24.75in
BARREL LENGTH 247mm/9.75in
WEIGHT UNLOADED 4,140g/146oz

MP40

The MP40 was a revised version of the MP38 which made substantial use of pressed-steel parts. It could therefore be produced in much greater numbers than the MP38. It became the definitive submachine gun of the German Army during World War II. The rate of fire and recoil of the weapon were lower than contemporary submachine guns, making it very manageable. It also had an improved safety device. The weapon had a folding metal stock and incorporated plastic furniture instead of wood, which was advanced for its day.

SPECIFICATION

MANUFACTURER Erfurter Maschinenfabrik Berthold Geipel GmbH. (Erma Werke)/Various
CALIBRE 9mm Parabellum
MAGAZINE CAPACITY 32
ACTION Blowback
TOTAL LENGTH (STOCK EXTENDED) 833mm/32.80in
TOTAL LENGTH (STOCK RETRACTED) 630mm/24.8in
BARREL LENGTH 251mm/9.9in
WEIGHT UNLOADED 3,970g/140oz

"The Schmeisser"

The MP40 was often called the Schmeisser by the Allies, after weapons designer Hugo Schmeisser. However, he did not design the weapon, but only the magazines for the MP40, which bear his name.

Heckler & Koch MP5A3

SPECIFICATION

MANUFACTURER Heckler & Koch GmbH.

CALIBRE 9mm Parabellum

MAGAZINE CAPACITY 15 or 30

ACTION Delayed blowback

TOTAL LENGTH (STOCK EXTENDED) 660mm/26in

TOTAL LENGTH (STOCK RETRACTED) 490mm/19.3in

BARREL LENGTH 225mm/8.85in

WEIGHT UNLOADED 2,550g/88.18oz

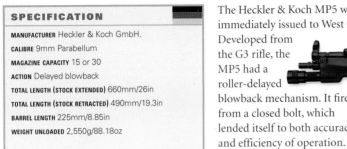

The Heckler & Koch MP5 was first introduced in 1966 and was immediately issued to West German police and border-guard units. Developed from the G3 rifle, the MP5 had a roller-delayed blowback mechanism. It fired from a closed bolt, which lended itself to both accuracy and efficiency of operation. Different variants of the weapon are produced: the MP5A2 had a rigid plastic butt while the MP5A3 had a telescopic metal stock. The MP5 was used by the world's elite forces.

SPECIFICATION

MANUFACTURER Heckler & Koch GmbH.

CALIBRE 9mm Parabellum

MAGAZINE CAPACITY 15 or 30

ACTION Delayed blowback

TOTAL LENGTH 550mm/21.65in (SD1)

BARREL LENGTH 146mm/5.75in (SD1)

WEIGHT UNLOADED 2,900g/102oz

Heckler & Koch MP5SD

This was a silenced version of the MP family. The mechanism was exactly the same as the standard MP5 but the barrel was shorter and drilled, and was surrounded by a large silencer casing. The MP5SD was produced in various configurations: the MP5SD1 had a cap at the end of the receiver and no stock, the MP5SD2 had a retractable stock and a fixed butt. The MPSD4, MPSD5 and MPSD6 all had three-round bursts and were variations of earlier versions.

SPECIFICATION

MANUFACTURER Heckler & Koch GmbH.

CALIBRE 5.56mm

MAGAZINE CAPACITY 25

ACTION Delayed blowback

TOTAL LENGTH (STOCK EXTENDED) 755mm/29.72in

TOTAL LENGTH (STOCK RETRACTED) 563mm/22.17in

BARREL LENGTH 211mm/8.31in

WEIGHT UNLOADED 3,050g/107.56oz

Heckler & Koch MP53

Produced from 1975 onwards, this weapon could be used as a submachine gun, or an assault rifle. It had the same roller mechanism that typified the Heckler & Koch submachine-gun range. The HK33 rifle was also unusual because it worked by a delayed blowback mechanism. Similar in appearance to the HK33K rifle, the MP53 was shorter and could be fitted with a fixed or a telescoping butt. A switch could be used to select single shots, automatic fire or full safety.

SPECIFICATION

MANUFACTURER Heckler & Koch GmbH.

CALIBRE 9mm Parabellum

MAGAZINE CAPACITY 15/30

ACTION Delayed blowback

TOTAL LENGTH 325mm/12.80in

BARREL LENGTH 115mm/4.53in

WEIGHT UNLOADED 2,100g/74oz

Heckler & Koch MP5K

Introduced in 1976, the MP5K was essentially the same weapon as the standard MP5. The major difference was its more compact size, with a smaller barrel and magazine (the K stands for *kurz* in German, which means "short"). This version was not fitted with a stock and instead had an additional forward grip, plus a guard to prevent fingers from sliding over the muzzle. It was easily concealed but its size meant that it had a limited range of fire.

Heckler & Koch MP7

This weapon was developed to meet new requirements for a personal defence weapon, as broadly laid down by NATO. It was produced from 2001 onwards and designed for close combat as well as for mid-range personal defence. In view of advances in body armour technology, a new calibre of high-penetration round was formulated. The round was unique to the weapon, reducing recoil and increasing accuracy and penetration, The light weight of the MP7 was achieved through the use of polymers in its construction.

SPECIFICATION	
MANUFACTURER Heckler & Koch GmbH.	
CALIBRE 4.6mm H&K	
MAGAZINE CAPACITY 20 or 40	
ACTION Gas	
TOTAL LENGTH (BUTT EXTENDED) 640mm/25.2in	
TOTAL LENGTH (BUTT RETRACTED) 420mm/16.4in	
BARREL LENGTH 180mm/7.09in	
WEIGHT UNLOADED 1,800g/63.49oz	

Heckler & Koch UMP40

The HK UMP (Universal Machine Pistol) was developed in the 1990s as a replacement for the HKMP5 and was available from 2002. Constructed largely of polymers, it was lighter than the MP5. It was produced in three different versions, according to calibre (.40 S&W, .45 ACP and 9mm Parabellum). To allow for the range of calibres it had a reduced rate of fire, but a longer range than comparable weapons. The UMP had a side-folding buttstock. It could be fitted with optional extras, such as flashlights, optical sights or laser sights.

SPECIFICATION	
MANUFACTURER Heckler & Koch GmbH.	
CALIBRE .40 S&W, .45 ACP, 9mm Parabellum	
MAGAZINE CAPACITY 30	
ACTION Recoil	
TOTAL LENGTH (STOCK EXTENDED) 600mm/27.17in	
TOTAL LENGTH (STOCK RETRACTED) 450mm/17.72in	
BARREL LENGTH 200mm/7.87in	
WEIGHT UNLOADED 2,100g/74oz	

Dux 53 (modified)

non-standard barrel

The Dux 53 was derived from the Finnish Model 44 submachine gun. The promoter of the weapon, Willi Daugs, fled from Finland at the end of World War II. Eventually he took the designs to the Oviedo Arsenal in Spain and the Dux 51 was produced. After weapons were supplied to Germany and a new order was received from Germany to develop various models of the Dux, it was designated the Dux 53 and made at Oviedo in Spain.

SPECIFICATION	
MANUFACTURER Auschütz/Oviedo Arsenal	
CALIBRE 9mm Parabellum	
MAGAZINE CAPACITY 50 box	
ACTION Blowback	
TOTAL LENGTH (STOCK EXTENDED) 825mm/32.5in	
TOTAL LENGTH (STOCK RETRACTED) 615mm/24.25in	
BARREL LENGTH 249mm/9.8in	
WEIGHT UNLOADED 3,490g/123.1oz	

Walther MPK

The MPK was first produced in 1963 and was deployed by police and some naval units until production ceased in 1987. The MPK was a conventional blowback weapon. The stock could be folded away and used as a forward hand grip. The MPK had a selector for single shots, automatic fire or full safety. There was a cocking handle on the right of the receiver, which could be locked into the bolt if necessary to clear stoppages.

SPECIFICATION	
MANUFACTURER Carl Walther, Ulm, Donau	
CALIBRE 9mm Parabellum	
MAGAZINE CAPACITY 32	
ACTION Blowback	
TOTAL LENGTH (STOCK EXTENDED) 653mm/25.71in	
TOTAL LENGTH (STOCK RETRACTED) 368mm/14.5in	
BARREL LENGTH 171mm/6.7in	
WEIGHT UNLOADED 2,800g/98.77oz	

 Italy

After the production of the famous Villar Perosa (OVP) in the 1920s, much of the manufacture of Italian submachine guns was undertaken by Beretta.

More recently, some attempts have been made by smaller firms to enter the submachine-gun market, one of the most successful of which was the Spectre.

Beretta Model 1918

SPECIFICATION

MANUFACTURER Pietro Beretta SpA.
CALIBRE 9mm Glisenti
MAGAZINE CAPACITY 25
ACTION Delayed blowback
TOTAL LENGTH 850mm/33.5in
BARREL LENGTH 305mm/12in
WEIGHT UNLOADED 3,260g/115oz

This submachine gun went into service with the Italian armed forces. It was based on the Villar Perosa (OVP) mechanisms as no other submachine gun designs existed at that time. The receiver and barrel were the same as the Villar Perosa and a wooden stock was added. Some versions of the Model 1918 had two triggers, one for single shots and the other for automatic fire. The design proved to be successful and some examples of the Beretta Model 1918 were still in use during World War II.

Beretta Model 1938A

SPECIFICATION

MANUFACTURER Pietro Beretta SpA.
CALIBRE 9mm Parabellum
MAGAZINE CAPACITY 10, 20, 30 or 40
ACTION Blowback
TOTAL LENGTH 953mm/37.5in
BARREL LENGTH 318mm/12.5in
WEIGHT UNLOADED 4,190g/147.78oz

This proved to be a successful design and one that was derived from a semi-automatic carbine produced in 1935. The weapon had a conventional blowback mechanism and a double-trigger arrangement whereby one could be used for firing single shots and the other for automatic fire. There were various versions of the weapon, with slight modifications in design and manufacture. Earlier versions, for example, were made from largely machined parts while later versions incorporated a larger proportion of sheet metal. The Model 1938A was issued to Italian and German forces and saw extensive service. Further adaptations were made to produce the Model 38/42, Model 38/44 and Model 38/49 and the Beretta 5.

Beretta Model 1938/42

SPECIFICATION

MANUFACTURER Pietro Beretta SpA.
CALIBRE 9mm Parabellum
MAGAZINE CAPACITY 20 or 40
ACTION Blowback
TOTAL LENGTH 800mm/31.5in
BARREL LENGTH 216mm/8.5in
WEIGHT UNLOADED 3,260g/115oz

This weapon was a modified version of the Model 1938A, and immediately distinguishable due to the fact that the barrel was shorter. The wooden stock was less extensive and finished short of the magazine. In order to reduce the ingress of dirt, the bolt handle was fitted with a dust cover. Like the Model 1938A, the Model 1938/42 proved to be a highly successful design which was ordered in large numbers by the German Army as well as by the Romanian Army.

Beretta Model 1938/44

This weapon was a simplified version of the Beretta Model 1938/42 and was designed for ease of production at the end of World War II. In the internal mechanism, the bolt was reduced in length from 180mm/7.1in to 150mm/5.91in. The 38/44 was issued to the German Army and was designated the MP739.

SPECIFICATION

MANUFACTURER Pietro Beretta SpA.
CALIBRE 9mm Parabellum
MAGAZINE CAPACITY 20 or 40
ACTION Blowback
TOTAL LENGTH 800mm/31.5in
BARREL LENGTH 216mm/8.5in
WEIGHT UNLOADED 3,260g/115oz

Beretta Model 4

This weapon was a development of the Beretta Model 1938A and was originally designated Model 1938/44. It came with a range of options to suit the requirements of different customers – either a wooden stock or a folding metal one, and an option for a grip safety in addition to the conventional safety. Essentially, the Beretta Model 4 was a simplified version of its predecessor, produced in the somewhat straitened circumstances at the end of World War II.

SPECIFICATION

MANUFACTURER Pietro Beretta SpA.
CALIBRE 9mm Parabellum
MAGAZINE CAPACITY 20 or 40
ACTION Blowback
TOTAL LENGTH 800mm/31.5in
BARREL LENGTH 216mm/8.5in
WEIGHT UNLOADED 3,260g/115oz

Beretta Model 5

The Beretta Model 5, introduced in 1957, was mainly a series improvement on the Beretta Model 1938/49 (a modified version of the Model 1938/44). A new safety system was designed and fitted, which comprised a grip safety that had to be depressed to allow the weapon to fire. This device was located in the wooden furniture on the side of the receiver and it was operated by the forward hand. The spring-loaded catch freed the bolt when it was depressed. It was produced until 1959.

SPECIFICATION

MANUFACTURER Pietro Beretta SpA.
CALIBRE 9mm Parabellum
MAGAZINE CAPACITY 20 or 40
ACTION Blowback
TOTAL LENGTH 800mm/31.5in
BARREL LENGTH 216mm/8.5in
WEIGHT UNLOADED 3,260g/115oz

Beretta Model 12S

silencer   selector-safety

Although the submachine guns derived from the Model 1938/44 proved to be successful they also became dated in design and, with their solid wood stocks, were comparatively heavy. The Model 12 submachine gun, first produced in 1958, proved to be a novel and successful design. The Model 12 was adopted by the Italian Army in 1979 and was also sold widely in Africa and South America. In 1983 a revised model was introduced, designated the 12S. Changes were made in areas such as the safety mechanism, fire selector and the sights. A silencer could also be fitted.

SPECIFICATION

MANUFACTURER Fabbrica D'Armi P. Beretta SpA.
CALIBRE 9mm Parabellum
MAGAZINE CAPACITY 32
ACTION Blowback
TOTAL LENGTH 418mm/16.47in
BARREL LENGTH 200mm/7.87in
WEIGHT UNLOADED 3,000g/105.80oz

FNAB Model 1943

SPECIFICATION

MANUFACTURER Fabbrica Nazionale d'Armi
CALIBRE 9mm Parabellum
MAGAZINE CAPACITY 20 or 40
ACTION Delayed blowback
TOTAL LENGTH (STOCK EXTENDED) 790mm/31.10in
TOTAL LENGTH (STOCK RETRACTED) 527mm/20.75in
BARREL LENGTH 198mm/7.79in
WEIGHT UNLOADED 3,250g/114.64oz

This rare weapon was developed and produced during World War II in small numbers. Unusually, it went against the trend of the time, which was to produce inexpensive and easily assembled weapons. It was a finely engineered product with high manufacturing quality.

SPECIFICATION

MANUFACTURER Luigi Franchi SpA.
CALIBRE 9mm Parabellum
MAGAZINE CAPACITY 20/40
ACTION Blowback
TOTAL LENGTH (STOCK EXTENDED) 688mm/27in
TOTAL LENGTH (STOCK RETRACTED) 419mm/16.5in
BARREL LENGTH 203mm/8in
WEIGHT UNLOADED 3,170g/111.81oz

Franchi LF57

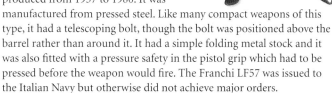

The Franchi LF57 was produced from 1957 to 1980. It was manufactured from pressed steel. Like many compact weapons of this type, it had a telescoping bolt, though the bolt was positioned above the barrel rather than around it. It had a simple folding metal stock and it was also fitted with a pressure safety in the pistol grip which had to be pressed before the weapon would fire. The Franchi LF57 was issued to the Italian Navy but otherwise did not achieve major orders.

TZ45

SPECIFICATION

MANUFACTURER Giandoso
CALIBRE 9mm Parabellum
MAGAZINE CAPACITY 40
ACTION Blowback
TOTAL LENGTH (STOCK EXTENDED) 850mm/33.46in
TOTAL LENGTH (STOCK RETRACTED) 545mm/21.45in
BARREL LENGTH 230mm/9.05in
WEIGHT UNLOADED 3,260g/114.99oz

Developed at the end of World War II, the TZ45 was a basic design and had low manufacturing costs. It had a retracting metal stock and was equipped with a grip safety. Although some of these weapons were exported, it failed to impress in terms of either quality or performance and it was soon discontinued in Italy.

SPECTRE M-4

SPECIFICATION

MANUFACTURER SITES SpA.
CALIBRE 9mm Parabellum
MAGAZINE CAPACITY 30 or 50
ACTION Blowback
TOTAL LENGTH (STOCK RETRACTED) 350mm/13.78in
BARREL LENGTH 130mm/5.1in
WEIGHT UNLOADED 2,900g/102.29oz

Introduced in 1984, this weapon had a closed-bolt system and a double-action trigger that incorporated a de-cocking lever. A pull on the trigger cocked the hammer and a round was chambered. In this mode it could still be carried safely. The magazine had a four-column design which allowed a greater number of rounds in a reduced-length magazine. The Spectre was the only submachine gun on the market to have a double-action system in the mid-1980s.

Socimi Type 821

The Socimi (named after the manufacturer Societa Construzioni Industriali Milano) was said to be influenced by the Israeli Uzi submachine gun. Introduced in 1984, it had a rectangular steel receiver, and a pistol grip protruded from the centre of the weapon giving it good balance. The magazine was inserted into the base of the pistol grip. The pistol grip was covered in plastic furniture, as was the forward underpart of the receiver where the front hand would grip. It had a retracting stock that pivoted from the base of the receiver. A pressure safety was located at the back of the pistol grip, which needed to be pressed before the weapon was fired. The Socimi was produced for about five years until the late 1980s.

SPECIFICATION

MANUFACTURER Societa Construzioni Industriali Milano SpA.
CALIBRE 9mm Parabellum
MAGAZINE CAPACITY 32
ACTION Blowback
TOTAL LENGTH (STOCK EXTENDED) 600mm/23.6in
TOTAL LENGTH (STOCK RETRACTED) 400mm/15.7in
BARREL LENGTH 200mm/78.4in
WEIGHT UNLOADED 2,450g/86.42oz

Twin Villar Perosa

feed for curved box magazines
twin barrels
rear grips
bipod mount

This somewhat strange-looking weapon is not instantly recognizable as a submachine gun. Early versions were produced between 1915–17 and so the earliest model was designated as "the first submachine gun". It was also known as the "Fiat" (when manufactured from Revelli factories in Italy). It came with a bipod (or tripod) mount for ground use and a shield which could be used in fixed positions or on the move. The Villar Perosa had double barrels and also double magazines firing 9mm cartridges and a delayed-blowback mechanism. Although it was an original design, the Villar Perosa was somewhat clumsy as a personal weapon and poor tactical handling meant that it soon gave way to more conventional designs.

SPECIFICATION

MANUFACTURER Various (in Italy and Canada)/Oficina di Villar Perosa
CALIBRE 9mm Glisenti
MAGAZINE CAPACITY 25
ACTION Delayed blowback
TOTAL LENGTH 953mm/37.5in
BARREL LENGTH 318mm/12.5in
WEIGHT UNLOADED 4,190g/147.8oz

Villar Perosa (OVP)

This weapon, unlike its predecessor, the twin Villar Perosa, was an entirely conventional design with a wooden stock and single, extended barrel. It was developed after World War I and introduced in the early 1920s. The weapon was directly derived from the Twin Villar Perosa, being based round a single barrel of the older weapon. The cocking mechanism was adapted so that it could be operated when firing from the shoulder. The trigger setup incorporated two triggers: the front one was used for automatic fire and the rear for single shots. The OVP was used during World War II.

SPECIFICATION

MANUFACTURER Various (in Italy and Canada)/Oficina di Villar Perosa
CALIBRE 9mm Glisenti
MAGAZINE CAPACITY 25
ACTION Delayed blowback
TOTAL LENGTH 776mm/35.5in
BARREL LENGTH 280mm/11in
WEIGHT UNLOADED 3,670g/129.45oz

Denmark

Danish submachine-gun design and manufacture has been largely centred on the Madsen M45 and M46 models. The first model did not prove to be successful due to its complexity, but the second was an original design that caught the imagination, especially because of the novel way of opening the side of the weapon so that the internal workings were visible. The Madsen M50 and M53 were developments of this gun.

Madsen M46

SPECIFICATION	
MANUFACTURER	Dansk Industri Syndikat, Madsen
CALIBRE	9mm Parabellum
MAGAZINE CAPACITY	32
ACTION	Blowback
TOTAL LENGTH (STOCK EXTENDED)	780mm/30.71in
TOTAL LENGTH (STOCK RETRACTED)	550mm/21.65in
BARREL LENGTH	200mm/7.87in
WEIGHT UNLOADED	3,150g/111.11oz

The first Madsen model to be produced at the end of World War I was the M45, but it had little commercial success. The M46, introduced a year later (designated the P16), was far more successful. It was made of two sheet-steel frames, hinged at the rear. The frame could open to allow access for cleaning, maintenance or replacement. It was blowback operated and had an open-bolt mechanism. It had a folding stock, partly covered with leather, which folded to the right. It also had a grip safety to the rear of the magazine holder. The weapon proved successful in South America.

Madsen M53

SPECIFICATION	
MANUFACTURER	Dansk Industri Syndikat, Madsen
CALIBRE	9mm Parabellum
MAGAZINE CAPACITY	32
ACTION	Blowback
TOTAL LENGTH (STOCK EXTENDED)	800mm/31.5in
TOTAL LENGTH (STOCK RETRACTED)	530mm/20.87in
BARREL LENGTH	200mm/7.8in
WEIGHT UNLOADED	3,200g/112oz

The M50 (designated the P56) was a slightly modified version of the M46. In 1953, the M53 was introduced, followed very shortly after by the Mark II, in a variety of models. As with all Madsens the frame was sheet-steel, hinged at the rear and fired from the open-bolt position. The Mark II had a fire-selector lever above the left-side rear pistol grip and wood or heat-insulating pistol grips (to prevent oveheating by the sun). The stock folded to the right. Apart from the curved frame of the magazine, the M53 and the Mark II were almost identical to the M46 and M50.

SPECIFICATION	
MANUFACTURER	Haerens Vabenarsenalet
CALIBRE	9mm Parabellum
MAGAZINE CAPACITY	36
ACTION	Blowback
TOTAL LENGTH (STOCK EXTENDED)	810mm/31.9in
TOTAL LENGTH (STOCK RETRACTED)	550mm/21.65in
BARREL LENGTH	216mm/8.5in
WEIGHT UNLOADED	3,500g/123.45oz

M49 Hovea

Originally designed in Sweden in the mid-1940s, it was a blowback-operated automatic weapon with a cylindrical receiver. It had a folding metal stock and a wooden hand grip behind the trigger guard. It was similar to the Carl Gustaf, and in trials for the Swedish armed forces the Carl Gustaf model won the contract. The Hovea won a competition held by the Danish armed forces and it was then produced under licence in Denmark.

Austria

In Steyr Mannlicher GmbH, Austria has one of the world's leading small-arms manufacturers, providing leading-edge designs to armed forces throughout the world. The Steyr Aug Para submachine gun, developed from the Steyr Aug rifle, is just one example in this impressive line up.

Steyr MPi 69

Introduced in 1969, the Steyr MPi 69 was a simplified version of the world-renowned Uzi submachine gun. It was issued to a number of security forces around the world but has since been replaced by the Steyr Aug. It was a blowback-operated selective-fire weapon with a wrap-around bolt. The weapon fired either single shots or automatic fire depending on the pressure exerted on the trigger. The safety catch located above the trigger had three positions. The magazine was inserted into the vertical pistol hand grip. The stock could be folded. The receiver fitted into a plastic hand grip. The sling strap could be attached to the cocking handle. The MPi 81 was an updated version with a higher rate of fire and a conventional cocking handle.

SPECIFICATION

MANUFACTURER Steyr Mannlicher GmbH.
CALIBRE 9mm Parabellum
MAGAZINE 25 or 32
ACTION Blowback
TOTAL LENGTH (STOCK EXTENDED) 670mm/26.38in
TOTAL LENGTH (STOCK RETRACTED) 465mm/18.3in
BARREL LENGTH 260mm/10.24in
WEIGHT UNLOADED 2,930g/103.35oz

Steyr Aug Para

The Steyr Aug family of weapons was first introduced in the 1970s. The Para was a submachine gun version of the Aug assault rifle, the main difference being a new 9mm barrel, a closed-bolt firing system and a magazine adaptor. The length produced a higher muzzle energy as well as greater accuracy. The weapon had a blowback operating system and the bolt was one-piece, whereas the rifle had a bolt and a carrier system. The barrel was threaded and could accept a range of silencers. The rifle could be turned into a submachine gun by the use of a conversion kit.

SPECIFICATION

MANUFACTURER Steyr-Mannlicher GmbH.
CALIBRE 9mm Parabellum
MAGAZINE 25
ACTION Blowback
TOTAL LENGTH 665mm/26.18in
BARREL LENGTH 420mm/16.54in
WEIGHT UNLOADED 3,700g/130.51oz

Steyr TMP (Tactical Machine Pistol)

The design brief for the Steyr TMP was for an easy-to-handle weapon with significant firepower and a pistol-type grip. It was manufactured in 1993 from composite materials and had a very smooth, moulded design to minimize snagging. It had a delayed-blowback, closed-bolt system and a rotating barrel. The trigger was automatically selective and adjusted from single shots to automatic fire according to pressure. The mode could also be controlled with the safety catch. The Steyr TMP was designed to take a silencer as well as a variety of sights.

SPECIFICATION

MANUFACTURER Steyr-Mannlicher GmbH.
CALIBRE 9mm Parabellum
MAGAZINE 15, 20 or 25
ACTION Delayed blowback
TOTAL LENGTH 270mm/10.6in
BARREL LENGTH 150mm/5.9in
WEIGHT UNLOADED 1,400g/49.39oz

🇸🇪 Sweden

Although Sweden has only produced one submachine gun of its own design, it has become a classic. The Carl Gustaf M45 was used by the US Army during the Vietnam War and, when supplies ran out, the US produced their own copy. The Egyptians copied it in two homemade versions. The M45 was rugged, simple, effective and, almost as important, it had the right look.

Carl Gustaf M45

SPECIFICATION 🇸🇪	
MANUFACTURER	Carl Gustaf Arms Co.
CALIBRE	9mm Parabellum
MAGAZINE CAPACITY	36 or 50
ACTION	Blowback
TOTAL LENGTH (STOCK EXTENDED)	806mm/31.7in
TOTAL LENGTH (STOCK RETRACTED)	552mm/21.7in
BARREL LENGTH	203mm/7.99in
WEIGHT UNLOADED	3,430g/121oz

This weapon was designed by Gunnar Johnsson of Carl Gustaf Arms Company. He is said to have been inspired by the German Bergmann MP35 used widely during World War II. The M45 was issued to the Swedish Army after 1945. It was also later issued to US special forces and was used in service in Vietnam. It was a blowback-operated weapon firing from an open bolt. Due to the comparatively low rate of fire and small amount of recoil, the M45 was relatively easy to handle. Early versions did not have a magazine support, but this was rectified in later versions. The design of the magazine itself was widely acclaimed.

Suomi/Husqvarna M37-39

SPECIFICATION 🇸🇪	
MANUFACTURER	Husqvarna Vapenfabriks AB
CALIBRE	9mm Parabellum
MAGAZINE CAPACITY	36 box or 71 drum
ACTION	Blowback
TOTAL LENGTH	831mm/32.7in
BARREL LENGTH	249mm/9.8in
WEIGHT UNLOADED	2,900g/102oz

A licenced model of the Finnish Suomi M31 was made by the Husqvarna factory in Sweden, where it was designated the M37-39. Sweden also exported their version to other countries, including their neighbours, Norway and Denmark, and countries farther afield such as Indonesia and Egypt. The main design differences between the Suomi M/31 and the Husqvarna M37-39 were the stock, the barrel and the sights.

Hovea prototype

SPECIFICATION 🇸🇪	
MANUFACTURER	Husqvarna Vapenfabriks AB
CALIBRE	9mm Parabellum
MAGAZINE CAPACITY	71 drum
ACTION	Blowback
TOTAL LENGTH (STOCK EXTENDED)	845mm/33.27in
TOTAL LENGTH (STOCK RETRACTED)	590mm/21.65in
BARREL LENGTH	212mm/8.46in
WEIGHT UNLOADED	3,000g/105.82oz

This weapon was one of a series of prototype submachine guns made by Husqvarna for the submachine-gun trials held during late 1944 and 1945. This was a blowback-operated automatic weapon with a cylindrical receiver similar to that of the Sten. It had a folding metal stock and a wooden hand grip behind the trigger guard. The design lost out to the Carl Gustaf, which was a similar design, in Swedish military trials. The rights of manufacture were sold to Denmark.

Czech Republic

Czech industry has produced a variety of highly regarded armaments over the years and most of these have been manufactured by Ceskoslovenská

Zbrojovka (sister company to Ceská Zbrojovka). Pioneering designs include the CZ23–26 series of submachine guns, with their wraparound bolts.

ZK 383

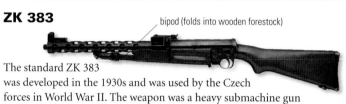

bipod (folds into wooden forestock)

The standard ZK 383 was developed in the 1930s and was used by the Czech forces in World War II. The weapon was a heavy submachine gun that is sometimes described as a light automatic rifle and it is heavy enough to be deployed as a squad submachine gun. Characteristics that are more typical of a heavy submachine gun include a bipod and an interchangeable barrel. There were variations on the design, including the ZK 383H and ZK 383P. The ZK 383 was issued to German troops and to the Bulgarian Army, and also appeared in parts of South America.

SPECIFICATION

MANUFACTURER Ceskoslovenská Zbrojovka
CALIBRE 9mm Parabellum
MAGAZINE CAPACITY 30
ACTION Blowback
TOTAL LENGTH 902mm/35.5in
BARREL LENGTH 325mm/12.8in
WEIGHT UNLOADED 4,250g/150oz

CZSA 25

This submachine gun was developed in 1948 and was possibly the most successful version among a series of submachine guns that included the SA23, SA24, SA25 and SA26. The action was blowback with an open-bolt system that wraps around the rear end of the barrel – one of the first designs to incorporate this system. There is a fire-selection system in the trigger, whereby the gun will fire single shots or automatic fire according to finger pressure. The magazine was inserted in the hand grip, which helped to balance the weapon. The earlier versions, CZ 23 and CZ 24, were distinguished by a wooden stock, whereas the CZ 25 had a metal stock.

SPECIFICATION

MANUFACTURER Ceskoslovenská Zbrojovka
CALIBRE 9mm Parabellum
MAGAZINE CAPACITY 24 or 40
ACTION Blowback
TOTAL LENGTH (STOCK EXTENDED) 686mm/27in
TOTAL LENGTH (STOCK RETRACTED) 445mm/17.5in
BARREL LENGTH 284mm/11.2in
WEIGHT UNLOADED 3,817g/134.39oz

Skorpion M61

The Skorpion submachine gun had a somewhat iconic design that has appeared in different versions with different calibres. Most notable were the vz.61 and vz.62, in both .32 ACP and 9mm calibre. It is characterized by small dimensions and light weight. It has been deployed successfully by specialist paramilitary and police units who have to operate in confined spaces, such as buildings, aircraft and other vehicles. The weapon had a retractable shoulder stock and it could be carried in a holster if necessary. The pressure-sensitive trigger allowed for the firing of single shots or automatic fire.

SPECIFICATION

MANUFACTURER Ceskoslovenská Zbrojovka
CALIBRE .32 ACP, 9mm Parabellum
MAGAZINE CAPACITY 10 or 20
ACTION Blowback
TOTAL LENGTH (STOCK EXTENDED) 517mm/20.35in
TOTAL LENGTH (STOCK RETRACTED) 270mm/10.63in
BARREL LENGTH 113mm/4.45in
WEIGHT UNLOADED 1,440g/50.79oz

Poland

Apart from the PM-63 submachine gun developed in Poland in the 1960s, the Polish armed forces relied largely on a copy of the classic Soviet PPS-43 submachine gun in the immediate post-war years. In the 1980s the PM-84 and PM-98 were developed as replacements for the PM-63.

Sudaev PPS-43

SPECIFICATION

MANUFACTURER State Arsenals

CALIBRE 7.62mm Tokarev

MAGAZINE CAPACITY 35

ACTION Blowback

TOTAL LENGTH (STOCK EXTENDED) 808mm/32.25in

TOTAL LENGTH (STOCK RETRACTED) 606mm/24.25in

BARREL LENGTH 269mm/10.75in

WEIGHT UNLOADED 5,625g/198.42oz

This weapon was designed by Soviet engineer Aleksei Sudaev in 1942 and it proved to be one of the most effective submachine guns used by the Russians in World War II. It was based on the PPSh-41 and PPSh-42 designed by Georgii Shpagin but was less expensive to produce. The PPS-43 was a modified and standardized version of the PPS-42. It had a blowback operation, firing from an open bolt, and it was set to permanent automatic fire. The folding stock made it a handy weapon for paratroop units and tank crews. The Polish armed forces were issued with copies after 1945.

PM-63 (Pistolet Maszynowy wz.63)

SPECIFICATION

MANUFACTURER State Arsenals

CALIBRE 9mm Makarov

MAGAZINE CAPACITY 15 or 25

ACTION Blowback

TOTAL LENGTH (STOCK EXTENDED) 583mm/22.95in

TOTAL LENGTH (STOCK RETRACTED) 333mm/13.11in

BARREL LENGTH 152mm/5.98in

WEIGHT UNLOADED 1,800g/63.49oz

This weapon was designed by Peter Wilniewczyc in 1963 and was issued to the Polish armed forces in 1965. It was a blowback-operated weapon with an open-bolt mechanism. For single shots, the weapon was cocked by pulling back the slide until it locked. After the firing action, the slide returned to the cocked position, ready for the next round to be fired. A more firm pressure on the trigger enabled automatic fire. Otherwise, the PM-63 was designed in much the same way as a pistol. It could be fired single-handedly, like a pistol, with varying degrees of accuracy, or the shoulder stock could be used to improve control.

PM-84P

SPECIFICATION

MANUFACTURER State Arsenals (Radom)

CALIBRE 9mm Makarov

MAGAZINE CAPACITY 15 or 25

ACTION Blowback

TOTAL LENGTH (STOCK EXTENDED) 575mm/22.64in

TOTAL LENGTH (STOCK RETRACTED) 375mm/14.76in

BARREL LENGTH 185mm/7.28in

WEIGHT UNLOADED 2,170g/76.54oz

The PM-84 (sometimes called the "Glauberyt") was developed in the early 1980s as a replacement for the PM-63. The weapon had a higher proportion of stamped parts over its predecessor as technology had improved. It was a conventional blowback design, fired from an open bolt. The weapon could be cocked from either side of the receiver and there was a fire selector and safety switch above the hand grip. A further development of the weapon in the 1990s was the PM-98. The new model could also be fitted with a laser-pointer or flashlight.

Croatia

A number of submachine guns have been produced in Croatia over the years, including the Agram 2000, the Sokacz, said to be influenced by the Russian PPSh-41 (and often built by local machine shops) and the Ero, which was a version of the Israeli Uzi submachine gun with minor differences.

Ero

The Ero was a 1994 Croatian version of the Israeli Uzi submachine gun, which was first designed by Major Uziel Gal at the end of the 1940s. The Ero is almost entirely manufactured from stamped steel and has a minimum number of parts. The magazine is inserted into the hand grip, which is placed at the centre of the weapon. This makes for optimum balance and also makes it easier to reload in dark conditions. Other than differences in weight and size, the main difference between the Ero and the Uzi is the grip safety at the top of the pistol grip.

SPECIFICATION	
MANUFACTURER	Local Croatian manufacturer
CALIBRE	9mm Parabellum
MAGAZINE CAPACITY	32
ACTION	Blowback
TOTAL LENGTH (STOCK EXTENDED)	650mm/25.59in
TOTAL LENGTH (STOCK RETRACTED)	470mm/18.5in
BARREL LENGTH	260mm/10.24in
WEIGHT UNLOADED	3,730g/131.57oz

Sokacz

The Sokacz was effectively a copy of Soviet Georgii Shpagin's PPSh-41. It was produced in the mid-1990s entirely from stamped metal parts, which were relatively cheap and easy to produce. The receiver was hinged and could be opened easily for maintenance of the internal working parts. The weapon had a very high rate of fire, making it a formidable tool. It had a built-in compensator to reduce muzzle lift while firing. Designed originally for internal security forces, the weapon began to be used throughout Europe after the break-up of Yugoslavia.

SPECIFICATION	
MANUFACTURER	Local Croatian manufacturer
CALIBRE	9mm Parabellum
MAGAZINE CAPACITY	32 or 40
ACTION	Blowback
TOTAL LENGTH (STOCK EXTENDED)	880mm/34.65in
TOTAL LENGTH (STOCK RETRACTED)	605mm/23.82in
BARREL LENGTH	300mm/11.81in
WEIGHT UNLOADED	3,580g/126.28oz

Agram 2000

The Agram was developed for the Croatian Army from the Italian Beretta PM12-S submachine gun. It was primarily intended for personal defence or for use by troops in armoured vehicles. It was a recoil-operated weapon with an open-bolt system. The bolt wrapped round the rear of the barrel so as to reduce the overall length. There was an automatic safety incorporated in the grip and a three-position safety and fire selector. A modified 2002 version of the Agram was also available, designed without the foregrip.

SPECIFICATION	
MANUFACTURER	Local Croatian manufacturer
CALIBRE	9mm Parabellum
MAGAZINE CAPACITY	22, 32 or 40
ACTION	Recoil
TOTAL LENGTH	482mm/18.98in
BARREL LENGTH	200mm/7.87in (various)
WEIGHT UNLOADED	1,800g/63.49oz

 South Africa

The BXP submachine gun is produced by Vektor, part of the large Denel corporation, which produces a wide range of armaments. It was designed in the 1980s when international sanctions against South Africa led to a shortage of arms. It was similar to the US Ingram MAC 10 submachine gun.

BXP

SPECIFICATION	
MANUFACTURER Vektor	
CALIBRE 9mm Parabellum	
MAGAZINE CAPACITY 22 or 32	
ACTION Blowback	
TOTAL LENGTH (STOCK EXTENDED) 607mm/23.9in	
TOTAL LENGTH (STOCK RETRACTED) 387mm/15.2in	
BARREL LENGTH 208mm/8.2in	
WEIGHT UNLOADED 2,500g/88.18oz	

Developed in the mid-1980s, this was a compact design with a conventional blowback mechanism firing from an open bolt. It was small enough and well-balanced enough to be fired like a pistol with one hand. The bolt overlapped the rear end of the barrel, which contributed to the compact size and provided better balance. The cocking handle was located on the top of the receiver and there were fire-selector and safety levers on both sides of the receiver. The weapon had a folding shoulder stock and, when folded, the buttstock could be used as a front hand grip.

 Finland

Finland produced one of the most famous and reliable submachine guns before World War II, the Suomi Model 31. It was extremely well made and proved to be highly effective in the Finnish defence of their country against Soviet invasion forces. The Suomi was adopted by Denmark, Sweden and Switzerland.

Jati-Matic

SPECIFICATION	
MANUFACTURER Tampereen Asepaja Oy	
CALIBRE 9mm Parabellum	
MAGAZINE CAPACITY 20 or 40	
ACTION Blowback	
TOTAL LENGTH 400mm/15.74in	
BARREL LENGTH 249mm/9.8in	
WEIGHT UNLOADED 1,650g/58oz	

The Jati-Matic was introduced in the 1980s. It was a blowback-operated weapon with a select-fire mechanism. There was an upward incline at the rear which had the effect of braking the bolt on recoil. The rear hand grip could be positioned higher than on standard designs. It had a pressure-selective trigger which could fire either single shots or automatic. A forward handle acted as a safety when locked and also doubled as a cocking handle. A new model, the GG-95, was introduced in 1995.

Suomi Model 1931

Designed during the 1920s, the Suomi was still being used in the 1980s. Part of the reason for its longevity was the quality of its manufacture. The bolt was similar to that of a rifle and the drum magazine was similar to that of the Thompson submachine gun. The Suomi played a major role for the Finnish Army in fighting between Finland and the Soviet Union in 1940. It was exported widely, and manufacturing licences were granted to Denmark, Sweden and Switzerland.

SPECIFICATION	
MANUFACTURER Tikkakoski Oy	
CALIBRE 9mm Parabellum	
MAGAZINE CAPACITY 20, 36, 40, 50 or 70	
ACTION Blowback	
TOTAL LENGTH 870mm/34.25in	
BARREL LENGTH 314mm/12.36in	
WEIGHT UNLOADED 4,600g/162.26oz	

M44

This weapon was essentially a copy of the Soviet PPS-43 submachine gun. Considerable numbers were manufactured in Finland in 1944 and it was the standard submachine gun of the Finnish Army. In the 1950s production was restarted in Spain, when the manager of the Tikkakoski Arsenal moved to Oviedo. The Model 1944 could take either a Carl Gustaf box magazine or a Thompson-style drum magazine.

SPECIFICATION

MANUFACTURER Tikkakoski Oy
CALIBRE 9mm Parabellum
MAGAZINE CAPACITY 36 box or 71 drum
ACTION Blowback
TOTAL LENGTH (STOCK EXTENDED) 831mm/32.71in
TOTAL LENGTH (STOCK RETRACTED) 622mm/24.49in
BARREL LENGTH 249mm/9.8in
WEIGHT UNLOADED 2,900g/102oz

Romania

In 1941 the Cugir Arsenal, based in the Transylvanian part of Romania, produced a submachine-gun design known as the Orita. It was quite similar in general appearance to the German MP41, but was a sturdier weapon. It had a limited production but was used extensively by Romanians in Soviet territory.

Orita M41

This weapon was designed by Leopold Jaska and was manufactured to a high standard using machined parts. It normally had a solid wooden butt. It had a blowback operation and bolt mechanism similar to the one used in the Thompson submachine gun. The cocking handle was located on the left of the receiver and the fire selector on the right of the receiver, for either single shots or automatic fire. The weapon was used by pro-German Romanian forces in the invasion of Russia.

SPECIFICATION

MANUFACTURER Cugir Arsenal
CALIBRE 9mm Parabellum
MAGAZINE CAPACITY 25 or 32
ACTION Blowback
TOTAL LENGTH 894mm/35.2in
BARREL LENGTH 287mm/11.3in
WEIGHT UNLOADED 3,460g/122oz

Russia

The Soviets had few doubts about the effectiveness of submachine guns when the Finnish Suomi was used against them to devastating effect in 1940. During the Siege of Leningrad (1941–44), the war industry produced the rugged PPS-43. More recently produced models were adaptations of the AKS-74 rifle.

Makarov Bizon

This submachine gun was designed by a team that included Victor Kalashnikov and Alexei Dragunov, and introduced in 1995. The design is said to have been influenced by the US Calico submachine gun, especially the helical magazine, located under the receiver on the Bizon. The weapon fired from a closed bolt. Many of the working parts were similar to those found on Kalashnikov rifles. The heavy-duty buttstock folded to the side when not in use.

SPECIFICATION

MANUFACTURER Izhevsk Mechanical Plant (IZHMECH)
CALIBRE 9mm Makarov
MAGAZINE CAPACITY 64 **ACTION** Blowback
TOTAL LENGTH 660mm/25.98in
BARREL LENGTH 425mm/16.7in
WEIGHT UNLOADED 2,470g/87oz

PPD 1934/38

SPECIFICATION

MANUFACTURER State Arsenals

CALIBRE 7.62mm Tokarev

MAGAZINE CAPACITY 25 box or 71 drum

ACTION Blowback

TOTAL LENGTH 779mm/30.6in

BARREL LENGTH 269mm/10.75in

WEIGHT UNLOADED 3,730g/131.57oz

This submachine gun was designed by Russian arms-designer Vasily Degtyarev and produced in 1934. He was influenced by the German Bergmann MP28 and the Finnish Suomi Model 31. It was manufactured to a high standard using machined steel parts, and the inside of the barrel was chromium plated. The weapon was fitted with a drum magazine, located underneath the receiver. First introduced in 1935, the weapon proved to be too complex to produce in great numbers and it saw only limited service in World War II.

SPECIFICATION

MANUFACTURER State Arsenals

CALIBRE 7.62mm Tokarev

MAGAZINE CAPACITY 71

ACTION Blowback

TOTAL LENGTH 790mm/31in

BARREL LENGTH 260mm/10.5in

WEIGHT UNLOADED 3,630g/128oz

PPD 1940

The PPD 1940 was a modification of the PPD 1934/38 and was designed for greater ease of manufacture. It retained the high-quality levels of the PPD 1934/38 and was also a better weapon. It became the standard Soviet service issue in 1940. However, despite the efforts to simplify the manufacturing process, the weapon could still not be produced in sufficient numbers to satisfy the requirements of the Soviet Union on a war footing, and it was not long before an alternative was sought.

PPSh-41

SPECIFICATION

MANUFACTURER State Arsenals

CALIBRE 7.62mm Tokarev

MAGAZINE CAPACITY 35 box or 71 drum

ACTION Blowback

TOTAL LENGTH 838mm/33in

BARREL LENGTH 266mm/10.5in

WEIGHT UNLOADED 3,640g/128.4oz

This weapon answered the requirement of the Soviet Union for a reliable and effective submachine gun that could also be produced in large numbers. Designed by Russian engineer Georgii Shpagin, the PPSh-41 was produced entirely from stamped metal parts, which were relatively cheap and easy to produce. The receiver was hinged and could be opened easily for maintenance of the internal working parts. The weapon had a very high rate of fire, making it a formidable tool in the hands of large numbers of troops.

PPS-43

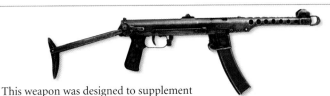

SPECIFICATION

MANUFACTURER State Arsenals

CALIBRE 7.62mm Tokarev

MAGAZINE CAPACITY 35

ACTION Blowback

TOTAL LENGTH (STOCK EXTENDED) 808mm/32.251in

TOTAL LENGTH (STOCK RETRACTED) 606mm/24.25in

BARREL LENGTH 254mm/10in

WEIGHT UNLOADED 5,625g/198.41oz

This weapon was designed to supplement existing supplies of weapons during the Siege of Leningrad. Designed by Russian engineer Aleksei Sudaev and based on earlier models such as the PPSh-41, it proved to be one of the most effective submachine guns of World War II. One major difference was that it had a folding stock, which made it a handy weapon for paratroop units and tank crews. The PPS-43 had blowback operation, firing from an open bolt, and it was set to permanent automatic fire.

AKS-74U

This gun was developed from the AK-74 rifle, used by the Soviet Union in place of submachine guns. It had a short barrel and gas tube. The receiver has been altered so that it is hinged at the top. There is an expansion chamber on the top of the receiver which was designed to release the gas pressure. The internal mechanism remained identical to the AK-74 rifle. The stock folded round and could be locked into the side of the receiver. The plastic magazine was strengthened. Developed in the 1970s, the weapon is said to have been first used in Afghanistan in 1983.

SPECIFICATION

MANUFACTURER State Arsenals
CALIBRE 5.45mm
MAGAZINE CAPACITY 30
ACTION Gas
TOTAL LENGTH (STOCK EXTENDED) 675mm/26.6in
TOTAL LENGTH (STOCK RETRACTED) 420mm/16.5in
BARREL LENGTH 200mm/7.87in
WEIGHT UNLOADED 2,710g/95.6oz

Egypt

Egypt chose, along with the US armed forces, to adapt a version of the Swedish Carl Gustaf submachine gun. This was a simple, robust and effective weapon and also proved to be the inspiration for two separate Egyptian derivatives, the Port Said and the Akaba, a simpler version of the Port Said.

Port Said

The Port Said was a close copy of the Swedish Carl Gustaf, which was issued to the Swedish armed forces after World War II, and was also used by US forces in Vietnam in the 1950s and 1960s. The Carl Gustaf was a development of the German submachine guns, the Bergmann MP35 and the Bergmann MP18. It was a fully automatic weapon, firing from an open bolt. The simplicity and efficiency of the design, allied to its sheer robustness, contributed to its success and explains why it was produced under licence not only in Egypt but also in Indonesia and the United States.

SPECIFICATION

MANUFACTURER Local Egyptian manufacturer
CALIBRE 9mm Parabellum
MAGAZINE CAPACITY 36 or 50
ACTION Blowback
TOTAL LENGTH (STOCK EXTENDED) 811mm/31.9in
TOTAL LENGTH (STOCK RETRACTED) 552mm/21.7in
BARREL LENGTH 212mm/8.35in
WEIGHT UNLOADED 3,900g/137.57oz

Maadi Akaba

This submachine gun was developed in the 1970s as a simpler version of the Port Said. It is immediately recognizable due to the fact that the barrel jacket was removed, and the barrel itself reduced in length to only 150mm/5.9in. The sights were also rearranged, the foresight having been removed from the end of the barrel jacket. Instead of a folding stock, the Akaba had telescoping wire stock not unlike that of the American M3. Otherwise, the basic configuration of the weapon remained the same as the original Carl Gustaf and the Port Said. The model was produced in the 1970s and again in the mid-1990s.

SPECIFICATION

MANUFACTURER Local Egyptian manufacturer
CALIBRE 9mm Parabellum
MAGAZINE CAPACITY 36 or 50
ACTION Blowback
TOTAL LENGTH (STOCK EXTENDED) 737mm/29in
TOTAL LENGTH (STOCK RETRACTED) 482mm/19in
BARREL LENGTH 150mm/5.9in
WEIGHT UNLOADED 3,900g/137.57oz

✡ Israel

There is only one word for submachine gun in Israel: that word is Uzi. The same name is instantly recognizable around the world. By using a wraparound bolt, the gun was very compact and easily concealed for covert operations. An even smaller variety, the Mini-Uzi, was also produced, as well as a Micro-Uzi, which is sometimes categorized as a pistol.

Uzi

SPECIFICATION	✡
MANUFACTURER Ta'as Israel Industries Ltd.	
CALIBRE 9mm Parabellum	
MAGAZINE CAPACITY 25 or 32	
ACTION Blowback	
TOTAL LENGTH (STOCK EXTENDED) 650mm/25.59in	
TOTAL LENGTH (STOCK RETRACTED) 470mm/18.5in	
BARREL LENGTH 260mm/10.2in	
WEIGHT UNLOADED 3,500g/123oz metal stock	

The Uzi submachine gun, introduced in the 1950s, has become a byword for efficient weapons of this type. It was designed by Major Uziel Gal at the end of the 1940s, influenced by Czech designs. The design was simple and effective, being made up of steel pressings, spot-welded and riveted together. It was a blowback-operated weapon which used a system whereby the round is fired while the bolt is still in forward motion. The bolt surrounded the rear end of the barrel at the moment of firing. The selector could be positioned for automatic fire, single shots or full safety. The was a grip safety and an extra safety was also located in the cocking-handle slide.

Parabellum Mini-Uzi

SPECIFICATION	✡
MANUFACTURER Ta'as Israel Industries Ltd.	
CALIBRE 9mm Parabellum	
MAGAZINE CAPACITY 20, 25 or 32	
ACTION Blowback	
TOTAL LENGTH (STOCK EXTENDED) 600mm/23.6in	
TOTAL LENGTH (STOCK RETRACTED) 360mm/14.1in	
BARREL LENGTH 197mm/7.8in	
WEIGHT UNLOADED 2,700g/95oz metal stock	

As its name suggests, the Mini-Uzi, introduced in 1980, was essentially a more compact version of the standard Uzi submachine gun. One major difference in more recent versions of the Mini-Uzi was that it incorporated a closed-bolt firing mechanism with a floating firing pin. This weapon was ideal for any form of covert operation as it can be easily concealed. As it was a well-balanced weapon, it could be fired easily "from the hip" or, with the stock extended, from the shoulder.

Micro-Uzi

SPECIFICATION	✡
MANUFACTURER Ta'as Israel Industries Ltd.	
CALIBRE 9mm Parabellum	
MAGAZINE CAPACITY 20	
ACTION Blowback	
TOTAL LENGTH (STOCK EXTENDED) 460mm/18.1in	
TOTAL LENGTH (STOCK RETRACTED) 250mm/9.84in	
BARREL LENGTH 117mm/4.6mm	
WEIGHT UNLOADED 1,950g/68.78oz metal stock	

The Micro-Uzi was introduced in the 1990s. It was, again, essentially the same as the Mini-Uzi in operation but in a smaller package. There was a tungsten insert in the bolt which was designed to increase the mass and reduce the rate of fire. The Micro-Uzi was intended for covert operations which required a weapon that can be easily concealed and deployed, while providing an effective rate of fire and accuracy. Another role intended for the Micro-Uzi was as a Personal Defence Weapon (PDW) for airborne and armoured crews in the Israeli Defence Forces.

 China

Early Chinese guns were based on foreign designs such as the Soviet PPS-43, the American "grease gun" and the Russian Kalashnikov. The major producer of submachine guns for the Chinese armed forces is China North Industries Corporation, otherwise known as Norinco.

Type 36

The Type 36 (sometimes known as M36) was identical to the the American M3A1 (the "grease gun"), which was developed in the US during World War II as a cheaper version of the Thompson. It is thought that it was also produced at Mukden Arsenal in China during and after World War II. Although it was adopted by the Chinese in 1947, it never reached large-scale production because the factory was taken over by Chinese Communist forces in the late 1940s. Production started again on the island of Formosa (Taiwan) in 1950 where the model continued to be made, in 9mm Parabellum.

SPECIFICATION

MANUFACTURER Local Chinese manufacturers
CALIBRE .45 ACP
MAGAZINE CAPACITY 30
ACTION Blowback
TOTAL LENGTH (STOCK EXTENDED) 755mm/29.7in
TOTAL LENGTH (STOCK RETRACTED) 545mm/21.8in
BARREL LENGTH 203mm/8in
WEIGHT UNLOADED 3,375g/119oz

Type 50

The Type 50 was a Chinese copy of the Soviet PPSh-41. It was used extensively by Chinese forces in close combat. Designed by Russian Georgii Shpagin, it was a simple but rugged design that was both effective and reliable. The Type 50 was designed specifically for ease of manufacture, and was slightly lighter than the PPSh-41. Produced from two or three plants in China, production started in 1950, shortly before the Korean War began, and continued until the mid-1950s.

SPECIFICATION

MANUFACTURER State Arsenals/local Chinese manufacturers
CALIBRE 7.62mm Tokarev
MAGAZINE CAPACITY 35 box or 71 drum
ACTION Blowback
TOTAL LENGTH 843mm/33.75in
BARREL LENGTH 269mm/10.75in
WEIGHT UNLOADED 3,630g/128oz

Type 54

SPECIFICATION

MANUFACTURER State Arsenals/local Chinese manufacturers
CALIBRE 7.62mm Tokarev
MAGAZINE CAPACITY 35
ACTION Blowback
TOTAL LENGTH (STOCK EXTENDED) 808mm/32.25in
TOTAL LENGTH (STOCK RETRACTED) 606mm/24.25in
WEIGHT UNLOADED 3,330g/118oz

The Type 54 (also known as the M54) was a direct copy of the Soviet PPS-43. It went into production in China in 1953 with a distinguishing mark "K" on the grip. It had been designed by Russian Aleksei Sudaev in order to meet demand at the time of the Siege of Leningrad and was itself a stripped-down and simplified version of the PPSh-41. With its folding stock, it was adaptable for use in confined spaces. The PPS-43 was a blowback-operated weapon firing from an open bolt. The Type 54 quickly earned itself a good reputation under difficult circumstances. It was produced until 1956.

Type 64

SPECIFICATION

MANUFACTURER State factories
CALIBRE 7.62mm Tokarev
MAGAZINE CAPACITY 30
ACTION Blowback
TOTAL LENGTH (STOCK EXTENDED) 843mm/33.3in
TOTAL LENGTH (STOCK RETRACTED) 635mm/25in
BARREL LENGTH 244mm/9.6in
WEIGHT UNLOADED 3,400g/120oz

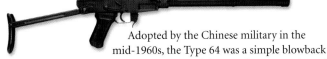

Adopted by the Chinese military in the mid-1960s, the Type 64 was a simple blowback gun with an open-bolt system. It borrowed features from a number of other weapons, including the Soviet PPS-43 and the British Bren gun. Unusually for this type of weapon, it came with an integral steel silencer. Another unusual characteristic of the Type 64 was its high rate of fire, which could make the weapon difficult to control. The magazine was inserted into the receiver forward of the trigger guard. The bullet used was heavy and had a distinctive point. If standard rounds were used in this gun, it could suffer wear and be as loud as a standard weapon.

SPECIFICATION

MANUFACTURER State factories/Norinco
CALIBRE 7.62mm Tokarev
MAGAZINE CAPACITY 20
ACTION Gas
TOTAL LENGTH (STOCK EXTENDED) 740mm/29.1in
TOTAL LENGTH (STOCK RETRACTED) 470mm/18.5in
BARREL LENGTH 225mm/8.86in
WEIGHT UNLOADED 1,900g/67oz

Type 79

The Type 79 submachine gun was first produced in 1979 and issued in large numbers to the People's Liberation Army and other Chinese security forces in 1983. Unlike many other weapons in its class, it was gas operated rather than blowback operated. It had a rotary bolt system and the gas piston is located above the barrel. The weapon had a fire-mode selector which could be set to full safety, single shots or automatic fire. The weapon had a foldable buttstock and could be fitted with both a tactical light and laser indicator.

SPECIFICATION

MANUFACTURER State factories/Norinco
CALIBRE 7.62mm Tokarev
MAGAZINE CAPACITY 30
ACTION Blowback
TOTAL LENGTH (STOCK EXTENDED) 628mm/24.7in
TOTAL LENGTH (STOCK RETRACTED) 444mm/17.48in
BARREL LENGTH 275mm/10.83in
WEIGHT UNLOADED 1,900g/67oz

Type 85

The Type 85 was essentially an improved version of the Type 79, developed during the 1980s. Both the barrel and the bolt-carrying mechanism were redesigned to reduce noise and fit into a cylindrical receiver. It had a traditional blowback design with an open-bolt mechanism and a steel stock that could be folded. There was a selector above the trigger guard which allowed for selection of full safety, single shots or automatic fire. The magazine was the same as that used on the Type 79.

SPECIFICATION

MANUFACTURER Jian Sheng
CALIBRE 9mm Parabellum
MAGAZINE CAPACITY 50
ACTION Blowback operated
TOTAL LENGTH 588mm/123.15in
TOTAL LENGTH 405mm/116in
BARREL LENGTH 250mm/19.84in
WEIGHT UNLOADED 2,100g/174oz

Chang Feng

Developed during the 1990s, this was a compact submachine gun with a blowback operation. The bolt wrapped around the barrel. The primary feed was from helical magazine made of polymer. The magazine was situated at the top of the weapon and is similar in design to the magazines of US Calico submachine guns. The gun had open sights and was also designed to take a night sight behind the main sight block. The barrel of the weapon was threaded to accept an optional detachable silencer.

Australia

Australia produced both its adaptation of the English Sten gun, known as the Austen, and a completely home-grown weapon, the 9mm Owen. The Owen proved to be popular with the troops and remained in service through to the 1960s, since when Australia has bought an adapted version of the Steyr Aug.

Austen

This submachine gun was an Australian version of the Sten gun, which had been imported into Australia in 1941, but failed to impress. The Lithgow Small Arms Factory in New South Wales set about developing the gun, borrowing some of the features of the German MP40. The weapon was given a folding stock and two plastic pistol grips. The mainspring was also an MP40 design. The Austen could be set to either selective or automatic fire. Despite all the improvements, the Austen did not prove very popular. The required level of performance was to be achieved by another Australian weapon, the Owen.

SPECIFICATION

MANUFACTURER Small Arms Factory, Lithgow, NSW
MAGAZINE 28
ACTION Blowback
TOTAL LENGTH (STOCK EXTENDED) 845mm/33.25in
TOTAL LENGTH (STOCK RETRACTED) 552mm/31.75in
BARREL LENGTH 290mm/11.41in
WEIGHT UNLOADED 3,980g/140oz

F1

The F1 was developed by the Lithgow Small Arms Factory and first produced in 1962. It proved to be a successful replacement for the Owen submachine gun and remained in service until the late 1980s, when it was replaced by a Steyr Aug adaptation, the F88. The F1 was a blowback-operated selective-fire weapon. The trigger mechanism included a lever that could be set in single-shot, automatic or safe modes.

SPECIFICATION

MANUFACTURER Small Arms Factory, Lithgow, NSW
CALIBRE 9mm Parabellum
MAGAZINE 34
ACTION Blowback
TOTAL LENGTH 714mm/28.1in
BARREL LENGTH 213mm/8.38in
WEIGHT UNLOADED 3,270g/115oz

Owen

The Owen submachine gun was designed by Lieutenant Evelyn Owen and developed privately. It took some time for the weapon to be accepted by the Australian military, partly in view of the fact that the Austen was the official submachine gun programme. Once adopted, however, it proved to be both reliable and popular, with better performance than the Austen. The production run was 45,000, finishing in 1944. It was a select-fire, open-bolt design that carried the 9mm Parabellum round.

sealed receiver

SPECIFICATION

MANUFACTURER John Lysaght (Australia) Ltd.
CALIBRE 9mm Parabellum
MAGAZINE 33
ACTION Blowback
TOTAL LENGTH 813mm/32in
BARREL LENGTH 250mm/9.84in
WEIGHT UNLOADED 3,980g/140oz

South Korea

Production of a version of the American M3 "grease gun" was undertaken by the Daewoo Corporation, resulting in the K1, which was updated to the K2 and is in use today by military forces. Otherwise the country does not have a history of indigenous submachine-gun manufacture.

SPECIFICATION

MANUFACTURER Daewoo Telecom Ltd.
CALIBRE 5.56mm
MAGAZINE CAPACITY 20 or 30
ACTION Gas
TOTAL LENGTH 838mm/33in
BARREL LENGTH (WITHOUT STOCK) 653mm/25.7in
WEIGHT UNLOADED 2,870g/10oz

Daewoo K1A

The K1A was the first modern submachine gun developed by the Republic of Korea (South Korea) in the early 1980s. This was a gas-fired, selective-fire gun with an aluminium alloy receiver and a rotating-bolt locking system. It had a selection system that can be set on safety, full automatic, semi-automatic, and burst-fire. The K1A was the upgraded version of the K1, a version of the American M3 or "grease gun". All K1s in the South Korean military have been modified to K1A.

● Japan

Japanese production of submachine guns was limited by the weak 8mm Nambu cartridge. Japanese manufacture of such weapons was in many respects the opposite of the manufacturing excellence that was to characterize Japanese industry in the post-World War II period.

SPECIFICATION

MANUFACTURER Kokura Arsenal/Nagoya Arsenal
CALIBRE 8mm Nambu
MAGAZINE CAPACITY 30
ACTION Blowback
TOTAL LENGTH 890mm/35in
BARREL LENGTH 228mm/9in
WEIGHT UNLOADED 3,830g/135oz

Nambu Type 100

This submachine gun, developed by the Imperial Japanese Army, was based on the Bergmann submachine gun. It was air cooled, blowback operated and fully automatic. The Type 100 was designed primarily for use by paratroops. Although it was robust, the weapon had some problems with stoppages and the cartridge it fired was relatively weak. A modified version was introduced in 1944, which had a higher rate of fire.

SPECIFICATION

MANUFACTURER Shin Chuo
CALIBRE 9mm Parabellum
MAGAZINE CAPACITY 30
ACTION Blowback/selective fire
TOTAL LENGTH (STOCK EXTENDED) 762mm/30in
TOTAL LENGTH (STOCK RETRACTED) 501mm/19.72in
BARREL LENGTH 140mm/5.5in
WEIGHT UNLOADED 4,080g/14.39oz

SCK Models 65 and 66

The SCK Model 65 was similar to the Swedish Carl Gustaf submachine gun and was introduced in 1965. A modified version was introduced in 1966 with a lower rate of fire. It had a conventional blowback operation. The weapon had a grip safety which had to be held down if the gun was to be either cocked or fired. The cocking handle had a safety system incorporated which would not allow it to be slip forward and fire the weapon unless it had first been pulled fully to the rear. The weapon had a buttstock that could be swung open or closed.

Manufacturers

Where information is available, listed below are details of the manufacturers whose arms are featured in the directories.

CANADA

Para-Ordnance Founded in 1985, its original products were based on adaptations of the Colt M1911. Now it produces a wide range of handguns for security forces, self-defence and target shooting.

UNITED STATES

Auto-Ordnance Corp. Founded in 1916 by John T. Thompson and others. Their products included various models of Thompson machine gun. The company was associated with Savage Arms Corp. from 1939 and then merged with Maguire Industries in 1944.

Calico Based in Oregon. Calico produces firearms that use the top-mounted, helical-feed magazine that can take between 50 and 100 rounds.

Colt Manufacturing Co. Founded in the 1840s in Connecticut, initially to produce revolvers. Products include the .45 Colt Single Action Army, Colt M1911 pistol and M4 Carbine. In 2002 the company was split between Colt Defense and Colt Manufacturing Company.

Harrington & Richardson Founded in 1871 as Wesson and Harrington. The major production is of single-shot shotguns. The company went out of business in 1986. The new company H&R 1871 was formed in 1991. It was sold to Marlin Firearms in 2000.

High Standard Mfg. Co. Founded in Connecticut in 1926. In 1932 the company purchased Hartford Arms and Equipment Company. It was purchased by Leisure Group in the 1960s and bought out by the management in 1978. In 1993, the company was acquired by High Standard Manufacturing Company Inc. of Houston, Texas.

Intratec Founded as a subsidiary of Interdynamic AB, then Interdynamic USA. Intratec produced the Tec-9 submachine gun. It folded in 2001.

Marlin Firearms Co. Founded in 1870 by John M. Marlin. In 1915 a New York syndicate bought the company and named it Marlin Rockwell Corporation. In 2000 Marlin bought the assets of H&R 1871, a US manufacturer of shotguns and rifles.

Remington Arms Co. Founded in 1816 by Eliphalet Remington. The first production was flintlock rifles. It continues to produce both arms and ammunition. It is one of the oldest manufacturing concerns in the United States.

Savage Arms Corp. Founded in 1894 by Arthur Savage, it manufactured pistols, rifles and ammunition. The company grew through the acquisition of Stevens Arms, Page Lewis Co., Davis-Warner Arms, Crescent Firearms and A.H. Fox. In 1995 it became a private company.

Smith & Wesson Inc Its origins lie in the partnership between Horace Smith and Daniel Wesson, dating from 1852. First success came in 1856 with manufacture of the .22 rimfire revolver. It was an important producer of firearms during the American Civil War and later during World Wars I and II. It is now the largest producer of handguns in the United States.

Sturm, Ruger & Co Inc. The company was founded in 1949 by William B. Ruger. The product line covers hunting, target shooting, self-defence and law enforcement. It is now the largest manufacturer of firearms in the United States.

Taurus International Manufacturing Inc. Forjas Taurus was established in Brazil in Porto Alegre in 1937. It opened an affiliated company in Miami, USA, in 1968. Taurus began to produce Beretta pistols under licence. From the 1990s it began to produce its own range of pistols and revolvers in both countries.

MEXICO

Productos Mendoza S.A. This company was established in 1911 and manufactures submachine guns and other products.

CHILE

Las Fábricas y Maestranzas del Ejército (FAMAE) Founded in 1811, this is the oldest defence company in South America. It produces a wide range of assault rifles and submachine guns.

ARGENTINA

Bersa S.A. Founded in the 1960s. Its product line consists of pistols for various purposes, including self-defence and target shooting.

Portatiles "Domingo Matheu"
This company used to produce weapons for FN Herstal of Belgium, under licence.

BRAZIL
Indústria de Material Bélico do Brasil (IMBEL) This is a publicly owned company administered by the Brazilian Ministry of Defence, said to have strong ties with the Brazilian military establishment. From 1985 IMBEL entered into association with Springfield Armory of the United States.

Mekanika Indústria e Comércio Lda This company was set up to produce the Uru submachine gun from 1979 to 1988. It has made an arrangement with Rossi for continued production of the Uru.

Rossi Founded in 1889. From 1997, Rossi firearms were imported into the United States by BrazTech International. Forjas Taurus SA bought the rights to produce Rossi handguns.

PORTUGAL
Fábrica Militar de Braço de Prata
One of the major armaments manufacturers in Portugal. It manufactured the Heckler & Koch G3 under licence, among others.

Indústrias Nacionais de Defesa (INDEP) This company is the main ordnance factory in Portugal, and produces a wide range of military equipment, including mortars, artillery and small arms.

SPAIN
Astra-Unceta y Cia. Unceta was founded in 1908 in Eibar, Spain, and then moved to Guernica in the Basque country. Today it is known by the name of Astra.

Indústria de Guerra de Cataluña
This industry grew up during the Spanish Civil War when many manufacturing industries were given over to arms production.

Star Bonifacio Echeverría S.A.
Manufacturer of small arms in the Basque region 1905 to 1997.

UNITED KINGDOM
Birmingham Small Arms Company (BSA) This company was founded in 1861 in the Gun Quarter of Birmingham. During World War I, the gun business grew exponentially. In World War II, production was focused on the Lee Enfield rifle as well as on military folding bicycles and on motorcycles. In 1986 BSA Guns was liquidated and now trades as BSA Guns (UK) Ltd.

Royal Small Arms Factory, Enfield Founded in 1804 as one of the factories of the Board of Ordnance. Privatized in 1984 as part of Royal Ordnance Plc. Production included Bren and Sten guns as well as a modified version of the Webley service revolver.

Royal Ordnance This was formed as a public corporation in 1985 but its roots in the Royal Ordnance factories extend back to the middle of the 16th century. The company was bought by British Aerospace, later BAE systems, and became part of BAE Systems Land and Armaments.

Webley & Scott Founded around 1834 by Philip Webley as Webley & Sons. Production moved from percussion rifles to revolvers. In 1897 the firm amalgamated with W&C Scott & Sons. Production increased during the World Wars, but fortunes declined post-war and the company closed in 2005. It was bought by Airgunsport in 2006, which has kept the famous Webley name.

FRANCE
Hotchkiss et Cie. This company was set up by Benjamin B. Hotchkiss of the United States in 1867 to produce a wide range of weaponry for both the

French and the American armed forces. By the beginning of the 20th century, Hotchkiss was also manufacturing cars.

Manufacture d'Armes de Bayonne (MAB) Founded in 1920 by Leon Barthe. Initial production of pistols was based on the Browning M1906.

Manufacture d'Armes de Châtellerault (MAC) Founded 1819 on the banks of the River Vienne. Initial production was of tools and swords. In 1822 the factory began to produce firearms and this was to continue until 1968.

Société Alsacienne de Construction Mécanique (SACM) Founded in 1839. The company was mainly concerned with manufacture of locomotives.

BELGIUM
Anciens Établissements Pieper
Located at Herstal, Belgium, Pieper was a manufacturer of small arms between 1907 and 1939. During this time it manufactured Bayard pistols.

Charles Ph. Clement
A manufacturer based in Liège that patented an automatic pistol with no fixed cylinder head. The company ceased trading from the beginning of the German occupation of Belgium in 1914.

Fabrique Nationale (FN) Herstal
This firm was first established in 1889 near Liège. The company began a successful association with John Moses Browning at the end of the 19th century which resulted in the famous Browning GP35 High-Power, among other designs. The firm continues to produce world-class small arms and also owns the US Repeating Arms Company (Winchester) and the Browning Arms Company.

SWITZERLAND
Hispano-Suiza S.A. (Suisse) The company was founded in 1899 by Mark Birkigt in Catalonia and formed an alliance with Spanish banker Damian Mateu. It made famous cars and aircraft. It is now part of the huge SAFRAN Group.

SIG Founded in 1853 by Friedrich Peyer im Hof, Heinrich Moser and Conrad Nehrer. It won an order for the Prelaz-Burnand rifle from the Swiss Ministry of Defence. In the 20th century, the company developed a range of pistols, beginning with the P49. It had acquired J.P. Sauer by the early 1980s. SIGARMS was formed in the United States in 1985.

GERMANY
Carl Walther Waffenfabrik GmbH. This business was first founded in 1886 by Carl Walther to make hunting and target-shooting rifles. The first semi-automatic pistol was produced in 1908. The factory closed down at the end of World War II and re-opened again in West Germany.

Heckler & Koch GmbH. This firm began business in January 1950 and was first concerned with making parts for bicycles and sewing machines. In 1956 the company won the bid for the new West German general service rifle, the G3. In the mid-1960s, the MP5 was developed. In 1991 the company was bought by British Aerospace/ Royal Ordnance. It produces the whole range of small arms, from pistols to grenades and machine guns.

J.P. Sauer & Sohn GmbH.
Founded in 1751, the company received its first major order from the German Army in 1870. In 1976 SIG of Switzerland acquired the majority of Sauer's stock and completed acquisition at the beginning of the 1980s. The company continues to produce pistols and hunting rifles today.

Korth GmbH. This company was founded in 1940s by Willi Korth. The company is now Korth Germany and Korth USA. Korth manufactures revolvers and semi-automatic pistols.

Rheinische Metallwaaren und Maschinefabrik This company was established in 1889 by Heinrich Erhardt. Production increased during World War I. In 1941, the company was taken over by the German state. In 1997 weapons and ammunition division became Rheinmetall W&M GmbH. In 2002 the company acquired Oerlikon Contraves Pyrtotec AG.

Waffenfabrik Mauser AG. Oberndorf This company was founded in 1811 as a royal weapons factory in Oberndorf. In 1867 Wilhelm and Paul Mauser developed a rifle with a rotating bolt system. In 1912 the company started producing pistols. In 1897 the factory became Waffenfabrik Mauser AG. It supplied rifles to the German Army through both

World Wars. The factory was dismantled by French authorities at the end of World War II but the firm was then re-established in the 1950s. In 2004 Mauser-Werke Oberndorf Waffensysteme GmbH incorporated into Rheinmetall Waffe Munition, GmbH. Mauser is a highly regardedmanufacturer of quality hunting rifles.

ITALY
Benelli Armi SpA. The company was founded in 1911 with production focused on motorcycles. In the mid-1960s the firearms business was started. The company manufactures shotguns, rifles and pistols.

Fabbrica d'Armi P. Beretta SpA.
This company had its roots in the early 16th century, beginning with the forging of arquebus barrels. Today it is one of the leading firearms producers in the world, providing issue service pistols to the United States, French, Italian and other armed forces.

Fabbrica Nazionale d'Armi Brescia This firm was launched in 1935 and began producing sports and hunting rifles. In World War II, production was focused on military weapons. In 1958 the factory was bought by Beretta.

Luigi Franchi SpA. Founded in 1868 and now part of the Beretta group. Current production is devoted to shotguns and sporting rifles.

DENMARK
Dansk Industri Syndikat, Madsen This company was first established in 1900 for the production of light machine guns. In 1959 the shipping company Maersk acquired a controlling interest in the company. By 1963 arms production had ceased.

AUSTRIA
Glock GmbH. Founded in 1963 by Gaston Glock in Deutsch-Wagram, near Vienna. The product line consists of pistols, knives, and various typs of tools and accessories.

Steyr Mannlicher GmbH. & Co. KG This firm incorporated the designs of Ferdinand Ritter von Mannlicher, who joined Steyr in 1866. It currently produces some of the most highly regarded assault rifles on the international market today as well as sniper rifles and pistols.

SWEDEN
Carl Gustaf Arms Co. Formed as part of the original agglomeration of small arms producers that began in 1620 and centred on certain designated towns. The company itself dates from 1812. It is now part of Bofors.

Husqvarna Vapenfabriks AB. The company was founded in 1689 to produce muskets.

CZECH REPUBLIC
Ceská/Ceskoslovenská Zbrojovka Established in 1919 as part of the famous Skoda Works. Post-World War II products carried the BRNO designation. In the 1990s it was re-established on a free-trade basis. It established a US subsidiary, CZ-USA.

POLAND
Fabryka Broni Radom Founded in 1922, the company became independent in 2000. Early production included the Nagant 95 pistol.

HUNGARY
Fegyver es Gepgyar (FÉG) Founded in 1891, the company produced Frommer pistols and also hunting and sports weapons. In 2003 the company was privatized and at this present time still continues to produce small arms.

SERBIA
Zastava Arms Co. Founded in 1853 to manufacture cannons. It is the sole arms producer in Serbia and Montenegro, with production largely based around Kalashnikov designs.

FINLAND
Valtion Kivaaritehdas (VKT), Jyvastalyla A state factory which produced the Lahti pistol.

ROMANIA
Cugir Arsenal This arsenal has been producing small arms from World War II to the present day. It is now part of the Romaru National Company.

RUSSIA
Izhevsk Machanical Plant (IZHMECH) This is the state-owned Russian plant at Izhevsk.

Tula Arsenal Founded in 1712 by Peter the Great. It has produced arms throughout Russia's modern history. Production has included the Mosin-Nagant rifle and the AK-47.

ISRAEL
Israeli Military Industries (IMI) The company said to have roots in the period of the British Mandate in Palestine. Small Arms Division privatized in 2005 as Israel Weapons Industries. The product line includes Uzi submachine guns and the Galil assault rifle.

Ta'as Israel Industries Ltd. Established in 1933 and is the country's oldest defence industry. It grew substantially after the 1973 Middle East wars and produces a wide range of advanced defence equipment.

CHINA
China North Industries Corp. (Norinco) Established in 1980, Norinco makes a wide variety of equipment for defence, including submachine guns.

AUSTRALIA
John Lysaght Ltd. This firm was established in 1921, initially as a wholly owned subsidiary of a firm of the same name in England. Mainly concerned with the production of sheet steel, during World War II the company produced the Owen submachine gun.

Lithgow Small Arms Factory Opened in 1912, having been set up with the assistance of exports from US-based Pratt & Whitney. The factory produced Lee-Enfield rifles during World War I and the Bren machine gun in World War II. The factory later diversified to produce sporting rifles, tools and other manufactured items.

SOUTH KOREA
Daewoo Telecom Ltd. This corporation was first founded in 1967 and is one of South Korea's leading industrial concerns, including cars in one of its product divisions.

JAPAN
Nagoya Arsenal This arsenal was opened in 1923 and ceased manufacture in 1945.

Kokura Arsenal Consisted of an extensive collection of military industries. It began operating in 1935 and was the intended target for the second atomic bomb to be dropped on Japan. Due to bad weather over Kokura Nagasaki suffered devastation instead.

Glossary

ACP Abbreviation for "Automatic Colt Pistol". Used to designate certain cartridges that were first chambered in Colt pistols.

Action The working mechanism of the firearm which determines the way it is cocked, fired and reloaded.

Arquebus An early matchlock pistol which preceded the musket. It was the forerunner of the rifle and other longarm firearms.

Assault rifle An automatic or semi-automatic rifle with a magazine.

Backstrap The part of the frame of a firearm that is exposed at the rear of the grip.

Baffles Devices that impede the movement of gas within a silencer. Baffles deflect and slow the flow of gas emerging from the expansion chamber of a gun. When the gases emerge from the silencer, their flow is cooler, at low velocity and quieter.

Barrel The metal tube of a firearm. The bullet accelerates through it when the firearm is fired.

Beavertail Describes the shape of some forms of trigger, safety catch or hammer guard.

Blackpowder The earliest type of firearms propellant used in muzzleloaders and older breech-loading guns. Modern firearms use smokeless powder.

Blish lock system A breech-locking mechanism designed by John Bell Blish used in the original Thompson submachine gun. It was a form of retarded blowback based on the principle of static friction.

Blowback An operation system which the slide or breech block is driven to the rear by direct gas pressure on the cartridge case head.

Bolt Normally a mobile device that closes the breech of a weapon.

Bolt action A gun mechanism activated by manual operation of the breech block.

Bore The inside of the barrel of a gun, excluding the chamber. It is the channel through which the bullet is fired from the weapon.

Box lock A system whereby the firing mechanism (and sometimes the trigger) is concealed in the body of the pistol and only appears once the trigger is pulled.

Box magazine A rectangular compartment attached to, or placed into a firearm that holds cartridges stacked on top of one another ready for feeding into the chamber.

Bramit device A special silencer that was designed by Mitin brothers for the Nagant M1895 revolver and was mounted on the barrel.

Breech The rear part of the barrel of the firearm, sometimes used as an area for reloading.

Breech block The part of the firearm action that closes the breech of a weapon at the moment of firing.

Breech loader A gun that is loaded through the rear or breech.

Bullet The projectile expelled from a firearm.

Burr-type hammer A rounded, grooved hammer, rather than the more well-known spur shape.

Butt/buttstock In a handgun, the butt is the bottom part of the grip or grip frame. In submachine gun, it is the rear or shoulder end of the stock.

Butt plate A plate put on the butt end of a stock. May be used for comfort, positioning or may be purely decorative.

Calibre Measurement of the interior diameter of a gun barrel (the size of the bore). It also refers to the size of firearm. This is determined by the diameter of the cartridge, measured either in millimetres in the European system or in hundredths of an inch in the American system.

Cam A mechanical device that uses a rotating motion in order to move another part of a mechanism in a particular way.

Carbine A lightweight rifle with a short barrel, which developed from muzzle-loading muskets.

Cartridge case A cylindrical case containing primer, charge and bullet. As the powder burns, the case expands to seal against the side of the chamber, forcing the expansion of gas down the barrel.

Centrefire A cartridge with its primer located in the centre of the base of the case.

Chamber The area of a firearm where a round rests prior to firing. A revolver has several chambers.

Charger A device that is used to load a magazine.

Clip A device for holding cartridges together, usually to facilitate loading. Technically, a magazine has a feeding spring, but a clip does not.

Cocked and locked The practice of carrying a semi-automatic pistol with a round in the chamber, the hammer cocked and the safety engaged.

Cocking handle A handle which compresses the spring behind the bolt.

Combat range The range at which a firearm is effective against a target.

Crane The swinging unit hinging the cylinder of a revolver with the frame.

Cutts compensator A device invented by Colonel Richard Malcolm Cutts that reduces the shock and rise of the muzzle when firing a firearm.

Cyclic rate The rate at which an automatic weapon goes through the full reload cycle after a round is fired.

Cylinder The part of a revolver that holds the chambers where rounds are inserted prior to firing.

Delayed blowback A variant of the blowback principle in which the blowback operation is deliberately retarded by some means.

Discharge To cause a firearm to fire.

Disconnector Part of trigger mechanism in a semi-automatic pistol that disconnects the trigger from the firing mechanism after each shot.

Dot system A system of marking fixed sights on semi-automatic handguns so that there is greater contrast between the sight and the target, especially in low light conditions.

Double action A type of lockwork in either a revolver or semi-automatic pistol that permits the hammer to be cocked either by direct manual action or by a long pull on the trigger.

Double-action only Double-action only handguns function in much the same way as double-action handguns, except it is not possible to manually cock the hammer.

Double-barrel A firearm with two barrels, either side by side or one above the other.

Drop safety Designed to prevent the unintentional discharge of a handgun if it is dropped on the hammer.

Dum-dum bullet Originally referred to the British military jacketed .303 bullet with an exposed lead core, developed in India's Dum-Dum Arsena. It is also the name given to several types of expanding bullets.

Ejection port The opening through which spent cartridge cases are ejected.

Ejector Mechanism that ejects the spent cartridge case.

Extractor Normally a claw-like mechanism that pulls the empty cartridge case from the chamber so that it can be ejected by a separate mechanism (the ejector).

Feed mechanism/system The mechanism that feeds the new round into the chamber.

Field stripping The act of taking apart a firearm for regular maintenance and cleaning.

Fire selective system A system by which single shots or automatic fire can be manually selected by pushing a lever or button normally located on the side of the receiver.

Firing pin The mechanism that strikes the rear of the cartridge.

Flash hider A device attached to a gun to reduce the muzzle flash which occurs upon firing. The flash is caused by incandescence of the expanding gases produced by burning gunpowder.

Flintlock The action of early firearms where a piece of flint was held by the cock. When the trigger was pulled, the cock/flint struck the steel "frizzen" causing a shower of sparks to ignite fine gunpowder in a small pan next to the "touch-hole" in the barrel. The flash in the pan travelled through the touch hole and ignited the powder charge in the base of the barrel under the ammunition.

Folding stock Usually a metal shoulder piece that can be folded back against the main body of the weapon when not in use.

Frizzen The metal arm of a flintlock mechanism. The flint strikes the frizzen to create sparks in the flash pan.

Full metal jacket A bullet enclosed in copper or steel, which helps prevent damage and misfires.

Full cock The position of the hammer or striker when the firearm is ready to fire.

Full-moon clip A clip designed to hold ammunition to fill the cylinder in a revolver.

Fulminate of mercury A highly sensitive explosive used as a primer compound.

Furniture Parts of the weapon that facilitate handling – such as stock, butt and pistol grip.

Gas-operation An operating system in a firearm. Gas being bled off from the barrel and used against the bolt to drive it backwards and prepare the gun for the next round.

Grip The handle of a handgun.

Grip safety A device that prevents a handgun from being fired unless the handle is firmly gripped.

Half-moon clip A clip designed to hold ammunition to fill half of the cylinder in a revolver.

Hammer Part of a weapon that drives the firing pin forward.

Hammer spur The extension on an exposed hammer that acts as a cocking aid.

High-capacity magazine A non-technical term for a magazine that holds more rounds than average.

LAM (laser aiming module) A laser module set on a weapon to emit a laser beam parallel to the barrel. When fired, the bullet will hit the spot made by the laser.

Loading gate The hinged cover over the opening through which cartridges are inserted into the magazine or chamber on a revolver.

Lock plate A metal plate mounted on the stock of a firearm and on which the firing mechanism (traditionally in flintlock and percussion firearms) is attached.

Locked breech A firearms action in which the barrel and breechface remain locked together during the initial part of the firearm's discharge. Most powerful semi-automatic pistols use the locked-breech principle; most low-powered ones are blowbacks.

Long recoil A method of recoil in which the barrel and bolt recoil for a greater length than that of the entire cartridge.

Magazine A holder for cartridges prior to their being fed into the weapon chamber.

Magazine catch The catch that releases to open a firearm in order to insert the magazine.

Magazine safety A device that prevents a firearm from being discharged when the magazine has been removed.

Magnum A type of firearm that fires a heavily loaded metallic cartridge.

Mainspring The source of the energy needed to fire the gun. Cocking the hammer compresses the mainspring, generating potential energy.

Match A long cord soaked in saltpetre (potassium nitrate), which burns slowly and was used to ignite powder in an early firearm.

Matchgrade trigger A trigger found in some guns used for competitive shooting. The trigger is smoother and lighter than standard triggers.

Matchlock The action of early firearms that relied on an S-shaped (serpentine) piece of metal to hold a smouldering match. Once activated, the burning end of the match, held by the upper end of the serpentine, drops to the priming powder in the pan and ignites the powder charge in the barrel though the touch hole.

Musket A muzzle-loaded smoothbore gun, fired from the shoulder.

Muzzle The opening at the end of the barrel from which the projectile exits.

Muzzle brake A device attached to the muzzle which softens the recoil of the firearm.

Muzzle climb Upward movement of a firearm as a result of recoil.

Muzzle velocity The speed at which the bullet leaves the muzzle of a firearm.

Needle gun A rifle where the primer, placed against the bullet beyond the powder, was detonated by a needle passing through the powder when the trigger was pulled.

Open bolt A semi or fully automatic firearm fires from an "open bolt" when the bolt and working parts are held at the rear when ready to fire. When the trigger is pulled the bolt goes forward, feeding a round from the magazine into the chamber and firing it. The action is cycled by the energy of the shot; this sends the bolt back to the rear, ejecting the empty cartridge case and preparing for the next shot.

Pan The small container located on the side or top of a matchlock, wheel-lock or flintlock pistol, used to hold the priming powder.

Parabellum A type of 9mm ammunition used in some pistols and submachine guns. The word derives from a German arms manufacturer, who used the Latin maxim – *si vis pacem, para bellum*. This means "If you want peace, prepare for war."

PDW (personal defence weapon) A firearm designed for close-quarters defence rather than a firearm designed for active assault.

Percussion cap A small metal explosive-filled cup, which is placed over the nipple of a percussion firearm. The compound explodes when fired igniting a secondary charge of gunpowder or other explosive.

Pinfire cartridge A 19th-century cartridge where a pin would ignite the priming mixture and the explosion would cause the brass sheath containing the gunpowder and ball to expand, closing the breech.

Ported barrel The holes that are precision drilled in the forward part of the barrel of a revolver (and the slide on pistols) to divert gases and so reduce the upward flip of the firearm.

Primer The ignition part of a cartridge, usually made up of a metallic fulminate or, currently, lead styphnate.

Proof-mark Official mark placed on a firearm after the barrel has been tested by a proof house.

Rail attachment A rail fixed to a firearm or integral to the frame that enables attachments such as lights or laser pointers to be fitted.

Ramrod A rod used to ram the charge and bullet into a muzzle-loading firearm.

Receiver Major part of the body of a firearm that houses its internal workings, including the barrel and bolt.

Recoil The rearward movement of internal parts of a gun as a result of the explosive force of the cartridge.

Recoil operated Operating system in which the firearm is cycled by the recoil-propelled force of the bolt and barrel when the firearm is fired. The bolt and barrel recoil together before the barrel stops and the bolt moves forwards to perform reloading and chambering.

Repeater A firearm which loads a new round as a result of the action created by the explosive force of the previous round.

Revolver A firearm with a revolving cylinder that holds the rounds. The cylinder is turned automatically after each round is fired to present a new round to the hammer.

Rifled barrel A barrel with a spiral pattern of grooves cut into its bore. This puts a spin on the projectile (bullet) as it is forced through it.

Rim The edge on the base of a cartridge case. The rim is the part of the case that the extractor grips in order to remove the cartridge from the chamber.

Rimfire A cartridge that has its primer located inside the rim of the case.

Round One shot fired by a gun. It is also one complete unit of ammunition or a cartridge which has all the parts needed to fire one shot.

Safety A device on a firearm designed to prevent accidental firing.

Sear A lever or catch connected to the trigger that holds back the firing pin.

Select-fire trigger A trigger mechanism that will allow either single shots or automatic fire..

Selective fire The ability of a firearm to be fired fully automatically, semi-automatically or in burst-fire mode at the option of the shooter.

Self-loading Operating system in which one pull of the trigger allows the gun to fire and reload in a single action. A semi-automatic pistol is self-loading. An automatic firearm would continue to fire.

Semi-automatic A firearm that loads a new round automatically after firing and just requires another squeeze of the trigger to fire the next round.

Sight Any of a variety of devices, mechanical and optical, designed to assist in the aiming of a firearm.

Silencer A device attached to a firearm's muzzle to suppress sound. The bullet emerges at a lower speed and the firearm makes less noise. Reducing the speed avoids a sonic crack as the speed is below the speed of sound.

Single action Mechanism by which the hammer is cocked, either manually or by the action of recoil and then released by the trigger.

Single shot A gun mechanism lacking a magazine. Separately-carried ammunition must be manually placed in the gun's chamber for each firing.

Slide Upper part of a gun that literally slides back, under the force of recoil, or by being manually pulled back in order to service the weapon.

Slide safety A device that blocks the firing mechanism of a firearm.

Slide stop This indicates when a handgun has expended all loaded ammunition, and helps reloading by removing the step of pulling back the slide to advance the first round of a new magazine.

Small bore Generally refers to a .22 firearm or rimfire ammunition (called a .22 calibre firearm).

Smokeless powder Propellent powder for cartridges normally containing mainly nitrocellulose or both nitrocellulose and nitroglycerine.

Smooth bore A firearm with a bore that is not rifled, such as a shotgun.

Stock (wooden or wire) The part of a firearm that is held against the shoulder to steady it for aiming and to absorb the force of recoil.

Striker An axially mounted, spring-propelled firing pin. A firing pin is an alternative term for striker used mainly when a firing pin is axially mounted and spring-propelled.

Subcompact pistol A pistol that is even smaller than the compact size.

Submachine gun A fully automatic firearm commonly firing pistol ammunition intended for close-range combat.

Suppressor Similar to a silencer, but it only muffles the noise rather than affect the bullet's velocity.

Telescopic mount The means of attaching a telescopic sight to a firearm.

Telescopic sight An optical sight attached to a firearm that magnifies the user's view of a target.

Three-dot sights The part of the firearm used to line up a target. A white dot painted on the front sight is lined up between a dot on each side of the rear sight notch. These are the three-dot sights.

Touch-hole A small hole, through which the propellant charge of a cannon or muzzle-loading gun is ignited.

Tumbler A steel cam attached to the axis shaft of the cock of a gun. It holds and releases the power of the mainspring and transmits it to the hammer.

Toggle-lock pistol A sophisticated device by which the bolt or breech lock of the Luger pistol is locked by a two-lever link. It is also found in the Maxim machine gun.

Top-break system A mechanism by which a revolver is broken open and hinges forward to reveal the cylinder for reloading.

Trigger The part of the firearm mechanism that releases the part of the action that fires the cartridge.

Trigger guard The metal loop around the trigger made to protect it and prevent the user accidentally touching the trigger.

Wadcutter A type of bullet used in target shooting. It is designed to make a clean hold in the target at the range, without ragged edges.

Wheel-lock An early firearm mechanism. A wheel with serrated edges is spun against a piece of iron pyrites.This sends sparks into the pan to ignite the charge.

Windage An allowance given in taking aim in order to compensate for the effect of wind on the bullet's flight. The rear sight adjustment is known as "windage."

Index

Picture credits

The publisher would like to thank the following for kindly supplying photos for this book: Aaron Littlefield: 116t; Corbis: 17t, 34b, 36, 54b, 90t, 94, 95t, 95b; Gary Cooke: 105, 111t; Getty Images: 43, 79b, 37t; Horst Held: 49t; iStockphoto: 26b, 33b, 39t, 39tm, 65bl, 82b, 83t, 86m, 86b, 89b, 89t, 90b, 91r, 92; JupiterImages 33r, 39, Peter Newark's Military Pictures: 11t, 13b, 16b, 19b, 27b, 27t, 28bl, 29t, 31b, 31t, 37b, 38, 42, 47b, 63t, 75mr, 11b; Royal Armouries Picture Library: 15t, 17b, 18t, 20t, 21b, 21t, 22t, 24t, 25t, 26t, 33t, 35b, 41b, 44bl, 45b, 48, 53t; The Bridgeman Art Library: 6b, 23, 41t; The Kobal Collection: 87b; The Research House: 78b, 83b, 85t, 85b; TopFoto: 10, 15b, 19tr, 28t, 29b, 40t, 47t, 52b, 63b, 68bl; Will Fowler: 58b, 60b, 62b, 64b, 66b, 67b, 70b, 71b, 72b, 76b, 51b.

All other images are commissioned. With thanks to the Royal Armouries, Leeds in England for allowing access to their extensive collection of firearms for photography.

With thanks to the following companies for supplying images: Browning-Winchester, Glock, Heckler & Koch, Para-Ordnance, Ruger, Tangfoglio, Taurus International Manufacturing, Inc.

All commissioned pictures by Gary Ombler. All artwork by Peters & Zabransky Ltd., and Richard Peters.

With thanks to Cybershooters for their invaluable information about gun mechanics.

Every effort has been made to obtain permission to reproduce copyright material, but there may be cases where we have been unable to trace a copyright holder. The publisher will be happy to correct any omissions in future printings.

NOTES

NOTES

NOTES

NOTES

NOTES

NOTES

NOTES

THE ILLUSTRATED ENCYCLOPEDIA OF

RIFLES
and MACHINE GUNS

THE ILLUSTRATED ENCYCLOPEDIA OF

RIFLES
and MACHINE GUNS

WILL FOWLER & PATRICK SWEENEY

LORENZ BOOKS

This edition is published by Lorenz Books,
an imprint of Anness Publishing Ltd, 108 Great Russell Street,
London WC1B 3NA; info@anness.com

www.lorenzbooks.com; www.annesspublishing.com;
twitter: @Anness_Books

Anness Publishing has a new picture agency outlet for images for
publishing, promotions or advertising. Please visit our website
www.practicalpictures.com for more information.

© Anness Publishing Ltd 2015

All rights reserved. No part of this publication may be
reproduced, stored in a retrieval system, or transmitted
in any way or by any means, electronic, mechanical,
photocopying, recording or otherwise, without the
prior written permission of the copyright holder.

A CIP catalogue record for this book is available from
the British Library.

Designed and produced for Anness Publishing by
THE BRIDGEWATER BOOK COMPANY LIMITED.

Publisher: Joanna Lorenz
Editorial Director: Helen Sudell
Editor: Rosie Gordon
Project Managers: Sarah Doughty & Cath Senker
Photography: Gary Ombler
Designer: Alistair Plumb
Art Director: Michael Whitehead
Production Controller: Pirong Wang

PUBLISHER'S NOTE
Although the advice and information in this book are believed to
be accurate and true at the time of going to press, neither the
authors nor the publisher can accept any legal responsibility or
liability for any errors or omissions that may have been made.

Contents

Introduction

Firearms have exerted a fascination since medieval times, and today's weapons are more accurate and effective than the first designers could have imagined. The rifle has been developed for use both in target shooting and for hunting, while the machine gun was exclusively developed for major conflict – and has demonstrated its devastating efficiency.

This book explores the earliest firearms, through to the ultra-modern assault rifles and machine guns of today, and introduces the small arms designers who have shaped history, such as Samuel Colt, Hiram Maxim, Pietro Antonio Beretta and Mikhail Kalashnikov.

The first muskets

The history of rifle development goes back to 14th-century Europe, when firearms using gunpowder as a propellant first appeared. These hand cannons, which could be loaded and fired by one man, were hazardous and not very effective. In the first section, "Early rifles", discover the designs that were successful and those that failed, and the many developments leading to selection of certain weapons for major conflicts. For example, flintlock muskets and pistols were used during the American Revolutionary Wars of 1775–83 and in the Napoleonic Wars of 1792–1815. Soldiers were drilled to fire in short-range volleys, waiting (often under artillery fire) until they could see the whites of the eyes of the approaching enemy

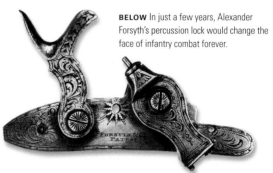

BELOW In just a few years, Alexander Forsyth's percussion lock would change the face of infantry combat forever.

infantry – difficult to imagine today. Following the volley they launched a bayonet charge against their shocked and battered opponents. In the American Civil War (1861–65), M1816 flintlock muskets were still in use with some of the Confederate forces.

From the American Civil War to World War I

Flintlocks may have been an incredible innovation in the 1700s, but as the second section of the book, "Rifles from 1800–2000" shows, 1807 saw a huge step forward. The Reverend Alexander Forsyth developed the first percussion ignition system for sporting guns. Forsyth's system was rather cumbersome, but, unlike flintlock weapons, it was weatherproof. About seven years later an English gunsmith, Josef Egg of London, invented the percussion cap, which was made of copper and filled with black blasting powder and potassium chlorate. These developments ultimately led to the modern magazine- and belt-fed weapons detailed in these pages. By World War I most combatants had equipped their soldiers with a magazine-fed bolt-action rifle, which could be fired fast, in all weather conditions, from the prone position.

Early machine guns

The inspiration for the world's first machine gun is said to have been a visitor to the Paris Electrical Exhibition of 1881, who said to the American engineer

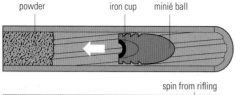

ABOVE The Minié rifle bullet system revolutionized firearm developmment. When the propellant charge exploded, the lead bullet expanded and cut into the twists of the rifling. This produced a spin that made it travel in a straight line and so gave it accuracy over a long range – which had never been achieved before.

powder · iron cup · minié ball

spin from rifling

and inventor Hiram Maxim, "If you want to make a lot of money, invent something that will enable these Europeans to cut each other's throats with greater facility." The gun he showed the British Army four years later had the firepower of all the riflemen in an infantry company. The potential of firearms in warfare, which we take for granted today, was just being dreamed of. Section three, "The machine gun age 1883–2000" charts the incredibly fast-paced development of machine guns – once that potential had been spotted, arms manufacture exploded into a race of innovation.

By the end of World War I, the first submachine guns (SMGs) had been developed. These compact, fast-firing weapons fired a pistol-calibre bullet and were ideal for the confined spaces of the trench systems of the Western Front. The book explores the ways that warfare conditions, allies and enemies alike influenced each country's weapons development, coming up with ever more devastating armories – for example, problems with cumbersome SMGs in World War I led the Germans to develop the MG34, the world's first General-Purpose Machine Gun (GPMG). This versatile new weapon was widely copied by all armies after World War II, and classics such as the AAT-52 and RPD are introduced on these pages.

The final development in the story of infantry weapons came just before World War II, but "New developments" shows how modern weapons designers are still drawing upon past guns, such as the Russian PK and the 19th century Gatling, to produce today's awesome fire power.

ABOVE The Maxim gun was the world's first true machine gun. For mobility on the battlefield it could be mounted on a light gun carriage, with the crew protected by a shield.

ABOVE In developing the MG34 (above) between the wars the Germans came up with a wholly new concept – the General-Purpose Machine Gun – a weapon that could be used as a light or medium machine gun. The MG42 that followed was an improvement.

The directories

There are two directories; the first devoted to rifles and carbines from around the world, the second to machine guns. The history of arms manufacture within each country is briefly introduced, then each weapon entry includes a concise description of the firearm and its key specifications, listed by country and manufacturer. Many weapons are pictured.

Readers will discover firearms from the 19th century "Brown Bess" flintlock musket to the Short Magazine Lee-Enfield, which, in the hands of the British Expeditionary Force (BEF) at Mons, shattered German infantry attacks. In the machine gun directory it becomes clear how the World Wars, and warfare generally, were shaped by machine gun development. World War I was dominated by the designs of American Hiram Maxim. Inventive German weapons designers gave the world the assault rifle, an automatic rifle firing intermediate calibre rounds. The directories bring readers right up to date with the weapons used today.

The history section and the detailed directories enable enthusiasts to identify firearms and fully appreciate their unique features, funtionality and designs.

LEFT Cadets of the Confederate Army with the Model 1841 Mississippi rifle, as photographed in 1861. By the end of 1863 most Federal infantrymen were armed with the Mississippi rifle or the Enfield.

Early rifles

The first firearms developed in Europe in the 14th century were hand cannon. These crude weapons were refined during the following century through a series of modifications such as the hackbut and arquebus, some fitted with snapping matchlocks or sear-lock matchlocks. In some regions of the world, including Japan and India's North-West Frontier, matchlocks would survive for centuries, and in the hands of trained marksmen prove very effective weapons. The development of the wheel lock and snaphance in the 16th century led to the production of the flintlock, a weapon that was used until the American Civil War. During this period, sights and rifling were developed, which greatly improved the accuracy of rifles. In the 17th and 18th centuries, new technologies were introduced to allow soldiers to carry gunpowder more safely. The section also covers the muskets of the 18th century, which also saw service in the American Civil War (1861–65) and the British Army in its conquest of colonies around the world.

BELOW The Mauser Model 1871 was the first Mauser rifle to be manufactured in 1871, and after the introduction of an adequate safety, it was adopted by the German Army in 1872. Millions of rifles were subsequently manufactured to the Mauser design.

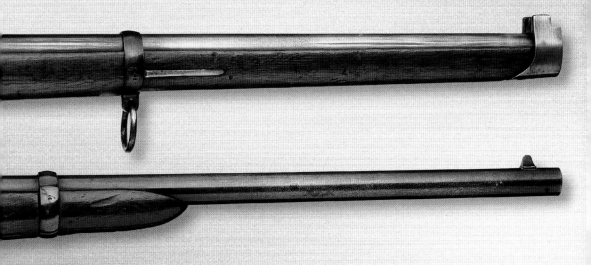

ABOVE The Remington Model 1871 carbine was a single-shot weapon, which was produced only in the 1870s and early 1880s before the advent of repeating rifles made it obsolete. The advantage of the Remington was its flexibility; it could be adapted to take a variety of rifle cartridges.

Hand cannon

The first firearms that appeared in the late 14th century in Europe were simply miniature cannon that were fired from horseback or from ships and fortifications. They were noisy and had a very short effective range. The invention of gunpowder was the kickstart for this new type of weapon, and although it was only gradually introduced, the use of gunpowder would change the character of war on land and at sea forever.

Before gunpowder

Before gunpowder came on the scene, combat weapons were implements that could stab, cleave or batter an enemy to death, and so had to be used at close quarters. The only weapons that allowed combatants to engage at range were the crossbow and longbow. In the 15th century, skilled English and Welsh archers armed with longbows could deliver plunging fire at targets such as massed horsemen at about 180m/200yd. This type of fire was similar to that delivered by a machine gun firing at long range. As the range shortened, the fire would be direct, and the metal arrowhead with the mass of the shaft or stele behind it would take on the characteristics of a modern anti-tank shell with its long rod penetrator.

The invention of gunpowder

In 1242, however, an English monk named Roger Bacon wrote down the formula for the preparation of gunpowder as an anagram or cipher. Not only did

ABOVE The Welsh longbow (shown without string here) was adopted by the English and used with lethal effect against French mounted knights at the Battle of Agincourt of 1415. The longbow was actually more accurate than most firearms until the introduction of rifled percussion-cap fired weapons in the mid-19th century.

Bacon name the ingredients and the proportions then used (saltpetre: charcoal: sulphur 7:5:5) but he also described the explosive properties of the mixture. Although he gave no indication that it could be employed as a propellant, by around 1300 muzzle-loading cannon were beginning to appear. By 1364, there was documented evidence of hand-held firearms in Perugia, Italy; and ten years later firearms had become common in Europe. One of the earliest

BELOW Two early hand cannons. The lip allowed the barrel of the weapon to be hooked over a parapet before it was fired. The upper weapon has a metal hook-type handle, while the lower has a more conventional butt.

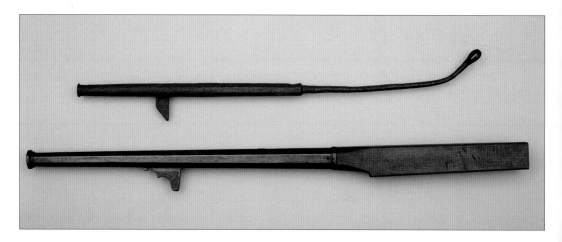

examples is in the Tøjhus Museum in Copenhagen, Denmark. Constructed from iron with a long handle and simple hook, the weapon could be secured to a wall or palisade or even a tripod, so that when the operator fired it the recoil would have been absorbed by the solid structure. Another version, made from iron in the second half of the 15th century (found in the Bernisches Historisches Museum in Switzerland), has both a hook as well as a D-shaped grip for easy carriage and deployment.

Hand cannon design

Early firearms that appeared around 1375 were often called "hand cannon"; they consisted of a simple iron or brass tube with a touchhole at the top fixed in a straight stock of wood, the end of which passed under the right armpit when the gun was ready to be fired. Some versions used by mounted soldiers had a ring at the end of the stock with a cord attached, which allowed the gun to be hung over the shoulder, leaving both hands free. When the rider wished to fire it he used a forked rest, fitted into a ring on the saddle, to steady the gun. When the fork rest was not in use, it hung down in front of the rider's right leg. An example of a cavalry hand cannon dating from 1400–50, and now in the Bernisches Historisches Museum, was found in the River Tiber in Rome. It has a wrought-iron barrel with a ring to allow it to be slung from a strap over the shoulder. The wooden stock had long disappeared and has been restored.

The slow match

The match was made from cotton or loosely spun hemp, which was boiled in a strong solution of saltpetre or in the lees of wine. Kindled by a flint and steel, the match, or slow match, would remain an important piece of equipment while gunpowder weapons were in use. Ideally, the match should not burn quickly or produce sparks, nor should it be blown out by a breeze. Like a conventional cannon, the touchhole was first placed on top of the gun barrel, but afterwards it was moved to the side, with a small pan underneath to hold the priming, and held in place by a pivoted cover.

Firearms training

Although the hand cannons produced a spectacular, and no doubt terrifying bang and cloud of white smoke, the longbow and crossbow were more accurate

ABOVE This early 15th-century illustration depicts the firing of hand cannons in battle. The stock is held firmly under the firer's arm, and the man in the foreground is holding the slow match in his left hand. Burning gas from the gunpowder is emitted from the muzzle and the touchhole.

and deadly – and far less dangerous to use. They would remain so until the American Civil War during the mid-19th century. Yet even early, inaccurate firearms had a distinct advantage: it was easy to train soldiers to use them, whereas the skill of using a longbow could be mastered only after expert tuition and long and regular practice. Soldiers were trained to use firearms by a series of drills, which taught them to load, aim and fire the musket. This ensured that in the smoke, noise and confusion of the battlefield they would keep up a steady volume of fire.

Sometimes in 18th- and 19th-century actions a soldier forgot under pressure that one of the drills was to remove his ramrod after loading his weapon. If the ramrod was fired off, the musket lacked this vital component and became useless. In some European armies there were severe punishments for men who lost their ramrods.

Since muskets were smoothbore (with no rifling to direct the shot) and only accurate over short ranges, soldiers were taught to fire in volleys, at short range, delivering a blast of musket balls that produced an effect similar to a giant shotgun.

The matchlock

The 15th century saw improvements in firearm design such as the matchlock, which looked less like a miniature cannon and more like our familiar rifle with a butt and trigger. Further developments in design produced the arquebus, some versions of which were fitted with snapping matchlocks or sear-lock matchlocks.

The matchlock

The first design improvement came in about 1411 with the first matchlock; a simple trigger was linked into a curved metal clamp called a serpentine, which held a match. When the trigger was pressed, the serpentine tipped forwards and pushed the match into the priming pan containing gunpowder. The flash passed through the touchhole to the main charge and the shot was fired. Refinements included a hinged cover for the pan that kept the powder dry and reduced the risk of an accidental discharge. By the late 15th century, these weapons were being fitted with shoulder stocks.

The English idiom "a flash in the pan", to describe an event that looks spectacular but is of no consequence, probably dates from the time of flintlocks (16th century), although men armed with matchlocks would also have been familiar with the phenomenon. Although there would be a flash of exploding powder and a cloud of smoke, the burning gas would not pass into the barrel and set off the main charge because the touchhole was fouled with burned gunpowder residue. It would be a "flash in the pan" or non-event.

The arquebus

The hackbut was the first gun fired from the shoulder. It was a smoothbore matchlock (without rifling) and had a stock resembling that of a modern rifle. The arquebus, invented in Spain in the mid-15th century, was a medium-weight gun that evolved from the heavy and awkward hackbut. Instead of the recoil from firing being directed against the soldier's shoulder, some of it was absorbed by the support; however the hook was needed to prevent the gun sliding off the support. (The name "arquebus" may come from the Low German for "hooked gun".)

The arquebus was the first firearm to resemble a modern gun, with lock, stock and barrel. As technology advanced, the arquebus was fitted with

The gunsmith's craft

Firearms were a "must-have" weapon for the monarchs and rulers of Europe. In addition to their beautifully crafted armour and edged weapons, these leaders had firearms made to order, and gunsmiths came up with some ingenious designs that were pointers to the future. A revolving matchlock was presented to King Louis XIII of France. This gun had multiple chambers, each of which had its own priming pan. To fire it, the user rotated each chamber into place and opened the pan and fired as a conventional matchlock.

RIGHT The beautifully engraved breech-loading matchlock used by Henry VIII; his crest featuring a rose can be seen on the barrel. The carefully engineered breech was designed to give an effective gas seal for the exploding powder.

King Henry VIII of England had a custom-made breech-loading matchlock. This gun was loaded through the rear by lifting the breech block, placing the shot followed by gunpowder into the barrel and then closing the breech block. The pan was then primed and the gun fired as a conventional matchlock.

more advanced forms of ignition. There were three major types of arquebus: those with serpentine locks, those with snapping matchlocks and those with sear-lock matchlocks. The caliver was a more advanced form of arquebus with a standardized bore size. The caliver used either a trigger lever or a conventional trigger to operate the matchlock mechanism.

The snapping matchlock

By about 1475 the snapping matchlock had appeared. It was operated by cocking a spring-powered serpentine and pushing a button on the lock plate (a trigger was used on later guns) to release the

ABOVE A good idea of the very short effective range of an arquebus can be gauged from this 15th-century German woodcut. The knights equipped with firearms have sensibly retained their swords. Reloading an arquebus would take up too much time, which would have been in short supply during close combat.

serpentine, allowing it to snap into the priming pan. This type of matchlock lost popularity in Europe because the slow match was often extinguished when it was snapped hard into the powder. The sear-lock matchlock operated by squeezing a trigger attached to a sprung sear inside the lock, allowing the serpentine to be lowered into the priming pan as the hand squeezed, then retracted when pressure was released.

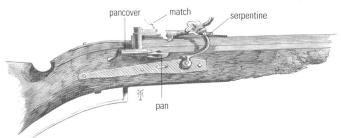

pancover   match   serpentine

pan

LEFT The slow match smoulders, ready to be lowered into the pan of a caliver. The caliver was an advanced version of the arquebus, which was an improvement on the inaccurate hand cannon.

New users of the matchlock

The simplicity of the matchlock led to its adoption by indigenous warriors wherever it was taken by European traders and soldiers. The Japanese learned how to build matchlocks from Portuguese traders, while the Indians and Afghans adopted the technology from the British. On India's North-West Frontier, warlike tribesmen used their Jezail matchlocks, designed for easy fire from horseback, with ruthless efficiency against the British.

Japanese matchlocks

Although based on matchlocks introduced by the Portuguese traders in 1543, Japanese Tanegashima weapons never progressed beyond the basic snapping matchlock mechanism; most European designs used flintlocks. In the 1860s, percussion locks were imported from the West, and this ignition system was the first departure from the matchlock.

All Japanese matchlocks of this type were handmade, varying greatly in calibre, size, length and styles and rarely had interchangeable parts. Unlike European muskets, the stocks had no shoulder supports with a butt plate, but at the rear they had a distinctive cheek piece, described as a "cheek stock".

In feudal Japan the Tanegashima matchlock styles were classified by the shooting schools where the gun makers taught and worked, and by the fiefdoms of the ruling lords. The country was divided among almost one hundred lords, each with his own distinctive ideas or policies about the manufacture of every kind of civil or military product. Records suggest that in the late

ABOVE Warriors on the Afghan–Baluch frontier in the 1890s armed with their Jezail muskets; the stocks and other simple components were often handmade. These men were formidable marksmen, capable of hitting human targets at a considerable range.

LEFT The Japanese had been introduced to the matchlock by Portuguese traders. They were quick to grasp its utility as a weapon. Here, warriors use a modified version; however, like European soldiers they retain their swords for personal protection.

18th century there may have about 250 shooting schools in Japan; shooting, or *Houjyutu*, was classed as a martial art along with techniques such as karate.

Indian and Afghan matchlocks

A form of matchlock musket used in India until the 20th century was known as the Bandukh Torador. British soldiers also adopted the name, referring to their rifles as "Bondooks" well into the 20th century.

The Jezail, which came from the area of the Pashto-speaking people of Afghanistan and the North-West Frontier of British India (now Pakistan), was a matchlock or flintlock musket fired from a forked rest. The Jezail used the unusual curved Sind stock, which made the gun easier to fire from horseback. Many of these guns were later converted to percussion. The Jezail, although long and awkward to carry, was reputedly accurate up to 730m/800yd; Afghans picked off sheep and horses at 550m/600yd with a single shot.

In his poem "Arithmetic on the Frontier", Rudyard Kipling writes about the death of a young British officer:

A scrimmage in a Border Station –
A canter down some dark defile –
Two thousand pounds of education
Drops to a ten-rupee jezail –
The Crammer's boast, the Squadron's pride,
Shot like a rabbit in a ride.

War on the North-West Frontier

A series of conflicts known as the Anglo–Afghan Wars took place during the imperialist struggle for domination in Afghanistan between Britain and the Russian Empire in the 19th century.

On 1 January 1842 the besieged British garrison at Kabul, commanded by General William Elphinstone, made an agreement that safe passage for the soldiers and their dependants from Afghanistan would be granted. Five days later, the retreat began. The British column, more than 16,000-strong, was composed of about 4,500 British and Indian soldiers, along with as many as 12,000 camp followers. As they struggled through the snowbound passes, the British were picked off in a series of ambushes by Ghilzay tribesmen armed with Jezails. They were then massacred in close combat while moving through the 50km/30 miles of treacherous gorges and passes lying between Kabul and Gandamak.

After further wars, in 1893 the British succeeded in imposing control up to the Durand Line, a border that ran through the Afghan tribal lands between Afghanistan and what was then British India and thus divided Afghanistan.

BELOW The last stand of the 44th Regiment at Gandamak, during the retreat from Kabul in 1841. Cold was as much a killer as Afghan fire, but together they eventually killed more than 16,000 soldiers and camp followers in what became a Victorian military disaster.

16th century technology

The 16th century saw great developments in weapons technology, much of which remains in use today. These innovations included the wheel lock, which was invented around the turn of the century, although the actual inventor is unconfirmed. In addition, sights and rifling were major advances, and ensured that weapons could be aimed accurately and that the bullet had a straight flight path to the target.

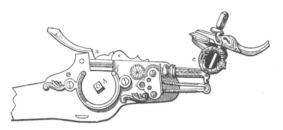

ABOVE The ingenious clockwork mechanism of the wheel lock introduced in the 16th century was complex, but more reliable than earlier systems. However, the flintlock that would replace it would remain in widespread use for more than two hundred years.

The wheel lock

Many scholars believe that the Italian genius Leonardo da Vinci invented the wheel lock, in which a gun's firing mechanism was activated by sparks produced by friction between a small steel wheel and a flint. This belief is based on drawings of a wheel-lock mechanism which da Vinci made between the 1490s and 1510. However, there is a strong possibility that the inventor was actually an unknown German craftsman because a drawing dated 1505 has been found in a German book of inventions as well as a reference in 1507 to the purchase of a wheel lock in Austria.

By 1515 it appears that wheel locks were in widespread use. A young man from Augsburg in Bavaria, southern Germany is reported to have invited a "handsome whore" to his room where, perhaps showing off his new "self-igniting pistol", he pulled the trigger and it went off, hitting her in the chin. During the plague of 1526 in Italy, Ben Vinito Cellini noted in his diary that he survived by shooting pigeons to eat with his wheel-lock rifle. It was either a good rifle or he was an excellent shot, since he rarely missed.

Across the Atlantic, inventories of public stores from the 1660s and archaeological sites show that a large number of wheel locks had reached America.

Rifling

The spiral grooving in the bore of a firearm, which was used to spin-stabilize the projectile and so improve its accuracy after leaving the barrel, had been developed by the early 16th century. Rifling can have either an even or odd number of grooves that produce either a clockwise or anti-clockwise spin on the projectile. Modern handguns also usually have rifled barrels.

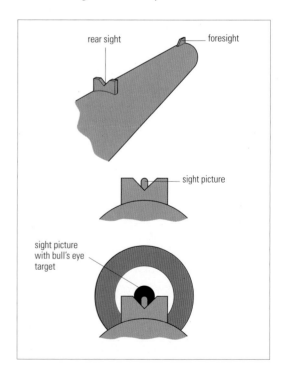

ABOVE The oldest and most basic form of sight consists of a foresight at the end of the barrel and a V-shaped rear sight close to the firer's eye. To aim the weapon, the firer positions the two sights so that the centre of the target is at the top of the foresight, which in turn bisects the V-shaped notch of the rear sight.

Matchlock drill

In 16th-century European armies, there was a strict set of orders for firing a musket. On the command "Handle your piece", the musketeer placed the weapon on the rest, near the point of balance. On receipt of the order "Take forth your match", he transferred the burning match from the left hand to the right hand. On the order "Blow off your coal", he blew off any loose ash from the burning end of the slow match. On the command "Cock your match", he clamped the burning end of the slow match between the jaws of the serpentine.

He flipped the pan cover over the priming powder and on the order "Try your match", operated the serpentine to ensure that the match would hit the powder. On the command "Guard your pan", he placed two fingers over the pan to ensure that random sparks did not fire it prematurely as he followed the order "Blow off the coal". He would then blow the match to make it glow.

On receipt of the last order "Present and give fire", he would swing the stock into his shoulder, open the pan cover and slowly pull the trigger to ensure that the match was not stubbed out as it was lowered into the pan. What followed was a spectacular bang and cloud of white smoke, and the lead ball went on its short and inaccurate journey.

RIGHT This illustration indicates the complexity of firing a 16th-century musket correctly; the musketeer was required to follow no less than 16 precise steps.

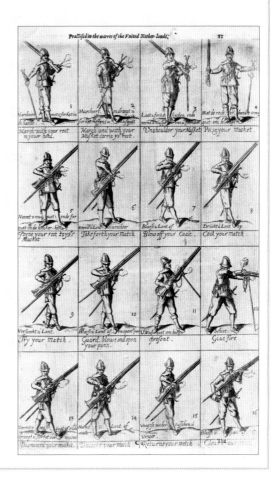

Sights

Matchlocks with simple sights appeared around 1537. Sights are the fittings on a firearm that help the user align the weapon accurately when it is pointed at a target. The first sights were in two parts: the foresight, a vertical post mounted at the muzzle, and the rear sight, a V-shaped notch mounted as far to the rear as possible and close to the firer's eye. To aim the weapon, the firer had a sight picture with the foresight in the centre of the notch and the target at the top of the foresight. However, with adjustable sights a weapon could be zeroed or adjusted to suit the individual shooter. With modern adjustable rear sights, to move the shot right, the firer moves the rear sight to the right. The sight is normally adjusted by two screws that can be loosened and tightened. Usually, sights have right-hand threads on their adjusting screws.

With adjustable foresights, the firer moves the sight adjuster in the opposite direction that he or she wishes the shot to go on the target. Optical sights are more accurate since they magnify the sight picture; they may have a crosshair, pointer or dot that the firer should place in the centre of the target.

Although electronic aids have been developed to provide training for soldiers, there is still a place for the range coach – a marksman who can observe a soldier as he or she fires on the range and adjust or zero the sights through various techniques to ensure accurate shooting.

Classic 16th century designs

In 1517 and 1518, the first gun-control laws were introduced by Holy Roman Emperor Maximilian I, when he attempted to ban the manufacture or possession of matchlocks; being compact and more reliable than earlier firearms, they were seen as an ideal assassin's weapon. The matchlock nevertheless remained popular as a sporting arm and weapon. Meanwhile, the new Spanish musket became a common weapon of war for nearly a century.

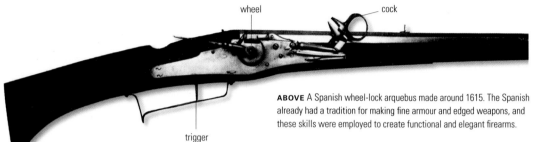

wheel   cock

trigger

ABOVE A Spanish wheel-lock arquebus made around 1615. The Spanish already had a tradition for making fine armour and edged weapons, and these skills were employed to create functional and elegant firearms.

Spanish muskets

Around 1521 the Spaniards constructed the large and heavy musket, which gave them military superiority. The Spanish musket quickly gained popularity throughout Europe owing to its power and reliability. Early types fired a ball about 160m/175yd and were no more accurate than the arquebus. However, later types of Spanish musket proved to be far more lethal weapons than the arquebus at long range, with the ability to reliably penetrate armour at 90m/100yd and kill an unprotected man or horse at 460m/500yd.

This advantage was to some extent gained by sheer size. A 16th-century arquebus was big, weighing around 4.5kg/10lb with a bore diameter of about 60 calibre (sixty-hundredths of an inch). Spanish muskets, however, were even bigger, weighing at least 8.2kg/18lb and with a bore diameter of 70–85 calibre, with some virtually the size of a cannon at 90 calibre. The large calibres meant that the ammunition was proportionately bigger; while an arquebus fired a ball that weighed about 12g/0.5oz, the musket fired a full 50g/2oz lead ball.

The penalty for firing such a powerful weapon was a huge recoil. Some of this was absorbed by the weight of the weapon. However, to be effective, these muskets required big, muscular men to fire them. This restricted their use and produced a new military elite – the musketeer. The Spanish musket was excellent in

ABOVE Big men were needed to carry and fire the Spanish musket. It required a forked rest to spread the weight when the musketeer moved it into the aim. The musketeer has gunpowder reloads slung in a bandolier across his chest.

Wheel lock and snaphance

The wheel-lock mechanism used a fluted or grooved steel wheel located above the priming pan and held under tension by a strong spring. The cock was also regulated by a spring and fitted with a piece of iron pyrite. To fire the gun, the lock was wound up with a key, then the cock was let down on the priming pan, so that the pyrite rested on the wheel. To ignite the powder in the pan, the trigger was pressed which caused the wheel to be released and spin round

quickly. The sparks produced then ignited the powder. The lock was not only complicated and expensive but also prone to damage, which prevented its wider adoption. Wheel-lock and matchlock combinations were fairly common because many wheel-lock mechanisms were unreliable. Such a gun would function as a regular wheel lock, but if the wheel lock broke or malfunctioned the user would still be able to fire the gun using the matchlock.

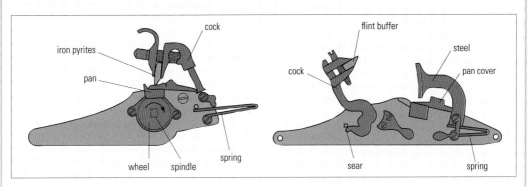

ABOVE The wheel lock was an efficient but complex mechanism that never entirely replaced the much more basic matchlock in military use. The wheel lock was popular with aristocratic hunters and sportsmen as an obvious demonstration of their wealth.

ABOVE The snaphance marked a new innovation since it used flint and steel to ignite the powder. When the trigger was pulled, the pan covering the powder opened mechanically as the flint scraped down the face of the steel to produce sparks.

siege warfare and aboard ships, where the weight presented less of a problem. (Ottoman shoulder arms, similar in proportion to Spanish muskets, proved very effective in sieges.) The Spanish musket soon came into general use throughout Europe and was introduced into England in the early 16th century.

Elegant wheel locks

The wheel lock was first used in action at the siege of Parma in 1521 and was brought to England in 1530, where it continued in partial use until the reign of Charles II (1660–85). It had actually been developed for hunting, and some elegant weapons were made for wealthy clients.

The Metropolitan Museum, New York has an early multi-shot wheel-lock pistol made by Peter Peck of Munich, who worked as a watchmaker and gunsmith between 1503 and 1596. It was made for Emperor

Charles V c.1540–45. Each barrel had separate ignition which was achieved by two locks being combined in one mechanism. Made from cherry wood, staghorn and steel, the .46-calibre pistol was decorated by Ambrosius Gemlich with the emperor's dynastic and personal emblems: the pillars of Hercules with the Latin motto *Plus ultra* ("More beyond") and the double-headed imperial eagle.

The National Maritime Museum in Greenwich, England has an elegant wheel-lock rifle made in Dresden, Germany in 1664. The stock is made from dark brown wood, partially decorated with inset ivory or bone panels, and the calibre is approximately .33. Utility combines with beauty where, on the right side of the rifle, a sliding trap covers a patch or toolbox let into the side of the butt. The rifle has a horn butt plate and is decorated with pieces of bone or ivory.

Tools of the trade

Men in the 17th and 18th centuries armed with muzzle loaders such as the doglock, miquelet and flintlock required a number of essential pieces of equipment in the field. These would enable them to carry gunpowder securely and maintain their weapons sufficiently when on campaign in all weather conditions.

Powder, flasks and horns

Gunpowder or black powder (also known as *poudre N*, or *poudre noir*) becomes useless with even the slightest amount of moisture, so it had to be kept absolutely dry. It was therefore normally carried in a powder horn or flask often made from a cow's horn. Horn has been described as the equivalent of today's plastic: it was light, strong and completely waterproof.

The flask or horn was designed so that at the wider end black powder could be poured in and then closed off with a cap. At the narrow end there was a spout with a cap. To load his weapon, the muzzle loader tipped the horn forwards to allow sufficient powder

ABOVE A 17th-century musketeer uses his powder horn to load an exact amount of gunpowder into the barrel of his weapon. The powder horn was strong, light and waterproof and could be slung over the soldier's shoulder when not in use.

into the barrel before ramming wadding and the ball home and then pouring powder into the pan. From around the late 16th century, musketeers carried individual loads in wooden containers attached to a belt slung across their shoulders. Later soldiers carried powder loads in waxed paper cartridges. (Even in the 21st century, good-quality writing paper is still known as cartridge paper.)

Just as many sporting and early military weapons were elaborately engraved, powder flasks and horns were also carved and had elegant metal fittings.

Bullet moulds and flints

Besides the horn or flask an essential item was a bullet mould. This looked a little like a pair of pliers but had a dimple into which molten lead could be poured. When it had filled the mould the excess was removed with a simple cutter.

Soldiers might also carry a simple metal tool that incorporated several implements for cleaning and servicing their muskets. Today such a tool, called a combination tool, is found in all modern military cleaning kits.

Finally, spare flints were essential, since flint can split or shatter, and without a flint to strike a spark, weapons such as the snaphance, flintlock or miquelet would be useless. Most flints had a useful life of about twenty shots.

The doglock

Named after the dog safety catch behind the cock, the doglock musket replaced the Jacobean English lock of the early 17th century and was a transitional design between the snaphance and flintlock. A "dog" or safety catch was engaged to hold the heel of the hance in a half-cock position.

The doglock entered widespread use around 1640 and was popular with the British Army until about 1715. It remained in use as a regular issued weapon in the Royal Navy for many years after this and eventually evolved into the Sea Service musket of the 1730s. This musket was very popular in the colonies from the Caribbean to Canada. The common early British trade gun with the serpentine side plate was modelled after this musket as well. Many of these rugged muskets were used right up to the Revolutionary War in America by colonial troops as well as Native Americans.

By 1700 the doglock had evolved into a beautiful and sleek weapon complete with brass hardware that was unique to Britain and its colonies. While flintlocks without dog catches started to surface at this time, the doglock would have been one of the principal weapons in Marlborough's army when he defeated the French at the Battles of Blenheim in 1704, Ramillies in 1706, Oudenaarde in 1708 and Malplaquet in 1709, during the War of the Spanish Succession (1701–14).

Excavations of 17th-century Native American burial sites have unearthed doglock muskets. The doglock long fowler – a long-barrelled hunting weapon – was the most popular trade gun from 1625 to 1675. Native Americans valued it not only for hunting but also as a prestige item and for use in self-defence. These later doglocks had vertically attaching sear springs, and often the tumbler had notches for half- and full-cock positions. The cock (or hammer) was long and slender in style.

ABOVE The dog safety catch can be seen holding the cock back on this doglock musket. The hammer that held the flint was called a cock because it looked like a bird's beak and snapped forwards in a pecking action. Even today soldiers "cock" their rifles when they operate the bolt.

The miquelet and flintlock

The miquelet lock was named after Catalan militia leader Miquelot de Prats. Popular in the Mediterranean area from the 16th to 19th centuries, it was a distinctive flint-on-steel ignition mechanism. The design is attributed to an anonymous Italian gunsmith working for a Madrid gunmaker, Pedro Marquart, in the mid-1570s. This prototype was refined by Madrid gunsmiths into the Spanish patilla style now commonly known as the miquelet. A distinctive Italian miquelet lock was also developed.

With its combined battery and pan cover, the miquelet was the final innovative link that would be both the precursor and companion to the flintlock. The

flintlock was a refinement in which the steel and pan cover were made in one piece. When the trigger was pressed, the cock scraped the flint down the length of the steel, simultaneously uncovering the pan and exposing the prime charge to a stream of sparks. It was a simple and effective mechanism that would remain in use for over two centuries.

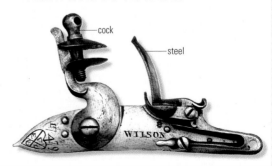

RIGHT A military flintlock from the late 18th century. Though it bears the maker's name and would have been handmade, it was no elaborately engraved work of art but rather a utilitarian weapon suitable for the new mass armies of the Napoleonic Wars.

Three special muskets

The Kentucky rifle was made famous as the weapon carried by "Hawkeye", the colonial trapper Nathaniel Poe, in James Fenimore Cooper's novel *The Last of the Mohicans*. The blunderbuss was a short-range weapon that fired a load of heavy gauge shot (not scrap metal, as has been suggested). In the 18th century the British Army received the "Brown Bess" musket, a reliable weapon that would serve it well through the Napoleonic Wars and the colonial campaigns around the world.

The Kentucky rifle

The American Pennsylvania Kentucky rifle, produced in 1700, was much longer than an ordinary musket and very cumbersome to load while in battle. An expert rifleman could load and fire a shot in 1.5 minutes. However, the rifling provided greater range and accuracy and made the Kentucky ideal for sniping.

The blunderbuss

In the early 18th century, the blunderbuss (also called the blunderbess) was a popular weapon for close range fighting. Like a shot gun, it produced a lethal blast of shot or ball. In the mid-1700s, it was in widespread use by soldiers, sailors and civilians for close-quarter defence and its popularity lasted for nearly forty years. It is reported that George Washington proposed that instead of the carbine, Continental Dragoons should

ABOVE The Kentucky long rifle might have been cumbersome but its rifling and long barrel made it very accurate. The settlers in North America found it an invaluable weapon for hunting, though it was also a very effective military arm.

carry a blunderbuss because this weapon was not only easy to handle but actually more accurate with its spread of shot.

Blunderbusses were manufactured with both brass and steel barrels during the 18th century. On board ship, often the steel barrels were japanned (covered with a heavy black lacquer); this protected them against salt corrosion. A typical Royal Navy boarding blunderbuss was 775mm/30.5in long with a 370mm/14.5in brass barrel, 64mm/2.5in diameter at the muzzle. In the American colonies, settlers armed themselves with blunderbusses. Across the Atlantic, by the late 18th century the blunderbuss had gained fame as the weapon carried by British coachmen to thwart attacks by highwaymen. It was also the weapon of choice of pirates and privateers at sea.

The Brown Bess

The origin of the nickname "Brown Bess" is unknown but it was the affectionate name for the British Army's Land Pattern musket and its derivatives. It entered British service in 1722 and became as important symbolically as it was in practical terms in the field, since this was a period of global expansion. The Long Land Pattern musket and its derivatives, all in .72 and .705 calibre flintlock, were the standard infantry weapons from 1722 until 1838, although there were many incremental changes in its design. These versions include the Sea Service musket, New Land Pattern,

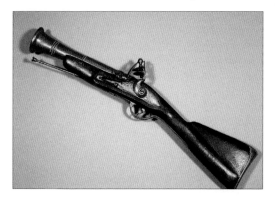

ABOVE The blunderbuss, with its short barrel and bell-shaped muzzle, delivered the same sort of lethal punch as a sawn-off shotgun. As such it was favoured by naval boarding parties for its shock effect at close range.

ABOVE A re-enactor from the Coldstream Regiment of Foot Guards in the uniform of the late 18th century takes aim with his "Brown Bess" musket. With some minor modifications the Brown Bess would be a great survivor, remaining in service into the early 19th century.

Short Land Pattern, India Pattern and new Long Land Pattern musket. The earliest models had iron fittings but after 1736 these were replaced by brass, which did not rust. Wooden ramrods were also replaced by more robust iron ones. However, up until 1765, muskets with wooden ramrods were still issued to troops on American service and those fighting for the Crown in the Revolutionary War. Wooden ramrods were also used in the Dragoon version produced from 1744 to 1771 and to reduce problems of corrosion for the Royal Navy and Marine muskets.

Muskets in action

Infantry soldiers were armed with a musket and a bayonet. The musket was muzzle loading with a flintlock mechanism at the butt end of the barrel. The soldier's normal ammunition load was 24 cartridges. Each cartridge contained a single load of gunpowder and a spherical lead ball. When loading, the soldier ripped open the paper cartridge with his teeth and poured a small quantity of powder into the firing pan. He poured the remainder of the charge into the muzzle of the musket, followed by the cartridge paper as a wad, and poked the charge to the bottom of the barrel with the ramrod.

The soldier then put the musket ball into the barrel so that it rolled to the bottom (or he pushed it down with the ramrod), on top of the charge of gunpowder. The soldier cocked the flintlock mechanism, aimed the weapon at the target and pulled the trigger. This caused the flint to strike, producing sparks and igniting the powder in the firing pan, which flashed through the touchhole and set off the charge. The musket discharged the ball with a flash, a considerable quantity of smoke and a roar. A well-trained soldier was able to fire his musket two or three times in a minute.

Guns of the Revolution

In 1776 the United States was locked in war with Britain, the colonial power, and was desperate for muskets. In the spring of that year, the US Congress sent a secret agent to France to ask the king for help in the form of weapons, equipment and financial support. The 1766 musket, shipped over by France, would later be replaced by the home-produced US 1795 musket, made at the Springfield Armory.

pan

trigger

button ram rod

Safety muskets

On 18 July 1775 the Continental Congress passed the following resolution: "that it be recommended to each colony to appoint a Committee of Safety to superintend and direct all matters necessary for the security and defence of their respective colonies, in the recess of their assemblies and conventions". Several colonies had already begun to acquire muskets from private contractors and builders. Many are signed, and others are attributed to known makers based on similarities to signed muskets or guns made by builders who had connections with the various Committees of Safety.

ABOVE A re-enactor dressed as a civilian soldier in the War of Independence. His simple hunting clothes would have been comfortable and have given him a tactical edge over British troops dressed in the cumbersome uniforms favoured by European armies. He would also have been a skilled hunter and an accurate shot.

ABOVE The French were responsible for supplying many of the muskets used by the colonists against the British in the American War of Independence. Their Model 1766 was a simple and reliable weapon that was copied by the US Armory at Springfield, Massachusetts.

Musket drill 1764

Musket drill in the mid-18th century was based around a series of commands. On the order "Poise your Firelocks", the soldier took his musket in his right hand, and turned the lock outwards, while keeping the musket upright. He then swung the musket off his shoulder and grasped it with his left hand just above the lock with the little finger resting upon the spring, and the thumb on the stock.

At the command to "Cock your Firelocks", he turned the barrel towards his face, placed his thumb upon the cock, with his elbow square in this position. He then cocked the action and positioned his thumb on the breech pin and fingers under the trigger guard.

On the command "Present", he moved his right foot about six inches to the rear. At the same time the musket butt was moved to shoulder height, with the left hand on the wooden stock, and the right-hand forefinger on the trigger or "Tricker". The muzzle was lowered a little to compensate for the recoil.

When the order to "Fire" was given, the soldier pulled the trigger. As soon as his musket had fired he moved into the priming position ready to reload.

Genuine Committee of Safety muskets are rare, since they were mostly used up in the early days of the war. During the American War of Independence, a veteran militiaman armed with a Committee of Safety musket could load and fire three shots per minute.

French Model 1766 Musket

Three years after it was introduced in 1763, several modifications were made to the new French Infantry musket to create the French Model 1766 Musket. It was lighter in weight, with a smaller lock and a ramrod shaped like a flat button, known as the button-head ramrod design. Vast numbers of these muskets were produced for the French Army by an arsenal in Charleville in the Champagne–Ardennes region of north-eastern France.

When the request for arms came from the United States, the French, happy to wage a proxy war with Britain, provided the rebellious colonists with shiploads of muskets. Since France was not at war with Britain, various ploys were adopted that now seem very modern: a fake corporation had to be set up to mask the French government's direct involvement; in addition to this, ship's logs were falsified to conceal the ultimate destination of the muskets. Because the Royal Navy dominated the high seas, some French ships sailed to the West Indies and dropped off their cargo of muskets, where American vessels then collected them.

The Model 1766 had a powerful influence on the United States. Most of the surviving French-made muskets that have US markings are the Model 1766 and, in 1795, the United States used this musket as the template when it started mass production of its own at the Springfield arsenal.

The US 1795 musket

Colonel Henry Knox of General George Washington's staff decided that the area near Springfield, Massachusetts would be an ideal location for an ordnance depot to store arms and ammunition during the American Revolution.

A small depot was created in 1776, and Congress established it as a national armoury in 1794. The Springfield Armoury went on to produce arms for the United States for nearly 175 years.

When it began operations, Springfield had only 40 workers available, but in its first year managed to make 245 muskets. The first musket produced was the

ABOVE At the height of the Napoleonic Wars, a grenadier of Napoleon's Imperial Guard protects the emperor. The grenadier has a Charleville 1777 musket supported in the crook of his arm.

Model 1795, which was almost a direct copy of the French Model 1766 Charleville musket. Eventually, Springfield Armory would make 80,000 muskets and the armoury at Harpers Ferry in eastern West Virginia a further 70,000. The Model 1795 was carried during the ground-breaking Lewis and Clark expedition in 1803–06 and used in action during the 1812 war between the United States and Britain.

Art and utility

Two types of firearm used in the 19th century are at the extreme end of weapons design. The miquelet, produced in Turkey, was more a work of art than a weapon. By contrast, the Baker rifle, used by British riflemen in the Peninsula War, was a functionally efficient weapon, and the soldiers who used it were trained to make the most of its potential.

The miquelet

An example of a Turkish miquelet from around 1760 that came up for sale in 2006 on an internet site, with an asking price of £1300 ($2,500), shows how beautiful the work was on these weapons. It has a .60 calibre, 117cm/46in Damascus barrel that has a little silver inlay work. The gunsmith took the Ripoll pistols of Catalonia for his inspiration for the brass overlay decoration of the stock and copied a Spanish mechanism for the lock. Using a punch, the lockplate was signed in Arabic script and was extensively inlaid and overlaid with silver. The barrel may have come from a 17th-century Persian matchlock, since barrels

ABOVE As a weapon the miquelet was becoming obsolescent by the 18th century when Europeans soldiers and sailors encountered it. However, as a trophy it was exquisite, since the workmanship and designs were now no longer produced in an increasingly utilitarian European arms industry.

and other parts were often reused. Miquelets like this reached Europe through trading contacts in the Balkans, part of the Ottoman Empire at the time.

A Turkish miquelet was bequeathed by Admiral Lord Nelson to Alexander Davison, his friend and prize agent, together with a water canteen and scimitar. It is a beautiful weapon with an inscription on the butt: "This gun together with a skymetar and canteen were presented by the Grand Signor to Horatio Viscount Nelson and by will bequeathed to his friend Alexander Davidson 10 May 1803." It has a Turkish variant of the Spanish miquelet lock with gold *koftgari* decoration. The stock is ivory and is decorated with silver and gilt studs with bands of gilt brass and mother-of-pearl. It has been suggested that the rifle, scimitar and canteen may have been gifts from the Sultan of Turkey to this successful and charismatic sailor. In 1873 Davison's son gave the rifle to Greenwich Hospital, and it was originally displayed with other Nelson relics in the Painted Hall at the National Maritime Museum in Greenwich, London.

The Baker rifle

This weapon was designed and made by Ezekiel Baker, who was not an innovator but took all the best features in the current European designs. With a seven-groove

LEFT A print produced in 1813 shows riflemen of the 60th and 95th Regiments armed with the superb Baker rifle. Their camouflaged dark-green uniforms and dedicated personal weapon marked them out as an elite within the British Army.

Napoleonic Wars 1792–1815

The wars fought by Britain and European powers against the nationalistic and ambitious French leader Napoleon Bonaparte marked a significant change in the practice of land warfare.

Although there were few innovations in weapons design, the French employed conscription to produce huge armies, and had a flexible form of command that allowed forces to concentrate on the battlefield and achieve overwhelming superiority. The British, who were leaders of the Industrial Revolution, fielded comparatively small armies but had an industrial power base that allowed them to supply arms to many of the allies facing Napoleon. The effects of combining the mass production of weapons and the mass conscription of military-age men began a devastating, grand-scale brand of warfare, which would next be demonstrated in the American Civil War and later in the two world wars.

BELOW The critical moment in the Battle of Waterloo, when Napoleon committed the Old Guard in the last hours of 18 June 1815. Massed volley fire followed by a savage bayonet attack would break their ranks and lead to the British victory.

quarter-turn 76cm/30in rifled barrel, the Baker rifle was robust, soldier-proof and relatively easy to load. The rifle was originally produced in .705, the same calibre as the "Brown Bess" infantry musket in order to standardize ammunition supplies. It was later reduced to .615in, the standard ammunition used for cavalry carbines. This made the rifle lighter and easier to handle. The final innovation was specially designed ball ammunition cartridges.

Most riflemen were permitted to practise with live ammunition. They aimed to accurately fire two shots per minute against human-sized targets at ranges of around 137–183m/150–200yd, a remarkable degree of accuracy given that the ordinary soldier fired his musket in volleys and was not accurate over 68m/75yd. The barrel of the rifle was browned to prevent sunlight reflecting and giving away the camouflaged rifleman's position. In his toolbag, each man carried a supply of cleaning patches, new flints, a worm and tommy bar to service his rifle as well as a turnscrew and ballpuller.

The Baker rifle of the Peninsular War period came with a 60cm-/24in-long sword bayonet. Although handy for camp tasks, it was rarely used in combat.

The last flintlocks

The Prussian Jäger rifle and the Mississippi rifle were examples of weapons built by countries that did not have a large industrial base. The British, by contrast, who were entering the Industrial Revolution, embarked on more systematic weapons production and design rationalization with their Short Land Pattern and India Pattern muskets.

flint   ram rod   bayonet

The Prussian Jäger rifle

The German states built their own weapons for their armed forces, and the compact 14.7mm calibre Prussian rifle was widely copied in the 18th century. The Swiss, with a long tradition of marksmanship, produced a longer-barrelled .72 Jäger rifle with two triggers. One was set for accurate shooting and required only the lightest pressure to operate.

The Mississippi rifle

In 1846–48, before the American Civil War, the United States was at war with Mexico. American forces under Zachary Taylor campaigned against substantial Mexican forces, using the Mississippi rifle. Produced around 1841, it would later see service with the Southern armies. It was distinctive as the first rifle, as opposed to musket, to be adopted by the US Army.

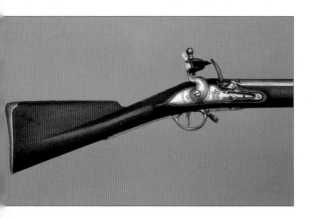

ABOVE The British Short Land Pattern musket was developed as part of a programme of rationalization for kit and clothing for the British Army in the mid-18th century.

ABOVE The India Pattern musket was a remarkable survivor. Developed in the mid-1790s, it was a good weapon that remained in service with some regiments of the British Army – particularly with the volunteer militia based on the British mainland – as late as the 1850s.

The first formation to go into action with the rifle was composed of men from Mississippi and so it became known as the Mississippi rifle. One example that came up for sale in 2006 showed that it had enjoyed a varied military career. The lock plate was marked "Tryon U.S." and rear of the lock "Philada PA 1847". The gun was in good condition with excellent plum-brown wood with two cartouches, one to indicate it had seen action in the Mexican war, the other the Civil War, as it was altered to a .58in calibre. It had its original sites, and despite some pitting, it had strong rifling.

Short land and India pattern muskets

In 1768, the Clothing Warrant was introduced to lighten the load that infantrymen had to carry. As a result a new musket called the Short Land Pattern Flintlock was issued to the British Army, which had a shorter overall length of 107cm/42in. In addition, swords were abolished for private soldiers (the exception being the Highland and Grenadier regiments) and uniforms were made less bulky.

The Short Land musket was widely used during the American Revolution and its popularity was such that a number of these black-powder muzzle loaders continued to be used by some regiments until the end of the Napoleonic Wars. Captured weapons were also added to the stocks of the American Continental Army. In addition, it was the most common rifle in the British Army until the 1790s, when it was replaced by the 3rd Model, or India Pattern.

ABOVE A group of Charleston Zouave cadets of the Confederate Army photographed in 1861, armed with the Model 1841 Mississippi rifle. The rifles had already seen service against the Mexicans before it became one of the many weapons fielded in the American Civil War.

Introduced during the mid-1790s, the India Pattern was a new pattern of flintlock musket that was slightly lighter than the Short Land, at under 4kg/9lb, and slightly shorter at 1m/39in. It had no thumb plate, and only three pipes for the ramrod. Developed and adopted by the East India Company in 1795, two years later the India Pattern was accepted by the Board of Ordnance of the British Army. The only modification to the three million or more muskets that were eventually made was the replacement in 1809 of the swan-necked cock by a more robust version. By 1839 the British had adopted a .75-calibre percussion musket, a transitional weapon built mostly from flintlock musket components. However, with so many Short Land and India Pattern muskets having been made, they were still in use by the British Army and the militia as late as 1850.

Volley firing

Throughout the 17th, 18th and 19th centuries, when smoothbore muskets were slow to load and inaccurate, short-range volley firing was an essential tactic. A trained soldier could fire a shot about every twenty seconds but could not expect to hit a human target beyond 73m/80yd. To accommodate this limitation, infantry soldiers fired in closely disciplined volleys, in which one rank would fire while the second reloaded. The firing rank might take place from the standing or kneeling position, while reloading was conducted from a standing position. A variation of this drill had a row of kneeling men with muskets and bayonets at a 45-degree angle, presenting a formidable barrier to enemy infantry or cavalry. A volley could also be fired by all the soldiers simultaneously, producing a crushing weight of fire which would then be followed up with a bayonet charge.

LEFT British soldiers, forming part of the Territorial Army, carrying Lee-Metford rifles just before World War I. In various versions, the Lee-Metford was the British Army's standard service rifle for over 60 years.

Rifles from 1800–2000

The birth of modern weapons begins with the development of the percussion cap at the start of 19th century. Initially, this did away with the problems of priming with loose powder and the unreliability of the flint striking a steel plate to produce a spark. Paper cartridges had already been developed to hold a fixed charge of gunpowder, and once a reliable breach-loading system was developed in 1812, the cartridge and percussion cap could be married up with the bullet to produce a self-contained round. This was the work of Frenchman Eugène Lefaucheux with his pinfire cartridge in 1835, and in turn led to efficient feed systems for rifles. Black powder was the next significant invention. From black powder came smokeless powder, and the battlefield was no longer enveloped in the "fog of war" – clouds of white smoke. Cartridges were loaded with this powder in magazines, fired initially from bolt-action rifles and later from rifles with self-loading mechanisms. This chapter looks at developments in rifles up to the sniper and assault rifles of the late 20th century.

LEFT The AK-74 fitted with a grenade launcher. This enhancement copied from the United States proved very popular during the Soviet intervention in Afghanistan in the latter years of the 20th century.

BELOW The Springfield M1903 would equip the US Army in World War I and many units in World War II. It was one of a range of rifles produced by the Springfield Armory for the US Army that have the generic title Springfield rifle.

An inventive century

The mid-19th century saw two major developments in small arms technology: the Pauly cartridge and the Dreyse needle gun. Just as the percussion cap had advanced weapons technology in its day, so these two inventions would take it further and point to modern small arms of the 20th century. While the British 1853 Enfield rifle did not mark any significant technological advances, it did demonstrate ruthless commercial enterprise, since the British sold it to both sides in the American Civil War.

ABOVE The percussion lock of the British 1853 pattern Enfield rifle musket was used and copied in large numbers by both the Confederate and Union Armies in the American Civil War. The musket fired a big .577 bullet.

Jean-Samuel Pauly

In 1812–16 a Swiss inventor, Jean-Samuel Pauly, experimented with the production of a breech-loading rifle. For some time, firearms designers had hoped to produce an efficient breech-loading mechanism because allowing the soldier to load from the breech end reduces exposure to enemy fire and greatly increases his own rate of fire.

Pauly's solution was to fit a brass base to the cartridge case. This meant the base could expand to seal the breech, then contract when the gas pressure in the barrel fell after firing. The Pauly system was adopted by almost every firearm from the 1850s onwards. It did suffer from some technical problems however; the quality of the seamless drawn-brass cartridge tubing was inconsistent, and the cost made it too expensive except for specialist shooters. Another of his inventions was a centrefire primer, a percussion cap set into the middle of the rear end of the cartridge.

The needle gun

In 1824 Johann Nikolaus von Dreyse, a Prussian inventor, began experiments with breech-loading firearms. Dreyse's solution to the problem was to design the first bolt-action rifle. To load it, the soldier opened the breach to insert a cartridge made of stiff paper, containing a .61-calibre bullet and powder charge. He then closed the bolt home and turned it to lock the breech. When he pulled the trigger, a firing pin about 12mm/0.5in long penetrated the paper cartridge and set off a percussion cap inside it, just below the bullet. It was this firing pin, or needle, that gave the rifle its name.

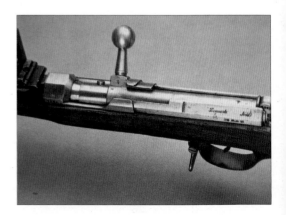

ABOVE The bolt-action, breech-loading rifle developed by the Prussian Nikolaus von Dreyse became widely known as the needle gun. It allowed soldiers to load and fire from the prone position and consequently remain undercover.

1807 percussion cap

One of the problems of flintlock weapons was that sometimes the priming powder didn't ignite because the lock wasn't able to keep it entirely dry. The solution was found in 1807 by Alexander John Forsyth who patented a priming powder made from an unstable mix of chlorate of potash, sulphur and charcoal, which exploded when it was struck. He saw it as a useful development for sportsmen who were wild fowling on wet days. It took 30 years for the technology to be recognized and adopted by the military authorities. In the meantime, it was gradually improved by gunmakers and private individuals, who developed the copper percussion cap.

Conservative Prussian soldiers disliked the new weapon despite its advantages. Unlike a muzzle loader, it did not require a complicated drill to reload. In the pressure of combat, a soldier with a muzzle loader might double load his weapon and then when he fired, it would explode in his face. The Dreyse design made this impossible since two rounds would not fit into the breach. Most significantly, the rate of fire increased from two rounds a minute for a muzzle loader to 10 to 12 rounds per minutes for the needle gun.

In time, weaknesses in the design were revealed. Gas often leaked through the bolt when the needle passed through, and the power of the explosion caused the needle to wear out rapidly or even break.

Made in Britain

In 1842 a new model percussion musket with a block or back sight set for 137m/150yd was issued to the British Army. It weighed 5.17kg/11.4lb, was 1.4m/1.5yd long without bayonet and 1.8m/1.9yd with bayonet fixed. It had a larger calibre than weapons issued to the soldiers of France, Belgium, Russia and Austria, which meant that British troops could fire continental ammunition but European soldiers could not fire British ammunition. The 1842 Pattern percussion musket was the final development of the "Brown Bess," which was used in the British Army until it was completely superseded by the Enfield rifle in 1855.

Although made in Britain, the .577-calibre 1853 Enfield rifle had the distinction of being the second most common infantry weapon of the American Civil

ABOVE The soldier armed: a New York State militiaman with his percussion lock musket, which has a fixed long-sword bayonet. The bayonet is still issued for modern combat rifles but is now used more as a multi-functional tool.

War (1861–65). Weighing 4kg/9lb and measuring 140.5cm/55.3in, it was imported by Confederate and Union ordnance officers to meet the sudden increase in demand for small arms at the outbreak of war. It is estimated that 900,000 Enfields were eventually bought by both sides. The rifle was so named because it was originally produced at the Royal Small Arms Factory in Enfield, England, where it was the standard firearm of the British Army at the time. Several contractors later provided arms for export. Its .577 calibre made it compatible with .58-calibre ammunition, which was very common in the American armies.

Mid-19th-century wars

Although the combatants in the American Civil War bought arms from Great Britain, such as the Whitworth .451, they also had stocks of their own weapons, such as the Model 1842 percussion musket and the Model 1865 Spencer carbine. However, it was the bullet designed by Frenchman Claude-Etienne Minié that would play a major part in the war. Meanwhile in France, his fellow national Antoine Alphonse Chassepot had produced the innovative Modèle 1866 breech-loading rifle.

The Model 1842 rifled musket

The Harpers Ferry and Springfield Armories produced large numbers of the robust US Model 1842 rifled Percussion musket between 1844 and 1855. The Model 1842 was the last .69 calibre musket, but in addition it was the first weapon made at both the Harpers Ferry and Springfield Armory that had entirely interchangeable parts – an invaluable feature in the field. Harpers Ferry produced 103,000, while Springfield produced 172,000. As many of the muskets had been delivered to militias in the late 1850s, they were prominent in the early years of the American Civil War. About 14,000 were upgraded between 1856 and 1859 with rifling and around 10,000 were then fitted with rear sights.

The M1855 rifle and rifle-musket produced by the Union was copied by the Confederates at their Fayetteville Armory in North Carolina. The British even produced a version for export to the Union. Designated the P1856, it had a 33-inch long barrel and only two bands to secure the barrel to the stock. The rifles came with a sword rather than a spike bayonet; however as

RIGHT Private Thomas Taylor of the 8th Louisiana Infantry holds his Model 1842 musket. Taylor is well equipped with pack, canteen, ammunition pouches and a Bowie knife tucked into his belt.

BELOW The British Whitworth short rifle enjoyed a reputation for considerable long-range accuracy and was one of the first sniper weapons to be developed fitted with a telescopic sight.

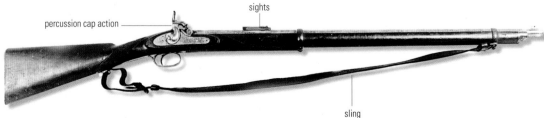

sights

percussion cap action

sling

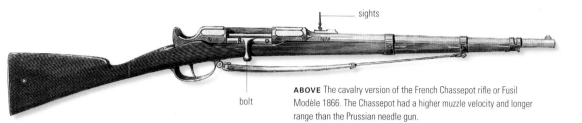

sights

bolt

ABOVE The cavalry version of the French Chassepot rifle or Fusil Modèle 1866. The Chassepot had a higher muzzle velocity and longer range than the Prussian needle gun.

the blockade on the Confederacy began to bite, the factory at Fayetteville abandoned the sword bayonet in favour of the spike – a design that harked back to the Napoleonic Wars. The angled spike would survive into the 20th century with the Russian Mosin-Nagant rifle and be revived in a slightly different form with the British Lee-Enfield No. 4 rifle. However, soldiers preferred the sword bayonet, which was a practical tool rather than a weapon, handy for prising open tins and preparing food.

The Whitworth .451 short rifle

In 1863 the British Whitworth .451in short rifle was produced and bought by the Confederate government. It was an unusual weapon with a hexagonal barrel that fired a special hexagonal bullet. This made it more accurate than many modern sniper rifles, with a maximum reported range of around 1,830m/2,000yd. The Whitworth was equipped with a British-made mounted Davidson telescopic sight.

The Model 1865 Spencer carbine

In the Union, Christopher Spencer, noted as one of the leading engineers in the machine-tool industry, produced in 1860 a seven-round carbine that was accurate over long ranges. Spencer asserted that the seven rounds in his percussion carbine models could be loaded and capped and fired in less time than any other rifle. His carbine could fire faster than a revolver and be reloaded in a tenth of the time it would take to reload a Colt revolver. In 1865, Spencer modified and corrected the design flaws in the original weapon and produced the Model 1865 Spencer carbine.

Chassepot Modèle 1866

The "Chassepot", officially known as Fusil Modèle 1866, was the breech-loading rifle with which French forces were equipped in the Franco-Prussian War of 1870–71. It took its name from its inventor, Antoine Alphonse Chassepot (1833–1905), who, from 1857 onwards, had designed and developed various

experimental forms of breech loader. The Modèle 1866 became the French service weapon in 1866. At the battlefield at Mentana, Italy on 3 November 1867, soldiers using the Chassepot inflicted severe losses upon the forces of the Italian nationalist leader, Giuseppe Garibaldi. This action fought during the Risorgimento (Italian unification) involved Garibaldi's forces, which had invaded the papal territory, facing the papal army and a French expeditionary force. Napoleon's empress Eugenie was keen on defending the papacy against the Republican threat.

In the Franco-Prussian War the Chassepot proved greatly superior to the Prussian Dreyse needle gun, although it had a smaller calibre of 11mm. The French rifle used more propellant and had a 33 per cent higher muzzle velocity; it also had a longer barrel and thus produced a longer range. The effective range was about 595m/650yd.

1849 Minié bullet

The innovative gunsmith Claude-Etienne Minié was born in 1814 in Paris. After serving as an officer in the French Army, in 1849 he developed the Minié rifle and bullet.

Inaccurately pronounced *minnie* and incorrectly called a ball, the bullet was a cylindro-conoidal (i.e., bullet-shaped) lead projectile fired from a muzzle-loading rifle. It was small enough to fit down the barrel of a rifle even when fouled with burned powder. When the rifle was fired, expanding gases entered the bullet's hollow base, pushing the outer edges into the rifling of the barrel. Since it greatly improved the accuracy, range and rate of small-arms fire, the Minié ball was rapidly adopted by the US Army. During the American Civil War, the Minié became one of the most widely used types of ammunition by the armies of the Confederacy and the Union.

Conversion rifles

The successful Snider P/53 was a converted rifle produced in Enfield from 1866. It was replaced by the 1871 Martini-Henry single-shot rifle, which was used by the British Army for 30 years and could truly be called the gun that served the empire. However, another conversion rifle – the American "trapdoor" Springfield – was a cost-cutting conversion that would prove unsatisfactory when tested in war.

The 1867 Snider rifle

It was an American, Jacob Snider, who invented the .577 weapon adopted by the British Army. The rifle that bore his name was adopted by the British Army to replace the Pattern 1853 rifled musket that had served in the Indian Mutiny and Crimea. However, to keep costs down, the muzzle-loading P/53 was altered to use the Snider system. The modified weapon was more accurate than the P/53 and soldiers could also fire it much faster. The ordnance factory in Enfield, London converted large numbers, beginning with the initial pattern, the Mark I in 1866. The conversion involved fitting a new breech block/receiver assembly but retaining the original iron barrel, furniture, locks and hammer. This rifle was replaced by the Martini-Henry rifle, which was adopted by the British Army in 1871.

The 1871 Martini-Henry

The British had taken an American idea for the Snider and in 1871 would now turn to the Swiss in the shape of Friedrich von Martini. Unlike the Snider-Enfield it replaced, the Martini-Henry rifle was Britain's first service rifle to be designed from the outset as a breech-loading rifle for metallic cartridges. Martini designed the falling block, self-cocking, lever-operated, single-shot action. It was an American, Henry Peabody, who had originally designed this action; however, his had an external hammer that struck the firing pin. Martini's refinement consisted of conversion to an internal

BELOW The 3rd Gurkhas in the 1880s skirmishing with the 1867 Snider-Enfield rifle. Elite troops from Nepal, the Gurkhas would serve with distinction in the British Army.

ABOVE A clear view of the slot through which a round was loaded into the breach in the Martini-Henry action. It allowed trained soldiers to keep up a high rate of fire, providing ammunition was readily available.

coiled spring-activated striker, which was much more soldier-friendly. The barrel used the rifling system designed by Alexander Henry.

It was the Martini-Henry that would save the day at Rorke's Drift on 22 January 1879, when 137 men, largely from the British 24th Regiment, held off about 4,000 Zulu warriors who had just scored a crushing victory over the British at Isandhlwana. The tiny garrison lost 25 men but won 11 Victoria Crosses.

The Springfield Model 1873

At the close of the American Civil War, the US recognized the need to obtain a reliable breech-loading rifle. Funds were tight, however, and the army had huge numbers of muzzle-loading weapons left from the war that it did not want to waste. The "trapdoor" rifle, denoting the method of opening the rifle at the top of the breech to load a cartridge, was developed as a result, and about 30,000 of the left-over rifles were converted to trapdoor models or, as they were more formally known, Allin Conversions.

Smokeless propellants

Poudre B or *poudre blanche* (white powder, to distinguish it from black powder), was the first smokeless propellant, developed around 1885 by Paul Vieille. Made up from nitrocotton and ether-alcohol, unlike black powder it did not produce clouds of white smoke when it was detonated. Subsequently, the prolific Swedish inventor Alfred Nobel added to the growing list of smokeless powders a substance called ballistite.

Ballistite contained two powerful explosives: a low-nitrogen content nitrocotton, gelatinized by nitro-glycerine. Meanwhile in Britain, Sir Frederick Abel and Sir James Dewar used acetone to produce probably the most effective and widely used smokeless powder propellant – cordite made from highly nitrated guncotton and nitro-glycerine. Mineral jelly was added to act as a lubricant. Now when rifles were fired the battlefield would no longer be enveloped in "the fog of war".

By 1868, instead of converting old weapons into trapdoor models, a new rifle was developed using the Allin action. This weapon was designated the Rifle Model 1868. It went through a series of minor modifications (1870, 1873, 1879, 1880, 1884 and 1889, as well as a few more specialized cadet and officer varieties), and was used for 30 years. The modification that represented the major difference between the M1873 and the M1889 was the replacement of the triangular bayonet with a rod bayonet; there were also a few other very minor modifications.

At the outbreak of the Spanish–American War, the current model was the Model 1889, which was used by the volunteer troops, despite being outdated in comparison with the widely available smokeless powder weapons.

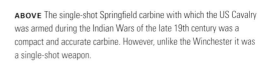

ABOVE The single-shot Springfield carbine with which the US Cavalry was armed during the Indian Wars of the late 19th century was a compact and accurate carbine. However, unlike the Winchester it was a single-shot weapon.

Historic guns

The American Winchester 1873 was not the first gun bearing the Winchester name, but its popularity earned it the nickname of "The Gun That Won the West". The British Lee-Metford had only a short operational life with the British Army, while the Italian Carcano 91/94 had a long and ultimately notorious history, due to its most famous owner. On 22 November 1963, Lee Harvey Oswald used a Mannlicher-Carcano serial number C2766 with an Ordnance Optics 4x18 scope to kill the US President John F. Kennedy in Dallas, Texas.

bolt action

cleaning ro

box magazine

ABOVE The Mannlicher-Carcano Modello 91 was the standard bolt-action rifle used by the Italian Army in World War I. Like the SMLE with the British, it would carry on with the Italian infantry into World War II.

The Winchester

The first real Winchester was the Model 1866. The major change was the incorporation of a totally round magazine tube. Winchester's plant foreman, Nelson King, designed it to replace the slotted-tube design. There was a marked improvement in the reliability of the rifle since there was no ingress of dirt into the working parts. Frames were initially made of brass and then replaced by iron; this version had the model number 1867. Eventually steel was adopted in 1884. The Winchester was popular because the .44-centrefire

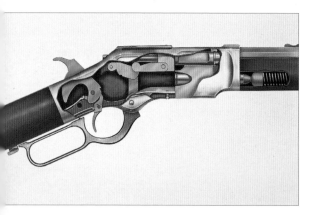

ABOVE The spring-loaded tube magazine on the Winchester Model 1866 fed rounds backwards when the lever was operated and as it was closed loaded them into the breach. It was a quick, reliable mechanism.

ammunition was compatible with some handguns, and a man could carry a Winchester and a revolver and use the same rounds of ammunition for both weapons.

The Lee-Metford

Introduced in 1888, the Lee-Metford rifle, also known as the Magazine Lee-Metford or MLM by British soldiers, was a breech-loading service rifle. It combined James Paris Lee's rear-locking bolt system and ten-round magazine with a seven-groove rifled barrel designed by William Ellis Metford. Although nine years of development followed before it replaced the Martini-Henry rifle, it remained in service for only a short time until replaced by the similar Lee-Enfield.

At a time when most military rifles used smokeless powders, the Lee-Metford used a black powder-loaded rimmed .303in cartridge. It had been intended to fire a smokeless cartridge, but this was not available to the War Department when it entered service. The MLM design went through several variations; the main changes were to the magazine (from eight-round single stack to ten-round staggered), sights and safety catch. In 1914 some Territorial Army battalions were still equipped with the MLM.

Mannlicher-Carcano rifles

The Italian Carcano 6.5mm Fucile Modello rifle went through many modifications in the 1890s. The 1892 rifle was the first of the Mannlicher-Carcano rifles to

ABOVE Soldiers of the Civil Service Rifles, a British Territorial Army formation, armed with Lee-Metford rifles. The bolt action developed by James Lee would be incorporated into the Lee-Enfield rifle that was in service with the Regular Army.

be accepted by the Italian Army. The Mannlicher-Carcano system was based on the bolt action of the Mauser Model 1889 with the addition of the Carcano bolt-sleeve mechanism; the Mannlicher six-round clip-loading magazine was retained. The name of General Parravicino is often linked with this rifle; he headed the commission that introduced the rifle to the Italian Army. The Modello 91 was the standard Italian Army rifle during World War I and was still in use in 1940 in large numbers. The Germans took some over in 1943 to arm several of their units in Italy, and these were designated the Gew 214(i). During 1944 some were rebored for the German calibre of 7.92mm/0.31in.

In World War I, Italian soldiers fought Austro-Hungarian forces armed with the Mannlicher Model 1895. Made in Budapest in Hungary as well as Steyr in Austria, the Mannlicher M1895, also known as the Repetier Gewehr M95, was the principal Austro-Hungarian rifle. After World War I, the Italians received large numbers of Mannlichers as reparations from Austria and used them in large numbers. In World War II it was also used by the Bulgarians, Yugoslavs and to some extent by the Greeks.

A Winchester by any other name

In 1848 American small arms designer Walter Hunt developed the concept of the first repeating rifle, giving it the grand name of "Rocket Ball and Volition Repeater." A lever-action, tube-loading repeater, it eventually evolved into the Winchester Model 1873. A US patent was granted in 1849 for an improved design by a machinist named Lewis Jennings and Hunt's partner George Arrowsmith.

A large number of people were involved in improving on the original design, among them Benjamin Tyler Henry and Courtland Palmer. Henry later teamed up with two men whose names would become legendary – Horace Smith and Daniel Wesson of handgun fame – and together they further refined the design. The Volcanic Arms Company was formed in 1855 by Smith, Wesson and Henry to market the rifle. Among their investors was Oliver F. Winchester. He had no knowledge of firearms and was more of an expert on sewing machines. Yet he was a shrewd investor; two years after buying stock he owned the majority holding in Volcanic Arms. So in 1866 the name was officially changed to Winchester Repeating Arms Company and thus Winchester gave his name to "The Gun that Won The West".

World War rifles

The excellent bolt-action rifles produced at the close of the 19th and beginning of the 20th century, such as the German Gewehr 98, British SMLE and American M1903, were used in World War I and, with some modifications, remained in service during World War II.

sights

sling swivel

inline magazine

ABOVE The German Gewehr 98 had an excellent bolt action, but its five-round magazine put a soldier at a disadvantage when he was up against a man armed with the SMLE and its ten-round box magazine.

The Gewehr 1898 and Kar 98k

The 7.92mm Gewehr 98, introduced into service with the Imperial German Army on 5 April 1898, was designed by Paul Mauser and became the standard German infantry weapon in World War I. While the Mauser action is superb (there are about 102 million rifles with the Model 98 bolt action worldwide), the rifle suffered from having a five-round magazine.

Massacre at Mons

In the hands of a trained soldier, the British Short, Magazine-Loaded Lee-Enfield was easily capable of 15 rpm of accurate fire. In the 1930s, a Small Arms School Corps Warrant Officer managed a rate of 37 rpm. This fast rate of fire proved significant in World War I.

Britain declared war on 4 August 1914 and when, by mid-August, the Belgians had been mauled by the German Army, only one intact force stood in the way of the Germans: the British Expeditionary Force (BEF). The first shots fired on 23 August by the BEF were at Malplaquet. The advancing German infantrymen were pulled up short near Mons as the withering rifle fire of the British caused them heavy casualties.

Two days later at Le Cateau the story of Mons was repeated, only on a bloodier scale. Once again the Germans attacked in tightly bunched waves and again they were met with rifle fire so intense that they thought the British were equipped with machine guns.

In 1939 German infantry entered World War II armed with the bolt-action Karabiner 98 kurz (Kar 98k), or Short '98 Carbine, developed from the Gewehr 98. The Kar 98k, first produced in 1935, weighed 3.9kg/8.6lb, was 1.11m/1.21yd long, and in its ten-year production life it was manufactured in its thousands in Germany, by FN in Belgium and Brno in Czechoslovakia.

A trained soldier could fire 15 rounds per minute (rpm) from a Kar 98k. Like all the 7.92mm calibre rifles, the maximum effective range of the Kar 98k was 800m/874yd.

The SMLE

In 1939 the British Army had a rifle with the official designation Short, Magazine-Loaded Lee-Enfield; this cumbersome name was more commonly shortened to SMLE. This weapon had been the standard infantry rifle in World War I and would remain so for much of World War II. A bolt-action weapon that fired a .303-calibre round, the SMLE weighed 3.9kg/8.6lb, was 1.13m/1.23yd long and had a ten-round magazine. Sights were set out to 1,830m/2,000yd.

The sword bayonet fitted to the SMLE had a formidable 43cm/17in blade. In the Sinai and Palestine campaign in World War I, the SMLE bayonet was in fact wielded like a cavalry sabre by the mounted infantrymen of the Australian 4th Light Horse in the Battle of Beersheba on 31 October 1917. In what is often called the last successful cavalry charge, the fast-moving horsemen cleared the Turkish defences in front of the town by stabbing and slashing. At the close of the fighting, the 4th Light Horse Brigade had taken Beersheba and captured 738 Turkish soldiers as well as

ABOVE British infantry in World War I in a secure area behind the front line clean their SMLEs. The rifle was easy to strip, and the mechanism could be operated to clear any dirt that might have fouled it in combat.

four field guns. In the two Australian regiments, only 31 men had been killed and 36 wounded as a result of this unique action.

The M1903

After the Spanish-American War of 1898, Erskine Allin, the Superintendent of the Springfield Arsenal, developed the M1903. It was a magazine-fed rifle that used a modified version of the Mauser Gewehr action and was 1.12m/1.23yd long and weighed 3.6kg/8lb. The M1903 was used by the American Expeditionary Force in France in World War I and continued as the issue US Army rifle until 1936. It was also used in World War II, however, owing to production problems with the M1A1, its intended replacement. It was utilised by snipers as the M1903A4, although because the scope was positioned directly over the action, reloading the magazine with five-round stripper clips was impossible, so rounds had to be loaded singly. The M1903A4 remained in service in World War II and the Korean War.

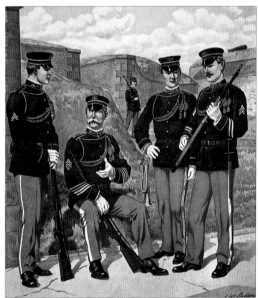

ABOVE US Infantry in dress blues, the full dress uniform worn in the early 20th century in a garrison base. The men are armed with the modern M1903 rifle, which was introduced following grim combat experience in the Spanish–American War.

Rifles far and wide

At the turn of the twentieth century some international rifle designs were conventional while others were innovative. The Mexican Mondragon was remarkably advanced, as was the philosophy proposed for its tactical employment. In Japan and Russia, two countries that had fought for dominance in the East, two reliable but conventional weapons, the Arisaka and the Mosin-Nagant, were produced for the infantry.

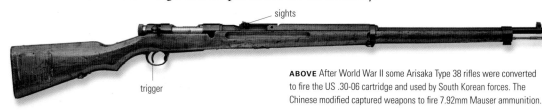

sights

trigger

ABOVE After World War II some Arisaka Type 38 rifles were converted to fire the US .30-06 cartridge and used by South Korean forces. The Chinese modified captured weapons to fire 7.92mm Mauser ammunition.

Japanese small arms

The 1905 Japanese 6.5mm Arisaka Rifle Type 38 was a development of the earlier Type 30 rifle designed by Colonel Arisaka and was often referred to by the Japanese as the Arisaka Sampachi (or Sampachi Shiki Hoheiju). It was fundamentally a Mauser rifle based on the Gew 98 but with changes to the safety and

cocking mechanisms. The combination of the light cartridge and the long barrel made the Type 38 a very easy rifle to fire because of its low recoil. At 127.5cm/50.2in long, however, it was a difficult rifle for some of the smaller Japanese soldiers to handle, particularly when fitted with its Type 30 sword

---

Marksmanship in battle

An American hero of World War I, Corporal (later Sergeant) Alvin Cullum York of the 328th Infantry was awarded the Medal of Honor for leading an attack on a German machine-gun nest during the battle of the Meuse-Argonne on 8 October 1918. Armed with the Springfield M1903 bolt-action rifle, he and his section killed 32 German soldiers and captured 132 others as well as 35 German machine guns, and took control of the fortified position.

As a corporal in the 328th Infantry 82nd Division, York had assumed command of his detachment after three NCOs had been killed. A semi-literate backwoodsman from the Tennessee mountains, he was a lay deacon in a Christian pacifist sect. However, he was persuaded that active service was sanctioned

by the Bible. While he is sometimes described as acting single-handedly, his official citation says he led seven others in a charge against the machine-gun position.

York's exploit is a clear demonstration that good weapons training and accurate shooting – whatever the weapon – can be devastating in battle. The South African Boers, who were natural marksmen, taught this lesson to the British in the Boer War of 1899–1902. Experienced hunters, they had bought excellent Mausers from Germany and had honed their marksmanship against wildlife targets. The British in turn learnt the lesson and taught it to the Germans in World War I. The accurate fire from their SMLEs did much to slow the German advance.

ABOVE The Springfield M1903 equipped the US Army in World War I and many units in World War II. A number of rifles produced by the Springfield Armory shared the generic title Springfield rifle.

bayonet. The Type 38 was exported to Thailand and also used by the Chinese. It had a five-round magazine and weighed 4.2kg/9.3lb. The Type 38 carbine was only 86.9cm/34.2in long, and some were produced with a butt that folded to the right for paratroopers.

Mexican invention

In the early 1890s the Mexican inventor, engineer and army officer Manuel Mondragon, a graduate of both the Mexican Military Academy at Chapultepec and the French Academy at Saint-Cyr received a request to design an advanced infantry rifle from President Porfirio Diaz.

By the close of 1891, the initial design had been completed and a year later, on 18 October, the first prototypes went for evaluation. The 25th Infantry Battalion received 50 improved versions for troop trials on 27 September 1894. This Model 1894 had a safety catch with three settings: "A" for automatic, "L" for safe and "R" for use in the manual straight-pull bolt-action mode. The rifles were intended to be fired as single-shot weapons but could be switched to automatic in the assault.

ABOVE A German soldier looks down the x 4 P.E. side-mounted telescopic sight on a captured Russian 7.62mm calibre Mosin-Nagant Model 1891/30 rifle during the first days of Operation Barbarossa, the Nazi invasion of the Soviet Union of 1941.

The rifles had a fixed eight-round magazine using an enbloc Garand-type clip of special 6.5 x 52mm/ 0.26 x 2in Mondragon cartridges made by SFM in Paris. They were made in Switzerland owing to the lack of indigenous production facilities. However, although the design was advanced, it was also overly complex, not entirely "soldier-proof" and ultimately the weapon was too costly to be issued to the entire Mexican Army.

Old and reliable

The Russian Mosin-Nagant Model 1891/30 bolt-action rifle weighed 4kg/8.8lb empty, had a muzzle velocity of 81m/s (metres per second)/2,661ft/s (feet per second) and, although an old design, was robust and reliable. Until 1930 the iron sights on the rifle were graduated in the archaic linear measurement of *arshins* (0.71m/2.3ft), but the Soviet government redesigned the rear sight in metres.

Self-loading rifles

As the prospect of World War II loomed in Europe, designers looked at systems for self-loading or semi-automatic rifles. The most famous and successful was, and remains, the US M1 Garand. However, the Soviet Tokarev 38 and 40 were imaginative designs that impressed the Germans. The French bolt-action MAS 36 would prove a rugged and reliable weapon in some of the toughest campaigns.

The Garand

The US Rifle, Caliber .30, M1 (known as the M1 Garand), designed by John Garand of the Springfield Arsenal in the late 1920s, was adopted by the US Army in 1936. It was a robust, semi-automatic, gas-operated rifle that weighed 4.3kg/9.5lb, was 110cm/43.5in long and had an eight-round box magazine. The effective

rate of fire was 16–24 rpm. Sights were set out to 1,100m/1,200yd, but the effective range was 420m/460yd. Although it had the minor tactical drawback that the clip was ejected with a loud "ping" that indicated when the last round had been fired, General George S. Patton described the M1 Garand as "the best battle implement ever devised" and "the most deadly rifle in the world". Over 5,400,000 M1 Garands were manufactured by the Springfield Armory as well as three private contractors, until production stopped in 1957. The Garand was the US infantryman's weapon throughout World War II, the Korean War and in the early years of the Vietnam War.

The MAS Mle 1936

In World War II the French Army had a rugged bolt-action rifle that fired a 7.5mm round from a five-round magazine built at Manufacture d'Armes de St Etienne (MAS). It was introduced in 1936 and so was designated the Fusil MAS 36. It soldiered on in Vietnam in the 1950s and was still being used during the war in Algeria in the 1960s. It weighed 3.7kg/8.2lb and was 102cm/40in long. A version with a metal folding butt was produced for airborne forces and saw action with French paratroops at the ill-fated battle of Dien Bien Phu in 1954.

The Tokarev SVT 38 and SVT40

It took 20 years of research before the SVT38 (Samozaryadnaya Vintovka Tokarevao 1938g – Tokarev's self-loading rifle) was adopted by the Soviet Army in 1938. The Russian arms designer Fedor Tokarev had developed the 6.5mm Avtomat in 1916, and in 1936 S. G. Simonov had produced the select-fire

LEFT Armed with an M1 Garand rifle, a GI looks at the body of a Waffen-SS soldier killed during the break out from Saint-Lô in July 1944, following the Normandy invasion.

ABOVE French and Vietnamese paratroopers in dense jungle north of Dien Bien Phu in February 1954. They are armed with the MAS Mle 1936 folding butt bolt-action rifle that was developed for airborne and Alpine troops. Late models of the rifle have an extended barrel with concentric rings to permit the launching of rifle grenades.

John C. Garand

Born on 1 January 1888 on a small farm in Quebec, Canada, John Cantius Garand was working as a floor sweeper at a Connecticut textile mill by the time he was 11, where he was fascinated with the machinery he saw around him. In his spare time, he learnt from the mechanics and by 18 he had taught himself enough to work as a machinist.

Garand had an inventive mind and by November 1919 was working at the Springfield Armory in Massachusetts, where he would eventually become the Chief Civilian Engineer. Garand invented a self-loading .30-calibre rifle, known as the M1 or "the Garand", which was adopted in 1936 after gruelling tests by the US Army. During the time that he took to develop the M1 and other small arms innovations, Garand received no more than his government salary. Some people felt he deserved compensation, yet when a bill was introduced in Congress to grant him $100,000, it did not pass. He received official recognition in the form of a Medal for Meritorious Service in 1941 and in 1944 the Government Medal for Merit. He retired in 1953 and died on 16 February 1974.

AVS-36. However, the Avtomat used Japanese ammunition, so it was declared obsolete, while the AVS-36 had defects, including dirt ingress and excessive muzzle blast that necessitated fitting a compensator/muzzle brake. Therefore, the SVT38 was adopted. The SVT38 was issued to the Soviet Army, but experience in the Winter War with Finland in 1939–40 led to modifications. In 1940 the updated and re-adapted new rifle went into service as the SVT40.

Like the SVT38, the SVT40 or 7.62mm Samozaryadnaya Vintovka Tokarevao 1940g had a ten-round box magazine. It weighed 3.9kg/8.5lb. Nearly two million SVT40s were manufactured. When German soldiers captured them, they were quick to put them back into use against their former owners, redesignating them A1Gew259(r). The drawback with the SVT40 was that it had heavy recoil. Other versions of the rifle were the SNT sniper's rifle and the fully automatic AKT40. Although it was an innovative design, it demanded too many man-hours from skilled machinists and was phased out in 1943–4.

cocking handle   cooling slots

magazine release catch

ABOVE Tested in the Winter War with Finland in 1939–40, the Russian SVT38 rifle proved too fragile for front-line service. Limited numbers were captured by the Germans in 1941 and used by second-line and auxiliary troops on the Eastern Front.

The pressure of war

War pressures produced some very successful designs, such as the American M1 carbine; some very innovative designs, such as the German FG42; and some rugged, conventional but battle-worthy weapons, such as the British bolt-action No. 4 rifle. The German Gewehr 41, by contrast, was unreliable and too heavy to be popular.

The M1 Carbine

The American-designed M1 carbine was used in World War II by US forces, by the British in Malaya during the Emergency (1948–60) and by the French in Indo-China in the 1950s. It was described by one veteran as "one of the most appealing of weapons, light, handy, easy to shoot and totally useless over 200 yards [183m] since it fired a pistol bullet". The US Carbine Cal .30 M1 was produced with a folding stock for airborne forces as the M1A1; it weighed 2.7kg/6lb with a loaded magazine and folded down to a compact 630mm/25in. The wooden-stock M1 weighed a little less at 2.5kg/5.5lb, but it folded down to only 890mm/35in. Both weapons had a cyclic rate of 750 rpm and fired from a 15- or 30-round box magazine. A popular practice was to attach a two-magazine webbing pouch to the wooden stock, which gave the soldier two ready-to-use magazines with his weapon.

sights

flash eliminator

folding bipod

ABOVE The German FG-42 developed for parachute troops was an innovative weapon, but was too light to fire successfully in full automatic mode and too costly to produce.

The Gewehr 41

At the start of World War II, German Army commanders knew that they needed a self-loading semi-automatic rifle to replace the bolt-operated Karabiner 98k. A specification was issued for the weapon in 1940, which resulted in the Mauser Gewehr 41(W). But it was not a success in the field. The main problem was the complex gas-blowback system, which proved unreliable in the dust and dirt of the front line, primarily on the Eastern Front. It was also very heavy, weighing around 5kg/11lb, and the manufacturing costs were unacceptably high.

The paratrooper's rifle

The FG-42 (Fallschirmjägergewehr-42), also known as the Paratrooper's rifle, Model 1942, was designed for German airborne soldiers. Powerful yet light, the FG-42 was air cooled and gas operated, and sturdy – despite the widespread use of stamping and the minimum use of metal to reduce weight. It also had a unique spike bayonet, fitted as an optional extra. The ammunition feed was from a side-mounted 20-round box magazine, which could be loaded separately or from standard five-round Mauser clips with the action open.

No more than 2,000 examples of the original weapon, also known as the FG-42 1st model or FG-42-1, were delivered. This was because the lightweight rifle didn't

ABOVE A US Army squad leader briefs his patrol in Normandy. Most of the men are armed with the M1 Carbine, which was a handy weapon although it fired a short range .30 (7.62mm) pistol bullet and was useless at long range.

ABOVE Allied soldiers in street fighting in north-western Europe. The man in the foreground is armed with a .303in No. 4 rifle while the lance corporal has equipped himself with a captured German MP40 SMG.

Intermediate 7.92mm ammunition

During World War II, German after-action analysis in 1939–40 established that most firefights took place at comparatively short ranges, around 400m/437yd – not the 800–875m/1,005–1,100yd for which weapons such as the Kar 98K rifle had been designed.

Therefore, the ammunition firm Polte developed the 7.92mm K or short round for this type of combat. With a muzzle velocity of 650m/s/2,133ft/s, it was almost twice as powerful as 9mm submachine-gun ammunition. With a round that was more compact and ideal for automatic weapons, the ground had been prepared for the development of the assault rifle.

particularly when compared to the StG44 assault rifle. By the end of the war in 1945, some 5,000 FG-42-2 models had been built. The mechanism of the FG-42 reappeared as the basis of another flawed weapon: the US M60 machine gun.

The Lee-Enfield No.4

A new bolt-action rifle, the Lee-Enfield No. 4 replaced the SMLE during World War II, was less expensive to manufacture and had improved tangent sights. The No. 4, which would arm British and Canadian infantry at D-Day and through numerous post-war campaigns including Korea, the Malayan Emergency and Suez, was replaced only in the 1960s, by the 7.62mm SLR. At 3.9ft/1.2m long, the No. 5 or Jungle Carbine was shorter than the No. 4 at 1.4m/1.5yd and lighter at 3kg/6.6lb compared to 4kg/8.8lb. It looked a handsome weapon but suffered from a wandering zero, pronounced kick and a muzzle flash, which made a flash eliminator necessary. As the 7.62mm L42A1 sniper's rifle, the modified No. 4 was used by the British Army until the early 1980s. All weapons had a ten-shot detachable box magazine.

have enough strength to handle powerful rifle ammunition in full automatic mode. In addition, the manufacturing cost was too high.

A redesigned weapon, the FG-42-2, was introduced in early 1944. It was heavier and longer but even so it was still too light to be fired accurately on full automatic – even from the prone position using the bipod. Just as importantly, it was too expensive,

The first assault rifles

In the latter years of World War II, the German small arms industry came up with the assault rifle, which fired an intermediate round – smaller than a rifle round but bigger than a pistol. This was a weapon that would change the whole philosophy of rifle design. Meanwhile, at the end of the war, the AK-47, which would become the weapon of the late 20th century, was designed by Mikhail Kalashnikov.

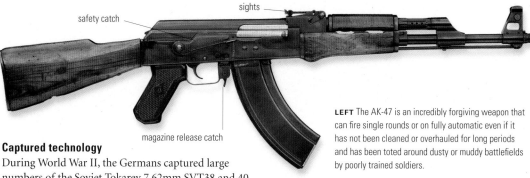

safety catch

sights

magazine release catch

LEFT The AK-47 is an incredibly forgiving weapon that can fire single rounds or on fully automatic even if it has not been cleaned or overhauled for long periods and has been toted around dusty or muddy battlefields by poorly trained soldiers.

Captured technology

During World War II, the Germans captured large numbers of the Soviet Tokarev 7.62mm SVT38 and 40 semi-automatic rifles. The simpler gas-operated bolt system was adapted to the Gewehr 41 and the resulting weapon, the Gew 43, was an immediate success. It weighed 4.4kg/9.6lb and at 1,120mm/44in was slightly shorter than the Gew 41. It was easier to produce and incorporated features such as laminated wood furniture, simple forgings and a minimum of machined parts. The detachable magazine made loading, with two five-round clips, much easier. A bracket for the Zf41 telescopic sight was a standard fitting.

The SturmGewehr-44

In the light of combat experience on the Eastern Front in World War II, the German Army issued a specification to the small arms designers Haenel and Walther for a new machine-carbine. The two resulting gas-operated designs were remarkably similar, using the same straight-line butt and barrel arrangement, pistol grip and curved 30-round box magazine. The Haenel-designed weapon was known as the Maschinkarabiner 42 (H) or MKb42(H) and the Walther as the MKb42(W). Both were designed to be manufactured quickly and cheaply using plastic and stamped and die-cast metal components.

The MKb42(H), which had been designed by the prolific Louis Schmeisser, was 94cm/37in long, weighed 4.9kg/10.8lb and had a cyclic rate of fire of

500 rpm. About 8,000 were produced for troop trials on the Eastern Front, where they were very successful, and this was the weapon selected by the army.

Despite the success of the MKb42(H), Hitler decided that further development of assault rifles should be halted. Fortunately for the soldiers in the field, the German Army and Haenel changed the designation of the improved MKb42(H) to MP43 and so for documentation purposes made the weapon a *Maschinenpistole*, or submachine gun. In this guise it went into mass production. Further modifications to the weapon, including the facility to launch rifle grenades, produced a weapon that weighed 5.2kg/11.5lb and had a cyclic rate of 500 rpm.

When Hitler finally approved the MP43, he gave it a new name, the SturmGewehr-44 (StG-44) or "Assault Rifle". It was a name that would later be used for all post-war infantry automatic weapons designed to fire the compact intermediate cartridge. The total number of German assault rifles of all designs produced was about 500,000.

The Kalashnikov AK-47

The AK-47, in all its numerous versions, is probably the most widely used weapon in the world. The original assault rifle, designed by Mikhail Kalashnikov at the end of World War II, entered service with the

Mikhail Timofeyevich Kalashnikov

In 1938 Mikhail Kalashnikov, a self-taught inventor, joined the Soviet Army in Kiev and went to a tank mechanics school. There, among other useful tactical devices for armoured vehicles, he designed a device to count the shots fired by a tank.

Serving as a tank commander, Kalashnikov survived the fierce battles following the German invasion in 1941. Suffering from serious wounds and battle fatigue, he was sent to the rear to recover in hospital. He began to work on the idea of a new lightweight machine gun that could provide a high volume of fire for soldiers in mechanized infantry. While convalescing at Matai he had access to the workshop facilities and began work on the prototype of his weapon. In 1944 his first prototype was accepted for further development, and finally in 1949 the Soviet Army adopted the Automatic Kalashnikov design of 1947 or AK47. As of 1990, more than 70 million Kalashnikovs had been produced.

Soviet Army in 1951. It was 1.07m/42in long with a wooden butt. The folding metal-butt version was 870mm/34.2in long open and 635mm/25in closed. It fired a 7.62 x 39mm round weighing 122 grains and had a muzzle velocity of 717m/s/2,352ft/s at a cyclic rate of 600 rpm. The AKM, a modernized version of the AK-47, was lighter and weighed 2.9kg/6.4lb empty or 3.6kg/8lb with a fully loaded 30-round steel magazine. The effective range of both the AK-47 and AKM was 400m/437yd.

The AK family of assault rifles were well designed, easy to use even by unskilled men and had very few working parts. AK weapons were produced throughout the Warsaw Pact countries and in China and North Korea.

ABOVE A German soldier armed with a StG-44 assault rifle plods through mud churned up by tanks on the Eastern Front in the spring of 1945. The StG-44 was a remarkable and very advanced weapon.

cocking handle

compensator

pistol grip

LEFT The AKM was essentially an improved lighter version of the AK-47, with the addition of a compensator that reduced muzzle climb when the weapon was fired in full automatic mode.

Post-war assault rifles

In the 1950s new rifles were developed in the United States, Soviet Union and Europe. The American M14 had a short operational life, as did the Soviet SKS. The French MAS-49 soldiered on for many years, but the Belgian FN FAL was a real winner, widely built and used.

The MAS-49

The 7.5mm MAS-49 rifle, developed by the French state arms factory Manufacture Nationale d'Armes de St Etienne (MAS), was based on the direct gas-impingement system developed by the French designer Rossignol early in the 20th century. MAS-1949 (as it was stamped on the receiver) saw heavy combat in French Indo-China and Algeria, where it proved accurate and reliable.

The MAS-1949/56, an improved pattern rifle, was adopted by the Armée de Terre (French Army) in 1956. The MAS-49/56 retained the ten-round magazine but was lighter, had a shorter barrel and forend. It also had different grenade launcher sights and, unlike the MAS-49, the weapon could be fitted with a spike-shaped bayonet. The MAS-49/56 was not replaced in front-line service until 1979, when the French Army adopted the futuristic-looking 5.56mm FAMAS assault rifle.

The SLR

The British 7.62mm L1A1 self-loading rifle (SLR) was based on the Belgian Fabrique Nationale (FN) FAL. It entered service with the British Army in the mid-1960s and remained in use until 1985. Early weapons had wooden furniture, but this was later replaced with black plastic. It was a single-shot gas-operated weapon that had an effective range of 303m/328yd with iron sights. The flow of gas back on to the working parts could be adjusted, so if there was a malfunction, a simple drill was to close down the gas port at the front of the rifle. The cocking handle on the left side allowed the right hand to remain on the trigger.

The Samozaryadnyj Karabin Simonova

The 7.62mm SKS Samozaryadnyj Karabin Simonova, or Simonov Self-loading Carbine, designed by the famous Russian arms designer Simonov in 1949, was a

FN Fusil Automatique Léger

Developed by the Belgian Fabrique Nationale company, the FN FAL (Fusil Automatique Léger – light automatic rifle) is one of the most widely known rifle designs of the 20th century. Its popularity is reflected in the fact that more than 70 countries have used it and at least ten countries made it themselves.

Canada was the first country to adopt the FAL in 1955 with a slightly modified version designated the C1. The C1 and heavy-barrelled C2 squad automatic rifles were made at the Canadian Arsenal. Belgium followed in 1956, Britain a year later with the British-built L1A1 SLR (self-loading rifle), which was often issued with a x4 SUIT Trilux optical sight. When Austria adopted the rifle in 1958, it was designated Stg.58 and built at the Steyr arms factory. The FAL was adopted in various types by Argentina, Brazil, Turkey, Australia, Israel, Rhodesia (modern-day Zimbabwe) and South Africa.

RIGHT The FN FAL has the distinction of being adopted by more than ninety countries and has been used in action in almost every continent in the world. Models are available in automatic and semi-automatic fire form.

gas-operated, magazine-fed, self-loading weapon. It utilized a short-stroke gas piston with its own return spring, and a tilting bolt locking, where a bolt tips down to lock on to the floor of the receiver. The cocking handle was attached to the right side of the bolt carrier and moved when the gun was fired. The receiver was machined from steel. The SKS was fed from the integral ten-round magazine, which could be loaded from the top through the open bolt by loose cartridges or by using special ten-round clips. Adopted by the Soviet Army as the 7.62mm Samozaryadnyj Karabin Simonova obr. 1945 goda – SKS, it entered service alongside the Kalashnikov AK-47.

The M14

The M14 rifle, or United States Rifle, Caliber 7.62mm, M14, is a selective-fire 7.62mm rifle that has now been largely superseded in military use by the M16. After trials against other rifles, including the FN FAL, the US Army adopted the M14 in 1957. A production line was set up at the Springfield Armory in 1958, and the first

ABOVE A Royal Marine takes aim with his SLR during arctic warfare training in Norway in the 1970s. This rifle has black plastic furniture but has not been upgraded by being fitted with a SUIT optical sight.

rifles were delivered in 1959. However, owing to long production delays, the 101st Airborne Division was the only army unit fully equipped with the M14 by the end of 1961.

In Vietnam, although its length and weight made it unwieldy in the jungle, the powerful 7.62mm NATO round penetrated cover quite well and had a good range. The weapon also proved to be very reliable and continued to function even under adverse conditions. However, there were several drawbacks to the M14. Soldiers soon realized that in the heavy humidity of the tropics in Vietnam, the wooden stock swelled and expanded, which affected the zeroing on the sights. Fibreglass stocks were developed to compensate for this defect, but by then the M14 had been withdrawn from service. The M14 was replaced by the M16 in Vietnam in 1966–8.

sights

box magazine

sling swivel

ABOVE The M14 represented a logical development of the M1 Garand, although it fired the NATO standardized 7.62mm round. The M14 saw action in Vietnam before it was replaced by the M16.

Outstanding models

The German G3 rifle is one of the small arms success stories of post-war Europe. An excellent and reliable design, the weapon has been widely exported and manufactured under licence. The American M16 has enjoyed even greater success, and this rifle and its derivatives are in use across most of the world. The Russian SVD's claim to fame is that it is the only semi-automatic sniper's rifle with bayonet fittings.

tunnel sights · drum sights · change lever

RIGHT The 7.62mm German Heckler & Koch G3 selective fire rifle has been adopted throughout the world. It is a rugged and reliable weapon that has been made under licence in five countries.

The Heckler & Koch G3

At the close of World War II, engineers at the German Mauser-Werke small arms factory were working on a revolutionary design for a selective-fire, magazine-fed rifle. After the war, the design was refined by CETME in Spain, and in 1959 the Bundeswehr (West German

ABOVE Gurkha soldiers board a truck in Borneo in the 1960s. They are armed with the Colt Armalite rifle – at the time it was a unique weapon in the unusual calibre of 5.56mm – it would later become the M16.

Army) adopted the rifle as the Gewehr 3 or Rifle model 3, better known simply as the G3. In 1959 Germany bought the manufacturing licence for the rifle and transferred it to Heckler & Koch at Oberndorf. The first G3s, although modified, were quite similar to the CETME rifles and until 1961 had CETME stamped on the receiver.

The G3 is cheaper to produce than the FAL or M14 since it uses as many stamped parts as possible. To speed production and reduce costs, the rifle uses sheet steel stampings for the receiver, trigger unit and pistol-grip frame. The pistol grip is hinged to the receiver with a cross-pin behind the magazine housing and in front of the trigger unit. The weapons have distinctive drum-type rear diopter sights, marked from 100–400m/109–438yd.

Since its adoption by the Bundeswehr, the G3 in various modifications has gone global. Foreign users include Greece, Iran, Mexico, Norway, Pakistan, Portugal, Sweden and Turkey. In the past forty years more than fifty countries have issued the G3 to their armed forces. The G3 has been manufactured in Greece, Pakistan, Iran, Turkey and Portugal.

The Armalite and M16

The Colt AR-15 Armalite, which became the M16 when it was adopted by the US Army in Vietnam in 1966, was an innovative weapon when it was first introduced. It was made from alloys and plastic and fired an M193 5.56mm round with a 55-grain bullet

M16 controversy

The first M16 rifles, issued to US troops in Vietnam in the mid-60s, were loathed because men were killed or wounded when they jammed in combat. One of the major causes for these malfunctions was that the US Army replaced the originally specified Dupont IMR powder with standard ball powder, used in 7.62 x 51mm NATO ammunition. This produced much more fouling, which rapidly caused the actions of the M16 to jam unless the weapon was cleaned thoroughly. However, the initial M16 rifles had been promoted as "low maintenance", requiring no cleaning, and therefore no cleaning kits were issued and soldiers received no instructions in weapons cleaning.

In 1967–70 new 5.56mm ammunition was loaded using a different propellant. Cleaning kits were produced and issued to troops, and the M16 barrel,

chamber and bolt were chrome-lined to enhance their resistance to corrosion. At first, the cleaning kits had to be carried separately from the rifle, but since 1970 a cavity was included in the buttstock of all M16A1 rifles to hold the kit, and 30-round magazines replaced the original 20-round magazines.

RIGHT The M16 in use during the Vietnam War. It has gone through many stages of improvements and remains a general-issue rifle with the US armed forces.

with a muzzle velocity of 975m/s/3,198ft/s. This made the M16 much lighter than big 7.62mm rifles such as the M14 and a more practical weapon for the jungle.

The weapon that is currently in service is the M16A1/2, which is 99cm/39in long, weighs 3.2kg/7lb and fires a 20- or 30-round magazine. On automatic it has a cyclic rate of 700–950 rpm. The M16A1 has a manual bolt-closing device on the right side of the receiver, which allows extra pressure to be applied if there is dirt in the chamber or a cartridge case jams. The M16A2, which fires the NATO SS109 round – a 62-grain bullet with a muzzle velocity of 823 m/s /2,700ft/s – has a heavier barrel and a case deflector. This allows left-handed soldiers to handle the weapon. The M16A3 is an A2 with a removable carrying handle, which, when removed, allows a telescopic sight to be fitted.

The Dragunov SVD

The gas-operated, short-stroke, rotating-bolt, semi-automatic SVD (Snaiperskaya Vintovka Dragunova, or Dragunov Sniper Rifle) was adopted by the Soviet military in 1963. It can use any kind of standard 7.62 x 54R ammunition, but a primary round specially developed for the SVD sniper-grade cartridge has a steel-core bullet. The SVD is extremely reliable in all conditions, and has seen action in Afghanistan and Chechnya. In the mid-2000s, insurgent groups in Iraq and Afghanistan used it against US and Coalition forces. If the PSO-1 optical sight with illuminated reticle is damaged, the soldier has back-up adjustable iron sights. Unusually for a sniper weapon, it takes the standard AK-47 bayonet. The rifle has a ten-round detachable box magazine that gives a maximum rate of fire of 30 rpm or aimed fire of three to five rounds.

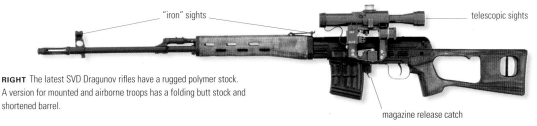

"iron" sights

telescopic sights

magazine release catch

RIGHT The latest SVD Dragunov rifles have a rugged polymer stock. A version for mounted and airborne troops has a folding butt stock and shortened barrel.

Modern assault rifles

Modern assault rifles, such as the Austrian Steyr AUG rifle, are commonly made from polymers and GRP (glass-reinforced plastic, or fibreglass). They are made in weapons "families": individual parts are interchangeable between models, and a rifle can be converted into a light support weapon in minutes. The Israeli Galil came from a different family that took design ideas from the Finnish Valmet, which itself had adopted them from the Soviet AK-47. The Soviet AK-74 is an update on the AK-47.

The Galil

During the late 1960s the Israel Defence Force (IDF) tested two replacements for the FN FAL rifles used by its soldiers. One weapon was designed by Uziel Gal and the other by Israel Galili, chief weapons designer for IMI (Israeli Military Industries). Drawing on the Finnish Valmet Rk 62 assault rifle, an improvement of the Soviet AK-47, Galili placed his rifle in competition with the M16A1, the Stoner 63, the AK-47, the HK 33 and a design by Uziel Gal. Galili's weapon eventually won the competition. It was selected as a new IDF assault rifle in 1973, but the Yom Kippur War of 1973 delayed its introduction.

The Galil is a versatile design that is available in several configurations. The full-sized AR and ARM, the compact SAR carried by vehicle crews and the MAR or Micro-Galil subcompact assault rifle are all in 5.56mm. An AR is available in 7.62mm NATO, while the Galatz is a 7.62mm semi-automatic sniper weapon. Most of the weapons fire at a cyclic rate of 650 rpm, the exception being the MAR, which fires 600–750 rpm. The 7.62mm AR/ARM has an effective range of 500–600m/550–655yd, while that of the 5.56mm AR/ARM is 450m/490yd. The little MAR has an effective range of 150–200m/165–220yd.

Galil rifles were exported to various Central American, African and Asian countries. In the first years of the 21st century, Estonia also took delivery of some Galils. In South Africa, Vektor (part of the DENEL defence and aerospace group) manufactures a modified Galil as the R4 and R5.

The AK-74

Chambered for a smaller 5.45 x 39mm round, the AK-74 is a modernized version of the 7.62mm AKM. Initially, NATO intelligence analysts thought that the AK-74 was a specialist weapon for airborne units of Special Forces. Produced from 1976, it was updated as the AK-74M, with a new muzzle brake and gas return cylinder, and since the early 1990s has been issued to the forces of the Russian Federation.

Like the AK-47 and AKM weapons, the AK-74 is a magazine-fed, selective-fire, intermediate-calibre assault rifle with a rigid-piston gas system and rotating bolt-locking mechanism. In addition, it uses the stamped sheet-metal receiver of the AKM. However, the AK-74 differs from the AKM in several ways, notably with its distinctive muzzle brake, which drastically cuts the already mild recoil and muzzle climb of the AK-74 when it is firing on fully automatic at 600–650 rpm – although the muzzle brake does

sights

cocking handle

hinged butt

LEFT The Galil was a superb weapon, rugged and soldier friendly; however, because the Israel Defence Force was offered the US M16 rifle at almost bargain prices, it adopted that instead.

flash eliminator

telescopic sights

RIGHT The Austrian AUG assault rifle adopted by the Austrian Army in 1979 is made under licence in Australia as the F88. The weapon shown here has the longer barrel; however, this can be changed in minutes.

hinged grip

moulded polymer

flash eliminator

grenade launcher

plastic magazine

LEFT The AK-74 fitted with a grenade launcher. This enhancement copied from the United States proved very popular during the Soviet intervention in Afghanistan in the latter years of the 20th century.

increase noise and muzzle blast. Current production versions of the AK-74M have a mounting rail on the left side of the receiver for fixing a telescopic or night-vision sight in place of the adjustable iron sights. It has an effective range of 457m/500yd.

The Steyr AUG
The futuristic-looking Austrian Steyr AUG rifle, with a distinctive green polymer frame and integrated Swarovski x1.5 scope, is actually one of a family of firearms first introduced in 1977 by Steyr Mannlicher. AUG stands for Armée Universal Gewehr, or "Universal Army Rifle", but is often used for the initial version – the 5.56mm NATO bullpup assault rifle. The family includes related weapons such as a submachine gun, sniper's rifle and LMG. Firing from a 30- or 42-round magazine, the rifle has an effective range of 450–500m/490–550yd and a cyclic rate of fire of 650 rpm. The weapon pioneered the use of translucent magazines, which allow the firer to make a quick visual check on how many rounds are available.

The Australian and New Zealand version of the weapon, the F88, fires in semi-automatic mode when the trigger is pressed to a clearly felt point and then in fully automatic when it is fully depressed. Other modifications to the AUG include three-round or fully

Plastic guns
Although the Germans had pioneered the use of early plastics such as Bakelite in automatic weapons prior to World War II, it was in the late 1960s that the American M16 rifle first caught the general public's attention. It used black polymers for the "furniture" (the butt and stock), where wood would traditionally have been used. Materials such as polymers and ceramics have considerable advantages over more traditional wood and steel: they do not corrode and deform in wet and humid conditions, which makes them ideal in a maritime or tropical environment; they are often lighter and actually stronger; and polymers can be cast in a colour that suits the theatre in which they are likely to be used – black, sand or olive drab.

automatic fire. Besides Austria, Australia and New Zealand, users include Indonesia, Luxembourg, Oman, Pakistan, Republic of Ireland, Saudi Arabia, Tunisia and Malaysia. The AUG has seen action with Australian forces in East Timor, Afghanistan and Iraq.

France and Britain

While the British L96A1 PM sniper rifle enjoys an excellent reputation, this cannot be said for the L85A1 rifle – the British soldier's issue rifle. The French FAMAS has had its critics too, but it is in wider use around the world. The French FR F2 sniper rifle is well regarded, but lacks the unique features of the L96A1.

cocking handle

ejection port

folding bipod

ABOVE The French F1 FAMAS is a comfortable weapon to fire with its built-in bipod and ambidextrous cocking handle. It is in service with the French armed forces as well as those of Djibouti, Gabon, Senegal and the United Arab Emirates.

The FAMAS

In 1967, development started on the Fusil d'Assaut de la Manufacture d'Armes de St Etienne or FAMAS. The new weapon was designed to replace both the MAS Mle 49/56 semi-automatic rifle and the veteran MAT-49 submachine gun. Paul Tellie, who headed the design team, came up with a radical design. The first prototype was completed in 1971, trialled in 1972–3 and adopted by the French Army in 1978. It has a delayed blowback action, and although the magazine can hold 30 rounds it is normally loaded with 25 rounds. On automatic it fires at 900–1,000 rpm. The FAMAS has an effective range of 300m/330yd. It has been exported to Djibouti, Gabon, Senegal and the UAE. The FAMAS G2 is intended for export, takes the 3-round M16-type magazine and is rifled for M193 or SS109 ammunition.

The L85A1 rifle SA80

In the late 1960s, the British Army realized it required a new rifle and began the development of the Small Arms for the 80s, or SA 80 system. The system was concentrated on two systems: the Individual Weapon, or SA80 IW and the Light Support Weapon, or LSW. The LSW was mechanically similar to the SA80 but had a bipod and longer barrel.

The L85A1 rifle that finally reached the soldier was not well received. Although it was chambered for 5.56mm, it was the heaviest weapon in this calibre in service. Being a bullpup design, the rifle had a long barrel, but with most of the weight located towards the butt this did not help to control muzzle climb during automatic fire. In the upgrade programme undertaken by Heckler & Koch in 2000–02, about 200,000 rifles were upgraded into the L85A2 configuration out of a total of about 320,000 original L85A1 rifles produced. The rifle is gas-operated with a rotating bolt. It has a 30-round box magazine and a cyclic rate of fire of 650 rpm. In general, the best feature of the L85 is its SUSAT x4 telescopic sight, which allows for accurate shooting out to 500m/550yd.

The L96A1 PM (Precision Marksman) sniper rifle

The Accuracy International, Bolt Action 7.62 x 51mm NATO sniper rifle entered service with the British Army in 1985 and was given the designation L96. With a ten-round box magazine, it is designed to achieve first-round hit at 600m/660yd and harassing fire out to 1,100m/1,200yd. The L96 was upgraded with a new sight and spotting scope to L96A1. The infantry version of the rifle has 6 x 42 Schmidt & Bender

ABOVE Gurkha soldiers armed with the L85A1 rifle and LSW negotiate with Indonesian Special Forces in East Timor in September 1999. The Indonesians are armed with an M16 and a Chinese-made SKS.

telescopic sights as well as iron sights. A covert version of the rifle folds down to fit into a suitcase and is fitted with a suppressed barrel. In ideal conditions the subsonic ammunition is accurate up to 300m/330yd.

Among the distinctive features of the L96A1 are a tool kit of three Allen wrenches and a screwdriver, which means the sniper is able to carry out all but the most major repairs by himself in the field, and a stainless-steel barrel that can be changed in five minutes. The L96A1 is in service with the British Army and with several armies in Africa, the Middle East and Far East.

The FR F2 sniper rifle

The French Army FR F2 sniper rifle is a modernized version of the earlier FR F1. The main differences are that it has been re-chambered from 7.5mm Lebel to 7.62 x 51mm NATO and the barrel design has been changed. FR F2 has a thermal-shielded barrel consisting of a polymer envelope enclosing most of the barrel. This ensures ballistic consistency, since the barrel stays at the same temperature, and it reduces the infrared signature and any heat haze from hot metal that could interfere with target location. FR F2 is a bolt-action weapon with iron sights and a x4 optical sight; it has a ten-round box magazine. It has been in service with the French Army since 1984.

SUSAT

The success story of the L85A1 rifle is the compact Sight Unit Small Arms Trilux (SUSAT), developed by the Royal Armaments and Research Department (RARDE). Weighing 417g/14.5oz, it is only 14.5cm/6in long and can be fitted or removed quickly using its universal mount on rifles, machine guns and recoilless rifles. It has a magnification of x4 and a field of view of ten degrees. The sight has been adopted by several armies including those of Sweden, Oman, Spain, Cameroon and, of course, Britain.

ABOVE Though the L85 rifle has been modified and improved as the L85A1, it still has its critics. Yet the x4 SUSAT sight has proved a huge success and has been adopted by other countries for their rifles.

Classic versus innovation

The United States' M24 sniper weapon and the Beretta SC-70/90 assault rifle are well established, classic designs. By contrast, the Barrett M82 .50in calibre rifle, known as the "Light Fifty", and the Heckler & Koch G-36 are more innovative weapons, and both have attracted great interest outside their countries of origin.

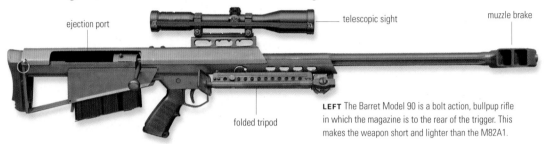

ejection port — telescopic sight — muzzle brake

folded tripod

LEFT The Barret Model 90 is a bolt action, bullpup rifle in which the magazine is to the rear of the trigger. This makes the weapon short and lighter than the M82A1.

The Barrett M82 "Light Fifty"

The American Barrett Firearms Company was founded in the early 1980s by Ronnie Barrett, who designed and built semi-automatic rifles chambered for powerful .50BMG ammunition, fired by Browning M2HB heavy machine guns. Barrett's first working rifles were available in 1982; four years later came the improved M82A1 rifle. The semi-automatic rifle has a ten-round detachable box magazine and a x10 scope.

ABOVE The M24 sniper rifle (right), which replaces the M21 rifle seen on the left, is an entirely new system. The M21 is based on the M14 and, despite its vintage, has proved a very effective sniper rifle in numerous conflicts around the world.

At this stage the "Light Fifty" was seen as something of a novelty, but in 1989 the Swedish Army purchased about 100 M82A1s. Major success followed in the US led international operations Desert Shield (1990) and Desert Storm (1991). The US Marine Corps ordered 125 "Light Fifty" rifles, and the US Army and air force also put in orders. It was given the designation SASR – Special Applications Scoped Rifle.

The weapon is used against targets such as the optical equipment on crew-served weapons, radar cabins, trucks and parked aircraft or in an Explosive Ordnance Disposal (EOD) function against unexploded munitions. Its long effective range of 1,800m/1,980yd, powerful muzzle velocity of 854m/s/2,800 ft/sec and capability to use different natures of ammunition such as API make it a potent tool. As with so many concepts, once Barrett had proved the principle of .50 long-range sniping weapons, other small arms manufacturers soon followed suit and produced their own designs.

The M24 sniper weapon

By the mid-1980s, the US Army M21 sniper rifles needed to be replaced, and conflicts in the deserts of the Middle East and mountains of Afghanistan meant that ranges for snipers jumped to distances of up to 1,000m/1,095yd. The US Army set the specifications for a bolt-action rifle, requiring a stainless-steel barrel rifle and a stock made from Kevlar-graphite (a tough man-made material used for body armour). After a final shoot-off between the Steyr SSG rifle and the

Remington model 700BDL, the latter was standardized in 1987 as the US Army's M24 sniper rifle. The M24 fires 7.62 x 51mm NATO from a five-round internal magazine. It has a 10x42 Leupold Ultra M3A telescope sight (Mil-Dots) and detachable emergency iron sights. The maximum effective range is 800m/875yd.

The Beretta SC-70/90

Beretta had already produced the AR70/223, a 5.56mm weapon for the export market, when the Italian Army decided to replace its 7.62mm Beretta BM59 rifles. The AR70/223 had been accepted by Italian Special Forces and exported to several countries including Jordan and Malaysia. Beretta produced an upgraded version in 1985, and following trials against similar calibre rifles, it was accepted as the AR-70/90. A folding butt version, the SC-70/90, was produced for Special Forces and a carbine version with a shorter barrel, the SCP-70/90, was made for paratroops. Finally, a squad automatic, the AS-70/90, was produced with a heavy fixed barrel and detachable bipod. The Beretta AR-70/90 weighs 4kg/9lb empty and has a cyclic rate of 670 rpm. The effective range of the AR-70/90 is 500m/550yd, while for the SCP-70/90 it is 350m/380yd.

The Heckler & Koch G-36

What came into being as the HK-50 project in the early 1990s became the the Heckler & Koch G-36 assault rifle. After the cancellation of the G11 (the futuristic caseless ammunition rifle), the Bundeswehr had no modern 5.56mm NATO-compatible rifle. So Heckler & Koch set out to develop a new assault rifle for the Bundeswehr and export markets. The brief was to produce a new rifle that was flexible, affordable and extremely reliable.

SS109 ammunition

During the 1970s, NATO members signed an agreement to select a smaller-calibre cartridge to replace the 7.62mm round. While there was agreement within NATO on the 5.56mm calibre, the M193 round used by US forces was rejected in favour of the more powerful Belgian FN SS109.

The M193 had proved appropriate for short-range engagements during the Vietnam war, but the SS109 had a heavier bullet but lower muzzle velocity, which gave better performance and greater penetration at the longer ranges likely to be found in Europe. When this powerful round is fired in long bursts from a fully automatic weapon such as the FN Minimi, its destructive power is phenomenal; it is capable of firing holes through brick walls that would not be penetrated by a 7.62mm round.

The G-36 uses a short-stroke gas piston above the barrel, a square-shaped bolt carrier and a rotating bolt with seven locking lugs. In these respects, it has similarities to the American AR-18. However, the receiver and most of the external parts of the G-36 are made from polymers reinforced with steel inserts in load-bearing areas.

The G-36 has a cyclic rate of 750 rpm and even though it can fire from standard M16 30-round magazines, the company has also decided to produce translucent magazines that allow the firer to make a quick visual check of the available ammunition. The rifle has an ambidextrous cocking handle and empty-case deflector for left-handed shooters.

carrying handle — built in sight — change lever — clear magazine

RIGHT The Heckler & Koch G-36 has been described as the weapon that may replace the L85A1 in British service. It is a rugged, well-priced weapon that can be fired comfortably by left-handed soldiers.

ABOVE When the Allies first encountered the superb German MG42 GPMG in Tunisia in 1943, they were intrigued by the stampings and brazings that were used in its construction – these were intended to speed mass production.

ABOVE An American M1917 Browning water-cooled machine gun with the unusual modification of a carrying handle around the water jacket. This allowed the crew to move the complete weapon short distances.

The machine-gun age 1883–2000

The search for a faster rate of fire led to the machine gun, and this crucial weapon will be covered in this section. Interestingly, prior to the demonstration of a recoil-operated belt-fed machine gun by Hiram Maxim, there had been earlier attempts to produce fast-firing weapons.

Heat is the challenge for all automatic weapons designers. It is generated by the exploding cartridges, by the machinery of the weapon and principally by the rounds passing rapidly up the barrel.

If a weapon overheats it will jam or may become a "runaway gun" that keeps firing even though the trigger is not being pressed. The solution for many machine-gun designs was to enclose the barrel in a water jacket; later weapons had barrels that could be changed quickly so that they did not overheat. It was vital for the machine-gun crew to follow the drills for their weapon as conscientiously as a Napoleonic soldier did for his flintlock musket. Skip a drill or fail to complete it properly and the weapon would malfunction.

ABOVE A German 7.92mm Maschinengewehr 08 water-cooled machine gun in a trench system on the Western Front in the latter years of World War I. The gun commander looks for targets while the crew are ready with belted ammunition.

Machine guns

Without the percussion cap and the self-contained round, the machine gun would never have been developed. As a minister, the Reverend Alexander Forsyth would perhaps have been horrified to discover his major part in this innovation. It was the method of ignition he invented to make wild fowling less vulnerable to the vagaries of the weather that became a key element of the machine gun. Rounds – the bullet and cartridge with its percussion cap and powder – could be fed on a belt or from a spring-loaded magazine into a rapid-firing and brutally effective weapon of war.

The Somme

World War I seems almost synonymous with the machine gun. On 1 July 1916, the first day of the Battle of the Somme, German artillery and machine-gun crews hunched behind their Maxim '08s killed or wounded about 60,000 British soldiers as they advanced across no-man's-land.

However rapid-fire weapons in the shape of multiple-firing flintlocks and muzzle-loaders had existed in the 18th and 19th centuries. The Puckle gun – a sort of large mounted revolver – was introduced in 1718 and was said to have fired 63

ABOVE The Gardner machine gun looks like a conventional weapon but it was operated by the crank handle on the right-hand side. Ammunition feed was by single rounds fed in from the top.

shots in seven minutes. In the American Civil War (1861–5), the .50/12mm-calibre Gatling gun (1862) with a reported rate of up to 1,000 rounds per minute (rpm), and the Agar "Coffee Mill" (1860), with a rate of 120 rpm, were used in some numbers. These guns were followed by other hand-cranked multi-barrelled models such as the Gardner, the Lowell and the Nordenfelt. In the period 1870–90 the British and Russian armies adopted the Gatling gun, while the Royal Navy used three makes – the Gatling, the Gardner and the Nordenfelt.

But none of these weapons was a truly automatic machine gun. All required some form of cranking and/or manipulation; a later model of the Gatling had its barrels rotated by an electric motor. This manipulation, combined with the effect of the recoil, meant that the accuracy of these rapid-firing guns was generally unpredictable. The French and Belgians developed similar weapons – *les mitrailleuses*, the principal product being a 37-barrelled weapon invented in 1870 by Joseph Montigny.

Fully automatic

At the close of the 19th century an American, Hiram Maxim, demonstrated a fully automatic weapon – a machine gun. This weapon would change the character of land warfare and dominate the skies when the first combat aircraft took off in World War I. The machine gun would heavily influence infantry tactics, requiring men to move in short dashes and employ "fire and movement", with the machine gun giving covering fire as rifle-armed soldiers closed with the enemy. As rates of fire increased the infantry would almost become ammunition carriers for the machine gun, advancing with belts or boxes of ammunition.

ABOVE A German MG34 in use in World War II on its sustained fire mount. This turned it from a light machine gun (LMG) into a medium machine gun (MMG), creating the general purpose machine gun (GPMG).

The GPMG

The inter-war years saw German arms designers learn the lessons of World War I and produce a machine gun that fulfilled the functions of both the long-range Medium Machine Gun (MMG) and the Light Machine Gun (LMG). In the MG34 they created the General-Purpose Machine Gun (GPMG). The United States, Great Britain and the USSR fought World War II with both MMGs and LMGs. The British used the superb Bren LMG, a weapon that was still in service with second-line troops in 1990–91 during the First Gulf War. The staggering volume of fire from the MG34 and 42,

respectively 900 and 1,500 rpm, was intimidating but could also be inaccurate. A machine gunner would often aim at an area target and produce a lethal "beaten zone" where falling rounds would make movement very risky.

Modern machine guns, such as the Belgian FN 5.56mm Minimi have become lighter and faster firing. Interestingly, the US electrically powered multi-barrelled M134 Minigun and GAU-19/A Gatling-type weapons incorporate technology first used in the designs of the 1860s. However, this development of a proven technology is not new. The Belgian FN MAG – in service with more than eighty armies across the world – uses the double-feed pawl system and the quick-change barrel that replaced the water jackets and cooling fins developed by the Germans for their superb MG42 machine gun in World War II.

BELOW The Belgian FN MAG is the most successful GPMG in service in NATO. It has a rate of fire of around 850 rounds per minute.

carrying handle

sights

gas regulator

cocking handle

trigger

Early multi-shot weapons

The 18th and 19th centuries saw the first multi-shot weapons, such as the English Puckle gun. They were not machine guns, but they pointed to future wars in which heavy volumes of fire could dominate the battlefield. The industrial base of the Union forces in the American Civil War gave inventors the facilities to develop these weapons, notably the multi-barrelled Organ gun and hopper magazine-fed Agar "Coffee Mill".

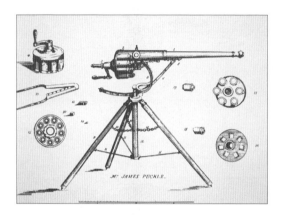

ABOVE The Puckle gun was a futuristic concept in the early 18th century and, unfortunately for its inventor, James Puckle, as was the case with many innovations, conservative British soldiers and government failed to see its military potential.

Puckle's gun

Born in 1667, James Puckle was an English lawyer, inventor and author. He is credited with two military inventions: a sword of which there is no record and his "portable gun or machine called a defence".

The Puckle gun was a tripod-mounted, single-barrelled flintlock gun fitted with a multi-shot revolving cylinder. At a time when a well-trained soldier could fire three shots a minute from his musket, one man with a Puckle gun could fire nine rounds. In a macabre marketing ploy Puckle offered two versions of the basic design. One gun, intended for use against Christian enemies, fired conventional round balls, while the second weapon, to be used against the Muslim Turks, fired square bullets that were believed to cause more severe wounds.

In 1717, after trials at Woolwich in front of senior officers, the gun was rejected by the British Government. Despite this, Puckle obtained a patent on 15 May 1718, and three years later set up a company to market it. An issue of the *Daily Courant* published in March 1722 carried an advertisement for "Several sizes in Brass and Iron of Mr. Puckle's Machine or Gun, called a Defence . . . at the Workshop thereof, in White-Cross-Alley, Middle Moorfields". At the end of the same month the *London Journal* reported that at a demonstration of one of the guns, "one Man discharged it 63 times in seven Minutes, though all the while Raining; and that it throws off either one large or sixteen Musquet Balls at every discharge with very great Force".

Despite the publicity, Puckle failed to attract backers, and when in 1718 his business went bust, a newspaper of the period ruefully noted that "those are only wounded who hold shares therein".

The 1860 Agar "Coffee Mill"

This is the earliest machine gun known to have been used by the United States Army. Designed by Wilson Agar, it was demonstrated to President Lincoln in 1861, and he was so impressed that he ordered ten at a price of $1,300 a gun; 51 were purchased a year later. They are known to have seen action in a limited number of arenas, and those include the battles of Petersburg, Virginia (1864–5). The machine gun earned its nickname from the hopper magazine feed, which resembled the feed for a coffee grinder. The "Coffee Mill" was mounted on a conventional artillery carriage with a small armour plate to protect the gunner. He had to stand, feeding .58in Minié bullets into the magazine and cranking a handle to fire. The weapon had an effective range of 915m/1,000yd and fired at 120 rpm. The gunner could increase this rate by cranking the handle faster, but because the Agar had only one barrel he ran the risk of overheating it. To obviate this, two spare barrels were always carried with the gun.

Billinghurst-Requa battery

Although the Gatling gun, patented on 4 November 1862, would prove a superior weapon, the Billinghurst-Requa battery, an advanced organ gun patented on 16 September 1862, predates it and is widely regarded as the first "practical" machine gun to be used during the American Civil War. It was the invention of the self-contained metal cartridge that made the organ gun (also known as the volley gun) a practical weapon. The cleverly arranged breech, which closed on a piano hinge, allowed for the ammunition strips to be loaded, fired, extracted, and reloaded quickly by the crew of three.

When the side-mounted loading levers were up, the breech was open. A powder train was laid behind the ammunition strip. Pushing the levers forward secured the breech. A musket cap was placed on the central priming nipple and fired with a simple flip-over hammer mechanism. The barrels, each 700mm/24in long, fired sequentially from the centre out with a characteristic rippling effect.

ABOVE A Billinghurst-Requa battery gun from around 1862. The weight of the 25 musket barrels meant that the gun had to be mounted on a light artillery carriage, and many armies therefore mistakenly considered weapons on gun carriages as light artillery and not a support weapon for the infantry. The idea of a multi-barrelled weapon had first appeared in a design by the Italian Leonardo da Vinci in the late 15th century.

ABOVE The Agar "Coffee Mill" was so-named because the ammunition feed was a hopper that looked very like the one that fitted to a coffee mill. It was hand cranked and capable of 120 rounds a minute.

The Organ gun

Also known as a volley gun or ribaldequin, this was a multi-barrelled gun designed to fire a number of shots simultaneously. Some volley guns could also fire their barrels in sequence. They were not machine guns because they did not load and fire automatically and were restricted by the number of barrels bundled together. The weapon was known as an organ gun because the bank of barrels resembled the pipes in a church organ.

In practice, the large organ guns had little more use than as a cannon firing canister or grapeshot. Mounted on a carriage, they were still as hard to aim and manoeuvre as a cannon, and the many barrels took as long or longer to reload. They also tended to be relatively expensive since they were more complex than a cannon; all the barrels had to be individually maintained, cleaned, loaded and primed. Despite this, the Requa battery, a 25-barrel organ gun, was used by Union forces in 1863 in the American Civil War. A three-man crew could fire seven volleys a minute.

Weapons of war

In the mid-19th century, weapons such as the Gatling were used in action by the Americans in the Civil War, while the French used the Montigny mitrailleuse, one of the first secret weapons, in the Franco-Prussian War. The Swedish-designed Nordenfelt was adopted by the British for use by the Royal Navy.

The Gatling gun

Patented in 1862 by Richard Jordan Gatling, a dentist from North Carolina, this gun was a variation on the revolver principle, with six to ten barrels revolved around a central axis, firing one barrel at a time. The main advantage of having many barrels was that they cooled in between shots, so maintaining their accuracy and preventing "cook-off": the premature ignition of a charge. In 1865 the US Army bought its first Gatling. The first weapons used paper cartridges, but a year later, metallic ones were introduced. Other types of automatic weapons were used in the Civil War but only the Gatling remained in service afterwards.

The Gatling was improved and served with a number of armies around the world as an infantry support or a light artillery weapon. Usually chambered

ABOVE The Gatling gun is one of the iconic weapons of the American Civil War. Soldiers were still unsure whether it was an artillery or infantry weapon, and the wheeled carriage makes it look like a field gun.

for the contemporary general issue rifle cartridge, some naval Gatlings, however, had calibres up to 1in, and some derivatives, such as the Hotchkiss, were up to 2in in calibre. To fire the Gatling, a handle at the back was cranked, which rotated the barrels and fired them in turn. Each barrel had its own bolt that reloaded with each turn. A competent gunner could reach rates of fire of over 200 rounds a minute – a far higher rate than with a single-shot muzzle-loaded or even magazine-fed bolt-action rifle. By 1890, the first true recoil-operated machine guns had been developed but some Gatlings remained in service until 1914.

ABOVE The mitrailleuse used by the French Army in 1870–71 in the Franco-Prussian War was regarded as light artillery even though it used rifle ammunition. Its lethal potential was not fully realized in that war.

The Montigny mitrailleuse

The mitrailleuse was designed in Belgium by Captain T. H. J. Fafschamps in 1851 and manufactured by Joseph Montigny of Fontaine-l'Evêque near Brussels. It was deployed in Belgium in the 1850s, apparently only on a limited basis as a defensive weapon to protect Belgian fortresses.

The Montigny mitrailleuse entered service with the French Army in 1869. Although it looked similar to a modern machine gun, it was strictly speaking a volley-fire gun. It had 26 barrels enclosed in a brass cylinder. A plate pre-loaded with ammunition was inserted into the breach, and to fire it, the gunner cranked a handle. He could fire all 26 barrels in one blast.

At the outbreak of war between France and Prussia in July 1870, the French Army had approximately 190 of these weapons available. Each division was issued with one battery of six guns, issued as replacement for the *Canon de 4* (86.5mm) battery. However, the tactical philosophy behind the deployment of the mitrailleuse was unsuccessful in practice. The guns were ideal at short range against cavalry and infantry, and on one occasion a single mitrailleuse stopped a charge by 500 Prussian cavalry in a murderous 90-second fusillade. Yet French gunners assumed the mitrailleuse was an artillery piece and attempted to use it in long-range duels with very efficient Prussian artillery, a role for which it was entirely unsuited.

The Nordenfelt

This machine gun was of Swedish design and consisted of four to ten barrels mounted on a tripod and fitted with a hopper magazine, with a hand lever to operate the mechanism. It was adopted by the Royal Navy and used as an anti-torpedo boat weapon and by naval landing parties.

There were several designs, including a ten-barrelled Nordenfelt machine gun in .45 calibre, a four-barrelled Nordenfelt 1in-calibre gun with a rate of 200 rpm (introduced into service by the British in 1880, replacing the Gatling .45-calibre machine gun and five-barrelled Gardner machine gun), and the five-barrelled Nordenfelt .45-calibre, 600-rpm gun introduced in 1882.

Torsten W. Nordenfelt

The Swedish engineer Torsten Wilhelm Nordenfelt (1842–1920) teamed up with his fellow countryman and inventor Palmcrantz to produce the M1877 25mm/1in four-barrelled semi-automatic weapon for the Royal Swedish Navy. The gun was gravity fed and fired at 120 rpm. As the Royal Navy was the largest in the world in the late 19th century, Nordenfelt set up a factory in London to supply guns. He teamed up with Maxim to produce guns that were supplied to the Ottoman and German navies. In 1906 the US Navy adopted its first light automatic anti-aircraft gun, the Maxim-Nordenfelt 1 pdr Mark 6.

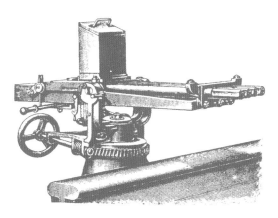

ABOVE The Nordenfelt was produced in several calibres with one to twelve barrels. The weapon shown here is a naval mounting designed to combat torpedo boats.

The first machine guns

Hiram Maxim's invention at the close of the 19th century dominated the 20th century. Colt and Browning, two American small arms giants, combined to produce a machine gun, the Colt-Browning "Potato Digger", while the Danish produced the Madsen – significantly, the first light machine gun (LMG) – which has often been overlooked.

The Maxim machine gun

In 1883–85 US-born Hiram S. Maxim developed the first fully automatic machine gun. After cocking the weapon and pressing the firing button, a round was fired. The recoil energy from firing operated the breech-block; the spent cartridge was expelled, a new round fed into the breech, the firing pin cocked, and a new round fired. As long as the button was depressed a Maxim would fire until the entire ammunition belt was expended. Trials showed that the machine gun could fire 500 rounds per minute. Maxim was knighted for his work after becoming a British citizen.

The Maxim machine gun was adopted by the British Army in 1889. In the following year the Austrian,

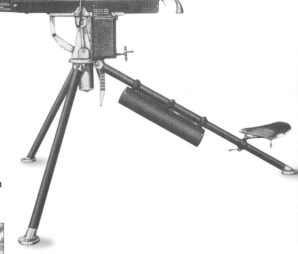

ABOVE The Colt-Browning "Potato Digger" received this nickname during the Irish Civil War in 1922, when combatants likened the action of the swinging lever to a farmer digging for potatoes.

German, Italian, Swiss and Russian armies also purchased Maxim's gun. The gun was first used by Britain's colonial forces in the Matabele War in southern Africa, in 1893–4. In one engagement, 50 soldiers fought off 5,000 Matabele warriors with just four Maxim guns.

The success of the Maxim machine gun inspired other inventors. The German Army's Maschinengewehr and the Russian Pulemyot Maxima were both based on Maxim's invention.

The Colt-Browning "Potato Digger"

The 1895/1914 Colt-Browning .3 machine gun was initially adopted by the American Expeditionary Force (AEF) at the start of World War I pending delivery of other weapons, including the Browning M1917. The Colt-Browning, which weighed a little over

ABOVE Under the watchful eye of a British officer and the inventor Hiram Maxim, Henry M. Stanley experiments with a Maxim gun. Unlike earlier weapons the maxim did not require a hand crank and was belt fed.

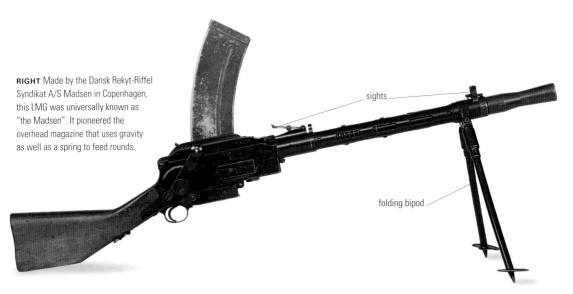

RIGHT Made by the Dansk Rekyt-Riffel Syndikat A/S Madsen in Copenhagen, this LMG was universally known as "the Madsen". It pioneered the overhead magazine that uses gravity as well as a spring to feed rounds.

sights

folding bipod

45.9kg/101lb, had a maximum cyclic belt-fed firing rate of 500 rpm. It is regarded as the first successful gas-operated machine gun, designed by John Moses Browning and offered to the Colt company towards the close of 1890.

Originally designed to use .3 Krag Jorgenson cartridges, the gun was modified in 1914 and chambered for .30/60 cartridges. Italy purchased a number of Colt-Browning 1895/1914 guns in 6.5mm calibre for use by its army as a supplement to the home-grown Fiat-Revelli gun. This machine gun got its nickname "potato digger" because of the action of the swinging lever below the gun.

The Madsen LMG
The Danish 8mm Madsen light machine gun (LMG) was first introduced in 1902 and was the first true light machine gun. A recoil-operated weapon, it was fed from a 20-round curved box magazine. It has been said of the Madsen that the remarkable thing about it was not that it worked well, but that it worked at all. It had a complex mechanism built around the Martini breech-block action. The breech was opened by a recoil-driven cam, and then a separate rammer pushed the cartridge into the chamber before it closed and the round was fired. The Madsen has a long operational history; it first saw action with Russian cavalry squadrons in the Russo–Japanese War of 1904–05. In World War I Germany, Britain and France used it in limited numbers. The German Army formed the first light machine-gun units based on the Madsen; the

Musketen Battalions. They went into action in the Champagne sector in September 1915. Yet the German Army failed to realize their potential. The three Musketen Battalions were used in a defensive role, and so did not demonstrate the advantages of an LMG in the attack. Later, when the utility of an LMG became apparent, the Germans ignored the Madsen and instead developed the MG08/15 water-cooled gun.

Hiram S. Maxim

Born in Sangersville, Maine, USA in 1840, Hiram Maxim became a coachbuilder in an engineering works in Fitchburg, Massachusetts. When he was 26, he obtained the first of many patents for a hair-curling iron. This was rapidly followed by a machine for producing illuminating gas and a locomotive headlamp.

Maxim was employed by the United States Electric Lighting Company as chief engineer and designed a method of producing carbon filaments. At the Paris Electrical Exhibition in 1881 he found the inspiration to develop a machine gun. Maxim moved to London, and in 1884 produced the first working model of an automatic portable machine gun. His Maxim Gun Company, founded the same year, was later absorbed into Vickers Ltd, and he became a director. Maxim was knighted by Queen Victoria in 1901.

Machine guns of World War I

Prior to World War I, Austria-Hungary had an established small arms industry in what is now the Czech Republic as well as in Austria, where it produced the Schwarzlose MG07/12. In France, Hotchkiss, a firm established by an American, produced two reliable machine guns, while the German Maschinengewehr 08 was used to great effect against British and French forces on the Western Front.

grips   sights   water filler cap   flash eliminator

The Schwarzlose MG07/12

Designed by Andreas Wilhelm Schwarzlose in 1902, the MG07/12 would be the standard MMG (Medium Machine Gun) with Austro-Hungarian forces during World War I. It was widely sold or delivered as war reparations after 1918. Many were used by the Italians in World War II. The water-cooled machine gun had a distinctive cone-shaped flame damper and pistol grip. It had a cyclic rate of fire of 400–500 rpm and fired from a 250-round fabric belt.

ABOVE A German MG08 machine gun crew in the latter years of World War I. The gun was rugged and reliable, but heavy, which meant that it was not suitable for infantry actions involving the tactics of fire and manoeuvre, and were largely used for defence.

ABOVE The Austrian Schwarzlose MG07, produced by Steyr, was so rugged that guns that were nearly forty years old were still in service in Yugoslavia, Bulgaria, Holland, Romania, Hungary, Italy and Greece as well as Austria at the outbreak of World War II.

This weapon had a fixed barrel, few moving parts and rugged construction. The breech was at no time truly locked. When the gun fired, the rearward thrust of the exploding gases actually started the action opening at the same instant as it caused the bullet to move down the barrel. However, by using a very short barrel and a combination of extremely heavy recoil parts and springs, Schwarzlose produced a machine gun that permitted the use of powerful military rifle cartridges without an impossibly heavy breech mechanism to absorb the recoil energy from these rounds.

The Maschinengewehr 08

The German Maschinengewehr 08, or MG08, was virtually a direct copy of the 1884 Maxim, and was the German Army's standard machine gun in World War I. At the start of the war, about 12,000 MG08s were available. The British assumed that the Germans had large numbers of guns; in fact they had learned that machine guns proved more effective when concentrated together. The Maschinengewehr 08 remained in service in static positions even after the outbreak of World War II, until it was replaced by the MG34 in about 1942.

The 7.92mm MG08, based on the 1901 model but named after 1908, its year of adoption, was water cooled by about 4.5 litres/1 gallon of water in a jacket around the barrel. It fired from a 250-round fabric belt and had a cyclic rate of 400 rpm, although sustained firing would lead to overheating. The MG08 had a range of about 2,010m/2,200yd up to a maximum of 3,660m/4,000yd. It was moved on a cart, or dismantled and carried by the crew on their shoulders to a new position.

The Benet-Mercie 1909
The Benet-Mercie Machine Rifle, Calibre .30 US Model of 1909 was a .30 machine gun, adopted by the US Army in 1909 and used throughout World War I. The same basic pattern was also used by the French and British: with the French as the Hotchkiss M1909 chambered for 8mm Lebel ammunition and with the British as the Hotchkiss Mark I. The French and British designs proved longer lived; used in tanks and aircraft, they served on into World War II. The US design was fed from 30-round strips, as were other types, although there were also belt-fed versions and others with enhanced barrel cooling. The US types had a bipod, while some others used a small tripod.

ABOVE During a visit by a politician to France in World War I, a Canadian officer explains the workings of the Hotchkiss Mark 1. The gun would remain in service into World War II in light armoured vehicles.

Benjamin Hotchkiss

Born in Watertown, Connecticut, in 1826, Benjamin Berkeley Hotchkiss became a skilled designer in the family's engineering business, working on new weapons designs. When he failed to interest the US Government, he moved to France and set up the Hotchkiss Company in 1867.

Hotchkiss began producing weapons and explosives for the French armed forces at his factory near Paris. After his death in 1885, work continued, and the first working model of an automatic machine gun was produced by 1892.

In 1897 it was adopted by the French Army. A series of improvements and modifications followed, and by 1914 the definitive Hotchkiss gun had been created. Reliable and simple, it became one of the standard gas-operated heavy machine-gun designs to be adopted for use by the British, French and Japanese armies during World War I.

Machine gun veterans

Three machine guns that were the cornerstones of infantry operations in World War I – the Russian PM1910, British Vickers MMG and French Hotchkiss M1914 – were still in use during World War II. Indeed, the Vickers was still in use in the mid-1960s, before the British Army switched to 7.62mm NATO calibre ammunition.

The Pulemyot Maxima PM1910

The Russian Pulemyot Maxima na stanke Sokolova (Maxim's machine gun on Sokolov's mount), was also known as the Maxim machine gun 1910 (or Pulemyot Maxima PM1910). This variant of the Maxim machine gun was chambered for the standard Russian 7.62 x 54mm R ammunition. It served as the medium machine gun in the Imperial Russian Army during World War I and the Red Army during World War II. The gun fired at 600 rounds per minute from a 250-round fabric belt. The water-cooling jacket had a screw cap normally fitted to tractor radiators; it was large enough that snow could be packed into the jacket during the bitter Russian winters when all water was frozen. For a degree of mobility, the M1910 could be installed on the wheeled Sokolov mount. By 1943 it was replaced by the excellent SG-43 Gorunov. Maxims were often bolted together on a high-angle mount as anti-aircraft guns.

ABOVE Soviet sailors fighting as infantry in World War II man a triple PM1910 anti-aircraft machine gun. The guns would have put up 1,800 rpm and made an effective low-altitude anti-aircraft system.

ABOVE A sergeant of the British Gloucestershire Regiment, whose ribbons indicate that he is a veteran of World War II, supervises two Vickers MMG detachments in the 1950s in a display of infantry weapons.

The Vickers MMG

The first Vickers machine gun, the Vickers .303in Medium Machine Gun Mark 1, entered service in 1912 and soldiered on with the British Army until 1974. It was a Maxim mechanism that had been inverted and improved. With water in the cooling jacket, the gun weighed 18kg/40lb and the tripod 22kg/48.5lb, while the total weight of the gun was 40.2kg/88.5lb. The Vickers machine gun had a muzzle velocity of 744m/s/2,440ft/s and a rate of fire of 450–500 rpm, and it was fired from a 250-round fabric belt. The introduction of the Mark 8z round added a further 915m/1,000yd to the 550m/3,600yd maximum range. Using a dial sight, which was introduced in 1942, the gun could be used for indirect fire.

During World War I the Vickers MMG gained a reputation as the "Queen of the battlefield" with men of the British Machine Gun Corps (founded in October 1915). It is a measure of the effectiveness and reliability of the weapon that, during the British attack upon High Wood on 24 August 1916, it is estimated that ten Vickers fired in excess of one million rounds over a 12-hour period.

The Hotchkiss M1914

The St Etienne Mle 1907 was the standard machine gun of the French Army at the outbreak of World War I. However, it performed badly in the field. It had so many deficiencies that although guns were captured by the Germans and given the designation 8mm sMG256(f), they were never used, even in fixed fortifications.

There were several modifications until the gas-operated, air-cooled Hotchkiss 8mm M1914 machine gun was produced in 1914, when gas operation was still a relatively new concept. It was a very distinctive gun, with five large circular cooling fins and a metal strip ammunition feed. The Hotchkiss became the French army's standard heavy tripod-mounted MMG in World War I. Twelve divisions of the American Expeditionary Forces (AEF) in France were equipped with the Mle 1914 Hotchkiss in 1917–18.

ABOVE The French mitrailleuse St Etienne Mle 1907 had evolved from the earlier Mle 1905 produced by the State Arsenal Puteaux. It was gradually replaced in service during World War I.

cooling fins

seat

LEFT The French Hotchkiss Mle 1914 was the standard French medium machine gun during World War I. It remained in widespread use during World War II.

The gun was heavy at 23kg/50lb (44kg/88lb with its mounting), but reliable. The main drawback was the ammunition feed, a cumbersome 24- or 30-round metal magazine strip that fired 8mm Lebel rounds. In 1917 a 250-round belt feed was introduced, enabling effective sustained fire. The Hotchkiss had a muzzle velocity of 701m/s/2,299ft/s and a cyclic rate of 450 rpm.

Machine-gun tactics in World War I

In 1914 a German Army battalion had six Maxim MG Modell 1908 machine guns; in contrast, a British battalion had only two Vickers Mark 1s, or Maxims. However, from the outset of the fighting, the Germans tactically concentrated these already co-ordinated battalion teams into batteries and thus gave the appearance, and effect, of having even more machine guns than was actually the case. They gave this impression at Loos, where German machine-gun crews opened fire at 1,400m/1,530yd on the advancing British infantry on the afternoon of

26 September 1915. They inflicted 8,000 casualties (50 per cent) on just two British New Army Divisions (21st and 24th). One German single machine-gun crew is said to have fired 12,500 rounds.

In 1917–18 the British and Germans made a change from the defensive to a more offensive role for the machine gun. The British Machine Gun Corps undertook highly co-ordinated offensive and defensive tactics, including barrages. The infantry then concentrated on the deployment, with much success, of the lighter Lewis machine guns at the platoon level.

The good and the bad

The Italian Fiat-Revelli M1914 must have been a gunner's nightmare, with a complex mechanism that was prone to jamming. The unreliable French Chauchat LMG was designed by three men – Chauchat, Suterre and Riberolle – and as such has been called a gun designed by committee. The American-designed British-built Lewis gun, however, would be one of World War I's success stories.

water filler cap — sight

The Fiat-Revelli M1914

This was Italy's first mass-produced machine gun. It was designed in 1908 and bought for use by the Italian Army in 1914, as Army Chief of Staff Luigi Cadorna prepared the Italian Army for its 1915 entry into World War I.

The 6.5mm calibre Fiat-Revelli was water cooled and fired from a 50-round (later 100-round) magazine composed of ten columns of five rounds feeding from the left. Unsurprisingly, given such a loading method, it jammed frequently, but despite this it remained in service for the duration of the war.

It bore a superficial resemblance to both the Maxim and Vickers machine guns but had an entirely different mechanism. Using a delayed blowback mechanism, the barrel and bolt recoiled a short distance, held in place by a swinging wedge. As the

ABOVE The Italian Fiat-Revelli had a complex mechanism, which included a feed system that consisted of a magazine with ten compartments.

latter opened, the bolt was released so that it could be blown back by the spent case's recoil. The overly complex design of this mechanism led to cartridge extraction difficulties; consequently, an oil reservoir was used to lubricate cartridges before they were loaded into the gun. However, oil attracts dirt and dirt can jam mechanisms.

Isaac Newton Lewis

In 1911, a serving American officer and amateur inventor, Colonel Isaac Newton Lewis, perfected a light machine gun originally designed by another American, Samuel Maclean. The American Army showed no interest in its production, so Colonel Lewis retired and moved to Belgium in January 1913, where the Belgians undertook its manufacture. Surprisingly, its calibre was 7.7mm or .303, the calibre of the standard British rifle round.

When Germany invaded Belgium in 1914, the German forces who came up against the weapon

called it "the Belgian rattlesnake". Many of Lewis's Belgian workers fled to Britain, where they were given employment by the Birmingham Small Arms Company (BSA), which bought the licence to manufacture the gun. From 1915 it entered service in increasing numbers with the British Army. By 1916 approximately 50,000 had been produced. In 1915 each British battalion on the Western Front had just four Lewis guns, but by 1917 each infantry section boasted its own Lewis gunner and number two, with battalions by now deploying 46 Lewis guns.

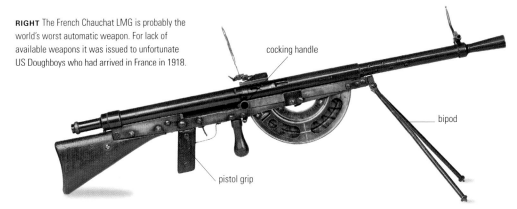

RIGHT The French Chauchat LMG is probably the world's worst automatic weapon. For lack of available weapons it was issued to unfortunate US Doughboys who had arrived in France in 1918.

cocking handle

bipod

pistol grip

The Fiat-Revelli was theoretically capable of firing 400–500 rpm out to 1,500m/1,640yd, but in practice it fired approximately 150–200 rpm. It was modified for use in aircraft in 1915 before British-supplied Vickers and Lewis guns were fitted to Italian aircraft in 1917. The Fiat-Revelli nevertheless held a place within the Italian Army's armoury, albeit with modifications including a 300-round belt feed, until the end of World War II.

The Chauchat LMG
The Chauchat was the light machine gun used principally by the French Army and also by seven other nations, including the USA, during and after World War I. Its formal designation in the French Army was Fusil-Mitrailleur Mle 1915 CSRG. It was also known as the CSRG or Gladiator. More than 260,000 were produced, making it the most widely manufactured automatic weapon of World War I. It was among the first light machine-gun designs of the early 1900s, with

BELOW Although the Lewis LMG was designed by an American, during the two world wars it became a truly international weapon. Lewis guns accounted for 20 per cent of the Luftwaffe aircraft shot down around London in 1940.

novel features, such as a pistol grip, an in-line stock and select fire lever, that are now standard in modern assault rifles. To speed production it was made from stampings and tubular and lathe-turned components. It fired from a 20-round magazine at 250 rpm and had a rather complex long barrel recoil and gas-assisted mechanism. The Chauchat was designed and built in a hurry during World War I and had numerous faults, and it is recognized today as one of the least reliable automatic weapons ever issued to armed services.

The Lewis LMG
In 1911, Colonel Isaac Lewis of the US Army adapted the complex light machine-gun design of another American engineer, Samuel McLean, and produced the Lewis gun. This early light machine gun was widely adopted by the military forces of Britain and its empire from 1915 onwards. The M1914 air-cooled Lewis gun had a 47-cartridge circular magazine, or a 97-round cartridge for aircraft. The adjustable clockwork recoil spring allowed the gunner to adjust his rate of fire between 500 and 600 rpm, although most gunners preferred to fire short bursts. The gun had adjustable sights and a bipod for firing from the prone position. This gave it an effective range of 600m/655yd.

drum magazine

sights

cooling jacket

World War I survivors

The heavy weight of the German MG 08/15 (a "light" machine gun) must in part have been the inspiration to produce the genuinely light MG34 and later the well-designed MG42. The American Browning M1917 would serve through two world wars, but the Browning .50 would be a true survivor; it remains in service in the 21st century.

sights

improvised carrying handle

RIGHT The Browning M1917 was under development as far back as the 1890s, but the US Army expressed little interest in it until World War I.

The Browning M1917

Like the MG08 the Browning M1917 was a water-cooled machine gun. It was superficially similar to the Maxim and Vickers machine guns, although its pistol grip and internal mechanism differentiated it from both. It was adopted by the US Army following the entry of the United States into World War I in April 1917. Before the war ended on 11 November 1918, some 57,000 recoil-operated, belt-fed, M1917 machine guns had been manufactured for use by the American Expeditionary Force (AEF). Weighing some 24kg/53lb, the Browning .3 was actually developed in 1910 from an 1890s design. The M1917 fired from a 250-round fabric belt and was capable of firing 450–600 rpm. The basic Browning mechanism in the M1917 would remain virtually unchanged in all future Browning designs.

Immediately following US entry into World War I, the M1917 was not initially available. In the interim, while production was increased, the AEF deployed the French Chauchat LMG. The M1917A1,

The Maschinengewehr MG08/15

The MG08/15 was an attempt by the Germans to produce a lighter version of the MG08 for use by assault troops. It retained the mechanism of the MG08 but in place of the heavy tripod had a bipod with a pistol grip and shoulder stock. Despite this attempt to lighten the gun, it still weighed 18kg/40lb. It fired from 50-, 100- or 250-round fabric belts at 450 rpm. The gun was used by Belgium and Yugoslavia in the inter-war years, and in World War II was still in service with German formations, albeit with second- and third-line units. It was used in an anti-aircraft (AA) role and perhaps most notoriously in the watchtowers of concentration and prisoner-of-war camps. At the close of the war, MG08/15 guns were issued to Volkssturm formations.

water jacket

LEFT The MG08/15 was an attempt by the Germans to turn the big MG08 into a weapon that could be used as an LMG. The water jacket required to cool the barrel meant that the gun still weighed 18kg/40lb.

bipod

cocking handle

barrel change handle

spade grips

cooling vents

LEFT The Browning M2 .50in Heavy Machine Gun "Big Fifty" in a ground mount is heavy at 37.8kg/84lb, but the powerful 12.7mm rounds are effective against lightly armoured vehicles.

produced in 1936, had changes to the feed, sights and tripod. It continued to be used into World War II with US and Allied forces. A total of 53,854 of these guns were built.

The Browning M2 HMG

The US Browning .50 M2HB machine gun, or "Big Fifty", is one of the longest-serving weapons in the world, having entered service with the US Army in 1923. Some water-cooled guns were produced, but most relied on the heavy barrel to absorb the heat of firing. Although the sights are graduated up to 2,600m/2,845yd the big rounds are effective beyond this range. The M2HB's ammunition was developed from the German anti-tank rifle rounds captured at the end of World War I and is effective against lightly armoured vehicles. The French-made Société Française de Munitions (SFM) armour-piercing ammunition weighs 47.6g/1.68oz and will penetrate 2.49cm/0.98in of steel at 300m/330yd and 1.29cm/0.51in at 1,300m/1,420yd. Among the types available are ball, tracer, incendiary and armour-piercing incendiary. The slow cyclic rate of 450–600 rpm ensures accuracy.

It was firing a Browning M2 HMG mounted on a knocked-out US tank destroyer armoured vehicle that won 21-year-old Lieutenant Audie Murphy the Medal of Honor on 26 January 1945 during the Battle of the Bulge. He pushed the dead tank commander out of the way and used the machine gun to cut down advancing German infantry. At the same time, he called down artillery fire on the tanks supporting them. At one stage, in order to convince the distant gunners that the enemy attack had come dangerously close, he held the field telephone next to the machine gun as he fired.

Post-World War II improvements on the battle-tested Browning .50 include the RAMO and Saco .50 M2HB quick-change kit and the M2 lightweight machine gun, which weighs 27kg/59lb compared to the 38kg/83.7lb of the M2HB. The rate of fire on the lightweight gun can be adjusted from 550–750 rpm to allow it to be used in ground-support or air-defence roles. The quick-change kits only allow hot barrels to be changed quickly and safely after prolonged firing and eliminate the time-consuming task of headspace adjustment.

Machine gun deployment

Machine guns were deployed in three ways in World War I: direct fire, indirect fire and firing from fixed points.

• In direct fire the gunner could clearly see his target and he pressed the trigger, firing bursts of fire in the direction of the enemy infantry.

• Indirect fire was rather like artillery fire with rounds being "dropped" over enemy territory at unseen targets, beyond the effective cone of fire for the weapon. The gunner would adjust the weapon to fire skywards and shoot across the battlefield with a long curving trajectory. Although random, like any harassing fire it could suppress the troops at the other end by killing, injuring or simply dispersing them.

• Firing from fixed points worked by providing a dense, compact cone of fire at the enemy, which could have an end result similar to that of indirect fire.

Browning and Kijiro's designs

The diversity and durability of the small arms designed by John Moses Browning are remarkable. His BAR and M1919 machine gun would see US forces through World War II and the Korean War, and in the case of the M1919, were still used by armies around the world in the 21st century. While never in the Browning league, General Kijiro Nambu was also a very talented designer, producing pistols, rifles and machine guns.

The Browning Automatic Rifle

Late in World War I, John Moses Browning received a request from the US Expeditionary Corps in France to design the 0.3 Browning Automatic Rifle, or BAR. It had a 20-round box magazine and was initially a selective-fire weapon. Since the standard machine guns were heavy and not very manoeuvrable, it was intended for use by infantry firing from the shoulder or the hip when advancing on enemy positions, and to provide mobile firepower to every squad. However, the BAR M1918 proved to be twice as heavy as a bolt-action Springfield M1903 rifle.

In 1939, after several modifications, the final version of the BAR appeared as the M1918A2. Manufactured by Colt, Marlin-Rockwell and Winchester, it became the section or squad automatic weapon for US troops during World War II and the Korean War. M1918A1 guns, converted to M1918A2, had a skid-footed adjustable bipod under the flash hider, M1917 sights, smaller forend and a metal heat shield between barrel

and cylinder/spring. The single-shot capability was replaced by two fully automatic modes, with fast at 650 rpm and slow at 450 rpm. The bipod, however, was rather impractical, so many M1918A2 gunners dispensed with it. The BAR remained in service with US Allies into the 1970s.

The M1919 Browning machine gun

The .3in Browning M1919 machine gun was essentially an M1917 but with an air-cooled barrel. The M1919A4 was used on a ground mount by infantry, the M1919A5 worked coaxially in tanks, and the M2 was used in aircraft and as an AA gun by US and Allied forces in World War II. The M1919A6 was fitted with a bipod, butt and carrying handle. As an infantry squad weapon it looked a little odd, but was very popular, and 43,479 were manufactured in World War II. The M1919 remained in service in the Korean War and was even used in Vietnam. Towards the end of the 1960s it began to be superseded by newer designs. Even so, in the late 1990s (as the 7.62mm NATO M2) it formed part of the arsenals of the armies of Canada, Denmark, the Dominican Republic, Guatemala, Haiti, Iran, Israel, Italy, Liberia, Mexico, South Africa, South Korea, Spain, Taiwan and Vietnam.

US Navy Brownings were converted to 7.62mm during the Vietnam War and designated Mark 21 Mod 0. These guns were fitted to river patrol craft which were operating on the Mekong Delta. A reliable recoil-operated gun, the Mark 21 Mod 0 fired from a 250-round belt at 400–600 rpm. The maximum effective range was 1,370m/1,500yd.

The Type 11 LMG

Commonly known by the Allies as the Japanese Nambu and by the Japanese as the Taisho 11 Nen Shiki Kikanju, the Type 11 LMG was designed by the prolific General Kijiro Nambu and entered service in 1922.

ABOVE US soldiers in training with the Browning Automatic Rifle (BAR) after World War I. The BAR was a heavy but reliable squad automatic weapon that served through World War II and during the Korean War of 1950–53, with greater range and power than the opponents' weapons.

ABOVE The Browning M1919 machine gun would prove almost as long lived as the bigger .50 Browning. Here it is on an improvised mount on a US jeep in the bitter winter of 1944–45 in Europe.

It was the standard light machine gun (LMG) in 1941, although later in the war it was replaced by the Type 96 and the Type 99. It drew on Hotchkiss principles but had an unusual hopper feed mechanism. Up to 30 rounds in standard clips of rifle ammunition could be

ABOVE Japanese troops wearing gas masks man a Type 11 LMG during fighting in the streets of Shanghai in the Sino-Japanese War of the 1930s, later becoming part of World War II.

dropped into it, but the complex mechanism could not handle the powerful rounds, so it required its own lower-powered 6.5mm ammunition to operate. Only capable of automatic fire, the gun fired at 500 rpm.

John Moses Browning

The son of a Mormon gunsmith, John Moses Browning was born in Ogden, Utah in 1855. Working with scrap metal, he produced his first gun when he was 13. At the age of 24 he patented a breech-loading single-shot rifle.

In the 1890s Hiram Maxim's invention inspired Browning to develop his own automatic weapon. Instead of using the recoil forces, Browning drilled a hole in the gun barrel and used this to tap some of the gas from the propellants in the cartridge back into a cylinder to drive a piston. This piston extracted the cartridge case, reloaded and fired the gun. In 1895 the Browning machine gun was purchased by the US Navy.

From a slow start, demand for Browning machine guns took off when the USA entered World War I and ordered them for the US Army on active service in France.

Light firepower

Light machine guns developed in the 1930s played a profound part in World War II, as well as in conflicts for years afterwards. The French Chatellerault was fielded by paratroops in the doomed battle of Dien Bien Phu, Vietnam in 1954, while numerous liberation armies in Africa and Asia used the Soviet-supplied DP LMG. The Czech ZB vz/26 was used by all the combatants in World War II and forms the model for the British Bren gun.

The Mitrailleuse de 7.5mm Mle 1924/29

Also known as the Chatellerault, this gas-operated light machine gun was first introduced in 1924 and modified in 1929. It was used by the French armed forces from 1930 until the mid-1950s, when it was replaced by the AAT-F1 light machine gun. Adjusting the gas regulator along with the buffer allowed the gunner to vary his cyclic rate. What set the Chatellerault apart, however, was the new 7.5mm round that it had been developed to fire – a round that was as good as the German 7.92mm. Many Chatelleraults were captured after the fall of France in 1940 and were used by the Germans in coastal defences and in improvised AA mountings.

The M1924/29 had a top-loading 25-round box magazine and a cyclic rate of 500 rpm. It was easy to use in the roles of both LMG and SAW. It had two triggers: the rear one for fully automatic fire and the other for semi-automatic. The Model 31, which had a 150-round drum magazine, was a version of the Chatellerault built specifically for the Maginot Line fortifications.

The ZB vz/26 LMG

Soon after World War I, at the newly formed Czech armaments firm of Ceskoslovenska Zbrojovka at Brno, the talented small arms designer Vaclav Holek was charged by the Czechoslovakian Army to produce a new light machine gun. Holek was assisted by his brother Emmanuel, as well as other experts.

Work on what would become the 7.92mm ZB-vz.26 began in 1923. Within a year Holek's team had produced a prototype light machine gun. Following modifications, the Czechoslovakian Army quickly adopted the ZB as the vz.26, and many other countries later adopted the ZB or similar designs. The main users were China, Czechoslovakia, Lithuania, Yugoslavia, Romania, the Soviet Union, Spain, Sweden, Turkey and Japan. After World War II, guns seized from the Nationalist Chinese by their Communist Chinese opponents entered the arsenal of North Vietnam and were used in the Vietnam War.

The ZB-vz/26 fired from a 20- or 30-round box magazine at 500–550 rpm. It had an effective range of 1,000m/1,095yd.

RIGHT The French Chatellerault LMG was an excellent weapon that served with French and colonial forces in the conflicts in Indo-China and Algeria as well as in World War II.

box magazine

flash eliminator

double trigger

bipod

butt strap

magazine release catch

cooling fins on barrel

LEFT The Czech ZB vz/26 LMG fired from a 20- or 30-round box magazine. It was normally used in the light role with the gunner using the bipod mounted near the muzzle. The gun illustrated has the less widely used tripod.

RIGHT In the front line in the summer of 1942 a Soviet soldier spoons stew from his mess tin. His DP LMG rests on its bipod, ready to hand. His comrades are armed with the ubiquitous PPSh-41 SMG.

Vasily Alekseyevich Degtyarev

Born on 2 January 1880 at Tula, south of Moscow, Vasily Alekseyevich Degtyarev was to become a prolific Russian weapons engineer. For this work his titles and honours would include Major General of the Engineers and Artillery Service, Doctor of Technical Sciences in 1940, and two weeks after Joseph Stalin had been awarded Hero of Socialist Labour that year, Degtyarev received the second such award in its history. Interestingly for a man so closely involved with the Soviet Union, he did not become a Communist Party member until 1941.

Degtyarev was the first head of a Soviet small arms bureau. The bureau designed and developed the DshK1938 and DT machine guns, the PPD 34/38 and 40 submachine guns and the PTRD-41 anti-tank rifle. For this work Degtyarev received the State Award of the USSR in 1941, 1942 and 1944. He was also awarded the Order of Lenin three times, along with numerous medals and awards. After his death on 16 January 1949 in Moscow, he was posthumously awarded his fourth State Award of the USSR.

The DP LMG

The Ruchnoy Pulemyot Degtyareva pekhotnyi – Degtyarev hand-held infantry machine gun, or simply the DP, was a gas-operated light machine gun adopted by the Red Army in 1928. It fired the powerful 7.62 x 54R round and was cheap and easy to manufacture: early models had fewer than 80 parts and could be built by unskilled labourers. The DP had only six working parts and was especially able to withstand dirt. Indeed, Soviet soldiers joked that the gun fired better if sand were thrown on it. However, the bipod was weak, the pan-shaped drum magazine (normally loaded with 47 rounds) took time to fit on to the gun, and each magazine was slow to load. Its positive points were an inherent lower rate of continuous fire (500–600 rpm), which reduced the risk of the barrel overheating and it had an effective range of 800m/875yd. An improved version of the gun, the DPM, was introduced in 1944, and the gun was not replaced in service until the 1960s, when the PK machine gun was introduced.

Defective designs

The Italian Mitriaglice Fiat 1914/35 has the appearence of a good medium machine gun, just as the Breda Modello 30 has the look of a good light machine gun. However, appearances can be deceptive. Both guns had some troublesome design defects that only came to light when the unfortunate soldiers were in action in the front line. The German Flugzeugmaschinen-gewehr MG 15 and 17 were tested in action in Luftwaffe bombers, before they were modified for a ground role.

The Mitriaglice Fiat 1914/35

From 1935 onwards the Italians modernized the old Fiat 1914. The new machine gun, the Mitriaglice Modello 1914/35, had a 300-round belt feed. The water jacket had been removed and replaced with a heavy

air-cooled, quick-change barrel. The gun was rebarreled for the larger calibre of 8mm, and engineers at Fiat hoped that this would mean that they could dispense with the oiler. However, the old violent blow-back mechanism (the way that the recoil from the exploding cartridge pushes back the bolt and a new round is fed in) had been retained from the Revelli-designed Fiat 1914. To reduce wear and tear from this violent action, the oiler had to be reintroduced. Despite all these modifications, the gun was not a success; in fact, many old soldiers said it was worse than the Fiat 1914. Among the undesirable features was the tendency for the barrel to overheat and, as always in the desert, the oiler attracted dust and dirt that clogged the mechanism. The Germans, who were always keen to use any available weapons, gave the Fiat 1914/35 the designation 8mm sMG255(i). Although it was widely available from captured stocks in 1943, they do not appear to have used it. They were probably aware of its deficiencies. The complete gun with its tripod weighed in at 36.6kg/81.25lb. It fired 500 rounds per minute and could be used both in a ground role and as a light anti-aircraft gun.

The Fucile Mitragliatore Breda modello 30

This was the standard light machine gun of the Italian Army during World War II. It was widely regarded as a poor weapon: it had fired the underpowered 6.5 x 52mm cartridge in 20-round clips that were inserted into a fragile hinged magazine, and the gun was prone to jamming. It had a cyclic rate of fire of 450–500 rounds per minute.

LEFT Here the Mitriaglice Fiat 1914/35 appears on a high-angle anti-aircraft mount during the Italian campaign in the Balkans of 1939–41. While one man keeps the mount stable, the other holds the belted ammunition so that it will feed smoothly when the gunner fires.

sights

butt strap

bipod

sling

The weapon fired from a closed bolt and had a small lubricating device that sprayed oil on each cartridge as it entered the chamber. However, this caused the chamber and barrel to heat rapidly, which in turn caused rounds to fire prematurely, or "cook off", before they were fully in the chamber. The oil from the lubrication also quickly picked up dust and debris, making the weapon highly prone to jamming during fighting in North Africa.

Some Bredas were modified to fire the new 7.35mm cartridge that was being introduced into service and designated modello 38. However, production problems with the new ammunition meant that this was a short-lived programme.

The Flugzeugmaschinengewehr MG15 and 17
Based on the system of the Rheinmetall MG30, the Flugzeugmaschinengewehr MG15 and MG17 were the standard aircraft machine guns fitted to most German combat aircraft in 1939. The MG15 was developed by Rheinmetall in Borsig as a flexible-mounted defence machine gun for bombers, and the MG17 was the fixed forward-firing armament for fighters such as the Messerschmitt Bf 109E. Both weapons were air cooled and recoil operated. The MG15 firing at 850 rpm was magazine fed from Doppeltrommel (double-drum) magazines containing 75 rounds, while the MG17 was belt fed. Both used Mauser 7.92mm ammunition.

When, later in World War II, the Luftwaffe concentrated on 13 and 15mm machine guns, the MG15 was distributed to ground troops – mainly the field units of the Luftwaffe. Since production of the MG34 and MG42 could never meet the demand from

ABOVE The Italian Fucile Mitragliatori Breda modello 30 was one of the first air-cooled machine guns with a quick-change barrel. It had evolved from the Breda modello 1924 via the modello 1928.

Anti-aircraft ammunition

Machine guns firing rifle-calibre ammunition were only effective against low-flying aircraft if they were used en masse. Weapons such as the heavy Browning .50 and DshK1938 were capable of taking down aircraft. Yet one of the most effective features of these weapons was the deterrent value of the tracer ammunition. For the gunner, the burning tracers allowed him to correct his aim against moving targets. For the pilot of a bomb-laden aircraft diving towards a target on the ground, the sky filled with flashing tracer, which could put him off his aim. Tracers proved effective against aircraft as late as the Falklands War in 1982.

ground forces, reworking the aircraft machine guns for a ground role began in 1942. The modifications involved new sights, a shoulder stock, a tripod or bipod mount, a spent cartridge deflector and a carrying sling. It was widely used in garrison and guard units and issued to formations of the German Volksturm, the home guard, at the end of the war. Four MG17s could be mounted together in an anti-aircraft role, and with a combined rate of fire of 4,400 rpm they were a potent low-level anti-aircraft weapon deployed as a stop-gap in the last two years of the war.

SAS guns

The light .303 drum-fed Vickers-Berthier machine gun would prove an ideal weapon for the Special Air Service Regiment (SAS) jeeps in World War II – armed with these machine guns they caused chaos behind German lines in North Africa and Europe. Sometimes the jeeps came under fire from German MG34s, their weapons firing almost twice as fast as the VB guns. In contrast, the Japanese Type 92 had a slow rate of fire.

ABOVE US Marines on Iwo Jima with a captured Japanese Type 92 machine gun. The 30-round stripper clip feed can be clearly seen.

The Type 92 machine gun

It is unusual for weapons to be given nicknames by the men who are their targets, but the Type 92 Shiki Kikanju Heavy Machine Gun (HMG) had such a low rate of fire at 450–500 rpm and curious stuttering effect that it was known as the "Woodpecker" by Allied soldiers. Allied troops under fire from the Type 92 always recognized it.

In the 1930s, the Japanese had realized that the small 6.5mm round fired by their soldiers was not powerful enough, and a new 7.7mm round was produced. It was introduced into new weapons, including the Type 92, a variation on the Hotchkiss design. Unlike the Hotchkiss, however, the Type 92 was heavy (over 54.5kg/120lb with the tripod; the tripod legs had holes drilled through the "feet" to take poles so that two men could carry it more easily.) The new gun bore was similar to the Type 3, including the oil dispenser required to ensure a smooth feed for the ammunition that was fed from 30 round metal clips.

The Vickers-Berthier

The Vickers "K" or VGO or CO gun was a gas-operated machine gun based on a French Berthier design that Vickers had bought in 1925. It had a cyclic rate of fire of 950–1,000 rpm and a 100-round magazine, although it was normally loaded with 96 rounds to prevent over-compression on the spring. It had a muzzle velocity of 745m/s/2,444ft/s and weighed 11.1kg/24.4lb. The guns were mounted in RAF Hawker Hart aircraft, and when these aircraft became obsolete this was the source of armament for SAS jeeps in North Africa and Europe. K guns were mounted in

ABOVE The Vickers-Berthier K gun had been designed for inter-war RAF fighters. The SAS took surplus weapons and mounted them on jeeps to produce fast, compact vehicles with an awesome firepower.

pairs on the front and rear of SAS jeeps. Such a vehicle therefore had the potential firepower of nearly 4,000 rounds of tracer and ball ammunition per minute.

ABOVE A German grenadier with an MG34 scans the surroundings from a lookout post. The barrel of the gun was air cooled through the holes in the protective metal sleeve, but it could also be changed quickly.

The MG34

To many Allied soldiers the German infantry appeared less as riflemen and more as ammunition carriers for the formidable 7.92mm MG34 machine gun, known by the Allies as the Spandau after its place of manufacture. This gun was 1,220mm/48in long with a 625mm/24.6in barrel, weighed 11.9kg/26.2lb in the light role and 31.1kg/68.5lb on the sustained fire mount. With a muzzle velocity of 755m/s/2,477ft/s, it had a maximum range of 2,000m/2,190yd and a cyclic rate of 800–900 rpm. It fired from a 75-round saddle-drum magazine or 50-round non-disintegrating belts. It was a remarkable design that drew on experience in World War I, during which heavy water-cooled weapons were difficult to handle.

One of the other spurs for the development of the revolutionary air-cooled weapon was accidental. According to the 1919 Treaty of Versailles, Germany was forbidden to construct water-cooled machine guns like the cumbersome MG08.

The MG34 was the world's first General-Purpose Machine Gun (GPMG) that could be used in a light role in the attack and in defence as a medium machine gun. When used in defence, it was mounted on the MG-Lafatte 34, a lightweight folding tripod that could be set at two positions – high and low. The tripod could also be converted into an anti-aircraft mount.

SAS jeep attack

In July 1942, Major David Stirling of the British Special Air Service Regiment (SAS) decided to attack Landing Ground 21, the airfield at Sidi Haneish, Egypt, using a V-shaped formation of two columns of seven jeeps commanded by Earl George Jellicoe and Paddy Mayne, with Stirling leading. They were to drive down the runway, engaging the lines of aircraft with their Vickers K guns, a total firepower of 68. To ensure surprise, the attack would be on a night with a full moon.

On the night of 26 July they set off. They hit the airfield at speed, the machine guns opened fire and Stirling fired a green Very light, the signal for the V formation. Recalling it afterwards, the men told Virginia Cowles, the author of *Phantom Major.* "The planes took longer to catch fire than the men had imagined. It was perhaps thirty seconds before the interior of the aircraft suddenly glowed red, followed by the dull thud of exploding petrol, which turned the whole body into a sheet of flame. Some planes did not burn but seemed literally to crumble and disintegrate as the bullets ploughed into them from less than fifty yards."

A hero's gun

The Japanese Type 96 light machine gun (LMG) drew on some of the design features of the earlier Czech ZB 26. The Bren gun, also based on the Czech ZB 26, became the British and Commonwealth section LMG in World War II. Even as late as 21 November 1965 it was the weapon with which brave junior NCOs such as L. Naik Rambahadur Limbu of the 2/10th Gurkha Rifles won the highest award for gallantry: the Victoria Cross. Another Czech weapon, the ZB vz/53, was fielded by both the Germans and the British in World War II.

The Type 96 LMG

The Japanese 6.5mm Type 96 LMG was introduced in 1936. A number of ideas were taken from the Czechoslovakian ZB 26 (an LMG design manufactured at the small arms factory in Brno, Czechoslovakia) and the Hotchkiss machine gun. The Type 96 LMG had a curved 30-round box magazine and a cyclic rate of 550 rpm. The reduced-power Meiji 30 cartridge produced a muzzle velocity of 730m/s/2,394ft/s; this cartridge should not have caused a feed problem but in fact the gun still needed an oil dispenser to ensure a smooth feed. The Type 96 had a quick-change barrel and drum or telescopic sights. It could be fitted with a Model 30 sword bayonet, although launching a bayonet charge carrying a 9kg/20lb LMG would have been rather challenging to slightly built Japanese soldiers.

ABOVE A Japanese paratrooper armed with the 6.5mm Type 96 LMG. The gun drew on a number of Western design concepts. A typical Japanese feature was that it could be fitted with a bayonet for close combat.

Corporal Tom Hunter VC

In the last weeks of World War II on 2 April 1945, Corporal Tom Hunter's troop from 43 Royal Marine Commando came under heavy and constant fire from three German MG42s dug in close to a group of houses near to Lake Comacchio in northern Italy.

Picking up his Bren gun, Hunter charged the houses single-handedly across 183m/200yd of open ground. He came under intense fire but so determined was his charge that six German gunners surrendered and the rest fled. Changing magazines as he ran, he cleared the house of the enemy. He drew heavy incoming fire but continued until the rest of his troop found safety. Shortly after, Cpl Hunter was killed still firing his Bren gun.

He is buried in the Argenta Gap Cemetery in Emilia-Romagna, Italy.

The Bren gun

The British Bren gun was initially built in 1937 at the Royal Small Arms Factory at Enfield and was based on the Czechoslvakian-designed ZB vz/26 light machine gun. It was tested by British Army officials in the 1930s. A licence to manufacture was obtained and the Czech design modified to British requirements. The two factory names (Brno and Enfield) were combined to produce the name Bren, and the gun continued in use from World War II to the Gulf War of 1991.

The Bren was an air-cooled gas-operated weapon that fired a .303 round from a 30-round box magazine. It had a slow rate of fire – 500 rpm – but was extremely accurate, with sights set out to 1,830m/2,000yd. It was also light, weighing only 10kg/22.1lb, and measured 1,155mm/45.5in in length.

flash eliminator

foresight

carrying handle

barrel

magazine

magazine catch

gas regulator

return spring

piston

trigger

bipod

It was easy to strip, and experienced gunners could change magazines or barrels in less than five seconds. Bren guns were also made in Australia, Canada and India during World War II. When, after the war, the British Army standardized its rifle ammunition with NATO and adopted 7.62mm, the versatile Bren was re-engineered to take the cartridge and with it a magazine with a flatter curve that was interchangeable with the L1A1 SLR magazine. This meant that, in a contact, riflemen in a section could resupply ammunition to the LMG crew. The Bren could be mounted on a bipod, tripod or vehicle mounted.

The ZB vz/53 medium machine gun

The Czech ZB vz/53, designed by Vaclav Holek, was first produced in Brno in 1937 and entered service with the Czechoslovakian Army as the Kulomet vz/37. Captured guns were designated by the Germans as the 7.92mm MG 37 (t) and issued widely, often to Waffen-SS units. The British had obtained a production licence before the war and produced it as the Gun, Machine, Besa, building 59,322 of them, which were fitted to tanks. Among the British tanks that fielded the Besa were the Churchill, Valentine, Matilda and Cromwell.

The ZB vz/53 was unusual, with a quick-change barrel (normally fitted to LMGs) and two rates of fire: 500 or 700 rpm, firing from a 100- or 200-round metal link belt. The Besa was a very reliable gun which had a tripod mount that could be adjusted as an AA mount as well as a fortress mount for embrasures in fortifications.

ABOVE The later Bren featured a curved box magazine, conical flash eliminator and barrel that could be quickly changed. In the 1950s the Bren was rebarrelled to accept the 7.62 x 51mm NATO cartridge. It could be fitted on a bipod, or mounted on a vehicle.

BELOW The .303 Bren, with its characteristic curved magazine, remained in service with the British Army after the war. When 7.62mm ammunition was standardized by NATO, the gun was rebarrelled and fitted with a new magazine.

Enduring designs

The German MG42 and Soviet DShk and SG43 are three machine guns that have enjoyed a remarkable operational life. The MG42 has been the basis for numerous automatic weapons and remains the touchstone for all general purpose machine guns.

sights

cocking handle

bipod

plastic pistol grip

plastic butt

ABOVE The German Maschinengewehr MG42 machine gun had a practical rate of fire of 250 rounds per minute in the light role and 500 in the medium.

The Degtyarev DShk 1938

The large Krupnokaliberny Pulemet Degtyareva-Shpagina, DShK or "Degtyarev-Shpagin, large calibre" 12.7mm/.50 entered service with the Red Army in 1939 and remained in production until 1980. Soviet soldiers nicknamed it the "Dushka". Although it has been compared to the .50 Browning HMG, it was not a recoil-operated gun but used a gas system developed by Georgiy Shpagin that has a three-positions gas regulator. The Dushka was used throughout World War II as an anti-aircraft weapon on tanks like the

ABOVE The Soviet DshK 1938 12.7mm/.50 in service as an anti-aircraft gun aboard a Soviet naval craft. The gun had an effective range of 1,500m/1,641yd.

heavy IS-3, in twin and quad AA mounts and even on river craft. As a formidable heavy infantry support gun it was mounted on a modified version of the Maxim Sokolov mount.

After the war, the modernized version DShK Modernized (DShK-M), also known as DShKM-38/46, was mounted on Soviet tanks such as the T-55 and T-62, and armoured reconnaissance vehicles and personnel carriers. The DShKM was also manufactured in China, Iran, Yugoslavia and Pakistan. It was widely used in numerous post-1945 conflicts including Vietnam, the Arab-Israeli wars, and more recently, the Soviet and NATO campaigns in Afghanistan. The DShKM was one of the most successful designs of its time.

The muzzle velocity is 850m/s/2,788ft/s, and the gun fires at 600 rpm from a 50-round belt. The AP rounds can pierce 15mm/0.6in of armour at 500m/547yd.

The MG42

The MG42 replaced the MG34 during World War II. Designed by Dr Grunow of Grossfuss-Werke, it used stamping and spot-welding to speed the manufacturing process. When the Allies captured their first MG42s in Tunisia, they thought that stamping and spot welding indicated a cheap and shoddy weapon. Nothing could have been further from the truth. The MG42 entered service in 1942 and by 1945 some 750,000 had been produced. The gun introduced the quick barrel change that was essential for fast firing air-cooled weapons.

LEFT A Waffen SS soldier cleans his MG34. It has been said that many automatic weapons have been worn out not by constant firing but by constant cleaning; it is essential to keep weapons clean. Gas-operated weapons can foul up with hard carbon that builds up around narrow apertures such as the gas regulator, which can cause stoppages and jams.

The gun was 122cm/48in long with a 53.3cm/21in barrel and weighed 11.8kg/26lb in the light role and 29.7kg/65.3lb on the sustained fire mount. With a muzzle velocity of 755m/s/2,746ft/s, it fired 50- and 250-round metal-belted ammunition and had a maximum range of 2,000m/2,188yd and a cyclic rate of 1,550. A US Army Intelligence Bulletin identified the drawback of this high rate of fire: "the gun has a tendency to 'throw off', so that its fire stays on target for a much briefer time than does that of the slower firing MG34". German gunners were therefore instructed to fire bursts of between five to seven rounds when firing in the light role. The gunners also aimed low and the Intelligence Bulletin noted a comment from a GI who remarked, "German machine gun fire is usually so low – often about a foot and a half above the ground – that we call it 'grass cutting.'"

The SG43 and SGM MMG

In the early 1940s the Red Army realized that the old PM1910 machine gun was being outclassed by the German MG34 and later MG42 machine guns. The need for a new weapon was addressed by the talented Goryunov brothers, who produced the Stankovii Pulemet Goryunova Obrazets 1943G, or simply the SG43. This gun combined in its mechanism features from Degtyarev, Browning and other weapons. It was a robust and reliable weapon that fired at 500–640 rpm to a maximum effective range of 1,000m/1,094yd from a 50-round metal-link belt. The gun was 40.7kg/89.5lb on its two-wheel mount, which compared favourably to the complete weight of a PM1910: a staggering 74kg/163lb.

Among the variants of the SG43 were the SGMT co-axial tank gun and the SGMB vehicle-mounted gun. As late as the mid-1990s the SG43 was still in service in Egypt, China, the Middle East and Southeast Asia.

The MG42 in war

US soldiers who encountered the MG42 in the wooded cover of the bocage of Normandy in June and July 1944 said that the ripping sound of the fast-firing MG42 resembled the sound of a sheet of calico being torn apart.

Sydney Jary, a young British infantry platoon commander in Normandy, recalled "I remember my first reaction to actual infantry warfare in July 1944 was one of amazement at the crushing fire-power of these rapid-firing guns . . . firing long sustained bursts, the object of which seemed to me to keep us pinned to the ground regardless of the ammunition expenditure. Typically German – protracted and discordant."

BELOW The Soviet SGM machine gun developed during World War II could be fired from a wheeled ground mount by infantry or was mounted in armoured fighting vehicles both as a co-axial and an AA gun.

spade grips   ejection port

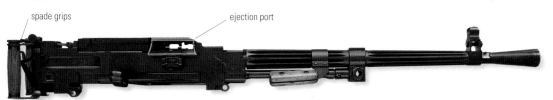

General-Purpose Machine Guns

The GPMG (general-purpose machine gun), which was exemplified by the MG42, would be regarded as an essential weapon by all armies after the war, and widely copied. The French had their AAT-52 and the Belgians their highly successful MAG, while the Russian belt-fed RPD LMG was a step towards the GPMG concept.

sights — barrel change handle

The AAT 52 GPMG

Designed by the French MAS company in the early 1950s, the Arme Automatique Transformable modèle 52 machine gun, better known simply as the "cinquante-deux", was adopted by the French Army in 7.5mm and later, after conversion to fire the 7.62mm NATO round, as the AAT F-1. It uses stampings wherever possible for ease and speed of production.

The AAT-52 uses 50- or 200-round belts and has a delayed blowback action and a rate of fire of 900 rpm. The quick-change barrel has a fluted chamber to assist extraction. In the light role the gun has a 50cm/20in, 2.9kg/6.4lb barrel, while in the sustained fire role it has a heavier 4.3kg/9.5lb barrel that is 60cm/2ft long.

The gun gave good service in Algeria in the 1960s and in numerous operations around the world. It is still in service with the French Army.

ABOVE The French AAT-52 in medium machine-gun role mounted on a US M2 tripod fitted with a heavy barrel. It has a practical range of 1,200m/1,320yd.

The RPD

The RPD 7.62mm light machine gun was designed by Vasily Degtyarev in the USSR in 1943 and introduced into service in the Soviet Army shortly after the end of World War II. It was adopted by Warsaw Pact forces and copied by China as the Type 56 and North Korea as the Type 62. The RPD weighs 7.1kg/15.6lb empty and fires a 7.62 x 39mm round from a 100-round disintegrating link belt housed in a drum clipped below the weapon. It fires only on automatic and has a cyclic rate of 700 rpm and an effective range of 800m/875yd. It works well in adverse conditions and is very easy to strip and assemble.

The FN MAG GPMG

The Belgian 7.62mm FN Mitrailleuse à Gaz, or MAG, is one of the most successful GPMGs to be manufactured since World War II. An FN design, it uses the feed mechanism developed by the Germans for the MG42 during the war. This gives it a rate of fire of 650–1,000 rpm, which can be adjusted by opening or closing the gas regulator controlling the flow of gas from the barrel back on to the cupped piston head. Gunners learn to "balance" their weapon so that this gas flow gives an optimum performance.

The MAG can be used in the light role with a bipod or on a sustained fire (SF) spring-buffered tripod.

ABOVE An Egyptian soldier taking part in a joint exercise with US Forces takes aim with an RPD LMG fitted with the 100-round magazine. The rugged weapon has performed well in the jungles of Asia as well as in the desert.

In the SF role a butt plate is fitted, and the rear sight flips up and shows ranges of 800–1,800m/ 875–1,970yd. An optical sight, similar to that on a mortar, can also be fitted; this allows the gun to be fired on pre-registered targets that may be obscured by darkness or smoke. In the light role the sights lie flat and are graduated between 200–800m/220–875 yards in 100m/110-yd intervals. The GPMG/MAG weighs 11.7kg/25.7lb empty and has an overall length of 126cm/50in. The rate of fire is 650–1,000 rpm and the

ABOVE An Israeli soldier in Lebanon in 1984 lounges by an M151 fitted with two MAGs. The one in the rear has had the butt removed and replaced with the butt plate for ease of operation in the confined space.

muzzle velocity is 840m/s/2,755ft/s. The MAG is probably the most successful general-purpose machine gun in the world. It is manufactured under licence in Argentina, Egypt, India, Singapore, the United States, and the UK.

GPMG hero

At 04.45 on 27 April 1965, in Plaman Mapu, Sarawak, a position held by 34 men from the British B Company HQ 2nd Battalion, the Parachute Regiment and a platoon of young soldiers fresh from the depot came under three attacks by a Javanese Para-Commando Regiment. Company Sergeant Major (CSM) Williams and other officers were with them, along with cooks, mortar crews and radio operators.

The Javanese gained a lodgement in the position. With the situation deteriorating, Williams grabbed a GPMG and clipped on two more belts to the one already on the gun. He recalls thinking,

"this is it, this is the end of the story anyway, so I'll give them a bit of rapid fire". He stood firing from the hip as a corporal led a counterattack. Several Indonesian commandos charged straight at Williams, the nearest being killed only 2m/2.2yd from him.

When the second assault came in, Williams brought another GPMG up and mortar bombs fired by the Paras fell only 30m/33yd away. This broke up the second assault.

The third attack, just before dawn at about 05.45, was not pressed home with great vigour. When Williams took out a clearing patrol he found one Indonesian, whom he killed.

Old concepts, new designs

Originating from the MG42, the German MG3 machine gun can truly be called an old soldier in the world of small arms design. The Russian RPK-74 is in concept a 7.62mm RPK scaled down to 5.45mm ammunition. The American M60, however, was a machine gun that caused considerable problems and was therefore very unpopular with its users.

optical sights

gas feed

change lever

ABOVE The RPK-74 is similar in concept to the British light support weapon: an infantry rifle with a longer barrel and bipod to give a squad an automatic weapon for engaging targets at longer range.

The Maschinengewehr MG3

The MG3 is a modified version of the German MG42 belt-fed, air-cooled machine gun adapted to fire 7.62mm NATO M13 or DM 6 disintegrating link or German DM 1 continuous link. (When continuous link has been fired, the empty belt hangs off the gun for reloading later; disintegrating link unclips itself as it is fired.) It is in service in many countries including Chile, Denmark, Saudi Arabia, Norway, Austria and Portugal. The Sarac, an MG3 copy, is built in the former Yugoslavia, and the MG3 is made under licence

in Greece, Iran, Italy, Pakistan, Spain and Turkey. The MG3 began life as the MG42/59 in 1959, and after 1968 went into mass production as the MG3.

The MG3 fires from an open bolt and has a short recoil barrel with the bolt locking into the barrel extension via two rollers. Like the MG42, the MG3 has a quick change barrel. The normal drill is to replace it after a 150-round burst. However, in contact this rate can be increased to 200 to 250. As a GPMG the MG3 has a very high rate of fire – between 700 and 1,300 rpm.

The RPK-74

The Soviet Ruchnoi Pulemet Kalashnikova-74, or RPK-74, was developed along with the AK-74 assault rifle as a ten-man squad-level light-support weapon firing the new, small-calibre 5.45mm ammunition. The RPK-74 was adopted by the Soviet Army in the late 1970s and is still in use with the Russian Army today. The RPK-74 has a cyclic rate of 600–650 and a practical rate of 150 rpm. The maximum effective range is 460m/503yd.

LEFT Bundeswehr soldiers with the MG3. The gunner is using the trigger extension grip for the gun's sustained fire mount. The litter of empty cases shows that this post-war clone of the MG42 has a high rate of fire. Its quick-change barrel is replaced after 150 rounds.

Internally the RPK-74 is almost the same as the AK-74 rifle – a select-fire, gas-operated, rotating bolt-locked weapon – but it has a heavier and longer fixed barrel with a bipod, and redesigned buttstock. The RPK-74 can be fed from 45-round box magazines or standard AK-74 30-round magazines. Drum magazines holding 75 rounds similar in design to those of the RPK were also developed. They are much in demand with Russian troops in Chechnya.

Versions of the RPK-74 with a side-mount for the 1LH51 night-vision scopes are called RPK-74N. The first RPK-74s were manufactured with wooden pistol grips and fixed buttstocks, but current guns have polymer grips and side-folding polymer buttstocks.

M60 GPMG

Entering service in the late 1950s, the American M60 GPMG was designed towards the end of the 1940s. Its design drew on a number of German wartime developments including the MG42 machine gun and FG 42 automatic rifle. It had no gas regulator, which sometimes resulted in the gun jamming if fouled or, less usually, in a "runaway gun". This occurred when the working parts went back far enough to feed, chamber and fire a round but not far enough to be engaged by the sear, so that even if the pressure is taken off the trigger the gun keeps on firing. In these conditions the only option is to hold on to the belt to prevent it from feeding.

The M60 can be mounted as a sustained fire gun or on vehicles and has a quick-change barrel and integral bipod. Both the M60 and M60E3 have a cyclic rate of 550 rpm.

ABOVE A grizzled US soldier in Vietnam has belts of 7.62mm ammunition ready for use for his M60, draped over a tree trunk to ensure that they do not foul in the mud on the jungle floor.

The M60 – "The Pig"

The M60 machine gun was a weapon that seemed fine in theory but for soldiers in Vietnam terrible design defects were obvious. The bipod and the gas cylinder were permanently attached to the barrel, so quick barrel changes after firing bursts of 200 rounds proved extremely difficult during a contact. To handle the barrel, the Number 2 on the gun required a heat-protecting mitten, which was often lost on patrol or in a contact. Finally, key components in the operating group, such as the firing pin, were prone to fracturing. Unsurprisingly, the gun came to be known by frustrated soldiers in Vietnam as "the Pig". A lighter version of the gun, designated the M60E3, was subsequently produced but it was actually no great improvement. It did have a non-removable gas cylinder supporting the bipod, and the new barrel had a carrying handle so barrel changes were quicker and easier. However, the new lightened gun was actually less reliable; the light barrel would burn out if 200 to 300 rounds were fired on fully automatic, so it had to be changed after 100 rounds in rapid fire.

New developments

While the Soviet PK machine gun and even the Belgian FN Minimi are significant improvements on the concept of a General-Purpose Machine Gun; the M134 and M61 look back to the Gatling concept.

ABOVE The first American female aerial gunner, photographed in 2002, appears in the door of an HH-60G Pave Hawk helicopter, equipped with a 7.62 M134 minigun.

M134 minigun

In Vietnam in the 1960s the US Army realized it was essential to arm its helicopters. It was necessary to deliver a heavy weight of fire over a short period of time, so designers at General Electric scaled down the proven M61 gun to enable it to fire 7.62 x 51mm NATO ammunition. The weapon designated the M134 Minigun had a phenomenal rate of fire of 4,000 rpm. It was normally mounted in chin turrets or wing pods on AH-1G Cobra attack helicopters. Usually, the AH-1G Cobra carried one or two miniguns in its chin turret, with 2,000–4,000 rounds of ammunition. The guns were also installed on door, pylon and pod mounts on UH-1 Huey helicopters, and on fixed-wing gunships such as the A/C-47 Dakota, nicknamed "Puff the Magic Dragon" after a children's television show.

PK machine gun

The development of a new 7.62mm General-Purpose Machine Gun (GPMG) for the Soviet Army began around 1953, and the lead was taken by the Nikitin-Sokolov (NS) machine gun. The Kalashnikov design bureau submitted a design in 1958, at the request of the Soviet Ministry of Defence, to provide a competitor for the NS gun. After extensive trials the Kalashnikov design was adopted as a new general-purpose machine gun, replacing the DPM light, RP-46 medium/company and SGM heavy machine guns in service. The PK fires from 100-, 200- or 250-round belts at a cyclic rate of 650 rpm.

A tank version that replaced the older SGMT was later developed by Kalashnikov with the designation PKT. Following user reports from the Soviet Army, a modified version of the PKM was adopted in 1969. It had an improved barrel and shorter flash hider, a stamped belt feed and was overall a lighter weapon. The sustained-fire PKMS had a new simple, lighter tripod. The PKM and its variants are still in production in Russia and it is in service in the Russian Army, former Warsaw Pact forces and many other forces worldwide. Copies – both licensed and pirated – have been made in Bulgaria, China, Poland, Romania and the former Yugoslavia.

ABOVE PK machine guns captured by US forces in Grenada in 1983. The gun has been exported throughout the world and copied by manufacturers in Europe and China. It is in widespread use in Iraq and Afghanistan.

RIGHT The FN Minimi is a light weapon that is comfortable to fire and has proved popular with soldiers because its belt feed allows it to deliver a high volume of fire.

cocking handle

gas regulator

ammunition box feed

Kalashnikov later developed a tank version, designated as PKT, which replaced in service older SGMT machine guns. Based on the initial experience, in 1969 the Soviet Army adopted the modified PKM machine gun, which had an updated barrel with shorter flash hider, stamped belt feed and a generally lightened construction. The PKMS (tripod-mounted) version also had a new, lighter tripod of simpler design. The PKM series of machine guns are still manufactured in Russia and are used by the Russian Army and armies of several other ex-USSR republics. In addition, PK/PKM copies are made in Bulgaria, China, Poland, Romania and Yugoslavia.

The FN Minimi

The Minimi light machine gun, designed by the Belgian Fabrique Nationale (FN), can fire, feeding from the left, either belted disintegrating link SS 109 NATO or US M193 5.5mm ammunition or it can fire from 30-round box magazines that are compatible with the American M16 and most NATO rifles. A 200-round box of belted ammunition can be clipped directly to the Minimi, making it a formidable close-quarter battle (CQB) weapon. Gas operated, the Minimi is normally fired from its bipod, though a sustained fire tripod is available. The gun has a gas regulator with two settings: normal and adverse. The latter ensures a sufficient flow of gas against the piston to clear a malfunction. The adjustment can be made even with a hot barrel. It does not have the recoil forces of a full-size 7.62mm round and so consequently it can be fired with greater accuracy.

The Minimi has been adopted by the Australians as the F89, the US as the M249 Squad Automatic Weapon (SAW), and also by the Belgian, Canadian, Indonesian and Italian Armed forces.

Back to the Gatling

By the early 1950s, the newly formed US Air Force realized that the speed of new jet fighters had made conventional gas or recoil-operated machine guns or cannon obsolete. The General Electric Company was approached to produce a new fast-firing gun under the project name "Vulcan". Multi-barrelled weapons seemed a promising research path, since between shots the barrels would have time to cool. In trials, 19th-century Gatlings were fitted with electrical drive instead of the manually operated crank. No longer reliant on muscle power, the gun had a staggering rate of fire of about 4,000 rounds per minute.

Further development resulted in some experimental, electrically driven, six barrelled .60-calibre machine guns, and in 1956, the six-barrelled 20mm T171 gun was officially adopted as the M61 aircraft gun capable of 4,000–6,000 rpm. M61 became the main aircraft gun for USAF fighters, and is also used by the US Army on the M161 and M163 Vulcan ground anti-aircraft gun mounts. The US Navy also returned to the Gatling with the Vulcan-Phalanx CIWS (Close-In Weapon System) designed to shred fast sea-skimming anti-ship missiles.

BELOW US soldiers on exercise in West Germany in the 1980s with a M161 Vulcan air defence system. The high rate of fire would be lethal against helicopters and low-flying ground attack aircraft.

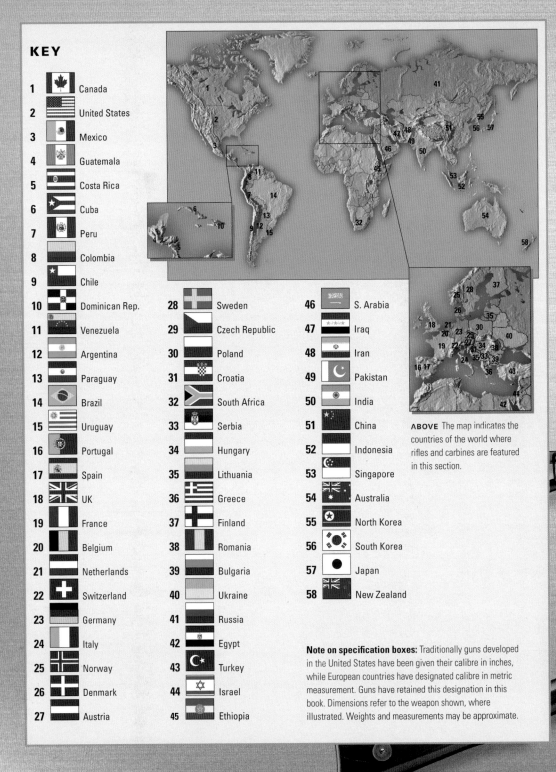

KEY

1. Canada
2. United States
3. Mexico
4. Guatemala
5. Costa Rica
6. Cuba
7. Peru
8. Colombia
9. Chile
10. Dominican Rep.
11. Venezuela
12. Argentina
13. Paraguay
14. Brazil
15. Uruguay
16. Portugal
17. Spain
18. UK
19. France
20. Belgium
21. Netherlands
22. Switzerland
23. Germany
24. Italy
25. Norway
26. Denmark
27. Austria

28. Sweden
29. Czech Republic
30. Poland
31. Croatia
32. South Africa
33. Serbia
34. Hungary
35. Lithuania
36. Greece
37. Finland
38. Romania
39. Bulgaria
40. Ukraine
41. Russia
42. Egypt
43. Turkey
44. Israel
45. Ethiopia

46. S. Arabia
47. Iraq
48. Iran
49. Pakistan
50. India
51. China
52. Indonesia
53. Singapore
54. Australia
55. North Korea
56. South Korea
57. Japan
58. New Zealand

ABOVE The map indicates the countries of the world where rifles and carbines are featured in this section.

Note on specification boxes: Traditionally guns developed in the United States have been given their calibre in inches, while European countries have designated calibre in metric measurement. Guns have retained this designation in this book. Dimensions refer to the weapon shown, where illustrated. Weights and measurements may be approximate.

A directory of rifles and carbines from around the world

A variety of countries around the world produce and manufacture firearms. Some produce arms that are unique, while others produce or import versions of firearms from other countries under licence, sometimes with different fittings and specifications. Rifles are long guns, with rifled barrels, that can be fired from the standing, kneeling and prone position. Carbines are shorter, lighter and more portable than rifles. This directory is a cross-section of selected countries of the world – west to east – and some of the rifles and carbines that are available in those countries and their main features. Within each country guns are organized alphabetically by manufacturer except where its historical development is shown more clearly chronologically or a company changes its name. Each firearm has a description and a specification that lists its vital measurements, including its calibre and operating method.

ABOVE Light and compact, this modern carbine, the AKS-74U, is not much larger than the shoulder-stocked handguns of World War I.

ABOVE This assault weapon, the Stg 44, could have changed Germany's fortunes on the Eastern Front in World War II had it been in full production before autumn 1942.

ABOVE The .303 No. 4 Mk 1 was the best bolt-action rifle of World War II. Despite its speed of use, no soldier with a bolt-action rifle could deliver as much firepower as with a semi-automatic.

 Canada

Canada primarily used Commonwealth firearms, but also had numerous designers and manufacturing plants. In both World Wars Canada produced its own small arms. In 1903 it adopted the Canadian-designed Ross rifle. The failure of that rifle led to the use of SMLE Mark III* (Lee-Enfield) in 1916. Manufacture of military rifles in Canada re-started with the Long Branch Arsenal in Ontario making arms in 1940. After World War II Canada adopted the Fusil Automatique Léger (FAL), also made in Ontario.

Diemaco C7

The C7 was the Canadian version of the American M-16 rifle, the primary military rifle of the United States in the 1960s. When the United States upgraded the Colt M-16 to the M-16A2 in the late 1980s, it made sense for Canada to adopt a similar rifle. The C7 was an M-16 clone built by the Diemaco Corporation in Ontario. The barrel was upgraded and the lower receiver (which houses the operating parts of the gun) reinforced to prevent cracking at weak points. The M-16A1 sights were retained on the C7. The C7 was adopted in 1986 and is used to the present day.

SPECIFICATION	
MANUFACTURER Diemaco Corporation	
CALIBRE 5.56 x 45mm	
MAGAZINE CAPACITY 20, 30	
ACTION Gas operated/rotating bolt	
TOTAL LENGTH 1,016mm/40in	
BARREL LENGTH 508mm/20in	
WEIGHT UNLOADED 3.85kg/8.5lb	

Diemaco C8A1

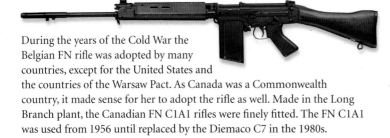

Trijon Acog scope

Along with the M-16A2, Canada adopted the American M4, an M-16 carbine. The M4 was intended to be a carbine for support troops, but it proved so successful that it was sought after by troops and units at all levels. As with the C7, the C8A1 was an improvement on the M4 rather than just a clone. The C8A1 uses a hammer-forged barrel, like the C7, for greater accuracy and longevity. However, like the M4, the C8A1 suffers from loss of velocity due to the barrel being shorter than the M-16. This is a common feature of all carbines, but a particular problem with the 5.56 x 45mm cartridge, which needs high bullet velocity to be effective. The Diemaco C8A1 was adopted immediately after Colt developed the M4 in 1995 and is still in use.

SPECIFICATION	
MANUFACTURER Diemaco Corporation	
CALIBRE 5.56 x 45mm	
MAGAZINE CAPACITY 20, 30	
ACTION Gas operated/rotating bolt	
TOTAL LENGTH 838mm/33in	
BARREL LENGTH 370mm/14.5in	
WEIGHT UNLOADED 2.52kg/5.55lb	

FN C1A1

During the years of the Cold War the Belgian FN rifle was adopted by many countries, except for the United States and the countries of the Warsaw Pact. As Canada was a Commonwealth country, it made sense for her to adopt the rifle as well. Made in the Long Branch plant, the Canadian FN C1A1 rifles were finely fitted. The FN C1A1 was used from 1956 until replaced by the Diemaco C7 in the 1980s.

SPECIFICATION	
MANUFACTURER Long Branch	
CALIBRE 7.62 x 51mm	
MAGAZINE CAPACITY 20	
ACTION Gas operated/tilting lock	
TOTAL LENGTH 1,136mm/44.75in	
BARREL LENGTH 533mm/21in	
WEIGHT UNLOADED 4.3kg/9.5lb	

Ross Mark 3

SPECIFICATION	
MANUFACTURER Ross Rifle Co.	
CALIBRE .303 British	
MAGAZINE CAPACITY 5	
ACTION Straight-pull bolt action	
TOTAL LENGTH 1,279mm/50.36in	
BARREL LENGTH 768mm/30.25in	
WEIGHT UNLOADED 4.47kg/9.85lb	

Canadian Sir Charles Ross patented the Ross rifle at the turn of the 20th century. The Mark 3 Ross, developed a decade later, was fast and accurate. Yet the fine machining necessary for the design made it less than reliable when used in combat during World War I. When it was used in the mud, grit and ice of the trenches, the debris caught in the bolt bound the mechanism, and the Ross would quickly stop working. When the rumour spread that it could be reassembled incorrectly causing the bolt to blow out of the rifle, injuring the shooter, it quickly faded from use. The Ross Mark 3 was used from 1911 to 1914, when it was withdrawn from service except as a sniper rifle, and replaced with the SMLE Mark III* rifle.

Ross Mark 3 sniper

SPECIFICATION	
MANUFACTURER Ross Rifle Co.	
CALIBRE .303 British	
MAGAZINE CAPACITY 5	
ACTION Straight-pull bolt action	
TOTAL LENGTH 1,279mm/50.36in	
BARREL LENGTH 768mm/30.25in	
WEIGHT UNLOADED 4.87kg/10.75lb	

The accuracy of the Ross, coupled with the more thorough maintenance a sniper would be expected to give his rifle than a soldier in military combat, kept the Ross in use for precision shooting even after it had been withdrawn from general issue. The stripper clip (a device that holds several rounds of ammunition together in a single unit for easier loading) projected vertically from the action. The optical sights were mounted to the side of the rifle to clear the stripper clip guide or the rifle could not be loaded. The rifles were very accurate, but were soon withdrawn. The rifle was developed in 1914, but dropped by 1916.

United States

Proud of the title "a nation of riflemen", the United States has a long history of making accurate and powerful rifles. Deciding on which one was best suited to the needs of the Army, however, has not always been easy and attempts to replace rifles such as the M-16 have often failed because of the costs involved.

M1 Carbine, commercial

SPECIFICATION	
MANUFACTURER Alpine	
CALIBRE .30 carbine	
MAGAZINE CAPACITY 5, 15, 30	
ACTION Gas operated	
TOTAL LENGTH 905mm/35.65in	
BARREL LENGTH 457mm/18in	
WEIGHT UNLOADED 2.44kg/5.4lb	

The M1 military carbine was a compact and lightweight shoulder arm that was developed before World War II and issued to the US Army. Military production of the M1 had ceased by the 1960s. Although it took a while for surplus supplies to dwindle, the supply of military carbines was running low in the years after production stopped. This led to commercial manufacturers producing the carbine for civilian use. Most new manufacturers of the carbine were under-capitalized, however. As a result, short-cuts in manufacturing adversely affected quality of the production.

Armalite AR-50

The Armalite AR-50 is a single-shot long-range sniper rifle, first produced in the 1990s. It was designed for civilian use rather than for the military. It has unique octagonal receiver that is fixed into a stock of aluminium. Typically, a rifle loaded with .50 Browning Machine Gun (BMG) ammunition is light and easy to transport. Recoil (backward momentum) caused by firing is very mild because it is fitted with an excellent muzzle brake (designed to reduce recoil). This is essential, otherwise it could not be fired safely.

SPECIFICATION

MANUFACTURER Armalite
CALIBRE .50 BMG
MAGAZINE CAPACITY No magazine
ACTION Single shot
TOTAL LENGTH 1,499mm/59in
BARREL LENGTH 787mm/31in
WEIGHT UNLOADED 18.61kg/41lb

Barrett M82A1

The Barrett M82 is a semi-automatic rifle used by a marksman for long range sniper work. The M82A1 is the latest version, and represents the limit of portable rifle power. If it was any larger it would require either an entirely different recoil-control system, or become a low-velocity grenade launcher. Used in Iraq and Afghanistan, the Barrett has set new records for the range of successful sniper engagements. It has been in production since 1982.

SPECIFICATION

MANUFACTURER Barrett Manufacturing
CALIBRE 12.7 x 99mm
MAGAZINE CAPACITY 10
ACTION Recoil operated
TOTAL LENGTH 1,448mm/57in
BARREL LENGTH 737mm/29in
WEIGHT UNLOADED 12.9kg/28.4lb

Stoner 63

The 63 is the second of three rifle designs by Indiana-born military arms designer Eugene Stoner. It was produced between 1963 and 1969. The Stoner 63 differed from most other assault rifles in having "components". The basic receiver could be assembled by the user as a carbine, Light Machine Gun (LMG), belt-fed or sniper rifle. Although it was popular with the United States Navy Sea, Air and Land (SEAL) special forces in Vietnam, the model required more research and development. However it was in competition with the M16 which had been adopted by the US military in the 1960s.

SPECIFICATION

MANUFACTURER Cadillac Gage
CALIBRE 5.56 x 45mm
MAGAZINE CAPACITY 20, 30, belt-fed
ACTION Gas operated
TOTAL LENGTH 1,022mm/40.25in
BARREL LENGTH 508mm/20in
WEIGHT UNLOADED 4.37kg/9.65lb

Colt AR-15 Mod 08

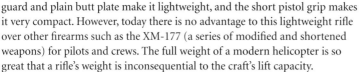

SPECIFICATION

MANUFACTURER Colt
CALIBRE 5.56 x 45mm
MAGAZINE CAPACITY 20
ACTION Gas operated
TOTAL LENGTH 787mm/31in
BARREL LENGTH 330mm/13in
WEIGHT UNLOADED 2.67kg/5.9lb

The Colt AR-15 was produced between 1964 and 1966 as a survival rifle for pilots and helicopter crews. The simple tubular hand guard and plain butt plate make it lightweight, and the short pistol grip makes it very compact. However, today there is no advantage to this lightweight rifle over other firearms such as the XM-177 (a series of modified and shortened weapons) for pilots and crews. The full weight of a modern helicopter is so great that a rifle's weight is inconsequential to the craft's lift capacity.

XM-177E2

SPECIFICATION

MANUFACTURER Colt

CALIBRE 5.56 x 45mm

MAGAZINE CAPACITY 20, 30

ACTION Gas operated

TOTAL LENGTH 787mm/31in

BARREL LENGTH 342mm/13.5in

WEIGHT UNLOADED 2.76kg/6.1lb

flash hider

As light and handy as the Colt M16 was in its earliest version, there was always a perceived requirement for something lighter and more compact. The XM-177 series went through several stock configurations, two barrel lengths and moderator designs. The moderator was designed to keep the short barrel from deafening the firer. However, conflicting regulatory definitions prevented Colt from exporting the moderator, and this meant that the model itself could not be sold abroad. As a result, Colt went on to perfect the M16 carbine in the form of the M4. The XM-177E2 was produced between 1966 and 1969.

AR-15 Heavy Barrel Mod 01

SPECIFICATION

MANUFACTURER Colt

CALIBRE 5.56 x 45mm

MAGAZINE CAPACITY 30

ACTION Gas operated

TOTAL LENGTH 990mm/39in

BARREL LENGTH 508mm/20in

WEIGHT UNLOADED 3.40kg/7.5lb

Armalite sold the rights of the AR-15 to Colt. The AR-15 Mod 01 was an attempt to provide armed forces with a light machine gun based on the Colt M16 in the 1970s. Colt made their rifle with a heavy barrel and bipod, and fastened together three magazines side by side. However, this approach had its limitations. The AR15 was not popular and this was reflected in poor sales.

SPECIFICATION

MANUFACTURER Colt, FNH-USA

CALIBRE 5.56 x 45mm

MAGAZINE CAPACITY 30

ACTION Gas operated

TOTAL LENGTH 1,005mm/39.6in

BARREL LENGTH 508mm/20in

WEIGHT UNLOADED 3.85kg/8.5lb

M16A2

The predecessor of the M16-A2 was the M16A1, a slightly-modified M16. However, it was not popular with the army and it was decided that it should be improved. The barrel was made heavier and with a faster twist to allow the use of heavier bullets. The plastic of the stock and forearms was strengthened. The sights were made click-adjustable. The result was a superb target rifle. The M16A2 was produced from 1985 to the present. However, it proved just too long and heavy for many types of combat.

SPECIFICATION

MANUFACTURER Colt

CALIBRE 5.56 x 45mm

MAGAZINE CAPACITY 30

ACTION Gas operated

TOTAL LENGTH 863mm/34in

BARREL LENGTH 368mm/14.5in

WEIGHT UNLOADED 3.4kg/7.5lb

M4

The M4 carbine differs from the M16A2 rifle only by having a shorter barrel and a telescoped buttstock. However research and development by Colt led to significant improvements. The M4 has greatly increased reliability, durability and accuracy. This progress has made it very difficult for the Army to justify its desire to replace the M16. The short barrel length exists for one reason: it is the distance needed between the front sight housing and the muzzle to mount a bayonet. The M4 was produced from the 1990s to the present.

FN T48

The FN T48 (the Belgian FN FAL) was one of
the competitors in the US Army rifle trials.
These were held after World War II to find a replacement for the M1 Garand,
the main rifle used by the United States since the 1930s. The T48 competed
against the T44 rifle, a modified version of the M1 Garand. Testing proved
them to be similar in performance, but the T44 was the winner. However, the
FN T48 was the rifle that most other countries found to be most suitable.

SPECIFICATION

MANUFACTURER FN, Liège
CALIBRE 7.62mm T65
MAGAZINE CAPACITY 20
ACTION Gas operated
TOTAL LENGTH 1,089mm/42.9in
BARREL LENGTH 533mm/21in
WEIGHT UNLOADED 3.88kg/8.56lb

FN SCAR

In searching for a replacement rifle to the M16A2 and M4, the US Army
Special Operations Command asked for a Special Operations Combat Rifle.
The result was a polymer-shell encased, piston-driven M16 replacement.
Two basic versions of SCAR system were produced – the SCAR-light
(SCAR-L), and the SCAR-heavy (SCAR-H). The heavier model would be
available in significantly more powerful chambering. Both models are easily
adaptable in the field. They are designed to have the same control, handling
and maintenance procedures. Intended to be quickly reconfigurable, and
have barrels of various lengths, the SCAR is difficult to list in a "standard"
configuration. Given the US Army's stringent testing procedures, the FN SCAR
may never be used by the military. It was produced between 2000 and 2006.

SPECIFICATION

MANUFACTURER FNH-USA
CALIBRE 5.56 x 45mm (SCAR-light) and
7.62mm NATO (SCAR-heavy)
MAGAZINE CAPACITY 30 (light) 20 (heavy)
ACTION Gas operated
TOTAL LENGTH 850 to 620mm/33.4 to
24.4in (light) 997 to 770mm/39.25
to 30in (heavy)
BARREL LENGTH 280 to 508mm/
11 to 20in
WEIGHT UNLOADED 3.5kg/7.7lb (light)
3.68kg/8.11lb (heavy)

Heckler & Koch XM-8

Produced between 1999 and 2005, the US Army considered the XM-8, (a
derivative of the Heckler & Koch G36) as a suitable replacement for the Colt
M16. However, the changes they made to materials and mechanism of the rifle
were not a sufficient improvement to make it viable. The costs of the war in
Iraq consumed any budget for research and development that might have
improved it further. The failure of the XM-8 has not changed the desire of
the US army to find something "better".

SPECIFICATION

MANUFACTURER Heckler & Koch
CALIBRE 5.56 x 45mm
MAGAZINE CAPACITY 30
ACTION Gas operated
TOTAL LENGTH 838mm/33in
BARREL LENGTH 318mm/12.5in
WEIGHT UNLOADED 2.67kg/5.88lb

Armalite AR-18

Eugene Stoner was the
designer of the AR-15 and its
later competitor, the AR-18. Whereas the AR-15
uses a direct impingement gas system the AR-18 was designed to use the short
piston gas system. The AR-15 was designed to use aluminium forgings, the
AR-18 is fabricated by the use of sheet metal pressings. But by the time Stoner
designed the rifle, the US government had settled, however reluctantly, on the
AR-15/M16. The AR-15 ended up being made in three countries, but was not
commercially successful. The AR-18 was manufactured from 1969 to 1978. It
was resurrected by the Armalite company as the AR-180B in 2002.

SPECIFICATION

MANUFACTURER Howa, Sterling,
Costa Mesa
CALIBRE 5.56 x 45mm
MAGAZINE CAPACITY 20, 30
ACTION Gas operated
TOTAL LENGTH 965mm/38in
BARREL LENGTH 470mm/18.25in
WEIGHT UNLOADED 3.08kg/6.8lb

Johnson Model 1941

SPECIFICATION

MANUFACTURER Johnson
CALIBRE .30-06
MAGAZINE CAPACITY 10
ACTION Recoil operated
TOTAL LENGTH 1,155mm/45.5in
BARREL LENGTH 558mm/22in
WEIGHT UNLOADED 4.31kg/9.5lb

A relative latecomer to the semi-automatic rifle market in the 1930s, the Johnson had several unique features. Its internal, rotary magazine could be topped off at any time via stripper clips and the barrel could be removed for compact storage, such as in parachute jumps. However, it was not as robust as the Garand and found few buyers. One fault was the short recoil action. The barrel had to move a short distance with the bolt, in order to actuate the system. Therefore anything that interfered with the barrel's movement could cause a malfunction. Used by the US Marine Corps in 1941 and found wanting, it stayed in service due to wartime needs until 1945. It was declared surplus afterwards and sold off.

SPECIFICATION

MANUFACTURER Knight's Armament
CALIBRE 7.62mm NATO
MAGAZINE CAPACITY 20
ACTION Gas operated
TOTAL LENGTH 1,174mm/46.25in
BARREL LENGTH 508mm/20in
WEIGHT UNLOADED 4.42kg/9.75lb

Stoner SR-25 sniper

The desire for a medium- to long-range sniper rifle that was also a semi-automatic stemmed from the success of the M-21 sniper rifle used in the Vietnam war. The SR-25 is essentially an AR-10 rifle with the carry handle replaced by a slotted rail for scope attachment. The SR-25 is made by Knight's Armament, but there are a number of other manufacturers of AR-10-type rifles who also make a sniper rifle. The US Army and Marine Corps are currently purchasing the Knight's. It has been produced from the 1990s to the present.

SPECIFICATION

MANUFACTURER Marlin F.A. Co.
CALIBRE 9 x 19mm
MAGAZINE CAPACITY 15, 25
ACTION Blowback
TOTAL LENGTH 901mm/35.5in
BARREL LENGTH 419mm/16.5in
WEIGHT UNLOADED 3.06kg/6.75lb

Marlin Model 9

The Model 9 carbine is a popular choice for casual shooting and training indoors as some indoor ranges cannot take the regular impact of rifle cartridges. The Marlin was a simple carbine that used common pistol magazines and fired 9mm ammunition (often used in handguns), which makes it easy to switch between using handguns and this carbine. It has a low recoil which makes it comfortable to handle. It was produced between the 1970s and 1990s.

McMillan M-87 sniper

muzzle brake

SPECIFICATION

MANUFACTURER McMillan
CALIBRE .50 BMG
MAGAZINE CAPACITY 5
ACTION Bolt action
TOTAL LENGTH 1,448mm/57in
BARREL LENGTH 736mm/29in
WEIGHT UNLOADED 11.8kg/26.01lb

Where other long-range sniper rifles often look like a piece of industrial equipment, the McMillan looks like a sporting rifle. As with all .50 BMG rifles, the muzzle brake is a requirement, to reduce recoil. With proper ammunition and a good shooter, a McMillan can be expected to deliver its bullets within a 130mm/51in circle at 1,000m/3,200ft. It has been produced from the mid-1990s to the present.

M-40

Faced with the pressing need for a sniper rifle for use in the Vietnam War during the 1960s, the US Marine Corps rebuilt the sporting rifle Remington 700 and issued it as an accurate and durable military weapon. Unlike other services, the Marine Corps trains its own armourers, who build these rifles up from factory configuration. The result is a well designed sniper rifle that is still in use today. Some Vietnam-era M-40 rifles with new barrels, stocks and scopes are now called M-40A1. They are still in service. The M-40 has been produced from 1967 to the present.

SPECIFICATION

MANUFACTURER Remington Arms
CALIBRE 7.62mm NATO
MAGAZINE CAPACITY 5
ACTION Bolt action
TOTAL LENGTH 1,117mm/44in
BARREL LENGTH 660mm/26in
WEIGHT UNLOADED 6.57kg/14.5lb w/scope
    and mount

Krag-Jorgensen 1898

side-opening magazine

At the end of the 19th century the US Army was still armed with single-shot black powder rifles, when the rest of the world was transitioning to smokeless repeaters. Due to the mechanical limitations of the Krag (such as the inability to be recharged using stripper clips) it was soon replaced by the Springfield 1903. It was produced between 1898 and 1903. The new rifle was not common issue during the Spanish-American War. Many conflicts, such as that at San Juan Hill, Cuba had American troops with black powder single shots assaulting Spanish positions which were defended by Mauser rifles.

SPECIFICATION

MANUFACTURER Springfield
CALIBRE .30-40
MAGAZINE CAPACITY 5
ACTION Bolt action
TOTAL LENGTH 1,248mm/49.15in
BARREL LENGTH 762mm/30in
WEIGHT UNLOADED 4.08kg/9lb

Krag-Jorgensen 1898 carbine

A shorter Krag than the rifle, this carbine was light, handy, convenient and short-lived. It was produced between 1898 and 1903. The 1898 carbines received the 1898 rifle sights. Then, they were recalled and rebuilt in the very early 1900s to receive improved 1899 pattern stocks and new sights. The carbine, along with the rifle, was replaced by the Springfield 1903, the "one size fits all" length rifle. The carbines were greatly prized by hunters in the first half of the 20th century, for being light, handy, accurate and powerful enough for American big game.

SPECIFICATION

MANUFACTURER Springfield
CALIBRE .30-40
MAGAZINE CAPACITY 5
ACTION Bolt action
TOTAL LENGTH 1,054mm/41.15in
BARREL LENGTH 559mm/22in
WEIGHT UNLOADED 3.51kg/7.75lb

Springfield M-1903

The US Army developed and adopted the Springfield M-1903 in the early 20th century because the Krag was not a powerful enough weapon. However, it used many patented features created by the German company Mauser. Mauser sued Springfield and won, collecting royalties until 1917. The M-1903 illustrated is the earliest model, with a rod bayonet beneath the barrel, where a cleaning rod is usually kept. President Theodore Roosevelt was so outraged by the rod bayonet he ordered it changed to a blade bayonet. It was in service through World War II.

SPECIFICATION

MANUFACTURER Springfield, Remington,
    Winchester
CALIBRE .30-06
MAGAZINE CAPACITY 5
ACTION Bolt action
TOTAL LENGTH 1,102mm/43.4in
BARREL LENGTH 615mm/24.2in
WEIGHT UNLOADED 3.85kg/8.5lb

Springfield M-1903 Mark 1

SPECIFICATION

MANUFACTURER Springfield
CALIBRE .30-06
MAGAZINE CAPACITY 5
ACTION Bolt action
TOTAL LENGTH 1,102mm/43.4in
BARREL LENGTH 615mm/24.2in
WEIGHT UNLOADED 3.85kg/8.5lb

The Mark 1 was the "solution" to the stalemate of trench warfare in World War I. With enough firepower, the Allies could keep the Germans in their trenches while covering the gap of no-man's land. The Mark 1 differed from the M-1903 in having an ejection port on the left side for the Pedersen Device (an optional attachment that allowed it to shoot a pistol-sized round in semi-automatic mode) cases to exit the rifle. It also had a slightly altered trigger mechanism. While production was underway the war ended. The rifles were simply used as regular bolt-action rifles, until they were replaced by the M1 Garand and M-14. They were then sold as surplus. It was produced in 1918.

Pedersen Device

The Pedersen Device was designed to convert the 1903 Springfield to a semi-automatic rifle for assaults across no-man's land. It replaced the bolt of a 1903 Springfield, and converted that rifle (the Mark 1) into a semi-automatic rifle firing a cartridge of submachine gun power. It was thought that the conversion was lighter, and avoided the need to issue two weapons. World War I ended before the futility of the approach could be demonstrated and almost all the devices were destroyed. However, the cartridges left behind became the basis of the French M-1935 .32 pistol.

Springfield M1903A4 sniper

ABOVE A 3-power commerical hunting scope is attached to the Springfield M1903A4.

SPECIFICATION

MANUFACTURER Springfield
CALIBRE .30-06
MAGAZINE CAPACITY 5
ACTION Bolt action
TOTAL LENGTH 1,098mm/43.25in
BARREL LENGTH 609mm/24in
WEIGHT UNLOADED) 4.00kg/8.83lb

Faced with the need for more accurate fire in World War II, the US Army simply mounted commercial scopes in commercial bases on production 1903A3 rifles. The A4 designation simply means that the rifle never received iron sights at the factory, and always had a scope mount installed. Factory-produced A4 sniper rifles even had the receiver marking location moved, so they would be visible when the scope mount was attached. As a more accurate rifle in infantry use, it was good enough. But as a special-purpose sniper rifle it was not as effective as its Mauser counterparts. It was adopted in 1942 and, despite the development of the M1C and M1D Garand sniper variants, the Springfield remained in service through the Korean War.

T44E4

SPECIFICATION

MANUFACTURER Springfield
CALIBRE 7.62mm T65
MAGAZINE CAPACITY 20
ACTION Gas operated
TOTAL LENGTH 1,117mm/44in
BARREL LENGTH 559mm/22in
WEIGHT UNLOADED 3.88kg/8.56lb

This Springfield rifle was one of the rifles that took part in the US trials between the wars. The US Army was so keen for their own design to be adopted that the tests were all but a sham. (The FAL was rejected in one phase for not passing a field combat test.) Every time the T44 series rifles failed a test, the test was rescheduled. The competing T48 (an FAL made by Harrington & Richardson) and FN-FAL from Liège never stood a chance. The T44E4 was produced in 1955 and went on to become the M-14.

M-14

Based on World War II experience, the US Army needed more ammunition, increased firepower and greater adaptability. Unfortunately, the Americans spent twelve years and millions of dollars and ended up with a barely improved Garand. Worse still, they proposed to replace everything in inventory with one rifle: the M-14. It was supposed to replace the M1 Garand, the BAR and the M1 submachine gun. It was, however, too light to be a light machine gun (LMG), too large to be a submachine gun and not much improvement on the Garand. As a Designated Marksman Rifle (SDM-R), it saw a resurgence in Iraq. The M-14 was officially adopted in 1957 but production was slow at first. In the early 1960s, the US Congress held hearings to find out why it was not being issued in greater numbers, and found the Springfield Armoury alone (a government arsenal) an insufficient production base for its requirements.

SPECIFICATION

MANUFACTURER Springfield, H&R, TRW
CALIBRE 7.62mm NATO
MAGAZINE CAPACITY 20
ACTION Gas operated
TOTAL LENGTH 1,117mm/44in
BARREL LENGTH 558mm/22in
WEIGHT UNLOADED 3.88kg/8.56lb

Ruger Mini-14

Made in the 1970s as a sporting rifle to emulate the M-14 and M1 Garand, the Mini-14 proved to be useful as a semi-automatic rifle. Ruger originally marketed it as "The world's most expensive plinker". Plinking refers to shooting at chance targets, such as tin cans, using a .22 LR (Long Rifle) rifle or handgun. Despite using the much more expensive .223 ammunition, it sold very well. As a select-fire rifle for military or police use, the Ruger Mini-14 proved to be just a bit too lightly constructed, and not accurate enough.

SPECIFICATION

MANUFACTURER Sturm, Ruger & Co.
CALIBRE .223
MAGAZINE CAPACITY 5, 20, 30
ACTION Gas operated
TOTAL LENGTH 943mm/37.15in
BARREL LENGTH 470mm/18.5in
WEIGHT UNLOADED 3.06kg/6.75lb

Pedersen

This was another contender for the US Army semi-automatic research and testing between the wars. The Pedersen had a similar mechanism to the German Luger. The cartridges were coated with wax for easy extraction, although the wax could attract debris that would cause malfunctions. The .276 cartridge proved very effective in terminal ballistic testing, but the Army Chief of Staff, General Douglas MacArthur, vetoed any calibre change mainly due to conversion costs. The Pedersen was produced between 1932 and 1934.

SPECIFICATION

MANUFACTURER Vickers
CALIBRE .276 Pedersen
MAGAZINE CAPACITY 10, en bloc clip
ACTION Gas operated
TOTAL LENGTH 1,117mm/44in
BARREL LENGTH 558mm/22in
WEIGHT UNLOADED 4.12kg/9.1lb

Lee Navy

This rifle was produced from 1895 to 1902. Unhappy with the slow progress the Army was making in adopting a smallbore rifle, the US Navy adopted the Lee Navy in .256 calibre. Unlike other straight-pull actions, the Lee tips the bolt (in a similar way to the FAL bolt function) instead of rotating the bolt like the Steyr or Swiss M-31. While a reliable action, this did not allow for the high-velocity performance using 6mm ammunition without problems. The bullets fouled the inside of the barrel quickly, and the fast powders of the time quickly eroded the bore despite regular cleaning of the fouling.

SPECIFICATION

MANUFACTURER Winchester
CALIBRE .256
MAGAZINE CAPACITY 5
ACTION Straight-pull bolt action
TOTAL LENGTH 1,212mm/47.75in
BARREL LENGTH 711mm/28in
WEIGHT UNLOADED 3.77kg/8.32lb

M-1917 Enfield

SPECIFICATION

MANUFACTURER Winchester, Remington, Eddystone

CALIBRE .30-06

MAGAZINE CAPACITY 5

ACTION Bolt action

TOTAL LENGTH 1,176mm/46.3in

BARREL LENGTH 660mm/26in

WEIGHT UNLOADED 4.08kg/9lb

With Springfield and Rock Island Arsenals unable to increase production of the Model 1903 prior to World War I, the US Army had the British-designed and American-produced Enfield altered for their purposes. They were produced between 1917 and 1920 and their calibre was changed from .303 to .30-06. After World War I, the 1917s were put in storage while the more popular Springfield M-1903 was retained as the standard service rifle. Early in World War II, desperate for rifles, the British accepted many of the 1917s as part of an arrangement called the Lend-Lease Program. They had to be clearly marked as using non-standard .303 ammunition, with a large red stripe around the handguards, to avoid mistakes.

M2 Carbine

SPECIFICATION

MANUFACTURER Inland & Winchester

CALIBRE .30 carbine

MAGAZINE CAPACITY 15 & 30

ACTION Gas operated

TOTAL LENGTH 905mm/35.65in

BARREL LENGTH 457mm/18in

WEIGHT UNLOADED 2.45kg/5.42lb

This was the M1 carbine modified for selective fire and produced between 1943 to 1945. It was standardized in October 1944, along with the 30-round magazine to go with it. The conversion kit designated T17 could be installed in any M1, and so produce a select-fire weapon. In wartime, many were converted in this way. Those made specifically as select-fire were marked "M2" on the receiver ring. Removing the select-fire parts from an M1 makes it a semi-automatic only rifle again, with no modifications to show it was ever a "machine gun".

M3 Carbine

SPECIFICATION

MANUFACTURER Winchester

CALIBRE .30 carbine

MAGAZINE CAPACITY 15 & 30

ACTION Gas operated

TOTAL LENGTH 905mm/35.65in

BARREL LENGTH 457mm/18in

WEIGHT UNLOADED 2.45kg/5.42lb

scope powered by a pack of batteries

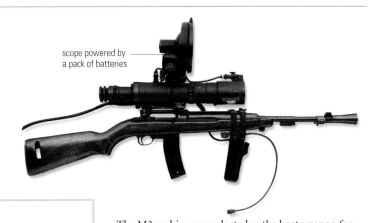

Sight, Night, M3 Carbine
This was an active scope, in that it projected a beam of infra-red light, so that the operator could then use the scope to see in the dark and fire. Modern electronics have made passive night vision equipment the new standard. Passive scopes, like the "Starlight", need no illumination but stars and moon, while Thermal Imaging detects the heat of the target against the background.

The M3 carbine was selected as the host weapon for the new infra-red sniper scope. Allowing the operator to see and aim in darkness, the scope was the future in hardware and promised to revolutionize warfare. The M3 was chosen as it was the lightest available rifle because the scope was very heavy and bulky. The M3 was produced from 1945 to the early 1950s.

M1 Garand

operating rod (lower gas tube)

The product of almost twenty years of research and development, and controversial for almost all that time, the finished Garand was not much like the prototypes that preceded it. It uses an en bloc, Mannlicher-type clip, but the Garand clip is inserted from the top, and ejects out of the top when firing the last round. The "ping" of ejection was viewed as a problem by some, but few, if any, combat veterans had a problem with it between 1936 and 1957. The Garand was also used as a target rifle for many years, but the long, unsupported operating rod could cause problems for armourers as they tried to fit it without it degrading target accuracy.

SPECIFICATION	
MANUFACTURER	Various US
CALIBRE	7.62 x 63mm
MAGAZINE CAPACITY	8, en bloc clip
ACTION	Gas operated/rotating bolt
TOTAL LENGTH	1,105mm/43.5in
BARREL LENGTH	609mm/24in
WEIGHT UNLOADED	4.31kg/9.5lb

Garand M1C sniper

The big obstacle to mounting optics on the Garand was the clip: it was inserted and ejected vertically. The scope mount on the C and D models were attached to the side of the receiver, and the scope offset from the line of the bore as a result. To effectively shoot the Garand, the sniper required a leather cheek piece lashed to the stock. The C and D model differed only in the maker of the mount. It was adopted in 1942, and lasted until the Garand was replaced by the M-14 in 1959.

SPECIFICATION	
MANUFACTURER	Various US
CALIBRE	7.62 x 63mm
MAGAZINE CAPACITY	8, en bloc clip
ACTION	Gas operated/rotating bolt
TOTAL LENGTH	1,105mm/43.5in
BARREL LENGTH	609mm/24in
WEIGHT UNLOADED	4.62kg/10.2lb

Mexico

Before World War I, Mexico purchased rifles abroad. Between 1913 and the 1950s, it produced its own bolt-action Mauser rifles. In the late 1970s, Mexico obtained a licence from Heckler & Koch to produce the G3. It is now being replaced by the Mexican-designed and manufactured FX-05.

Arisaka Type 38 carbine

The Mexican Revolution was a period of social and military conflict, beginning in 1911. The government placed an order with Japan for 40,000 Type 38 carbines. They were standard Japanese Type 38 rifles except for the calibre, and for the nosecap being modified to take standard Mexican-pattern bayonets. As with other last-minute orders, most were not delivered before the revolution was over, and the manufacturers had to sell them elsewhere. Manufactured from 1910 to 1911, few of the Arisaka Type 38 were delivered and most now reside in museums or collectors' vaults.

SPECIFICATION	
MANUFACTURER	Koishikawa
CALIBRE	7 x 57mm
MAGAZINE CAPACITY	5
ACTION	Bolt action
TOTAL LENGTH	869mm/34.2in
BARREL LENGTH	505mm/19.9in
WEIGHT UNLOADED	3.31kg/7.3lb

Mondragon M-1908

SPECIFICATION

MANUFACTURER SIG, Neuhausen
CALIBRE 7 x 57mm
MAGAZINE CAPACITY 8
ACTION Gas operated
TOTAL LENGTH 1,248mm/49.15in
BARREL LENGTH 620mm/24.4in
WEIGHT UNLOADED 4.74kg/10.45lb

The M-1908 was designed by a Mexican Army officer in the early 20th century. It was patented in the United States and built in Switzerland. The rifle was not only used in Mexico, but some were issued to the fledgling German air service, with drum (round) magazines, for air-to-air combat. The M-1908 was one of the first successful self-loading rifles. While it did not work particularly well, the fact that it worked at all in that period of time was a marvel. Some rifles went to Mexico in 1909; the leftovers were sold to Germany and served in the Luftwaffe (air force) to 1915. The Mondragon M-1908 was obsolete before World War I ended and is now found only in museums.

Mauser Model 1912

SPECIFICATION

MANUFACTURER Steyr
CALIBRE 7 x 57mm
MAGAZINE CAPACITY 5
ACTION Bolt action
TOTAL LENGTH 1,242mm/48.9in
BARREL LENGTH 739mm/29.1in
WEIGHT UNLOADED 4.11kg/9.06lb

The Mexican Revolution of 1911 made the availability of rifles an important concern for the Mexican government. The supply of Mausers from Germany was not forthcoming, so Mexico turned to Steyr in Austria for Mauser rifles from 1911. Apart from being made in Austria, these models were no different from other Mauser bolt-action rifles. Unfortunately, they were in use on the losing side of the revolution.

 # Guatemala

Like many countries in Central America, Guatemala has suffered from civil war and unrest within its own borders. Internal strife, police duties and plantation protection all required arms. Lacking local manufacture, Guatemala has purchased and imported small arms from abroad.

Mauser CZ Model 1924

Between the World Wars, Guatemala chose to introduce a German Mauser rifle to its country. They settled on the 1924 short rifle, in 7mm. Made for Guatemala and so-marked, it has served from 1924 to the present day. While they were all purchased for military and police use, almost all are probably in use guarding plantations, factories and other interests. The military and police have since moved to using assault rifles. The Mauser CZ was replaced in the Guatemalan Army by the Galil, purchased from Israel.

SPECIFICATION

MANUFACTURER CZ Brno
CALIBRE 7 x 57mm
MAGAZINE CAPACITY 5
ACTION Bolt action
TOTAL LENGTH 1,100mm/43.3in
BARREL LENGTH 565mm/22.23in
WEIGHT UNLOADED 4.1kg/9.2lb

Costa Rica

Like many Caribbean islands, Costa Rica has few threats from outside its borders, and abolished its army in 1949. However, all countries need a defence force, and all governments in the Caribbean have to deal with smugglers, drug dealers and, despite relative stability, the possibility of internal strife.

Mauser Model 1910

Manufactured in Oberndorf, the Costa Rican Mauser was virtually identical to the Gew 98, a model made by Mauser through World War I. Unlike other buyers, Costa Rica ordered its rifles enough in advance of World War I to be sure of delivery. Deliveries took place from 1911 to 1914, and the rifles were in service until 1949. In the same year Costa Rica abolished its Army. All rifles either went to the police or were sold on the world surplus market.

SPECIFICATION

MANUFACTURER Mauser
CALIBRE 7 x 57mm
MAGAZINE CAPACITY 5
ACTION Bolt action
TOTAL LENGTH 1,239mm/48.8in
BARREL LENGTH 740mm/29.15in
WEIGHT UNLOADED 3.97kg/8.75lb

Cuba

With no indigenous arms-making capacity, Cuba relied on outside sources before, through and after the revolution in the 1950s. For the last century Cuba has depended on a mélange of rifles from various sources. The Spanish 1896 Mauser, US Krags, Remington-Lee and even some Winchester 1895 lever-action rifles could all be found in various military and police units. The acquisition of FN-FAL rifles as the revolution was in progress was not perceived as a help to the government and, after the revolution, Soviet-pattern small arms were the order of the day. The fall of the Soviet Union has stopped the subsidies of material and money, greatly reducing the size of the Cuban Army.

FN FAL

SPECIFICATION

MANUFACTURER Fabrique Nationale, Liège
CALIBRE 7.62 x 51mm
MAGAZINE CAPACITY 20
ACTION Gas operated/tilting lock
TOTAL LENGTH 1,100mm/43.3in
BARREL LENGTH 533mm/24.3in
WEIGHT UNLOADED 4.45kg/9.81lb

This is a standard, select-fire Belgium FAL. The rifles were purchased from Fabrique Nationale (FN) in Belgium, shipped to Cuba and are probably used to this day. The reliable FAL was a prudent choice, as the cash-strapped Cuban economy could hardly afford spare parts and regular overhauls. The FAL seen on the shoulder of a Cuban policeman today probably has the same springs in it that it had when shipped from the manufacturers in Liège in 1958–9. It will have seen regular carry, if little firing, since then.

Trial rifles
Cuba only ordered three trial rifles before placing their order.

 # Peru

Peru purchased Mauser rifles from many of the companies licensed to make Peter Paul Mauser's designs beginning in 1892. Those earlier purchases had to be rebuilt and brought up to a new standard each time Mauser unveiled an improvement. By the 1930s, the improvements had stopped coming and

Peru could purchase rifles without need of further upgrades. After approaching the United States, France and Israel for arms without success, Peru contracted with the Soviet Union for armour in the 1970s. Today, small arms are purchased on the international market, products of the United States rather than Russia.

CZ M-1932

SPECIFICATION	
MANUFACTURER CZ Brno	
CALIBRE 7.65 x 53mm	
MAGAZINE CAPACITY 5	
ACTION Bolt action	
TOTAL LENGTH 1,099mm/43.25in	
BARREL LENGTH 591mm/23.25in	
WEIGHT UNLOADED 4.14kg/9.13lb	

Peru purchased CZ M-1932 rifles made at Brno in Czechoslovakia in 1934. They were simply standard Mauser-pattern export rifles, chambered in the Belgian 7.65mm cartridge. They have the Peruvian crest on the receiver ring. After World War II, many were rebuilt and re-barrelled to .30-06 to use readily available American surplus ammunition. The CZ Model 1932 was used until the late 1950s. Having reorganized the factory, and upgraded their products for the world market, Czechoslovakian rifle output was "appropriated" in order to provide the same rifle to Wehrmacht units during World War II. Built under German supervision it was known as the Gew 24(t).

 # Colombia

The Colombian Army dates its inception to 1819, when the "Army of the Commoners" was formed to achieve independence from Spanish rule.

To provide firearms for the armed forces, Colombia has negotiated foreign contracts with companies such as DMW, Loewe, Steyr, CZ and FN.

Mauser Steyr Model 1912

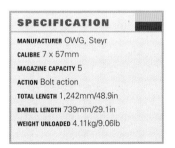

SPECIFICATION	
MANUFACTURER OWG, Steyr	
CALIBRE 7 x 57mm	
MAGAZINE CAPACITY 5	
ACTION Bolt action	
TOTAL LENGTH 1,242mm/48.9in	
BARREL LENGTH 739mm/29.1in	
WEIGHT UNLOADED 4.11kg/9.06lb	

National crest
Colombian rifles have the "Ejercito de Colombia" national crest on top of the chamber.

The Mauser Steyr Model 1912 was identical to the Mexican Model of 1912 except for its markings. The Mexicans had long had an excellent relationship with the German company Mauser. Their Mexican Model 1912 was an indigenous Mexican-built rifle based on the some of the earlier military rifles (such as the Model 1902) supplied by Germany and later by similar models from Austria-Hungary (such as the Model 1907). The Mexican and Colombian rifles were in the process of being manufactured by Steyr in Austria when World War I broke out. Once the war began, all outside contracts were suspended in Europe. Many of the German rifles were seized by the Austro-Hungarian government before they could be shipped to Mexico and Colombia and issued to Austro-Hungarian troops on the front line. When they appeared on the surplus market after the war, hunters and gunsmiths rapidly bought them up, as they were beautiful examples of pre-war craftsmanship. The Mauser Steyr Model 1912 was manufactured in 1913.

 Chile

With Chile's long coastline, the navy has had a greater importance than the army. Chile has had only one conflict – war with Bolivia in 1884, which was won by Chile and long over before Chile started buying modern arms. Like so many other countries in South America, lacking an industrial base, Chile purchased modern small arms beginning with the adoption of repeating rifles, at the end of the 19th century.

Johnson M1941

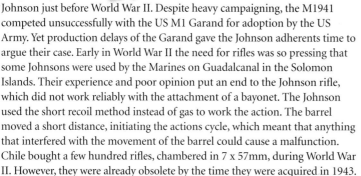

rotary magazine

The M1941 rifle was designed by Melvin Johnson just before World War II. Despite heavy campaigning, the M1941 competed unsuccessfully with the US M1 Garand for adoption by the US Army. Yet production delays of the Garand gave the Johnson adherents time to argue their case. Early in World War II the need for rifles was so pressing that some Johnsons were used by the Marines on Guadalcanal in the Solomon Islands. Their experience and poor opinion put an end to the Johnson rifle, which did not work reliably with the attachment of a bayonet. The Johnson used the short recoil method instead of gas to work the action. The barrel moved a short distance, initiating the actions cycle, which meant that anything that interfered with the movement of the barrel could cause a malfunction. Chile bought a few hundred rifles, chambered in 7 x 57mm, during World War II. However, they were already obsolete by the time they were acquired in 1943.

SPECIFICATION

MANUFACTURER Johnson Arms
CALIBRE 7 x 57mm
MAGAZINE CAPACITY 10
ACTION Recoil operated/rotating bolt
TOTAL LENGTH 1,156mm/45.5in
BARREL LENGTH 559mm/22in
WEIGHT UNLOADED 4.31kg/9.5lb

CZ Mauser M1935

The M1935 was a carbine-sized rifle designed for the Chilean police forces. It proved easier for a policeman to carry around than the longer M1912. It was bought in 1935 and used until the adoption of the Sig 540 in 1986. The Chilean contract called for some minor design changes to the original Mauser model: the sling swivels (for carrying) were placed on the left side of the stock, the bolt handle was turned down and the stock relieved at the bolt handle to make it easier to grasp.

SPECIFICATION

MANUFACTURER Mauser-Werke AG
CALIBRE 7 x 57mm
MAGAZINE CAPACITY 5
ACTION Bolt action
TOTAL LENGTH 1,057mm/41.6in
BARREL LENGTH 545mm/21.45in
WEIGHT UNLOADED 3.63kg/8.0lb

Mauser Model 1912

The Mauser Model 1912 was first purchased in 1912. Managing to acquire some 20,000 rifles before the outbreak of World War I, Chile used this rifle for military and police services. It was a standard Mauser rifle of the time in terms of its length, bolt handle and calibre. Chile, with a lengthy coast and few large cities, had little need of a compact arm for military and police work, so a full-size rifle worked well for it. The Mauser was officially dropped in 1986 when Chile adopted the Sig 540 as their issue rifle.

SPECIFICATION

MANUFACTURER Steyr
CALIBRE 7 x 57mm
MAGAZINE CAPACITY 5
ACTION Bolt action
TOTAL LENGTH 1,243mm/48.9in
BARREL LENGTH 735mm/28.95in
WEIGHT UNLOADED 4.11kg/9.06lb

 Dominican Republic

The Dominican Republic is not normally associated with arms production. However, it started an arms manufacturing base in the 1940s at San Cristobal using the expertise of émigrés from Hungary and Italy. The first effort by Armeria San Cristobal small arms factory was a copy of the Italian Beretta M-1938 submachine gun. The company went on to produce a light semi-automatic rifle, the Christobal, that used the M1 carbine cartridge. The Christobal Model 2 was mainly used by the Dominican military and the rest exported to other countries in the Caribbean, including neighbouring Cuba.

Cristobal Model 2

SPECIFICATION	
MANUFACTURER Armeria San Cristobal	
CALIBRE .30 carbine	
MAGAZINE CAPACITY 30	
ACTION Delayed blowback	
TOTAL LENGTH 945mm/37.2in	
BARREL LENGTH 411mm/16.2in	
WEIGHT UNLOADED 3.56kg/7.85lb	

The Cristobal Model 2 was designed by a Hungarian exile, Pal Kiraly, who established the Cristobal company in 1948. Popular in Central and South America, this rifle sold in hundreds of thousands. Its popularity may have owed as much to buyers not wanting the American or Soviet strings attached to USA-supplied or Warsaw Pact-supplied small arms, as to the reliability of the Cristobal carbine. However, once Central America became flooded by US and Soviet weapons, it was no longer possible for competitors to sell other designs, and the Model 2 faded from production. Examples may still be seen in out-of-the-way police barracks. The Cristobal Model 2 was manufactured from the mid-1950s to the mid-1960s, remained in service long after, and is perhaps still used today.

 Venezuela

On the north coast of the South American continent, Venezuela did not enjoy great economic significance until the discovery of large oil deposits in 1917. The Venezuelan army today mainly uses AK rifles, and the country has entered into production licensing with the Russian Federation.

SAFN M-49

SPECIFICATION	
MANUFACTURER FN, Liège	
CALIBRE 7 x 57mm	
MAGAZINE CAPACITY 10	
ACTION Gas operated	
TOTAL LENGTH 1,110mm/43.7in	
BARREL LENGTH 589mm/23.2in	
WEIGHT UNLOADED 4.30kg/9.48lb	

This was simply the Belgian SAFN M-49 chambered in 7 x 57mm, and marked with the Venezuelan crest on the receiver ring. The SAFN M-49 (which was similar to a Russian Tokarev rifle) was produced by FN in Belgium in 1949 and used in many countries around the world including Brazil, Argentina, Colombia and Venezuela. The rifle had a short front-line service life, from 1951 to 1954. Within a few years after purchase the FAL became available, and Venezuela purchased many FALs in 7 x 49mm. Soon afterwards the FALs were converted to 7.62 x 51mm, as Venezuela updated small arms to recognize the near-universal shift to 7.62 x 51mm cartridges. As a result, the SAFN-M49 rifles were most likely to have gone to police units. Since then, some have occasionally surfaced in the surplus market.

Argentina

The State-owned Argentine ordnance factory is called Fabrica Militar de Armas Portatiles (FMAP). The factory produces and maintains the FAL rifles.

A programme of conversion of 7.62mm rifles to 5.56mm was undertaken and work on the replacement design was abandoned.

FN SAFN M-1949

Manufactured in Liège in Belgium, the SAFN M-1949 was produced for Argentina in 7.62 x 63mm calibre. This calibre was dictated by the availability of surplus US ammunition after World War II. Most SAFN rifles were issued to the Navy. They were only in main-line service for a short while, from 1951 to 1959, and were then replaced by locally produced FN-FAL "metric" versions in 7.62mm NATO. The SAFN could be retro-fitted to use the magazine from the Browning Automatic Rifle (BAR), for a capacity of 20 rounds of .30-06 cartridges. The Argentinian SAFN is the result of that amalgam.

SPECIFICATION

MANUFACTURER FN, Liège
CALIBRE 7.62 x 63mm
MAGAZINE CAPACITY 10
ACTION Gas operated/tilting lock
TOTAL LENGTH 1,116mm/43.9in
BARREL LENGTH 590mm/23.2in
WEIGHT UNLOADED 4.31kg/9.5lb

Mauser Model 1891

protruding magazine

The Mauser Model 1891 was an evolutionary development of the 1889 rifle. Argentina bought some 180,000 Mauser Model 1891 rifles from Loewe, Berlin, in Germany. The 1891 model is distinctive, with its protruding single-stack magazine. While the design is entirely serviceable, the magazine is directly at the point of balance, making one-handed carry difficult. The 1891 model was used as a military rifle from 1891 until it was replaced by the 1909 Mauser. Once the army shifted to using the SAFN 49, all remaining 1891 Mausers were transferred to the police, who used them until the early 1950s.

SPECIFICATION

MANUFACTURER Ludwig Loewe, Berlin
CALIBRE 7.65mm Argentine
MAGAZINE CAPACITY 5
ACTION Bolt action
TOTAL LENGTH 1,234mm/48.6in
BARREL LENGTH 739mm/29.1in
WEIGHT UNLOADED 3.89kg/8.58lb

Mauser Model 1891 carbine

In the 1890s the flat grasslands of the Argentine Pampas was controlled by the cavalry. The standard rifle was too long for mounted use, so a shortened version of the 1891 was produced. Calibre remained the same, but the sights were re-calibrated for the shorter barrel and thus reduced muzzle velocity (the speed at which a bullet travels when it leaves the barrel of a weapon). The protruding magazine, with all rounds in a direct stack instead of staggered in the magazine, was less of a hindrance to cavalry than infantry. The carbines had an identical service life to the rifles. They were used by the military from 1891 to 1909, then became a police-issue rifle until the early 1950s.

SPECIFICATION

MANUFACTURER Ludwig Loewe, Berlin
CALIBRE 7.65mm Argentine
MAGAZINE CAPACITY 5
ACTION Bolt action
TOTAL LENGTH 940mm/37in
BARREL LENGTH 447mm/17.6in
WEIGHT UNLOADED 3.28kg/7.25lb

Paraguay

The German company Mauser succeeded in selling rifles to all sides in almost every South American conflict. They even sold rifles to peaceful countries such as Paraguay. Since a war lasting from 1865 to 1870, Paraguay has had internal security problems but has been at peace with her neighbours.

Mauser Model 1907

SPECIFICATION	
MANUFACTURER	DMW
CALIBRE	7.65 x 53mm
MAGAZINE CAPACITY	5
ACTION	Bolt action
TOTAL LENGTH	1,247mm/49.1in
BARREL LENGTH	740mm/29.15in
WEIGHT UNLOADED	4.11kg/9.06lb

An almost exact copy of the standard German Army rifle of the time, the Mauser Model 1907 had minor differences in bands and nosecap. These modifications were something the manufacturer DMW could expect many customers to worry about. This model did not take the standard German cartridge. However, the different chambering was to be expected, and was just the standard Belgian cartridge in a South American contract rifle. Shipments began in 1907 and the service life of the rifle was well into the 1950s.

Brazil

Brazil imported mainly bolt-action rifles from the German company Mauser until 1945 when it set up its own arms industry. The rapid industrialization that took place after 1930 provided the infrastructure necessary for developing an arms industry. Today Brazil exports arms all over the world.

Mauser Model 1908

SPECIFICATION	
MANUFACTURER	DMW
CALIBRE	7 x 57mm
MAGAZINE CAPACITY	5
ACTION	Bolt action
TOTAL LENGTH	1,248mm/49.15in
BARREL LENGTH	740mm/29.1in
WEIGHT UNLOADED	4.02kg/8.88lb

This was simply an export version of the Gew 98, the standard German military rifle throughout World War I. At the time a serviceable rifle, it was replaced soon after the war by many other armies because of its length. The Brazilians also bought carbine versions of this rifle, as well as other Mauser models from 1894 through the 1930s. Brazil had a large order with CZ at the time Germany invaded Czechoslovakia, and the loss of this order provided the impetus to develop its own arms industry. The Mauser Model 1908 was used from 1908 to the 1930s as a military rifle, then used as a police arm until the late 1950s and early 1960s. It was replaced by the M964 when it became available.

M954

SPECIFICATION	
MANUFACTURER	Fabrica de Armas de Itajuba
CALIBRE	.30-06
MAGAZINE CAPACITY	5
ACTION	Bolt action
TOTAL LENGTH	1,111mm/43.75in
BARREL LENGTH	599mm/23.6in
WEIGHT UNLOADED	4.17kg/9.2lb

The 08/34 was the first military rifle produced in Brazil. The M954 was an improved variant of this rifle, based on a German design, the G/K43. It differed in having a steel bolt installed in order to strengthen the buttstock and a threaded muzzle to attach a grenade launcher. Prototypes were made after World War II and the calibre was changed to use US ammunition (from 7 x 57mm to .30-06). Production began in 1954 and continued until the early 1960s, when it began to be replaced by the M964.

Imbel M964

The Imbel M964 is a licence-built FAL made at its Imbel factory. The original FN FAL was produced in Belgium by FN from 1955–74. The design of the Imbel M964 is slightly stronger, and easier to machine than the Belgian FAL. The Imbel M964 uses a "type 3" receiver, designed by Imbel in 1964, which is well designed and well finished. Brazil produced the Imbel M964 with such vigour that they soon competed with FN in sales to Central and South American markets. As with all FAL designs not made in the Commonwealth, it is a "metric-pattern" and not an "inch-pattern" rifle and so the measurements were in metric. It was produced in high volume from 1964 to the mid-1990s, when it began to be replaced by the Imbel MD-2.

SPECIFICATION

MANUFACTURER Imbel
CALIBRE 7.62mm NATO
MAGAZINE CAPACITY 20
ACTION Gas operated/tilting lock
TOTAL LENGTH 1,100mm/43.3in
BARREL LENGTH 533mm/21in
WEIGHT UNLOADED 4.45kg/9.8lb

Imbel MD-2

Faced with the world-wide switch (at least in the non-Warsaw Pact countries) to the 5.56mm cartridge, the Brazilian arms industry could not let market share slip away. The MD-1 and then MD-2 were scaled-down FAL rifles in 5.56 x 45mm. Like the Belgian company FN, Imbel first tried a tilting-bolt design. The tilting-bolt design of the FAL proved to be unreliable in extracting fired cases of the 5.56mm cartridge, so the MD-2 was changed from the tilting block of the FAL (in the MD-1) to a rotating bolt like the M16. In addition to the M16 type bolt, the MD-2 uses M16 magazines. This was the same step taken by FN when they changed from the CAL to the FNC. Production began in 1985 and continues to the present.

SPECIFICATION

MANUFACTURER Imbel
CALIBRE 5.56 x 45mm
MAGAZINE CAPACITY 20 & 30
ACTION Gas operated/rotating bolt
TOTAL LENGTH 1,010mm/39.7in
BARREL LENGTH 453mm/17.8in
WEIGHT UNLOADED 4.4kg/9.7lb

Uruguay

The South American country of Uruguay is not a world military power. It currently fields a mix of American, European and Soviet armoured vehicles, and is still using FN-FAL rifles, many decades after most other armies have switched to another assault rifle in 5.56mm calibre.

Daudeteau carbine

The Mauser M71 single shot rifle was cutting-edge when first made in Germany in 1871. By the time the rifles were sold to Uruguay in 1887 – where they were known as the Daudeteau carbine – they were already obsolete. The carbines were sent to the French Armoury at St Denis for conversion to the 6.5mm Daudeteau cartridge, and may have acted as an emergency stop-gap rifle. They remained in service until 1895, and Uruguay purchased 10,000 M1895 carbines less than ten years later.

SPECIFICATION

MANUFACTURER OWG-Steyr
CALIBRE 6.5 x 53mm Daudeteau
MAGAZINE CAPACITY Single shot
ACTION Bolt action
TOTAL LENGTH 994mm/39.15in
BARREL LENGTH 505mm/19.9in
WEIGHT UNLOADED 3.42kg/7.54lb

Portugal

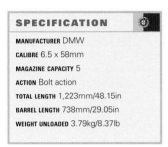

Leaving it a little late in upgrading its rifles, Portugal adopted a single shot Guedes in 1885. It immediately abandoned the Guedes, and then the Kropatschek in 1886, a tube-magazine rifle that was obsolete almost as soon as it was fielded. Finally, Portugal settled on a bolt-action magazine repeater, the Mauser-Verguiero, in 1904. That rifle was then produced in Portugal under licence.

Mauser-Verguiero 1904

SPECIFICATION

MANUFACTURER DMW
CALIBRE 6.5 x 58mm
MAGAZINE CAPACITY 5
ACTION Bolt action
TOTAL LENGTH 1,223mm/48.15in
BARREL LENGTH 738mm/29.05in
WEIGHT UNLOADED 3.79kg/8.37lb

Mannlicher-Schoenauer rifles and carbines were first manufactured by Steyr in Austria in 1903. However, the Mannlicher-Schoenauer was rejected by Portugal as too expensive for an issue rifle. A Portuguese officer, Verguiero, designed a rifle with a collection of features, using the split bridge (where the bolt handle is in front of the rear bridge) of the Mannlicher-Schoenauer, a dual half-cocking action (half on opening, half on closing) and a Mauser magazine. However, Portugal found it could not manufacture the rifle itself, so it was made in Germany. The Mauser-Verguiero was produced from 1904 to 1909 and used through the 1950s.

G3

SPECIFICATION

MANUFACTURER Fabrica de Braco de Porta
CALIBRE 7.62mm NATO
MAGAZINE CAPACITY 20
ACTION Roller-delayed blowback
TOTAL LENGTH 1,021mm/40.2in
BARREL LENGTH 450mm/17.7in
WEIGHT UNLOADED 4.49kg/9.9lb

After World War II, in the early stages of the Cold War, Portugal caught up with the rest of Europe and selected the excellent West German Heckler & Koch rifle as their issue rifle. Made under licence in Portugal, it is identical to the West German G3, which in its day competed with rifles such as the FAL. Production commenced in the early 1960s and the rifles are in use to the present day. The G3 was the standard infantry weapon of the German Bundeswehr until 1997, and is still being used by several armed forces around the world. Portuguese troops on peacekeeping missions can be seen with licenced G3 rifles.

Guedes M-1885

SPECIFICATION

MANUFACTURER Steyr
CALIBRE 8 x 60R
MAGAZINE CAPACITY Single shot
ACTION Tilting block
TOTAL LENGTH 1,218mm/47.9in
BARREL LENGTH 845mm/33.25in
WEIGHT UNLOADED 4.10kg/9.04lb

The Guedes was an Portuguese single-shot rifle, developed by Portuguese Lieutenant (later General) Luis Guedes Dias. The M-1885 was an example of how not to go about acquiring a rifle: the rifle was designed in Portugal, and a few tool room samples were made in 11mm calibre. However, Portugal was unable to mass-produce the rifles so Austrian manufacturer Steyr was asked to make them. Even before production could begin, smokeless powder and smaller cartridges were adopted in firearms across Europe. Portugal requested Steyr to change the calibre rifle from 11mm to 8mm. By the time they were finally made in 1885–6, single-shots were obsolete, so they were put in storage while the Kropatschek was being developed. This rifle was built for Portugal by Steyr in lieu of the short-lived Guedes M-1885.

Kropatschek M-1886

SPECIFICATION

MANUFACTURER Steyr

CALIBRE 8 x 60R

MAGAZINE CAPACITY 8-round tube

ACTION Bolt action

TOTAL LENGTH 1,319mm/51.95in

BARREL LENGTH 801mm/31.55in

WEIGHT UNLOADED 4.88kg/10.07lb

Having become obsolete in 1885, the Guedes was replaced with the Kropatscheck, a blend of the French Mle. 1878 and the German Gew 71/84 with an improved cartridge lifter. While the Guedes was obsolete before it was adopted, the Kropatschek had just over 20 years of use before it became obsolete. It was in service from 1886 to 1904.

Mannlicher-Schoenauer, Trials pattern

SPECIFICATION

MANUFACTURER Steyr

CALIBRE 6.5 M-S

MAGAZINE CAPACITY 5

ACTION Bolt action

TOTAL LENGTH 1,225mm/48.25in

BARREL LENGTH 725mm/28.55in

WEIGHT UNLOADED 3.76kg/8.31lb

Austrian manufacturer Steyr pushed the Mannlicher-Schoenauer on to the market, but found few buyers. It was made only in 1901 for the Portuguese Trials, and never adopted by the country as it was too expensive. Portugal decided to choose the Vergueiro instead.

Spain

Spain suffered internal military strife in the 20th century, during the Civil War (1936–9) that saw the overthrow of the monarchy and the establishment of the Republic. After World War II, German engineers emigrated to Spain, and brought with them their ideas, leading to CETME and the rifles that followed.

Destroyer carbine

SPECIFICATION

MANUFACTURER Ayra Duria, Eibar

CALIBRE 9mm Largo

MAGAZINE CAPACITY 5

ACTION Bolt action

TOTAL LENGTH 1,003mm/39.5in

BARREL LENGTH 495mm/19.5in

WEIGHT UNLOADED 2.72kg/6lb

The original Destroyer carbines were simple to the point of being crude, where the bolt handle was the only locking lug of the bolt to the receiver. However, that was strong enough for the handgun cartridge it was chambered in (the 9mm Largo). It was made from 1920 until the Civil War in 1936. After the Republic was established, the police force of Spain was reorganized. They also turned in their Winchester M-92 lever-action rifles for a new police carbine. The new Destroyer was a bolt-action carbine much like a scaled-down Mauser. The magazine was detachable, and held five rounds, although a good gunsmith could no doubt have fabricated one of greater capacity. For a police officer, armed with even lesser weapons, it was sufficient. And if stolen or turned against the government, it would prove less useful than a modern rifle. First issued in the mid-1930s, the carbines continued to be used until they were replaced by Star submachine guns in the late 1960s.

Police weapons
With rare exceptions, police officers need a firearm only as a badge of office. A bolt-action rifle using pistol ammunition was adequate until the late 20th century.

CETME Model A

SPECIFICATION

MANUFACTURER CETME
CALIBRE 7.62 x 51mm
MAGAZINE CAPACITY 20
ACTION Roller-delayed blowback
TOTAL LENGTH 1,015mm/39.95in
BARREL LENGTH 450mm/17.7in
WEIGHT UNLOADED 4.48kg/9.88lb

The Model A was the earliest version of the CETME (Centro de Estudios Técnicos de Materiales Especiales), before German manufacturers Heckler & Koch became involved in the design and production of a blueprint version of the CETME, the G3. The Model A fired from an open bolt in fully automatic fire, and a closed bolt in semi-automatic fire. The CETME Model A was built in 1955 and remained in service for only a short time. The initial models of the CETME used an under-powered dimensionally identical version of the 7.62mm NATO cartridge.

CETME Model C

SPECIFICATION

MANUFACTURER CETME
CALIBRE 7.62mm NATO
MAGAZINE CAPACITY 20
ACTION Roller-delayed blowback
TOTAL LENGTH 1,015mm/39.95in
BARREL LENGTH 450mm/17.7in
WEIGHT UNLOADED 4.58kg/10.1lb

The CETME Model C was strengthened to accept the full-power 7.62mm NATO instead of the lower-powered 7.62mm Spanish cartridge that used the same case. Heckler & Koch were involved and the CETME and the G3 were in parallel development. It was made in the late 1950s, as part of the final development process towards the G3/G33 and CETME production rifles.

SPECIFICATION

MANUFACTURER CETME
CALIBRE 5.56 x 45mm
MAGAZINE CAPACITY 30
ACTION Roller-delayed blowback
TOTAL LENGTH 925mm/36.42in
BARREL LENGTH 400mm/15.75in
WEIGHT UNLOADED 3.4kg/7.50lb

CETME Model L

This was the final derivation of the CETME. It was built to use the widely accepted 5.56mm cartridge fed from near-ubiquitous M16 magazines. It differed cosmetically from the Heckler & Koch G3/G33 series, but the design was the same even if parts did not interchange. It was replaced in Spanish service by the Heckler & Koch G36 because it was too heavy to use a 5.56mm cartridge. It was also showing its age, especially in comparison with the new G36. The Model L was in service from 1984 to 1999.

Mauser Model 1943

SPECIFICATION

MANUFACTURER La Coruña
CALIBRE 7.92 x 57mm
MAGAZINE CAPACITY 5
ACTION Bolt action
TOTAL LENGTH 1,105mm/43.5in
BARREL LENGTH 599mm/23.6in
WEIGHT UNLOADED 3.90kg/8.62lb

A standard Mauser action, this rifle was built in Spain for local use. The rifle calibre was changed to 7.92 x 57mm from the earlier 7 x 57mm to allow for easier supply, as most machine guns had also been changed to this calibre. When sold as surplus, a rifle manufactured by La Coruña was highly desired by custom gunsmiths, as a base on which to build hunting rifles. Thousands were stripped down to bolt and receiver, the rest of the parts discarded. The Mauser Model 1943 remained in use until the mid-1950s.

FR-8

The FR-8 was made by converting M-1896 Mauser rifles already in Spanish armouries. This bolt-action rifle was re-barrelled to 7.62mm, gained an aperture rear sight, a flash hider (a device to reduce muzzle flash), grenade launcher, and used the CETME/G3 bayonet. The idea was to build it into a reserve rifle that would use G3 ammunition, grenades and bayonets, but not cost as much as new G3 rifles. It was converted, put into storage, then sold as surplus decades later. The conversion work lasted from the mid 1950s to the early 1960s. The FR-8s were sold off at the beginning of the 1980s.

SPECIFICATION

MANUFACTURER La Coruña
CALIBRE 7.62mm NATO
MAGAZINE CAPACITY 5
ACTION Bolt action
TOTAL LENGTH 989mm/38.95in
BARREL LENGTH 470mm/18.5in
WEIGHT UNLOADED 3.75kg/8.27lb

Remington Rolling Block Model 1871 carbine

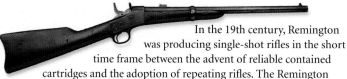

In the 19th century, Remington was producing single-shot rifles in the short time frame between the advent of reliable contained cartridges and the adoption of repeating rifles. The Remington Rolling Block was used around the world. It was adaptable to just about any rifle cartridge, for a price, and could be custom made to order. Spain bought the Remington Rolling Block in 1871 and it was in action until 1885 before becoming obsolete.

SPECIFICATION

MANUFACTURER Remington
CALIBRE 11 x 58R
MAGAZINE CAPACITY Single shot
ACTION Single shot
TOTAL LENGTH 962mm/37.9in
BARREL LENGTH 588mm/23.15in
WEIGHT UNLOADED 3.27kg/7.23lb

United Kingdom

Historically a dominant military power, Britain has a long history of weapons design, manufacturing and export. Britain was unique in the "sealed pattern" method of fixing dimensions and features. Once a firearm was finalized, a single sample would be selected and "sealed", or marked, as the definitive sample against which all others would be compared or measured. British rifle designs have always been driven by the needs of the army rather by the export market, as exemplified by Mauser.

Accuracy International suppressed

In the early 1980s the L42 sniper rifle was showing its age and so the British Army embarked on a search for a replacement. The

bedding block

Accuracy International (AI) design has a bedding block. (Bedding is the fitting of the metal parts of the barrel and receiver to the wood stock.) The receiver is bolted to the bedding block and the two halves of the stock are bolted to the block from the sides. Although heavy, the design eliminates loss of accuracy through stock warping. Accuracy of sniper and target rifles are usually measured by the "minute of angle" (MOA) which is approximately a 60th part of a degree (or an inch of group size at 100yd). The AI delivers sub-MOA accuracy (i.e. below the minute of an angle). It has been in service since 1986.

SPECIFICATION

MANUFACTURER Accuracy International
CALIBRE 7.62mm NATO, 7mm Rem Mag, .300 Win mag, .338 Lapua
MAGAZINE CAPACITY 5
ACTION Bolt action
TOTAL LENGTH 1,270mm/50in w/o suppressor
BARREL LENGTH 686mm/27in
WEIGHT UNLOADED 6.8kg/15lb w/o scope

EM 2

optical sight in carry handle

SPECIFICATION

MANUFACTURER Chambons Tool Co., Enfield, BSA, Long Branch
CALIBRE .280/30
MAGAZINE CAPACITY 20
ACTION Gas operated/pivoting flaps
TOTAL LENGTH 884mm/34.8in
BARREL LENGTH 609mm/24.6in
WEIGHT UNLOADED 3.65kg/8.06lb

The EM 2 was made as a prototype in the late 1940s and had a bullpup design. This means that rather than placing the receiver and magazine in front of the grip and trigger, they were placed behind them. This design was not new, but all the other features of the EM 2 were. The sights were in the carry handle, high over the bore, and the bore was directly in line with the stock. The calibre was the low-recoil .280/30. The US Army insisted on a cartridge no less powerful than the .30-06. The EM 2 could not compete with the Belgian FN FAL and languished both as a design and a concept.

Martini-Metford carbine

SPECIFICATION

MANUFACTURER Enfield
CALIBRE .303 British
MAGAZINE CAPACITY None
ACTION Single shot/tilting block
TOTAL LENGTH 947mm/37.3in
BARREL LENGTH 543mm/21.4in
WEIGHT UNLOADED 2.97kg/6.56lb

With old rifles on hand, the new .303 cartridge in production and many troops to equip, it made sense to rebuild old rifles in the late 19th century. The Martini was strong enough to take the new cartridge, and plentiful enough to be widely distributed. From front-line use to colonial, the boy scouts and drill rifles, the Martini could be found at every gun club and many armouries. Some even came out of storage for issue to the Home Guard during World War II. Unfortunately, this carbine was obsolete even when brand new in 1885.

Martini-Enfield Mark 1

SPECIFICATION

MANUFACTURER Enfield
CALIBRE .303 British
MAGAZINE CAPACITY None
ACTION Single shot/tilting block
TOTAL LENGTH 1,181mm/46.5in
BARREL LENGTH 767mm/30.2in
WEIGHT UNLOADED 3.77kg/8.31lb

The Metford rifling system (the grooves cut into the inside of the barrel to stabilize a projectile) was short-lived due to erosion caused to the inside of the barrel by new cordite gunpowder. The Enfield rifling proved to have a longer service life and was used when rebuilding Martini rifles. The manufacture of Enfield-rifled barrels would provide plenty of jobs at the Enfield factory. The rifle was very suitable for issue to indigenous troops in the colonies – it was durable, single-shot and with a fine bayonet mount. It was never used apart from in the colonies.

SPECIFICATION

MANUFACTURER Enfield
CALIBRE .303 British, black powder load
MAGAZINE CAPACITY 8
ACTION Bolt action
TOTAL LENGTH 1,266mm/49.285in
BARREL LENGTH 767mm/30.19in
WEIGHT UNLOADED 4.73kg/10.43lb

Lee-Metford Mark 1

Adopted in 1888, the Lee-Metford first fired .303 British cartridges loaded with compressed charges of black powder. The extreme length of the Lee-Metford reflects 19th century tactical use. The lack of a clip-charging guide until later would prove a problem when facing Boers in South Africa. While the Lee-Metford was only in service a short time in the late 1880s and early 1890s, long rifles, and the bayonets mounted on them, would later be found wanting in the trenches of World War I.

Lee-Speed carbine

SPECIFICATION	
MANUFACTURER	Enfield
CALIBRE	.303 British
MAGAZINE CAPACITY	10
ACTION	Bolt action
TOTAL LENGTH	1,013mm/39.9in
BARREL LENGTH	527mm/20.75in
WEIGHT UNLOADED	3.47kg/7.65lb

Joseph Speed, the assistant manager at Enfield during the adoption of the Lee-Metford rifle, made a number of improvements to the Lee, as well as patenting some features. These improvements included the wooden handguard above the barrel, the magazine cut-off and the patented magazine attachment to the receiver. Previously, barrels had often been left bare, and could burn the user after rapid firing. The radical magazine cut-off kept ammunition in reserve, a key concern for almost every military establishment in the world in the late 19th century. Continued updating of the Lee-Enfield makes this 1890 Speed carbine quite rare.

Lee-Enfield Mark 1*

SPECIFICATION	
MANUFACTURER	Enfield
CALIBRE	.303 British
MAGAZINE CAPACITY	10
ACTION	Bolt action
TOTAL LENGTH	1,257mm/49.5in
BARREL LENGTH	767mm/30.19in
WEIGHT UNLOADED	4.19kg/9.25lb

The Lee action was certainly fast and accurate enough for the British Army at the beginning of the 20th century. It had been proved that the rifling eroded in the earlier Lee-Metfords, so the Enfield-pattern rifling was immediately adopted. The Lee-Enfield Mark 1* had a long way to go before it became the standard pattern – for example, it needed a charging guide, so the magazine could be quickly reloaded with clips of ammunition. The Mark 1* was only current for a few years in the 1890s, being replaced by newer marks.

Lee-Enfield Cavalry Mark 1

SPECIFICATION	
MANUFACTURER	Enfield
CALIBRE	.303 British
MAGAZINE CAPACITY	6
ACTION	Bolt action
TOTAL LENGTH	988mm/39.3in
BARREL LENGTH	527mm/20.75in
WEIGHT UNLOADED	3.37kg/7.44lb

The Lee-Metford carbine lasted two years, and was replaced by the Lee-Enfield Cavalry Mark 1 carbine in 1896. The only changes from Metford to Enfield were the rifling pattern and the elimination of the sling bar on the right side of the buttstock. The sling bar was an attachment point for a hook so the cavalry rider stayed attached to the carbine even if he let go to handle the reins. It was replaced by a scabbard which moved the weight of the rifle from the trooper to the mount and also protected the rifle from the elements. In a little less than twenty years the cavalry unit to which this rifle was issued would become obsolete.

Lee-Enfield RIC

modified bayonet mount

SPECIFICATION	
MANUFACTURER	Enfield
CALIBRE	.303 British
MAGAZINE CAPACITY	6
ACTION	Bolt action
TOTAL LENGTH	1,016mm/40in
BARREL LENGTH	527mm/20.75in
WEIGHT UNLOADED	3.37kg/7.43lb

This rifle was made from the Lee-Enfield carbine specifically for the Royal Irish Constabulary (RIC) from the 1890s to the 1920s. The nosecap was modified to take the pattern 88 bayonet. At this time handguns were the weapons of military officers, and police constables, if they needed arms, used rifles or carbines. As the police rarely needed weapons, they spent more time in racks at the station than out with the constables. The RIC is as compact as other bolt-action rifles, but by today's standards is it not compact enough to be a carbine. After World War I, standard-issue rifles would be as compact.

No. 1 SMLE Mark III

SPECIFICATION

MANUFACTURER Enfield

CALIBRE .303 British

MAGAZINE CAPACITY 10

ACTION Bolt action

TOTAL LENGTH 1,130mm/44.5in

BARREL LENGTH 640mm/25.19in

WEIGHT UNLOADED 3.91kg/8.62lb

Adopted in 1907, the Mark III was the issue rifle when Great Britain entered World War I. Beautifully built by the best craftsmen and armourers of the time, it was smooth in function, balanced, accurate and suitable for combat. It was, however, too costly to make in wartime volume, and hand-fitting by trained craftsmen slowed production. The demands of wartime production diminished the rifle's surface appearance but not its performance. It was made from 1907 to 1915, when it was replaced with the Mark III*.

No. 1 SMLE Mark III*

SPECIFICATION

MANUFACTURER Enfield, BSA, Nottingham

CALIBRE .303 British

MAGAZINE CAPACITY 10

ACTION Bolt action

TOTAL LENGTH 1,130mm/44.5in

BARREL LENGTH 640mm/25.19in

WEIGHT UNLOADED 3.91kg/8.62lb

Manufacture of the Mark III* lasted from 1915 to 1918. In gaining its star (*), the Mark III* lost the long-range sight on the side of the rifle, the magazine cut-off, and less attention was given to polishing out tool marks. Despite the changes, the new Mark III* was rugged, durable and accurate enough for trench warfare. It was made in the millions and is still in use around the world. The durability of the design and the quality of manufacture means many are still standing in rifle racks today, as reliable as the day they were made.

No. 4 Mark 1

aperture sight

The No. 1 Mark III* served heroically through World War I, but it had some shortcomings. It was time-consuming to machine the receiver and the sights were only adequate at best. The re-design and testing process continued until adoption of the No. 4 Mark 1 in 1931. The No. 4 was designed with mass-production in mind, and incorporated a better sighting system as well as a heavier barrel. The receiver was altered to allow for manufacturing with fewer machine operations, lowering production costs. When World War II made even greater demands; the design was simplified further for mass production and became the No. 4 Mark 1*, made in Britain, Canada and the United States. The No. 4 action was strong enough to survive the adoption of the 7.62mm NATO cartridge, and has been built by some custom gunsmiths for even larger cartridges. Many No. 4s were still in use in the late 1950s, especially in former countries of the Empire.

SPECIFICATION

MANUFACTURER Enfield, Long Branch
(Canada), Stevens Arms (USA)

CALIBRE .303 British

MAGAZINE CAPACITY 10

ACTION Bolt action

TOTAL LENGTH 1,130mm/44.5in

BARREL LENGTH 640mm/25.2in

WEIGHT UNLOADED 3.99kg/8.8lb

Sniper No. 4 Mark 1 (T)

SPECIFICATION

MANUFACTURER Enfield, Holland &
Holland, London

CALIBRE .303 British

MAGAZINE CAPACITY 10

ACTION Bolt action

TOTAL LENGTH 1,130mm/44.5in

BARREL LENGTH 640mm/25.2in

WEIGHT UNLOADED 4.62kg/10.2lb

Like many armies between the wars, Britain dropped sniper rifles from inventories and removed sniper training from schedules. The new aircraft and tanks were thought to be the future. The needs of World War II changed that outlook, and the result was the No. 4 Mark 1. Each was a standard rifle with a telescopic sight affixed and a cheekpiece on the stock to make aiming more comfortable. The production and quality of sniper rifles quickly improved. When Britain changed to the 7.62mm NATO, the No. 4 Mark 1 (T) rifles that had served since 1942 were retired, and new 7.62mm versions built.

No. 5 Mark 1

flash hider

For all of its strengths, the No. 4 Mark 1 was too long and heavy for use in the jungle and by support troops. The No. 5 used a shorter and lighter barrel and had lightening cuts made to the receiver. The foresight assembly incorporated a flash hider. However, it suffered accuracy problems, maybe as a result of the cuts. To dampen the recoil of a lighter rifle using the .303 cartridge, the No. 5 was made with a rubber recoil pad. After a few years, the pads were usually rock-hard and did little to dampen felt recoil. However, the No. 5 was well thought of by those who used it. The No. 5 Mark 1 was a late-war introduction in 1944, kept in service to the end of the 1950s.

SPECIFICATION
MANUFACTURER Enfield
CALIBRE .303 British
MAGAZINE CAPACITY 10
ACTION Bolt action
TOTAL LENGTH 1,003mm/39.5in
BARREL LENGTH 475mm/18.7in
WEIGHT UNLOADED 3.24kg/7.15lb

DeLisle silent carbine

suppressor covering entire barrel

Despite camouflage, the sound of the shot can give away a sniper's position. The DeLisle carbines (designed by William DeLisle) were fitted with an integral suppressor. The suppressor dampens the sound of the shot, even at close range. As a .45 ACP "rifle", however, it was not intended for long-range shooting, being more of a sentry removal or commando weapon. The initial order of 500–600 was reduced to just over 100, making it quite rare. As a close-range quiet weapon, it was state-of-the-art in World War II, and used from 1942 to 1945. By the 1960s it was almost quaint.

SPECIFICATION
MANUFACTURER Enfield
CALIBRE .45 ACP
MAGAZINE CAPACITY 7 (using M-1911 magazines)
ACTION Bolt action
TOTAL LENGTH 895mm/35.25in
BARREL LENGTH 184mm/7.25in
SUPPRESSOR LENGTH 267mm/10.5in
WEIGHT UNLOADED 3.74kg/8.25lb

L1A1

Once adopted, the new British Service Rifle of the 1950s would be made at Enfield. The result was a licensed version of the Belgian FAL rifle, rugged enough to serve around the world for over 30 years. The Commonwealth FALs are known as "inch pattern" rifles, as the dimensions were in imperial rather than metric. British magazines also differed in the attachment blocks on the tube, making them unusable in metric rifles, but metric magazines were usable in British rifles. The L1A1 remained in service from adoption in 1956 until replaced by the dismal SA80 in 1985.

SPECIFICATION
MANUFACTURER Enfield
CALIBRE 7.62mm NATO
MAGAZINE CAPACITY 20
ACTION Gas operated/tilting bolt
TOTAL LENGTH 1,054mm/45in
BARREL LENGTH 533mm/21in
WEIGHT UNLOADED 4.33kg/9.56lb

No. 4 Enfield Target

target sights

The No. 4 action proved to be strong enough to be converted to 7.62mm NATO/.308 Winchester. Enfield converted many No. 4 rifles by replacing the extractor, barrel and magazine. A few smaller parts needed modification or replacement, and the end result was an accurate rifle for target shooting. With a heavier barrel, the same conversions were used by the British Army as the L42A1 sniper rifle. The No. 4 Enfield was used as a target rifle from the 1950s to the end of firearms ownership in England in the 1990s.

SPECIFICATION
MANUFACTURER Enfield
CALIBRE 7.62mm NATO/.308 Winchester
MAGAZINE CAPACITY 10
ACTION Bolt action
TOTAL LENGTH 1,181mm/46.5in
BARREL LENGTH 698mm/27.5in
WEIGHT UNLOADED 4.42kg/9.75lb

LSW prototype

SPECIFICATION

MANUFACTURER Enfield

CALIBRE 5.56 x 45mm

MAGAZINE CAPACITY 30

ACTION Gas operated/rotating bolt

TOTAL LENGTH 899mm/35.4in

BARREL LENGTH 645mm/25.4in

WEIGHT UNLOADED 5.28kg/11.65lb

The Squad Automatic Weapon (SAW) was tested using the 4.85mm cartridge system, developed by British designers in the mid-1970s searching for ideal small bore ammunition. The Light Support Weapon (LSW) had a long and heavy barrel, a bipod and was issued with a 30-round magazine. It lacked a quick-change barrel, leaving it prone to overheating in extended use. It did, however, evolve into the L85/86 series of SAWs using the American 5.56mm NATO cartridge. The LSW was made in the late 1970s only as a prototype.

EWS Experimental

SPECIFICATION

MANUFACTURER Enfield

CALIBRE 4.85mm

MAGAZINE CAPACITY 20 & 30

ACTION Gas operated/rotating bolt

TOTAL LENGTH 769mm/30.3in

BARREL LENGTH 518mm/20.4in

WEIGHT UNLOADED 4.13kg/9.1lb

An evolutionary step in the L85, the small 4.85mm cartridge was one of the attempts at producing high volumes of fire with decreased recoil. The idea was that a soldier could fire much faster and with greater accuracy than with larger calibres. This was perhaps correct, but it failed against the 5.56mm NATO cartridge and ended up as the L85A1 in 5.56 x 45mm. Given the half-century of wrangling over the performance of the 5.56mm cartridge, anything smaller in calibre would have caused a storm of controversy. The Enfield Weapon System (EWS) was made as a prototype in the late 1970s.

L85A1

SUSAT optical sight

In 1967, the British Army began a programme to find a new rifle to replace the L1A1. Initially tested with a new compromise cartridge, the 6.25 x 43mm, the rifle evolved from that through the 4.85mm cartridge and finally, in 1976, was adopted in the near-ubiquitous 5.56mm chambering. Initially known as the SA80, unlike the earlier EN 2, the L85 used the Stoner rotating bolt. It had, however, several major design flaws, and suffered from manufacturing problems. Apparently, bits and pieces fell off the rifle in hard use. It has since been overhauled by Heckler & Koch, to no avail. While some insist it is good enough, many users want a different weapon. The L85A1 was fielded in 1980 and is still in use.

SPECIFICATION

MANUFACTURER Enfield, Nottingham

CALIBRE 5.56 x 45mm

MAGAZINE CAPACITY 30

ACTION Gas operated/rotating bolt

TOTAL LENGTH 785mm/30.9in

BARREL LENGTH 518mm/20.4in

WEIGHT UNLOADED 4.13kg/9.1lb

SPECIFICATION

MANUFACTURER Enfield

CALIBRE 5.56 x 45mm

MAGAZINE CAPACITY 30

ACTION Gas operated/rotating bolt

TOTAL LENGTH 780mm/30.7in

BARREL LENGTH 518mm/20.4in

WEIGHT UNLOADED 4.13kg/9.1lb

L85A2, Heckler & Koch Models

After years of improvement, modifications, adjustments and upgrades, the SA80 was still not reliable. Heckler & Koch was given the contract to rebuild all SA80 rifles and improve their reliability. Some 200,000 of the 320,000 in inventory were serviced. The serviced weapons were tested, and approved. The Afghanistan campaign of 2002 proved that the efforts had not been successful. Some units were insisting on being issued other weapons instead of the L85. The rifles suffered from numerous malfunctions, and accuracy was often poor. They were issued first in 1985 and are still used today.

FN FAL Prototype

The initial prototype rifles had some unusual features. There was an optical sight and the top cover in one form or another was a type of stripper clip guide. They also had grenade launchers fitted during the consideration phase. The idea of an optical sight was radical in the early 1950s, as optics were rightly deemed as being too fragile for general issue. It was some time, however, before designers gave up on rifle-launched grenades as more than an emergency tool. The prototypes were made in the very early 1950s, and tested by the British Army.

SPECIFICATION

MANUFACTURER FN, Liège
CALIBRE 7.62 x 51mm T65
MAGAZINE CAPACITY 20
ACTION Gas operated/tilting bolt
TOTAL LENGTH 1,054mm/41.5in
BARREL LENGTH 533mm/21in
WEIGHT UNLOADED 4.13kg/9.12lb

FN FAL Trials Model

After the failure of the 4.85mm and the FN .280 for NATO adoption, the FAL was redesigned to use the US 7.62 x 5mm cartridge, as the T65. The trials model eliminated the grenade launcher and optical sight of the prototypes and incorporated sand cuts to increase reliability in desert conditions. The sand cuts were locations in the action rails where sand, mud or dirt could collect and not interfere with the rifle's operation. While the US Army rejected the FAL, it went on to be widely used. Curiously, the shortcomings the US Army found were not noted by other testers. The Trials models were made in 1954.

SPECIFICATION

MANUFACTURER FN, Liège
CALIBRE 7.62 x 51mm T65
MAGAZINE CAPACITY 20
ACTION Gas operated/tilting bolt
TOTAL LENGTH 1,054mm/41.5in
BARREL LENGTH 533mm/21in
WEIGHT UNLOADED 4.03kg/8.9lb

P-14 Mark 1*

Before World War I, Britain set out to improve or replace the Lee Enfield with an accurate long-range rifle. The P-13 did away with the two-piece stock of the Lee-Enfield, and featured a greatly improved rear sight. Chambered in a new 7mm cartridge, it was undergoing testing when World War I broke out. Rather than have two calibres in the supply system, Britain contracted with American firms to make the P-13 in .303 British. Called the P-14, or Enfield, it proved robust, accurate and reliable. When the United States entered World War I, they simply ordered it re-chambered in .30-06 and had millions more made. Used from 1914 through 1918, they went into storage after the war.

SPECIFICATION

MANUFACTURER Remington, Winchester, Eddystone
CALIBRE .303 British
MAGAZINE CAPACITY 5
ACTION Bolt action
TOTAL LENGTH 1,174mm/46.25in
BARREL LENGTH 660mm/26in
WEIGHT UNLOADED 4.35kg/9.6lb

M-1903 Springfield conversion prototype

Faced again with a critical shortage of small arms at the outset of World War II, Britain sought to have the American company of Remington Arms re-tool the US M-1903 Springfield rifle for the .303 cartridge (which were much larger than those of the .30-06 and unlikely even to accommodate five rounds.) For the amount of work the task would have involved, the fact that more than one prototype was made is amazing. With existing designs better suited to the .303 cartridge already in production, the idea was abandoned. The .303 Springfield was manufactured in 1940, only as a prototype.

SPECIFICATION

MANUFACTURER Remington
CALIBRE .303 British
MAGAZINE CAPACITY 5
ACTION Bolt action
TOTAL LENGTH 1,097mm/43.2in
BARREL LENGTH 609mm/24in
WEIGHT UNLOADED 3.94kg/8.69lb

Armalite AR-18

SPECIFICATION

MANUFACTURER Sterling, Costa Mesa,
Howa

CALIBRE 5.56 x 45mm

MAGAZINE CAPACITY 20, 30

ACTION Gas operated/rotating bolt

TOTAL LENGTH 965mm/38in

BARREL LENGTH 470mm/18.25in

WEIGHT UNLOADED 3.26kg/7.18lb

After Armalite sold the rights to the AR-15 to Colt, Eugene Stoner designed several new rifles. The AR-18 differed from his earlier AR-15 in several respects. Instead of aluminium forgings the AR-18 used steel pressings. The gas system of the AR-18 was basically that of the AK-47 and the stock could be designed and made as a folding unit as the recoil springs were not in the buttstock. The AR-18 did not achieve military acceptance (due partly to the United States giving free M16s to any country that asked and partly to the AR-18 not passing any military tests) and had a limited commercial production. It was made in three countries: United Kingdom, United States and Japan. Shooters and collectors still argue over which was the better made of the three, but all are extremely reliable and sought after by collectors. Production lasted from 1967 to 1979, occasionally in two of the three locations at the same time. The shorter barrel seen here is a non-factory modification to make the AR-18 more compact when the stock is folded.

Sterling Mark 6 Semi-automatic

SPECIFICATION

MANUFACTURER Sterling

CALIBRE 9mm Parabellum

MAGAZINE CAPACITY 34

ACTION Blowback

TOTAL LENGTH 914mm/36in (711mm/28in
police version)

BARREL LENGTH 406mm/16in (203mm/8in
police version)

WEIGHT UNLOADED 2.95kg/6.5lb

The semi-automatic-only versions of the L2A1 submachine gun were made for two different markets: police and sportsmen. Neither version accepts the internal parts of the submachine gun, while both accept the L2A1 magazines. As heavy as the Sterling carbine is, the recoil of the 9mm Parabellum is almost inconsequential. The submachine gun fires from an open bolt, while the semi-automatic version fires from a closed bolt. As an inexpensive practice rifle, or one for use indoors, the Sterling Mark 6 is fine. As a military or police weapon, the lack of full-automatic fire is something of a hindrance. The Sterling Mark 6 was made for a short time in the 1980s, and has been in service since then.

Pedersen Vickers

SPECIFICATION

MANUFACTURER Vickers

CALIBRE .276 Pedersen

MAGAZINE CAPACITY 10

ACTION Gas operated/toggle lock

TOTAL LENGTH 1,148mm/45.2in

BARREL LENGTH 520mm/20.5in

WEIGHT UNLOADED 4.13kg/9.1lb

The search for a viable self-loading rifle was quite vigorous between the World Wars. John Pedersen designed a rifle in his proprietary cartridge, the .276 Pedersen that used 10-shot en bloc clips. The action is basically a gas-operated version of the toggle lock of the German Luger. One concern of testers was that the toggle, breaking open and pivoting up, might strike the hat brim or helmet of a shooter. As good as the design was, it needed waxed cartridges to work. Any rifle or machine gun needing extra lubrication for its cartridges is simply not robust enough for combat. The .276 Pedersen cartridge preceded, by a decade, other attempts at a controllable assault weapon and cartridge, even though the Pedersen was meant as a battle rifle. Prototypes and a few production runs were made between 1930 and 1935, as Vickers vigorously promoted it.

France

With the development of Poudre B in around 1885, the first useful smokeless powder, France made all existing military rifles in their own, and all other armouries, obsolete. Combined with the new repeating rifles the change swept all military organizations. The last two decades of the 19th century saw all existing rifle designs continuously replaced, owing to the French policy of retaining and reworking existing designs rather than adopting new and improved ones.

Lebel Model 1886 M93

The Model 1886 M93, with its tubular magazine, was found to be more durable than the M-1916 when used in the rifle-grenade launching role. As a result, it was retained for that service even after World War I. The combination of pointed bullets and a tubular magazine required an odd rim design on the Lebel cartridge, with a groove machined in it to catch the bullet tip. Otherwise recoil might initiate a chain-fire in the magazine. The M93 was in service with France from 1886 to the 1930s.

SPECIFICATION

MANUFACTURER St Etienne and others
CALIBRE 8mm Lebel
MAGAZINE CAPACITY 10
ACTION Bolt action
TOTAL LENGTH 1,303mm/51.3in
BARREL LENGTH 798mm/31.4in
WEIGHT UNLOADED 4.24kg/9.35lb

Lebel Mannlicher-Berthier Model 1890 Cuirassier

The Mannlicher-Berthier is the amalgam of the Berthier bolt action and the Mannlicher magazine feed. The Mannlicher clip drops free when empty, and thus requires an opening in the magazine bottom plate. Most other Mannlicher-magazine rifles had a five-shot capacity, but the large rim of the Lebel cartridge made more than three difficult. The 1890 Cuirassier model has a buttstock shaped for use by heavy cavalry when wearing their steel back and breastplate. The incongruity of cavalry and repeating rifles had not yet become apparent in 1890. The rifle was in service from 1890 to 1914, when cavalry (and breastplates) became obsolete.

SPECIFICATION

MANUFACTURER St Etienne
CALIBRE 8mm Lebel
MAGAZINE CAPACITY 3
ACTION Bolt action
TOTAL LENGTH 945mm/37.2in
BARREL LENGTH 454mm/17.85in
WEIGHT UNLOADED 3.02kg/6.66lb

Mannlicher-Berthier Model 1916

larger magazine capacity

Despite the need for huge wartime production, France actually improved the basic Model 1907/15 design in 1916, based on operational experience. The magazine capacity of the Mannlicher clips was raised to five (although what having two different Mannlicher clips in the supply system did can only be imagined) and the ejection port for the expended clips was given a hinged cover. The Model 1916 was still in service in 1939, even though the planned upgrades (sights and handguards) in the 1920s and early 1930s had not all been done.

SPECIFICATION

MANUFACTURER St Etienne
CALIBRE 8mm Lebel
MAGAZINE CAPACITY 5
ACTION Bolt action
TOTAL LENGTH 1,305mm/51.4in
BARREL LENGTH 802mm/31.6in
WEIGHT UNLOADED 4.27kg/9.24lb

Mannlicher-Berthier M16 Artillery

SPECIFICATION

MANUFACTURER St Etienne and others
CALIBRE 8mm Lebel
MAGAZINE CAPACITY 5
ACTION Bolt action
TOTAL LENGTH 945mm/37.2in
BARREL LENGTH 453mm/17.85in
WEIGHT UNLOADED 3.24kg/7.16lb

A modified M92, using the M1916 Mannlicher clip for greater capacity, this was issued to artillery, as well as mounted and motorized infantry machine gun crews and bicycle troops. The sling hardware was moved to the side of the rifle for greater ease of carry. It was used in military service until 1939 and used by gendarmerie, customs and prison guards into the 1960s.

MAS Model 1936

SPECIFICATION

MANUFACTURER St Etienne
CALIBRE 7.5 x 54mm
MAGAZINE CAPACITY 5
ACTION Bolt action
TOTAL LENGTH 1,022mm/40.25in
BARREL LENGTH 575mm/22.65in
WEIGHT UNLOADED 3.75kg/8.27lb

Decades after the Mauser design had proven superior, France designed a new bolt-action rifle. The action was compact, with the locking lugs at the rear of the bolt. That necessitated angling the bolt handle forward to avoid striking the firer's hand during recoil. At least it was chambered for the M1929 short cartridge, and not the 8mm Lebel of earlier French bolt-action rifles. The rifle was obsolete the moment it was unveiled. It was manufactured from 1937 to 1940, and again from 1945 to 1953.

MAS Model 49

SPECIFICATION

MANUFACTURER St Etienne
CALIBRE 7.5 x 54mm
MAGAZINE CAPACITY 10
ACTION Gas operated/direct
  impingement
TOTAL LENGTH 1,075mm/42.35in
BARREL LENGTH 580mm/22.85in
WEIGHT UNLOADED 4.06kg/8.97lb

When the St Etienne region of France was liberated after World War II, the French introduced the MAS Model 44. The MAS Model 49 was an improved auto-loading rifle. While experimental models were made in .30-06, the Model 49 was designed in the standard French calibre, with improved gas system, and it dispensed with the Model 36 bayonet. It was rather awkward in handling, but reasonably reliable in function. The magazine catch, unique to the French, is on the side of the magazine, not the front and rear as other designs use. The MAS Model 49 was in service from 1949 to the early 1970s.

FR F-1 Type A

SPECIFICATION

MANUFACTURER MAS
CALIBRE 7.5 x 54mm, 7.62mm NATO
MAGAZINE CAPACITY 10
ACTION Bolt action
TOTAL LENGTH 1,136mm/44.75in
BARREL LENGTH 705mm/27.75in
  w/integral muzzle brake
WEIGHT UNLOADED 5.44kg/12lb

A further refinement of the MAS-36/44/49/56 series, the F-1 is a purpose-built, bolt-operated sniper rifle. It has the regular stock replaced with a stock and pistol grip, the barrel is free-floated, and there is a scope base attached to the receiver. With the 3.8 x Mle L.806 sight attached, it is suitable for short to medium-range use, out to 500–600m/1,600–2,000ft. Standard equipment features a bipod whose legs may be folded forward into a recessed area at the front-end of the weapon. The FR F-1 has been in use from 1964 to the present. The FR F-2 sniping rifle is an updated version of the F-1.

Famas F1

charging handle

Known as *le clarion*, or the bugle, by the troops, this
bullpup design is unmistakable owing to the extended
carry handle. The Fusil Assault MAS (FAMAS) distinctive handle
is on top, inside the carry handle, as in the earliest Armalite
designs. The top-mount charging handle therefore avoids the biggest problem
left-handed shooters have with bullpups. The carry handle is also the mounting
point for the integral bipod. By reversing the bolt head and ejection port
cover/cheekpiece, the rifle can be converted from right- to left-hand use. While
the delayed blowback system is barely strong enough for the brisk 5.56 x 45mm
cartridge, and extraction and ejection problems are not rare, the Famas F1
remains in service, although only with the French forces; it has not been adopted
outside of the French Army or French Foreign Legion. The FAMAS F1 was
introduced in 1976 to replace the Model 49, and is in service to the present.

SPECIFICATION

MANUFACTURER	MAS
CALIBRE	5.56 x 45mm
MAGAZINE CAPACITY	20,30
ACTION	Delayed blowback
TOTAL LENGTH	757mm/29.8in
BARREL LENGTH	487mm/19.2in
WEIGHT UNLOADED	3.93kg/8.66lb

Hecate II

SPECIFICATION

MANUFACTURER	PGM Precision
CALIBRE	12.7 x 99, .50 BMG
MAGAZINE CAPACITY	7
ACTION	Bolt action
TOTAL LENGTH	1,380mm/54.3in
BARREL LENGTH	700mm/27.55in
WEIGHT UNLOADED	13.8kg/30.42lb

When snipers require a long range, and precision rifle fire is used to deal with
dangerous situations, the .50 BMG cartridge is finding more and more favour.
PGM Precision makes their Ultima Ratio bolt action in .50 BMG for long-
range precision shooting, and for engaging harder targets. The muzzle brake is
essential in order to enable snipers to shoot it more than once or twice. The
blast is quite impressive, and it has served France well (quite often in
formations of the Foreign Legion) from 1989 to the present.

Belgium

Belgium had no national arms source until the
formation of FN (Fabrique Nationale) in 1889. It
quickly became a powerhouse in the arms market.
When German weapons manufacturer Peter Paul

Mauser introduced his improved repeating rifle
designs at the end of the 19th century, FN procured
licensing to produce this rifle, first for themselves,
then for the world market.

M-1889

SPECIFICATION

MANUFACTURER	FN, Liège
CALIBRE	7.65mm Mauser
MAGAZINE CAPACITY	5
ACTION	Bolt action
TOTAL LENGTH	1,273mm/50.13in
BARREL LENGTH	780mm/30.69in
WEIGHT UNLOADED	4.03kg/8.88lb

The first of the modern Mauser rifles, using a
charging clip and a bolt bored from the rear, the Belgian 1889
was made in FN as well as other plants. Earlier (before Mauser) bolt-
action rifle designs lacked clip-charging, and some were made with detachable
bolt heads, like the Lee-Metford. The M-1889 was modern when unveiled, but
soon fell behind due to Mauser's own design advances. The sheet metal cover
on the barrel, designed for protection, was itself susceptible to denting and
quickly allowed moisture to rust the barrel underneath. It also did nothing to
protect the firer from the hot barrel. The M-1889 was used from 1889 to 1905,
when many were upgraded and rebuilt.

M-1889 carbine

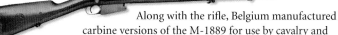

SPECIFICATION

MANUFACTURER FN, Liège
CALIBRE 7.65mm Mauser
MAGAZINE CAPACITY 5
ACTION Bolt action
TOTAL LENGTH 1,045mm/41.16in
BARREL LENGTH 550mm/21.65in
WEIGHT UNLOADED 3.51kg/7.75lb

Along with the rifle, Belgium manufactured carbine versions of the M-1889 for use by cavalry and bicycle troops. The only real difference was the barrel and overall length. While the protruding magazine of the 1889 looks very much like that of rifles with a Mannlicher-type magazine, the 1889 did not use enbloc clips. The cartridges were stripped off the charger into the rifle's internal magazine by the user. Thus, unlike the Mannlicher, the bottom of the M-1889 magazine was sealed against the elements. As with the rifles, the M-1889 carbine was used from 1889 until 1905.

Mauser FN M-1924

SPECIFICATION

MANUFACTURER FN, Liège
CALIBRE 7.92mm Mauser
MAGAZINE CAPACITY 5
ACTION Bolt action
TOTAL LENGTH 1,099mm/43.3in
BARREL LENGTH 589mm/23.2in
WEIGHT UNLOADED 3.85kg/8.5lb

After World War I, Belgium found the M-1889 and its variants to be increasingly obsolete. Since the FN plant was making Mauser 1898-type rifles for over 20 clients, it was easy to make more for the Belgian Army. The refined Mauser M-1924 became the essential military rifle for much of the world between the wars. Compared to previous models, the M-1924 was compact and handy, and still very reliable. FN not only equipped the Belgian Army with it, but sold great numbers around the world in a number of calibres, but mostly in 7.92mm. The M-1924 was made for Belgian and export use until 1940 and used by the German Army until the end of 1944.

Mauser FN M-1935

SPECIFICATION

MANUFACTURER FN, Liège
CALIBRE 7.65mm Mauser
MAGAZINE CAPACITY 5
ACTION Bolt action
TOTAL LENGTH 1,099mm/43.3in
BARREL LENGTH 589mm/23.2in
WEIGHT UNLOADED 3.85kg/8.5lb

This was essentially the M-1924 rifle in 7.65mm Mauser, developed in the 1930s in order to use up existing stocks of 7.65mm ammunition, which could not simply be discarded. After the 7.65mm ammunition supply was exhausted, the plan was to re-barrel rifles to the new standard 7.92 x 57mm calibre. The programme began in 1935 and was still going along slowly in 1940 when work stopped due to the invasion by Germany in World War II.

SPECIFICATION

MANUFACTURER FN, Liège
CALIBRE 7.65mm Mauser
MAGAZINE CAPACITY 5
ACTION Bolt action
TOTAL LENGTH 1,099mm/43.3in
BARREL LENGTH 601mm/23.7in
WEIGHT UNLOADED 3.94kg/8.7lb

M-1936

In the middle of the worldwide depression of the 1930s, Belgium sought to upgrade its arms, but not go to the full cost of new rifles. The M-1936 rifles were simply M-1889 rifles with the steel tube removed, re-stocked and with cocking pieces similar to the Mauser 1898 installed. The result was a rifle that looked and worked much like the M-1935 but which still used the ample supplies of 7.65mm ammunition stacked in warehouses. As with the M-1935, work began in 1936 and proceeded slowly until 1940.

FN SAFN M-1949

The experience of World War II made it clear that the days of the bolt-action rifle as a combat arm were over. As the first European-made self-loading rifle after the war, the M-1949 reflected designs from before the war. For a brief time after World War II, FN and Belgium sought to arm the world with M-1949 rifles. The basic design of the 1949 tilt-bolt action can be found in the FAL, the rifle FN developed and sold world-wide. The FAL replaced the M-1949, so sales were limited in volume and production of the M-1949 ceased in the late 1950s.

SPECIFICATION

MANUFACTURER FN, Liège
CALIBRE .30-06
MAGAZINE CAPACITY 10
ACTION Gas operated/tilting bolt
TOTAL LENGTH 1,109mm/43.7in
BARREL LENGTH 589mm/23.2in
WEIGHT UNLOADED 4.30kg/9.48lb

FN .280 prototype

Between 1949–53 FN addressed the wider need for short- to medium-range firepower for the infantry with the .280 prototypes. They did not have the full power of the .30-06, 7.92mm Mauser or .303 British, but no one except the US Army felt the need for a rifle that could kill at 914m/1,000yd. In the end the US Army won, and the .280 was relegated to museums. In less than 20 years, the US army would switch to the 5.56mm, and thus prove the wisdom of the FN approach. Had the US Army Ordnance experts not had their way, one of the FN .280 prototypes would probably be in service today.

SPECIFICATION

MANUFACTURER FN, Liège
CALIBRE 7 x 43mm
MAGAZINE CAPACITY 20
ACTION Gas operated/tilting bolt
TOTAL LENGTH 1,000mm/39.3in
BARREL LENGTH 500mm/19.68in
WEIGHT UNLOADED 4.3kg/9.47lb

FAL

During World War II many observers noted that the long range of a conventional rifle cartridge was not needed. More often, a high volume of fire at close to medium distances, large capacity and mild recoil were more useful. The FAL was originally conceived to fill that need. American insistence on the 7.62mm x 51 cartridge compelled other NATO countries to follow, and the FAL was scaled up to accept the 7.62mm. By modern standards the FAL fulfilled requirements for quite a long time. Starting with the required adoption of the T65 cartridge in 1953, the FAL was made as late as the 1980s.

SPECIFICATION

MANUFACTURER FN, Liège
CALIBRE 7.62mm NATO
MAGAZINE CAPACITY 20
ACTION Gas operated/tilting block
TOTAL LENGTH 1,090mm/42.9in
BARREL LENGTH 533mm/21in
WEIGHT UNLOADED 4.11kg/9.06lb

FAL-Para

By the middle of the 20th century airborne troops were the new elite. They required rifles that were both shorter and lighter. The FAL-Para features a folding stock, making it 245mm shorter than the standard weapon. It is not, however, much lighter unless the lower receiver is made of aluminium alloys. The FAL cannot be made much lighter as machined forgings are used in its upper receiver, the load-bearing part of the rifle. The Para version had a parallel service life to that of the standard FAL: 1958 to late 1980s. The aluminium-alloy version was half a kilo (one pound) lighter.

SPECIFICATION

MANUFACTURER FN, Liège
CALIBRE 7.62mm NATO
MAGAZINE CAPACITY 20
ACTION Gas operated/tilting block
TOTAL LENGTH 845mm/42.9in
BARREL LENGTH 533mm/21in
WEIGHT UNLOADED 4.11kg/9.06lb

FN CAL

SPECIFICATION

MANUFACTURER FN, Liège
CALIBRE 5.56 x 45mm
MAGAZINE CAPACITY 20 or 30
ACTION Gas operated/rotating bolt
TOTAL LENGTH 980mm/38.6in
BARREL LENGTH 467mm/18.4in
WEIGHT UNLOADED 3.31kg/7.3lb

The decision by the US army to adopt the 5.56mm cartridge prompted FN to develop and build the Carabine Automatique Légère (CAL) in the 1960s to replace the FAL. The CAL started as a tilting-bolt rifle, but extraction problems forced the designers to change to a rotating-bolt design. It was produced from 1966 to the early 1970s, and never adopted. Belgium found it too expensive to justify manufacture, and too unreliable to trust in combat. Plagued with problems, and with no apparent customers, FN eventually dropped the CAL. It was resurrected to some extent in the FNC, rushed to the market to compete in American rifle trials, but it differs markedly from the CAL.

SPECIFICATION

MANUFACTURER FN, Liège
CALIBRE 5.7 x 28mm
MAGAZINE CAPACITY 50
ACTION Blowback
TOTAL LENGTH 500mm/19.64in
BARREL LENGTH 263mm/10.35in
WEIGHT UNLOADED 2.54kg/5.6lb

FN P-90

In the late 1980s NATO expressed a need for a Personal Defence Weapon (PDW). The PDW was to be more than a handgun, but much handier than a rifle or carbine. Intended for use by support troops, the PDW is a new name for an old idea. The FN P-90 also introduced a new cartridge, the 5.7 x 28mm, which is vigorous enough to penetrate body armour. The P-90 comes with an optical sighting system as standard equipment. The P-90 was slowly adopted after 1990 and is presently in use, mostly in the law enforcement area.

SPECIFICATION

MANUFACTURER FN, Liège
CALIBRE 7.62mm NATO, .30 WSM
MAGAZINE CAPACITY 5 (7.62mm) 3 (WSM)
ACTION Bolt action
TOTAL LENGTH 1,118mm/44in
BARREL LENGTH 609mm/24in
WEIGHT UNLOADED 5.62kg/12.4lb
w/o scope

FN SPR

The FN SPR (Special Purpose/Police rifle) is a long-range precision rifle (or sniper) built on a "blueprinted" (machined to the exact dimensions of the drawings) Winchester M-70 action. The result is a rifle of great accuracy and durability. While the standard is 7.62mm NATO, those needing longer range (but losing two rounds in the magazine) can opt for the .300 Winchester Short Magnum, a cartridge no longer than the 7.62mm NATO which delivers performance of the much longer .300 Winchester Magnum. The FN SPR is a dual project by Winchester and FN, manufactured from 1998 to the present.

SPECIFICATION

MANUFACTURER FN, Liège
CALIBRE 5.56 x 45mm
MAGAZINE CAPACITY 20 & 30
ACTION Gas operated/rotating bolt
TOTAL LENGTH 694mm/27.32in
BARREL LENGTH 400mm/15.74in
WEIGHT UNLOADED 3.6kg/7.9lb

F2000

The FN bullpup solves the one glaring problem that all other bullpup rifles have – ejection of empty brass. Most are one-side-only rifles, as few can be reassembled to offer left-side ejection. The F2000 (introduced in the year 2000) ejects the empty brass forward through a tube. The shooter thus need not worry about empty brass being ejected into the face, nor an operating handle cycling on one side or the other. The mechanism of the F2000 is enclosed in a polymer shell, and can have optical sights mounted on the top rail. The forearm can be removed and replaced with a grenade launcher. A new design and product, it has already been purchased by Slovenia for military/police use.

Netherlands

The early Dutch rifles were entirely serviceable until the advent of self-loading rifles after World War II. By then, there were good ones to choose from, and more on the way. Except for the brief run of AR-10 rifles, the Netherlands has always purchased small arms as needed.

Armalite AR-10

stock in line with bore

Once the US company Armalite had perfected the AR-10 in the 1950s, they sought manufacturers. (Armalite was only a design, research and development company, not a manufacturing one.) Armalite granted manufacturing rights to Artillerie-Inrichtigen in the Netherlands in the hope that once there was a Dutch contract, other orders would follow, but this never came about. There was a brief interest around the world and Sudan and Portugal bought some rifles for their military, but then the US Army turned down the AR-10. The brief production period of 1959 to 1962 was enough to create a legend that weapons cognoscenti would not let go of for decades afterwards. Indeed, to this day the 7.62mm Armalite is still being offered by one company or another. But the Armalite of that time had a brief moment of interest, but little return for the investment placed in it.

SPECIFICATION

MANUFACTURER Artillerie-Inrichtigen, Zaandam
CALIBRE 7.62 x 51mm
MAGAZINE CAPACITY 20
ACTION Gas operated/rotating bolt
TOTAL LENGTH 1,049mm/41.3in
BARREL LENGTH 508mm/20in
WEIGHT UNLOADED 3.11kg/6.85lb

Mannlicher Model 1895

clip ejection port

Essentially the same as the Romanian M-1893 Mannlicher, the Dutch used the same style Mannlicher magazine, where the clip fell out when the last round in it was chambered. To reload the rifle, a new clip with cartridges had to be inserted, which was a simple and quick operation. While the 6.5mm Dutch cartridge is no powerhouse, it was good enough to serve as an infantry cartridge. The rifles served from 1895 to 1920.

SPECIFICATION

MANUFACTURER Steyr
CALIBRE 6.5 x 53R
MAGAZINE CAPACITY 5
ACTION Bolt action
TOTAL LENGTH 1,295mm/51in
BARREL LENGTH 790mm/31.1in
WEIGHT UNLOADED 4.30kg/9.48lb

Model 1895 carbine (Old Model)

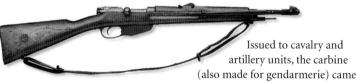

Issued to cavalry and artillery units, the carbine (also made for gendarmerie) came in a host of variants. The Old Model did not have the wooden fairing pinned on to the stock to preclude the magazine abrading uniforms. In a peacetime army, and with gendarmerie, the look of a uniform is very important. Despite the wear to uniforms, the carbine served well, from 1897 to 1920.

SPECIFICATION

MANUFACTURER Steyr, Artillerie-Inrichtigen
CALIBRE 6.5 x 53R
MAGAZINE CAPACITY 5
ACTION Bolt action
TOTAL LENGTH 952mm/37.5in
BARREL LENGTH 450mm/17.7in
WEIGHT UNLOADED 3.11kg/6.85lb

✚ Switzerland

Independent, neutral, and fiercely protective of her borders, Switzerland has a citizen army. All adults go through a period of active service and then remain in the Reserves all their lives. Annual rifle qualification is a requirement. While ready for action, the Swiss have avoided being in a war for centuries.

Schmidt-Rubin 1889 Experimental

safety ring

The original 1889 rifle was good when it was designed, but that period was one of intense rifle and cartridge development. The original 7.5mm cartridge could not be improved unless the 1889 rifle was improved, so Eidenossische Waffenfabrik (EW) in Bern strengthened the 1889 rifle. EW went on to make further improvements to the design, culminating in the M-1931. The experimental models were made only for a short time, between 1888 and 1897.

SPECIFICATION ✚
MANUFACTURER EW, Bern
CALIBRE 7.5 x 53.5mm
MAGAZINE CAPACITY 12
ACTION Straight-pull bolt action
TOTAL LENGTH 1,323mm/52.1in
BARREL LENGTH 780mm/30.7in
WEIGHT UNLOADED 4.5kg/9.94lb

Schmidt-Rubin M-1911 carbine

The rush to upgrade to repeating rifles of flat trajectory, high velocity and quick reloading led the Swiss to the Schmidt-Rubin straight pull. It was not quite as robust as a turnbolt in the mud of trench warfare, but this was unlikely to be required. It was also introduced in 1911 and served until the last upgrade of the Schmidt-Rubin, in 1931. Many simply went into the home rifle racks of the reservists to whom they were issued, and could be called on today.

SPECIFICATION ✚
MANUFACTURER EW, Bern
CALIBRE 7.5 x 55mm
MAGAZINE CAPACITY 6
ACTION Gas operated
TOTAL LENGTH 1,103mm/43.45in
BARREL LENGTH 592mm/23.3in
WEIGHT UNLOADED 3.92kg/8.65lb

Schmidt-Rubin M-1931

This rifle had a stronger lockup, shorter action and thus better accuracy. The improved action was shorter and stronger than the 1911 action. Note that the 1931 rifle was much the same size as the earlier carbine. Switzerland, along with many other countries, went to a shorter rifle as the standard for all units, and the few carbines manufactured were very compact. The M-1931 served until the mid 1950s, when they began to be replaced by the Stgw 57 in 1957.

SPECIFICATION ✚
MANUFACTURER EW, Bern
CALIBRE 7.5 x 55mm
MAGAZINE CAPACITY 6
ACTION Straight-pull bolt action
TOTAL LENGTH 1107mm/43.6in
BARREL LENGTH 651mm/25.65in
WEIGHT UNLOADED 4.01kg/8.85lb

BEW+F Mod SG E22

cold-weather trigger guard

When the Swiss Army decided to change from the 7.5mm to a smaller cartridge, it considered accuracy at 300m/984ft as well as at longer ranges. One cartridge tested used a shortened and necked-down 7.62mm NATO case: the 6.5 x 48mm, but the accuracy of heavier-bullet 5.56mm ammunition made the intermediate cartridge unnecessary. The Mod SG E22 was prototyped in the late 1970s.

SPECIFICATION ✚
MANUFACTURER EW, Bern
CALIBRE 6.45 x 48mm
MAGAZINE CAPACITY 20
ACTION Gas operated
TOTAL LENGTH 1,001mm/39.4in
BARREL LENGTH 528mm/20.8in
WEIGHT UNLOADED 4.1kg/9.04lb

Mannlicher Model 1893 carbine

The 1889 Schmidt action was too long to be turned into a carbine, so Switzerland, after trials, adopted the straight-pull design from Mannlicher as their carbine. The main problem with turning the 1889 Schmidt action into a carbine was the length of the bolt and action. In order to make the whole rifle compact enough, the barrel would have to have been shortened below a usable length. The Mannlicher only lasted a short time, and was in regular service from 1898 to 1905. The improved Schmidt-Rubin action could be made in carbine length.

SPECIFICATION	
MANUFACTURER	SIG, Neuhausen
CALIBRE	7.5 x 53.5R
MAGAZINE CAPACITY	6
ACTION	Straight-pull bolt action
TOTAL LENGTH	1,016mm/40in
BARREL LENGTH	550mm/21.65in
WEIGHT UNLOADED	3.08kg/6.8lb

Mondragon Model 1908

The Mondragon 1908 was built for Mexico, with only part of the order (400 rifles) delivered before the Mexican revolution of 1911. However, it was not until the 1930s that self-loading rifle designs became truly reliable enough for combat. Had the Mexican government not lost the war, SIG may well have continued development of the design. Left with the rest of the production run, SIG fitted Model 1908s with drum magazines and sold the rifles to Germany early in World War I. They were manufactured in 1911, and had all been shipped to Germany by 1915.

SPECIFICATION	
MANUFACTURER	SIG, Neuhausen
CALIBRE	7 x 57mm
MAGAZINE CAPACITY	8
ACTION	Gas operated
TOTAL LENGTH	1,239mm/48.8in
BARREL LENGTH	620mm/24.4in
WEIGHT UNLOADED	4.42kg/9.75lb

Mondragon German Air Service

drum magazine

Produced in 1915, the Mondragon was bought by the German Air Service for air-to-air combat before machine guns became common. Using a drum magazine, it was marginally more useful than a bolt-action rifle or a handgun. As soon as it became possible (and common) to mount machine guns on aircraft, the Mondragons went into storage.

SPECIFICATION	
MANUFACTURER	SIG, Neuhausen
CALIBRE	7 x 57mm
MAGAZINE CAPACITY	20
ACTION	Gas operated
TOTAL LENGTH	1,239mm/48.8in
BARREL LENGTH	620mm/24.4in
WEIGHT UNLOADED	4.58kg/10.1lb

SIG SG551-2

Called by some "the best-made AK-47 in existence", the Sig 551 uses an AK gas system, with a 5.56mm cartridge and proprietary magazines. The Special Weapons And Tactics (SWAT) version has a cheekpiece on the buttstock and an optics rail. The magazines are manufactured of polymer and have nubs and sockets on them that allow them to be snapped together side-by-side. They are not compatible with M16 magazines, as the Swiss felt the aluminium M16 magazines were far too flimsy for their use. Manufacturing began in 1986 and the 551 still stands as the issue rifle to Swiss forces.

SPECIFICATION	
MANUFACTURER	SIG, Neuhausen
CALIBRE	5.56 x 45mm
MAGAZINE CAPACITY	30
ACTION	Gas operated
TOTAL LENGTH	843mm/33.2in
BARREL LENGTH	358mm/14.1in
WEIGHT UNLOADED	4.1kg/9.04lb

Germany

Driven by the demands of two World Wars, German small arms inventiveness seems to have had no limits. Very few German designs can be said to be fragile or unreliable. However, the penalty for robust designs quite often seems to be weight. Some designs, although certain of action, are somewhat portly.

During World War II, the German small arms procurement system was not very centralized. The Luftwaffe, navy and Waffen-SS all procured their own weapons. Since the parachute units were part of the Luftwaffe, this added more confusion. The system proved to be very inefficient.

HK-CETME Prototype

curved 7.62 x 39mm magazine

SPECIFICATION

MANUFACTURER CETME
CALIBRE 7.62 x 39mm
MAGAZINE CAPACITY 20
ACTION Roller-delayed blowback
TOTAL LENGTH 939mm/37.4in
BARREL LENGTH 431mm/17in
WEIGHT UNLOADED 4.76kg/10.5lb

Derived from the Stg45(M) using the Vorgrimmler roller-delayed blowback action, the original CETME rifles were not designed for the full-power NATO cartridge. Early prototypes used the 7.92 x 33mm, 7.92 x 40mm and a lightly loaded 7.62 x 51mm cartridge. The lack of initial extraction (that is, no rotating bolt) means the CETME and all derivatives must use a fluted chamber to prevent case adhesion in the chamber and case breakage which leads to malfunctions. The refined design saw limited production in the late 1940s to mid 1950s.

Commission Model 1888

SPECIFICATION

MANUFACTURER Danzig, Erfurt, Spandau
CALIBRE 7.92 x 57mm
MAGAZINE CAPACITY 5
ACTION Bolt action
TOTAL LENGTH 1,244mm/49in
BARREL LENGTH 740mm/29.15in
WEIGHT UNLOADED 3.9kg/8.6lb

Designed by a committee, the 1888 rifle was intended as an improvement to replace the already obsolete Gew 71/84 rifles in service. The committee did not consult Peter Paul Mauser, nor was his firm awarded any contracts to build the new rifles. Some speculate that this oversight or slight drove him to design and refine his own rifle which ended up as the 1898. The 1888 rifle fired a 7.92 x 57mm cartridge using a .318 diameter round-nosed bullet. When the German military cartridge was updated to use a spitzer bullet, the diameter was increased to .323. It is generally unsafe to fire the later ammunition in earlier rifles. Production began in 1888 but by 1898 it was obsolete.

Cavalry Carbine, Commission Model 1888

SPECIFICATION

MANUFACTURER Danzig, Erfurt, Spandau
CALIBRE 7.92 x 57mm
MAGAZINE CAPACITY 5
ACTION Bolt action
TOTAL LENGTH 952mm/37.5in
BARREL LENGTH 435mm/17.15in
WEIGHT UNLOADED 3.08kg/6.8lb

The committee-designed M-1888 rifle was modified for cavalry service by shortening the barrel and bending the bolt handle down. As with the rifle, the carbine used the Mannlicher magazine system. Using the same 7.92 x 57mm cartridge with a .318 diameter round-nosed bullet as the rifle, the felt recoil of the much lighter carbine had to be quite stout. Likewise with the rifle, it is generally unsafe to fire the later ammunition (with its larger-diameter 8mm bullet) in these earlier-model carbines. Production began in 1890 but by 1898 it was obsolete and replaced by cavalry-version Model 1898 Mauser designs.

Kar 98 Cavalry

At the end of the 19th century the Mauser Model 98 action was robust, reliable, handy, and easy to train troops in its use. The cavalry, however, had not yet been replaced. Thus a short rifle for mounted use was designed, tested, and began issue in 1909. By the spring of 1915, there was no more need for cavalry, and short rifles went to artillery crews and machine gunners. After the war, rifles got shorter still, to the point of being almost as compact as pre-war carbines had been. The Kar 98 Cavalry was in service from 1909 to 1918.

SPECIFICATION	
MANUFACTURER	Danzig, Erfurt, Amberg
CALIBRE	7.92 x 57mm
MAGAZINE CAPACITY	5
ACTION	Bolt action
TOTAL LENGTH	1,079mm/42.9in
BARREL LENGTH	589mm/23.2in
WEIGHT UNLOADED	3.71kg/8.18lb

Luger Model 1902

shoulder stock detaches

Almost as soon as self-loading pistols were invented, designers attempted to make them into self-loading carbines. The drawbacks to the handy (for a carbine) size were lack of power and range, and decreased durability. For close-in work, especially in the trenches, however, a shoulder-stocked Luger carbine had a number of advantages. During World War I all Lugers were made to accept, and many fitted with stocks, which were issued to machine gun and artillery crews. After the war, with many submachine gun designs being developed, shoulder-stocked pistols fell out of favour. The Luger Model 1902 was popular from 1902 to 1918.

SPECIFICATION	
MANUFACTURER	DMW
CALIBRE	7.65 x 21mm
MAGAZINE CAPACITY	8, 32 round "snail" drum
ACTION	Recoil operated/toggle lock
TOTAL LENGTH	222mm/8.75in (longer with longer barrels)
BARREL LENGTH	101mm/4in (6, 8in also)
WEIGHT UNLOADED	0.875kg/1.93lb (stock adds 0.68kg/1.5lb)

FN FAL G1 sniper

optical sight

The Germans required rifles when they reorganized a defence force in the 1950s. The first rifle was a variant of the FN FAL known as the G1. The differences from the Belgian version were minor, with the sights on a slightly lower sighting plane, a sheet-metal handguard and integral bipod. The sniper version features optics for precise aim at longer ranges. Their request to build future G1 rifles themselves was brusquely turned down by FN. Their next rifle was the G3. Sniper variants are a standard model, once regular rifles have been provided in volume. It was produced from the late 1950s to early 1960s.

SPECIFICATION	
MANUFACTURER	FN, Liège
CALIBRE	7.62mm NATO
MAGAZINE CAPACITY	20
ACTION	Gas operated
TOTAL LENGTH	1,100mm/43.3in
BARREL LENGTH	533mm/20.98in
WEIGHT UNLOADED	4.45kg/9.81lb

Volksturm VG1-5

At the end of World War II, with central control crumbling, many local designs showed up. The *Volksturm* ("People's Force") needed weapons, and with no central supply, they manufactured what they needed whenever possible. The VG 1-5 uses the Stg44 magazines and ammunition, but the gas ports under the handguards bleed gas to delay the blowback action rather than initiate it. Crude but effective, it was far too little and too late to make any difference. The VG1-5 was made only in the spring of 1945 and could prove hazardous to fire.

SPECIFICATION	
MANUFACTURER	Gustloffwerke am Suhl
CALIBRE	7.92 x 33mm
MAGAZINE CAPACITY	30
ACTION	Gas-retarded blowback
TOTAL LENGTH	889mm/35in
BARREL LENGTH	374mm/14.75in
WEIGHT UNLOADED	4.61kg/10.18lb

Haenel MKb42(H)

SPECIFICATION

MANUFACTURER Haenel
CALIBRE 7.92 x 33mm
MAGAZINE CAPACITY 30
ACTION Gas operated
TOTAL LENGTH 939mm/37in
BARREL LENGTH 365mm/14.37in
WEIGHT UNLOADED 5.0kg/11.06lb

By the mid-1930s the German Army had finally concluded that the standard 7.92mm cartridge was too powerful, and settled on a new cartridge: the 7.92 x 33mm. Both Haenel and Walther were given contracts to develop carbines using this round. The Haenel design proved superior and, after extensive use on the Eastern Front, the design was refined and production increased. The project was kept from Hitler, who thought only full-power rifles were suitable for combat. When he found out about it, only personal intervention by Eastern Front combat veterans convinced him the new carbines were useful for combat. The Haenel MKb42(H) was made in 1942, and, once tested and improved, manufactured as the MP-43.

SPECIFICATION

MANUFACTURER Haenel, Mauser, Erma
CALIBRE 7.92 x 33mm
MAGAZINE CAPACITY 30
ACTION Gas operated
TOTAL LENGTH 939mm/37in
BARREL LENGTH 419mm/16.5in
WEIGHT UNLOADED 5.21kg/11.5lb

MP-43/1

The MP-43 series were the first assault rifles fielded in combat. The stamped-steel construction made manufacture fast and easy and the medium-powered cartridge made volume fire effective. Long-range rifle fire was no longer needed, and it was popular on the Eastern Front. At first, its issue was hidden from Hitler, who felt the only real rifle a soldier needed was a 98k. Only the incessant bombing of production facilities and rail lines prevented Germany from fielding this series in huge numbers. It was used from 1943–5.

Heckler & Koch G3

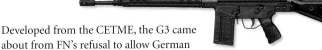

SPECIFICATION

MANUFACTURER Heckler & Koch
CALIBRE 7.62mm NATO
MAGAZINE CAPACITY 20
ACTION Roller-delayed blowback
TOTAL LENGTH 1,021mm/40.2in
BARREL LENGTH 450mm/17.7in
WEIGHT UNLOADED 4.5kg/9.9lb

Developed from the CETME, the G3 came about from FN's refusal to allow German production of the G1, the FAL in German service. To make the CETME work with the 7.62mm NATO cartridge, and give it the durability required, it ended up being heavy. (The officially-stated weight is less than any example weighed so far.) The roller-delayed blowback action requires a fluted chamber to be sure of certain extraction, and the resultant ejection is quite vigorous. Concealed soldiers could sometimes be spotted by the empty brass flying from their firing position. The rifle was used from 1959 to the early 1990s.

SPECIFICATION

MANUFACTURER Heckler & Koch
CALIBRE 20mm and 5.56 x 45mm
MAGAZINE CAPACITY 6, 30 respectively
ACTION Gas operated
TOTAL LENGTH 890mm/35in
BARREL LENGTH 460mm/18in (20mm cal)
250mm/9.8in (5.56mm cal)
WEIGHT UNLOADED 5.5kg/12.12lb

HK OICW

In an attempt to replace not only the M16 rifle but also grenade launchers, submachine guns and handguns, the US Army requested designs and trial models for the Offensive Individual Combat Weapon (OICW), a 20mm grenade-launching individual weapon with an attached (but detachable) 5.56mm carbine. The internal laser rangefinder was expected to set the fuses of each individual 20mm round electronically as it was fired. The OICW proved heavy, expensive, fragile and slow to use. Tested from the early 1990s to 2005, it was never fielded.

Heckler & Koch G36

optical sight

This was the replacement for the
G3. While Heckler & Koch made a variant of
the G3 in 5.56mm, it was not particularly
popular and it was also quite heavy for a 5.56mm rifle. The G36 is lighter than
the G3 and has a folding stock and built-in optical sight. It uses a variant of
the short-stroke gas system of the Armalite AR-18. With the collapse of
Communism, and the G11 project no longer needed, the Bundeswehr was
left with the G3. The G36 was the immediately available replacement as the
German service rifle, produced from the mid-1990s to the present.

SPECIFICATION

MANUFACTURER Heckler & Koch
CALIBRE 5.56 x 45mm
MAGAZINE CAPACITY 30
ACTION Gas operated
TOTAL LENGTH 998mm/39.24in
BARREL LENGTH 480mm/18.8in
WEIGHT UNLOADED 3.6kg/7.93lb

Heckler & Koch G41

This was the last in the line of roller-delayed blowback Heckler
& Koch weapons. The G41 was planned as the Reservist
weapon, backing up the G11. Using standard 5.56 x 45mm
ammunition, and M16 magazines, and working exactly like the familiar G3, it
would be a cost-effective reserve weapon to the more expensive G11. The lower
receiver was made of polymer and moulded, to reduce weight and cost. Where
the regular Army would be using G11s, the Reservists (who had mostly trained
on G3s) would be using the G41. The collapse of Communism threw all those
plans into disarray. It was produced in the mid-1980s, never fielded, was not
successful as an export weapon. Today it is found only in museums.

SPECIFICATION

MANUFACTURER Heckler & Koch
CALIBRE 5.56 x 45mm
MAGAZINE CAPACITY 30, NATO standard
ACTION Roller-delayed blowback
TOTAL LENGTH 997mm/39.2in
BARREL LENGTH 450mm/17.7in
WEIGHT UNLOADED 4.1kg/9.03lb

Heckler & Koch G11 prototype

Desiring a leap past the American
M16, Germany spent a great deal
of time (through Heckler & Koch)
developing a radical new rifle that
used caseless ammunition. The
magazine is above the bore and parallel to it. The rounds are
positioned nose-down and the bolt rotates ninety degrees to
cycle a round from the magazine. The bolt is also the chamber.
In full-auto fire the cyclic rate is 600 rpm, but in three-shot burst
mode the three shots are fired at a cyclic rate of 2,000 rpm. The idea is for all
three shots to be on target, and gone from the muzzle before the weapon can
move in recoil. The largest technical obstacle with caseless ammunition is
heat: the ejected brass of conventional cartridges takes a large amount of heat
with it. Caseless ammunition does not have that heat-loss option, and
the propellant had to be specially formulated to avoid cook-offs. (If an
over-heated weapon has a round left in the chamber, the heat can cause
combustion of the propellant, known as a cook-off.) When Communism
collapsed, the requirement and the funding disappeared. Germany suddenly
no longer needed them. The Heckler & Koch G11 was made in limited
numbers in the 1980s as test models, but never fielded.

SPECIFICATION

MANUFACTURER Heckler & Koch
CALIBRE 4.7mm
MAGAZINE CAPACITY 50
ACTION Recoil
TOTAL LENGTH 750mm/29.52in
BARREL LENGTH 540mm/21.25in
WEIGHT UNLOADED 3.6kg/7.93lb

The design
The futuristic design sealed the
mechanism from the elements
and reduced malfunctions.

Mauser M96

SPECIFICATION

MANUFACTURER Mauser

CALIBRE 7.65 x 25mm

MAGAZINE CAPACITY 10

ACTION Recoil operated

TOTAL LENGTH 508mm/20in
w/stock installed

BARREL LENGTH 133mm/5.25in

WEIGHT UNLOADED 1.25kg/2.75lb

The Mauser System, as the M96 was called, was more than just an autoloading pistol. The holster/stock also allowed its user to press it into service with aimed fire as a short-range carbine, or to deliver a great deal of firepower in a short time at close range. The internal magazine is reloaded using stripper clips, or chargers. Some models used external, or box, magazines which could be exchanged like any other pistol when more ammunition was needed. Manufacture began in 1896, and the M96 remained in use through the 1930s. Some were issued to motorcycle troops in Germany during World War II.

SPECIFICATION

MANUFACTURER Mauser

CALIBRE 7.92 x 57mm

MAGAZINE CAPACITY 10

ACTION Gas operated

TOTAL LENGTH 1,175mm/46.25in

BARREL LENGTH 552mm/21.75in

WEIGHT UNLOADED 5.10kg/11.25lb

G-41

The G-41 was an early attempt at a full-power self-loading rifle. Not very successful, the G-41 suffered from excessive size and weight, poor reliability and clumsy operation. For example, the charging handle worked very much like that of a bolt on a bolt-action rifle but did not reciprocate when fired. It was used solely to chamber the first round of a magazine. Field-testing proved its faults, and it was quickly replaced by improved designs such as the G-43. It was produced between 1941 and 1942.

FG 42

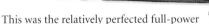

bipod, folded

SPECIFICATION

MANUFACTURER Rheinmettal-Borsig

CALIBRE 7.92 x 57mm

MAGAZINE CAPACITY 20

ACTION Gas operated

TOTAL LENGTH 940mm/37in

BARREL LENGTH 501mm/19.75in

WEIGHT UNLOADED 4.5kg/9.93lb

The German parachute units needed more firepower, but machine guns were too large and heavy for the limited Luftwaffe transport capacity to have as many as needed. The Luftwaffe sought self-loading rifles for their use. The two variants of the FG 42 were both select-fire box magazine fed rifles in the full power 7.92mm cartridge. Made of heavy-gauge steel stampings, they proved useful but not entirely satisfactory. As semi-auto rifles they worked fine, but when pressed into service as automatic weapons they recoiled quite briskly and overheated quickly. The FG 42 was in service from 1942 to 1945.

Walther G43

SPECIFICATION

MANUFACTURER Walther

CALIBRE 7.92 x 57mm

MAGAZINE CAPACITY 10

ACTION Gas operated

TOTAL LENGTH 1,117mm/44in

BARREL LENGTH 549mm/21.62in

WEIGHT UNLOADED 4.3kg/9.5lb

This was the relatively perfected full-power semi-auto rifle in German service during World War II. Using the bolt of the G41(W) and a gas system similar to the Tokarev M-1940, it was produced in large numbers. A quarter of a million semi-auto rifles in a war with millions of combatants, however, was not nearly enough. Typically it was issued with a low-power optical sight, mounted on the dovetail rail built into the right side of the receiver. The rifle was reliable and accurate, and saw service for a short time after the war in the Czech armed forces. It was in service in Germany from 1943 to 1945.

Wa 2000 Sniper

ejection port

This rifle was developed around the .300 Winchester Magnum cartridge, and was meant to be a long range sniper rifle of extreme accuracy. The bullpup design allowed for a high-performance cartridge in a relatively compact package. It was ultimately a failure, and whether this was due to high cost or continued mechanical problems is unknown. The Wa 2000 was built and offered for sale from 1982 to 1988.

SPECIFICATION	
MANUFACTURER	Walther
CALIBRE	7.5 x 55mm, 7.62mm NATO, .300 Winchester Magnum
MAGAZINE CAPACITY	6
ACTION	Gas operated
TOTAL LENGTH	905mm/35.65in
BARREL LENGTH	650mm/25.6in
WEIGHT UNLOADED	7.95kg/17.54lb

Gew 98

Adopted in April of 1898 to replace the Commission 1888 rifles, the new Mauser was a revelation. It was strong, fast, almost impossible to use incorrectly, and durable. It also reflected the idea of the time for infantry rifles: long, and suitable for a long bayonet. It was the rifle with which Germany entered World War I and it served her well in that conflict. In one form or another it is still in production today. In the depicted version, it served from 1898 to 1918, but was replaced after the war by shorter rifles. Some Gew 98 rifles were still in use by police officers when Allied troops entered Germany in 1944.

SPECIFICATION	
MANUFACTURER	Various
CALIBRE	7.92 x 57mm
MAGAZINE CAPACITY	5
ACTION	Bolt action
TOTAL LENGTH	1,249mm/49.2in
BARREL LENGTH	740mm/29.15in
WEIGHT UNLOADED	4.09kg/9.02lb

Gew 98 sniper

Germany appreciated earlier than other combatants the usefulness of snipers in trench warfare. It was some time before the British realized that the "random" deaths due to head wounds were in fact deliberate. By today's standards the Gew 98 is quite rough as a sniper rifle but it was certainly good enough to give its users a significant edge on the Western Front for some time. While Germany maintained some sniper training and equipment between the wars, even they were surprised at the large number of Soviet snipers, and had to revamp their programme significantly. The Gew 98 was in use from 1915 to 1918.

SPECIFICATION	
MANUFACTURER	Various
CALIBRE	7.92 x 57mm
MAGAZINE CAPACITY	5
ACTION	Bolt action
TOTAL LENGTH	1,249mm/49.2in
BARREL LENGTH	739mm/29.1in
WEIGHT UNLOADED	4.62kg/10.2lb

98k

After World War I, Germany realized that the best rifle was what had been considered a cavalry carbine before the war – namely something shorter, lighter and handier. The 98k was just such a rifle. The bolt handle was turned down to get it out of the way, and the sword bayonet was abandoned for a design half as long. In slow design changes from post-World War I, the 98k reached its final form in 1935 and was in service until 1945.

SPECIFICATION	
MANUFACTURER	Various
CALIBRE	7.92 x 57mm
MAGAZINE CAPACITY	5
ACTION	Bolt action
TOTAL LENGTH	1,109mm/43.7in
BARREL LENGTH	599mm/23.6in
WEIGHT UNLOADED	3.91kg/8.64lb

Stg 44

SPECIFICATION

MANUFACTURER Various

CALIBRE 7.62 x 33mm

MAGAZINE CAPACITY 30

ACTION Gas operated/tilting bolt

TOTAL LENGTH 940mm/37in

BARREL LENGTH 419mm/16.5in

WEIGHT UNLOADED 5.21kg/11.5lb

Made only in 1944 and 1945, this was the refined and battle-tested "storm rifle". With large magazine capacity, select fire, moderate recoil and greater range and accuracy than any submachine gun, it proved a highly effective weapon among the swarms of Soviet soldiers on the Eastern Front. The Stg 44 is a further product-improved MP-43, with production shortcuts intended to speed factory output. It came, however, too late to make much difference. Had the German trials boards in the 1930s reports been acted on, Germany could have had the whole army equipped with the MP-43/Stg 44 for the duration of the war. However, they were ignored until it was too late.

Volksturm VG1

SPECIFICATION

MANUFACTURER Various

CALIBRE 7.92 x 57mm

MAGAZINE CAPACITY VG1: 10, VK-1; 5, some single shots

ACTION Bolt action

TOTAL LENGTH 1,092mm/43in

BARREL LENGTH 589mm/23.2in

WEIGHT UNLOADED 3.76kg/8.3lb

no bayonet lug

This was another stopgap weapon made in the days of World War II. The VG1 used the magazine of the G43 semi-automatic rifle, with a Mauser action. A similar weapon was the VK98, a Mauser stripped to its simplest form: a board/stock with a bolt action rifle screwed or bolted to it, lacking even a magazine. On both weapons every possible machining operation that could be left undone was avoided. Parts were sub-contracted to any small shop that could make them. The rifle would not accept a bayonet. It did, however, fire the full-power 7.92mm cartridge, and would shoot for as long as its owners cared to use it. Produced in the spring of 1945 alone, the VG1 was probably unsafe to fire.

SPECIFICATION

MANUFACTURER Various

CALIBRE 7.62 x 39mm

MAGAZINE CAPACITY 30

ACTION Gas operated/rotating bolt

TOTAL LENGTH 867mm/34.2in

BARREL LENGTH 414mm/16.3in

WEIGHT UNLOADED 4.3kg/9.48lb

MPi-KM (AK-47)

As a Soviet satellite, East Germany was expected to provide troops and build weapons for the Soviets. The East-German AK is noted by the pebble texture of the synthetic furniture, in the pistol grip and buttstock. When Germany re-unified, they were of no use at all, and were either destroyed or their parts sold as surplus. The MPi-KM was made from the late 1950s to the late 1970s, when replaced by AK-74 variants. Many of the AK variants seen in news photos from Iraq are ex-East-German MPi-KM rifles.

SPECIFICATION

MANUFACTURER Various

CALIBRE 5.45 x 39mm

MAGAZINE CAPACITY 30

ACTION Gas operated/rotating bolt

TOTAL LENGTH 956mm/37.65in

BARREL LENGTH 415mm/16.35in

WEIGHT UNLOADED 4.85kg/10.7lb

MPi-KMS74

Production of the MPi-KMS74, the East-German variant of the AK-74, had barely begun to replace existing 7.62mm weapons when the Berlin Wall fell in 1989, and Germany became one country again. The East-German rifles had no place in the new, unified Germany because all service rifles had to be 5.56mm in calibre. As with the AK variants, the MPi-KMS74 was scrapped or its parts were sold as surplus. It was in service for only a brief time from 1983 to 1989.

Italy

Rather than simply adopt the Mauser that was sweeping the world in the late 19th century, Italy elected to go with an amalgamation of local features. The Carcano rifles used a Mauser-type bolt, but the receiver bridge was split, so the bolt handle could pass through the slot in the receiver. Without Mannlicher clips in the magazine, the rifle was a single-shot.

Unlike the M1 Garand clips, the Carcano clips were quite flimsy and easily damaged. The 7.35mm cartridge was introduced in 1938 after Italian troops found themselves out-ranged in Ethiopia, against troops armed with Mausers in 7.92mm. The 7.35mm was dropped two years later when Italy entered World War II.

Vetterli Model 1934

SPECIFICATION	
MANUFACTURER	Beretta
CALIBRE	6.5 x 52mm
MAGAZINE CAPACITY	5
ACTION	Bolt action
TOTAL LENGTH	919mm/36.2in
BARREL LENGTH	450mm/17.7in
WEIGHT UNLOADED	3.12kg/6.9lb

The Swiss-designed Vetterli rifle originated as a tube-magazine repeating rifle shooting a black powder 10mm cartridge. It was also made in Italy as a tube-fed then later as a magazine-fed rifle. In the 1930s, Italy had the 10mm barrels lined to accept the 6.5mm Carcano cartridge, altered the box magazine, and issued the Vetterli as training rifles. They were used from 1934 to 1940.

Garand

box magazine

SPECIFICATION	
MANUFACTURER	Beretta
CALIBRE	.30-06
MAGAZINE CAPACITY	8, en bloc clip
ACTION	Gas operated/rotating bolt
TOTAL LENGTH	1,103mm/43.4in
BARREL LENGTH	610mm/24in
WEIGHT UNLOADED	4.32kg/9.52lb

After World War II, Italy adopted the Garand, and Beretta started to produce it. Identical to the US-made Garand, it lasted only a short time in Italian service (1952–9) before being replaced by the BM-series of rifles. This transitional Garand had a box magazine rather than an en bloc clip.

BM59

SPECIFICATION	
MANUFACTURER	Beretta
CALIBRE	7.62mm NATO
MAGAZINE CAPACITY	20
ACTION	Gas-operated/rotating bolt
TOTAL LENGTH	945mm/37.2in
BARREL LENGTH	450mm/17.7in
WEIGHT UNLOADED	3.69kg/8.15lb

With Beretta set up to make Garands, and the United States switching to the M14, Italy decided to make the Garand into an M14. It perhaps cost Italy as much to convert every Garand on hand into their BM59 (and make more) as it cost the US to develop and test the M14. The BM59 magazine, however, was not the same as the magazine of the M14, and the magazines were not interchangeable. Quarter-masters had to be aware of this issue when North Atlantic Treaty Organization (NATO) forces were stationed in Italy during the 1950s and 1960s. All the Italian efforts were negated in less than ten years when the US switched again to the M16. The BM59 was issued at the beginning of 1959 and the rifles continued in service until the mid-1970s.

Beretta BM62

SPECIFICATION

MANUFACTURER Beretta
CALIBRE 7.62mm NATO
MAGAZINE CAPACITY 20
ACTION Gas operated/rotating bolt
TOTAL LENGTH 977mm/38.5in
BARREL LENGTH 447mm/17.6in
WEIGHT UNLOADED 3.96kg/8.75lb

This was an export version of the BM59 rifle. After only a short time in development, the BM59 rifle had gained a new and improved gas system and been offered in nearly a dozen versions. The BM62 was slightly shorter, with a new flash hider but without the built-in bipod of the BM59. It was produced as a semi-auto-only rifle from 1962 to the early 1980s. Large numbers were bought by the United States. The Italian version had a quick-detach muzzle brake to make it more compact for paratroopers.

M70

SPECIFICATION

MANUFACTURER Beretta
CALIBRE 5.56 x 45mm
MAGAZINE CAPACITY 30
ACTION Gas operated/rotating bolt
TOTAL LENGTH 955mm/37.6in
BARREL LENGTH 451mm/17.8in
WEIGHT UNLOADED 3.85kg/8.5lb

While the United States had switched to the M16, and other manufacturers were looking to get into the 5.56mm market, Beretta designed and produced the M70. Unlike the M16, the M70 does not use the Stoner gas system. The long-stroke piston above the barrel is a cross between the AK and the AR-18. The M70 was a contender in the Swedish rifle trials, but lost to the Fabrique Nationale Carbine (FNC) from FN. Continued development has changed some features, as Beretta keeps the design current and relevant. Production ran from 1972 to 1983, with improved models since then with different model numbers.

Model 1957 carbine

SPECIFICATION

MANUFACTURER Luigi Franchi
CALIBRE .30 US carbine
MAGAZINE CAPACITY 15 & 30
ACTION Gas operated
TOTAL LENGTH 925mm/36.4in
BARREL LENGTH 429mm/16.9in
WEIGHT UNLOADED 3.40kg/7.5lb

30-round magazine

A carbine made from sheet metal stampings, the Model 1957 was intended as a lightweight weapon for use by non-combat personnel. An interesting attempt at a compact, reasonably powerful close and medium-range weapon, it came too late, as the AK was already in production and the AR-15 was soon to arrive. The carbine was an early effort at a Personal Defence Weapon. Probably due to the US M1 carbines that were already widespread, it found no buyers and had only a short production life, between 1957 and 1958.

Model 1891

SPECIFICATION

MANUFACTURER Terni
CALIBRE 6.5 x 52mm
MAGAZINE CAPACITY 5
ACTION Bolt action
TOTAL LENGTH 1,290mm/50.8in
BARREL LENGTH 780mm/30.7in
WEIGHT UNLOADED 3.90kg/8.6lb

A typical late-19th-century bullet-launching bayonet mount, the Model 1891 was reasonably well designed for its time. Although long, it was not excessively heavy, and the recoil of the 6.5mm cartridge was moderate enough to make the rifle easy to shoot. By the beginning of World War I, however, it was dated. It would have been a relatively easy task to update it, and change the Mannlicher magazine for a Mauser type. Yet Italy did not take this route and instead stuck with it. First fielded in 1891, the Model 1891 was still in service in 1945.

Mannlicher-Carcano Ballila

folding bayonet

This training rifle for the Opera Nazionale Balilla, the Youth Fascist Organization, was neither intended for nor mechanically suited for use with standard ammunition. As a lightweight and compact rifle, it was suitable for teaching marksmanship basics at Mussolini's fascist youth camps. It was supplied with an attached, but hinged, bayonet, similar to the standard Model 91 carbines. It was used from the 1920s to 1945.

SPECIFICATION	
MANUFACTURER	Terni
CALIBRE	6mm
MAGAZINE CAPACITY	N/A
ACTION	Gas operated/tilting lock
TOTAL LENGTH	711mm/28in
BARREL LENGTH	366mm/14.43in
WEIGHT UNLOADED	2.04kg/4.5lb

Model 91/38 TS

A carbine version of the Model 1891, the TS uses a knife-type bayonet instead of the permanently attached bayonet of the 1891 carbine, which pivoted into place. A detachable bayonet was a useful tool. Production began in 1938 and service lasted until 1945. The 91/38 was the rifle Italy should have had from the early 1920s. When the rest of Europe was changing to the carbine-size Model 1924, Italy retained a long rifle until 1938.

SPECIFICATION	
MANUFACTURER	Terni
CALIBRE	6.5 x 52mm
MAGAZINE CAPACITY	5
ACTION	Bolt action
TOTAL LENGTH	919mm/36.2in
BARREL LENGTH	450mm/17.7in
WEIGHT UNLOADED	3.12kg/6.9lb

Model 1941

This was a new rifle, in the old calibre, for use in World War II. It was slightly shorter, but not otherwise markedly different from the Model 1891. Taking 100mm/4in off the excessive length of the 1891 did not make it much easier to handle or reduce the weight significantly. Model 1941s were, however, solidly made and reliable. Introduced in 1941, few were made before Italy changed sides in 1943 and dropped production.

SPECIFICATION	
MANUFACTURER	Terni
CALIBRE	6.5 x 52mm
MAGAZINE CAPACITY	5
ACTION	Bolt action
TOTAL LENGTH	1,171mm/46.1in
BARREL LENGTH	691mm/27.2in
WEIGHT UNLOADED	3.72kg/8.21lb

 # Norway

Once a province of Sweden, and later a sovereign country invaded by the Germans in World War II,

Norway has a long history of weapons manufacture. Reliable function in extreme cold, deep snow and the rains of coastal areas are important considerations when selecting a rifle for use in Norway.

1912/18 carbine

strengthened nosecap

As did many countries, Norway went towards a universal rifle – one short enough for cavalry while still long enough for infantry. The M1912/18 was their pre-war attempt at a one-size-fits-all rifle. Field use uncovered a stock weakness, so after 1916 rifles were made with a new nose cap with strengthening collar. The rifle was in service from 1912 to the 1950s.

SPECIFICATION	
MANUFACTURER	Kongsberg
CALIBRE	6.5 x 55mm
MAGAZINE CAPACITY	5
ACTION	Bolt action
TOTAL LENGTH	1,106mm/43.55in
BARREL LENGTH	610mm/24in
WEIGHT UNLOADED	4.01kg/8.86lb

Krag-Jorgensen Model 1925

rear target sight _____

SPECIFICATION

MANUFACTURER Kongsberg
CALIBRE 6.5 x 55mm
MAGAZINE CAPACITY 5
ACTION Bolt action
TOTAL LENGTH 1,260mm/49.6in
BARREL LENGTH 759mm/29.9in
WEIGHT UNLOADED 4.05kg/8.93lb

The Krag action has design features with advantages and drawbacks. The bolt has only one locking lug, which limits the strength of the cartridges it can use. But the action as a result is very smooth and fast to cycle. When all rifles were bolt-action rifles, a fast-working bolt action was an asset to any army. The magazine cover hinges open (down, on the Norwegian Krag) and can be easily topped off with single rounds. However, the Krag cannot be quickly reloaded with chargers or stripper clips, which is a drawback. The M1925 is an iron-sighted sniper or target model, with aperture rear sight, heavy barrel and protected front sight. It was a service rifle from 1925 to 1940 and used as a target rifle into the 1950s.

Krag-Jorgensen Model 1925 carbine

SPECIFICATION

MANUFACTURER Kongsberg
CALIBRE 6.5 x 55mm
MAGAZINE CAPACITY 5
ACTION Bolt action
TOTAL LENGTH 1,107mm/43.6in
BARREL LENGTH 610mm/24in
WEIGHT UNLOADED 3.99kg/8.8lb

For every rifle, there has to be a carbine. The M1925 carbine is simply a shortened Krag with a shortened version of the heavy barrel of the rifle. It was issued first in 1925 and lasted on the target ranges to the 1950s.

Krag experimental model

ABOVE The Krag magazine hinges open downwards for loading and unloading. It cannot take chargers for fast reloading.

SPECIFICATION

MANUFACTURER Kongsberg
CALIBRE 7.92 x 57mm
MAGAZINE CAPACITY 5
ACTION Bolt action
TOTAL LENGTH 1,106mm/43.55in
BARREL LENGTH 610mm/24in
WEIGHT UNLOADED 4.01kg/8.86lb

After World War II, with large quantities of 98k rifles and 7.92 x 57mm ammunition on hand, Norway put together M1912 carbine actions with surplus Colt 8mm machine-gun barrels. The Krag action, when made from the right alloys, had just enough strength to contain the 7.92 x 57mm cartridge. As a means of using up a surplus supply of non-standard ammunition and barrels, the process was a good one. It was not, however, meant for use as a military arm. The Krag experimental was sold commercially in Norway for target shooting from 1948 to 1951, and used in target competition for years afterwards.

Denmark

Denmark had an army complete with cavalry and artillery units by the 19th century. Some service rifles in the late 19th and first half of the 20th century were made in Denmark while others were acquired from the original manufacturers. A forward-looking country, Denmark adopted the Madsen M1896 rifle and was the first country to adopt a semi-automatic service rifle for general issue, but it did not last long.

Krag-Jorgensen Model 1889

Denmark was the first country to adopt the Norwegian rifle designed by Krag and Jorgensen in the late 19th century. The rifle was modified in Denmark for its later adoption by the United States and Norway. The magazine box on the Danish Krag opens horizontally, hinging towards the muzzle, while the US and Norwegian Krags have the box pivoting down. They all suffered from the same shortcoming of the Krag magazine: it could not be recharged via stripper clips. Rounds had to be individually handled and dropped into the open magazine well while the rifle was tilted to the left. The complexity of manufacturing this magazine was probably why many countries did not adopt the Krag-Jorgensen. Manufacture ran from 1889 to 1921.

SPECIFICATION

MANUFACTURER KT, Copenhagen
CALIBRE 8 x 58R
MAGAZINE CAPACITY 5
ACTION Bolt action/single-locking lug
TOTAL LENGTH 1,328mm/52.3in
BARREL LENGTH 950mm/37.4in
WEIGHT UNLOADED 4.58kg/10.1lb

Model 1889 Cavalry

Designed for the Danish cavalry, this was a shorter version of the Krag rifle. The single-lug Krag action was relatively weak. It had to be limited to the mild 8 x 58R cartridge. The mild cartridge did not lose as much velocity when fired in a carbine as more powerful cartridges would. The Model 8 x 58R Cavalry was manufactured from 1912 to 13 and was still in service when Germany invaded in 1940.

SPECIFICATION

MANUFACTURER KT, Copenhagen
CALIBRE 8 x 58R
MAGAZINE CAPACITY 5
ACTION Bolt action/single-locking lug
TOTAL LENGTH 1,100mm/43.3in
BARREL LENGTH 599mm/23.6in
WEIGHT UNLOADED 4.03kg/8.9lb

Bang Model 1927

muzzle cup

One of the first semi-automatic rifles to be tested and offered, the Bang Model 1927 was never adopted. The operating system used a cup around the muzzle to capture gases and power the action. The method was sensitive to powder-burn rates and charge weights, and the corrosive primers of the time prevented the system from working effectively. Heavy corrosion from the priming compound fouled the cup and operating system, leading to malfunctions. The Bang system was used later in the German Gew 41 and caused the same problem. While mechanically interesting, it was not reliable enough for military use, and was not adopted, even by the Danes. Development began in 1911 and continued until 1929 when the project was abandoned.

SPECIFICATION

MANUFACTURER Dansk Industri Syndikat
CALIBRE .256, .276 Pedersen, .30-06
MAGAZINE CAPACITY 6
ACTION Gas operated
TOTAL LENGTH 1,118mm/44in
BARREL LENGTH 508mm/20in
WEIGHT UNLOADED 4.08kg/9lb

Ljungman

SPECIFICATION

MANUFACTURER Dansk Industri Syndikat
CALIBRE 7 x 57mm, 7.92 x 57mm
MAGAZINE CAPACITY 10
ACTION Gas operated/tilting bolt
TOTAL LENGTH 1,205mm/47.45in
BARREL LENGTH 622mm/24.5in
WEIGHT UNLOADED 4.64kg/10.25lb

The Ljungman rifle is capable of causing significant injury to the user who does not know its peculiarities. The gas system functions by direct impingement: the gas is fed through a tube directly back to the bolt carrier. The pressure of the gas launches the carrier back, taking the bolt with it. The action requires a strong recoil spring to work reliably. The uncovered bolt and feedway allow unwary users to get their fingers in the bolt path while manipulating the action, and injury can result. Built as development for a Danish service rifle, with licensing from Sweden, the Madsen-Ljungman project began in 1946 and dragged on for a number of years before being abandoned in the early 1950s.

SPECIFICATION

MANUFACTURER Dansk Industri Syndikat
CALIBRE 7 x 57mm, 7.65 x 53mm,
.30-06, 7.92 x 57mm
MAGAZINE CAPACITY 5
ACTION Bolt action
TOTAL LENGTH 1,100mm/43.3in
BARREL LENGTH 596mm/23.45in
WEIGHT UNLOADED 3.85kg/8.5lb

Madsen M47

Built as an export item, the Madsen 47 was designed for the smaller military force. In a world awash with surplus arms from World War II, the Madsen bolt-action rifle found few buyers. The receiver had the rear bridge split, and the bolt handle passed through it as the bolt was worked. On closing, the bolt handle acted as a safety lug. Offered in a variety of calibres, the only large contract was to Colombia, for rifles chambered in .30-06. When manufactured in 1947, it was immediately obsolete. The largest of the world's armies had begun to re-equip with semi-auto rifles.

SPECIFICATION

MANUFACTURER Dansk Industri Syndikat
CALIBRE 7.62mm NATO
MAGAZINE CAPACITY 20
ACTION Gas operated/rotating bolt
TOTAL LENGTH 1,100mm/43.3in
BARREL LENGTH 523mm/20.6in
WEIGHT UNLOADED 4.64kg/10.23lb

LAR

Initially developed as an assault rifle for the Finnish trial of 1958, the Light Automatic Rifle (LAR) began as a rifle chambered in 7.62 x 39mm. As it evolved it grew to encompass the 7.62 x 51mm cartridge and adopted an alloy receiver, a free-floating barrel and chromium-plated operating parts. However, the LAR could not compete on the world market with products from Belgium, Germany, the United States and the Soviet Union. It was abandoned in 1965, just before Denmark adopted the G-3 as the new service rifle.

SPECIFICATION

MANUFACTURER Various US
CALIBRE 7.62 x 63mm
MAGAZINE CAPACITY 8, en-bloc clip
ACTION Gas operated/rotating bolt
TOTAL LENGTH 1,105mm/43.5in
BARREL LENGTH 609mm/24in
WEIGHT UNLOADED 4.31kg/9.5lb

Gavaer Model 1950

After World War II, the Danish armed forces wisely elected to use American M1 Garands as their service rifle. Although they were never manufactured in Denmark, Danish armouries rebuilt and overhauled them as needed. They manufactured small parts, stocks and handguards, but kept the barrelled receivers of the original rifles in service. The M1 Garand went into service in Denmark as the Gevaer Model 1950. It was retained until the adoption of the M/66 (G3) in 1966.

Austria

Austria and Austro-Hungary, positioned in the middle of Western Europe, spent many centuries struggling against their neighbours. They consequently have a long tradition of arms-making and armouries, as well as weapons design. Many of the armouries continued manufacture under the flag of their new countries.

Mannlicher 1888

The Mannlicher 1888 started as a rifle using black powder cartridges, but within two years had to be rebuilt with sights calibrated to the new smokeless cartridges. The magazine was a marvel of the time: each five-round clip was self-contained. The user simply opened the bolt, pressed in a new loaded clip and, once it locked in place, closed the bolt. The fast reload was a desirable feature. However, the bottom of the magazine housing had to be open for the clip to fall free when empty, and the opening allowed dirt, dust and mud to enter. Introduced in 1888, the Mannlicher 1888 was obsolete in ten years but was nevertheless still issued as late as 1918.

SPECIFICATION	
MANUFACTURER	Steyr
CALIBRE	8 x 50 M-88 black powder
MAGAZINE CAPACITY	5
ACTION	Straight-pull bolt action
TOTAL LENGTH	1,279mm/50.38in
BARREL LENGTH	765mm/30.14 in
WEIGHT UNLOADED	4.40kg/9.7lb

Mannlicher M1895

The Mannlicher M1895 was Austro-Hungary's principle arm during World War I. A bolt action of straight-pull design (the bolt handle was simply pulled back, instead of being turned up before retracting), it was easy and quick to manipulate. The disadvantage of this design was its poor performance in combat, particularly trench warfare. Mud bound the spiral grooves machined in the bolt, which stopped the rifle. As with all Mannlicher rifles, it needed a sheet-metal clip holding five rounds, or could be used as a single-shot rifle. The clip dropped out of the bottom of the rifle when the last round was chambered. Issued from 1895 to 1918, after World War I it was used by other countries formed from Austro-Hungary.

SPECIFICATION	
MANUFACTURER	Steyr
CALIBRE	8 x 50R
MAGAZINE CAPACITY	5
ACTION	Straight-pull bolt action
TOTAL LENGTH	1,270mm/50in
BARREL LENGTH	765mm/30.12in
WEIGHT UNLOADED	3.76kg/8.31lb

Mannlicher M1895 carbine

straight-pull bolt

Before World War I, cavalry units were highly regarded elite formations. No army was complete without a cavalry branch, and Austria was no different. The only differences between the carbine and M1895 rifle issued to the Austrian cavalry from 1895 to 1918 were overall length, barrel length and weight. In the cavalry, the problem of mud was less crucial than in the infantry, but by the spring of 1915 all Austrian cavalry units were relegated to an infantry role. Horses had no place in trench warfare, and the 1895 carbine was too short for bayonet combat. After the war, many carbines ended up as police weapons, due to their convenient size. They were rapidly made obsolete by the flood of Mauser rifles in the 1920s and 1930s.

SPECIFICATION	
MANUFACTURER	Steyr
CALIBRE	8 x 50R
MAGAZINE CAPACITY	5
ACTION	Straight-pull bolt action
TOTAL LENGTH	1,003mm/39.5in
BARREL LENGTH	500mm/19.65in
WEIGHT UNLOADED	3.17kg/7.0lb

Steyr SSG 69

hammer-forged barrel

SPECIFICATION

MANUFACTURER Steyr

CALIBRE 7.62mm NATO

MAGAZINE CAPACITY 5, 10 or 20

ACTION Bolt action

TOTAL LENGTH 1,143mm/45in

BARREL LENGTH 650mm/25.6in

WEIGHT UNLOADED 4.64kg/10.25lb

The bolt-action Steyr Scharf Shutzen Gewehrifle (SSG 69) was introduced in 1969 and is still used as a sniper rifle in military and police units. It has a smooth bolt movement, partly because of the locking lugs at the rear of the bolt. The lugs are cammed into and out of the bolt body as the bolt rotates, unlike other bolt actions where the locking lugs are fixed to the bolt body. Steyr hammer-forged barrels are accurate and durable. Within the range limitations of the 7.62mm NATO cartridge, the SSG 69 is a superb sniper rifle. The detachable box magazines allow different natures of ammunition.

Steyr AUG

quick-change barrel

SPECIFICATION

MANUFACTURER Steyr

CALIBRE 5.56 x 45mm

MAGAZINE CAPACITY 30 (M-16 magazines)

ACTION Gas operated/rotating bolt

TOTAL LENGTH 805mm/31.7in

BARREL LENGTH 508mm/20in

WEIGHT UNLOADED 3.8kg/8.4lb

The Steyr Armee Universal Gewehr (AUG) solved the problem left-handed shooters have with the bullpup design – the ejection port is usually right where their face would be, when firing. The bolt in the Steyr AUG can be switched from right- to left-ejection. The first polymer-constructed rifle, the AUG is also unique in other regards: the barrels are quickly exchanged, and the firing selector is incorporated in the trigger system. A clean press delivers a single shot. Clutch the trigger back briskly and the mechanism automatically goes to full-auto fire until released. Introduced in 1985, the Steyr AUG remains in use worldwide today.

SPECIFICATION

MANUFACTURER Steyr

CALIBRE 5.56mm flechette, plastic case

MAGAZINE CAPACITY 24

ACTION Vertical-lift bolt

TOTAL LENGTH 779mm/30.7in

BARREL LENGTH 540mm/21.25in

WEIGHT UNLOADED 3.23kg/7.12lb

ACR

In the 1980s, the United States Army sought a new combat rifle, in its ceaseless efforts to replace the M16. Steyr proposed the Advanced Combat Rifle (ACR), which incorporated several novel features, including a vertically lifting bolt and a 5.56mm flechette round. Yet the ACR did not meet the mechanical standards of durability, accuracy and lightness that the US Army demanded. In the end, none of the rifles under consideration delivered the 100 per cent hit improvement over the M16 that the US Army required. Prototypes and test rifles of the ACR were made from 1986 to 1990.

Steyr AUG Police

SPECIFICATION

MANUFACTURER Steyr

CALIBRE 9 x 19mm

MAGAZINE CAPACITY 32

ACTION Blowback

TOTAL LENGTH 533mm/21in

BARREL LENGTH 256mm/10in

WEIGHT UNLOADED 3.3kg/7.27lb

This is a 9mm Parabellum version of the Steyr Armee Universal Gewehr (AUG) for police and auxiliary unit use. It is also known as the "Para" version. The AUG can be converted between 5.56mm and 9mm in ten minutes. Since the AUG is already compact, changing it to 9mm to make it more compact is only useful for training rather than for tactical utility. Many indoor ranges cannot take the 5.56mm cartridge with safety because of its destructive power. The AUG Police was introduced in 1989 and is still in use today.

 Sweden

Sweden has always sought reliable and durable rifles. From the Mauser bolt actions to semi-automatic rifles of several origins, Sweden quickly transformed from purchaser to manufacturer. The country's century-long reputation for producing superb steel greatly assisted this transformation.

Mauser Model 1894 carbine

SPECIFICATION	
MANUFACTURER	Mauser, Oberndorf/ Carl Gustaf
CALIBRE	6.5 x 55mm
MAGAZINE CAPACITY	5
ACTION	Bolt action
TOTAL LENGTH	949mm/37.4in
BARREL LENGTH	439mm/17.3in
WEIGHT UNLOADED	3.31kg/7.3lb

This rifle used the Mauser M96 (Spanish M93) action. The first batch was purchased, and after upgrades and improvements was adopted in 1899. Production began in Sweden in 1900. It was used as a rifle in the reserves, and as a hunting rifle, long after it was dropped as the issue rifle of the Swedish Army. While in service from 1894 to the 1940s, it hung on in the reserves until the 1950s. As with many carbines, rapid fire can heat the forearm to a noticeable degree.

Mauser Model 41 sniper

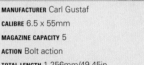
side-mount scope

SPECIFICATION	
MANUFACTURER	Carl Gustaf
CALIBRE	6.5 x 55mm
MAGAZINE CAPACITY	5
ACTION	Bolt action
TOTAL LENGTH	1,256mm/49.45in
BARREL LENGTH	739mm/29.1in
WEIGHT UNLOADED	4.37kg/9.65lb

This was a converted Model 1896 rifle. A sidemount with a mounting dovetail was fitted on to the receiver. With a scope installed, it was issued for sniper use. Even after self-loading rifles were introduced the Model 41 sniper was kept in service until a new sniper variant of the AK4 could be fielded. It was first issued in 1941 and was still in regular service until the early 1960s.

Carl Gustaf M/42 AT

vent nozzle

SPECIFICATION	
MANUFACTURER	Carl Gustaf
CALIBRE	20 x 180R
MAGAZINE CAPACITY	Single shot
ACTION	Semi-recoilless
TOTAL LENGTH	1400mm/55.11in
BARREL LENGTH	1050mm/41.33in
WEIGHT UNLOADED	11.2kg/24.69lb

In service during 1942–4, this weapon had a single-shot early recoilless design and was intended as an anti-tank weapon for the infantry. The M/42 used a 20mm solid projectile. The huge case had a blowout vent in the base, and gas venting to the rear combined with the muzzle brake to reduce recoil. A tolerable level of recoil was gained at the expense of a large backblast caused by firing a solid projectile. The backblast was a hazard to the assistant gunner and potentially lethal to anyone to the rear of the weapon. The weapon was outclassed in less than two years. However, the manufacturing and cartridge design experience lead Carl Gustaf to the recoilless 84mm calibre rifle, introduced in 1946 and still in use today.

Carl Gustaf M63 sniper

SPECIFICATION

MANUFACTURER Carl Gustaf

CALIBRE 7.62 x 51mm

MAGAZINE CAPACITY 5

ACTION Bolt action

TOTAL LENGTH 1,028mm/40.5in

BARREL LENGTH 510mm/20.1in

WEIGHT UNLOADED 4.19kg/9.25lb

The commercial variant of the M1896 rifle was the M63, fielded in the late 1950s. Many rifles were converted to sporting use, and some were built up as sniper rifles. The action, made of excellent Swedish steel, was strong enough to use the 7.62mm NATO cartridge, so early efforts at developing a sniper rifle in 7.62mm were focused on the Krag rifles at hand, and the Carl Gustaf M63 sniper was produced. Carl Gustaf was amalgamated with Husqvarna Waffenfabrik just before Sweden adopted the AK4, and once enough sniper-variant AK4s were on hand, Sweden dropped the M63 and earlier rifles. The Model 63 was in service from the late 1950s until the early to mid 1960s.

SPECIFICATION

MANUFACTURER Husqvarna, Carl Gustaf

CALIBRE 7.62mm NATO

MAGAZINE CAPACITY 20

ACTION Roller delayed blowback

TOTAL LENGTH 1,020mm/40.15in

BARREL LENGTH 450mm/17.7in

WEIGHT UNLOADED 4.39kg/9.68lb

AK4

The Automatkarbin 4 (AK4) was the Swedish version of the Heckler & Koch G3, built under licence in Sweden. Adopted when 7.62mm rifles were still in their ascendancy, they were replaced twenty years later by 5.56mm rifles. However, all useable AK4 rifles were overhauled and rebuilt, gaining rails for optical sights and placed in storage for Home Guard use in an emergency. The AK4 was in service from 1965 to 1985 with the regular army, and was then replaced by the Automatkarbin 5 (AK5). It has been maintained as a reserve rifle.

Ljungman AG42B

muzzle brake

SPECIFICATION

MANUFACTURER Husqvarna

CALIBRE 6.5 x 55mm

MAGAZINE CAPACITY 10

ACTION Gas operated

TOTAL LENGTH 1,205mm/47.45in

BARREL LENGTH 622mm/24.5in

WEIGHT UNLOADED 4.64kg/10.25lb

Production of the Ljungman was undertaken at the Husqvarna factory to avoid interfering with current-issue rifle production during World War II. The Ljungman uses a direct-impingement gas system, doing away with a piston or operating rod. It can be hazardous to the untrained. If the bolt is locked back, the feedway is open to finger access. If a user trips the bolt catch with a finger in the bolt path, a serious injury can occur. During the war the Ljungman was issued to rifle squads to increase firepower. The tooling was sold to Egypt in 1954. Despite being out of production and replaced in line units by the AK4, the Ljungman remained in Swedish reserves until the early 1970s.

AK5

SPECIFICATION

MANUFACTURER FFV

CALIBRE 5.56 x 45mm

MAGAZINE CAPACITY 30

ACTION Gas operated

TOTAL LENGTH 1,007mm/39.65in

BARREL LENGTH 460mm/18.1in

WEIGHT UNLOADED 3.90kg/8.6lb

When the AK4 began to show its age, and Sweden faced the shift to 5.56mm calibre, rifle trials were instituted in order to find a new rifle. The winner was the FN FNC, which Sweden modified. The trigger guard and cocking handle were made larger, to accommodate mittens, and the fore end was given cross-hatched grooves. As with the AK4, Sweden acquired licensing to build the rifles itself. Production and issue began in 1985, and the AK5 is the present standard-issue rifle of the Swedish Defence Forces.

 Czech Republic

After World War I, the new country of Czechoslovakia made and sold Mausers. After invading in 1939, Germany took over arms production. When World War II ended in 1945, the country became a Soviet ally and the Czech firearms industry mostly produced clones of the various Kalashnikovs.

Mauser VZ24

The Mauser VZ24 is basically a Kar 98k, but with slightly different fittings and furniture. The standard infantry rifle of Czechoslovakia, it was also an export item, competing successfully with FN for the world market. Upon their arrival in the spring of 1939, German supervisors simply changed the acceptance stamps and continued production to the end of the war. The Mauser VZ24 was produced between 1924 and 1945.

SPECIFICATION

MANUFACTURER	CZ Brno
CALIBRE	7.92 x 57mm
MAGAZINE CAPACITY	5
ACTION	Bolt action
TOTAL LENGTH	1,100mm/43.3in
BARREL LENGTH	589mm/23.2in
WEIGHT UNLOADED	4.07kg/8.98lb

Mauser G33/40

The G33/40 was made in Brno during 1933–45 for the German Army, specifically for paratrooper and mountain units. The receiver was extensively machined in an effort to reduce weight, the lightness somewhat offset by the steel reinforcing plate bolted to the buttstock. The idea was to produce as light and compact a rifle as possible without giving up durability. After the war, hunters stripped them down to build custom rifles for hunting.

SPECIFICATION

MANUFACTURER	CZ Brno
CALIBRE	7.92 x 57mm
MAGAZINE CAPACITY	5
ACTION	Bolt action
TOTAL LENGTH	993mm/39.1in
BARREL LENGTH	490mm/19.29in
WEIGHT UNLOADED	3.58kg/7.9lb

Mauser 98k

Called a carbine when first developed (because it was shorter than the then-standard Gew98 rifle by nearly 200mm/8in), the Mauser 98k was built in all German-occupied countries that had a factory set up to build Mauser-type rifles. Germany aimed to produce as many recognizable Mauser rifles as possible for use in the war. During 1939–45, CZ Brno took part in this project. After the war, no army wanted bolt-action rifles, and Brno turned to the hunting rifle market, to which the 98k action was well-suited.

SPECIFICATION

MANUFACTURER	CZ Brno
CALIBRE	7.92 x 57mm
MAGAZINE CAPACITY	5
ACTION	Bolt action
TOTAL LENGTH	1,107mm/43.6in
BARREL LENGTH	599mm/23.6in
WEIGHT UNLOADED	3.62kg/8.6lb

VZ52

side-folding bayonet

After World War II, designers continued apace to produce semi-auto service rifles. The VZ52 used the trigger mechanism of the Garand, the gas system of the Mkb42W and a box magazine designed in Czechoslovakia but similar to the German K43. Production of the VZ52 began in 1952 and continued to the early 1960s until AK production was great enough to replace it. The VZ52/57 was the same rifle chambered in the Soviet M43; large numbers were exported to aid "liberation fronts" around the world.

SPECIFICATION

MANUFACTURER	CZ Brno
CALIBRE	7.62 x 45mm
MAGAZINE CAPACITY	10
ACTION	Gas operated/tilting bolt
TOTAL LENGTH	1,000mm/39.37in
BARREL LENGTH	525mm/20.66in
WEIGHT UNLOADED	4.44kg/9.8lb

VZ58

SPECIFICATION

MANUFACTURER CZ Brno

CALIBRE 7.62 x 39mm

MAGAZINE CAPACITY 30

ACTION Gas operated/pivoting latch

TOTAL LENGTH 838mm/33in

BARREL LENGTH 401mm/15.8in

WEIGHT UNLOADED 3.31kg/7.3lb

At first glance the VZ58 appears to be an AK clone. Internally it is quite different, as the firing pin is a striker, not a hammer-struck pin. The VZ58 uses a pivoting locking block, attached to the bolt, to lock the action when fired. After the calibre was changed to that of the Soviet Union, the Czech-produced VZ58 was chambered in the Soviet M43, 7.62 x 39mm cartridge. Around a half kilo (1lb) lighter than most AKs, the recoil of the VZ58 must have been considerable in full-auto fire. Production began in 1958 and continued to the mid-1970s.

ZH29

SPECIFICATION

MANUFACTURER ZB

CALIBRE 7.92 x 57mm

MAGAZINE CAPACITY 5/10/25-round
magazines

ACTION Gas operated/tilting bolt

TOTAL LENGTH 1,156mm/45.5in

BARREL LENGTH 546mm/21.5in

WEIGHT UNLOADED 4.53kg/10lb

ten-shot magazine

Not to be left behind by the most advanced armies, Czechoslovakia designed and experimented with semi-automatic rifles. Designed by Emmanuel Holek, the ZH29 was not only a successful semi-automatic rifle, but also used box magazines. The design found limited interest, but was tested by the USA at the Aberdeen Proving Ground in .276 Pedersen calibre. The worldwide Depression and World War II turned it into a museum piece. Manufactured only as a prototype and trial rifle and never adopted for service use, it was made from the mid-1920s to the early 1930s. Although its appearance seemed odd, before the Depression the ZH29 was the epitome of a modern rifle. Had it been accepted in any number, the ZH29 might well have been the first general-issue semi-automatic rifle, beating the Garand by a decade.

 # Poland

After World War I, newly independent Poland began production for its own needs right away. Production continued under German and then Soviet control.

Production under Germany consisted of the speeded-up manufacture of Mauser rifles. Under the Soviets the emphasis was on manufacturing AKs.

SPECIFICATION

MANUFACTURER Panstwowa Fabryka

CALIBRE 7.92 x 107mm

MAGAZINE CAPACITY 4

ACTION Bolt action

TOTAL LENGTH 1,760mm/69.29in

BARREL LENGTH 1,200mm/47.24in

WEIGHT UNLOADED 9.5kg/20.94lb

Maroszek WZ35 A/T

Using a high-velocity hard-cored bullet, this anti-tank rifle could penetrate the light armour found on tanks at the beginning of World War II – at 100m/s/328ft/s it could penetrate about 30mm/1in of armour. The high pressure and velocity put great stress on the rifle, which had a frequent maintenance/ barrel replacement schedule of less than a thousand rounds. The Maroszek was used from 1935 until Poland was invaded in 1939. Soon after, armour development left all such rifles useless against armoured vehicles.

Mauser G98A/40

The G98A/40 was produced from 1930 to 1939 for Poland, and from 1939 to 1944 for the Germans. It was built as a copy of the short rifles many countries adopted at the time, such as the VZ-Brno 24, on Mauser-type receivers. The G98A/40 was similar to the VZ24 but designed and produced independently. Once Germany invaded in 1939, production continued for German use, but as the war progressed the fine craftsmanship and precise fitting were omitted. When the Soviets arrived, production stopped.

SPECIFICATION

MANUFACTURER Radom
CALIBRE 7.92 x 57mm
MAGAZINE CAPACITY 5
ACTION Bolt action
TOTAL LENGTH 1,102mm/43.4in
BARREL LENGTH 599mm/23.6in
WEIGHT UNLOADED 4.09kg/9.02lb

PMK-MS

The PMK-MS is simply the updated Soviet AK, with a sheet-metal receiver and under-folding stock instead of the fixed stock and forged receiver of the original. It was made in volume for use by Polish infantry and motorized infantry units that were to follow the East German and Soviet armoured divisions on an anticipated invasion of Western Europe. The PMK-MS was made from the early 1960s until the AK-74 variants came on line in the 1970s, and used as reserve weapons until the mid-1980s. After Polish entry to the EU and NATO, these rifles were sold as surplus. Many of the disassembled parts kits have been exported to the USA for use by collectors.

SPECIFICATION

MANUFACTURER Radom
CALIBRE 7.62 x 39mm
MAGAZINE CAPACITY 30
ACTION Gas operated/rotating bolt
TOTAL LENGTH 870mm/34.25in
BARREL LENGTH 415mm/16.33in
WEIGHT UNLOADED 3.14kg/6.92lb

KA wz/88 Tantal

heavy-gauge
wire stock

The KA wz/88 Tantal was a Polish-designed improvement of the AK-74S, with a three-shot burst setting and a side-folding stock of the East German heavy-gauge wire design. It was meant both as a Polish Army rifle and as an export item. While similar, the two cartridges in which it is available are not a close enough match to use the same magazines, and the receivers are not identical either. The selector is on the left side (convenient for a right-handed user's thumb), and the sights have tritium night-sight inserts, which glow in the dark. The KA wz/88 Tantal was produced between 1988 and 1997, when it was replaced by an improved model called the Beryl.

SPECIFICATION

MANUFACTURER Radom
CALIBRE 5.45 x 39mm, 5.56 x 45mm
MAGAZINE CAPACITY 30
ACTION Gas operated/rotating bolt
TOTAL LENGTH 943mm/37.1in
BARREL LENGTH 423mm/16.65in
WEIGHT UNLOADED 3.4kg/7.49lb

Wz/96 Beryl

Upon joining NATO, Poland needed a rifle that would use NATO ammunition; the wz/96 could take both SS109 and M193 ammunition. The Radom arsenal updated the Tantal/Onyks line with a new stock, new furniture, an optical sight rail and a new grenade launcher. It was also made in a short-barrel variant. Accurate and reliable, the rifle was made to endure tough environmental conditions. Production of the Beryl began in 1997 and continues to the present day.

SPECIFICATION

MANUFACTURER Radom
CALIBRE 5.56 x 45mm
MAGAZINE CAPACITY 30
ACTION Gas operated/rotating bolt
TOTAL LENGTH 943mm/37.1in
BARREL LENGTH 457mm/18in
WEIGHT UNLOADED 3.89kg/8.59lb

 # Croatia

Croatia became a nation after the break-up of Yugoslavia. With great experience in arms

manufacture and a need for defence owing to the tensions in the Balkans, Croatia makes small arms for its own use and for export. It has sold handguns to the United States and plans to offer rifles as well.

APS 95

SPECIFICATION

MANUFACTURER RH-Alan
CALIBRE 5.56 x 45mm
MAGAZINE CAPACITY 35
ACTION Gas operated/rotating bolt
TOTAL LENGTH 980mm/38.5in
BARREL LENGTH 450mm/17.7in
WEIGHT UNLOADED 3.8kg/8.37lb

The APS 95 was developed to replace the ageing Yugoslavian-made M70 rifles. It is a mechanical if not cosmetic licensed copy of the Israeli Galil but with an optical sight of 1.5x incorporated into the carrying handle. The carrying handle is almost as large as that of the French FAMAS, extending from the rear of the receiver cover to the receiver over the chamber. Although the basic AK system is old, the APS 95 has remained in production since 1995 and is unlikely to be replaced in the near future.

 # South Africa

As both a Dutch and British colony, and as an independent nation, South Africa has experienced many conflicts throughout its history. Given the wide

open spaces and the need for rifles for hunting and defence, South Africans have a well-earned reputation as top marksmen.

R4

SPECIFICATION

MANUFACTURER Lyttelton Eng Co.
CALIBRE 5.56 x 45mm
MAGAZINE CAPACITY 35
ACTION Gas operated
TOTAL LENGTH 979mm/38.55in
BARREL LENGTH 460mm/18.1in
WEIGHT UNLOADED 4.20kg/9.26lb

35-round magazine

Basically a Galil with minor changes owing to South African manufacturing necessities, the R4 was reliable, if heavy for its power. However, police and military units sometimes found the 5.56mm cartridge to be lacking, especially when attempting to penetrate the tough bush of South Africa. They therefore kept many FALs in reserve for the extra power the 7.62mm cartridge provided. Manufacture of the R4 began in 1982 and continues to the present day.

Mauser Model 1896

SPECIFICATION

MANUFACTURER Mauser, Oberndorf
CALIBRE 7 x 57mm
MAGAZINE CAPACITY 5
ACTION Bolt action
TOTAL LENGTH 1,250mm/49.2in
BARREL LENGTH 740mm/29.15in
WEIGHT UNLOADED 3.62kg/8lb

More commonly found with infantry, or non-mounted Boers, the Mauser Mod 1898 was handy and very accurate. The 7 x 57mm cartridge was relatively mild in recoil, accurate, and a suitable hunting cartridge for all but the largest game. During the Boer War (1899–1902), British troops found out just how useful the clip-charging feature of the Mauser could be. With Boer marksmen firing at high rates of speed, the British often found themselves at a severe disadvantage. The rifle was in service from 1896 to the mid-20th century.

Mauser Mod 1896 carbine

SPECIFICATION

MANUFACTURER Mauser, Oberndorf
CALIBRE 7 x 57mm
MAGAZINE CAPACITY 5
ACTION Bolt action
TOTAL LENGTH 944mm/37.2in
BARREL LENGTH 434mm/17.1in
WEIGHT UNLOADED 3.28kg/7.25lb

Commonly smuggled into South Africa during the Boer War, the Mauser Mod 1896 carbine was a constant companion to the mounted Boer and served until the middle of the 20th century. It was the same as the rifle but had a shorter 51cm/20in barrel. Typically, carbines had sling swivels on the side of the stock as well as a saddle loop on the rear sling swivel plate. The rifle could be carried by the trooper on his back or in a saddle loop hung off the saddlehorn.

Serbia

The Balkans have been a flashpoint and source of conflict for centuries. Serbia was once part of the Austro-Hungarian Empire and for a while part of

Yugoslavia. Starting with basic Mauser bolt actions and Kalashnikovs, the Yugoslavian arms industry produced an array of military and sporting products. It also extended the Kalashnikov action to include calibres its designer would not have thought of.

Mauser Koka Model 1884

SPECIFICATION

MANUFACTURER Mauser, Oberndorf
CALIBRE 10.15mm x 63R
MAGAZINE CAPACITY 5
ACTION Bolt action
TOTAL LENGTH 955mm/37.6in
BARREL LENGTH 465mm/18.3in
WEIGHT UNLOADED 3.75kg/8.27lb

tubular magazine under barrel

Basically a Gew 71/84 built for Serbia, the Koka had a tubular magazine similar to the German Kropatschek model, all in keeping with a transitional cavalry rifle/carbine of the late 19th century. Within a few years all such designs would be obsolete. Following advances in bullet construction and shape, smokeless powder and stronger actions, any country wishing to remain at the forefront of weapons development found it necessary to adopt these new technologies. The Koka was in service in the Serbian armed forces from 1884 to 1899.

Cavalry issue
The Koka is generally considered a cavalry-issue carbine, as there is no provision for mounting a bayonet, while the artillery carbines can take a bayonet.

Mauser Model 1910

SPECIFICATION

MANUFACTURER Mauser, Oberndorf
CALIBRE 7 x 57mm
MAGAZINE CAPACITY 5
ACTION Bolt action
TOTAL LENGTH 1,238mm/48.75in
BARREL LENGTH 740mm/29.15in
WEIGHT UNLOADED 4.11kg/9.06lb

With the purchase of the MM 1910, Serbia was as modern as anyone in Europe, and had a rifle fully capable of serving in any future war the Empire might call them up for. The calibre was also state-of-the-art for the time and popular around the world for good reason. That it was the standard export model of Mauser did not detract from its excellence. Within a few years the rifles and soldiers would be called up and sent off to the front. It was in service from 1910 to 1918. After that, there was no Austro-Hungarian Empire and Serbia was pretty much on its own.

Mauser Model 1924

SPECIFICATION

MANUFACTURER FN & CZ Brno
CALIBRE 7.92 x 57mm
MAGAZINE CAPACITY 5
ACTION Bolt action
TOTAL LENGTH 1,098mm/43.25in
BARREL LENGTH 590mm/23.25in
WEIGHT UNLOADED 4.14kg/9.13lb

The Mauser Model 1924 was the standard export model of Mauser design between the wars. The "short" rifle was universally popular. Yugoslavia purchased large numbers to replace the miscellaneous collection of rifles it possessed as a legacy of the Austro-Hungarian Empire and World War I. The Model 1924 was purchased in the late 1920s and remained in service to 1945. It was used in resistance to German occupation 1941–1945.

SPECIFICATION

MANUFACTURER Zastava
CALIBRE 7.62 x 39mm
MAGAZINE CAPACITY 10
ACTION Gas operated
TOTAL LENGTH 1,120mm/44.1in
BARREL LENGTH 519mm/20.45in
WEIGHT UNLOADED 4.01kg/8.85lb

M59/66

grenade launcher

The M59/66 was the SKS (a Russian carbine) with a twist, as the flash hider was also a grenade launcher. It was made as a reserve carbine, semi-automatic only, for the emergency inventory. Since there was no emergency, it became common on the surplus market. Manufacture began in 1959, and the rifles were updated with new barrels and grenade launchers from 1966. It remained in service until the late 1970s.

M70AB2

SPECIFICATION

MANUFACTURER Zastava
CALIBRE 7.62 x 39mm
MAGAZINE CAPACITY 30
ACTION Gas operated
TOTAL LENGTH 877mm/34.55in
BARREL LENGTH 415mm/16.35in
WEIGHT UNLOADED 3.58kg/7.9lb

The M70AB2 was the modernized AK, the AKM, with a sheet-metal receiver and folding stock. It was manufactured both for use in the Yugoslavian Army and as an export item, of which a number in semi-automatic only form ended up in the United States. It was manufactured from the early 1960s to 1990s. The parts were supplied to Iraq for assembly there as the Iraqi issue rifle.

M77B1

SPECIFICATION

MANUFACTURER Zastava
CALIBRE 7.62mm NATO
MAGAZINE CAPACITY 10
ACTION Gas operated
TOTAL LENGTH 1,135mm/44.7in
BARREL LENGTH 550mm/21.65in
WEIGHT UNLOADED 4.25kg/9.37lb

The M77B1 was a Kalashnikov extended to take the .308/7.62mm NATO cartridge. It was also made in 7.92 x 57mm where the calibre would sell better. The AK action is at its limit of cartridge size and durability when stretched to take the high-pressure 7.62mm NATO round, and recoil is heavy even given the rifle's weight. Produced between 1976 and the 1990s, it sold badly; buyers preferred rifles tailored to the NATO round.

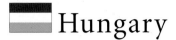 Hungary

From part of the Austro-Hungarian Empire, to an independent country, to an ally of Germany and then the USSR, Hungary is now charting its own course once again. During much of its history, Hungary had little choice in what it made or fielded. The cost of a modern army and the need for NATO inter-operability have severely restricted Hungarian choices in small arms design and issue in the current era.

Model 35

A Mannlicher-magazined bolt-action rifle, chambered for the rimmed 8mm Hungarian cartridge, the Model 35 had a short service life. It was designed and built in Hungary for use by the Hungarian Army. While sturdy and reliable, its production was questionable since Europe and most of the rest of the world was awash in Mauser rifles in the 1930s. After Germany occupied Hungary in 1944, the Model 35 was redesigned and the designation changed to G98/40. It was then issued as an alternate German rifle. The Model 35 was in production only from 1935 to 1942 but was used by Hungarian units until 1945.

SPECIFICATION

MANUFACTURER Danuvia Arms Works
CALIBRE 8 x 56mm M31
MAGAZINE CAPACITY 5
ACTION Bolt action
TOTAL LENGTH 1,107mm/43.6in
BARREL LENGTH 599mm/23.6in
WEIGHT UNLOADED 4.03kg/8.9lb

Mannlicher G98/40

split bridge for bolt handle

SPECIFICATION

MANUFACTURER Danuvia Arms Works
CALIBRE 7.92 x 57mm
MAGAZINE CAPACITY 5
ACTION Bolt action
TOTAL LENGTH 1,107mm/43.6in
BARREL LENGTH 599mm/23.6in
WEIGHT UNLOADED 4.03kg/8.9lb

The Mannlicher G98/40 was known as the Model 43 in Hungarian service. From a Mannlicher-magazine bolt action, the rifle was modified to take a Mauser-style magazine, and the calibre changed from 8 x 56 to 7.92 x 57mm. These modifications enabled it to be issued as an alternative rifle in German units during World War II. While not handsome, the action was strong enough for the task. Production of the new rifle lasted from 1943 to 1945.

AMD 65

muzzle brake

The distinctive sheet-metal hand guard and forward-angled front grip of the Automata Módosított Deszant (AMD 65) make it stand out in any photo of troops in the field. The intention was to keep the firer's hand away from the heat from the barrel, created by extensive shooting. This was a common problem in all AK-47 rifles. Made both with wooden and steel wire folding stock, the mild recoil of the M43 cartridge, combined with the control the front grip provides, makes the flimsy wire stock sufficient to the task. It was introduced in 1965 and remained in use until the early 1990s, despite the introduction of AK-74 variants.

SPECIFICATION

MANUFACTURER Fégyver es Gépgyár (FEG)
CALIBRE 7.62 x 39mm
MAGAZINE CAPACITY 30
ACTION Gas operated/rotating bolt
TOTAL LENGTH 870mm/34.25in
BARREL LENGTH 415mm/16.34in
WEIGHT UNLOADED 4.85kg/10.7lb

AMP-69, Grenade-launching

grenade launcher

SPECIFICATION

MANUFACTURER FEG

CALIBRE 7.62 x 39mm

MAGAZINE CAPACITY 5 or 30

ACTION Gas operated/rotating bolt

TOTAL LENGTH 914mm/36in

BARREL LENGTH 444mm/17.5in

WEIGHT UNLOADED 5.44kg/12lb

Fitted with a grenade-launching muzzle device, and with an adjustable sight for ranging and aiming, the AMP-69 was designed for launching grenades. Given the proliferation of the RPG and its much more effective (and further-ranging) warhead, its use was somewhat limited. It could, however, use standard M43 service ammunition, so an assigned grenadier could contribute to the firepower of a small unit. The AMP-69 was first issued in 1969, and although it was gradually replaced by the AK-74 from the early 1980s, it remained in reserve service until the early 1990s.

Lithuania

Achieving independence in 1918, Lithuania struggled between the wars to remain free from both the USSR and Poland. Occupied again in 1939, first by the USSR, then Germany, and again by the USSR,

Lithuania did not regain independence until 1990. Since then, Lithuania has become a member of NATO and produces high-quality ammunition that is NATO-accepted.

Mauser FN 1924

SPECIFICATION

MANUFACTURER FN, Liège

CALIBRE 7.92 x 57mm

MAGAZINE CAPACITY 5

ACTION Bolt action

TOTAL LENGTH 1,089mm/42.9in

BARREL LENGTH 591mm/23.25in

WEIGHT UNLOADED 3.80kg/8.4lb

The Mauser FN 1924 was the standard FN export short rifle that achieved huge sales in the 1920s and 1930s. Other than the Lithuanian crest and inspectors' marks, it was like any other 1924 short rifle. The FN 1924 was purchased first in 1924 and used until the initial occupation by Germany in 1939.

Lithuanian funded rifles
Many FN 1924 rifles are marked "Ginklu Fondas" on the receiver, which indicates they were purchased with funds donated by the Lithuanian people in 1937 to equip the army.

SPECIFICATION

MANUFACTURER Unk

CALIBRE 7.62 x 39mm

MAGAZINE CAPACITY 30

ACTION Gas-operated/rotating bolt

TOTAL LENGTH 877mm/34.55in

BARREL LENGTH 415mm/16.35in

WEIGHT UNLOADED 3.82kg/8.42lb

AKM

As a Soviet republic from 1944 to 1991, Lithuania produced the standard Soviet weapon, the Automat Kalashnikova Modernized (AKM) with sheet-metal receiver; indistinguishable from Soviet-produced rifles except for the inspectors' marks. When Lithuania became independent in 1991 and joined NATO and the EU, it began manufacturing new 5.56mm variants of its AK rifles, designated the AK-4MT. While building a NATO-compatible force, Lithuania is purchasing new equipment, although it also produces its own submachine gun as well as NATO-accepted 5.56mm and 7.62 x 51mm ammunition.

 Greece

Independent from the Ottoman Empire since 1831, Greece spent much of the 19th century struggling with its neighbours. The Balkans, then as now, were a source of international friction. At the dawn of the 20th century, Greece needed modern rifles with which to equip its army. Lacking an industrial base, Greece set out to purchase rifles from foreign manufacturers. Its first choices were perhaps more expensive than they should have been, but later models were more in line with contemporary designs and cost.

FN M1930

The new short rifle, wisely selected and purchased by Greece, was a carbine by pre-World War I standards. The M1930 was the rifle all the world was adopting: the Mauser/FN/98k Model of 1924. Greece simply purchased standard FN Model 1924 rifles, which were marked for the use of the Greek forces and renamed them the M1930. The rifle was in use from 1930 to the early 1950s, when it was replaced by the M1 Garand, which had served the Americans through World War II.

SPECIFICATION	
MANUFACTURER	FN, Liège
CALIBRE	7.92 x 57mm
MAGAZINE CAPACITY	5
ACTION	Bolt action
TOTAL LENGTH	1,099mm/43.3in
BARREL LENGTH	589mm/23.2in
WEIGHT UNLOADED	3.85kg/8.5lb

Mannlicher-Shoenauer Model

rotary magazine

The Mannlicher-Shoenauer Model was beautifully machined, very smooth and costly as a military weapon. The rotary magazine of the Mannlicher-Shoenauer action functioned so well that shooters and hunters sought it out for building expensive rifles. Greece bought M-S models as a combat arm, a role for which they were not well suited. Many were given up as war reparations after World War I and replaced by a miscellaneous collection of Austrian Mannlichers and Turkish Mausers. Purchased in 1903, this rifle remained in service until 1918.

SPECIFICATION	
MANUFACTURER	Steyr
CALIBRE	6.5 x 54mm
MAGAZINE CAPACITY	5
ACTION	Bolt action
TOTAL LENGTH	1,227mm/48.3in
BARREL LENGTH	724mm/28.5in
WEIGHT UNLOADED	3.76kg/8.31lb

Mannlicher-Shoenauer M1903 carbine

At the turn of the 20th century, police forces, mounted troops and people of high social status required a carbine. The police and mounted troops needed carbines for their short length and lighter weight than a rifle. Civilians seeking to enhance their status acquired carbines because they were less common than the rifle. Thus Greece purchased Mannlicher-Shoenauer (M-S) carbines as well as the rifles. The only difference between M-S rifles and carbines was the barrel and stock (forearm) length. The M-S M1903, like the M-S rifle, was in service from 1903 to 1918. It cost at least twice as much as any Mauser rifle Greece could have purchased.

SPECIFICATION	
MANUFACTURER	Steyr
CALIBRE	6.5 x 54mm
MAGAZINE CAPACITY	5
ACTION	Bolt action
TOTAL LENGTH	1023mm/40.3in
BARREL LENGTH	520mm/20.5in
WEIGHT UNLOADED	3.62kg/8lb

Final Mannlicher
The 1903 was the final design by Ferdinand Ritter von Mannlicher.

 Finland

Having fought for independence from Russia at the time of the 1917 Revolution, Finland naturally used Russian-pattern small arms. The Finns then began to produce their own weapons. Finnish-built and overhauled small arms tended to be better-fitted and finished than their Soviet counterparts.

Valmet M-82

SPECIFICATION

MANUFACTURER Lithgow
CALIBRE 5.56 x 45mm
MAGAZINE CAPACITY 30
ACTION Gas operated/tilting lock
TOTAL LENGTH 710mm/27.95in
BARREL LENGTH 420mm/16.5in
WEIGHT UNLOADED 3.3kg/7.27lb

The Valmet M-82 was an M-76 in a bullpup polymer shell, with the sights elevated to line up with the shooter's eye. It was an export item with almost no sales, and suffered from all the problems of an AK design in a bullpup shell: the stock is removed and the buttplate located on the rear of the receiver. The pistol grip goes in front of the magazine. However, the AK safety on a bullpup is out of sight and almost unreachable for the shooter. The M82 had a short production period, from 1978 to 1986.

Mosin-Nagant 28-30 Civil Guard

SPECIFICATION

MANUFACTURER Sako
CALIBRE 7.62 x 54R
MAGAZINE CAPACITY 5
ACTION Bolt action
TOTAL LENGTH 1,185mm/46.65in
BARREL LENGTH 685mm/26.95in
WEIGHT UNLOADED 4.35kg/9.61lb

improved rear sight

Sako, a new company at the time, produced its own barrels for the Mosin-Nagant 28-30 as well as a revised magazine and improved rear sight. Otherwise, the 28-30 was a standard Mosin-Nagant bolt-action rifle, of which Finland would need many during World War II. It was produced from 1931 to 1940.

Sako TRG

SPECIFICATION

MANUFACTURER Sako
CALIBRE .338 Lapua magnum
MAGAZINE CAPACITY 5
ACTION Bolt action
TOTAL LENGTH 1,200mm/47.24in
BARREL LENGTH 690mm/27.16in
WEIGHT UNLOADED 5.1kg/11.24lb

As infantry units get ever more powerful weapons, snipers need larger cartridges and rifles to reach their targets from further distances. The Sako TRG is available in the 22 and 42 models. The 22 is a standard 7.62 x 51mm chambering, but the 42 is available in the exemplary .338 Lapua magnum. A trained sniper can easily strike a point target 1,500m/1,640yd away, or a vehicle or radar array at 2,000m/2,187yd. As with all sniper rifles, scope selection can affect weight. Production began in 1995 and continues today.

Tikka Finlander M-68 sniper, silent

SPECIFICATION

MANUFACTURER Tikka
CALIBRE 7.62 x 51mm
MAGAZINE CAPACITY 5
ACTION Bolt action
TOTAL LENGTH 1,070mm/42.15in
BARREL LENGTH 570mm/22.45in
WEIGHT UNLOADED 3.65kg/8.05lb

full-length suppressor

An improved and refined Mauser action, the Tikka sniper rifle is also a hunting rifle modified for sniper use. More accurate than the Mosin-Nagant sniper rifles in the Finnish Defence Forces inventory, the Tikka also can use a suppressor, a feature the Mosin-Nagant is unable to use. Production began in 1968 and has continued until the present day.

Valmet M-62

tubular steel stock

An improved M-60 rifle, the M-62
lasted for 40 years as the standard Finnish Defence Force
rifle. Attempts to replace it with the M-76 were unsuccessful, as the
sheet-metal receiver of the M-76 was not as durable as the milled M-62 receiver.
A little less weight did not count as much as continued function in arctic
warfare. Despite its durability, the ageing M-62 required replacement, and the
low cost of imports made it possible to purchase Chinese-made AKs in the
late 1990s. The Valmet M-62 was in service from 1962 to the late 1990s, and
probably can still be found in an armoury or police station in Finland today.

SPECIFICATION

MANUFACTURER Valmet
CALIBRE 7.62 x 39mm
MAGAZINE CAPACITY 30
ACTION Gas operated/rotating bolt
TOTAL LENGTH 914mm/36in
BARREL LENGTH 420mm/16.55in
WEIGHT UNLOADED 4.09kg/9.02lb

Valmet M-76

This "improved" M-62 used a stamped
steel receiver like that of the AKM, and
was offered in both Soviet and American chamberings. Also, the
buttstock was synthetic instead of the steel tube of the M-62. Finland
found the stamped-steel receiver to be less durable than desired, something
other countries have not. It was offered as an export item as well, but the cost
of a Finnish-made rifle could not compete with those made in developing
countries on the international arms market. The Valmet M-76 was
manufactured from 1977 to 1990.

SPECIFICATION

MANUFACTURER Valmet
CALIBRE 7.62 x 39mm & 5.56 x 45mm
MAGAZINE CAPACITY 30
ACTION Gas operated/rotating bolt
TOTAL LENGTH 913mm/35.95in
BARREL LENGTH 420mm/16.55in
WEIGHT UNLOADED 3.66kg/8.09lb

Mosin-Nagant 1927 cavalry

This was a short rifle rather than a carbine, but
still better suited to mounted use than the full-sized rifle. In the
harsh winter climate of Finland, durability was more important than light
weight or quick handling. As a previous province of Russia, Russian-pattern
small arms such as the Mosin-Nagant were well-known, and Finns were
trained in using them. The Mosin-Nagant was used from 1927 to 1939.

SPECIFICATION

MANUFACTURER VKT
CALIBRE 7.62 x 54R
MAGAZINE CAPACITY 5
ACTION Bolt action
TOTAL LENGTH 1,110mm/43.7in
BARREL LENGTH 607mm/23.9in
WEIGHT UNLOADED 3.97kg/8.77lb

Mosin-Nagant M-39 sniper

Finnish optics

In the 1930s, the Finnish Defence Department
undertook a programme to consolidate all Mosin-Nagant production into a
single, improved design. The resulting M39 was issued in 1939. It had a more
robust stock – with re-contoured buttstock and pistol grip – and a heavier
handguard, made from Arctic birch, which was resistant to warping in the
extreme cold. It had higher-quality barrels than the standard Soviet version.
The M-39 was regularly overhauled and rebuilt, and used into the 1990s.

SPECIFICATION

MANUFACTURER VKT
CALIBRE 7.62 x 54R
MAGAZINE CAPACITY 5
ACTION Bolt action
TOTAL LENGTH 1,232mm/48.5in
BARREL LENGTH 729mm/28.7in
WEIGHT UNLOADED 5.12kg/11.3lb

Romania

The Romanians found themselves between Germany and Russia in both World War I and World War II. As with so many central European countries in World War II, they received the worst of both: siding with Germany, only to suffer great losses on the Eastern Front (reported as high as 200,000 at Stalingrad alone) and then occupation for decades as a satellite state of the Soviet Union.

VZ24

SPECIFICATION	
MANUFACTURER	CZ Brno
CALIBRE	7.92 x 57mm
MAGAZINE CAPACITY	5
ACTION	Bolt action
TOTAL LENGTH	1,100mm/43.3in
BARREL LENGTH	589mm/23.2in
WEIGHT UNLOADED	4.07kg/8.98lb

After World War I, with a large supply of Mannlicher 1893 rifles, French Berthier and Austrian 1895 rifles making the supply system nearly impossible to control, Romania tried to consolidate with the VZ24 short rifle, a standard Mauser. The first rifles arrived in 1928 and stayed in service as Romanian rifles until 1939. Having switched to a standard Mauser and 7.92mm cartridge, it was easy for the Germans to supply their Romanian allies with ammunition on the Eastern Front. Any surplus rifle production went to German units.

FPK

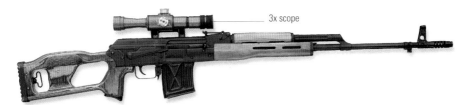

3x scope

SPECIFICATION	
MANUFACTURER	State armoury
CALIBRE	7.62 x 54R
MAGAZINE CAPACITY	10
ACTION	Gas operated
TOTAL LENGTH	1,225mm/48.22in
BARREL LENGTH	620mm/24.4in
WEIGHT UNLOADED	4.31kg/9.50lb

The FPK (as it is sometimes known) was a Romanian-produced rifle resembling the Dragunov and, like all the other versions, was meant not so much as a sniper rifle (for long-range precision shooting) as a squad Designated Marksman Rifle (DMR). The former fires on high-value targets at extreme range, while the DMR rifleman fires on close to medium-range targets in order to solve the immediate problems of his field commander. The FPK, like the Dragunov, is a solid and serviceable weapon that is quite dangerous to opponents when in capable hands. Manufacture began in the 1960s and the rifles are in service today.

AKM

SPECIFICATION	
MANUFACTURER	State armoury
CALIBRE	7.62 x 39mm
MAGAZINE CAPACITY	30
ACTION	Gas operated/rotating bolt
TOTAL LENGTH	870mm/34.25in
BARREL LENGTH	415mm/16.33in
WEIGHT UNLOADED	3.14kg/6.92lb

The Romanian AKM (an improved Kalashnikov with a sheet-metal receiver) is instantly recognizable by the foregrip. The forearm of the Romanian rifle has a vertical grip that is angled towards the muzzle. The AK, in sustained fire, makes the firer's forearm very hot. The foregrip, besides being more ergonomic, and allowing for greater control in full-auto fire, keeps the firer's hand further from the heat. Soon after manufacture commenced in Russia, client states such as Romania were making the new version, replacing the receiver of forged steel with a metal pressing. Production lasted from the early 1960s to the late 1970s, but the 7.62mm rifles remained in use for years afterwards.

AKS74

This was the improved (sheet-metal receiver) AK in the new Soviet cartridge. The "S" denotes the folding stock version. As the USSR found its military aspirations harder to achieve, it required its client states to assist. Some, such as Romania, made small arms for export to Soviet allies. This was a Romanian-produced clone of the standard Soviet assault rifle, fielded in the early 1980s to the present day.

muzzle brake

SPECIFICATION

MANUFACTURER State Armoury
CALIBRE 5.45 x 39mm
MAGAZINE CAPACITY 30
ACTION Gas operated
TOTAL LENGTH 943mm/37.12in
BARREL LENGTH 415mm/16.33in
WEIGHT UNLOADED 3.43kg/7.56lb

Mannlicher Model 1893 carbine

Differing in minor details, but essentially the Dutch 1895 Mannlicher, the Romanian 1893 Mannlicher carbine was a serviceable rifle for the trench warfare of World War I. Made for cavalry use, the carbine was particularly useful. After the war it was replaced with the VZ24 rifle, although undoubtedly many 1893 carbines remained in storage in 1939. The Model 1893 was in service in the Austro-Hungarian Empire from 1893 to the 1920s.

SPECIFICATION

MANUFACTURER Steyr
CALIBRE 6.5 x 53R
MAGAZINE CAPACITY 5
ACTION Gas operated
TOTAL LENGTH 952mm/37.5in
BARREL LENGTH 450mm/17.7in
WEIGHT UNLOADED 3.30kg/7.25lb

Bulgaria

Before World War I, Bulgaria manufactured rifles for the Austro-Hungarian empire of which it was part.

During World War II, Bulgaria was forced to supply Germany with war material. Post-war, as a member of the Warsaw Pact, Bulgaria manufactured Soviet-pattern rifles.

AK-47

As with all Soviet client states, Bulgaria adopted the AK-47 for its own use. Early-issue AK-47s for the Bulgarian Army came from Poland; Bulgarian manufacture began in 1965. The Bulgarian AK-47 is of excellent quality, enabling Bulgaria to compete with small arms sales from the Russian Federation after the break-up of the USSR in 1991. The rifle remained in service from 1965 until the early 1980s.

SPECIFICATION

MANUFACTURER FÉG, Budapest
CALIBRE 7.62 x 39mm
MAGAZINE CAPACITY 30
ACTION Gas operated/rotating bolt
TOTAL LENGTH 877mm/34.55in
BARREL LENGTH 415mm/16.35in
WEIGHT UNLOADED 3.82kg/8.42lb

AK-74

This modernized AK was essentially a clone of the Soviet AK-74 in a smaller calibre. Most Bulgarian AK-74 rifles were demilitarized – declared surplus and sold for parts. When Bulgaria joined the EU, it had to change to NATO-compliant small arms. It was easier to make new AK-74s in 5.56mm than to rebuild the old ones to the new calibre. The AK-74 was manufactured from the early 1980s to the mid-1990s.

SPECIFICATION

MANUFACTURER FÉG, Budapest
CALIBRE 5.45 x 39mm
MAGAZINE CAPACITY 30
ACTION Gas operated/rotating bolt
TOTAL LENGTH 956mm/37.65in
BARREL LENGTH 415mm/16.35in
WEIGHT UNLOADED 4.85kg/10.7lb

AKS-74S

SPECIFICATION

MANUFACTURER FÉG, Budapest
CALIBRE 5.45 x 39mm
MAGAZINE CAPACITY 30
ACTION Gas operated/rotating bolt
TOTAL LENGTH 643mm/26.55in
   (421mm/16.6in w/stock folded)
BARREL LENGTH 225mm/8.85in
WEIGHT UNLOADED 3.08kg/6.8lb

gas booster

This was the short-barrelled variant of the standard AK-74. A flash hider/gas booster was required for reliable function. The shortened barrel, without the special flash hider, would not supply enough gas to the action for reliable function. Typically, short-barrelled rifles not equipped like this fail to eject the empty case. The allure and apparent exclusivity of short rifles keeps them in service even when the compact design is not needed, but the loss of down-range performance is a real shortcoming. The 74S went the same path as the 74 when Bulgaria changed calibres, the 74S declared surplus, disassembled and the rifles and parts (with rare exception) are now all exported from Bulgaria.

Mannlicher Model 1895S

SPECIFICATION

MANUFACTURER Steyr
CALIBRE 8 x 50R
MAGAZINE CAPACITY 5
ACTION Straight-pull bolt action
TOTAL LENGTH 1,272mm/50.1in
BARREL LENGTH 765mm/30.1in
WEIGHT UNLOADED 3.78kg/8.35lb

Mannlicher magazine

Adopted in 1895 as an improvement over the older 1888 models, this model was taken up quickly. The complicated straight-pull action was unreliable in the mud of trench warfare and the relatively thin barrel would overheat in heavy combat. It was good enough, however, to be produced in the millions for World War I. Testing carried out since then shows that the light barrel "walks" (changes its zero) when it heats up and accuracy suffers. Adopted in 1895, it did not long survive the Austro-Hungarian Empire, being replaced in many countries (including Bulgaria) by one Mauser or another.

Ukraine

Absorbed into Russia under the Tsars, the Ukraine was independent from 1917 to 1921. Then it was divided between the new Poland and the Soviet Union. After the fall of the Soviet Union, the Ukraine became an independent country which needs to modernize and make its own arms without subsidies from Russia.

Vepr

SPECIFICATION

MANUFACTURER MOLOT
CALIBRE 5.45 x 39mm
MAGAZINE CAPACITY 30
ACTION Gas operated
TOTAL LENGTH 702mm/27.66in
BARREL LENGTH 415mm/16.35in
WEIGHT UNLOADED 3.45kg/lb

An upgraded AK, and manufactured since 2003, the Vepr is an AK-74 in bullpup configuration. Offered with an optional grenade launcher and built-in optical sight rail, the charging handle has been moved from the right side of the receiver to the left handguard, but the safety remains in the Kalashnikov location. While possibly a major improvement over the AK-74, it has all the faults of a bullpup: the safety lever is hard to reach, the magazine is difficult to exchange, and the trigger mechanism now incorporates a bar to reach from the new pistol grip location back to the receiver. The bar makes the AK trigger pull (which was always poor) worse.

Russia

With an army of millions, Russia needed plenty of rifles. In both world wars, initial losses and rapid expansion of the army entailed a frantic search for a sufficient volume to resupply the army. With many arsenals and designers available, there was often plenty of choice. Despite efforts to replace the elderly Mosin-Nagant rifle, the Soviet Army stuck with it, as all potential replacements had operational problems of one sort or another. After World War II, the army was completely resupplied with AK-47s.

Degtyarev PTRD41

An anti-tank rifle using the larger of the Soviet heavy machine-gun cartridges, the Degtyarev is unique: it is a self-activating single-shot bolt-action rifle. The recoil-reduction system is simple: the entire receiver recoils rearwards over the stock frame, similar to the Boys A/T rifle, but unlike the Boys, the PTRD includes opening the bolt and ejecting the empty case in its cycle. The advent of better armour enabled its use as a bunker-buster for infantry. Issued first in the 1930s, it served to the end of the war in 1945. All anti-tank rifles became obsolete when armour became thicker.

SPECIFICATION

MANUFACTURER Degtyarev
CALIBRE 14.5mm
MAGAZINE CAPACITY Single-shot bolt action
ACTION Gas operated
TOTAL LENGTH 2,000mm/78.74in
BARREL LENGTH 1,350mm/53.15in
WEIGHT UNLOADED 17.42kg/38.40lb

SKS 45

laminated stock

Having been type-defined in 1943, the Samozaryadniy Karabin sistemi Simonova (SKS) was finalized in 1945 but not put into mass production until 1949. It used the 7.62 x 39mm cartridge. The fixed magazine can be loaded with single rounds or via stripper clips of ten rounds. Many models made outside Russia are crude, but the SKS works with great reliability. China made several variants, mostly for export, that used detachable magazines. The SKS was made from 1949 to the late 1960s, and is presently still in use around the world. It was made obsolete in Soviet service as soon as there were enough AK-47s for all the armed forces.

SPECIFICATION

MANUFACTURER Izhevsk, others
CALIBRE 7.62 x 39mm
MAGAZINE CAPACITY 10
ACTION Gas operated
TOTAL LENGTH 1,121mm/44.15in
BARREL LENGTH 519mm/20.45in
WEIGHT UNLOADED 3.86kg/8.5lb

AK-47 1st Model

The initial production AKs were made with a receiver of a sheet steel pressing, in a "U" channel, with the front and rear trunnions rivetted to it. (The trunnions are steel castings used to secure the barrel in front and the stock in the rear to the receiver.) Sheet-metal stampings in Russia in 1949 were not up to the task, so production was shifted to a forged and machined receiver from 1951 to 1959, while the Soviets continued to study the sheet-metal pressing technologies they had obtained from Germany. The forged receiver added more than a pound of weight to the original design. The AK was produced between 1949 and 1975, in one form or another.

SPECIFICATION

MANUFACTURER Izhevsk, Tula, others
CALIBRE 7.62 x 39mm
MAGAZINE CAPACITY 30
ACTION Gas operated
TOTAL LENGTH 868.68mm/34.2in
BARREL LENGTH 414mm/16.3in
WEIGHT UNLOADED 4.3kg/9.48lb

AKM

"slant" muzzle brake

SPECIFICATION

MANUFACTURER Izhevsk

CALIBRE 7.62 x 39mm

MAGAZINE CAPACITY 30

ACTION Gas operated

TOTAL LENGTH 878mm/34.55in

BARREL LENGTH 415mm/16.34in

WEIGHT UNLOADED 3.38kg/7.45lb

This was an improved version of the Kalashnikov. Initially, the sheet-metal pressing receiver was not successful. Soviet technology was not up to the task of producing a rugged metal-pressing receiver, and the sheet-metal pressing machines were needed for higher-priority aircraft production. Once the problem was sorted out, the AKM was produced in large quantities. The AKM also introduced the "rate reducer", which is actually an anti-bounce device. It adds a few more parts to a simple and sturdy design, but not at any great cost in weight, complexity, reliability or manufacturing. The AKM was introduced in 1959 and remained in service to the late 1970s, when it was replaced by the AK-74.

SVD

cheekpiece for aiming

SPECIFICATION

MANUFACTURER Izhevsk

CALIBRE 7.62 x 54R

MAGAZINE CAPACITY 10

ACTION Gas operated

TOTAL LENGTH 1,226mm/48.25in

BARREL LENGTH 549mm/21.45in

WEIGHT UNLOADED 4.76kg/10.5lb

More a Designated Marksman Rifle (DMK) than a sniper rifle, the Snayperskaya Vintovka Dragunova (SVD) is a solid, if unspectacular, short-to-medium-range sniping rifle that is effective up to 500–600m/1,600–2,000ft. The cutaway buttstock, pistol grip and long barrel make it impossible to mistake the SVD for any other rifle on the battlefield. The rimmed Russian cartridge must have made designing a reliable magazine particularly problematic. The SVD has been manufactured since 1964 and is found in many areas that were under Soviet influence.

SPECIFICATION

MANUFACTURER Izhevsk

CALIBRE 5.45 x 39mm, 5.56 x 45mm

MAGAZINE CAPACITY 30

ACTION Gas operated

TOTAL LENGTH 947mm/37.15in

BARREL LENGTH 419mm/16.5in

WEIGHT UNLOADED 3.92kg/8.64lb

AN-94 Nikonov

Externally similar to the AK, the AN-94 Nikonov uses a cog and cable system to cycle some parts forwards and some rearwards, thus (theoretically, at least) negating recoil. On the two-shot burst setting, the Nikonov cycles at 1,800 to 2,000 rpm, letting off the second shot before the recoil of the first one can disrupt aim. Small arms experts outside the Russian system have reported that the Nikonov fails both in recoil reduction and cyclic rate. It may have been in in limited production from the mid-1990s or only produced as a prototype.

SPECIFICATION

MANUFACTURER Izhevsk

CALIBRE 7.62 x 39mm, 5.45 x 39mm,
5.56 x 45mm

MAGAZINE CAPACITY 30

ACTION Gas operated

TOTAL LENGTH 824mm/32.44in

BARREL LENGTH 314mm/12.36in

WEIGHT UNLOADED 3kg/6.61lb

AK-104

With the collapse of the Soviet Union, and many former Warsaw Pact countries manufacturing AK variants for the export market, Russian manufacturers have had to rapidly modernize. The AK-104 is a short-barrelled version of the Kalashnikov, with production and sighting improvements, burst setting as well as full-auto. Izhvesk intended it to compete well on the world small arms market. However, although the improvements are good they are not spectacular. The AK-104 was introduced in the late 1990s and production continues to the present day.

Federov Model 1916

The Federov Model 1916 was the first small arm that could be called an assault weapon. It was initially designed around a proprietary 6.5mm cartridge, but then changed to use the readily available 6.5 x 50mm Japanese cartridge. With a detachable magazine, selective fire and a vertical foregrip, it was far ahead of any other contender. The rifle was made in numbers large enough to see some action during World War I, and no doubt the 1917 Russian Revolution as well. Introduced in 1916, it remained in service until 1925.

SPECIFICATION	
MANUFACTURER	Sestroretsk
CALIBRE	6.5mm Arisaka
MAGAZINE CAPACITY	25
ACTION	Short recoil
TOTAL LENGTH	975mm/38.4in
BARREL LENGTH	519mm/20.45in
WEIGHT UNLOADED	4.45kg/9.8lb

Mosin-Nagant M-1891

With its distinctive spike bayonet (lacking a sheath), the Mosin-Nagant was the standard rifle for the Tsarist, and later Soviet, armies. Rugged and reasonably accurate, the army had enough on hand until war broke out. With the mobilized army several million men greater than the supply of rifles, the Tsar had to order additional rifles. Hence French- and American-made samples can be seen in many museums, collections and catalogues. The Mosin-Nagant was in service from 1891 to 1945. Despite its length, it is well balanced and handy, although the balance comes at the expense of barrel weight. Also, with sustained fire of 20 rounds in two–three minutes, the barrel and hand guards became too hot to handle.

SPECIFICATION	
MANUFACTURER	Russian & French arsenals, American arms companies
CALIBRE	7.62 x 54R
MAGAZINE CAPACITY	5
ACTION	Bolt action
TOTAL LENGTH	1,318mm/51.9in
BARREL LENGTH	820mm/32.3in
WEIGHT UNLOADED	4.06kg/8.95lb

Mosin-Nagant Mod 1891/30 sniper

3x scope

This was a standard Mosin-Nagant rifle, with the bolt handle turned down and the addition of a 3.5x PU optical sight, installed via a sidemount. The 3.5 power scope did not allow for effective long-range sniping, but on the Eastern Front there were plenty of opportunities to locate German officers, Non-Commissioned Officers (NCOs) or machine-gun crews at close to medium range. The rifle was developed in 1930 and served in the Red Army until 1945. During the war, the Tokarev M1938 was to be issued with optics and replace all Mosin sniper rifles. However, the Tokarev was insufficiently accurate and so Mosin sniper rifles were put back into production.

SPECIFICATION	
MANUFACTURER	Tula, Izhevsk, others
CALIBRE	7.62 x 54R
MAGAZINE CAPACITY	5
ACTION	Bolt action
TOTAL LENGTH	1,231mm/48.45in
BARREL LENGTH	730mm/28.75in
WEIGHT UNLOADED	4.4kg/9.7lb

Mosin-Nagant Carbine M-1907

Made for Tsarist cavalry and artillery, the first carbine had the stock extended so closely to the muzzle that the standard socket bayonet would not fit. When the 7.62 x 54R cartridge was upgraded in 1908, the sights on all Mosin-Nagant rifles and carbines had to be changed. While the Mosin-Nagant has an undeserved reputation as being rather awkward, the 1907 carbine is handy and well-balanced. It served from 1907 to 1918, and until all the models were used up.

SPECIFICATION	
MANUFACTURER	Tula
CALIBRE	7.62 x 54R
MAGAZINE CAPACITY	5
ACTION	Bolt action
TOTAL LENGTH	1,020mm/40.15in
BARREL LENGTH	509mm/20.05in
WEIGHT UNLOADED	3.41kg/7.51lb

Tokarev Model 1938

muzzle brake

SPECIFICATION

MANUFACTURER Tula, Izhevsk
CALIBRE 7.62 x 54R
MAGAZINE CAPACITY 20
ACTION Gas operated
TOTAL LENGTH 1,220mm/48.05in
BARREL LENGTH 635mm/25in
WEIGHT UNLOADED 3.95kg/8.7lb

The winner of the semi-auto rifle trials of the 1930s, the Tokarev Model 1938 was an entirely acceptable battle rifle. But the situation changed during World War II, when entire Russian units were armed with submachine guns. After the war, assault rifles like the AK-47 became the standard-issue weapon. The Tokarev has a very effective muzzle brake. However, while the firer experiences reduced recoil, anyone standing near him is blasted by high-pressure gases. The Model 1938 is a solid wartime weapon and served from 1938 to 1945. It was subsequently withdrawn from service.

Tokarev SVT 40

SPECIFICATION

MANUFACTURER Tula, Izhevsk
CALIBRE 7.62 x 54R
MAGAZINE CAPACITY 20
ACTION Gas operated
TOTAL LENGTH 1,220mm/48.05in
BARREL LENGTH 636mm/25in
WEIGHT UNLOADED 3.9kg/8.6lb

An improved M1938, the Samozaryadnaya Vintovka Tokareva (SVT) 40 replaced the fragile two-piece stock with a more durable single-piece stock. The cleaning rod was moved back to the traditional location under the barrel. It also incorporated design changes to make manufacturing less expensive and faster. Despite the improvements, it was still far more costly to manufacture than other rifles, and the decreased quality of wartime ammunition made it less reliable. The SVT 40s were so commonly captured that the German Army produced ammunition (which worked better than the Soviet type) and training manuals for it. Made and issued from 1940, production dwindled until in 1945 it ceased entirely.

Mosin-Nagant M44 carbine

SPECIFICATION

MANUFACTURER Tula, others
CALIBRE 7.62 x 54R
MAGAZINE CAPACITY 5
ACTION Bolt action
TOTAL LENGTH 1,020mm/40.15in
BARREL LENGTH 509mm/20.05in
WEIGHT UNLOADED 4.04kg/8.9lb

Modern warfare required shorter weapons with greater firepower than the Mod 1891/30 Mosin-Nagant, but the realities of production meant keeping that bolt-action rifle in full production. The M44 is merely a shortened rifle, the stock and metal furniture not even modified on the remaining length. After testing a number of bayonet designs, the USSR settled on a side-folding spike. Although relatively compact, the M44 carbine was as heavy as many other rifles. Entering service in 1944, it remained as a military rifle to the early 1950s, but was produced into the 1960s in some Communist bloc countries.

SPECIFICATION

MANUFACTURER Tula
CALIBRE 5.45 x 39mm
MAGAZINE CAPACITY 30
ACTION Gas operated
TOTAL LENGTH 730mm/28.74in
BARREL LENGTH 210mm/8.27in
WEIGHT UNLOADED 2.71kg/5.97lb

AKS-74U

stock fabricated from sheet steel

A short-barrelled assault rifle, the AKS-74U has a side-folding stock that reduces it to a compact package. The length of the barrel and the sight radius reduce power and accuracy, but this is thought to be an acceptable trade-off for the compactness of the weapon. It was made from the mid-1970s to the mid-1990s.

OC-14 Groza

This is a bullpup version of the modern Kalashnikov, with several additions or modifications, including a detachable grenade launcher. It can also be made in a special large-bore cartridge optimized for use with a suppressor. It can sometimes be difficult to insert magazines on AK bullpups. The AK magazine seats in place by catching the front lip in the receiver, then pivoting the rear back until it locks. Many bullpup designs have the pistol grip located in front of the magazine well, in the path of the tipped magazine. This rifle was produced in the late 1980s and remains in use today with the Russian Internal Affairs ministry.

SPECIFICATION

MANUFACTURER Tula
CALIBRE 7.62 x 39mm, 9 x 39mm
MAGAZINE CAPACITY 30
ACTION Gas operated
TOTAL LENGTH 700mm/27.56in
BARREL LENGTH 415mm/16.34in
WEIGHT UNLOADED 3.2kg/7.05lb

Winchester 1895

Unable to find or make enough Mosin-Nagant rifles in World War I, Russia contracted Winchester to provide its lever-action 1895 in the Russian calibre. Complete with stripper-clip guides and bayonet mounts, the Winchester was certainly up to the task of warfare. The fortunes of World War I went against the Tsar, and deliveries, which started in 1915, stopped in 1917. Out of 426,000 manufactured by Winchester over 300,000 were shipped to the Russian Army. The shipments were complete enough, however, for more of them to have been sent to Russia than remained in the United States, where for some time they were rare collectors' items.

SPECIFICATION

MANUFACTURER Winchester
CALIBRE 7.62 x 54R
MAGAZINE CAPACITY 5
ACTION Lever action
TOTAL LENGTH 1,160mm/45.65in
BARREL LENGTH 712mm/28.05in
WEIGHT UNLOADED 4.1kg/9.04lb

 Egypt

Egyptian firearms manufacture began with the production of Remington rolling-block rifles for the army in the late 19th century. Later, King Farouk (1936–52) upgraded the small arms inventory by purchasing from FN. After his overthrow, Egypt alternated between purchasing Soviet small arms and producing Soviet and other designs in-country, causing difficulties for the supply staff.

SAFN Model 1949

ten-shot magazine

SPECIFICATION

MANUFACTURER FN, Liège
CALIBRE 7.92 x 57mm
MAGAZINE CAPACITY 10
ACTION Gas operated/tilting lock
TOTAL LENGTH 1,110mm/43.7in
BARREL LENGTH 589mm/23.2in
WEIGHT UNLOADED 4.30kg/9.48lb

Produced for Egypt by FN, the SAFN Model 49 was certainly durable and reliable enough to cope with the climate and dust of the desert region. The 7.92 x 5mm cartridge had the range necessary for open-desert combat. Egyptian rifles can be recognized by the royal cipher of King Farouk above the chamber, and the Arabic numerals on the rear sight. The SAFN Model 1949 was purchased from 1950 to 1956, and continued in use for decades after. As a general-issue weapon it was replaced by the AK, which was produced in large quantities in Egypt. There may well be SAFNs still in use today, somewhere in the region.

Remington Rolling Block

SPECIFICATION

MANUFACTURER Remington Arms
CALIBRE 11.43 x 50R
MAGAZINE CAPACITY Single shot
ACTION Pivoting breechblock
TOTAL LENGTH 1,278mm/50.3in
BARREL LENGTH 889mm/35in
WEIGHT UNLOADED 4.15kg/9.15lb

single shot, no magazine

At the time Egypt purchased it, the Remington Rolling Block was a sensible choice of rifle, and certainly as good as any other single-shot breech-loading model. Within ten years, repeaters using smokeless powder were being manufactured and issued, but Egypt retained the Remington for a long time. At the time, many defence duties were undertaken by British Army units, which made armaments expenditure less pressing. The Remington Rolling Block was first obtained in 1876 and used well into the early 20th century.

Ljungman-Hakim

SPECIFICATION

MANUFACTURER State Factory 54
CALIBRE 7.92 x 57mm
MAGAZINE CAPACITY 10
ACTION Gas operated/tilting lock
TOTAL LENGTH 1,209mm/47.6in
BARREL LENGTH 590mm/23.25in
WEIGHT UNLOADED 4.82kg/10.63lb

muzzle brake

In July 1952, revolution erupted in Egypt and King Farouk, who had reigned since 1936, was forced to abdicate from the throne in favour of his son. The SAFN 49 was deemed unsuited for desert use, and the new rifle had to be of local manufacture. Husqvarna sold the tooling for the Ljungman-Hakim (LH) to Egypt. State Factory 54, in Port Said, was tasked with building the rifles. Longer and heavier than the SAFN Model 49, the Ljungman action was entirely unsuited to the combination of desert sand and dust and imperfect maintenance routines. The muzzle brake was difficult to fire when prone in the desert, and the resultant cloud of dust would have given away the firer's position. The LH was made from the mid-1950s to mid-1960s and sold as surplus in the 1980s.

Rasheed

SPECIFICATION

MANUFACTURER State Factory 54
CALIBRE 7.62 x 39mm
MAGAZINE CAPACITY 10
ACTION Gas operated/tilting lock
TOTAL LENGTH 1,077mm/42.4in
BARREL LENGTH 570mm/22.45in
WEIGHT UNLOADED 3.74kg/8.25lb

folding bayonet

Derived from the Ljungman designed by Erik Eklund, a Swedish engineer, the Rasheed was essentially a scaled-down and improved Hakim, without the muzzle brake and chambered for the Soviet M43 cartridge. In appearance a combination of the Hakim and the Soviet SKS, it is not clear why it was deemed necessary to design a different weapon. The Rasheed may have been manufactured to equip reserves or the police force. The local production of AK-47 rifles had already started when the Rasheed was being built; the Rasheed may have been produced to provide a weapon that would fire Soviet ammunition until AK production was sufficient to meet Egypt's needs. Only about 8,000 of the rifles were ever produced. The Rasheed was made between 1959 and 1960 and immediately became obsolete.

AK-47

Also known as the Maadi, the Egyptian AK-47 is made with Russian-supplied tooling and machinery. It is an example of the AKM as built in the Soviet Union from the late 1950s until the 1970s. While neither being as accurate as the SAFN Model 1949 nor as powerful as any of the rifles chambered in 7.92 x 57mm, the Maadi was more reliable in desert conditions than the Hakim. Manufacture began in the late 1950s and continues today. The Maadi was the first semi-auto-only AK made for export to the USA.

SPECIFICATION

MANUFACTURER State Factory 54
CALIBRE 7.62 x 39mm
MAGAZINE CAPACITY 30
ACTION Gas operated/rotating bolt
TOTAL LENGTH 870mm/34.25in
BARREL LENGTH 415mm/16.35in
WEIGHT UNLOADED 4.44kg/9.8lb

 Turkey

Before World War I the Ottoman Empire was on good terms with Germany and purchased many small arms from German firms. Once in Turkey, the local arsenals made modifications as needed. Often, the resulting rifle, while still named by its original designation, bore little resemblance to the factory blueprints.

Mauser Model 1905 carbine

The Mauser Model 1905 was an 1898 Mauser action in 7.65mm calibre, made for mounted troop and artillery unit use. Turkey was quite aggressive in requesting improved versions of the rifles it purchased, moving swiftly from the Gewehr 88 to M93 to 96 to 98 versions. With the collapse of the Ottoman Empire and the start of Kemal Atatürk's rule (1922–38), Turkey began converting many older rifles in 7.65mm to 7.92 x 57mm, for which they had a large supply of ammunition. The Mauser Model 1905 carbine was purchased in 1905 and served in the original or later calibre until the 1950s.

SPECIFICATION

MANUFACTURER Mauser, Oberndorf
CALIBRE 7.65 x 53mm
MAGAZINE CAPACITY 5
ACTION Bolt action
TOTAL LENGTH 1,045mm/41.15in
BARREL LENGTH 550mm/21.65in
WEIGHT UNLOADED 3.92kg/8.25lb

 Israel

Until it achieved independence in 1948, Israel had to make the best of whatever rifles were at hand. Afterwards, it bought and later produced its own arms. Israel's experience and reputation allowed it to enter the export market and sell small arms – and designs – to other countries.

NATO FN-FAL

The FN-FAL was issued from the early 1960s to 1990. The earliest rifles were FN-made, but later rifles were assembled in Israel using FN receivers and locally made parts. While robust and reliable, the FN-FAL was over 1m/3ft long and heavy. Much Israeli combat was urban, and the length of the rifle proved awkward. The IDF is a citizen force, and when the citizens complained about the weight of the issue weapon, a lighter model had to be found. The FN-FAL was standard issue until M16 rifles became common after 1973.

SPECIFICATION

MANUFACTURER FN, Liège
CALIBRE 7.62mm NATO
MAGAZINE CAPACITY 20
ACTION Gas operated/tilting lock
TOTAL LENGTH 1,016mm/40in
BARREL LENGTH 533mm/21in
WEIGHT UNLOADED 4.10kg/9.06lb

Galil

SPECIFICATION ✡

MANUFACTURER IMI

CALIBRE 5.56 x 45mm, 7.62mm NATO

MAGAZINE CAPACITY 35 (5.56) 25 (7.62)

ACTION Gas operated/rotating bolt

TOTAL LENGTH 970mm/38.2in

BARREL LENGTH 460mm/18.1in

WEIGHT UNLOADED 4.4kg/9.7lb

receiver milled
from a steel forging

Limitations
The Galil was a better version of the AK but was costly and heavy. The IDF limited issue to artillery and headquarters units, issuing M16s to all others.

An improved AK, the Galil features some updates to the basic Kalashnikov design. The rear sight is on the dust cover for a longer sighting radius, and is an aperture sight for more precise aiming. The safety/selector has a lever on the left side of the receiver, to be pushed by the thumb. The bipod incorporates a wire cutter. The folding stock is more solid and easier to fire with than the under folder of most AK-47s, and more durable than the side folder of the AK-74. The 7.62mm Galil was planned to replace the FAL and heavy-barrel FAL. However, the Galil turned out to be too heavy compared to the M16 and too expensive to manufacture. The Galil was first fielded in the early 1970s and has been in continued but diminished use to the present. Nowadays, it is found in only a few units of the IDF.

Galil sniper

SPECIFICATION ✡

MANUFACTURER IMI

CALIBRE 7.62mm NATO

MAGAZINE CAPACITY 25

ACTION Gas operated/rotating bolt

TOTAL LENGTH 1,115mm/43.9in

BARREL LENGTH 500mm/19.7in

WEIGHT UNLOADED 6.39kg/14.1lb

With a heavy barrel and muzzle brake, a match trigger, and the bipod moved back to the receiver to relieve stress on the barrel, the scoped Galil serves well as a semi-automatic sniper rifle, although it is more a tactical support rifle than a true sniper rifle. It was redesigned to fire 7.62mm NATO cartridges. Its weight, excessive for an infantry rifle, is not a hindrance as a sniper rifle, as snipers are seldom engaged in running gun battles. Additionally, Israel has them on hand to modify and use – an important consideration in military planning. The Galil sniper has been in use since the early 1980s and remains in service today.

TAR-21

SPECIFICATION ✡

MANUFACTURER IMI

CALIBRE 5.56 x 45mm

MAGAZINE CAPACITY 30

ACTION Gas operated/rotating bolt

TOTAL LENGTH 720mm/28.34in

BARREL LENGTH 460mm/18.11in

WEIGHT UNLOADED 2.8kg/6.17lb

The Tavor Assault Rifle (TAR-21) is the newest Israeli assault rifle, gradually being introduced to replace the M16 and all other rifles in service, including the AK and Galil. Basically an AK action in 5.56mm in a polymer bullpup shell, it is more compact, lighter and more durable than existing rifles. By 2007, it was still unclear whether the basic problems of the bullpup design would be solved by the TAR-21. (Bullpups are difficult and hazardous for left-handed shooters to use, and right-hand building corners are always a problem). Manufacture of the TAR-21 began in 1998 and continues to the present day.

 # Ethiopia

Ordering rifles from FN, Ethiopia (then Abyssinia) took delivery just before Italy invaded in October 1935. Although armed with the best rifles of the time, Ethiopian troops could not successfully resist the Italian Army. While Mussolini easily conquered the African state, he did not learn from this experience that his army was woefully equipped and trained, and his troops suffered in World War II as a result.

Mauser FN Model 1924 carbine

This was a standard export carbine of the mid-1930, in the standard calibre. The receiver bore the royal cipher of Emperor Haile Selassie (officially Emperor of Ethiopia from 1930 to 1974). It was purchased from 1933 to 1935 and used for decades afterwards. Using the standard 7.92mm Mauser cartridge, Ethiopia could acquire ammunition for rifles and light machine guns from any manufacturer in Europe, Britain or the United States. It made sense in a poor country for all rifles and machine guns to use a common calibre.

SPECIFICATION

MANUFACTURER FN, Liège
CALIBRE 7.92 x 57mm
MAGAZINE CAPACITY 5
ACTION Bolt action
TOTAL LENGTH 996mm/39.2in
BARREL LENGTH 493mm/19.4in
WEIGHT UNLOADED 3.67kg/8.1lb

Mauser Model 1933

The Mauser Model 1933 was the standard model short rifle as produced by FN in the mid-1930s. Except for the royal cipher and Lion of Juda markings, it would have been similar to any other country's Mauser-pattern rifle of the time. As with the carbine, the Mauser Model 1933 was purchased between 1933 and 1935 and in use for decades afterwards.

SPECIFICATION

MANUFACTURER FN, Liège
CALIBRE 7.92. x 57mm
MAGAZINE CAPACITY 5
ACTION Bolt action
TOTAL LENGTH 1,107mm/43.6in
BARREL LENGTH 600mm/23.62in
WEIGHT UNLOADED 3.99kg/8.8lb

 # Saudi Arabia

With no natural resources besides people and oil, Saudi Arabia initially purchased its small arms. With oil revenues after World War II, it began to invest in its own manufacturing. Saudi Arabia ranks among the world's most heavily armed nations, and it has plans to further upgrade its arsenal.

G3

Initially purchased from Hecker & Koch, Saudi Arabia bought manufacturing rights and began making its own G3s, which could be distinguished from West German G3s only by the markings. Once the 7.62mm NATO cartridge was replaced, the Saudis purchased the Steyr AUG. The G3 was produced from 1968 to the early 1980s. Since it is not practical to march through the desert, much of the patrolling by Saudi units would be vehicular, thus the weight of the G3 did not present a problem.

SPECIFICATION

MANUFACTURER H&K, al-Khardj Arsenal
CALIBRE 7.62mm NATO
MAGAZINE CAPACITY 20
ACTION Roller-delayed blowback
TOTAL LENGTH 1,021mm/40.2in
BARREL LENGTH 450mm/17.7in
WEIGHT UNLOADED 4.49kg/9.9lb

Iraq

From a miscellaneous collection of British arms, Iraq went mostly for Soviet-pattern rifles during the later stages of the Cold War. Given the dusty desert conditions in Iraq, the durability of the AK and its variants were an asset. France, China, Egypt and the United States have all supplied arms to Iraq.

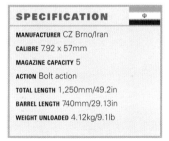

Tabuk M70

SPECIFICATION	
MANUFACTURER	Zastava/Iraq
CALIBRE	7.62 x 39mm
MAGAZINE CAPACITY	30
ACTION	Gas operated/rotating bolt
TOTAL LENGTH	869mm/34.25in
BARREL LENGTH	415mm/16.34in
WEIGHT UNLOADED	4.02kg/8.87lb

The Tabuk M70 was assembled in Iraq using the M70 Zastava AKM rifles as a pattern, and in many cases using Yugoslavian-manufactured parts such as the gas block. Other parts, such as the wood furniture, pins and springs, were locally made. Except for minor dimensional details, the Yugo/Iraqi AK is the same as any other sheet-metal receivered AK and works identically. It is made in both wood-stock and folding-stock versions. The M70 was assembled in Iraq from the early 1970s until 2003.

Iran/Persia

Iran became significant to the world economy after oil was discovered there in the early 20th century. After the price of oil increased in the early 1970s, Iran's export earnings increased, and the government was able to update much of its military equipment, including small arms. After the Iranian Revolution of 1979, Iran fought a war with Iraq (1980–90). Iran now has its own manufacturing base for small arms.

VZ 98/29

SPECIFICATION	
MANUFACTURER	CZ Brno/Iran
CALIBRE	7.92 x 57mm
MAGAZINE CAPACITY	5
ACTION	Bolt action
TOTAL LENGTH	1,250mm/49.2in
BARREL LENGTH	740mm/29.13in
WEIGHT UNLOADED	4.12kg/9.1lb

The standard VZ export rifle of 1930, the Persian 98/29 was at first made in Brno, Czechoslovakia. Production was increased in Iran once World War II began and supplies from the Czechs stopped. With VZ tooling on-site, the VZ 98/29 did not differ at all from the standard VZ/Mauser rifle, except for Iranian markings on the left rail in Farsi. Purchased rifles were issued in 1930, and local production began in Iran within a couple of years, lasting to the late 1960s. Iranian-produced rifles showed more alterations as time went on.

G3

SPECIFICATION	
MANUFACTURER	H&K, Mosalsalasi
CALIBRE	7.62 x 51mm
MAGAZINE CAPACITY	20
ACTION	Roller-delayed blowback
TOTAL LENGTH	1,021mm/40.2in
BARREL LENGTH	450mm/17.7in
WEIGHT UNLOADED	4.16kg/9.9lb

The G3 was provided at first by Hecker & Koch in the early 1970s, then built in Iran at the State Arms Factory at Mosalsalasi. Given the German attention to detail, the only difference between HK-produced and Iranian-produced rifles would have been the markings. Slightly modified and called the G3A6, it continued in production even after the Iranian Revolution. Purchased and locally manufactured rifles were first issued in the early 1970s and continue to serve to the present.

Model 49 carbine

SPECIFICATION

MANUFACTURER Iran
CALIBRE 7.92 x 57mm
MAGAZINE CAPACITY 5
ACTION Bolt action
TOTAL LENGTH 965mm/38in
BARREL LENGTH 454mm/17.91in
WEIGHT UNLOADED 3.8kg/8.4lb

The Model 49 was a carbine designed and produced only in Iran for Iranian use. It differed from the CZ-provided carbines in barrel band and sling-swivel configuration. The sling-swivel design was modified for local preferences and produced on Iranian designed and fabricated tooling and patterns, alongside the CZ tooling. Production of the new model began in 1949 and the rifles are no doubt in use somewhere to this day.

Pakistan

As part of the former British colony of India, it was natural for Pakistan to start with British-pattern rifles upon achieving independence in 1979. Pakistan then began its own arms industry. The long border with Afghanistan and the Soviet influence there brought extensive exposure to the AK system. Yet AKs have been phased out of service in Pakistan in favour of locally produced G3 rifles. Although many countries have switched to the 5.56mm or 5.45mm calibres, Pakistan sticks with the 7.62mm NATO and the G3.

SMLE No. 4 Mark 2

aperture rear sight

SPECIFICATION

MANUFACTURER Enfield
CALIBRE .303 British
MAGAZINE CAPACITY 10
ACTION Bolt action
TOTAL LENGTH 1,129mm/44.45in
BARREL LENGTH 640mm/25.2in
WEIGHT UNLOADED 4.11kg/9.06lb

The Mark 2 of the ubiquitous No. 4 SMLE had the trigger mounted to the underside of the receiver instead of on the frame around the magazine opening. This produced a more consistent trigger pull. Made at the end of World War II, it was kept longer in service in Pakistan solely due to a pressing need for rifles. It was first fielded in 1947 and was kept in service until the late 1960s.

AKMS

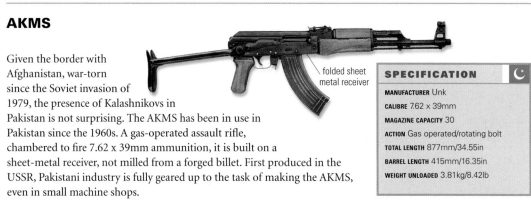

folded sheet metal receiver

SPECIFICATION

MANUFACTURER Unk
CALIBRE 7.62 x 39mm
MAGAZINE CAPACITY 30
ACTION Gas operated/rotating bolt
TOTAL LENGTH 877mm/34.55in
BARREL LENGTH 415mm/16.35in
WEIGHT UNLOADED 3.81kg/8.42lb

Given the border with Afghanistan, war-torn since the Soviet invasion of 1979, the presence of Kalashnikovs in Pakistan is not surprising. The AKMS has been in use in Pakistan since the 1960s. A gas-operated assault rifle, chambered to fire 7.62 x 39mm ammunition, it is built on a sheet-metal receiver, not milled from a forged billet. First produced in the USSR, Pakistani industry is fully geared up to the task of making the AKMS, even in small machine shops.

G3

SPECIFICATION

MANUFACTURER Wah
CALIBRE 7.62mm NATO
MAGAZINE CAPACITY 20
ACTION Roller-delayed blowback
TOTAL LENGTH 1,020mm/40.15in
BARREL LENGTH 450mm/17.7in
WEIGHT UNLOADED 4.08kg/9.68lb

A locally produced G3, made under licence from Heckler & Koch, the G3 has been the standard Pakistani Army rifle since its introduction there in 1967. The earliest rifles were purchased, but within a short time Pakistan was making its own. Except for the markings, this was a direct and exact copy of the G3, and equally unbreakable. Production began in 1967, and the rifles are still in regular use.

India

While India was a British colony, it was far enough away from Britain, and important enough, to warrant having its own armouries. Once independent after 1947, India continued making its own small arms. The Indian Army can count on more than 40 active armories and weapons manufacturers.

SMLE No.1 Mark III*

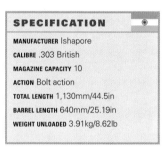

SPECIFICATION

MANUFACTURER Ishapore
CALIBRE .303 British
MAGAZINE CAPACITY 10
ACTION Bolt action
TOTAL LENGTH 1,130mm/44.5in
BARREL LENGTH 640mm/25.19in
WEIGHT UNLOADED 3.91kg/8.62lb

Produced in-country for local use, the Indian SMLE rifle was considered rough by some users but entirely serviceable. Many were produced during World War II. It was simply an Indian-made No.1 Mark III*. Production began at the Ishapore plant in 1907, and continued until 1955. After 1947 the imperial marking on the SMLE was replaced with the Indian Ashoka.

SMLE Mod2A1

7.62mm NATO magazine

Collectors' rifle
The Mod2A1 is popular with collectors.

SPECIFICATION

MANUFACTURER Ishapore
CALIBRE 7.62 x 51mm
MAGAZINE CAPACITY 10
ACTION Bolt action
TOTAL LENGTH 1,130mm/44.5in
BARREL LENGTH 640mm/25.19in
WEIGHT UNLOADED 3.91kg/8.62lb

India did not switch to the No. 4 action as Britain did in the 1940s. Therefore, in 1955, when it was necessary to convert rifles to the 7.62 x 51mm cartridge, it had none suitable for conversion. Instead, India used the No. 1 action blueprint to make new receivers out of a much tougher alloy, with better heat-treating. The new rifle, the SMLE Mod2A1, was deemed strong enough for the new cartridge. With an army of nearly 1.5 million men, a large number of rifles was required. The Mod2A1 was intended as an interim arm until the new FAL-derived rifle was made, but owing to the slow progress of the FAL project, was kept in service far longer than anticipated. The Mod2A1 is distinguished from the No. 1 by its square-profile magazine (the SMLE magazine is tapered). Manufacture began in the mid-1950s, and the rifles were in service until the mid-1980s.

FN 1A

A non-licensed version of the FAL, the Indian rifle was reverse-engineered and adapted to local tooling and dimensional practices, so parts did not easily interchange with any other FAL. Without the FN licensing and support, initial production was small, and the rifle was rough at first. However, the basic design was solid. After a few years, Indian FN 1As were solid, reliable, and coming off the production lines in sufficient numbers for domestic use. By the mid-1980s the FN 1A was showing its age, and India started the Indian Small Arms System (INSAS) programme. Delays in production led to the continued use of ageing FN 1A rifles and the interim purchase of AKM rifles from various ex-Warsaw Pact countries. Introduced in Indian service in 1963, the FN 1A did not replace the 2A1 for a number of years. It lasted in regular service to the mid-1990s until replaced by the INSAS, but probably remains in police service in distant provinces.

SPECIFICATION
MANUFACTURER Ishapore
CALIBRE 7.62 x 51mm
MAGAZINE CAPACITY 20
ACTION Gas operated/tilting lock
TOTAL LENGTH 1,089mm/42.9in
BARREL LENGTH 533mm/21in
WEIGHT UNLOADED 3.90kg/8.6lb

INSAS

An amalgam of three different rifles, built in India for use by its armed forces, the Indian National Small Arms System (INSAS) has the gas system and general layout of the AK, the gas regulator of the FAL, and a cocking handle on the upper left side like that of the Heckler & Koch G3. Adopted to replace the ageing stock of FAL rifles, it is a recent introduction and one intended for the usual triumvirate: rifle, carbine and squad automatic weapon. Production began in the late 1990s and the INSAS is the present issue weapon.

SPECIFICATION
MANUFACTURER Ishapore
CALIBRE 5.56 x 45mm
MAGAZINE CAPACITY 30
ACTION Gas operated/rotating bolt
TOTAL LENGTH 945mm/37.2in
BARREL LENGTH 464mm/18.26in
WEIGHT UNLOADED 3.2kg/7.05lb

China

Before the Communist Revolution of 1949, a variety of rifles were found in China, including imports, captured weapons and locally produced guns. After 1949 China settled on Soviet designs, principally the AK and Simonov rifles. China began to manufacture large numbers of both Soviet and Western designs for export. In recent years it has begun working on its own assault weapons system.

Kalashnikov Type 56

receiver milled from a steel forging

An early convert to the AK-47, China initially made forged-receiver Type 56 rifles. It switched to the stamped, AKM style in the mid-1960s. Chinese AKs have attached bayonets that are pivoted to deploy. Select-fire models are for military production. Via the Norinco Company, China has manufactured tens of thousands of semi-auto fire-only AKs for the United States market. Once production began in the late 1950s for Chinese needs, production did not slacken off for almost three decades. It picked up again to supply the US market, starting in the 1980s.

SPECIFICATION
MANUFACTURER Factory 66, Norinco
CALIBRE 7.62 x 39mm
MAGAZINE CAPACITY 30
ACTION Gas operated/rotating bolt
TOTAL LENGTH 870mm/34.25in
BARREL LENGTH 415mm/16.35in
WEIGHT UNLOADED 4.4kg/9.81lb

Model 311 (M16A1 copy)

SPECIFICATION	
MANUFACTURER Norinco	
CALIBRE 5.56 x 45mm	
MAGAZINE CAPACITY 20, 30	
ACTION Gas operated/rotating bolt	
TOTAL LENGTH 990mm/39in	
BARREL LENGTH 508mm/20in	
WEIGHT UNLOADED 2.85kg/6.31lb	

stock shape
unique to Model 311

Made as the 311 (semi-automatic fire only) and the CQ (select fire), the Norinco-made rifle is similar to an M16A1. Yet the pistol grip, handguards and stock are shaped differently and are made from a different formula plastic than US-made rifles. The rifling twist of the 311 is the old A1 rate (one turn in twelve inches), so it will not stabilize the newer SS-109 cartridge. As a result, firing SS-109 ammunition in a Model 311 is not advised. The Model 311 was produced from the early to late 1980s, for export sales only.

Model 305 (M14)

SPECIFICATION	
MANUFACTURER Norinco	
CALIBRE 7.62 x 51mm	
MAGAZINE CAPACITY 20	
ACTION Gas operated/rotating bolt	
TOTAL LENGTH 1,117mm/44in	
BARREL LENGTH 559mm/22in	
WEIGHT UNLOADED 3.8kg/8.56lb	

When the US Army dropped the M14 as a service rifle, target and sports shooters sought replacements. Curiously, China was in a position to make semi-auto only (the original M14 is select fire; semi and fully automatic) rifles for it. The US clients complained occasionally that the bolts were made of soft alloys and that the receivers had not been heat treated, but the shipments were nevertheless rapidly purchased. The Model 305 was produced throughout the 1990s. Target shooters found them an inexpensive alternative practice rifle. They could engage in lots of practice on the relatively cheap Chinese rifles, saving their expensive, hand-built target rifles for match use.

Type 86

SPECIFICATION	
MANUFACTURER Norinco	
CALIBRE 7.62 x 39mm	
MAGAZINE CAPACITY 30	
ACTION Gas operated/rotating bolt	
TOTAL LENGTH 667mm/26.25in	
BARREL LENGTH 438mm/17.24in	
WEIGHT UNLOADED 3.59kg/7.91lb	

This was an AKM variant built as a bullpup. While all bullpups have problems, the AK is particularly problematic. For one, the safety selector on the AK is a large lever on the right side of the receiver. An operator can only work the safety by removing his/her hand from the pistol grip and removing the rifle from the firing shoulder. The Type 86, produced in the 1990s, may have been built as a test-bed for the handling and operation of the new family of assault rifles that resulted in the Qing Buqiang Zu (QBZ-95).

QBZ-95

SPECIFICATION	
MANUFACTURER Unk	
CALIBRE 5.8 x 42mm	
MAGAZINE CAPACITY 20	
ACTION Gas operated/rotating bolt	
TOTAL LENGTH 760mm/29.9in	
BARREL LENGTH 520mm/20.47in	
WEIGHT UNLOADED 3.4kg/7.49lb	

China approached the question of a new assault rifle by first designing a new cartridge for it, the 5.8 x 42mm. Then, the type 95 rifle, a bullpup design, could be built around the cartridge. It was intended as part of a family of weapons, to include a compact version, a Squad Automatic Weapon (SAW) and a sniper rifle. China also makes the QBZ-97 variant, chambered in 5.56 x 45mm, for export. Production of the QBZ-95 began in 1995 and continues to the present. The QBZ-95 and its ammunition are so closely guarded that no rifles, and only a few dozen rounds of ammunition, are known to exist outside China.

Mosin-Nagant Type 53

The Mosin-Nagant Type 53 is identical to the Soviet model 1944 carbine, except for the Chinese armoury markings. The bayonet is attached to the rifle and pivots from alongside the handguard. A spike rather than a blade, the bayonet is more useful as a tent peg than as a cutting tool. However, by attaching the bayonet directly to the rifle, it could not be lost, so troops armed with the carbine were still armed even if they did not have ammunition. Production commenced in 1953 and continued until the early 1960s, when there were enough SKS carbines to replace them.

SPECIFICATION

MANUFACTURER Various
CALIBRE 7.62 x 54R
MAGAZINE CAPACITY 5
ACTION Bolt action
TOTAL LENGTH 1,020mm/40.15in
BARREL LENGTH 509mm/20.05in
WEIGHT UNLOADED 3.9kg/8.6lb

Simonov Type 56

Also known as the SKS, the Simonov carbine has a fixed magazine with a hinged floorplate for unloading. The magazine can be charged via stripper clips of ten rounds, or with individual rounds with the bolt locked back. It is semi-automatic only. Compact and handy, if somewhat heavy for a carbine, the SKS is rugged and reliable. Sturdy through design rather than materials, some Simonov carbines were made with steel that was not heat-treated yet still functioned properly. The Simonov could be repaired by blacksmiths if necessary. The Simonov Type 56 was produced from 1956 until the supply of AK-47s was sufficient for Chinese needs in the 1960s.

SPECIFICATION

MANUFACTURER Various
CALIBRE 7.62 x 39mm
MAGAZINE CAPACITY 10
ACTION Gas operated/tilting lock
TOTAL LENGTH 1,121mm/44.15in
BARREL LENGTH 519mm/20.45in
WEIGHT UNLOADED 3.8kg/8.5lb

Type 68

The Type 68 has a blend of features from the SKS Simonov Type 56 carbine and the AK-47 Kalashnikov Type 56. Externally the Type 68 appears to be an SKS with an AK magazine in place of the ten-shot SKS magazine. Internally, it uses a bolt similar to that of the AK instead of the tilting bolt of the Simonov. Additionally, the Type 68 has an adjustable gas regulator. It was built as an adjunct to AK production. First made in 1968, production of the Type 68 continued until the late 1980s.

SPECIFICATION

MANUFACTURER Various
CALIBRE 7.62 x 39mm
MAGAZINE CAPACITY 20 & 30
ACTION Gas operated/rotating bolt
TOTAL LENGTH 1,029mm/40.5in
BARREL LENGTH 520mm/20.5in
WEIGHT UNLOADED 3.5kg/7.7lb

Dragunov Type 85

The Dragunov Type 85 was an improved model of the Type 79 and a copy of the Dragunov sniper rifle. Soviet (and probably Chinese) sniper tactics are less concerned with long-range hits than short-to-medium range use to increase the effectiveness of the infantry in attack or defence. A self-loading rifle increases the sniper's rate of fire, and allows more targets of opportunity to be engaged. In Western military units, that niche is now filled by 5.56mm rifles, referred to as Designated Marksman Rifles. The Chinese Dragunov presents an equally serious threat at 600m/1,969ft as the Soviet model. Production has run since 1985, and no viable replacements have yet emerged.

SPECIFICATION

MANUFACTURER Various
CALIBRE 7.62 x 54R
MAGAZINE CAPACITY 10
ACTION Gas operated/rotating bolt
TOTAL LENGTH 1,220mm/48.0in
BARREL LENGTH 620mm/24.4in
WEIGHT UNLOADED 4.4kg/9.7lb

Indonesia

The Netherlands ruled Indonesia as a colony until it was occupied by Japan during World War II, primarily for its rich oil fields and rubber plantations. Indonesia gained independence in 1945. From the 1970s, the country purchased large numbers of M16s from the United States.

Arisaka Type 38

SPECIFICATION
MANUFACTURER Koishikawa, Tokyo
CALIBRE 6.5 x 50mm
MAGAZINE CAPACITY 5
ACTION Bolt action
TOTAL LENGTH 1,021mm/50.2in
BARREL LENGTH 799mm/31.45in
WEIGHT UNLOADED 4.11kg/9.08lb

After World War II, many Japanese rifles were left behind by the former occupation forces. In Japan during the struggle for independence, and as an independent country afterwards, the Type 38 was common. Other than cleaning them up, Indonesia did nothing to alter them from the original issue, even keeping the calibre. With large stocks of ammunition on hand, there was no reason to alter them. The Arisaka Type 38 was in regular use from 1940 to 1949.

Mannlicher Model 1895 conversion

SPECIFICATION
MANUFACTURER Steyr
CALIBRE .303 British
MAGAZINE CAPACITY 5
ACTION Bolt action
TOTAL LENGTH 1,272mm/50.1in
BARREL LENGTH 765mm/30.1in
WEIGHT UNLOADED 3.78kg/8.35lb

Given a ready supply of ammunition, the military need and a basic machine shop it is possible to convert a bolt-action rifle to another calibre. To do so on a large scale is more difficult. In the early stages of World War II, with no 6.5mm Dutch ammunition available, the Japanese had no choice but to convert the Mannlicher rifles to 7.7mm Japanese. After the war, the new government converted many others to .303 British. The Mannlicher Model 1895 conversion served in .303 from 1949 to the late 1950s.

Singapore

One of the very few city-states left in the modern world, Singapore has the economic muscle to make its own way in the Asian market. After occupation during World War II, Singapore joined briefly with the Federation of Malaya in 1963 to form Malaysia. It is now independent and builds its own small arms.

CIS Armalite M-16S1

SPECIFICATION
MANUFACTURER Chartered Industries of Singapore (CIS)
CALIBRE 5.56 x 45mm
MAGAZINE CAPACITY 30
ACTION Gas operated
TOTAL LENGTH 1,006mm/39.6in
BARREL LENGTH 508mm/20in
WEIGHT UNLOADED 3.7kg/8.15lb

This is a licensed copy of the Colt rifle, produced by the CIS for local use and export sales. Except for the markings, it is a Colt rifle, with all parts interchangeable. By establishing an offshore manufacturing presence, Colt could derive income from sales to entities the US State Department might otherwise deny them. CIS could earn cash for Singapore and supply the Singapore Defence Forces with small arms. The CIS Armalite was manufactured from 1970 to the early 1980s and was the standard rifle of the Singapore Defence Forces.

CIS SAR-80

Based on the US-designed Armalite AR-18 with improvements, the CIS produced the Singapore Assault Rifle (SAR)-80 for local use and export. It is a gas-operated, selective-fire rifle, which uses a short-stroke gas piston to push the large bolt carrier with a rotating bolt. The piston system allows the SAR-80 to be fitted with a folding stock. Used by the Singapore Army and exported to clients including Croatia, Sri Lanka and Somalia, there was stiff competition to the SAR-80 on the world market. It was manufactured from 1981 to the early 1990s.

SPECIFICATION	
MANUFACTURER	CIS
CALIBRE	5.56 x 45mm
MAGAZINE CAPACITY	30
ACTION	Gas operated
TOTAL LENGTH	970mm/38.18in
BARREL LENGTH	459mm/18.0in
WEIGHT UNLOADED	3.7kg/8.15lb

Australia

Australia did not have its own government rifle factory until the establishment of the Lithgow Arsenal in 1912. Between the world wars, rather than switch to the No. 4 design, as Britain did, Australia produced the No. 1 Mark III*, which remained in production until 1955.

SMLE No. 1 Mark III*

Manufactured in Lithgow, as all subsequent Australian service rifles have been, the No. 1 began production in 1912. Once the volume of rifles needed for combat in World War I became apparent, all Australian rifles, save an essential reserve, were shipped to Britain until the end of the war. Production for Australian needs continued until after the Korean War (1950–53). Lithgow looked into a short "jungle carbine" conversion and a conversion of the Mark III* to 7.62 NATO, but neither plan went ahead. The SMLE No. 1 was the standard Australian military rifle from 1912 until replaced by the Australian-made inch pattern FAL, the L1A1.

SPECIFICATION	
MANUFACTURER	Lithgow
CALIBRE	.303 British
MAGAZINE CAPACITY	10
ACTION	Bolt action
TOTAL LENGTH	1,130mm/44.5in
BARREL LENGTH	640mm/25.2in
WEIGHT UNLOADED	3.92kg/8.65lb

No. 6 Mark 1/1

shortened barrel with flash hider

During World War II, instead of changing production to the No. 4 series, Lithgow refined the No. 1 Mark III* which continued in production. When the call went out for shorter and lighter rifles for use in jungle and amphibious warfare, Lithgow refined the Mark III* into the No. 6 and the No. 6 Mark 1/1. The war ended, however, before the No. 6 could go into production. Later, tests to convert the Lithgow rifles to 7.62mm NATO proved unsatisfactory. The No. 6 missed both opportunities, and was thus never issued. The Mark 1/1 used an aperture rear sight instead of the notch rear sight of the Mark III*. The No. 6 Mark 1/1 was made only as a prototype in 1944–5 and was never adopted or issued as a regular item of the army.

SPECIFICATION	
MANUFACTURER	Lithgow
CALIBRE	.303 British
MAGAZINE CAPACITY	10
ACTION	Bolt action
TOTAL LENGTH	1,000mm/39.5in
BARREL LENGTH	482mm/19in
WEIGHT UNLOADED	3.40kg/7.5lb

L1A1

SPECIFICATION

MANUFACTURER Lithgow

CALIBRE 7.62 x 51mm

MAGAZINE CAPACITY 20

ACTION Gas operated/tilting lock

TOTAL LENGTH 1,136mm/45in

BARREL LENGTH 533mm/24.3in

WEIGHT UNLOADED 4.77kg/10.5lb

Manufactured by Lithgow, the L1A1 was an inch-pattern copy of the FAL, made under licence. The weight proved something of a hindrance in jungle fighting in the Vietnam War (1954–75). As a result it was not unusual for Australian Special Air Service to be seen with the lighter M16s. As with all inch-pattern FAL rifles, the L1A1 could be fitted with metric-pattern magazines in an emergency. The inch-pattern magazines use a large front block as an attachment point; the metric uses a small one. The rifle was produced and issued from 1955 to 1992, when the Australian Defence Force switched the Steyr AUG.

L2A1 Heavy Barrel

SPECIFICATION

MANUFACTURER Lithgow

CALIBRE 7.62 x 51mm

MAGAZINE CAPACITY 30

ACTION Gas operated/tilting lock

TOTAL LENGTH 1,136mm/45in

BARREL LENGTH 533mm/24.3in

WEIGHT UNLOADED 7.37kg/16.25lb

In order to increase the firepower of a squad, the Australian armies, like many others, attempted to turn a rifle into a light automatic weapon. The basic L1A1 was too light for the job, so the L2, with its heavier barrel, was pressed into the role. The bipod was built as a wood-covered handguard, and when folded appeared as just another L1A1. Unfolded, it exposed the heavy barrel for greater cooling and provided a shooting rest. Fewer than 10,000 were made and, being too light, they were not entirely successful. Even the BAR, at 8.2–8.6kg/18–19lb, was regarded as light for the role. However, had the L2A1 been employed as a semi-automatic sniper rifle, it probably would have been very successful. From adoption in 1958 to replacement by the F-89 in 1992, it was a good rifle in the wrong role.

F88

ejection can be changed from right to left

SPECIFICATION

MANUFACTURER Lithgow

CALIBRE 5.56 x 45mm

MAGAZINE CAPACITY 30

ACTION Gas operated/rotating bolt

TOTAL LENGTH 790mm/31in

BARREL LENGTH 508mm/20in

WEIGHT UNLOADED 3.6kg/7.9lb

F88 materials

Many of the major components of the F88 are made from non-corroding polymers.

In the early 1990s Australia adopted the 5.56mm cartridge, as used in the Austrian AUG. The F88 was manufactured under licence by Lithgow. Offered in the basic AUG form as the F88, it was also produced with a shorter barrel as a carbine, and as a model with an integral rail for mounting optics. When the army changed from the L1A1 to the F88, the decreased recoil and increased accuracy of the F88 produced high range-qualification scores, and the ratings had to be recalculated. It has been produced since 1992 and has been used by Australian forces in East Timor, Iraq and Afghanistan.

North Korea

North Korea, with assistance from the Chinese, has spent the last half-century manufacturing rifles and machine guns of the Soviet model for its 1.2 million-man army. While perhaps deficient in electronics, North Korea does not lack factories for producing small arms and ammunition.

AK-47

The AK-47 was a thoroughly standard AKM although it lacked the rate-reducer/anti-bounce mechanism. The bolt and carrier of the AK bounce when closing. This is an unavoidable result of the steel-on-steel impact of the carrier striking the front of the receiver when the bolt closes. Occasionally, in full-auto fire, an AK built without the anti-bounce feature will misfire. The cause is due to the hammer striking the bolt just as it has bounced away from the front of the receiver. It is not known why North Korea builds AKs lacking the anti-bounce parts, since they are not difficult to manufacture or to install. The AK-47 was produced and fielded from the 1950s to 1990s.

SPECIFICATION

MANUFACTURER N. Korea Arsenal
CALIBRE 7.62 x 39mm
MAGAZINE CAPACITY 30
ACTION Gas operated/rotating bolt
TOTAL LENGTH 877mm/34.55in
BARREL LENGTH 415mm/16.35in
WEIGHT UNLOADED 3.81kg/8.42lb

South Korea

After the Korean War (1950–53), South Korea built up a modern economy. While depending on the United States for support in defending against a potential North Korean attack, South Korea has developed its own arms manufacture. As well as rifles, South Korea produces ammunition.

Daewoo K2

Basically an M16 with the gas system of an AK-47 instead of the direct gas impingement system, the Daewoo K2 allows the user to have a folding polymer or a telescoping wire stock. The rifle uses standard M16 magazines, and the AK gas system avoids the gas fouling that causes problems in the Stoner system. Also, the Daewoo lacks the carry handle of the M16, and the charging handle of the Daewoo is on the right side, attached to the bolt carrier. While manufacture began in the early 1980s and the K2 remains in South Korean service to the present time, it has not been accepted as a service rifle outside of Korea.

SPECIFICATION

MANUFACTURER Daewoo
CALIBRE 5.56 x 45mm
MAGAZINE CAPACITY 30
ACTION Gas operated
TOTAL LENGTH 980mm/38.58in
BARREL LENGTH 465mm/18.30in
WEIGHT UNLOADED 3.26kg/7.19lb

Daewoo in the West
In the early 1990s the K2 was available in North America, but its simple sights and basic finish ensured that it was never popular with shooters.

 Japan

When the Japanese economy first opened up to the West in 1868, it was centuries behind the industrial economies. Starting with no industrial base or tradition of arms design and production, Japan adopted existing ideas. Later Japanese designs proved to be quite idiosyncratic, and in some cases were unreliable in the field. Compounding the design and production problems, during World War II, each Japanese Defence branch organized its own design, production and distribution of arms. Post-war Japan was forbidden from creating a defence force and so had no need of small arms. When a new force was established in the 1950s, Japan designed and produced its own small arms weapons.

Type 64

SPECIFICATION ●

MANUFACTURER Howa
CALIBRE 7.62 x 51mm
MAGAZINE CAPACITY 20
ACTION Gas operated/tilting lock
TOTAL LENGTH 989mm/38.95in
BARREL LENGTH 450mm/17.7in
WEIGHT UNLOADED 4.40kg/9.72lb

After 1957, when the post-war restrictions on Japanese military production were lifted, Japan started to design its own rifles. The first was the Type 64, produced from 1964 until 1985. With its gas regulator, the Type 64 could fire either reduced-power 7.62mm ammunition or full-power 7.62 NATO. While a 7.62 battle rifle in 1964 made a lot of sense, by the 1980s even the low-recoil ammunition was perceived to have too many shortcomings. There was still too much recoil, and the low velocity meant the trajectory was too arched. Despite the rifle's intrinsic accuracy, hitting targets beyond 300m/328yd was not possible. The Type 64 was replaced by the Type 89, which was in 5.56mm.

AR-180

hinge for folding stock

SPECIFICATION ●

MANUFACTURER Howa
CALIBRE 5.56 x 45mm
MAGAZINE CAPACITY 20 & 30
ACTION Gas operated/rotating bolt
TOTAL LENGTH 940mm/37.0in
BARREL LENGTH 464mm/18.26in
WEIGHT UNLOADED 3.09kg/6.81lb

The AR-180 was a Stoner design. Manufactured from sheet-metal stampings instead of the aluminium forgings of the earlier Stoner design, the M16, the AR-180 failed to compete with the M16 or AK-47. The design did lead to the Singapore SAR-80 and the SA-80, and some elements even appeared in the West German G36. When Japanese law banned the export of rifles that might be used for war, production moved to Costa Mesa, USA and Sterling, UK. Manufacture in Japan lasted from 1968 to 1972, while elsewhere it continued until 1979. While some parts are similar to those of the M16, no parts are interchangeable between the AR-180 and the M16.

SPECIFICATION ●

MANUFACTURER Howa
CALIBRE 5.56 x 45mm
MAGAZINE CAPACITY 20 & 30
ACTION Gas operated/rotating bolt
TOTAL LENGTH 864mm/34.0in
BARREL LENGTH 420mm/16.53in
WEIGHT UNLOADED 3.5kg/7.71lb

Type 89

Developed by Howa, and a descendant of the AR-18, the Type 89 solves the Type 64's problem of two 7.62mm ammunitions in supply. The Type 89 has a built-in bipod, folding stock and polymer furniture, and is up to date without being a bullpup. To make the Type 89 lighter, designers used aluminum forgings and polymers in place of the steel and wood of the Type 64 it replaced. It is capable of firing rifle grenades. Manufacture and issue commenced in 1989 and continues to the present.

Murata Type 22

The Murata Type 22, issued in 1889, used a
Japanese-designed 8mm rimmed round, and
fed from a tube magazine under the barrel. Although Japan's industrial
base was centuries behind Europe, this rifle was not particularly backward
compared to the magazine-fed repeating rifles that many European countries
were adopting at the time. When the Japanese became involved in conflict
in China in 1894, they discovered the Gewehr 1888 and learnt about clip
chargers and vertical magazines. The speed of reloading the 1888 made it
apparent that the Murata was obsolete, and by 1896 it was being withdrawn.

SPECIFICATION ●

MANUFACTURER Koishikawa

CALIBRE 8mm

MAGAZINE CAPACITY 8

ACTION Bolt action

TOTAL LENGTH 1,206mm/47.5in

BARREL LENGTH 749mm/29.5in

WEIGHT UNLOADED 3.93kg/8.68lb

Arisaka Type 38

With a split and solid bridge (the bolt
handle went ahead of one part of the
receiver but behind a solid ring of another) and a circular, rotating safety,
the Arisaka Type 38 is distinctive. It is also quite strong. The Arisaka cocks
on the forward movement of the bolt, like earlier Mauser designs. Many early
rifles were made with receiver covers, which rattled when the bearer walked.
The cover was meant to keep dust and debris off the bolt, and moved with the
bolt when the action was worked. The circular safety seemed odd at first, but
was easy to manipulate once understood. The Type 38 was manufactured in
volume from 1905 to 1945.

SPECIFICATION ●

MANUFACTURER Koishikawa

CALIBRE 6.5 x 50mm

MAGAZINE CAPACITY 5

ACTION Bolt action

TOTAL LENGTH 1,275mm/50.2in

BARREL LENGTH 799mm/31.45in

WEIGHT UNLOADED 4.11kg/9.08lb

Arisaka Type 97 sniper

2.5x scope

A sniper version of the Type 38, the
Type 97 was a 6.5mm rifle with an optical scope
attached, the bolt turned down and a wire monopod installed. No one knows
if there was special sniping ammunition made (for greater accuracy) or if the
snipers who used the Type 97 received any additional training. However, once
a shooter knew where his particular rifle hit, in relation to the optics reticle,
he was able to fire accurately in the jungle. As with almost all sniping duties,
fieldcraft and camouflage are quite often more important than pure
marksmanship. The rifle was in service from 1937 to 1945.

SPECIFICATION ●

MANUFACTURER Kokura, Nagoya

CALIBRE 6.5 x 50mm

MAGAZINE CAPACITY 5

ACTION Bolt action

TOTAL LENGTH 1,275mm/50.2in

BARREL LENGTH 799mm/31.45in

WEIGHT UNLOADED 4.44kg/9.81lb

Arisaka Type 2

Using an interrupted thread, like an artillery breech, the Type 2 paratroop rifle
could be taken down into two compact pieces. The idea was clever, but
foundered on two problems: there were no planes to transport parachutists,
and by the time it was developed and fielded, Japan was fighting a defensive
war. Production was limited to 1943–4, although the Type 2 has regularly
appeared as a sniper rifle in films. Apart from arms collectors and movie prop
houses, the Type 2 is now quite rare.

SPECIFICATION ●

MANUFACTURER Nagoya

CALIBRE 7.7 x 58mm

MAGAZINE CAPACITY 5

ACTION Bolt action

TOTAL LENGTH 1,150mm/45.3in

BARREL LENGTH 620mm/24.4in

WEIGHT UNLOADED 4.05kg/8.93lb

Arisaka Type 99

SPECIFICATION ●

MANUFACTURER Toriimatsu
CALIBRE 7.7 x 58mm
MAGAZINE CAPACITY 5
ACTION Bolt action
TOTAL LENGTH 1,149mm/45.25in
BARREL LENGTH 656mm/25.85in
WEIGHT UNLOADED 3.79kg/8.37lb

The Arisaka Type 99 was the 6.5 Arisaka action scaled up slightly to accommodate the larger 7.7 cartridge. It had the standard sliding dust/mud cover and a wire monopod to aid stability when aiming. Many covers were discarded in the jungles or on the islands to reduce the rattle and prevent revealing the owner's position, or to shed 0.2kg/0.5lb of weight. The wire monopod, while well intended, proved an illusory aid to aiming. Production began in 1939, just before the Japanese war machine turned against the USA, and continued until 1945.

Type 5 Garand copy

ten-shot magazine

SPECIFICATION ●

MANUFACTURER Yokosuka Navy Arsenal
CALIBRE 7.7 x 58mm
MAGAZINE CAPACITY 10
ACTION Gas operated/rotating bolt
TOTAL LENGTH 1,098mm/43.25in
BARREL LENGTH 588mm/23.15in
WEIGHT UNLOADED 4.14kg/9.13lb

In the 1920s Japan had an interest in self-loading rifles. Yet Japanese efforts did not lead to a rifle for adoption, and it was left with bolt-action rifles. During World War II, captured Garands were inspected, and a semi-auto rifle produced. However, it was the navy that made the Type 5, not the army. It used an internal magazine charged with two five-round stripper clips, instead of the Garand en bloc clip. Few Type 5s were produced, and most disappeared during the war. Those that still exist are found only in museums. The Type 5 was made only in 1945.

New Zealand

Having little local defence manufacturing, New Zealand purchases weapons from abroad, which allows it to choose the best for its needs. The country has a mixture of British, French, German, Norwegian and Australian equipment. The current rifle is the Australian F-88, a licenced copy of the Steyr AUG.

Charlton conversion

added gas system

RIGHT The outer housing keeps the firer safe.

SPECIFICATION

MANUFACTURER Charlton Motor
Workshops, NZ
CALIBRE .303 British
MAGAZINE CAPACITY 10, 30
ACTION Gas operated
TOTAL LENGTH 1132mm/44.55in
BARREL LENGTH 640mm/25.2in
WEIGHT UNLOADED 7.48kg/16.5lb

The New Zealand forces in World War II had a very improbable weapon: the Charlton conversion. The Charlton .303 Light Machine Gun (LMG) was a No. 1 Mark III* bolt-action rifle converted to a LMG. Besides adding a gas piston, cutting off the bolt handle and putting a sheet-metal cover over a new mechanism, New Zealand devised new magazines of more than ten-round capacity – although the conversion could still use standard rifle magazines. The sheet-metal cover kept the reciprocating parts from grabbing on to the shooter or his assistant. It was remarkable that the device worked at all; in fact, contemporary reports state that it worked well. The Charlton conversion was made only in 1941–2. As soon as BREN guns arrived in New Zealand from overseas, conversion work stopped, and the workshop was switched over to manufacturing Owen submachine guns, of which there was also a pressing need.

KEY

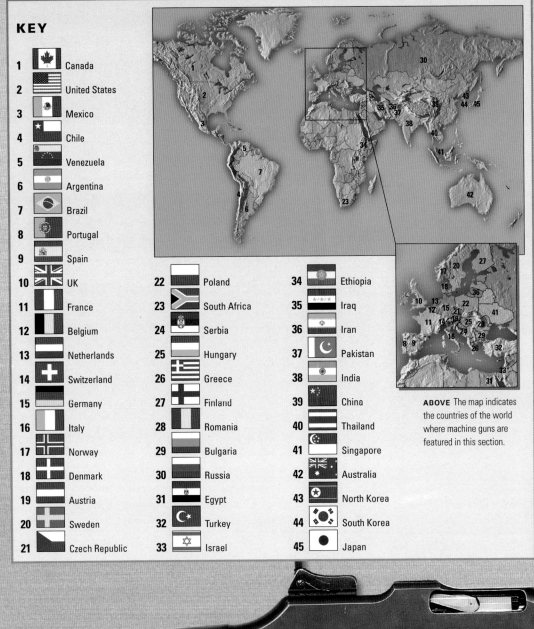

#	Country		#	Country		#	Country
1	Canada	22	Poland	34	Ethiopia
2	United States	23	South Africa	35	Iraq
3	Mexico	24	Serbia	36	Iran
4	Chile	25	Hungary	37	Pakistan
5	Venezuela	26	Greece	38	India
6	Argentina	27	Finland	39	China
7	Brazil	28	Romania	40	Thailand
8	Portugal	29	Bulgaria	41	Singapore
9	Spain	30	Russia	42	Australia
10	UK	31	Egypt	43	North Korea
11	France	32	Turkey	44	South Korea
12	Belgium	33	Israel	45	Japan
13	Netherlands				
14	Switzerland				
15	Germany				
16	Italy				
17	Norway				
18	Denmark				
19	Austria				
20	Sweden				
21	Czech Republic				

ABOVE The map indicates the countries of the world where machine guns are featured in this section.

A directory of machine guns from around the world

Machine guns are produced and manufactured across the world – some countries designing weaponry for their own armies, others producing or importing versions of machine guns from abroad, often modified or tailored to the importer's unique needs. This directory takes a look at the weapons from selected countries of the world, travelling from west to east, and details some of the machine guns that are available in those areas. Guns are organized alphabetically by manufacturer, except where their historical development is shown more clearly chronologically, or a company changes its name. Each machine gun has a description and a specification that lists its vital measurements, including length, unloaded weight, calibre, action and magazine capacity.

LEFT While the Hotchkiss Model 1914 had some minor faults, it was sufficient for France to manufacture tens of thousands of Hotchkisses during World War I.

BELOW Too late for more than the last few days of World War I, the Browning BAR Model 1921 was a solid design that sold well around the world, and was later used in all theatres during World War II.

Note on specification boxes: Traditionally guns developed in the United States have been given their calibre in inches, while European countries have designated calibre in metric measurement. Guns have retained this designation in this book. Dimensions refer to the weapon shown, where illustrated. Weights and measurements may be approximate.

# Canada

Manufacture of machine guns first began in Canada in 1938 when the Inglis firm signed a contract to manufacture BREN (from BRio/ENfield) guns for both Britain and Canada. Production started in 1940, and by 1943, some 60 per cent of all BREN guns that were being produced came from Inglis.

BREN Mark 2 Conversion

adjustable gas valve

Like so many countries after World War I, when faced with the prospect of converting to the new 7.62mm NATO cartridge, Canada first adapted older designs. Converting the BREN to 7.62mm required only a new bolt, barrel and magazines and it worked well in the new chambering. The most expensive part to make, the receiver, was simply re-marked to show the calibre change. They were only in use from the early 1950s to the early 1960s until replaced by the MAG 58, but were common in Canadian infantry units.

SPECIFICATION	
MANUFACTURER Inglis	
CALIBRE 7.62 x 51mm	
MAGAZINE CAPACITY 20	
ACTION Gas operated/tilting lock	
TOTAL LENGTH 1,158mm/45.6in	
BARREL LENGTH 635mm/25in	
WEIGHT UNLOADED 10.51kg/23.18lb	

Inglis Experimental

This was a simplified Oerlikon cannon meant for armoured and infantry use. Also known as the "Polsten" (Polish STEN), it was brought to Inglis by Polish engineers fleeing the German invasion. The Inglis was intended to be faster and cheaper to produce. Designed as light tank armament, it quickly became obsolete. Only the Finns found 20mm anti-tank guns transported by infantry to be useful for long. Introduced in 1939, it was quickly outclassed by armour advances, but stayed in service into the 1950s as a direct-fire infantry cannon.

SPECIFICATION	
MANUFACTURER Inglis	
CALIBRE 20mm	
MAGAZINE CAPACITY 30	
ACTION Recoil operated	
TOTAL LENGTH 2,210mm/87in	
BARREL LENGTH 1,397mm/55in	
WEIGHT UNLOADED 68kg/150lb	

United States

The United States was a power on the world stage before World War I, but the production requirements for World War II turned it into an arms-producing powerhouse, equalled only by the Soviet Union. Every rifle expert selling to the US government had his own machine-gun design.

Stoner 63/Solenoid

The Stoner 63 was designed to be a "one size fits all" weapon by building the components into the desired configuration using a single, multi-purpose receiver as the "building block". In this way, what was an assault rifle could be built as a belt-fed solenoid-fired fixed machine gun for mounting on a helicopter and fired forward. It could also be used as a top-fed BREN clone, or a belt-fed Light Machine Gun (LMG). The Stoner 63 system was used by the USA Navy's Sea, Air and Land (SEALS).

SPECIFICATION	
MANUFACTURER Cadillac Gage	
CALIBRE 5.56 x 45mm	
MAGAZINE CAPACITY Belt-fed	
ACTION Gas operated	
TOTAL LENGTH 762mm/30in	
BARREL LENGTH 508mm/20in	
WEIGHT UNLOADED 5.25kg/11.57lb	

Colt M1895

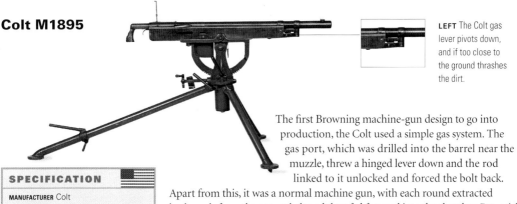

LEFT The Colt gas lever pivots down, and if too close to the ground thrashes the dirt.

SPECIFICATION

MANUFACTURER Colt
CALIBRE .30-06 & .303 British
MAGAZINE CAPACITY Belt-fed
ACTION Gas operated
TOTAL LENGTH 1,035mm/40.75in
BARREL LENGTH 711mm/28in
WEIGHT UNLOADED 15.87kg/35lb

The first Browning machine-gun design to go into production, the Colt used a simple gas system. The gas port, which was drilled into the barrel near the muzzle, threw a hinged lever down and the rod linked to it unlocked and forced the bolt back. Apart from this, it was a normal machine gun, with each round extracted backwards from the canvas belt and then fed forward into the chamber. Potentially, a gas-operated machine gun could be lighter than a recoil-operated one and the Colt was much lighter than the Maxim, Vickers and others, even when the water was left out of them. However, if the Colt gun was mounted too low to the ground the "flapper" would chew the earth, earning the nickname "potato digger". Introduced by Colt in 1895 and used in the Spanish-American War, it lasted to 1918, serving as a training and combat machine gun in World War I.

SPECIFICATION

MANUFACTURER Colt
CALIBRE .30-06
MAGAZINE CAPACITY 24- or 30-round trays
ACTION Gas operated
TOTAL LENGTH 1,232mm/48.5in
BARREL LENGTH 637mm/25.1in
WEIGHT UNLOADED 12.52kg/27.6lb

Benet-Mercie

This was the Hotchkiss light machine gun turned into an automatic rifle. Discarding the tripod for a rather tall bipod, the Benet-Mercié was used in training by the US Army. Between 1900–1914, the US Army owned less than 1,000 machine guns. Between not knowing which was best suited for their needs, and many officers thinking the army did not need machine guns at all, they only bought a few test samples of any one model. The Benet-Mercie was purchased in 1909 and used for training until 1918. It was popular outside the United States as a portable lightweight machine gun.

Browning M1917

water jacket for cooling

SPECIFICATION

MANUFACTURER Colt
CALIBRE .30-06
MAGAZINE CAPACITY Belt-fed
ACTION Recoil operated
TOTAL LENGTH 978mm/38.5in
BARREL LENGTH 610mm/24in
WEIGHT UNLOADED 14.78kg/32.6lb
w/o mount

trigger and pistol grip

Tasked with designing a new heavy machine gun for the US Army before World War I, John Moses Browning produced this design in record time. Designed as a recoil-operated water-cooled machine gun, it proved so adaptable that in World War II it was all things to all users: a water-cooled, air-cooled, infantry and air service capable machine gun produced in staggering numbers. For decades after World War II it was ubiquitous, found in all conflicts, sometimes on both sides. It was introduced in 1917 and had a service life in some areas beyond the 1960s.

Browning BAR M1918

SPECIFICATION

MANUFACTURER Colt
CALIBRE .30-06
MAGAZINE CAPACITY 20
ACTION Gas operated
TOTAL LENGTH 1,214mm/47.8in
BARREL LENGTH 610mm/24in
WEIGHT UNLOADED 8.79kg/19.4lb

As a Light Machine Gun (LMG) or Squad Automatic Weapon (SAW), the BAR proved useful enough to still be in service in World War II, Korea and Vietnam. Despite its name, the BAR 1918 went into service just before World War I, and lasted in one form or another to the 1960s. The improvements of the M1918 (the A1 followed by the A2) included the flash hider, bipod and carry handle. Typically, World War II GIs would discard the flash hider and carry handle and some even the bipod from the A2. The barrel is not user-changeable, and by modern standards exchanging magazines is slow. But an adversary armed with a BAR is not to be taken lightly.

Browning M1919A6

added shoulder stock

SPECIFICATION

MANUFACTURER Colt
CALIBRE .30-06
MAGAZINE CAPACITY Belt-fed
ACTION Recoil operated
TOTAL LENGTH 1,346mm/53in
BARREL LENGTH 610mm/24in
WEIGHT UNLOADED 14.74kg/32.5lb

This was essentially the Browning M1917, altered far beyond the designer's mission or intent. It was changed to air-cooled and given a pierced barrel shroud. By adding a shoulder stock to the rear and changing the trigger plate from a spade to a trigger system, the US Army produced a lighter machine gun that could be used by the infantry. Introduced in 1942, it stayed in inventory and in service until the early 1960s. Despite its weight, it was loved for its reliability and durability.

Chauchat (CSRG) M1918

recoil spring retainer

SPECIFICATION

MANUFACTURER C.S.R.G.
CALIBRE .30-06
MAGAZINE CAPACITY 20
ACTION Long recoil
TOTAL LENGTH 1,143mm/45in
BARREL LENGTH 470mm/18.5in
WEIGHT UNLOADED 8.61kg/19lb

The Chauchat was designed around the tapered and rimmed 8mm Lebel in 1918. In the .30-06 it was said to be almost as hazardous to the firer as to his target. The long, essentially straight .30-06 case was difficult to extract and the long-recoil mechanism was not up to handling the power of the cartridge, so it was relegated as a training weapon. It was so poor in .30-06 that after the war the army had them all destroyed.

M134 (GAU-2B/A)

SPECIFICATION

MANUFACTURER Dillon Aero
CALIBRE 7.62mm NATO
MAGAZINE CAPACITY Belt-fed
ACTION Electrically operated
TOTAL LENGTH 800mm/31.5in
BARREL LENGTH 533mm/21in
WEIGHT UNLOADED 18.8kg/41.44lb
w/o mount

The M134 GAU (Gun/ Automatic/Unit in US Air Force nomenclature) is the standard weapon on Blackhawk helicopters. It is essentially a multi-barrel Gatling gun powered by an electric motor, in a flexible mount. The firing rate is user-adjustable from 2,000 to 6,000 rpm. The weapon uses linked ammunition, but requires a de-linking feed system. It needs an electrical power supply and chutes to dispose of the links and brass, and thus is vehicular or aircraft bound. Developed in the 1960s and refined by Dillon, it is in use to the present day due to its staggering firepower.

Mark 48 Mod 0

SPECIFICATION

MANUFACTURER FNH-United States

CALIBRE 7.62mm NATO

MAGAZINE CAPACITY Belt-fed

ACTION Gas operated

TOTAL LENGTH 1,009mm/39.75in

BARREL LENGTH 470mm/18.5in

WEIGHT UNLOADED 8.2kg/18.1lb

Manufactured since 2000, the Mark 48 was developed to be a lightweight General-Purpose Machine Gun (GPMG) that could be handled like a squad automatic weapon by one operator. Developed for the United States Navy's Sea, Air and Land (SEALs) force, it is not in common use but heavily used by the special operations units that have it. Unlike the MAG 58/M240, the Mark 48 is (for a machine gun) light, handy and responsive. Light for a belt-fed, it is lighter than some models of the BAR, and lighter than the BREN gun.

XM312

SPECIFICATION

MANUFACTURER General Dynamics

CALIBRE .50 BMG

MAGAZINE CAPACITY Belt-fed

ACTION Gas operated, recoil dampened

TOTAL LENGTH 1,600mm/63in

BARREL LENGTH 980mm/38.5in

WEIGHT UNLOADED 19.28kg/42.5lb
tripod included

Introduced in 2000, the XM312 was meant to replace the M2HB, but General Dynamics has struggled to make it work. To control the forces of recoil, the XM312 fires each round as the action is moving forward. Recoil must first overcome the inertia of the moving action before the gas system can unlock the bolt and cycle to chamber another round. The design is soft in recoil but complicated, and has a slow rate of fire. Complaints arose during trials about its rate of fire: compared with the sedate 400 rpm of the M2HB, it reportedly fires at the dawdling pace of 240 rpm. It was still being pushed as an M2HB alternative in 2006.

Johnson M1941 LMG

SPECIFICATION

MANUFACTURER Johnson

CALIBRE .30-06

MAGAZINE CAPACITY 20

ACTION Recoil operated

TOTAL LENGTH 1,066mm/42in

BARREL LENGTH 558mm/23.14in

WEIGHT UNLOADED 6.48kg/14.28lb

Melvin Johnson felt his Light Machine Gun (LMG) was superior to the BAR. Although lighter, the recoil system of the LMG proved not to be as reliable in combat as the gas system of the BAR, and it only survived in service until 1945. The stock was designed to reduce muzzle rise in recoil, and the magazine could be charged with stripper clips while still in the weapon. While it showed promise in the mid to late 1930s, it was not made in any volume until 1941. It soon proved inadequate, and Johnson's prickly personality made improvements impossible.

M2HB

SPECIFICATION

MANUFACTURER Kelsey-Hayes

CALIBRE .50 BMG

MAGAZINE CAPACITY Belt-fed

ACTION Recoil operated

TOTAL LENGTH 1,656mm/65.2in

BARREL LENGTH 1,143mm/45in

WEIGHT UNLOADED 38.10kg/84lb
w/o mount

The massive Browning .50 machine gun was meant as an anti-tank weapon for World War I. By World War II, it had been worked over and turned into an air-cooled weapon with a heavy and (for the time) quick-change barrel. Just barely light enough for use by infantry, it could easily be mounted on any vehicle or aircraft. To move the M2HB, a tripod and a useful amount of ammunition would take an entire infantry squad or one jeep. It is so capable and durable that it is still in regular use today around the world, despite decades of work to replace it with an improved model.

M60

no handle for
changing a hot barrel

Developed by the
US Army Ordnance
as a General-Purpose
Machine Gun (GPMG), the M60 incorporated features of several machine guns
combined into one weapon. The bolt and barrel had a short service life because
the locking lugs would chip, reducing reliability. Once they were chipped, they
would gall the barrel cams. It also had a gas system that could be re-assembled in
the wrong way (turning it into a single-shot). Production began in 1960 after years
of testing and it remained in service until the late 1990s, when the US Marine
Corps persuaded the US procurement system to allow MAG 58s for purchase.

SPECIFICATION	
MANUFACTURER	Maremont Corp.
CALIBRE	7.62mm NATO
MAGAZINE CAPACITY	Belt-fed
ACTION	Gas operated
TOTAL LENGTH	1,111mm/43.75in
BARREL LENGTH	648mm/25.5in
WEIGHT UNLOADED	10.43kg/23lb

Marlin M1914

This was the version of the Colt/Browning M1895 produced by Marlin
between 1914 and 1918. It was purchased by the US Army for training
purposes before and during World War I. As with all air-cooled machine guns,
it could overheat if not used judiciously. It was made in two versions. While
the first was a copy of the Colt/Browning, the second involved improving the
"flapper" design of the Colt to a straight piston parallel to the bore, making it
better for use in tanks. Early teething problems almost kept it from service.

SPECIFICATION	
MANUFACTURER	Marlin-Rockwell
CALIBRE	.30-06
MAGAZINE CAPACITY	Belt-fed
ACTION	Gas operated
TOTAL LENGTH	1,028mm/40.5in
BARREL LENGTH	711mm/28in
WEIGHT UNLOADED	14.74kg/32.5lb

Lewis Mark 6 USN

SPECIFICATION	
MANUFACTURER	Savage Arms Corp.
CALIBRE	.30-06
MAGAZINE CAPACITY	47- or 96-round drums
ACTION	Gas operated
TOTAL LENGTH	1,283mm/50.5in
BARREL LENGTH	668mm/26.3in
WEIGHT UNLOADED	12.33kg/27.2lb

While the US Army was against adopting the Lewis gun, the US Navy was not.
Acquired during World War I, the naval Lewis guns served for years in relative
obscurity until the navy gunboats on the Yangtze River were attacked in the early
years of World War II, before the United States had even entered the war. As
local and light defence weapons, they served well on the gunboats, which were
shallow-draft vessels cruising up and down the
major Chinese rivers, unlikely to face artillery-
class weapons. The high quality of manufacture
of the Lewis guns kept them in service into the 1930s, when
other machine guns would have been scrapped long before.
It is shown here with the 47-round pan magazine.

forced-air
cooling jacket

M73

Developed as a replacement in tanks for the Browning and M60, the M73 turned
out to be less reliable than the M60 in training and service, and more expensive
than the Browning that the United States already had in inventory and wanted
to dispose of. One problematic design feature was the barrel-change method: the
barrel could be changed from inside the tank, a requirement that made the
design complex, expensive and which decreased accuracy and reliability. It was
later removed from (limited) service as unfixable and a waste of effort to continue.

SPECIFICATION	
MANUFACTURER	Springfield
CALIBRE	7.62mm NATO
MAGAZINE CAPACITY	Belt-fed
ACTION	Recoil, w/gas assist
TOTAL LENGTH	882mm/34.75in
BARREL LENGTH	559mm/22in
WEIGHT UNLOADED	12.70kg/28lb

 Mexico

For a long time, Mexico used imported arms. There were a few designs that Mexican nationals produced, however, and the Mendoza is the most prominent.

Mexico licensed manufacture of the Heckler & Koch 21E as its light and General-Purpose Machine Gun (GPMG). It uses the M2HB as its heavy machine gun.

Mendoza RM2

offset sights

SPECIFICATION

MANUFACTURER Mexico National Armoury
CALIBRE .30-06
MAGAZINE CAPACITY 20
ACTION Gas operated/rotating bolt
TOTAL LENGTH 1,100mm/43.3in
BARREL LENGTH 610mm/24in
WEIGHT UNLOADED 6.39kg/14.1lb

Offset sight
Some say the RM2 was the light machine gun the BAR should have been. A top-mounted magazine needs an offset sight so that the firer can aim.

Designed by Raphael Mendoza, while working for the National Arms Factory in Mexico, the RM2 was a refined version of the M1934. During World War II the US government commissioned more weapons, so Mendoza updated his M-1934, changing the calibre to .30-06 and removing the quick-change barrel feature. The war ended before he could fulfil the contract, and in 1947 he submitted 50 prototypes of the RM2 to the Mexican Marine Corps. The Mexican government declined to purchase any. As Mexican law prohibited the export of "instruments of war" he could not sell it outside Mexico. The M1934 served in the Mexican Army into the late 1950s, but the RM2 ended up in museums around the world.

 Chile

Many weapons systems in Chile, large and small, reached the end of their useful life at much the same time. From the mid 1960s, Chile's machine gun needs were filled by

the Rheinmettal MG3 and the FN M2HB. Since the turn of the century, it has been replacing a lot of equipment, from small arms through to frigates and F-16 fighters.

BAR Model 1925

SPECIFICATION

MANUFACTURER Colt
CALIBRE 7.62 x 63mm aka .30-06
MAGAZINE CAPACITY 20
ACTION Gas operated/toggle lock
TOTAL LENGTH 1,214mm/47.8in
BARREL LENGTH 609mm/24in
WEIGHT UNLOADED 8.79kg/19.4lb

Colt was eager to manufacture and export the BAR, as sales had not met expectations. As a result, they could be found in ones and twos in many armouries, both police and military, before World War II. Used as a Light Machine Gun (LMG) in Chilean service, the only problem would have been in keeping the .30-06 ammunition supply separate from the 7.7mm ammunition for the Nambu. After World War II, the US government gave BARs to any ally who asked for them. It was in service from 1918 until the 1960s.

Madsen M1946

Previous Madsen machine guns purchased by Chile had been in 7 x 57mm. After World War II, ammunition supply was easiest in .30-06, the American service cartridge, due to wartime production, and postwar American Cold War efforts. Chile used the .30-06 until the 1960s, when it adopted the G3 and MG3, both in 7.62mm NATO, the cartridge easiest to procure on the world market. It was in service from 1946 to the mid 1950s.

SPECIFICATION	
MANUFACTURER	Dansk Industri Syndikat
CALIBRE	7.62 x 63mm
MAGAZINE CAPACITY	20
ACTION	Recoil operated
TOTAL LENGTH	1,165mm/45.9in
BARREL LENGTH	477mm/18.8in
WEIGHT UNLOADED	9.97kg/22lb

Nambu Type 3, M1920

fins for air-cooling

SPECIFICATION	
MANUFACTURER	Various
CALIBRE	7.7 x 58R
MAGAZINE CAPACITY	24- & 30-round trays
ACTION	Gas operated
TOTAL LENGTH	1,155mm/45.5in
BARREL LENGTH	736mm/29in
WEIGHT UNLOADED	55.33kg/122lb w/tripod

This is one of the many Hotchkiss variants made by Japan. Between the wars, business was brisk in weapons, and Japan was active on the Pacific coast in selling. As the Nambu Type 3 was a sturdy, reliable machine gun, the Chilean Army could not have had any complaints about it other than the weight. It was produced between 1920 and 1936.

Venezuela

On the Caribbean coast of South America, Venezuelan forces could count on having to deal with piracy and drug running. Due to oil exports from 1935, Venezuela has had the economic reserves to buy modern weapons. After World War II, they were purchased mostly from FN in Liège, Belgium. Today, Venezuela makes its own AK rifles.

VZ37

dual sideways pistol grips

SPECIFICATION	
MANUFACTURER	CZ, BRio
CALIBRE	7 x 57mm
MAGAZINE CAPACITY	Belt-fed
ACTION	Gas operated
TOTAL LENGTH	1,104mm/43.5in
BARREL LENGTH	678mm/26.7in
WEIGHT UNLOADED	18.96kg/41.8lb

The VZ37 was the precursor to the BESA medium machine gun in British service, adapted here to fit on a tripod. As with many earlier designs, it was quite easy to adapt it to any calibre that would fit through the feed tray. For any customer willing to buy, BRio were happy to modify their products to the national calibre. The VZ37 was peculiar in that the pistol grip was the cocking handle to charge the weapon: the gunner would grasp the pistol grip and push forward until it caught the bolt and then draw it back until it stopped. It was bought from BRio at the start of 1937 and remained in service until the late 1950s.

FN M1950

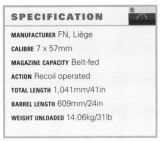

SPECIFICATION

MANUFACTURER FN, Liège

CALIBRE 7 x 57mm

MAGAZINE CAPACITY Belt-fed

ACTION Recoil operated

TOTAL LENGTH 1,041mm/41in

BARREL LENGTH 609mm/24in

WEIGHT UNLOADED 14.06kg/31lb

The Browning machine gun design was as adaptable to other calibres as any. For FN to produce it in 7mm Mauser was therefore straightforward. By 1950, FN had made improvements to the basic Browning machine gun. The sights had been changed, and the barrel jacket was given larger slots for better cooling. The M1950 also features the FN two-bolt mounting system, which FN have used on all machine guns since then. It was produced between 1950 and the 1960s.

 # Argentina

After World War II, Argentina licensed manufacture of firepower from FN in Liège, Belgium. The success of a proven design such as the Belgian FN MAG 58 meant that it has continued in service. In the Falklands War, both the Argentine and British sides used licensed copies of FN rifles and machine guns.

FN MAG 58

With FN taking over the world's arms markets after World War II, as Mauser had done before World War I, the MAG 58 became nearly ubiquitous. With the adoption of the FAL and MAG 58, Argentina dropped the 7.65mm Mauser cartridge in rifle and machine guns, sold all the older rifles on the surplus market, and adopted the 7.62mm NATO. Observers of the Falklands War commented on how the Argentine and British forces were using identical machine guns. With FN so vigorous in sales and licensing, this has been a regular occurrence since 1958. Argentina adopted the MAG 58 in 1960 and they are still in service today.

SPECIFICATION

MANUFACTURER FN, Liège

CALIBRE 7.62mm NATO

MAGAZINE CAPACITY Disintegrating belt

ACTION Gas operated/toggle lock

TOTAL LENGTH 1,257mm/49.5in

BARREL LENGTH 544mm/21.4in

WEIGHT UNLOADED 10.88kg/24lb

Maxim M1898

— long-range sight

firer's seat

SPECIFICATION

MANUFACTURER Simpson & Co.

CALIBRE 7.65mm Mauser

MAGAZINE CAPACITY Cloth belt

ACTION Recoil operated, gas boost

TOTAL LENGTH 1,193mm/47in

BARREL LENGTH 711mm/28in

WEIGHT UNLOADED 29.9kg/66lb w/o water

The Maxim was adaptable to almost any cartridge design, so chambering it for the 7.65mm Mauser was relative child's play for the Simpson & Company manufacturers. Known in North America as "7.65 Argentine", the 7.65 x 53mm cartridge is entirely suitable for military use, although little-adopted and thus not common today. The Maxim M1898 was in use from 1898 to the 1920s, when it was replaced by lighter machine guns.

Brazil

Being cut off from suppliers during both World Wars gave Brazil the impetus to form its own arms industry. Since 1954, Brazil has made sure it is self-sufficient in arms production. Today Mekanika Indutria e Comercio Ltd manufactures the 7.62mm "Uirapuru" for use by the Brazilian Armed Forces.

Madsen M1935

Introduced by Denmark in 1904, the Madsen is the only single-shot rifle action to ever be made into a machine gun. The bolt hinges on a rear pivot pin, in much the same manner as the Martini-Henry rifle. The feed mechanism is activated by a cam shuttling along a track in the side plate and each round is fed down out of the magazine. The Madsen depends on good-quality ammunition, but is essentially low maintenance. In Brazil, the Madsen was used in infantry units and on armoured cars until replaced in the late 1950s by Brazilian-made FALs and MAG 58s.

cooling jacket

SPECIFICATION

MANUFACTURER Dansk Industri Syndikat
CALIBRE 7 x 57mm
MAGAZINE CAPACITY 30-round magazine
ACTION Tilting bolt
TOTAL LENGTH 1,165mm/45.9in
BARREL LENGTH 477mm/18.8in
WEIGHT UNLOADED 9.98kg/22lb

Portugal

In World War I, Portuguese infantry fought with France and Britain, equipped with British SMLEs. INDEP, the Portuguese small arms manufacturer now produces a range of weapons under licence, including a copy of the Heckler & Koch-21 light machine gun (LMG).

Madsen M/956

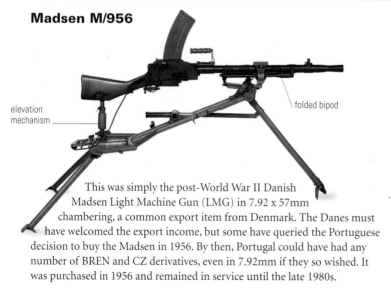

elevation mechanism

folded bipod

This was simply the post-World War II Danish Madsen Light Machine Gun (LMG) in 7.92 x 57mm chambering, a common export item from Denmark. The Danes must have welcomed the export income, but some have queried the Portuguese decision to buy the Madsen in 1956. By then, Portugal could have had any number of BREN and CZ derivatives, even in 7.92mm if they so wished. It was purchased in 1956 and remained in service until the late 1980s.

SPECIFICATION

MANUFACTURER Dansk Industri Syndikat
CALIBRE 7.92 x 57mm
MAGAZINE CAPACITY 30
ACTION Recoil operated
TOTAL LENGTH 1,166mm/45.9in
BARREL LENGTH 477mm/18.8in
WEIGHT UNLOADED 9.97kg/22lb

Reliable long-range fire
Shown here on a sustained-fire tripod, the Madsen was reliable and accurate enough for long-range fire. However, the box magazine limited fire volume, only holding 30 rounds each.

Dreyse M/938

SPECIFICATION

MANUFACTURER RM&M
CALIBRE 7.92 x 57mm
MAGAZINE CAPACITY Belt-fed from drums
ACTION Recoil
TOTAL LENGTH 1,194mm/47in
BARREL LENGTH 622mm/24.5in
WEIGHT UNLOADED 13.15kg/29.2lb

This was a modified Dreyse M1918, used by Germany as the MG13 and sold to Portugal in 1938. A select-fire (rare in an light machine gun) weapon, which can be fired in either semi or full auto settings, it was obsolete even before the Germans sold them. As Portugal was only involved in colonial campaigns, this was not an issue. The Dreyse M/938 was purchased in 1938, but was never used in a conflict, becoming obsolete before ever being accepted. It was a solid and dependable, albeit heavy, machine gun.

Spain

Lacking a major industrial base in the first half of the 20th century, Spain did not enter the world market for machine guns as an exporter. After World War II, Spain followed many other countries and began producing small arms for its own use. CETME currently manufactures the MG3 and the Ameli under licence.

SPECIFICATION

MANUFACTURER Alfa
CALIBRE 7.92 x 57mm
MAGAZINE CAPACITY Belt-fed
ACTION Gas operated
TOTAL LENGTH 1,448mm/57in
BARREL LENGTH 750mm/29.53in
WEIGHT UNLOADED 12.99kg/28.66lb
w/o tripod

Alfa M1944

Lacking access to German small arms (particularly machine guns) during World War II, Spain made its own. The Alfa closely resembled the Italian Breda in layout and function but was certainly a solid medium machine gun. Spain even exported a few to Egypt. The Alfa M1944 remained in service until the 1980s.

CETME Ameli

belt-feed only, no box magazines

Externally a scaled-down MG 42, and internally an HK 21 in 5.56mm instead of 7.62mm NATO, the Ameli has a reputation for being a bit obstinate. Some users report regular malfunctions, while others report flawless reliability. Research suggests that the buffer system may be the main problem and that replacing or rebuilding it turns the Ameli into a spectacularly good Squad Automatic Weapon (SAW). In that role it does not accept the box magazines of any rifle system, only using disintegrating belts. Experience has shown the "feature" of being able to use box magazines far less useful in a SAW than designers had thought. Given the fierce competition from other makers and their designs, the initial problems of the Ameli kept it from gaining market share. The CETME Ameli has been in service since 1982.

SPECIFICATION

MANUFACTURER CETME
CALIBRE 5.56 x 45mm
MAGAZINE CAPACITY Belt-fed
ACTION Roller-delayed blowback
TOTAL LENGTH 900mm/35.43in
BARREL LENGTH 400mm/15.74in
WEIGHT UNLOADED 5.3kg/11.68lb

United Kingdom

The British Army did not take machine guns in any numbers before World War I. But the high rate of fire of British-trained riflemen during the conflict led the Germans to under-estimate the number of machine guns in the British Army. After using one of the heaviest rifle-calibre machine guns (Vickers), after the war Britain adopted the BREN, one of best lightweight rifle-calibre squad automatic weapons (SAWs) ever made.

BESA Mark 2

Developed from the Czech ZB53, the BESA served as armament on tanks. The BESA fired its cartridge while the barrel was moving forward. Thus, part of the recoil was used up in stopping the forward travel of the barrel. This compact design made it useful in the crowded environment of tanks. The design was not changed from the Czech in 7.92mm as the Royal Armoured Corps had its own supply system, separate from that of the Infantry. It was deemed easier to produce and ship 7.92mm ammunition for the tanks than to re-design the BESA to use .303 ammunition. The War Office signed a contract with BRio for licensed manufacture of the BESA in 1936, placing their first order in 1938. They stayed in regular service until 1945, but new tank designs received the L7A1 after the war.

sliding the pistol grip forward and back cocked the BESA

SPECIFICATION

MANUFACTURER BSA
CALIBRE 7.92mm Mauser
MAGAZINE CAPACITY Belts, cloth or disintegrating
ACTION Gas operated
TOTAL LENGTH 1,105mm/43.5in
BARREL LENGTH 736mm/29in
WEIGHT UNLOADED 21.7kg/48lb

Colt M1914

Like the earlier 1895 Colt, this was called the "potato digger" due to the front actuating arm, and was a refined M1895, designed by John Moses Browning. Gas bled off the barrel and pivoted the actuator down. If the gun was too close to the ground, it would dig into the soil. Despite being air-cooled, the Colt had a good reputation for reliability and volume of fire. The slow cyclic rate (400 rpm) kept it cooler than other air-cooled machine guns. Despite its heavier barrel, the loss of the water and jacket made it lighter and more compact than the Vickers or Maxim, and popular with the troops. It was first used in American service in Cuba, but not kept after 1918.

SPECIFICATION

MANUFACTURER Colt
CALIBRE .30-06, .303 British, 7 x 57mm, 7.65 x 54mm
MAGAZINE CAPACITY Belt-fed
ACTION Gas operated
TOTAL LENGTH 1,035mm/40.75in
BARREL LENGTH 711mm/28in
WEIGHT UNLOADED 15.9kg/35lb

Browning Mark 2, Air Service

SPECIFICATION

MANUFACTURER Colt
CALIBRE .303 British
MAGAZINE CAPACITY Belt-fed
ACTION Recoil operated
TOTAL LENGTH 978mm/38.5in
BARREL LENGTH 610mm/24in
WEIGHT UNLOADED 14kg/31lb

The Browning is easily converted from one rifle calibre to another. As long as the cartridge length and rim diameter fit the receiver, the rest of the conversion job is simply detail. Thus, converting Browning machine guns from the American .30-06 to .303 British was easy. Britain purchased many Browning machine guns for air service to arm World War II aircraft. The cyclic rate on aircraft guns was typically increased, with hydraulic buffers and modified springs, from 500 rpm to 1,000 rpm. These guns were quite popular for infantry use. While .303 weapons were desired in 1940, within a few years all aircraft machine guns were .50 BMG.

Browning 1919 A4 conversion

SPECIFICATION

MANUFACTURER Colt, Savage, many others

CALIBRE 7.62mm NATO

MAGAZINE CAPACITY Belt-fed

ACTION Recoil operated

TOTAL LENGTH 1,041mm/41in

BARREL LENGTH 721mm/28.4in

WEIGHT UNLOADED 11.3kg/25lb

Given the durability, near-ubiquity and availability of spare parts for the Browning .30 machine guns in all their guises, it was no wonder than many countries sought to convert them. When NATO switched to the 7.62 x 51mm cartridge, it was easy enough to convert Brownings of all types to the new cartridge. Some conversions even went so far as to change the Browning from cloth to disintegrating belts. However, as soon as the new generation of general-purpose machine guns (GPMGs) were fielded, with their quick-change barrels, all the old Brownings went back into storage and were subsequently scrapped. However, between the adoption of the T65 (7.62mm NATO cartridge) in 1953 and the manufacture of increasing numbers of the Enfield L7A1, it was a machine gun in any inventory, including British.

BREN Mark 2

SPECIFICATION

MANUFACTURER Enfield

CALIBRE .303 British

MAGAZINE CAPACITY 30

ACTION Gas operated/tilting bolt

TOTAL LENGTH 1,158mm/45.6in

BARREL LENGTH 635mm/25in

WEIGHT UNLOADED 10.5kg/23.18lb

A joint development between BRio and Enfield, the BREN gun (a combination of the initials of BRio and Enfield) was adopted in 1937, when production for British use began in Enfield. Experience in World War I had shown that machine guns were an essential part of winning a war, and that troops simply could not move water-cooled guns fast enough to take advantage of any successful attack or breakthrough. The BREN fired from magazines, requiring assistant gunners to keep them fed. But the quick-change barrel allowed a BREN gunner to maintain a substantial rate of fire, for as long as cool barrels were available. The BREN was superbly accurate. In the 1950s many armies converted BRENS to 7.62mm NATO for continued use. From .303 in 1935 to 7.62mm NATO during the 1950s, the BREN was very popular with troops.

top-mounted magazine

carry handle, also barrel-change handle

L7A1

quick-change barrel

SPECIFICATION

MANUFACTURER Enfield

CALIBRE 7.62mm NATO

MAGAZINE CAPACITY Disintegrating belt

ACTION Gas operated/tilting bolt

TOTAL LENGTH 1,262mm/49.7in

BARREL LENGTH 629mm/24.75in

WEIGHT UNLOADED 10.88kg/24lb

This was the Enfield-produced version of the MAG 58. It was also manufactured in variants for tank use and tested as a fixed-mount aircraft machine gun. The L7A1 went on to aerial service in helicopters, where door gunners could use them to protect the aircraft during landings and takeoffs. It found its way into every infantry, marine and airborne unit as well as coastal craft. Other than the Enfield and British-service markings, it does not differ from the FN version. It was adopted in 1959 and is still in use.

L86A2 HK

long barrel,
but not quick-change

The L86A2 Squad
Automatic Weapon (SAW) proved
as unreliable as the L85A2 individual
weapon. Heckler & Koch undertook an upgrade but they were not successful:
the L86A2 had the same tactical shortcomings as all other SAWs with only a
magazine feed (no belt-feed, thus low sustained fire) and a barrel that was non-
interchangeable (limited firepower and fast overheating). The longer barrel gave
it more reliability than the similarly upgraded rifle. It was first issued in 1986.

SPECIFICATION	
MANUFACTURER Enfield	
CALIBRE 5.56 x 45mm	
MAGAZINE CAPACITY 30	
ACTION Gas operated	
TOTAL LENGTH 900mm/35.43in	
BARREL LENGTH 646mm/25.43in	
WEIGHT UNLOADED 7.3kg/16.1lb	

Rexer (Madsen)

The Rexer machine gun company made
Madsen light machine guns under
licence from Dansk Syndikat until
legal difficulties caused Rexer to
close their doors in 1910.
They managed to fulfil small
contracts to Natal, South Africa, and the Indian Army. Except for the
markings Rexer machine guns are Madsens, and any user familiar with a
Danish Madsen would have no problem using a Rexer.

SPECIFICATION	
MANUFACTURER Rexer	
CALIBRE .303 British	
MAGAZINE CAPACITY 30	
ACTION Gas operated	
TOTAL LENGTH 1,165mm/45.9in	
BARREL LENGTH 478mm/18.8in	
WEIGHT UNLOADED 10kg/22lb	

Lewis Mark 1

Arguably the best air-cooled light
machine gun of World War I, the
Lewis was used both as an aircraft
gun (fixed and flexible) and an infantry support weapon. Designed in the United
States and initially made there and in Belgium, the Lewis ended up being built
in quantity at BSA. Nicknamed "The Belgian Rattlesnake" by the Germans in
World War I, it was a complex and costly weapon, but very reliable. The pan
magazines were high-capacity, without belts to cause feeding problems. It was
not widely used after World War I, so its service life was from 1914 to 1918.

SPECIFICATION	
MANUFACTURER Savage, FN, BSA	
CALIBRE .303 British	
MAGAZINE CAPACITY 47- or 96-round drum	
ACTION Gas operated	
TOTAL LENGTH 1,282mm/50.5in	
BARREL LENGTH 668mm/26.3in	
WEIGHT UNLOADED 12.33kg/27.2lb	

Vickers No. 1 Mark 1, Air Service

A gas-operated Vickers (noted in inventory
as VGO), the No. 1 Mark 1 was intended as a defensive
weapon on observation planes and bombers. It had a
fairly high cyclic rate, 950 rpm. When the Browning machine gun was chosen for
that role, the Vickers went off to the Long Range Desert Group of the SAS. There,
mounted four or five to a jeep, they were used by scouts looking for the German
and Italians. With two or three jeeps positioned to bring all their guns to bear in
an ambush, the scouts could fire as many as 1,500 rounds in just over six seconds.
The weapons were declared obsolete and scrapped at the end of World War II.

SPECIFICATION	
MANUFACTURER Vickers	
CALIBRE .303 British	
MAGAZINE CAPACITY 60- & 100-round drums	
ACTION Gas operated/rotating bolt	
TOTAL LENGTH 1,016mm/40in	
BARREL LENGTH 508mm/20in	
WEIGHT UNLOADED 8.8kg/19.75lb	

France

From adopting the Hotchkiss, its first machine gun in 1897, France quickly settled for designs of limited usefulness and consequently suffered in World War I. Using mainly air-cooled machine guns, French troops could not maintain the sustained fire of the Germans, without assembling larger numbers of machine guns. Larger numbers of troops and guns simply meant larger targets for counter-battery machine gun and artillery fire.

Chauchat (CSRG) M1915

SPECIFICATION

MANUFACTURER Bayonne, others
CALIBRE 8mm Lebel
MAGAZINE CAPACITY 20 rounds
ACTION Recoil operated
TOTAL LENGTH 1,143mm/45in
BARREL LENGTH 470mm/18.5in
WEIGHT UNLOADED 8.6kg/19lb

curved magazine for rimmed cartridges

This is a long-recoil design, where the bolt and barrel recoil together down the length of the receiver, then reciprocate forward separately, the barrel first, followed by the bolt. The basic principle was first designed by John Browning and made in the Auto-5 shotgun. In a rifle calibre the parts have to travel a longer distance to avoid harsh internal impact and battering. It was made in massive numbers during World War I, where it was used as a portable, squad-level firepower weapon in trench warfare. The workmanship is at times quite rough, but the weapon was reasonably reliable, at least in 8mm Lebel.

SPECIFICATION

MANUFACTURER Bayonne
CALIBRE 7.5mm French M1929
MAGAZINE CAPACITY 36-round magazine and 100-round drum
ACTION Gas operated
TOTAL LENGTH 1,028mm/40.5in
BARREL LENGTH 596mm/23.5in
WEIGHT UNLOADED 12.47kg/27.5lb

M1931A

This was a tank and fortress gun pressed into service as an infantry weapon after World War II due to a lack of otherwise suitable machine guns. It was replaced by the AAT-52. The M1931A was unsuited as an infantry weapon for several reasons: it lacked a mechanical safety and fired from an open bolt. When unloading, a round would be left in the feed tray, and unless the operating rod was cycled again after removal of the magazine, it would fire a round even after it had been "unloaded". As a fortress gun, it served from 1931 to 1940. As a stop-gap infantry weapon, it was used until the late 1940s.

AAT-52

SPECIFICATION

MANUFACTURER Bayonne
CALIBRE 7.5mm French M1929
MAGAZINE CAPACITY Belt-fed
ACTION Delayed blowback
TOTAL LENGTH 1,166mm/45.9in
BARREL LENGTH 490mm/19.3in light, 600mm/23.6in heavy
WEIGHT UNLOADED 9.8kg/21.7lb light barrel, 10.6kg/23.38lb w/heavy barrel

Made as a General-Purpose Machine Gun (GPMG), the 52 is an amalgam of the MG 42 feed system and a variant of the CETME/Heckler & Koch roller-delayed blowback. With a light barrel and bipod, it is light enough to almost be a Squad Automatic Weapon (SAW). With the heavy barrel and tripod it is suitable as a heavy machine gun. The ejection is rough on empties, extracting them early in the firing cycle and making them unsuitable for reloading. Mangled brass is not usually a problem in military service, except that in the AAT-52 the metal is so abused it is sometimes ripped in half, causing a malfunction. Despite this, it served from 1953 to the late 1950s, when replaced by the AA F-1.

AA F-1

The AAT-52 was chambered in 7.62mm NATO, and
used a French adapter to fit the US M2 tripod. Despite the change in chambering
it was still harsh on the extracted and ejected brass, and prone to breaking it.
To ease extraction and hopefully prevent broken cases leading to malfunctions,
troops oiled the belt as it was feeding, but this could create other problems: the
oil attracted dust, dirt and other debris, which was then fed into the mechanism.
The Mod AA F-1 has been in service from the late 1950s to the present day.

SPECIFICATION

MANUFACTURER Bayonne
CALIBRE 7.62mm NATO
MAGAZINE CAPACITY Belt-fed
ACTION Delayed blowback
TOTAL LENGTH 1,166mm/45.9in
BARREL LENGTH 490mm/19.3in light,
600mm/23.6in heavy
WEIGHT UNLOADED 9.8kg/21.7lb light barrel,
10.55kg/23.38lb w/heavy barrel

Hotchkiss M1914

An updated version of earlier designs, primarily
the M1900, the M1914 was the primary machine
gun of France in World War I, and was still in
service at the beginning of World
War II. It was a reliable, if bulky
and heavy, air-cooled machine
gun. The feed system used
stamped steel or brass strips, each
holding 24 or 30 rounds. The strips could be linked by the assistant
gunner as the weapon fired, to provide continuous fire. In the sustained fire
of trench warfare, the barrel would glow red-hot but the Hotchkiss would still
work. Once overheated, it had to be left to cool as the barrels could not be
changed while hot. Hotchkiss machine guns with worn barrels had to be sent
back to rear areas for a new barrel. Production commenced in 1914, and
lasted through to 1918, while the weapon itself remained in service until 1940.

SPECIFICATION

MANUFACTURER Hotchkiss et Cie
CALIBRE 8mm Lebel
MAGAZINE CAPACITY 24- & 30-round trays
ACTION Gas operated
TOTAL LENGTH 1,270mm/50in
BARREL LENGTH 775mm/30.5in
WEIGHT UNLOADED 23.56kg/52lb w/o
tripod, which added 27.2kg/60lb

The Hotchkiss designs
The Hotchkiss machine guns
were based on a design by
Captain Baron A. Odkolek von
Augeza of Vienna in Austria.

Chatellerault M1924/29

This was the French answer between
the wars to the squad need for
firepower. The original M24 was
chambered in the 7.5mm 1924
cartridge. When the cartridge was
redesigned and shortened in 1929,

dual triggers for full and semi-fire

the old machine guns were rebuilt and the old and new alike were known as
M1924/29. It had selective-fire, with the front trigger for semi- and the rear
for full-auto fire. The M1924/29 was robust, reliable and popular with the
troops. Manufactured from 1924 to 1940, it is still found in use in former
French colonies. During the occupation, the Germans did not make any for
their use, which is surprising. They would have done well to switch it to
7.92mm and produce it as quickly as possible. However, they did use it to
arm their occupation troops, thus freeing other weapons for use on the Eastern
Front. It was used by the French Army after World War II into the late 1950s.

SPECIFICATION

MANUFACTURER MAC
CALIBRE 7.5 French M1929
MAGAZINE CAPACITY 25 rounds
ACTION Gas operated/linked bolt
TOTAL LENGTH 1,082mm/42.6in
BARREL LENGTH 500mm/19.7in
WEIGHT UNLOADED 11.1kg/24.51lb

St Etienne M1907

action spring around barrel
was prone to over-heating

SPECIFICATION

MANUFACTURER St Etienne

CALIBRE 8mm Lebel

MAGAZINE CAPACITY 24 & 30 round strips

ACTION Blow-forward/rack-and-pinion

TOTAL LENGTH 1,180mm/46.45in

BARREL LENGTH 710mm/27.95in

WEIGHT UNLOADED 25.73kg/56.7lb

In a contest of "worst machine gun ever made" the St Etienne is a definite finalist. The action is blow-forward, with the barrel going forward as the action cycles and the bolt (via a rack-and-pinion system) going backwards. While no doubt a design achievement and engineering tour de force, such extra complexity is always bad in a combat arm. The action spring is coiled around the barrel and if the barrel overheats, as it is sure to do in combat conditions, the spring suffers and eventually fails. Despite the urgent need for machine guns in World War I, the St Etienne was so bad it was removed from service and shipped to the colonies.

SPECIFICATION

MANUFACTURER Unk

CALIBRE 13.2 x 99mm

MAGAZINE CAPACITY 20-round strips

ACTION Gas operated

TOTAL LENGTH 1,371mm/54in

BARREL LENGTH 686mm/27in

WEIGHT UNLOADED 20.4kg/45lb

Hotchkiss

Developed between World War I and II, the design was licensed to Japan. The basic Hotchkiss design, while suitable for rifle-calibre cartridges, was strained when it was used in something so large. Curiously, while Hotchkiss was more than happy to license the design to the Japanese, the French Army saw no need for it. In Japanese service it lasted from the late 1930s to 1945. It did not see service in France.

Belgium

With the establishment of Fabrique Nationale (FN) Belgium was well suited to not only equip its own armed forces, but the world's as well. It has succeeded in this task. The Falklands War was not the only conflict waged where both sides used variants (or even identical versions) of FN weapons.

Hotchkiss

anti-aircraft tripod

SPECIFICATION

MANUFACTURER FN, Liège

CALIBRE 8mm Lebel, 6.5 Jap, .30-06, .303 British

MAGAZINE CAPACITY 24- or 30-round trays

ACTION Gas operated

TOTAL LENGTH 1,310mm/51.6in

BARREL LENGTH 787mm/31in

WEIGHT UNLOADED 25.26kg/55.7lb

The Hotchkiss was one of the first air-cooled machine guns. Early models used water to cool the barrel, as long bursts could quickly take it to red-hot. The Hotchkiss used cooling fins to partially deal with the heat produced. One peculiarity of the Hotchkiss was the feed mechanism: metal trays. Cloth belts were viewed as a necessary but awkward feed method, but they had drawbacks. The Hotchkiss trays could not rot or stretch. If they froze, they would still work. The assistant gunner could hook each tray on to the end of the feeding one, to keep up a continuous rate of fire, until the ammunition was exhausted or the barrel finally succumbed to the heat. It was made for export before World War I and used from 1896 to 1914, when the Liège plant was overrun.

Hotchkiss Export Model

odd-shaped but
comfortable stock

The Export, also known as the Portative,
as well as the M1909, was the Hotchkiss
effort at a light machine gun.
The locking system was changed
to make the weapon more compact,
and combined with a reshaped receiver, the weight loss was impressive. So
popular as a portable weapon, it even saw use as a Cavalry weapon. The Portative
was known in the US as the Benet-Mercie Machine Rifle. The Export could still
be found in armoury reserves in 1939, when it was hauled out for yet another
war. By 1945 it had been replaced by the BREN and BAR, and fell out of use.

SPECIFICATION

MANUFACTURER Hotchkiss
CALIBRE 8 x 50R Lebel, .30-06
MAGAZINE CAPACITY 30-round tray
ACTION Gas operated
TOTAL LENGTH 1,187mm/46.75in
BARREL LENGTH 597mm/23.50in
WEIGHT UNLOADED 12.25kg/27lb

FN Browning BAR D

quick-change barrel

In an effort to end the stalemate of trench warfare, the US Army
intended to introduce massive firepower into the hands of the
infantry. One approach was the Pedersen device, which
proved a failure. The other was the BAR, which was not.
A select-fire rifle-cartridge weapon that could be carried and used by one man, it
proved rugged, accurate, reliable and long-lived. The FN Model D differed from
the American version in having a finned barrel for greater cooling, and a pistol
grip. As an export weapon, it could be made in any cartridge that fitted the basic
BAR platform, and has been seen in eight different chamberings. Many armies
had the BAR as their machine gun, a Squad Automatic Weapon (SAW). FN sold
a great many between the wars and after World War II, until it developed the FAL
and MAG 58. It was a standard export item from the 1920s to 1940, and then
again in the early 1950s.

SPECIFICATION

MANUFACTURER FN, Liège
CALIBRE .30-06, 7.92, 7.65, 6.5 x 55
MAGAZINE CAPACITY 20-round magazines
ACTION Gas operated/toggle action
TOTAL LENGTH 1,194mm/47in
BARREL LENGTH 606mm/24in
WEIGHT UNLOADED 8.93kg/19.7lb

M2HB

anti-aircraft shooter's brace

When tanks appeared on the battlefields
of World War I, none of the armies
involved had the means to deal with
them. Artillery was too cumbersome, and rifle and machine
guns mostly ineffective. John Moses Browning scaled up
both his belt-fed machine gun and the .30-06 cartridge,
and produced the .50 calibre M2. The war ended
before it could be used on the Western Front,
but the M2 has been used ever since. The
HB is for "heavy barrel", a thicker-walled
and heavier barrel than the original, to do
away with the weight of a water-filled cooling jacket. Later FN improvements
included a quick-change barrel that did not require adjustment on installation.
For over a generation the US Army has been trying to replace the M2HB with
something lighter, but all efforts have failed to produce any weapon as rugged,
versatile and powerful. Production began in 1946 and continues today.

SPECIFICATION

MANUFACTURER FN, Liège
CALIBRE .50 BMG
MAGAZINE CAPACITY Belt-fed
ACTION Recoil operated
TOTAL LENGTH 1,656mm/65.2in
BARREL LENGTH 1,143mm/45.0in
WEIGHT UNLOADED 38.10kg/84lb

FN MAG

SPECIFICATION

MANUFACTURER FN, Liège
CALIBRE 7.62 x 51mm
MAGAZINE CAPACITY Belt-fed
ACTION Gas operated/toggle lock
TOTAL LENGTH 1,260mm/49.60in
BARREL LENGTH 545mm/21.45in
WEIGHT UNLOADED 12.0kg/26.45lb

Designed in the 1950s, the Mitrailleuse d'Appui General (MAG) was meant to be a truly General-Purpose Machine Gun (GPMG), with variants for ground, vehicle and aircraft use. It is an amalgam of designs: a Maxim/Browning-type receiver of riveted plates, the Browning BAR-style bolt as the action and an MG 42 feed mechanism to advance the belt and feed the rounds. It has become near-ubiquitous, and even adopted by the US Army and Marine Corps, replacing the American-designed M60. It is air-cooled, has two settings for the cyclic rate and a quick-change barrel.

FN Minimi

Almost from the moment of reluctantly adopting the 5.56mm cartridge, the US Army sought to replace it. One avenue explored was to find a Squad Automatic Weapon (SAW) that needed something other than the 5.56mm. After 15 years of experimentation and design dead-ends, the army gave up and adopted the FN Minimi, a 5.56mm SAW that used either belts or M16 magazines. The US Army could not simply adopt it, it had to "improve" it, though such endeavours were in fact digressions. The Minimi is now an integral part of many armies at the squad level, where a General-Purpose Machine Gun (GPMG) and the ammunition it consumes would be too heavy. FN sells or licenses the original, not a US Army-improved version. The Minimi, unlike many earlier light machine guns, can be mounted in a tripod as well as used on a bipod. It was introduced in 1982 and is now found worldwide.

SPECIFICATION

MANUFACTURER FN, Liège
CALIBRE 5.56 x 45mm
MAGAZINE CAPACITY Belt and 30-round magazines
ACTION Gas operated/rotating bolt
TOTAL LENGTH 1,040mm/40.94in
BARREL LENGTH 465mm/18.3in
WEIGHT UNLOADED 7.1kg/15.65lb

Netherlands

The Netherlands adopted the Schwarzlose in 7.92mm rimmed before World War I, opting for a lighter machine gun after the war. Lacking an armoury or manufacturer of their own has not kept the Netherlands from adopting the best rifles and machine guns to be found. They currently field the Minimi and FN MAG.

Lewis M20

SPECIFICATION

MANUFACTURER FN, Liège
CALIBRE 6.5 x 53R
MAGAZINE CAPACITY 47 or 96
ACTION Gas operated
TOTAL LENGTH 1,283mm/50.5in
BARREL LENGTH 660mm/26in
WEIGHT UNLOADED 12.24kg/27lb

96-round drum

Adopted in 1920, the Lewis gun had already proven its worth. Light, handy and reliable, albeit requiring maintenance, the Lewis served as well as any other. The Lewis was adaptable to many cartridges due to its pan magazine. Modifying the design to use the 6.5 x 53R cartridge probably did not take more than a day for the engineers. With proper maintenance, the Lewis worked under even extreme conditions, and continued to do so. It was in use from 1920 to 1940.

Switzerland

Despite a policy of neutrality for several centuries, Switzerland made and exported weapons for most of the 20th century. The mountainous countryside has meant Swiss armed forces have placed a premium on accurate, long-range fire. Switzerland has universal service, where every 18-year-old man goes through recruit training. Machine guns are stored in armouries, while service rifles are kept at home by each adult.

Furrer M1925

magazine on right side

SPECIFICATION

MANUFACTURER Bern
CALIBRE 7.5 x 55mm
MAGAZINE CAPACITY 30
ACTION Recoil operated
TOTAL LENGTH 1,163mm/45.8in
BARREL LENGTH 584mm/23in
WEIGHT UNLOADED 10.74kg/23.69lb

Developed by Colonel Furrer of the Bern Armoury, the Furrer (known as the M25 in Swiss service) uses a side-hinged toggle lock. As a light machine gun (LMG), the odd locking system added cost to production. However, the barrel was easily changed, the selector could be set to full or semi-automatic fire and each spare barrel, when exchanged, also came with a fitted toggle bolt. The side-mount magazine allowed the gunner to acquire a very low prone position. It was manufactured from 1925 to 1946 and remained in service until the 1970s.

The toggle system
The Borchardt/Luger toggle system is very efficient, and has been used on many machine guns. However, only the Furrer turns the toggle sideways.

Hispano HS820

SPECIFICATION

MANUFACTURER Hispano Suiza
CALIBRE 20 x 110mm
MAGAZINE CAPACITY 25
ACTION Gas-unlocked blowback
TOTAL LENGTH 2,517mm/99in
BARREL LENGTH 1,000mm/39in
WEIGHT UNLOADED 46kg/101lb w/o mount

As vehicles became more common, armour as well as heavy weapons for infantry became bigger. Especially for the Swiss, whose defensive operations called for many ambush and flanking manoeuvres, the 20mm HS820 could be relied upon to inflict extensive work on a vehicular column. It was in service from 1941 to the 1970s.

Maxim M1911

SPECIFICATION

MANUFACTURER Simpson & Co.
CALIBRE 7.5 x 55mm
MAGAZINE CAPACITY Belt-fed
ACTION Recoil operated
TOTAL LENGTH 1,077mm/42.4in
BARREL LENGTH 721mm/28.4in
WEIGHT UNLOADED 18.5kg/40.8lb w/o mount

An early adopter of the Maxim, Switzerland upgraded several times to the M1911. They were so satisfied with it that they kept it in service until after World War II. The conversion of their weapon to the Swiss 7.5mm cartridge was easy for Maxim engineers and, given the quality of Swiss ammunition, a Swiss Maxim could create an accurately aimed beaten zone (the area of the bullet's fall) even at the maximum range of the cartridge (which is 3,500m/3,800yd).

Solothurn M30

spring-loaded tripod

SPECIFICATION

MANUFACTURER Solothurn
CALIBRE 7.92 x 57mm
MAGAZINE CAPACITY 30-round box &
   50-round drum
ACTION Recoil operated
TOTAL LENGTH 1,085mm/42.7in
BARREL LENGTH 754mm/29.7in
WEIGHT UNLOADED 12.93kg/28.5lb

Designed by Rheinmetall but rejected by the German Army and prohibited from German manufacture by the Treaty of Versailles, the Solothurn was made in Switzerland. It was later adopted by the Luftwaffe as the MG15 in a flexible mount for bomber defence. The M30 had the option of full-automatic or semi-automatic firing rates, a feature many weapons designers worked on between the wars. It was in service between 1940 and 1945.

Solothurn S3200

SPECIFICATION

MANUFACTURER Solothurn
CALIBRE 7.92 x 57mm
MAGAZINE CAPACITY 30-round box &
   50-round drum
ACTION Recoil operated
TOTAL LENGTH 1,085mm/42.7in
BARREL LENGTH 754mm/29.7in
WEIGHT UNLOADED 12.93kg/28.5lb

A light machine gun (LMG) designed between World War I and World War II, the S3200 had many fashionable features. The trigger had two curves on its face. By pressing one curve the shooter could fire in semi-automatic mode. By placing his finger on the other and pressing, full-auto fire was delivered. Such designs were all the rage in the 1930s, despite the added complexity. The partnership of Rheinmetall and Solothurn produced many designs, and while they were all reliable, Switzerland chose to adopt native designs for their own use and sold a few S3200s on the export market.

Germany

In the decades before World War I, Germany was an enthusiastic adopter of the Maxim machine gun. After the war, the Treaty of Versailles greatly restricted the number and type of machine guns German armed forces could have. A great deal of design and manufacturing effort went into weapons that would get around the restrictions. Thus the General-Purpose Machine Gun (GPMG) was developed and first unveiled in the MG 34.

MG08

SPECIFICATION

MANUFACTURER DMW, Spandau, others
CALIBRE 7.92 x 57mm
MAGAZINE CAPACITY Belt-fed
ACTION Recoil operated/toggle lock
TOTAL LENGTH 1,175mm/46.25in
BARREL LENGTH 717mm/28.25in
WEIGHT UNLOADED 18.37kg/40.5lb (bare
   MG, no water)

Adopting the Maxim gun in 1899, Germany had perfected it for general use by 1908 (and named it the MG08 after its year of adoption). Robust to the point of being unstoppable, the Maxim was water-cooled and could therefore fire continuously until ammunition or water were exhausted. More commonly, the gun crew would be exhausted first. However, the price for that durability and sustained rate of fire was weight. With a water-filled jacket, the first belt of ammunition and a sledge-type mount which was ferried between locations, it weighed close to 68kg/150lb. The MG08 was in use from 1908 until 1918 as a heavy machine gun, and used as a "light" machine gun in fixed positions during World War II.

HK11

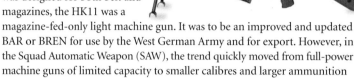

Unlike the HK21, which was designed for both belt and magazines, the HK11 was a magazine-fed-only light machine gun. It was to be an improved and updated BAR or BREN for use by the West German Army and for export. However, in the Squad Automatic Weapon (SAW), the trend quickly moved from full-power machine guns of limited capacity to smaller calibres and larger ammunition volumes. The HK11 was manufactured from the early 1960s until the 1990s.

SPECIFICATION	
MANUFACTURER	Heckler & Koch
CALIBRE	7.62mm NATO
MAGAZINE CAPACITY	20
ACTION	Gas operated
TOTAL LENGTH	1,020mm/40.1in
BARREL LENGTH	450mm/17.7in
WEIGHT UNLOADED	6.7kg/14.8lb

HK21A1

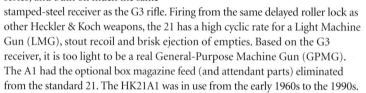

belt-feed tray

This was a development of the CETME and Heckler & Koch G3 series, and built on much the same stamped-steel receiver as the G3 rifle. Firing from the same delayed roller lock as other Heckler & Koch weapons, the 21 has a high cyclic rate for a Light Machine Gun (LMG), stout recoil and brisk ejection of empties. Based on the G3 receiver, it is too light to be a real General-Purpose Machine Gun (GPMG). The A1 had the optional box magazine feed (and attendant parts) eliminated from the standard 21. The HK21A1 was in use from the early 1960s to the 1990s.

SPECIFICATION	
MANUFACTURER	Heckler & Koch
CALIBRE	7.62mm NATO, 7.62 x 39mm,
	5.56 x 45mm
MAGAZINE CAPACITY	Belt-fed
ACTION	Recoil operated/roller-lock delay
TOTAL LENGTH	1,018mm/40.1in
BARREL LENGTH	575mm/22.63in
WEIGHT UNLOADED	6.66kg/14.7lb

MG 14/17

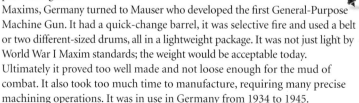

Also known as a "Zeppelin gun", the MG 14 derived from a need for automatic weapons for the Imperial Air Corps. The designers took a Maxim, lightened it to the extreme, took off the water jacket and turned the toggle lock upside down. By the end of World War I, the need for automatic weapons was so great that the MG 14 was fitted with a buttstock, bipod and forward handgrip. The resulting MG 14/17 was then handed to the infantry for use as a ground weapon and was not too heavy in the infantry role. It was in use from 1914 to 1918, obsolete at the end of the war and mostly confiscated in war reparations.

SPECIFICATION	
MANUFACTURER	Mauser
CALIBRE	7.92 x 57mm
MAGAZINE CAPACITY	Belt-fed
ACTION	Recoil operated/toggle lock
TOTAL LENGTH	1,422mm/56in
BARREL LENGTH	717mm/28.25in
WEIGHT UNLOADED	11kg/24.25lb

MG 34

dual trigger for full
and semi fire

With Versailles prohibiting new Maxims, Germany turned to Mauser who developed the first General-Purpose Machine Gun. It had a quick-change barrel, it was selective fire and used a belt or two different-sized drums, all in a lightweight package. It was not just light by World War I Maxim standards; the weight would be acceptable today. Ultimately it proved too well made and not loose enough for the mud of combat. It also took too much time to manufacture, requiring many precise machining operations. It was in use in Germany from 1934 to 1945.

SPECIFICATION	
MANUFACTURER	Mauser
CALIBRE	7.92 x 57mm
MAGAZINE CAPACITY	Belt, 50- and
	75-round drums
ACTION	Recoil operated/roller locked
TOTAL LENGTH	1,220mm/48in
BARREL LENGTH	623mm/24.6in
WEIGHT UNLOADED	12.02kg/26.5lb

MG 42/59

recoil
booster

SPECIFICATION

MANUFACTURER Rheinmettal
CALIBRE 7.92 x 57mm
MAGAZINE CAPACITY Belt-fed
ACTION Recoil operated
TOTAL LENGTH 1,220mm/48in
BARREL LENGTH 533mm/21in
WEIGHT UNLOADED 11.56kg/25.5lb

The first machine guns produced after the end of World War II, issued to the Border Police, were simply MG42s built on wartime machinery and still chambered in 7.92mm. During the 1950s the design was modified and the calibre changed to eventually become the MG 3. The changes gradually brought down the cyclic rate (as much as 1,300 rpm in the MG 42) and increased durability. It was produced from 1948 to the late 1960s and called the MG42/59.

Dreyse MG 13

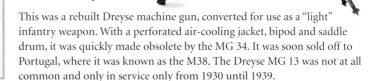

SPECIFICATION

MANUFACTURER RM&M
CALIBRE 7.92 x 57mm
MAGAZINE CAPACITY Drum, 25, 7, 50 round
ACTION Recoil operated
TOTAL LENGTH 1,220mm/48in
BARREL LENGTH 717mm/28.25in
WEIGHT UNLOADED 10.89kg/24.0lb

This was a rebuilt Dreyse machine gun, converted for use as a "light" infantry weapon. With a perforated air-cooling jacket, bipod and saddle drum, it was quickly made obsolete by the MG 34. It was soon sold off to Portugal, where it was known as the M38. The Dreyse MG 13 was not at all common and only in service only from 1930 until 1939.

MG 08/15

SPECIFICATION

MANUFACTURER Various
CALIBRE 7.92 x 57mm
MAGAZINE CAPACITY Belt, 50-round drum
ACTION Recoil operated/toggle lock
TOTAL LENGTH 1,435mm/56.5in
BARREL LENGTH 716mm/28.2in
WEIGHT UNLOADED 17.7kg/39lb without
    water

drum for
belted ammo

The Maxim MG 08 was a nearly indestructible engine of death in the trench warfare of World War I. What it was not, however, was portable. The MG 08/15 had the sledge removed, a bipod and butt stock affixed and a sling attached. The water jacket was left on, but it was a dull infantryman who failed to drain the water before exiting the trenches on an assault. Even with the reduction in weight, trying to wrestle it across a shell-churned battlefield had to be back-breaking. Still, anything that increased mobility was an improvement. It was used only in World War I from 1915 to 1918. Some were found in World War II in guard towers at armouries and death camps.

MG 42

SPECIFICATION

MANUFACTURER Various
CALIBRE 7.92 x 57mm
MAGAZINE CAPACITY Belt-fed
ACTION Recoil operated/roller locked
TOTAL LENGTH 1,220mm/48in
BARREL LENGTH 533mm/21in
WEIGHT UNLOADED 11.56kg/25.5lb

The MG 42 was made primarily of steel stampings and did away with the excesses of design of the MG 34: the 42 fed only from the left side, it was not select-fire, and it had no provision for magazine feed. It used a roller-lock, with a gas boost to the mechanism gained from the adjustable muzzle cone. The cyclic rate was 1,200 to 1,300 rpm, but the quick-change barrel was so easy to change that heating hardly mattered. It was produced in huge volumes from 1942 to 1945 and again after the war both for West Germany and for export.

Italy

Italy entered World War I with a motley collection of machine guns. Forces had to contend with machine guns made in two different locally produced rifle calibres (6.5 and 7.35mm) and a large supply of 8 x 50R Schwarzlose guns that were war reparations from Austria. Mussolini's emphasis on production did not help, as much effort went to political favourites instead of a few standard and debugged designs.

Breda M30

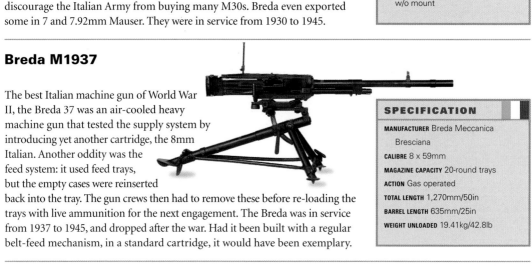

magazine on right side

A re-introduction of the Breda 1924, the M30 featured an Italian novelty: a permanently attached magazine which fed from the right, and was hinged to open when the gunner pushed it forward. He would recharge an empty magazine by means of a special charger with 20 rounds in it. The delayed blowback system produced a rather violent primary extraction, so the cases had to be oiled as they were fed, via a built-in cartridge oiler. These issues did not discourage the Italian Army from buying many M30s. Breda even exported some in 7 and 7.92mm Mauser. They were in service from 1930 to 1945.

SPECIFICATION

MANUFACTURER Breda
CALIBRE 6.5 x 52mm
MAGAZINE CAPACITY 20
ACTION Delayed blowback
TOTAL LENGTH 1232mm/48.50in
BARREL LENGTH 520mm/20.50in
WEIGHT UNLOADED 10.31kg/22.75lb
w/o mount

Breda M1937

The best Italian machine gun of World War II, the Breda 37 was an air-cooled heavy machine gun that tested the supply system by introducing yet another cartridge, the 8mm Italian. Another oddity was the feed system: it used feed trays, but the empty cases were reinserted back into the tray. The gun crews then had to remove these before re-loading the trays with live ammunition for the next engagement. The Breda was in service from 1937 to 1945, and dropped after the war. Had it been built with a regular belt-feed mechanism, in a standard cartridge, it would have been exemplary.

SPECIFICATION

MANUFACTURER Breda Meccanica
Bresciana
CALIBRE 8 x 59mm
MAGAZINE CAPACITY 20-round trays
ACTION Gas operated
TOTAL LENGTH 1,270mm/50in
BARREL LENGTH 635mm/25in
WEIGHT UNLOADED 19.41kg/42.8lb

Colt 1914

The 1914 was simply the Colt 1895 chambered in 6.5 Carcano, and manufactured in the early years of World War I. As an air-cooled machine gun it was prone to over-heating in the sustained fire of World War I tactical use. However, the medium-power 6.5 cartridge was a lesser heat source for the barrel, and the Italian guns were probably less prone to overheating than the more powerful .30-06 of the American versions. Despite the success of the Colt, they were not retained after the war, and were replaced by a steady succession of Italian designs of dubious reliability. They were in service during Italy's involvement in World War I, from 1915 to 1918.

SPECIFICATION

MANUFACTURER Colt
CALIBRE 6.5 x 52mm
MAGAZINE CAPACITY Belt-fed
ACTION Gas operated
TOTAL LENGTH 1,036mm/40.80in
BARREL LENGTH 711mm/28.0in
WEIGHT UNLOADED 18.14kg/40lb w/o mount

FIAT-Revelli 1914

As water-cooled heavy machine guns of the World War I period go, the Revelli was relatively lightweight. Chambered in the Italian 6.5mm cartridge, it should have been a steady performer, but any delayed blowback action had the potential to be unreliable with any ammunition that was not perfect. The bolt was not completely enclosed by the receiver, so it would cycle out of the rear, directly toward the firer. Also, the feed mechanism was a bottleneck in any sustained-fire situation. Instead of a belt, the Revelli used a sheet-metal contraption called a cage, holding 50 rounds in ten columns of five. The block of exposed cartridges was inserted into the left side. It would feed each column to the chamber, and then eject the empty feed cage out. The cages were not robust enough to survive many firings. The ammunition manufacturer would have to provide a new feed cage for each 50-round ammunition increment. It is hard to imagine why the designers thought the cage an improvement on a belt-fed system. Desperate for machine guns, the Italians bought the Revelli. After the war, they were put into storage and not seen again.

ammunition cage

SPECIFICATION

MANUFACTURER FIAT-Revelli
CALIBRE 6.5 x 52mm
MAGAZINE CAPACITY 50
ACTION Delayed blowback
TOTAL LENGTH 1,181mm/46.5in
BARREL LENGTH 654mm/25.75in
WEIGHT UNLOADED 17kg/37.5lb (no water)

FIAT M35

breechblock

SPECIFICATION

MANUFACTURER FIAT-Revelli
CALIBRE 8 x 59mm
MAGAZINE CAPACITY Belt-fed
ACTION Delayed blowback
TOTAL LENGTH 1270mm/50in
BARREL LENGTH 654mm/25.75in
WEIGHT UNLOADED 22.6kg/50lb

The Revelli 1914 was quite dated by 1935, so FIAT was asked to update its machine gun. It did so by changing from a water-cooled to an air-cooled barrel. It also increased the calibre, but kept the same delayed blowback action. The result was yet another machine gun that required lubricated cartridges to avoid broken cases and another seized-up machine gun in combat. Additionally, the 8mm cartridge further taxed the Italian production and supply system, which could only be charitably described as disorganized. It was in service only from 1935 to 1945, and immediately scrapped when the war was over.

Vickers Class C

SPECIFICATION

MANUFACTURER Vickers
CALIBRE 6.5 x 52mm
MAGAZINE CAPACITY Belt-fed
ACTION Recoil operated
TOTAL LENGTH 1,100mm/43.3in
BARREL LENGTH 720mm/28.34in
WEIGHT UNLOADED 33kg/72.75lb
(no water)

This was the export C model of the Vickers Company, shipped to Italy before and during World War I. The 6.5mm Carcano round would have made for a quiet, low-recoiling and slow-to-heat-up heavy machine gun. Italy would have done well to have simply retained the Vickers in 6.5mm, rather than try other designs such as the later short adoption of the 7.35mm cartridge. But had they stuck with it, their Vickers could have been converted for far less effort than designing and manufacturing a whole new machine gun. It was in service from 1910 to 1918.

Norway

When Norway separated from Sweden in 1905, it went to Denmark and the United States for machine guns: both countries were established and reliable performers. Between the wars, the choice of established machine guns to purchase was limited.

It was not that there were many contenders: the list of reliable machine guns was short and Norway was ill-equipped. The Danish Madsen was the standard machine gun and reasonably effective. The Browning MG M29 could be unreliable in cold weather.

Browning MG M29

clamp-adjustable tripod

SPECIFICATION	
MANUFACTURER	Colt
CALIBRE	7.92 x 57mm
MAGAZINE CAPACITY	Belt-fed
ACTION	Recoil operated
TOTAL LENGTH	1,155mm/45.5in
BARREL LENGTH	558mm/22in
WEIGHT UNLOADED	14.9kg/32.5lb

Tripods
After World War I, heavy machine guns were equipped with lighter tripods, as seen here. While heavier than a modern machine gun, the post-war tripods were light for the period.

Adopted in 1929 as the M29, this machine gun was simply the Colt-manufactured Browning-designed M1917 with the upgrades Colt had made to the design since 1917. The bottom plate was reinforced along with the feed. That the Norwegians elected to increase the calibre of the M29 over that of the light machine gun they chose was also wise. The 7.92mm has greater power and range than the 6.5mm. Chambered in a tripod-mounted, water-cooled machine gun, the extra recoil was of no concern to the crew operating it. During World War II, Norwegian and German units could use each other's ammunition, if not ammunition belts. It was replaced by the MG3 in the late 1950s.

Madsen M1922

While Norway offered many locations where a heavy machine gun could do great damage to an attacker, after World War I, all armies realized the

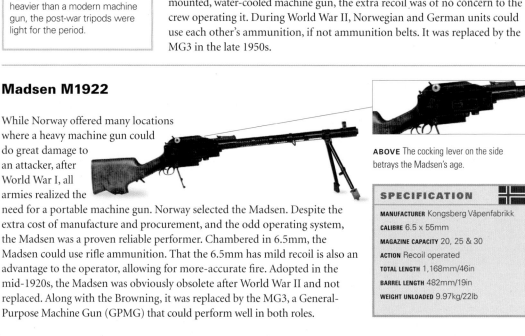

ABOVE The cocking lever on the side betrays the Madsen's age.

need for a portable machine gun. Norway selected the Madsen. Despite the extra cost of manufacture and procurement, and the odd operating system, the Madsen was a proven reliable performer. Chambered in 6.5mm, the Madsen could use rifle ammunition. That the 6.5mm has mild recoil is also an advantage to the operator, allowing for more-accurate fire. Adopted in the mid-1920s, the Madsen was obviously obsolete after World War II and not replaced. Along with the Browning, it was replaced by the MG3, a General-Purpose Machine Gun (GPMG) that could perform well in both roles.

SPECIFICATION	
MANUFACTURER	Kongsberg Våpenfabrikk
CALIBRE	6.5 x 55mm
MAGAZINE CAPACITY	20, 25 & 30
ACTION	Recoil operated
TOTAL LENGTH	1,168mm/46in
BARREL LENGTH	482mm/19in
WEIGHT UNLOADED	9.97kg/22lb

 Denmark

A peninsula in the Baltic, Denmark has a long history of fending off its neighbours, not always with success. Despite little in the way of natural resources, Denmark built a solid firearms production base. After World War II, Denmark left the arms-making field, in the face of increased competition from larger countries.

Madsen M1946

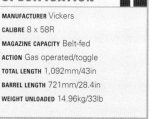

SPECIFICATION

MANUFACTURER Dansk Industri Syndikat
CALIBRE 7.62 x 63mm
MAGAZINE CAPACITY 20, 25, 30 &
40-round magazines (.30-06
were 30-round)
ACTION Recoil operated
TOTAL LENGTH 1,168mm/46in
BARREL LENGTH 482mm/19in
WEIGHT UNLOADED 9.97kg/22lb

The Madsen light machine gun was distributed widely from 1902. Although awkward in appearance it was easy to handle. The long-recoil design made for brisk, but manageable recoil. Relatively expensive to manufacture, and requiring good-quality ammunition, it worked well when treated well. That, combined with its relative light weight, made it popular around the world. Offered in a host of calibres, the M1946 was made in .30-06 for Denmark. Since it was using the American M1 Garand at the time, keeping the calibre supply simple was wise. It was used from 1946 until Denmark switched to the 7.62mm with the rest of Europe and was replaced by the Madsen-Saetter.

Madsen-Saetter

low-recoil tripod

SPECIFICATION

MANUFACTURER Dansk Industri Syndikat
CALIBRE 7.62 x 51mm
MAGAZINE CAPACITY 50, 7, 100-round
magazines, and belts
ACTION Gas operated/rotating bolt
TOTAL LENGTH 1,219mm/48in
BARREL LENGTH 660mm/26in
WEIGHT UNLOADED 11.61kg/25.6lb

The MG 42 had shown the way, and all countries after World War II wanted an air-cooled General-Purpose Machine Gun (GPMG), that could also serve in the support role. Development took until 1959, by which time the market was already claimed: the United States would make their own, the Soviets would make them for any client state, and FN would sell MAG 58s to the rest of the world. The Madsen-Saetter could be manufactured in any rimless cartridge from 6.5mm to 7.92mm. It fed from either belts or box magazines, unusual for this type of gun. The Madsen-Saetter was never a commercial success and it saw only limited production beginning in 1959.

SPECIFICATION

MANUFACTURER Vickers
CALIBRE 8 x 58R
MAGAZINE CAPACITY Belt-fed
ACTION Gas operated/toggle
TOTAL LENGTH 1,092mm/43in
BARREL LENGTH 721mm/28.4in
WEIGHT UNLOADED 14.96kg/33lb

Vickers Commercial C Model

As good as the Madsen machine gun proved to be, it was not a heavy, support-role machine gun. The only way to accomplish that, before World War II, was with a water-cooled machine gun. Thus, Denmark acquired a supply of Vickers heavy machine guns in the early 1920s. They were chambered in the Danish rifle calibre, 8 x 58R, a simple change for the Vickers Company to have made. Nearly all of them ended up being appropriated to feed the German war machine after the German occupation of Denmark.

Austria

Austrian inventiveness extended to machine guns as well as rifles. As the main supplier of small arms to the Austro-Hungarian empire, Steyr was heavily committed to manufacturing arms. After World War I weapons production in Steyr was next to prohibited, and in 1918, the company faced bankruptcy.

Solothurn Model 30S

This was a licensed Rheinmetall-designed Light Machine Gun (LMG), built in Solothurn, Switzerland to avoid restrictions on machine gun manufacture by Germany as laid down in the Treaty of Versailles. It was one of many contenders for the role of LMG, now called a Squad Automatic Weapon (SAW). Later design modifications in Germany led to the MG 15, a 75-round drum-fed, stockless machine gun for use as a defensive arm in bombers. The Solothurn Model 30S was a commercial export item from 1930, and used in World War II until 1945. After the war there were many LMGs to choose from, so production ceased.

SPECIFICATION	
MANUFACTURER	Solothurn
CALIBRE	7.92 x 57mm
MAGAZINE CAPACITY	50, beltless drum
ACTION	Gas operated
TOTAL LENGTH	1,389mm/54.7in
BARREL LENGTH	754mm/29in
WEIGHT UNLOADED	12.24kg/27lb

Skoda M1893

The 1893 Skoda was patented by Archduke Karl Salvator and Count George von Dormus. It fed on cartridges that were hand-laid into the feed chute by the assistant gunner. Blowback designs and rifle-calibre cartridges do not mix, so we also owe these two for the concept of the cartridge oiler. Oiled cartridges extract more easily, but the oil attracts dust and grit, causing malfunctions. A pendulum adjustment in the trigger mechanism allowed the operator to select the cyclic rate, from 180 to 250 rounds per minute. Upgraded marginally in the M1902, and greatly in the M1909. The 1893 lasted just long enough to reportedly be used in the Boxer Rebellion in 1900, before making its way into museums.

SPECIFICATION	
MANUFACTURER	Steyr
CALIBRE	8 x 50R
MAGAZINE CAPACITY	N/A
ACTION	Delayed blowback
TOTAL LENGTH	1153mm/45.4in
BARREL LENGTH	621mm/24.4in
WEIGHT UNLOADED	16.78kg/37lb

Schwarzlose M07/12

"tiller"-style dual grips

Adopted by several other countries, the Schwarzlose was used extensively during World War I by Austro-Hungarian empire units. It has a straightforward blowback mechanism. The bolt was not mechanically locked to the barrel or receiver when the chambered cartridge was fired. There was a lubricating pump in the original M07 to lubricate each cartridge for ease of extraction. The M07/12 update and rebuild changed the extraction timing and removed the need for the pump but the weapon still relied on a heavy bolt and very strong recoil spring. As with all World War I-era machine guns, the mount can weigh as much as or more than the weapon. The 8 x 50R was adopted in 1912 and used until the 1920s when it was replaced with locked-breech machine guns.

SPECIFICATION	
MANUFACTURER	Steyr
CALIBRE	8 x 50R
MAGAZINE CAPACITY	Cloth belt
ACTION	Blowback
TOTAL LENGTH	1,066mm/42in
BARREL LENGTH	527mm/20.75in
WEIGHT UNLOADED	19.95kg/44lb
	w/o mount

Steyr AUG A1 LMG

bipod attached to the barrel

SPECIFICATION	
MANUFACTURER	Steyr
CALIBRE	5.56 x 45mm
MAGAZINE CAPACITY	30 or 42
ACTION	Gas operated/rotating bolt
TOTAL LENGTH	900mm/35.4in
BARREL LENGTH	621mm/24.4in
WEIGHT UNLOADED	4.9kg/10.80lb

Belt-fed General-Purpose Machine Guns (GPMGs) are considered too heavy to be used as the integral weapon for a squad. Usually chambered in 7.62mm NATO or an equal, the GPMG needs a multi-man team to operate it. To increase the firepower of squads, the Squad Automatic Weapon (SAW) was re-invented near the end of the Cold War. The AUG A1 is the firepower base for the Austrian Army squad and is simply an AUG with a longer and heavier barrel and a bipod. The box magazine limits firepower, but the ease of barrel changes makes the AUG A1 a much more viable SAW than other assault rifles pressed into this role. The Steyr Aug has been used by the Austrian Army from 1985 to the present day.

▥ Sweden

By the 20th century Sweden's Baltic empire was long gone, but all countries need Armed Forces to defend themselves from would-be invaders. With a solid industrial base with world famous companies like FFV and Carl Gustav, Sweden had no problems with local manufacture, but also purchased guns from abroad.

Browning M1936

SPECIFICATION	
MANUFACTURER	Carl Gustav
CALIBRE	7.92 x 63mm
MAGAZINE CAPACITY	Belt-fed
ACTION	Recoil operated
TOTAL LENGTH	1,008mm/39.7in
BARREL LENGTH	610mm/24in
WEIGHT UNLOADED	14.51kg/32lb
	w/o mount

The M1936 was a water-cooled heavy Browning, chambered in the special Swedish heavy machine gun cartridge – the 7.92mm – which delivered a larger and heavier bullet than the 6.5mm, at a higher velocity. As a static machine gun in the kind of defensive positions found in World War I, a water-cooled machine gun in a heavier calibre makes sense. It remained in service to the late 1950s until it was replaced by the MAG 58.

Browning BAR M1921

6.5 x 55mm curved magazine

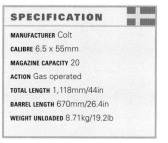

SPECIFICATION	
MANUFACTURER	Colt
CALIBRE	6.5 x 55mm
MAGAZINE CAPACITY	20
ACTION	Gas operated
TOTAL LENGTH	1,118mm/44in
BARREL LENGTH	670mm/26.4in
WEIGHT UNLOADED	8.71kg/19.2lb

This was bought from Colt and supplied to them in the Swedish calibre. The 1921 Swedish requirements added a pistol grip and dust covers over the ejection port and magazine port. Otherwise it was quite similar to the M1918 BAR. The M1921 served in Swedish Army units and Reserves between 1921 and the late 1950s.

219

SAV Model 40

curved gas tubes

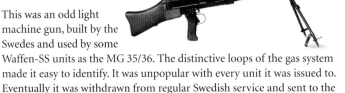

This was an odd light
machine gun, built by the
Swedes and used by some
Waffen-SS units as the MG 35/36. The distinctive loops of the gas system
made it easy to identify. It was unpopular with every unit it was issued to.
Eventually it was withdrawn from regular Swedish service and sent to the
Home Guard units, who also hated it. It was replaced after a short service
life between 1940 and 1945 by the M1921 Browning.

SPECIFICATION

MANUFACTURER SAV
CALIBRE 6.5 x 55mm
MAGAZINE CAPACITY 20
ACTION Gas operated
TOTAL LENGTH 1,257mm/49.48in
BARREL LENGTH 685mm/26.96in
WEIGHT UNLOADED 8.5kg/18.73lb

Czech Republic

After World War I, the Austro-Hungarian Empire was
divided into countries of similar ethnic backgrounds,
with the Czechs and Slovaks amalgamated into a new
country known as Czechoslovakia. After World War II,
the country was a Warsaw Pact ally. With the fall of the
Soviet Union, the two groups went their separate
ways. With many natural resources and a manufacturing
history, it is little wonder Czech designs are common.

VZ26

finned barrel for greater air-cooling

One of the first light machine guns, now
called a Squad Automatic Weapon (SAW),
the VZ26 (also ZB26) was popular enough to be made
on three continents and used by two dozen countries.
As a milled-receiver magazine-fed weapon,
it was relatively easy to produce in any
cartridge that fitted the basic receiver/bolt
dimensions. When built on contract, it
could be delivered in a variety of chambering choices. It was quickly improved
and upgraded. The VZ26 was the design and tactical forerunner to the BREN
gun. Production began in 1926 and it was used until the late 1940s.

SPECIFICATION

MANUFACTURER CZ BRio
CALIBRE 7.92 x 57mm, 6.5mm Jap
MAGAZINE CAPACITY 20
ACTION Gas operated/tilting bolt
TOTAL LENGTH 1,163mm/45.8in
BARREL LENGTH 602mm/23.7in
WEIGHT UNLOADED 9.65kg/21.28lb

VZ37

dual pistol grips/handles

The forerunner to the British BESA machine
gun, the VZ37 (also ZB37) was a heavy machine
gun meant to be used from a tripod. The barrel
moved fore and aft and the cartridge
was chambered and fired during
forward movement. The recoil of
firing had to thus overcome the forward inertia of the barrel. It was compact
for a heavy machine gun and used a pair of side-grasping/firing handles that
were pitched downwards. The Czechs manufactured them from 1937 until
Germany invaded, and then for the Germans until 1945. After the war, there
were many other designs found in greater numbers, so production ceased.

SPECIFICATION

MANUFACTURER CZ BRio
CALIBRE 7.92 x 57mm
MAGAZINE CAPACITY Belt-fed
ACTION Gas operated
TOTAL LENGTH 1,105mm/43.5in
BARREL LENGTH 678mm/26.7in
WEIGHT UNLOADED 18.96kg/41.8lb

VZ60

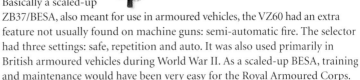

SPECIFICATION

MANUFACTURER CZ BRio
CALIBRE 15mm
MAGAZINE CAPACITY 25-round belt
ACTION Gas operated
TOTAL LENGTH 2,050mm/80.75in
BARREL LENGTH 640mm/25.2in
WEIGHT UNLOADED 56.9kg/125.5lb

Basically a scaled-up
ZB37/BESA, also meant for use in armoured vehicles, the VZ60 had an extra
feature not usually found on machine guns: semi-automatic fire. The selector
had three settings: safe, repetition and auto. It was also used primarily in
British armoured vehicles during World War II. As a scaled-up BESA, training
and maintenance would have been very easy for the Royal Armoured Corps.
It was manufactured from 1940 and declared obsolete in 1949.

VZ52/57

SPECIFICATION

MANUFACTURER CZ BRio
CALIBRE 7.62 x 39mm
MAGAZINE CAPACITY 25-round box,
100-round belt
ACTION Gas operated/tilting bolt
TOTAL LENGTH 1,041mm/41in
BARREL LENGTH 541mm/21.3in
WEIGHT UNLOADED 7.98kg/17.6lb

A new and improved post-war ZB26/30 or BREN gun, the VZ52 was designed
to be fed from a belt or box magazine. Complex and sophisticated, it pre-dated
the current SAWs such as the M249 or Minimi that also fed from either box or
belt. As a bonus, it featured a quick-change barrel. The VZ52 was chambered
in the new Czech intermediate cartridge, the 7.62 x 45mm. The 52/57 was the
designation given to the original light machine gun rebuilt to use the Soviet
M43 cartridge, the 7.62 x 39mm. The Czechs began making it in 1952 and,
after the calibre change, continued to manufacture it into the late 1960s.

UK 59

SPECIFICATION

MANUFACTURER CZ BRio
CALIBRE 7.62 x 54R
MAGAZINE CAPACITY Belt-fed
ACTION Gas operated/tilting bolt
TOTAL LENGTH 1,217mm/47.9in
BARREL LENGTH 693mm/27.3in
WEIGHT UNLOADED 19.23kg/42.4lb
w/heavy barrel, on tripod.
8.66kg/19.1lb in bipod

This was the Czech answer to the desire for a General-Purpose Machine Gun
(GPMG) that could be used on a bipod for squad use and on a tripod for
support fire. The feed mechanism is basically that of the ZB37 combined
with the quick-change barrel design of the ZB52. Chambered for the Soviet
rimmed .30, the 7.62 x 54R, it was manufactured from machined forgings,
and was thus somewhat heavy and expensive to manufacture. While production
was still underway, it was altered slightly (and the name changed to UK68)
when re-chambered for 7.62mm NATO. It is in current use with both the
Czech and Slovak armies.

Schwarzlose VZ7/24

lightweight
tripod

SPECIFICATION

MANUFACTURER Steyr
CALIBRE 7.92 x 57mm
MAGAZINE CAPACITY Belt-fed
ACTION Blowback
TOTAL LENGTH 1,066mm/42in
BARREL LENGTH 527mm/20.75in
WEIGHT UNLOADED 19.95kg/44lb

The Schwarzlose is perhaps
unique in belt-fed rifle-calibre
machine guns in not having a locked breech. Known
as a blowback action, the design needs a heavy bolt
and/or a stout recoil spring to contain the power
of the cartridge and to prevent battering and quick
weapon demise. The Schwarzlose has both.
Germany used Schwarzlose machine guns in World War I and World War II, the
latter chambered in the standard 7.92mm cartridge. The M07/24 was common
enough to have specialized equipment such as belt loaders and training manuals
printed for use by Wehrmacht troops in World War I. Production began in 1907.
It was rebuilt as the VZ7/24 in 1924, and used in German service until 1945.

Poland

Regaining independence after World War I, Poland did not have long on the world stage. Crushed between the Germans and Soviets in 1939, it was then fought over in the Russo-German war of 1941-5. Once it became a member of the Warsaw Pact, Poland supplied armaments and personnel to support the Red Army.

Browning BAR M28

Simply the American version in the German calibre, the Polish BAR was a vast improvement over its previous light machine gun, the Chauchat. It was purchased in 1928 and was in service until 1939.

SPECIFICATION	
MANUFACTURER Colt	
CALIBRE 7.92 x 57mm	
MAGAZINE CAPACITY 20	
ACTION Gas operated/toggle lock	
TOTAL LENGTH 1,214mm/47.8in	
BARREL LENGTH 610mm/24in	
WEIGHT UNLOADED 8.79kg/19.4lb	

Goryunov WZ43

This is the reliable, if heavy, Soviet-designed medium machine gun. After World War II, all Soviet client states converted to the Soviet pattern of small arms and produced weapons for their own use as well as for the Red Army. The Goryunov would have been issued to Polish infantry and mechanized infantry units, who were expected to be reserves to their Soviet and East German comrades for any offensive into Western Europe. It was replaced by the PKM in the mid 1960s.

SPECIFICATION	
MANUFACTURER Radom	
CALIBRE 7.62 x 54R	
MAGAZINE CAPACITY Belt-fed	
ACTION Gas operated	
TOTAL LENGTH 1,120mm/44.1in	
BARREL LENGTH 719mm/28.3in	
WEIGHT UNLOADED 13.15kg/29lb w/o mount	

DSHK M38/46

lower pawl-feed cover

The standard Soviet heavy machine gun, the 38/46 variant is a design improvement on the M38, where the rotating feed block is replaced with a conventional feed pawl to advance the belt. While rotating feed blocks or "spools" are seen by designers as an improvement, in the field the advantages are often illusory. Pawls and dog-leg shaped action tracks work just as well, as seen on the MG42 and other machine guns. Much as the American M2HB has outlived its replacements, the DSHK has outlasted lighter, "better" heavy machine guns. It was first placed into service with the Soviets in 1946, and with the Polish in the early 1950s, and is still in service to the present day.

SPECIFICATION	
MANUFACTURER Radom	
CALIBRE 12.7 x 108mm	
MAGAZINE CAPACITY Belt-fed	
ACTION Gas operated	
TOTAL LENGTH 1,588mm/62.5in	
BARREL LENGTH 1,070mm/42.1in	
WEIGHT UNLOADED 36.28kg/80lb w/o mount (approx 118kg/260lb)	

Replacement for DSHK
With Poland entering NATO, the DSHK may be at the end of its service, replaced by an even older heavy gun; the M2HB.

Kalashnikov PK

SPECIFICATION	
MANUFACTURER	Radom
CALIBRE	7.62 x 54R
MAGAZINE CAPACITY	Belt-fed
ACTION	Gas operated/rotating bolt
TOTAL LENGTH	1,199mm/47.2in
BARREL LENGTH	658mm/25.9in
WEIGHT UNLOADED	7.48–9.52kg/ 16.5–21lb

The Soviet General-Purpose Machine Gun (GPMG), the PK (Pulemyut Kalashnikov) is a Kalashnikov design with an additional belt-feed, scaled up to accept the larger 7.62mm Tsarist/Soviet cartridge. While the RPD has use at the squad level, the PK is meant for heavier work. In addition to the heavier cartridge, the PK has a quick-change barrel for use in sustained fire. It is a very versatile, dependable and long-lived GPMG, having been rebuilt in 7.62mm NATO and showing no signs of retiring. It was originally fielded in the late 1950s and is still going strong.

Chauchat CSRG

SPECIFICATION	
MANUFACTURER	St Etienne
CALIBRE	7.92 x 57mm
MAGAZINE CAPACITY	20
ACTION	Long recoil
TOTAL LENGTH	1,143mm/45in
BARREL LENGTH	470mm/18.5in
WEIGHT UNLOADED	8.61kg/19lb

Barely adequate in the French Lebel chambering and a disaster in the longer and more powerful .30-06, the Chauchat could not have been any better when chambered in 7.92 x 57mm than the .30-06. The long-recoil action had the bolt and barrel travelling the full cyclic distance backwards together, then the barrel recoiling forward, followed by the bolt as it chambered the next cartridge. When properly designed and built, it could be a reliable model. However, the Chauchat design was marginal at best: many were hastily assembled during World War I to dubious quality standards, and Polish use was entirely unsuited to the 7.92mm cartridge. Even a small amount of firing has been known to break the welded assemblies of the receiver. It was bought in 1920 and used until the late 1930s.

 South Africa

South African troops were involved in both world wars on the side of the British empire. Arms embargoes gave South Africa the impetus to build its own arms industry following the wars, eventually turning it into an arms exporting powerhouse. It manufactured and exported everything up to self-propelled artillery.

Vector SS77

SPECIFICATION	
MANUFACTURER	Lyttelton
CALIBRE	7.62 x 51mm
MAGAZINE CAPACITY	Belt-fed
ACTION	Gas operated
TOTAL LENGTH	1,155mm/45.47in
BARREL LENGTH	550mm/21.65in
WEIGHT UNLOADED	9.6kg/21.16lb

The SS77 was designed and built in South Africa as a General-Purpose Machine Gun (GPMG). With the examples of all other designs to draw from, and decades of experience in combat, the Vector SS77 is as good as any. The minimalist fore grip saves a pound or two of weight. Production commenced in 1977 and continued to the early 1990s. The SS77 is still in service.

Vector Mini SS

The Mini SS is the SS77
receiver built in 5.56mm
calibre. The Mini SS is
also found as a parts or conversion kit, containing all the parts needed to
rebuild a 7.62mm SS77 that uses 5.56mm ammunition. As a result it is only
a bit lighter but cannot be less durable than the larger calibre general-purpose
machine gun (GPMG). While 8.26kg/18.21lb is fairly heavy for a squad
automatic weapon (SAW), which is what most 5.56mm machine guns are,
the durability of such an approach cannot be faulted. Conversions began in
1994 and the Mini SS is presently in use.

SPECIFICATION

MANUFACTURER Lyttelton
CALIBRE 5.56 x 45mm
MAGAZINE CAPACITY Belt-fed
ACTION Gas operated
TOTAL LENGTH 1,000mm/39.37in
BARREL LENGTH 515mm/20.27in
WEIGHT UNLOADED 8.26kg/18.21lb

Vickers conversions

Not only were the Vickers rebuilt to 7.62mm by the South African forces, the
weapons were updated to the new calibre in the 1960s and served for several
decades. The conversions required new barrels, altering the feed system for the
shorter cartridge, and exchanging action springs. The Vickers would be fine
for vehicular or fortification use, but it was by no means a portable weapon
in the modern sense. Once a replacement was named, the machine guns
were dismantled and the parts were sold as surplus.

SPECIFICATION

MANUFACTURER Vickers
CALIBRE 7.62 x 51mm
MAGAZINE CAPACITY Belt-fed
ACTION Recoil operated
TOTAL LENGTH 1,158mm/45.6in
BARREL LENGTH 724mm/28.5in
WEIGHT UNLOADED 14.96kg/33lb

Serbia

As Yugoslavia, prior to the dissolution into five
independent countries in the 1990s, this region
produced many small arms for use by other Warsaw-
Pact or communist-aligned countries.
It also went further with the Kalashnikov design,
chambering it in calibres not found in the Soviet Union.

Maxim MG08

As part of the Austro-Hungarian
Empire before and during World
War I, it would be natural to find
Maxim machine guns in Yugoslavia.
Except for the markings required by
Yugoslavian purchase, they would
not have varied from German-issue
heavy machine guns of the period.
They also would have been
turned against the army of
their former manufacturers when
Germany invaded Yugoslavia in
1941. The Maxim MG08 was in
service from 1908 to 1945.

ABOVE The Maxim has more than just an
ejection port because a lengthy cloth belt had to
be expelled. The exit tray is to control the belt to
keep it from catching in the ejection port.

SPECIFICATION

MANUFACTURER Spandau
CALIBRE 7.92 x 57mm
MAGAZINE CAPACITY Belt-fed
ACTION Recoil operated
TOTAL LENGTH 1,175mm/46.25in
BARREL LENGTH 717mm/28.25in
WEIGHT UNLOADED 18.37kg/40.5lb
w/o water or mount

Sarac M53

SPECIFICATION

MANUFACTURER Zastava
CALIBRE 7.92 x 57mm
MAGAZINE CAPACITY Belt-fed
ACTION Recoil operated
TOTAL LENGTH 1,219mm/48in
BARREL LENGTH 533mm/21in
WEIGHT UNLOADED 11.56kg/25.5lb

This was the MG 42, built in Yugoslavia, and offered for export. While the 7.62 x 51mm version would be expected to work faultlessly, the proposed but never-seen .30-06 version probably would have had problems. It did not matter, as there were plenty of buyers and lots of ammunition available for the 7.92 x 57mm version. Buyers who were locked into the 7.62 x 51mm cartridge would find the Sarac altogether reliable. Manufacture of the M53 began in 1953 and continued until the dissolution of Yugoslavia in the 1990s.

M72 Kalashnikov

SPECIFICATION

MANUFACTURER Zastava
CALIBRE 7.62 x 39mm
MAGAZINE CAPACITY 30, 40
ACTION Gas operated
TOTAL LENGTH 1,040mm/40.94in
BARREL LENGTH 591mm/23.26in
WEIGHT UNLOADED 5kg/11.02lb

longer barrel than AK

Interchangeable parts
All parts of the RKP can be used with the AK or AKM, making the unit armourer's job easier.

This is simply the Yugoslavian RPK, in the standard Soviet chambering. The Yugoslavian manufacturing and design process of the M72 created a distinctive bulge in the receiver, caused by the bulged trunnion inside (the steel block securing the barrel and receiver). The longer barrel added little muzzle velocity but did add a significant sighting radius. The bipod was necessary, as the M72 (and other RPKs) were commonly issued with 40-round magazines. The bipod kept the magazine off the ground, although it also made the firer a slightly taller target. It was manufactured from the 1960s to the 1980s.

M84 PKM

SPECIFICATION

MANUFACTURER Zastava
CALIBRE 7.62 x 54R
MAGAZINE CAPACITY Belt-fed
ACTION Gas operated
TOTAL LENGTH 1,173mm/46.18in
BARREL LENGTH 658mm/25.90in
WEIGHT UNLOADED 8.99kg/19.81lb

stock specific to the M84

Modern Kalashnikov
PKM means "Machine-gun Kalashnikov Modernized".

The M84 was a clone of the Soviet PKM with very few differences. While the Soviet Union exported firearms at times for ideological reasons, the Yugoslavians did so only for cash. The Yugoslavian M84, like all PKMs, fired from an open bolt, and the cartridges must (the rims dictate it) be extracted rearwards from the belt on each firing cycle, before then being fed forward into the chamber. It was manufactured from the early 1960s to the 1990s.

Hungary

Prior to World War I, Hungary was a province of the Austro-Hungarian empire, and as such used the arms the Empire required. After World War I, with a communist revolution suppressed and territory lost, Hungary slowly allied itself with Germany. When Germany invaded the Soviet Union, Hungary became a full Axis ally. As with all countries occupied by the Soviet Union after World War I, Hungary adopted the Soviet pattern machine guns. They were manufactured at FÉG, the national arms factory.

PKM

Occupied by the Soviets after World War I, Hungary switched over to Soviet-pattern small arms. The PKM was made in Hungary, and except for markings denoting location of manufacture, it was identical to the Soviet version. The PKM was introduced in the early 1960s and remains in use to the present day. As with all ex-Warsaw Pact countries, Hungary is looking to upgrade her small arms, so the PKM may be replaced, or it might simply be made in a new version in 7.62mm NATO.

SPECIFICATION
MANUFACTURER FÉG, Budapest
CALIBRE 7.62 x 54R
MAGAZINE CAPACITY Belt-fed
ACTION Gas operated
TOTAL LENGTH 1,173mm/46.18in
BARREL LENGTH 658mm/25.9in
WEIGHT UNLOADED 8.99kg/19.81lb on bipod

Goryunov

shoulder stock added for use at squad level

The medium machine gun of the Soviet Union during Word War II, it was adopted by Hungary after the war. It was replaced by the PKM as supplies became available. It was in service only from 1945 until the mid 1960s.

SPECIFICATION
MANUFACTURER FÉG, Budapest
CALIBRE 7.62 x 54R
MAGAZINE CAPACITY Belt-fed
ACTION Gas operated
TOTAL LENGTH 1,150mm/45.27in
BARREL LENGTH 720mm/28.3in
WEIGHT UNLOADED 13.8kg/30.41lb (gun only, not carriage or shield)

Solothurn M31M

dual triggers for full and semi-fire

Denied possession of heavy machine guns by the Treaty of Versailles, Germany investigated light machine guns. Designed by Louis Schmeisser at Rheinmettal, the Solothurn M31M was rejected by the German Army, but produced in Switzerland and Austria for export. It was in use in Hungary from 1930 until 1945. Although the Hungarian Army served alongside German units on the Eastern Front and was often directed by German commanders, it retained its own small arms and calibre.

SPECIFICATION
MANUFACTURER Steyr-Daimler-Puch AG
CALIBRE 8 x 56R
MAGAZINE CAPACITY 30
ACTION Short recoil
TOTAL LENGTH 1,170mm/46.06in
BARREL LENGTH 600mm/23.6in
WEIGHT UNLOADED 9.5kg/20.93lb

 Greece

After separating from Turkey, Greece re-armed with "modern" small arms when it would have done well to retain the German small arms that Turkey had used.

Between the wars, Greece tried to remain neutral to ensure her security. When World War II broke out and this was no longer possible, Greece sided with the Allies.

Hotchkiss M1926

rear monopod for long-range fire

SPECIFICATION

MANUFACTURER St Etienne
CALIBRE 6.5 x 54mm
MAGAZINE CAPACITY Belt-fed
ACTION Gas operated
TOTAL LENGTH 1,180mm/45.5in
BARREL LENGTH 597mm/23.5in
WEIGHT UNLOADED 9.97kg/22lb

The Hotchkiss firm did not stop between the wars, and developed light machine guns for export. The Model 1926 for Greece was a belt-fed light machine gun that was greatly refined from the 1909 Portative. Hotchkiss could not find other export markets for such a well-made light machine gun due to the intense competition within the arms market between the wars. That competition, combined with the huge volume of surplus arms, made it a difficult time to make a living selling machine guns. They were only in service until World War II – after the war, Greece converted to American small arms and ammunition.

 Finland

Bristly about the independence it painfully acquired in 1917-1918, Finland has struggled to remain free of Russian control since. It sided with the Germans

against the Soviets in World War II at its cost. To protect its arms production capacity, it supplied maps without firearm-producing towns for decades.

SPECIFICATION

MANUFACTURER Tula, Russia
CALIBRE 7.62 x 54R
MAGAZINE CAPACITY Belt-fed
ACTION Recoil operated/toggle lock
TOTAL LENGTH 1,110mm/43.7in
BARREL LENGTH 720mm/28.3in
WEIGHT UNLOADED 24.0kg/52.9lb (tripod adds 27.6kg/60.8lb)

Maxim M09/21

rear sight folded

M-21 tripod, lighter in weight

This was one of three heavy machine guns, all Maxims, used by Finland. The 21 part of the model designation refers to the tripod. All Finnish heavy machine guns were Maxims, wrested from Russia or captured from armouries during Finland's break from the Russians. The M09/09 used the original wheeled mount whereas the 09/21 model used a tripod modelled after a pre-World War I Maxim tripod design, saving over 8kg/17.6lb from the 09/09 weight. From independence in 1918 to weapons retirement or upgrades in 1945, the Finnish Maxim could be counted on to keep Finnish borders intact.

Russian-based arms
It was not only logical that Finland's smaller army would use Russian-based small arms, it was also predictable that high-quality manufacturing standards would have been sought.

227

Valmet M-60 type B

Where it differs from the AK-47, the Valmet M-60 improves on it. The handguards are sturdier and actually protect the hands from heat (the AK and AKM handguards can get quite hot in sustained firing.) The rear sight is on the receiver cover, for better accuracy. The stock is a steel tube, stronger than the laminated wood of the AK. As an early rifle or Squad Automatic Weapon (SAW), it was a better rifle. Production began in 1960 and samples are still in use to the present day.

SPECIFICATION	
MANUFACTURER	Valmet
CALIBRE	7.62 x 39mm
MAGAZINE CAPACITY	30
ACTION	Gas operated/rotating bolt
TOTAL LENGTH	914mm/35.9in
BARREL LENGTH	420mm/16.5in
WEIGHT UNLOADED	4.3kg/9.47lb

Lahti M39/44

muzzle brake

At the start of World War II, 20mm anti-tank weapons were considered ineffective against all but the lightest tanks. The M39 was, however, a relatively portable weapon that the Finns put to good use besides shooting armoured vehicles. The 20mm explosive projectile did well on bunkers and the vehicles of supply convoys. The M39/44 was a full-auto variant that proved less successful in its designated role as an anti-aircraft gun: the receiver simply was not stout enough for full-auto fire. Original models were produced in 1939, the full-auto version five years later in 1944, lasting to retirement at the end of the war.

SPECIFICATION	
MANUFACTURER	VKT
CALIBRE	20 x 138mm
MAGAZINE CAPACITY	10
ACTION	Gas operated/tilting lock
TOTAL LENGTH	2,240mm/88.1in
BARREL LENGTH	1300mm/51.1in
WEIGHT UNLOADED	55.9kg/123.2lb

Sampo L41

This was a prototype machine gun: an attempt to produce a weapon lighter than a Maxim, fielded at the beginning of World War II. Only 50 were reported to be made. Some were sent to the front, for testing and to provide much-needed firepower to infantry units. At least one was captured by the Soviets, and is reported to be on display in the St Petersburg Artillery Museum. It required more work and, since existing designs worked as well, Finland used it for only a short time then dropped it from consideration.

SPECIFICATION	
MANUFACTURER	VKT
CALIBRE	7.62 x 54Rmm
MAGAZINE CAPACITY	Belt-fed
ACTION	Gas operated
TOTAL LENGTH	1,180mm/46.45in
BARREL LENGTH	500mm/19.6in
WEIGHT UNLOADED	14.9kg/32.8lb

Valmet KvKK 62

This is a Finnish-designed and produced light machine gun in the Squad Automatic Weapon (SAW) role. Unfortunately it is a heavy weapon and lacks a quick-change barrel, and even as a squad weapon this limits its firepower. Barrel overheating can be a problem even in the sub-zero climate of Finland. Despite local design and manufacture, it may soon be replaced with something with more power and greater reliability (such as the PKM). The Valmet KvKK 62 was first issued in 1966 and is still in use today.

SPECIFICATION	
MANUFACTURER	VKT
CALIBRE	7.62 x 39mm
MAGAZINE CAPACITY	Belt-fed
ACTION	Gas operated/tilting bolt
TOTAL LENGTH	1,080mm/42.5in
BARREL LENGTH	475mm/18.7in
WEIGHT UNLOADED	8.3kg/18.3lb

Romania

Newly independent after World War I, Romania found itself allied with Germany at the beginning of World War II. Romanian troops fought on the Eastern Front, where much of the army was destroyed at Stalingrad. When the Soviets rolled west, they invaded Romania and found a newly victorious pro-Soviet government waiting. From Austro-Hungarian Empire, to independent country, to Soviet client state in a generation, Romania had much the same rollercoaster ride that other Eastern European countries had.

PKM

SPECIFICATION	
MANUFACTURER	State Armoury
CALIBRE	7.62 x 54R
MAGAZINE CAPACITY	Belt-fed
ACTION	Gas operated
TOTAL LENGTH	1,173mm/46.18in
BARREL LENGTH	658mm/25.90in
WEIGHT UNLOADED	8.99kg/19.81lb

The standard post-war General-Purpose Machine Gun (GPMG) of the Soviet Bloc, the PKM (Pulemyot Kalashnikova Modernizirovanniy) is still in production. The PKM is the updated version of the PK. As with so many ex-Warsaw Pact countries, Romania must decide if it will change the PKM to 7.62mm NATO, leave it as it is, or replace it entirely. It has been in service from the late 1960s.

RPK

SPECIFICATION	
MANUFACTURER	State Armoury
CALIBRE	7.62 x 39mm
MAGAZINE CAPACITY	40 (can use standard magazines)
ACTION	Gas operated/rotating bolt
TOTAL LENGTH	1,040mm/40.95in
BARREL LENGTH	591mm/23.26in
WEIGHT UNLOADED	5.0kg/11.02lb

40-round magazine

This squad automatic weapon (SAW) was nothing more than an AK with a longer barrel, strengthened receiver, altered buttstock and larger magazine. Lacking a quick-change barrel, it had limited firepower before overheating. However, as a cost-effective means of getting a bit more firepower into a squad, the RPK made some sense. It was issued from the early 1960s until the to early 1980s.

RPK74

SPECIFICATION	
MANUFACTURER	State Armoury
CALIBRE	5.45 x 39mm
MAGAZINE CAPACITY	45 (can use standard magazines)
ACTION	Gas operated/rotating bolt
TOTAL LENGTH	1,060mm/41.73in
BARREL LENGTH	590mm/23.25in
WEIGHT UNLOADED	5.0kg/11.02lb

This was the successor to the RPK with a new Soviet calibre and minor changes such as polymer furniture, manufactured and issued from the early 1980s to the present day. Many AK-74 variants, including the RPK74, have an optics mount as a side rail. The 5.45mm cartridge is slightly less prone to overheating than the 7.62 x 39mm. If the RPK74 is issued with an optics mount, it would serve well as a squad-level sniper rifle (also known as the Designated Marksman Rifle). When Romania is fully a member of NATO, the AK-74s in 5.45 x 39mm will likely be withdrawn and replaced with AK-74s in 5.56 x 45mm calibre.

carry handle

Bulgaria

After World War I, Bulgaria found itself with less land than previously. In the years leading to World War II, they reluctantly worked more and more with Germany. After World War II, and a member of the Warsaw Pact, they manufactured Soviet-pattern rifles. Today, the army is undergoing a series of changes.

BREN ZB39

magazine curved differently for 8 x 56R

The ZB39 (made in 1939) was a BREN variant chambered in 8 x 56R. The cartridge was the standard Austro-Hungarian service round, the ZB39 from Czechoslovakia. The combination worked quite reliably. Hungary accepted the first ZB39 light machine guns in 1939. In 1941, Germany was at Bulgaria's border, and Bulgaria reluctantly accepted Germany's aid in recovering lost territories ceded after World War I. The ZB39 was used both by Bulgarian government troops and partisans until the end of World War I. After the war, Bulgaria reluctantly became a signatory of the Warsaw Pact, and began using Soviet-pattern machine guns.

SPECIFICATION

MANUFACTURER CZ BRio
CALIBRE 8 x 56R
MAGAZINE CAPACITY 20
ACTION Gas operated
TOTAL LENGTH 1,041mm/41in
BARREL LENGTH 541mm/21.3in
WEIGHT UNLOADED 7.98kg/17.6lb

Russia

Whether Tsarist, Soviet or as a Federation, Russia has always had a big army. Keeping it supplied means either a large purchase programme, a large number of arsenals at home and occasionally both. Under the Tsars they had both, but the Soviets insisted on home production. When Germany invaded in World War II, Russia packed up the arsenals that were too close to the front and shipped them to the Urals, where production continued.

Maxim M1905

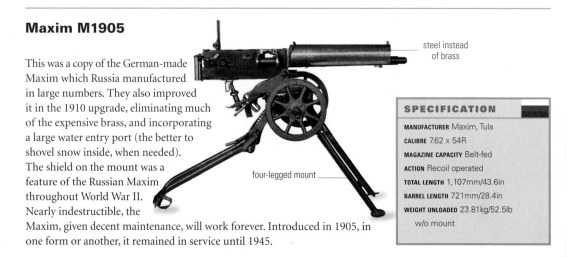

steel instead of brass

This was a copy of the German-made Maxim which Russia manufactured in large numbers. They also improved it in the 1910 upgrade, eliminating much of the expensive brass, and incorporating a large water entry port (the better to shovel snow inside, when needed). The shield on the mount was a feature of the Russian Maxim throughout World War II. Nearly indestructible, the Maxim, given decent maintenance, will work forever. Introduced in 1905, in one form or another, it remained in service until 1945.

four-legged mount

SPECIFICATION

MANUFACTURER Maxim, Tula
CALIBRE 7.62 x 54R
MAGAZINE CAPACITY Belt-fed
ACTION Recoil operated
TOTAL LENGTH 1,107mm/43.6in
BARREL LENGTH 721mm/28.4in
WEIGHT UNLOADED 23.81kg/52.5lb
w/o mount

Lewis LMG, Russian pattern

SPECIFICATION

MANUFACTURER Savage Arms
CALIBRE 7.62 x 54R
MAGAZINE CAPACITY 47-round drum
ACTION Gas operated
TOTAL LENGTH 1,282mm/50.5in
BARREL LENGTH 668mm/26.3in
WEIGHT UNLOADED 12.33kg/27.2lb

Using a drum, the Lewis was adaptable to almost any cartridge, as long as it was not too long for the drum radius. Adapting it to the Russian cartridge was a minor matter of drum shape, bolt face and recoil springs. Despite the complexity and cost, the Lewis LMG was so well made that it proved remarkably long-lived. While the Lewis guns were made for and shipped to Tsarist Russia in 1917, they may still be in warehouses in the Russian Federation as they use the standard 7.62mm rimmed cartridge.

DP

47-round drum

SPECIFICATION

MANUFACTURER Soviet State arsenals
CALIBRE 7.62 x 54R
MAGAZINE CAPACITY 47-round drum
ACTION Gas operated
TOTAL LENGTH 1,295mm/51in
BARREL LENGTH 604mm/23.8in
WEIGHT UNLOADED 9.29kg/20.5lb

Using the firing pin to actuate the locking flaps, the DP (Degtyarev Pechotnyi) is a solid Light Machine Gun (LMG). The feed pan is a necessity due to the rimmed cartridge and the first versions had the recoil spring around the barrel. Heat could cause problems with the spring temper, it was slightly redesigned in 1943-44 to move the spring away from the heat. It was named the DPM ("M" for modernized.) In 1946, a DP built for belt-feed was unveiled, called the RP-46. This and the DP served from 1928 to the late 1950s.

SPECIFICATION

MANUFACTURER Soviet State arsenals
CALIBRE 12.7 x 108mm
MAGAZINE CAPACITY Belt-fed
ACTION Gas operated
TOTAL LENGTH 1,587mm/62.5in
BARREL LENGTH 1,069mm/42.1in
WEIGHT UNLOADED 36.28kg/80lb
w/o mount

DSHK Model 1938

This was the Soviet heavy (large calibre) machine gun in service since 1938. The cartridge is so robust that the DSHK was designed and built with a muzzle brake to reduce felt recoil, but at the cost of increased blast to the gunner. The Soviets have tried unsuccessfully to replace their heavy machine gun with an improved, lighter version for decades. The Model 1938 was the original belt-fed version with a rotary feed mechanism. It was upgraded in 1946 with a regular pawl and dogleg track feed system.

SPECIFICATION

MANUFACTURER Soviet State arsenals
CALIBRE 7.62 x 54R
MAGAZINE CAPACITY Belt-fed
ACTION Gas operated
TOTAL LENGTH 1,120mm/44.1in
BARREL LENGTH 718m/28.3in
WEIGHT UNLOADED 13.15kg/29lb
w/o mount

Goryunov SGM

The Goryunov SGM ("M" for modernized) was intended as the wartime replacement for the Maxim. It ended up not being much lighter in combat-ready condition due to the various heavy mounts it was placed on. The standard Soviet/Tsarist wheeled mount weighed 27kg/60lb without the shield, so the end result was a medium, air-cooled machine gun that did not weigh much less than the Maxim. However, the Goryunov was made in large numbers. It entered service in 1943 where it remained until the late 1950s.

PKM

Only with the arrival of the PK did the Soviets have the General-Purpose Machine Gun (GPMG) they desired. The original PK was modified to the PKM with a few mechanical changes, and a smooth barrel instead of the fluted (and thus more costly) barrel it began with. With the quick-change heavy barrel and mounted in a tripod, it can be used in support. The lighter barrel and bipod weighs only 0.5kg/1lb more than an RPD (a much less effective weapon), and is far more mobile for use by infantry units. It has been in service since 1969.

SPECIFICATION

MANUFACTURER Soviet State arsenals
CALIBRE 7.62 x 54R
MAGAZINE CAPACITY Belt-fed
ACTION Gas operated
TOTAL LENGTH 1,198mm/47.2in
BARREL LENGTH 658mm/25.9in
WEIGHT UNLOADED 7.48kg/16.5lb

RPK

Designed as a Squad Automatic Weapon (SAW), the Ruchnoi Pulemet Kalashnikova (RPK) is an AK with a stiffer receiver, longer barrel and a larger magazine. However, the AK itself overheats too quickly, so the RPK is not nearly as useful as it might first appear. As an interim weapon to supply the squad with more firepower, it was an obvious step in the mid 1950s. That it continued in service until the 1970s can only be attributed to either parsimony or extreme need. For a little more weight, the RPD is far more useful to an infantry squad. However, even the RPD overheats too quickly.

SPECIFICATION

MANUFACTURER Soviet State arsenals
CALIBRE 7.62 x 39mm
MAGAZINE CAPACITY 40 rounds
ACTION Gas operated
TOTAL LENGTH 1,039mm/40.9in
BARREL LENGTH 589mm/23.2in
WEIGHT UNLOADED 5.58kg/12.3lb

RPK-74

optical sight for squad use

This was the RPK automatic rifle translated to the AK-74 and its new 5.45mm cartridge, which does not overheat the RPK quite as quickly as the 7.62mm does. The end result is still the same: the small-unit commander has to work with an inefficient system. The RPK would be more useful if issued with optics, and used as a squad designated marksman rifle, delivering accurate semi-automatic fire at close-to-medium range. It has been in service from 1974.

SPECIFICATION

MANUFACTURER Soviet State arsenals
CALIBRE 5.45 x 39mm
MAGAZINE CAPACITY 45 rounds
ACTION Gas operated
TOTAL LENGTH 1,060mm/41.73in
BARREL LENGTH 590mm/23.22in
WEIGHT UNLOADED 5kg/11.02lb

Pecheneg

A modernized and improved PKM, the Pecheneg features forced-air cooling, a concept not used since the Lewis gun of World War I. The gas pressure of cycling the mechanism also forces air down the covering of the barrel, cooling the barrel with each shot. The designers are so sure of its function that the barrel is not one with a quick-change design built in. Only severe testing or field experience will show if the manufacturer's assertions are true. Offered as a replacement for the PKM and for export, production began in the late 1990s and continues today.

SPECIFICATION

MANUFACTURER TNTM
CALIBRE 7.62 x 54R
MAGAZINE CAPACITY Belt-fed
ACTION Gas operated
TOTAL LENGTH 1,145mm/45.07in
BARREL LENGTH 600mm/23.6in
WEIGHT UNLOADED 8.2kg/18.07lb

 Egypt

Until receiving Soviet machinery, Egypt did not have an indigenous arms making capacity for machine guns and had to buy them elsewhere. The Husqvarna machinery used to make the Hakim only provided a service rifle for a short time. Since the late 1950s Egypt has been able to produce arms for itself and even export some.

Alfa

During World War II, Spain found outside sources for machine guns unavailable. Their previous suppliers were all busy making arms for the war, so they designed and produced an air-cooled heavy machine gun of their own. Initially produced in 7.92mm, the Alfa was later manufactured in 7.62mm NATO. Not surprisingly, fierce competition for post-war sales worldwide ended any chances of it being an export success. Egypt bought a few, but soon after this, they began to convert to Soviet-pattern small arms and did not need Spanish machine guns. The Alfa was produced in Spain from 1943 and used in Egypt from 1953 to 1962.

German-type low-recoil tripod

SPECIFICATION

MANUFACTURER Alfa
CALIBRE 7.62 x 51mm
MAGAZINE CAPACITY Belt-fed
ACTION Gas operated
TOTAL LENGTH 1,118mm/44in
BARREL LENGTH 610mm/24in
WEIGHT UNLOADED 14.96kg/33lb

Goryunov Aswan

SPECIFICATION

MANUFACTURER State Factory 54
CALIBRE 7.62 x 54R
MAGAZINE CAPACITY Belt-fed
ACTION Gas operated/side-tipping bolt
TOTAL LENGTH 1,150mm/45.27in
BARREL LENGTH 720mm/28.34in
WEIGHT UNLOADED 13.8kg/30.42lb

An air-cooled heavy machine gun built on Soviet-supplied machinery, the Aswan is simply a 1960s-era Goryunov SGM. Soviet charity had nothing to do with it; they were planning to replace the SGM with what would become the PK series and giving away tooling was simply smart politics. The Egyptians had nothing like it, so the tooling was a double blessing for them: they could both equip their army, and create jobs. The SGM is durable enough to have lasted from the early 1960s to the present day.

VZ26 copy

carry handle and quick-change handle

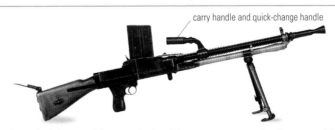

SPECIFICATION

MANUFACTURER Unk
CALIBRE 7.92 x 57mm
MAGAZINE CAPACITY 20
ACTION Gas operated/tilting bolt
TOTAL LENGTH 1,163mm/45.8in
BARREL LENGTH 602mm/23.7in
WEIGHT UNLOADED 9.65kg/21.28lb

Given the history of the area, it should come as no surprise that something as common as a VZ26 or a copy of it should be found in Egypt. Despite being a British protectorate before and during World War II, weapons could come in from all points of the compass.

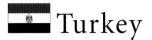

Turkey

Despite being aligned with Germany, Turkey bought small arms from many sources, including France, where there was a large volume of surplus weapons available after World War I. The resulting mix of German and French machine guns and calibres could not have been easy on the Turkish supply system.

Hotchkiss MA4

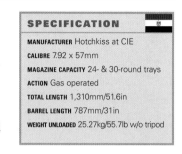

SPECIFICATION	
MANUFACTURER Hotchkiss at CIE	
CALIBRE 7.92 x 57mm	
MAGAZINE CAPACITY 24- & 30-round trays	
ACTION Gas operated	
TOTAL LENGTH 1,310mm/51.6in	
BARREL LENGTH 787mm/31in	
WEIGHT UNLOADED 25.27kg/55.7lb w/o tripod	

In the 1920s, Hotchkiss developed what could have been a viable General-Purpose Machine Gun (GPMG), ten years before the German MG34. The Model 1922 (called the MA4 in Turkish service) could be manufactured to feed from a vertical box magazine, a belt or the peculiar Hotchkiss feed trays. For Turkey, Hotchkiss made it in 7.92mm calibre, but it could also be made in others. Unfortunately Hotchkiss only sold a few, mostly to Greece and Turkey. The model was scrapped after World War II.

Israel

Israel had to start out with managing with whatever could be obtained from the miscellaneous collection of German and British small arms before independence. Only after establishing a sufficiently large production base could Israeli Military Industries manufacture what was both needed and desired.

Browning

built, or rebuilt to the FN two-post tripod mount

SPECIFICATION	
MANUFACTURER Colt, others	
CALIBRE 7.62mm NATO	
MAGAZINE CAPACITY Belt-fed	
ACTION Recoil operated	
TOTAL LENGTH 1,041mm/41in	
BARREL LENGTH 610mm/24in	
WEIGHT UNLOADED 14.06kg/31lb	

Tripod advantages
The benefits of a tripod are such that troops are willing to transport the extra weight. Using the control knobs on the traverse and elevation mechanism, the shooter can fire to extreme distances with accuracy, or return the gun back to a previous setting, to resume fire at a particular extreme range.

During World War II the Browning air-cooled machine gun was to be found everywhere and performed well. The basic weapon is so durable and versatile (although heavy) that it can be used in almost every role where the weight can be withstood. Inevitably, Israel converted it to 7.62mm. It was used in the War for Independence (1947–48) and can still be seen on vehicles to this day. Lighter machine guns than the Browning may be available, but few have had a longer service life.

Negev

SPECIFICATION	✡
MANUFACTURER IMI	
CALIBRE 5.56 x 45mm	
MAGAZINE CAPACITY 30, and belt-fed	
ACTION Gas operated	
TOTAL LENGTH 1,020mm/40.15in	
BARREL LENGTH 460mm/18.11in	
WEIGHT UNLOADED 7.6kg/16.75lb	

The Negev is the Israeli answer to the need for a Squad Automatic Weapon (SAW) in its modern army. The Negev looks a great deal like the FN Minimi. Like the Minimi, the Negev uses either linked belts of ammunition, or can be fed from magazines. The Negev magazine is the same as the Israeli Galil, and IMI makes adapters for the Negev allowing it to use M-16 magazines. Unlike other armies, Israel plans to replace all belt-fed machine guns with the Negev, retiring all their MAG-58s in service. Its advantages are its weight and lighter ammunition; its disadvantages are its lack of range and power. The Negev was first issued in the mid-1990s and is in use to the present day.

DROR (Johnson)

.30-06 ammunition used here

After World War II, Israel purchased the tooling for the Johnson light machine gun. Israel wanted production in-country, to avoid the problems any blockade might bring. The DROR is listed in references as having been re-designed to use .303 British ammunition. However, there are samples of the DROR in existence in .30-06, so the Israelis clearly manufactured both. As both calibres were common, and easily purchased, having weapons in both ensured Israel of being able to acquire ammunition for the Israeli Defence Force. The DROR was only in the testing phase during the battle for independence. It served from 1948 to an unknown date. The main obstacle in converting the DROR to the .303 was in accommodating the rim of the latter. It required a magazine with both a greater curvature, and a larger gap in the feed lips, than required for the American .30-06.

SPECIFICATION	✡
MANUFACTURER Johnson/Israeli	
CALIBRE .303 British,.30-06	
MAGAZINE CAPACITY 20	
ACTION Recoil operated	
TOTAL LENGTH 1,070mm/42.12in	
BARREL LENGTH 560mm/22.04in	
WEIGHT UNLOADED 10kg/22lb	

Ethiopia

A backwater in world events, Ethiopia still had to defend itself from its neighbours, and later, the aspirations of Italy under Mussolini. With no indigenous arms manufacturing, it had to import everything. That it chose the VZ30 should come as no surprise: it was the best at the time and would still be a good choice today.

VZ30

SPECIFICATION	
MANUFACTURER CZ BRio	
CALIBRE 7.92 x 57mm	
MAGAZINE CAPACITY 20	
ACTION Gas operated/tilting lock	
TOTAL LENGTH 1,163mm/45.8in	
BARREL LENGTH 602mm/23.7in	
WEIGHT UNLOADED 9.65kg/21.28lb	

An improved VZ26, the VZ30 only added to the sales and lustre of CZ and the reputation of their products. It was purchased by Ethiopia in the early 1930s, and used for decades until stocks were exhausted. Ethiopia wisely declined to design a proprietary cartridge. As the standard export light machine gun, the VZ30 in 7.92mm could be fed ammunition from any source of reliable and common 7.92 x 57mm.

 Iraq

In the Cold War struggle for dominance of the Middle East and its oil, Iraq elected to go with the Soviets for small arms, military vehicles, and command and staff structure. This did not keep Saddam Hussein from accepting Western aid in the Iran-Iraq War, something Iran has not forgiven. While still purchasing weapons from non-aligned countries, the basic small arms stock was Soviet, although locally produced.

Al Quds

This was a local version of the RPD. Iraqi small arms tended to have a glossier finish than their Soviet counterparts, whether an aesthetic selection or simply a result of the steel stock selected for use is unknown. As with all belt-fed squad automatic weapons lacking a quick-change barrel, the Al Quds overheats if not used carefully. Given the extreme desert environment, over-heating and weapons maintenance was an ongoing problem for Iraqi soldiers. Also, trying to deal with Iranian MG 3s, while armed with an Al Quds in 7.62 x 39mm, had to be a real challenge. The Iraqi soldiers were out-ranged, and did not have the sustained fire capability of the MG 3. Manufacture began in the 1970s and the Al Quds can still be seen in use to the present day.

SPECIFICATION

MANUFACTURER Iraqi armouries
CALIBRE 7.62 x 39mm
MAGAZINE CAPACITY 30, 40 and 75
ACTION Gas operated
TOTAL LENGTH 1,037mm/40.8in
BARREL LENGTH 520mm/20.47in
WEIGHT UNLOADED 7.4kg/16.3lb

Magazines
The Al Quds accepts 30 and 40 magazines, but has been seen with 75-round drum magazines.

 Iran/Persia

Persia was useful to Europe (and Britain) primarily as a block to Russian attempts to gain a warm-water port. However, the discovery of oil made it a much larger player on the world stage. During World War II, Iran was a transportation route for materials to the Soviets from the United States. So it did, for a brief time, have a warm-water port. With the post-war oil boom, Iran became a power in the Middle East. However, the revolution, followed immediately by the long war with Iraq, kept them isolated until recently.

MG 3

When Iran purchased Heckler & Koch G3 rifles in the early 1970s, it made sense to only purchase machine guns in the same calibre. They replaced their US .30 and .50 Brownings and the ZB 30 light machine guns they had on hand with the updated German MG42, aka the MG 3. One of the updates to the MG 3 was the ability to use disintegrating belts as well as the German continuous ones. Those machine guns no doubt went on to serve in the Iran-Iraq War in the early 1980s. The MG 3 was purchased in the early 1970s and has remained in service to the present. As they are entirely serviceable and nearly indestructible, they will probably remain in service for quite some time.

SPECIFICATION

MANUFACTURER Rheinmettal Borsig
CALIBRE 7.62mm NATO
MAGAZINE CAPACITY Belt-fed
ACTION Recoil operated
TOTAL LENGTH 1,219mm/48in
BARREL LENGTH 533mm/21in
WEIGHT UNLOADED 11.56kg/25.5lb

 Pakistan

As part of the pre-war British Indian Empire, Pakistan had the same selection of rifles, machine guns, spares and training as India. After independence from India, Pakistan has had almost continual friction with its neighbour, having both the border to patrol, and its own fractious north-west provinces to oversee.

MG 1A3

SPECIFICATION

MANUFACTURER POF

CALIBRE 7.62mm NATO

MAGAZINE CAPACITY Belt-fed

ACTION Recoil operated

TOTAL LENGTH 1,219mm/48in

BARREL LENGTH 533mm/21in

WEIGHT UNLOADED 11.56kg/25.5lb

Belts
The MG 1A3 accepts disintegrating and non-disintegrating belts.

The MG 1A3 is an improved (by Germany) MG 42, built under licence from Rheinmettal. The "1" denotes conversion to the NATO standard rifle cartridge of 7.62mm NATO, while the "A3" indicates the minor changes which collectively increase durability, reliability and service life of the already exemplary design. Typically, MG 1 machine guns can be made or issued with two bolt-buffer combinations. One produces a cyclic rate of 1,100 to 1,300 rpm, while the other produces 700 to 900 rpm. The MG 1A3 has been produced in Pakistan from the mid 1950s, with manufacture continuing to the present day.

 India

From a British colony to independent country, India has had a long history of martial strife and arms making. The British set up armouries in India to make British-pattern small arms for their own use. After independence, India simply kept the armouries open, while upgrading to designs it saw fit for its own needs.

BREN Model 1B

SPECIFICATION

MANUFACTURER Enfield

CALIBRE 7.62 x 51mm

MAGAZINE CAPACITY 30

ACTION Gas operated/tilting lock

TOTAL LENGTH 1,156mm/45.5in

BARREL LENGTH 635mm/25in

WEIGHT UNLOADED 10.03kg/22.12lb

As with many countries post-war, converting BREN guns from .303 to 7.62mm was an attractive proposition. For a small investment, India could keep its existing weapons going long enough to find a better replacement. It has been in use from 1953 to the present day, although all conversions were completed within a few years of the start of the process. Given the wide-open spaces of India, and the long distances from one ridgeline to another in various border skirmishes, the superb accuracy of the BREN had to be an asset. Along with the BREN, India made a copy of the MAG 58. The BREN is destined to be retired as soon as the INSAS Light Machine Gun (LMG) is fielded.

7.62mm magazines are straighter than .303 magazines

China

By the modern era, China had suffered the indignity of being apportioned between the occupying powers. Combined with internal strife from competing warlords, pre-World War II, Chinese small arms lists could only be described as "eclectic". Warlords and the central government bought arms from whomever they could or whichever sales agent offered the best bribes. What

could not be bought was made. With Mauser vigorous in sales, most rifles and light and medium machine guns were chambered in 7.92 x 57mm. After the revolution, China had a huge army and People's Militia to equip. It chose Soviet-pattern weapons, built at home. The volume of its production made export an attractive prospect once the Cold War had thawed somewhat.

MG Browning

sight

condensor cap

SPECIFICATION	
MANUFACTURER	Colt
CALIBRE	7.92 x 57mm
MAGAZINE CAPACITY	Belt-fed
ACTION	Recoil operated
TOTAL LENGTH	1,041mm/41in
BARREL LENGTH	610mm/24in
WEIGHT UNLOADED	14.06kg/31lb

The Browning machine gun was a natural for the Chinese market. All it needed was a supply of barrels chambered in 7.92 x 57mm and the receiver would work forever. While making one in a local workshop would have been a daunting task, Colt found it easy to produce a model in that calibre. It was made by Colt from 1919 to 1939, and used until 1949.

VZ26 copy

SPECIFICATION	
MANUFACTURER	Unk
CALIBRE	7.92 x 57mm
MAGAZINE CAPACITY	20
ACTION	Gas operated/tilting lock
TOTAL LENGTH	1,163mm/45.8in
BARREL LENGTH	602mm/23.7in
WEIGHT UNLOADED	9.52kg/21lb

The progenitor of the BREN, the VZ26 would have been a natural choice to copy once imported. Light, handy and reliable, it would have been the centrepiece of any warlord's armoury. While China did not have a large industrial base prior to the 1960s, it did have a lot of local armouries and workshops before World War II. The design of the VZ26 is not so complicated that it could not be copied. From its introduction in 1926 to the Communist takeover in 1949, a workshop could have produced quite a few.

Manufacturing challenges
The barrel and magazine are the two hardest parts of an automatic weapon to be made. Drilling a barrel needs costly machinery or excruciating labour and magazines must be bent out of sheet steel.

Maxim Type 24

SPECIFICATION

MANUFACTURER Various
CALIBRE 7.92 x 57 & 7.62 x 54R
MAGAZINE CAPACITY Belt-fed
ACTION Recoil operated
TOTAL LENGTH 1219mm/48in
BARREL LENGTH 605mm/23.8in
WEIGHT UNLOADED 23.8kg/52.5lb
  w/o mount

The Type 24 was both purchased from Germany, and Chinese-manufactured copies of the Maxim. The Type 24, like all Maxim-type machine guns, is heavy by the standards of today, but when reliability matters the Maxim can hardly be faulted. The originals were doubtless made in 7.92mm, but converting each to 7.62 x 54R would have been a simple operation when time for an overhaul. They were first purchased in 1924 and in use throughout the 1950s.

Robust design

Given the lack of maintenance any weapon could expect in Chinese service, the Maxim was a good choice. Short of allowing it to rust, anyone could keep a Maxim running, once they had been given a day's instruction.

VZ26

SPECIFICATION

MANUFACTURER Various
CALIBRE 7.62 x 39mm
MAGAZINE CAPACITY 20
ACTION Gas operated/tilting lock
TOTAL LENGTH 1,156mm/45.5in
BARREL LENGTH 635mm/25in
WEIGHT UNLOADED 10.03kg/22.12lb

7.62 x 39mm magazines much more curved

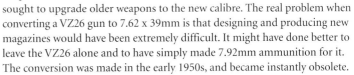

Faced with equipping an army in the millions and a People's Militia, China sought to upgrade older weapons to the new calibre. The real problem when converting a VZ26 gun to 7.62 x 39mm is that designing and producing new magazines would have been extremely difficult. It might have done better to leave the VZ26 alone and to have simply made 7.92mm ammunition for it. The conversion was made in the early 1950s, and became instantly obsolete.

DSHK Type 54

SPECIFICATION

MANUFACTURER Various Chinese
  heavy industries
CALIBRE 12.7 x 109mm
MAGAZINE CAPACITY Belt-fed
ACTION Gas operated/locking flaps
TOTAL LENGTH 1,587mm/62.5in
BARREL LENGTH 1,069mm/42.1in
WEIGHT UNLOADED 35.6kg/78.5lb

After the revolution, China made its own small arms, either based on or exact copies of Soviet designs. The DSHK Type 54 is the Soviet and Chinese heavy machine gun, chambered in the Soviet equivalent of the .50 Browning. The feed mechanism uses a sprocket, rotating the belt and cartridges to the chamber. A sprocket is more robust and less complicated than a pawl and dog-leg channel to move the belt, but a sprocket makes the receiver taller. Given even the least amount of care, the DSHK is completely reliable. It is typically manufactured with a muzzle brake that produces a ferocious back-blast. The DSHK Type 54 has been made from 1954 to the present day.

Degtyarev Type 56

SPECIFICATION

MANUFACTURER Various

CALIBRE 7.62 x 39mm

MAGAZINE CAPACITY Belt-fed

ACTION Gas operated/locking flaps on bolt

TOTAL LENGTH 1,037mm/40.8in

BARREL LENGTH 520mm/20.8in

WEIGHT UNLOADED 7.2kg/15.9lb w/o mount

This Chinese-built Soviet RPD is an air-cooled belt-fed machine gun that fills the role of the squad automatic weapon (SAW). The belt is held in a drum attached to the receiver. Belts can be used without the drum. Lacking a quick-change barrel, the gun can and will overheat if not fired with restraint. Overheating will cause myriad problems, including failure to extract or runaway firing. Otherwise the Type 56 it is quite reliable, relatively light, portable and quite formidable when used properly. In production since 1956 to the present day, it faces replacement by the new Chinese small arms family.

Chinese Type 57

anti-aircraft sights

SPECIFICATION

MANUFACTURER Various

CALIBRE 7.62 x 54R

MAGAZINE CAPACITY Belt-fed

ACTION Gas operated, side-shift bolt-lock

TOTAL LENGTH 1120mm/44.09in

BARREL LENGTH 720mm/28.35in

WEIGHT UNLOADED 13.83kg/30.5lb w/o mount

As with so many other small arms, the Communist Chinese took advantage of the manufacturing and combat experience of their Russian counterparts. The Type 57 was simply the Goryunov SG43/SGM built in China. While it was certainly adequate as a war-time medium machine gun in World War II, by the late 1950s, it was clearly not ageing well. The Goryunov was relatively light for a medium machine gun when it was designed in 1943. By 1958, when it was adopted by the Chinese, it was portly. In addition, it could not be used without a mount, the lightest of which weighed another 20kg/44lb. Despite its age, the Type 58 served until replaced by the Type 80 in 1980.

Kalashnikov Type 80

SPECIFICATION

MANUFACTURER Various

CALIBRE 7.62 x 54R

MAGAZINE CAPACITY 20

ACTION Gas operated/rotating bolt

TOTAL LENGTH 1,192mm/46.9in

BARREL LENGTH 605mm/23.8in

WEIGHT UNLOADED 12.6kg/27.8lb

Based on the Soviet PKMC 7.62 general-purpose machine gun, the Type 80 was adopted in 1980 and issued in the early 1980s. In the Soviet Union, the PKM replaced a slew of medium machine guns. In China, the Type 80 replaced the locally designed Type 67, which had proven less than satisfactory. Simple in design, tough as an anvil, and not requiring special alloys to be constructed, the Chinese PKM did not hurt the weapon's reputation for reliability. It was first made in 1980 and there are no plans to replace it.

 # Thailand

One of the many customers of Dansk Syndikat, the Kingdom of Thailand simply bought what it needed.

In the post-war period, the US and China have been Thailand's main source of military equipment. Russia, the Czech Republic, Spain, and Sweden are its European arms suppliers.

Madsen

SPECIFICATION

MANUFACTURER Dansk Industri Syndikat
CALIBRE 7.92 x 57mm
MAGAZINE CAPACITY 30
ACTION Gas operated
TOTAL LENGTH 1,168mm/46in
BARREL LENGTH 482mm/19in
WEIGHT UNLOADED 9.97kg/22lb

This was the standard export version of the Madsen, in the standard calibre, for customers who did not insist on their own proprietary cartridge. As with all export models, customers could have their order in any calibre, kitted out with any accessories they wished. Except for the markings denoting Thai ownership, the Thai Madsen could be any other Madsen. It was in service from the 1920s, through to World War II, where it may well have been used against the Japanese.

 # Singapore

As a centre of heavy industry in the modern world, it has not been a problem for Singapore to invest in arms

production in the modern era. Attracting designers is also straightforward. Its efforts in getting designs adopted abroad have not met with great success due mostly to the huge volume of small arms available.

SPECIFICATION

MANUFACTURER Chartered Industries of Singapore
CALIBRE 5.56 x 45mm
MAGAZINE CAPACITY 30, 100-round drum
ACTION Gas operated
TOTAL LENGTH 1,024mm/40.31in
BARREL LENGTH 508mm/20in
WEIGHT UNLOADED 4.9kg/10.80lb

CIS Ultimax 100

The Ultimax 100 is a Light Machine Gun (LMG) or Squad Automatic Weapon (SAW) that reduces felt recoil by a simple method: the receiver is long enough internally to prevent the cycling bolt from striking the rear of the receiver. The firer only feels the spring compression, never the bolt bottoming out against the rear of the receiver. As a result, it is very smooth in operation. Manufacture began in the early 1980s and continues to the present day. The Ultimax is a regular contender in SAW and LMG trials, but has yet to see much acceptance outside Singapore.

SPECIFICATION

MANUFACTURER Chartered Industries of Singapore
CALIBRE .50 BMG
MAGAZINE CAPACITY Belt-fed
ACTION Gas operated
TOTAL LENGTH 1,670mm/65.74in
BARREL LENGTH 1,141mm/44.92in
WEIGHT UNLOADED 30kg/66.13lb

CIS .50

This is another contender to try and throw the Browning M2HB off the throne. The CIS .50 has dual-feed, right and left. The feed is selectable, and the firer can switch from one to the other and use either type being fed. It is lighter than the M2HB. The barrel is a quick-change design, and the firing mechanism offers semi- and full-auto firing. The bolt rotates to lock, and features 24 small locking lugs, arranged in three rows. The advantage of such a design is that it allows for a more compact receiver, as the bolt is kept to the minimum size needed for safe function. It was introduced in the 1990s.

 Australia

Australia did not have its own government rifle factory until the establishment of the Lithgow Arsenal in 1912. Production of Vickers began in 1925, and subsequently that of BREN guns in 1938. Once World War II was underway, the Lithgow Arsenal worked day and night to meet demand.

BREN Mark 1

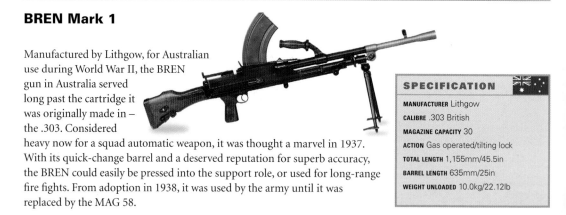

Manufactured by Lithgow, for Australian use during World War II, the BREN gun in Australia served long past the cartridge it was originally made in – the .303. Considered heavy now for a squad automatic weapon, it was thought a marvel in 1937. With its quick-change barrel and a deserved reputation for superb accuracy, the BREN could easily be pressed into the support role, or used for long-range fire fights. From adoption in 1938, it was used by the army until it was replaced by the MAG 58.

SPECIFICATION

MANUFACTURER Lithgow
CALIBRE .303 British
MAGAZINE CAPACITY 30
ACTION Gas operated/tilting lock
TOTAL LENGTH 1,155mm/45.5in
BARREL LENGTH 635mm/25in
WEIGHT UNLOADED 10.0kg/22.12lb

Vickers Mark 1

SPECIFICATION

MANUFACTURER Lithgow
CALIBRE .303 British
MAGAZINE CAPACITY Cloth belts
ACTION Recoil operated, water cooled
TOTAL LENGTH 1,092mm/43in
BARREL LENGTH 721mm/28.4in
WEIGHT UNLOADED 14.96kg/33lb
w/o water

In 1925 the Lithgow plant was expanded and tooling installed to begin production of the Vickers machine gun, in addition to the manufacture of Lee-Enfield rifles. With the extra weight of the tripod (50lb), and water in the jacket, a World War I-era machine gun is not exactly a portable weapon. However, neither jungle operations nor amphibious assaults in the Pacific were exemplars of fluid warfare. A completely dependable, if heavy, machine gun, it was highly valued. It was adopted in 1925 and used (along with the BREN) until it was replaced by the MAG 58.

Water-cooler can
The can that is often seen with a water-cooled machine gun is the condenser. In addition to supplying additional water for cooling, it cools and condenses the steam produced by the heat of firing. Without it, the machine gun could be quickly spotted by the plume of steam coming out of the water jacket vent.

long-range sight

condenser can, to cool steam

wood ammunition box, with 100 rounds in a belt

F89

SPECIFICATION

MANUFACTURER Lithgow
CALIBRE 5.56 x 45mm NATO
MAGAZINE CAPACITY 30 and belt-fed
ACTION Gas/rotating bolt
TOTAL LENGTH 1,038mm/40.9in
BARREL LENGTH 465mm/18.3in
WEIGHT UNLOADED 6.90kg/15.2lb

This was the Australian-built version of the FN Minimi, adopted in 1989 and still in use today. The F89 has a picatinny rail on which can be mounted a 1.5 power optic sight. The combination allows a gunner to engage targets at the extreme range of the 5.56mm cartridge, and the rail allows the gunner to mount night-vision optics if necessary. The F89 uses either belted ammunition in 100 and 200-round disintegrating belts, or 30-round M-16 magazines.

 # North Korea

North Korea makes copies of the standard Soviet arms. The Korean People's Army (KPA) was expanded during the 1970s and 1980s from half a million men to its present size of 1.2 million men, and a force that large needs many arms. Given the extremes of climate and terrain, simple but durable guns are a wise choice.

RPD

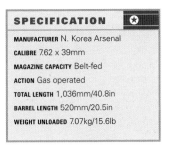

SPECIFICATION

MANUFACTURER N. Korea Arsenal
CALIBRE 7.62 x 39mm
MAGAZINE CAPACITY Belt-fed
ACTION Gas operated
TOTAL LENGTH 1,036mm/40.8in
BARREL LENGTH 520mm/20.5in
WEIGHT UNLOADED 7.07kg/15.6lb

The quality of manufacture of North Korean small arms is reported to be quite good internally, even if the exteriors are reported to be rough. The roughness may be more a matter of a harsh service environment, and the rigours that led to their capture, than a lack of concern for exterior finish. Other than the Korean markings, this weapon is a standard RPD, with all the strengths and weaknesses of the gun. It has been manufactured from the late 1950s to the present day.

 # South Korea

In 1950 the North invaded, and since the stalemate of 1953 Korea has been divided between North and South. The South Korean Army is only half the size of the KPA facing it from the North, but determined to resist an invasion. Daewoo is an an industrial giant; makers of a wide variety of products besides small arms.

Daewoo K3

SPECIFICATION

MANUFACTURER Daewoo
CALIBRE 5.56 x 45mm
MAGAZINE CAPACITY M-16 magazines
    & belt-fed
ACTION Gas operated
TOTAL LENGTH 1,030mm/40.55in
BARREL LENGTH 533mm/21in
WEIGHT UNLOADED 6.85kg/15.10lb

An aspirant for the Squad Automatic Weapon (SAW) market and clearly inspired by the FN Minimi, the Daewoo K3 is a solid light machine gun in use by the South Korean Defence Forces. It has not yet been accepted elsewhere but, as large as Daewoo is, contending with FN is not an easy task. Issue to South Korean Army units began in 1990 and the K3 remains in service in Korea, if not elsewhere. With a quick-change barrel and able to use either belt or box magazines, the K3 would serve as well as the FN Minimi. The fact that the FN Minimi was on the market first should not be held against the K3.

 Japan

Not only did Japanese machine guns use 6.5 and 7.7mm cartridges, there were further complications: some were rimmed, some were semi-rimmed, and none were interchangeable. Add to this a few foreign makes such as the Japanese-made Lewis Gun in .303 British, and the fact that the Army, Navy and Air Force selected models without consulting each other, then supplying troops with ammunition must have been very challenging.

Nambu Type 11

Another modified Hotchkiss, the Nambu Type 11 used the same 6.5mm cartridges as Japanese rifles and the same stripper clips. The feed "system" was a hopper that held the stripper clips. The operator would lift the hinged feed paddle and drop loaded stripper clips in, horizontally, and point forward. He would also have to operate the cartridge oiler. The machine gun would feed the rounds off the stripper clips, and eject empty brass and stripper clips. Contemporary shooters say that the oiler system was effective. The Type 11 was introduced in 1922 and used until 1945.

feed hopper on left side

SPECIFICATION	●
MANUFACTURER Kokura Arsenal	
CALIBRE 6.5 x 50mm	
MAGAZINE CAPACITY 25	
ACTION Gas operated	
TOTAL LENGTH 1,104mm/43.5in	
BARREL LENGTH 482mm/19in	
WEIGHT UNLOADED 10.20kg/22.5lb	

Hotchkiss-designed Type 93

Licensed from the French (who never built any), the Hotchkiss-designed Type 93 met a need the Japanese experienced after their invasion of China: long range and power. The 6.5mm machine guns that they had were not up to long-range machine gun duels, but the Type 93 with its powerful 13mm cartridge solved that problem. Built in the late 1920s and early 1930s, it was not made in particularly large numbers and served until the end of World War II.

SPECIFICATION	●
MANUFACTURER Tokyo Arsenal	
CALIBRE 13 x 99mm	
MAGAZINE CAPACITY 20-round trays	
ACTION Gas operated	
TOTAL LENGTH 2,413mm/95in	
BARREL LENGTH 1,651mm/65in	
WEIGHT UNLOADED 96.61kg/213lb w/tripod	

Lewis Type 92

96-round drum

This was a Japanese-built copy of the Lewis for flexible mounting in aircraft for use by the Japanese Imperial forces. It is not be confused with the Nambu/Hotchkiss Type 92. Curiously, the copy was also made in British .303, rather than the Japanese 7.7mm, which the Lewis mechanism could easily have handled. Consequently, the Imperial Air Force added yet another calibre to the ammunition supply chain. It was manufactured for the Air Force from 1924 until 1945.

SPECIFICATION	●
MANUFACTURER Tokyo Arsenal	
CALIBRE .303 British	
MAGAZINE CAPACITY 47- or 96-round drums	
ACTION Gas operated	
TOTAL LENGTH 940mm/37in	
BARREL LENGTH 660mm/26in	
WEIGHT UNLOADED 9.97kg/22lb	

Type 89

SPECIFICATION ●

MANUFACTURER Tokyo Arsenal

CALIBRE 7.7 x 58mm

MAGAZINE CAPACITY Belt-fed

ACTION Recoil operated

TOTAL LENGTH 1,051mm/41.4in

BARREL LENGTH 686mm/27in

WEIGHT UNLOADED 16.78kg/37lb

This was a copy of the Vickers machine gun, which had a reputation for being solid and reliable. The Type 89 was close enough as to almost have interchangeable parts. It was used as an aircraft gun and also would have been pressed into use on the ground. At least infantry units using salvaged Type 89 machine guns could count on them using the standard 7.7mm rifle cartridge, as long as they saved the belts and reloaded them. It was manufactured and used from 1928 until 1945.

Type 92

SPECIFICATION ●

MANUFACTURER Tokyo Arsenal

CALIBRE 7.7 x 58SR

MAGAZINE CAPACITY Tray feed,
    30 rounds each

ACTION Gas operated

TOTAL LENGTH 1,156mm/45.5in

BARREL LENGTH 731mm/28.8in

WEIGHT UNLOADED 28.12kg/62lb (tripod
    another 27.21kg/60lb)

The Type 92 is a heavy machine gun of Hotchkiss-type design, that required a new cartridge – a semi-rimmed 7.7mm: Type 92. When a new cartridge and machine gun are introduced into service the old ones should be withdrawn. The new Type 92 ammunition was more powerful than the 7.7mm, and rifles could not fire it. Conversely, the Type 92 could fire rifle ammunition. The tripod was fitted with sections of pipe, allowing it to be carried, stretcher-like, for short distances. It was introduced in 1932 and remained in service until the end of World War II.

Nambu Type 96

SPECIFICATION ●

MANUFACTURER Tokyo Arsenal and others

CALIBRE 6.5 x 50mm

MAGAZINE CAPACITY 30

ACTION Gas operated

TOTAL LENGTH 1,054mm/41.5in

BARREL LENGTH 552mm/21.75in

WEIGHT UNLOADED 9.07kg/20lb

The Type 96 is reported to be an improved Type 11, but it is simply the Czech ZB in 6.5 x 50mm, built for the Imperial Navy. Doing away with the cartridge oiler, the hopper feed of the Type 11 and changing to a quick-change barrel and magazine feed, the Type 96 is a much superior Light Machine Gun (LMG) to the Type 11. The Type 96 often had a 2.5x optical sight attached to the receiver, a first for an LMG. It entered service in 1936 and lasted until 1945.

Nambu Type 99

SPECIFICATION ●

MANUFACTURER Tokyo Arsenal

CALIBRE 7.7 x 58mm (could also use
    7.7 x 58SR)

MAGAZINE CAPACITY 30

ACTION Gas operated

TOTAL LENGTH 1,187mm/46.75in

BARREL LENGTH 549mm/21.6in

WEIGHT UNLOADED 10.43kg/23lb

bayonet
mounting
stud

This was another Czech ZB copy, in 7.7mm rimless for use at the squad level. The fact that the Type 99 looks very much like the Type 96 only increased the confusion over ammunition (and in this case, magazine) supply. The Type 99 and Type 92 both used 7.7mm ammunition, but with different rim diameters on the case heads. The Nambu Type 99 was an excellent model, but the Japanese never had enough of them. Initially built for the army, it also entered service with Naval garrison units, often mistakenly called "Marines". Production began in 1939 and lasted to 1945.

Manufacturers

Here are details of the manufacturers whose arms are featured in both directories, where information is available.

LEFT The Lebel Mannlicher-Berthier Model 1890 Cuirassier (France).

CANADA

Diemaco Diemaco produces the Canadian version of the Colt M16 and M4, for use in the Canadian armed forces and for export. In 2005 Colt purchased Diemaco, re-naming it Colt Canada.

Inglis A marine engine and water pump company at the beginning of World War II, Inglis produced a huge number of rifles, pistols and BREN guns during the war. After the war they transitioned completely into manufacturing household appliances.

UNITED STATES

Armalite The original Armalite was a division of the Fairchild Aircraft Company, and developed the AR-15. They sold the rights of that rifle to Colt. The current Armalite company makes AR-15, AR-180 and AR-10 rifles.

Barrett This company was established to manufacture and sell the Barrett Light Fifty (known as the M82A1 in military use.) The company now also makes Ar-15 rifles in 6.8mm, and a prototype semi-automatic 20mm grenade launcher.

Cadillac Gage An automotive manufacturer, Cadillac Gage made small arms components during World War II, and was still trying to

market small arms 20 years later. The Stoner was their final attempt. They continued making armoured cars.

Colt Established in 1836 by Samuel Colt to manufacture his handgun design, Colt went on to automatic rifles, pistol and machine guns, and produced huge volumes of all for the US military in World War I and II, Korea and Vietnam. Colt is the main producer of the M16 and M4 today.

Dillon Aero A new manufacturer to the small arms business, Dillon Aero re-designed and manufactured new parts for existing miniguns, and then went on to produce new ones when the US government found there were not enough of the old ones.

FNH-USA US Government regulations require that any producer of small arms have production facilities in the United States. So FN opened a business office, plant and hired staff in the US to be able to manufacture for the government.

General Dynamics A huge defence manufacturer, mostly in the heavy industrial sector (vehicles, aircraft, naval vessels) G-D has sought small arms contracts for decades with small success.

Johnson Arms Formed to manufacture and market the rifle and light machine gun of Melvin Johnson,

Johnson Arms was in existence only for a few years during World War II, manufacturing the rifle and machine gun.

Kelsey-Hayes During World War II, every machine shop, large or small, made something for the war effort. Kelsey-Hayes was an automotive components manufacturer that produced heavy machine guns.

Knight's Armament The largest manufacturers of AR-10 type rifles (known as the SR-25 in US service) Knight's huge plant is so busy with military orders they cannot fulfill all their commercial requests.

Maremont Corp. A diversified manufacturing corporation that had a speciality division to manufacture the M-60 machine gun for the US armed forces.

Marlin A sporting arms manufacturer, Marlin stepped up to produce small arms during World War I and II.

Remington Established in 1816, Remington manufactured military rifles for both US and foreign contracts in both World Wars.

Savage Arms Founded in 1894. As with many sporting goods manufacturers, Savage manufactured weapons for the war effort, in both World War I and World War II. Their primary product in peacetime was (and still is) a lever-action hunting rifle, although they produce arms for other activities such as law enforcement.

Stevens The hunting rifle and shotgun manufacturer fulfilled contracts in both World Wars for military arms for the US.

Sturm, Ruger & Co. The late Bill Ruger was a weapons' designer in World War II. He founded his firm in 1949, and pioneered the use of stampings and investment castings in US arms production.

Springfield Armory Established in 1794 as the official government arsenal, Springfield was closed in 1968 when then Secretary of Defense Robert McNamara changed the government acquisition process from government-designed weapons to private industry.

MEXICO

Productos Mendoza Formed to produce the LMG designed by Mendoza himself, it produces firearms and accessories for the Mexican military.

CHILE

Las Fábricas y Maestranzas del Ejército (FAMAE) Founded in 1811, Fábricas y Maestranzas del Ejército manufactures licenced copies of the FAL, as well as the Swiss SG540, in 5.56mm and 9mm. They also produce a 7.62mm variant, called the SG542.

DOMINICAN REPUBLIC

Armeria San Cristobal Begun in 1950, the Armeria produced the Model 2 carbine. After the assassination of Trujillo in 1961, the government of the Dominican Republic decided to leave the armaments business. By 1966, production had ceased and the factory closed.

ARGENTINA

FMAP One of the Argentine arsenals, devoted to small arms. FMAP produced a licence-built FN-FAL until it became necessary for Argentina to use the 5.56mm cartridge. In the 1980s they developed their own rifle.

BRAZIL

Indústria de Material Bélico do Brasil (IMBEL) Manufactured under licence FAL rifles for the Brazilian Army. They have also fulfilled contracts elsewhere in the Western hemisphere. When the 7.62 fell from favour, they re-engineered the FAL into the MD-2 and MD-3. They also manufacture copies of the M-1911 pistol, and an impressive array of cutlery.

PORTUGAL

Indústrias Nacionais de Defesa (INDEP) The main ordnance factory in Portugal, which produces a wide range of equipment, including mortars, artillery and small arms.

Fábrica Militar de Braço de Prata One of the major armaments manufacturers in Portugal. It produced the Heckler & Koch G3 under licence.

SPAIN

CETME The Spanish Design and Manufacturing Centre, set up after World War II, refined the Vorgrimmler lock system to become the HK G3.

Fabricas de Armas Oviedo was Spain's main armoury and manufacturing site for the first half of the 20th century, overtaken after World War II by CETME.

UNITED KINGDOM

Birmingham Small Arms Company (BSA) This company was founded in 1861 in the Gun Quarter of Birmingham. During World War I, the gun business grew exponentially. In World War II, production was focused on the Lee Enfield rifle as well as on military folding bicycles and on motorcycles. In 1986 BSA Guns was liquidated and now trades as BSA Guns (UK) Ltd.

Royal Small Arms Factory, Enfield Founded in 1804 as one of the factories of the Board of Ordnance. Privatized in 1984 as part of Royal Ordnance Plc. Production included

Bren and Sten guns as well as a modified version of the Webley service revolver.

Royal Ordnance This was formed as a public corporation in 1985 but its roots in the Royal Ordnance factories extend back to the middle of the 16th century. The company was bought by British Aerospace, later BAE systems, and became part of BAE Systems Land and Armaments.

FRANCE

Hotchkiss et Cie. This company was set up by Benjamin B. Hotchkiss of the United States in 1867 to produce a wide range of weaponry for both the French and the American armed forces. By the the beginning of the 20th century, Hotchkiss was also manufacturing cars.

Manufacture d'Armes de Châtellerault (MAC) Founded 1819 on the banks of the River Vienne. Initial production was of tools and swords. In 1822 the factory began to produce firearms and this was to continue until 1968.

St Etienne One of the first French armories to convert to the system of interchangeable parts (during the Napoleonic era) St Etienne manufactured small arms through World War II.

Tulle One of the main French armories, kept busy for decades starting with the manufacture of the Lebel 1886 rifle.

LEFT The Nambu Type 96 (Japan).

BELGIUM

Fabrique Nationale (FN) Herstal In 1888 the Belgian government offered a contract for 150,000 rifles, if a Liège firm could be found large enough to fulfill the order. The arms makers of Liége organized a corporation which would be large enough, and filled the order. Thus began one of the largest arms manufacturing companies in existence.

LEFT The VZ37 (Czech Republic).

NETHERLANDS

Artillerie Inrichtigen This company had a brief period of success with the AR-10. When contracts failed to appear they went back to heavy equipment.

SWITZERLAND

SA Hispano-Suiza While primarily an aircraft engine manufacturer, Hispano-Suiza worked on various small-arms designs.

SIG Formed in the middle of the 19th century, SIG has produced small arms for Swiss use and export ever since.

GERMANY

Carl Walther Waffenfabrik GmbH. This business was first founded in 1886 by Carl Walther to make hunting and target-shooting rifles. The first semi-automatic pistol was produced in 1908. The factory closed at the end of World War II and re-opened again in West Germany.

Heckler & Koch GmbH. This firm began business in January 1950 and was first concerned with making parts for bicycles and sewing machines. In 1956 the company won the bid for the new West German general service rifle, the G3. In the mid-1960s, the MP5 was developed. In 1991 the company was bought by British Aerospace/ Royal Ordnance. It produces the whole range of small arms, from pistols to grenades and machine guns.

Waffenfabrik Mauser AG. Founded in 1811 as a royal weapons factory in Oberndorf. In 1867 Wilhelm and Paul Mauser developed a rifle with a rotating bolt system. In 1912 the company started producing pistols. In 1897 the factory became Waffenfabrik Mauser AG. It supplied rifles to the German Army through both World Wars. The factory was dismantled by French authorities at the end of World War II. The firm was re-established in the 1950s. In 2004 Mauser-Werke Oberndorf Waffensysteme GmbH incorporated into Rheinmetall Waffe Munition, GmbH. Mauser is highly regarded in the field of hunting rifles.

ITALY

Fabbrica d'Armi P. Beretta SpA. One of the oldest manufacturing firms in the world, Beretta has been making sporting and military weapons since the 16th century.

Fabbrica Nazionale d'Armi Brescia A cooperative of gunmakers, located in the north of Italy, and beginning manufacture of military small arms in 1935. Bought in 1955 by Beretta.

DENMARK

Dansk Industri Syndikat A manufacturing conglomerate, of which small arms was a small part. Despite the success of the Madsen light machine gun, the post-war rifles were not greeted with enthusiasm, and in spite of good engineering and design, by 1963 there was no market share left to be had, and small arms production ceased.

AUSTRIA

Steyr Founded in 1864, the firm entered the military market with their breech-loading Werndl rifle of 1867. From then to the end of World War I, Steyr supplied small arms to the Austro-Hungarian Empire. Afterwards they supplied them to anyone in the market for small arms. Today they make select-fire rifles, sniper rifles and submachine guns.

SWEDEN

Carl Gustaf Arms Co. Formed as part of the original agglomeration of small arms producers that began in 1620 and centred on certain designated towns. The company itself dates from 1812. It is now part of Bofors.

Husqvarna Vapenfabriks AB. The company was founded in 1689 to produce muskets.

CZECHOSLOVAKIA (FORMER)

CZ-Brno Located in Strakonice, Czechoslovakia, the CZ Brno factory produced Mauser-pattern rifles after World War I, and through World War II. After World War II, the bolt-action rifles were produced for the sporting market while CZ-Brno developed and produced military rifles.

POLAND

Fabryka Broni Radom Founded in 1922, the company became independent in 2000.

SOUTH AFRICA

Lyttelton Engineering Works For decades this has been a small arms and artillery manufacturing centre.

CROATIA

RH-Alan In addition to the APS-95, RH-Alan manufactures pistols, submachine guns, grenades and mortars.

SERBIA

Zastava Arms Co. Founded in 1853 to manufacture cannons. Although it mainly produces cars, it is the sole arms producer in Serbia and Montenegro, with production largely based around Kalashnikov designs.

HUNGARY

Fegyver es Gepgyar (FÉG) Founded in 1891, the company produced Frommer pistols and also hunting and sports weapons. In 2003 the company was privatized and continues to produce small arms.

FINLAND

Valmet The State-owned weapons manufacturer, Valmet produced Kalashnikov-based weapons for the Finnish Defence forces from the early 1960s to the mid-1990s. The company now makes machinery for handling paper products. Before the 1960s, it was known as VKT; State Rifle Factory.

ROMANIA

Cugir Arsenal The State Arsenal located in Transylvania has manufactured small arms to the present. It is now known as the Romaru National Company.

BULGARIA

Arsenal Co. A government arsenal until 1999, when it was sold to the employees as part of the Bulgarian privatization programme, Arsenal is a vigorous exporter of small arms.

Long Branch Established to produce No 4 rifles during World War II to augment the production of other factories. Long Branch also produced STEN sub machine guns. Rifle production continued through the 1950s, switching to FAL production. After the Canadian army was converted to the FAL the plant was closed, and decades later the buildings torn down.

Ross The Ross rifle Company, Quebec, began production of their straight-pull rifles in 1905. In the mud of the trenches the action was found to not be reliable enough, and replaced by SMLEs in 1916. The company folded in 1917.

RUSSIA

Izhmech The State-owned Izhevsk Mechanical Plant, now manufacturing Kalashnikov-pattern small arms.

Tula Established in 1712 by Peter the Great, the Tula arsenal has produced small arms ever since.

EGYPT

State Factory 54, "Aswan" Established in Port Said to produce small arms for the Egyptian Army, Factory 54 began with the production of the Ljungman rifle. The tooling, bought from Husqvarna, armed the Egyptian Army and gave the factory production experience. Then, they went on to manufacture their own design, the Rasheed, then Soviet designs in the Goryunov and AK-47.

ISRAEL

Israeli Military Industries (IMI) IMI was formed as a State-owned company to manufacture weapons. The small arms division was privatized in 2005.

INDIA

Ishapore Located outside Calcutta, this was converted from a powder factory to a rifle factory in 1902. From SMLE to L1A1 rifles, the Ishapore factory now manufactures the INSAS rifle.

AUSTRALIA

Lithgow Established in 1909, production began in 1912 to produce the SMLE No.1 Mk III rifle for Commonwealth use. Production of BREN guns and Vickers (1937 and 1925, respectively) machine guns meant the Lithgow plant was able to supply impressive numbers of weapons in World War II.

CHINA

Norinco Also known as China North Industries Corp, Norinco is the exporter of Chinese-made small arms to the world. They offer military as well as non-military firearms.

State Factories Chinese State factories are only known by their factory number. Thus, the "location" of manufacture can often only be noted as "Factory 26" "Factory 36" or "Factory 66".

SINGAPORE

ST Kinetics Formerly known as Chartered Industries of Singapore, this company grew from a small arms manufacturer to a heavy-industry and integrated defence manufacturer.

SOUTH KOREA

Daewoo Founded in 1967, and an industrial giant, the corporation manufactures cars, ships, heavy construction and weapons.

JAPAN

Kokura This factory began in 1935. It was such a hub of production it was selected as the second target for atomic bombing, but bad weather brought the alternate city, Nagasaki to the history books.

Nagoya Opened in 1923, closed in 1945. It was not reopened after World War II.

ABOVE The HK-CETME Prototype (Germany).

Glossary

Air cooled Using ambient air as the cooling medium to deal with the heat of cartridge combustion.

Ammunition A supply of fully assembled cartridges ready for firing, sometimes abbreviated to "ammo".

Aperture sight Also a "peep" sight. The rear-aiming element of the sight is a device with a circular hole through it. The eye automatically centres the field of view in the middle of the aperture. The shooter then places the tip of the front sight in the centre of the view, and thus aims correctly.

Armour-piercing A bullet made with a hard core, used to penetrate light armour and chance obstacles.

Arquebus An early matchlock that preceded the musket, the forerunner of the rifle and other shoulder-fired weapons.

Assault rifle An automatic or semi-automatic rifle with a magazine feed now commonly firing small calibre ammunition.

Assault weapon A class of firearm which is a shoulder-fired, select-fire individual weapon chambered in a moderate-power cartridge.

Automatic A firearm with only one firing mode; where the weapon fires at its cyclic rate until the trigger is released. Also known as full-auto.

Backblast The backward blast created by igniting the propellant in a weapon designed to be as recoilless as possible.

Barrel The metal tube of a gun. The bullet, shot or projectile accelerates through it when the gun is discharged.

Battle rifle A self-loading rifle that uses full-power cartridges. It may or may not be select-fire and will generally be more than a metre/yard long and weigh over 4kg/8.9lb.

Bayonet A knife or spike that attaches to the muzzle of a weapon, for use in combat. Some are attached semi-permanently, and hinge into place while others are removable.

Beaten zone The area in which a burst of bullets fired from a machine gun will fall.

Belt A series of cartridges, parallel to each other, in a feeding mechanism. Belts can be reloaded with fresh ammunition and re-used. Metal belts can be continuous and disintegrating.

Blowback A breeching system that depends on the weight of the bolt and the force of the recoil spring to keep the bolt closed when the cartridge is fired.

Blowout vent Recoilless weapons dampen recoil by venting the gases of combustion to the rear, as well as launching the projectile forward.

Body The part of the weapon containing the bolt and return spring. The barrel is located forward of the butter, and the end cap at the rear. In the US, it is known as the receiver.

Bolt A mass of metal that feeds the round from the magazine into the chamber and supports it during firing.

Bolt-action The locking mechanism that works much like a deadbolt on a door. The firer lifts the bolt handle, pulls it back, then pushes it forward and turns the handle down.

Bore The inside of a barrel of a gun excluding the chamber. It is the channel through which the projectile passes when the gun is discharged.

Breech The open rear part of a firearm's barrel.

Breech loader A gun that is loaded via the rear or breech.

Bullpup A rifle design that has the trigger (and usually a pistol grip) forward of the magazine and receiver.

Burst-fire Either a set number of rounds fired by a mechanism designed to limit fire, or a small number of rounds fired by the operator.

Butt or stock The rear part of a firearm that may be made from wood, polymer or a metal frame that fits against the firer's shoulder.

Calibre Used both to describe the diameter of the bore, and a descriptor of the cartridge itself (in metric or imperial measure). The original Russian rifle cartridge of the Mosin-Nagant is both .30 calibre and the 7.62 x 54R calibre.

Carbine A shortened rifle. When rifles were bolt-action or large-calibre semi-automatics, a carbine was created by shortening the barrel and otherwise making the rifle lighter.

Cartridge A self-contained unit, comprising case, powder, primer and bullet. Each cartridge can be fed into the chamber, discharged, and the empty one extracted.

Centrefire A cartridge with the primer in the centre of the base.

Chamber The area of a gun where the round rests prior to firing.

Change lever The lever that controls the mode of fire i.e. single shot or automatic.

Clip Used correctly, a reloading tool, or an essential part of the mechanism. Used incorrectly to describe a magazine.

Closed bolt A design that when ready to fire has the bolt closed and locked, and a round chambered. Each cycle typically ends with the bolt closed on a fresh cartridge.

Cocking lever (or handle/retracting handle) A lever used to draw back the bolt in an automatic weapon.

Cook off The ignition of the propellant charge due to heat conducted from the chamber walls.

Combat/effective range The distance at which rounds are effective against a human target.

ABOVE The FN SAFN M-1949 (Belgium).

RIGHT The Imbel M964 (Brazil).

Cyclic rate The rate at which an automatic weapon fires (this is measured in rounds per minute).

Direct fire Firing at a target the operator can see. The operator can see the effect and correct fire himself.

Direct gas impingement The gas tapped off the barrel is not directed against a piston, but is ported via a tube directly to the bolt carrier. The carrier is pushed by the gas, and rotates the bolt, then reciprocates. Also called the Stoner system.

Discharge To cause a firearm to fire. A negligent discharge or ND is the accidental firing of a weapon.

Disconnector A part of the mechanism that intercepts the hammer or striker, preventing full-auto fire.

Disintegrating link Interlocking metal clips that hold machine gun ammunition. Upon firing the links separate and fall from the weapon.

Double-barrel A firearm with two barrels, which may be side by side or over/under. Used in shot guns.

Drop safety A safety device that prevents a weapon firing if it is accidentally dropped.

Dum dum/hollow point A bullet where the lead core has been exposed to cause the bullet to expand when it hits soft tissue.

Ejection port The opening normally on the side of the receiver through which spent cartridges are ejected after the bullet as been fired.

Ejector The spring-loaded plunger, or tab in the receiver, that ejects the cartridge from the mechanism when the action is cycled.

En bloc clip A package of cartridges in a metal clip. The firearm feeds the rounds when cycling, and ejects the clip when ammunition is exhausted.

Extractor A way of removing a cartridge by grasping the rim and pulling it rearward to remove it.

Feed tray On a belt-fed weapon, the flat section of the feeding area that the belt rides over as it enters the receiver. On the Hotchkiss design of machine gun, the flat sheet metal trays that hold cartridges.

Firing cycle The eight steps necessary for a mechanism to function. They are: feed, chamber, lock, fire, unlock, extract, eject, cock. Not all designs use all eight, but they do all use them in that order.

Firing pin The mechanism that strikes the percussion cap on a cartridge.

Flash hider A device attached at the muzzle to diminish the visible incandescent gases produced when firing to assist in concealing the user.

Flintlock The action of early firearms where a sliver of flint was held by a cock. When the trigger was pulled the spring-loaded cock holding the flint struck the steel "frizzen" producing sparks that ignited powder in the flash pan adjoining the "touch hole". The flash from the exploding powder passed through the hole to ignite the main charge in the barrel.

Fluted chamber A chamber manufactured with longitudinal slots, called flutes, to assist extraction.

Folding stock Normally a metal shoulder piece that folds back against the main body of the weapon when not in use. Stocks may also be telescopic.

Foresight A small blade or pillar above the muzzle. It may be adjusted laterally and sometimes vertically for "zeroing".

Frizzen The metal arm of a flintlock. The flint strikes the frizzen to create sparks in the flash pan.

Fullering Longitudinal grooves pressed into the magazine body to increase strength and let dirt drop to the bottom.

Gas The flame produced by an exploding cartridge – the pressure generated by the gas can be used to operate automatic weapons.

Gas operated A mechanism that utilises some of the propellant gases to activate the mechanism. Typically, gas is bled out of the barrel via a port, which then pushes a piston, attached to the carrier or bolt.

GPMG General purpose machine gun. A design intended to be versatile enough that it could be used in support, as an infantry weapon or as an aerial weapon.

Grenade launcher A weapon that fires or launches a grenade to longer distances than a soldier could throw by hand. Modern grenade launchers are separate tubes mounted under the rifle barrel, firing self-contained grenades.

Grip/spade/pistol The handle on a weapon. A pistol grip is behind the trigger. There are two spade grips with the button trigger between them.

Grooves The series of helical spirals cut into the bore of the barrel.

Hammer A spring-loaded, usually pivoting part of the mechanism, used to strike the firing pin and initiate the firing sequence.

Hammer-forged barrel A method of barrel making where a very hard mandrel, which is the exact shape and dimension of the desired bore, is inserted into the reamed and polished "blank". Powerful hydraulic hammers peen the blank down around the mandrel, shaping the interior so closely to the mandrel as to produce rifling.

Handguards A resting place and insulation against the heat of the barrel.

HMG Heavy machine gun. In the early years, a heavy machine gun was any that used water as a cooling method. With the development of the GPMG and larger calibres, "heavy" came to mean a larger-calibre machine gun.

Hold-open device A device operated by the magazine, to hold the breech block to the rear after the magazine is emptied.

Indirect fire The operator cannot see the target himself or the effect of his fire. The use of radios has made artillery so effective that machine guns are no longer used in this way.

LEFT The Armalite AR-18 (United Kingdom).

Lands The raised portions between the grooves of the rifling. The jacket of the bullet is engraved by the lands to provide spin and stability and to prevent gas escaping past the bullet.

Link The metal clips holding machine gun ammunition.

LMG Light machine gun. When machine guns were new, any model that did not require water as a cooling medium was considered a "light" machine gun. Later, the designation shifted to cover those fed from a box magazine instead of a belt.

Long recoil In the long recoil design, the bolt and barrel stay locked together after firing. They recoil, locked together, for a distance greater than that of the loaded cartridge length. Then, the mechanism unlocks and the barrel returns to battery followed by the bolt. Movement of the bolt and barrel activates the feed mechanism.

Lug/locking lug The shoulders of the bolt that lock into or against a surface on the receiver.

Magazine Either a sheet-metal box external to the firearm containing a cartridge lifter or follower and a spring, or a design internal to the rifle.

Mainspring/return spring The source of the energy required to fire a gun. The helical spring, generally behind the bolt, is placed under compression as the bolt moves to the rear. The compression is used to drive the bolt forward again.

Malfunction An unwanted interruption in the firing cycle.

Match A length of cord soaked in saltpetre, which was used to ignite gunpowder in early firearms.

Matchlock Early firearms fitted with an S-shaped metal lever holding a smouldering match. The lever can be operated to tip the smouldering end of the match into the powder in the priming pan and set off the main charge via the touchhole.

Musket A muzzle-loaded smoothbore weapon fired from the shoulder.

Muzzle brake A device attached to the muzzle of a weapon to re-direct the flow of the muzzle blast.

Muzzle climb The upward movement of a weapon as a result of recoil. A significant problem with automatic weapons.

Nose cap The steel or brass reinforcement at the front end of a stock, to support the stock and provide a bayonet-mounting attachment point.

Open bolt A design where the mechanism, cocked and ready to fire, has the bolt held back from the chamber, and the chamber is ready. When fired, the bolt will be pressed forward by the action spring, feed a round, close, fire and then retract, extracting the case and ejecting it.

Open sight A sighting system where the rear element is a notch, V-shaped, U-shaped or a rectangular slot.

Operating handle/rod The grasping handle or knob the firer uses to hand-cycle the action.

Optics Previously, magnifying optics used as an aiming aid. Now, red-dot optics, using a view screen and a reflected laser dot as an aiming aid.

Pan The small container located on the side or stop of a matchlock, wheel-lock or flint-lock firearm used to hold the priming powder.

Parabellum One of the terms used to describe the 9 x 19mm cartridge; it is also known as the 9mm Luger.

PDW Personal defence weapon. A compact weapon designed for close-quarters defence, rather than assault.

Percussion system A system in which a substance such as sodium chlorate is detonated by the impact of a hammer, setting off the main charge.

Percussion cap A small soft metal cup containing explosive that is placed over the nipple of a percussion firearm. In the days of muzzle loaders it allowed a gun to be loaded in all weathers. In breechloaded cartidges it was a primer.

Pinfire cartridge A 19th-century cartridge where a pin would ignite the priming mixture and the explosion would cause the brass sheath containing the gunpowder and ball to expand, closing the breech.

Pistol grip A grasping structure, looking much like the butt of a pistol that projects below a shoulder weapon. It is there solely to locate the firing hand near the trigger.

Primary extraction A movement of the bolt that frees the case from adherence to the chamber walls, but does not move the case out of the chamber.

Proof-mark Official mark placed on a firearm after the barrel has been tested by a proof house.

Propellant The charge of chemical energy which when burnt, produces a large volume of hot gas to force the bullet up the bore.

Quick-change barrel A design that allows an operator to change barrels to cool an overheated air-cooled machine gun quickly.

Rail attachment A rail either fixed onto the firearm or integral to the frame to which telescopic sights, laser pointers or lights can be attached.

Rear sight A "V" or an aperture placed over the breech, which with the foresight, allows aligning of the barrel.

Receiver The heart of a firearm. The receiver is the structure to which all other parts of the firearm are joined.

Recoil The rearward movement of integral parts of a gun as a result of the explosive force of the cartridge.

Reload To recharge a weapon with a fresh supply of ammunition. Also, to take empty cartridge casings and replace the consumed portions: primer, power and projectile.

Rifling A series of helical grooves cut in the interior of the barrel to give the bullet the required spin needed for stability in flight.

Rim The edge on the base of a cartridge case. The rim is the part of the case that the extractor grips in order to remove the cartridge from the chamber.

Rim-fire A cartridge that has its primer located inside the rim of the case.

Rimless Not truly rimless, but called so. The rim of the extractor groove (where the extractor grasps the cartridge) is not larger in diameter than the base, or head, of the cartridge case.

Rimmed Where the rim of the cartridge is larger in diameter than the base, or head, of the case it is on.

Round One shot fired by a gun. It is also one complete unit of ammunition or a cartridge which has all the parts required to fire one shot.

Sear A lever/catch connected to the trigger that holds back the firing pin.

Selector The lever that sets the rate of fire for a weapon from safe, through single shots to automatic.

Select-fire A firearm where more than a single firing mode may be selected.

Semi automatic A firearm where each pull of the trigger produces only one shot, but the mechanism operates to eject the empty and feed a fresh round into the chamber. Also known as a self-loading rifle (SLR).

Short recoil In a short recoil firearm the movement of the bolt and barrel are locked together, to actuate the mechanism. The distance moved is less than the cartridge's overall length. When the barrel movement stops, the bolt continues rearward enough to activate the feeding mechanism.

Sidemount A mount secured to the side of the receiver for designs that do not allow optics to be mounted above the bore.

Silencer or suppressor A device attached to a gun's muzzle that suppresses the sound of firing. Also known as a moderator or "can".

Single shot A gun mechanism without a magazine that requires rounds to be loaded manually.

Smooth bore A firearm with a bore that is not rifled, now only found with shotguns.

Sniper A trained precision marksman who uses a rifle of above-average accuracy to engage high-value targets or individuals at extreme range. In slang, anyone who takes a pot-shot at an individual or group.

Sniper rifle A rifle built or tuned for use as a sniper's tool. Typically it is a bolt-action rifle, and full-calibre (.30) or larger.

SAW Squad automatic weapon. A machine gun of moderate calibre, used by one or two men as an integral part of a squad.

Squad designated marksman An individual of above-average skill, tasked with precision marksmanship in service at the squad level.

Straight-line recoil To control semi and full-auto firing, the stock is placed directly behind the bore. The forces of recoil have no leverage, and the muzzle does not rise when fired.

Straight-pull bolt action Instead of the operator needing to lift the bolt handle, he just grasps the handle and pulls it directly to the rear. Camming surfaces machined into the bolt unlock the bolt from the receiver, and lock it again when the bolt is shoved straightforward.

Stampings/pressings A firearm's receiver made from stampings is created by large hydraulic machines pressing sheet steel into shape. By selecting the correct alloy, the steel is strengthened.

Stripper clip Also known as a charger, and used to quickly reload magazines. The clip is only a sheet metal strip that attaches to fresh cartridges on the rims. Submachine gun A select-fire rifle or carbine, chambered in a calibre typically considered a pistol cartridge.

Sustained fire In the early days, this meant the native cyclic rate of the weapon until a stated time period or number of rounds were fired. These days, it is the firing rate at which the weapon will not overheat, but which is needed at that moment.

Telescopic sight An optical sight attached to a firearm that magnifies the user's view of a target.

Telescoping stock A design that is made smaller for transport or storage by having the stock collapse in on itself, without the need for a hinge.

Tilting bolt A bolt that cams to lock and unlock, by means of the rear being tilted up or down into the locking recess.

Toggle lock A hinged lock, identical in operation to the human knee. When the hinge is in line or over-rotated into battery, it is incredibly strong. A small lateral force will pivot the hinge out of line, and the bolt then unlocks and collapses.

Tracer A bullet manufactured with a hollow base, which is filled with a combustible compound. The heat of firing ignites the compound, which burns with a visible light.

Water-cooled A cylinder filled with water to cool the barrel of early machine guns. This allowed for incredible sustained-fire volume but the weight made movement prohibitive.

Wheel lock An early firearm mechanism. Developed in the early 16th century it was the next major development in firearms technology after the matchlock. A spring-loaded wheel with serrated edges spins against a piece of iron pyrites producing a stream of sparks into the pan, and so igniting the powder.

Windage The adjustment or adjusting mechanism that moves the projectile's point of impact along the horizontal plane.

Zeroing The adjusting of sights to ensure that each of a firer's shots coincide with the point of aim.

RIGHT The Vickers No. 1 Mark 1, Air Service (United Kingdom).

Index

ABOVE The Mauser
Model 1910 (Costa Rica).

RIGHT The FAL-Para (Belgium).

ABOVE The Mondragon Air Service (Switzerland).

Picture credits

The publisher would like to thank the following for kindly supplying photos for this book: Cody Images/TRH Pictures: 34b, 45t, 46t, 47, 49t, 58b, 78, 79b, 86b, 88b, 90b, 92b, 94t; David Ezrets: 175 (www.israeli-weapons.com); The Lordprice Collection: 6t, 11, 18t, 65t, 68t, 90t; Peter Newark's Military Pictures: 7t, 8t, 13t, 14b, 15, 18b, 20, 22, 23, 25, 26b, 27, 29, 32, 33, 34t, 36, 37, 38t, 41b, 52t, 53t, 61, 63t, 64, 65b, 67t, 70b, 84t, 93; Royal Armouries Picture Library: 10, 14t, 17, 21, 26t, 30c, 51b, 54, 55b, 58t, 76b, 89b; TopFoto: 12, 13b, 28, 35, 53b; Will Fowler: 30t, 39, 41t, 43, 44, 46b, 51t, 52b, 57t, 71, 72, 79t, 81b, 82, 84b, 85, 87b, 89t, 91, 94b, 95b.

All other images are commissioned. With thanks to the Royal Armouries, Leeds in England for allowing access to their extensive collection of firearms.

All commissioned pictures by Gary Ombler. All artwork by Peters & Zabransky Ltd.

Every effort has been made to obtain permission to reproduce copyright material, but there may be cases where we have been unable to trace a copyright holder. The publisher will be happy to correct any omissions in future printings.

NOTES

NOTES

NOTES

NOTES

NOTES

NOTES

NOTES

NOTES